AREA HANDBOOK
for the
REPUBLIC OF KOREA

Co-Authors

Kenneth G. Clare

Gerald J. Foster
Robert C. Hannus
William Hrabko
Carolyn Knapp
Kyung Lee
Robert T. Mott
Yung Park

#85

Prepared for

The American University

by

Westwood Research, Incorporated

Research and writing were completed on
November 1, 1968

Published August 1969
(This pamphlet supersedes DA Pam 550–41, November 1964)

DA Pam 55–041

Library of Congress Catalog Card Number: 70-608 542

For sale by the Superintendent of Documents, U.S. Government Printing Office
Washington, D. C. 20402—Price $3.75

FOREWORD

This volume is one of a series of handbooks prepared under the auspices of Foreign Area Studies (FAS) of The American University, designed to be useful to military and other personnel who need a convenient compilation of basic facts about the social, economic, political and military institutions and practices of various countries. The emphasis is on objective description of the nation's present society and the kinds of possible or probable changes that might be expected in the future. The handbook seeks to present as full and as balanced an integrated exposition as limitations on space and research time permit. It was compiled from information available in openly published material. Extensive bibliographies are provided to permit recourse to other published sources for more detailed information. There has been no attempt to express any specific point of view or to make policy recommendations. The contents of the handbook represent the work of the authors and FAS and do not represent the official view of the United States Government.

An effort has been made to make the handbook as comprehensive as possible. It can be expected, however, that the material, interpretations and conclusions are subject to modification in the light of new information and developments. Such corrections, additions and suggestions for factual, interpretive or other change as readers may have will be welcome for use in future revisions. Comments may be addressed to —

The Director
Foreign Area Studies
The American University
5010 Wisconsin Avenue, N.W.
Washington, D.C.   20016

PREFACE

Since the publication in 1964 of a revision of the *Area Handbook for Korea* originally published in 1958, events have altered the situation in Korea significantly, necessitating a complete revision of many chapters. The present edition concerns the Republic of Korea. An Area Handbook for North Korea is published in a separate volume.

The original 1958 version was researched and written by a team made up of Robert J. Feldman, Mary W. Herman, Peter Malof, Florence K. Nierman, Otto R. Reischer, and Egon R. Tausch, under the chairmanship of Clifford R. Barnett. The 1964 version was produced by a team made up of Frederica Muhlenberg, Frances Chadwick Rintz, and Rinn-sup Shinn, under the leadership of Harvey H. Smith. The present revision was researched and written by Gerald J. Foster, Robert C. Hannus, William Hrabko, Carolyn Knapp, Kyung Lee, Robert T. Mott and Yung Park, under the chairmanship of Kenneth G. Clare.

This book is an attempt to provide, in compact, convenient, balanced, and objective form, an integrated exposition and analysis of the dominant social, political, and economic aspects of the society. It is a book of and about people as individuals and as members of the society, and how they live. It is designed to give readers, both within and outside of government, an understanding of the dynamics of the component elements of the society and an insight into the ideas and feelings, the goals, and the hopes and fears of its people.

At the time of publication of the 1964 edition, the Republic of Korea was recovering from a prolonged period of political instability following the devastation caused by the Korean conflict (1950–1953) and inflation had only recently been checked. There were emerging signs of vitality within the generally lethargic economy, particularly as a result of government investment in industrial production, and a democratically elected government headed by retired General Park Chung-hee had been installed in December 1963. These indications of increasing stability, however, had appeared too recently to permit assessment.

In the intervening 4 years, the Republic has seen a marked and sustained industrial expansion. The people's assent to the domestic and foreign policies of the government has been confirmed by the 1967 reelection of Park Chung-hee. In general, the mid-1960's have been a period of increasing political stability and accelerating economic growth. Drawing upon a long heritage of national pride, the people of the Republic of Korea—which was created as a political entity only a score of years ago—have made notable progress towards achieving economic and political viability.

The present handbook, then, is an attempt to analyze the social, political, and economic aspects of a society that is still experiencing great growth and change. Certain chapters, particularly in the Economic, Political, and National Security sections, have been largely or entirely rewritten, with the inclusion of much new material. A number of other chapters, concerning the social aspects of the country, incorporate information from the 1964 handbook with appropriate updating.

For place names, particularly on maps and charts, the Board on Geographic Names of the United States Department of the Interior has been used as final authority. The McCune-Reischauer system of transliteration has been used except in those few cases where a conventional form is mandatory for clarity or an official transliteration is available.

COUNTRY SUMMARY

1. COUNTRY: Republic of Korea. From 1392 until the end of World War II known as Chosŏn; from mid-19th century on, also known as Korea; officially changed to Korea after World War II.
2. GOVERNMENT: A kingdom until 20th century but often under foreign domination and annexed by Japan 1910–1945. Partitioned in 1945 into north (under Soviet control) and south (United States control) to facilitate Japanese surrender; Soviet authorities considered division permanent. Military occupation, trusteeship and United Nations debate eventuated in 1948 in formation of Republic of Korea, controlling Korean peninsula south of 38th parallel. After Korean conflict (1950–1953) demarcation line remained essentially the same. A democratic republic with actual power in 1968 centralized in office of President Park Chung-hee. President directs executive functions through Prime Minister and State Council; legislative power rests in unicameral National Assembly.
3. CONSTITUTION of First Republic adopted 1948, amended 1960 for Second Republic; Constitution of present Third Republic embodies amendments adopted 1963.
4. POPULATION: About 29 million; annual growth approximately 2.8 percent, density averaging about 750 per square mile; less than 25 percent of total land is arable and density in this portion is 4000 per square mile. *Composition*: Single ethnic group, Koreans, similar to northern Asians. Most numerous minority in 1968, about 34,000 Chinese. More or less steady emigration of students and skilled workers to United States and other industrialized nations. About 3 million refugees from north and repatriates from Japan since 1945; recent heavy internal rural-to-urban migration.
5. SIZE: Area, 38,175 square miles; greatest north-south distance, 300 miles; east-west, 150 miles.
6. TOPOGRAPHY: Mostly hills and low mountains, only about 15 percent plains. Five natural regions: Eastern Littoral, a coastal strip about 25 miles wide between T'aebeck Range and Sea of Japan; Central Region, the largest area, west of T'aebeck Range to Yellow Sea, mountainous in east and hilly to flat in extreme west; Southern Mountains and Valleys, consisting mainly of So-

beck Mountains and intervening valleys; Southern Littoral, a series of basins where Sobeck foothills reach sea; and Naktong River Basin, extensive delta east of Southern Littoral.

7. LANGUAGES: Official language since 1945 is Korean, spoken by all Koreans, indigenous to entire country; contains many borrowed Chinese words. Several mutually understandable dialects. Japanese language enforced 1910–1945 but no longer used. English a secondary language in cities; Chinese characters extensively used in newspapers.

8. RELIGIONS: Constitution guarantees religious freedom. Traditional Chu Hsi Confucian ethical system still influences most; other religions are Buddhism, Christianity, an indigenous monotheism (Ch'ŏndogyo), and animism in rural areas.

9. EDUCATION: Literacy rate in 1964 approximately 95 percent of those over 12 years. Government education program calls for expanded vocational training. Public school system comprises approximately 5400 primary, 1000 secondary, 25 vocational schools, 18 junior colleges, 2 colleges. In addition many private schools and universities.

10. HEALTH: Living conditions and public health improved since end of Korean conflict but still meager. Expanding governmental programs taking over more of relief and rehabilitation work formerly conducted by agencies of United Nations, United States and private organizations. In 1967 average life expectancy was up to 63.25 years but infant mortality was 67.9 per 1000 births. Leading causes of death in 1960's: tuberculosis, typhoid fever, encephalitis, leprosy, digestive ailments; other common diseases, parasitic infestation, typhus, diphtheria.

11. CLIMATE: Monsoonal, with warm, moist summer and cool-to-cold winter. Average precipitation rarely below 30 inches in any region, usually over 40 inches.

12. JUSTICE: Judiciary independent of executive and legislature, headed by Supreme Court (Chief Justice and 11 justices in 1968); 3 appellate courts, 10 district courts, 1 family court and 36 branch courts. Jury system not used.

13. ADMINISTRATIVE DIVISIONS: Provinces (9) and 2 cities, Seoul and Pusan, with provincial status; counties (139) and cities over 50,000 not included in counties (30); towns 20,000–50,000 (91); townships (1376); all largely centrally directed from Seoul.

14. ECONOMY: Historically agrarian, with rice predominant crop. Marked industrial expansion since 1963 with private enterprise increasing in importance and rapid development of manufacturing, mining, transport and electric power.

15. EXPORTS: Rapidly growing, promoted by government. Major exports in 1967: manufactured goods (70 percent of total),

agricultural and fisheries products (20 percent), mining products (10 percent); major markets that year: United States (42 percent of total) and Japan (27 percent).

16. IMPORTS: Increasing amounts of machinery and transport equipment (24 percent of total in 1966 and 1967) due to government industrialization programs. Also crude materials and fuels, manufactured goods, chemicals and foodstuffs. Asian areas supply about half of imports, western hemisphere about one-third, Europe less than 10 percent.

17. FINANCE: *Currency*: Severe inflation following Korean conflict, brought under control since 1963. Unit is wŏn; official exchange rate was 275=U.S.$1 in 1968. Backed by gold, foreign exchange and securities. *Banks*, including commercial, function largely as instrument of central government. Central bank is Bank of Korea.

18. COMMUNICATIONS: *Telephone and telegraph*: Telephones numbered 313,331 in 1966, two-thirds in urban areas; 420 telegraphic circuits, 20 international and 400 telex. *Postal offices*: 1728 in 1966. *Radio*: In 1968 there were 5 broadcasting companies with 34 stations. One network government-owned, four privately owned. An estimated 2.7 million receiving sets, largely in urban areas. *Television*: In 1967, 1 government-owned network, 1 privately owned; approximately 39,000 receiving sets.

19. RAILROADS: Government-owned totaling approximately 2000 miles, mostly main-line standard gauge. All single track except 276 miles double between Seoul and Pusan. Large-scale plans for modernization. RIVERS: Only 3 navigable, by sail and motor boat: Han, for 186 miles; Naktong, 210 miles, and Kum, 80 miles. ROADS: Approximately 20,450 miles, only about 1200 miles paved (800 intercity). Maintenance generally poor. An additional 3000 miles to be paved or improved by 1971.

20. PORTS: Fourteen comparatively large harbors but only 3 (Pusan, Ulsan, Mokp'o) accommodate vessels over 10,000 gross tons. Over 200 smaller commercial and fishing ports. Stevedoring and warehouse facilities inadequate but expanding.

21. AIRFIELDS: Eight principal airports; only 3 (Kimpo Shil Seoul, Pusan, Cheju) operate at night. Facilities being expanded and improved.

22. AIRLINES: Government-owned Korea Air Lines provides most of domestic service. Privately owned Air Korea operates on charter basis. Kimpo airport served also by several foreign carriers.

23. MERCHANT MARINE: Highly developed coastal fishing industry; fleet includes about 4000 motorized vessels and probably 45,000 other craft. Deep sea fishing expanding rapidly, with 150 modern vessels operating in 3 oceans in 1967.

24. INTERNATIONAL AGREEMENTS: *Civil*: Normalization treaty with Japan establishing diplomatic and trade relations and providing reparation to Korea; economic aid agreement with United States. *Military*: With United States: agreement providing advisory support and mutual defense; Status of Forces Agreement concerning jurisdiction over United States forces in Korea. ROK forces, Vietnam Command, activated in 1965, in support of Republic of Vietnam, numbering 48,000 in 1968.

25. AID PROGRAMS: *Civil*: Numerous and varied, consisting of loans, grants and technical assistance. Biggest single donors are United States, largely through Public Law 480 and Agency for International Development (AID); United Nations Korean Reconstruction Agency, and Civil Relief in Korea (CRIK). Dependence on foreign aid decreasing. *Military*: United Nations forces from 15 nations, mainly United States, during Korean conflict. United Nations forces still stationed in country.

26. INTERNATIONAL OBLIGATIONS AND MEMBERSHIPS: Instrumental in forming Asian and Pacific Council (ASPAC) for economic, technical and cultural cooperation. Not yet admitted to United Nations but has joined almost all major agencies of UN and every major international organization.

27. ARMED FORCES: In mid-1968 total strength exceeded 600,000: Army, 550,000; Navy, 50,000 including 30,000 Marine Corps; Air Force, 30,000. National Police Force of 40,000 under Ministry of Home Affairs are to support armed forces in emergencies and in combatting subversion. Conscription: 2½ years; budget, about 30 percent of total government budget.

REPUBLIC OF KOREA
TABLE OF CONTENTS

SECTION III. ECONOMIC (Continued)   Page

LIST OF ILLUSTRATIONS

LIST OF TABLES

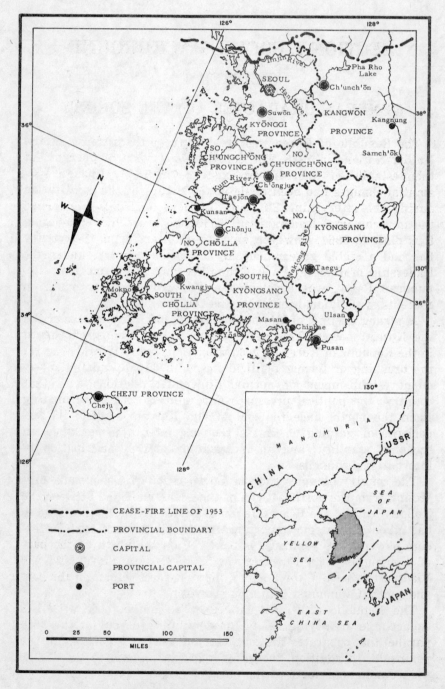

Figure 1. The Republic of Korea.

SECTION I. SOCIAL BACKGROUND

CHAPTER 1

GENERAL CHARACTER OF THE SOCIETY

The Republic of Korea was created under the auspices of the United Nations in 1948. The constitutional form of government then established was still in existence in 1968 although substantial changes had been made in the nature of the constitution during the intervening 20 years. Student uprisings overturned the governmental leadership in 1960 and a military revolution took place in 1961. However, since the military coup, the country has had a stable government. By 1968 the country, under the leadership of General Park Chung-hee and the Democratic Republican Party, was developing a democratic society based on concepts of individual initiative and freedom.

A strong feeling of national identity has long characterized the Korean people. This sense of unity has been strengthened in the Republic of Korea by events since the end of World War II: the breaking of former political ties with Japan and the subsequent establishment of normal diplomatic relations with that country; the political pressures and military threats emanating from the north since the end of the Korean conflict; the experience of gaining at first a tenuous, later a firmer, hold on economic stability; and an increasingly active participation in international councils.

The country occupies the southern portion of a peninsula projecting from the northeast rim of the Asian mainland between the Yellow Sea and the Sea of Japan, a position which for centuries has given it strategic importance in the rivalries of various foreign powers. The peninsula is bordered on the north by the part of Communist China which was formerly Manchuria and the Vladivostok area of the Soviet Union; it faces Japan on the east and south, Communist China on the west.

The Republic of Korea has effective control over a 38,175 square-mile area lying below the demilitarized zone at the 38th parallel that separates the southern and northern portions of the peninsula. In addition, the government lays claim to the 47,071 square mile area north of the parallel (see fig. 1).

1

In 1966 the country was one of the most densely populated in the world—about 29 million people, or an average of more than 750 per square mile. Less than a quarter of the total area is under cultivation, and density per square mile of cultivated land is almost 4,000. Moreover, the rate of population growth is relatively high. Urban centers are growing rapidly as a result of a heavy migration from rural areas.

The population is made up almost exclusively of persons of Korean ethnic origin, whose earliest forebears are believed to have come from Manchuria or northern China, probably during the third millennium B.C. Few countries of the world manifest such a high degree of ethnic homogeneity. Moreover, the language is virtually the same throughout the peninsula with regard to the written as well as the spoken word.

Though influenced in varying degrees by the culture of the peoples with whom they have come in contact, the people have preserved their own distinctiveness. For example, they have been able to share in the larger tradition of Chinese civilization while achieving and maintaining, through a process of selective adaptation, a unique social and cultural identity of their own. In terms of the contemporary scene, by far the most important element absorbed into the Korean culture in this manner was Confucianism. The Chu Hsi school of Confucianism, which originated in China, became the official Korean doctrine in the 14th century (replacing Buddhism to a large extent) and served as a unifying force in Korean society for several hundred years, continuing into the present century. With its emphasis upon social stratification, loyalty to authority, and reverence for scholarship, Confucianism has had a profound influence on the social and political life of the nation. The traditional Confucianist society has, however, been modified recently by powerful forces of change, notably by exposure to Western ideas. The effects of these forces have been much more evident in large urban centers than in rural areas.

Buddhism, imported from China in the fourth century, is still one of the principal religions, although its influence has been less than that of Confucianism. Among the minority religions in the country in the mid-20th century are Christianity and Ch'ŏndogyo. Christians represent only a small fraction of the population. Ch'ŏndogyo, a monotheistic religion stressing the equality of man and the unity of man and the universe, had several hundred thousand adherents in the mid-1960's.

The family system today, as in the past, affects all aspects of Korean life. Traditionally, the family was a large, extended patriarchal unit, economically self-sufficient and integrally related to the Confucian ethic system. Some lessening of the earlier rigidity and pervasiveness of the family system has taken place, particularly as a result of the disrupting influence of the Korean conflict and of urbanization. The small conjugal family is gradually replacing the extended family as the dwelling and consumption unit.

The traditional society was subjected to powerful new influences in the late 19th century when Korea was forced to open its doors to foreign trade, culture and religion. Goods and ideas were introduced from Japan and the West, paving the way for changes which eventually affected every aspect of society.

Japan formally annexed Korea as a colony in 1910. During the period 1910–1945 the Japanese colonial administration implemented a policy of systematic economic exploitation and political as well as cultural oppression.

With the Japanese surrender in 1945, the only effective military powers in the Far East were the United States and the Soviet Union. At the initiative of the United States, these powers agreed on a division of Korea at the 38th parallel as a temporary expedient for the sole purpose of accepting the surrender of Japanese forces then in the country. Soviet occupation authorities, however, interpreted this division as creating a permanent delineation between the two military zones.

The General Assembly of the United Nations adopted in November 1947 a resolution providing for election of representatives from the entire peninsula, who were to establish the conditions of unification and determine their own form of government. Elections were held in May 1948 only in the zone south of the 38th parallel and representatives were elected for a constituent assembly. Following adoption of a constitution, Syngman Rhee was elected the first president. The establishment of the Republic of Korea was formally proclaimed on August 15, 1948.

Communist guerrilla activities within the Republic were a problem facing the government from the outset. In June 1950 a full-scale attack was launched from the north across the 38th parallel. United Nations forces aided the Republic of Korea during the extended conflict, with Chinese military units intervening in support of the northern forces. An armistice was signed on July 27, 1953.

With the conflict ended, the Republic set upon the tremendous task of reconstruction, receiving substantial aid from the United Nations, the United States and others. By the late 1950's this task was essentially completed, though in 1960 the country still faced serious economic problems.

The Korean conflict contributed to the firm consolidation of power in the hands of Syngman Rhee, who asserted that only he was capable of leading the country. His regime, however, was

3

overthrown in 1960 after massive student demonstrations. Attempts were made by others to assume leadership but these were short-lived until Major General Park Chung-hee assumed leadership in a military coup in May 1961. A presidential election was held in 1963 and Park won by a narrow margin. He was reelected in 1967, receiving 10 percent more of the votes cast than his major opponent.

The presidential system of government in effect in 1968 was structured on the basis of principles established by the Constitution of 1948 with subsequent amendments put in force in December 1963. Sovereignty rests with the people, who are accorded a long list of civil rights and privileges. The executive is supreme over the legislature and judiciary with the actual locus of power in the office of the presidency. Delegates to the unicameral national assembly are elected by universal, direct and secret vote. In 1968, the assembly was under the control of Park's Democratic Republican Party. Among the other political parties the New Democratic Party had the greatest strength.

A basic political goal of the Park government was unification of all the people on the Korean peninsula. Other major objectives were to industrialize the country as rapidly as possible, to promote export trade, and to build an expanded and improved educational system geared to the needs of a modern industrial society.

Economic power in the Republic of Korea is not highly concentrated. The vast numbers of agricultural people collectively represent a large part of the productive capability of the country but they are not effectively organized and therefore do not, as a group, wield great influence. Industrialists are a small but growing and vigorous group, actively supported by a government that is eager to build a viable and diversified economy. Since 1963, industrialization has been increasing in tempo. Development has been encouraged in particular by the government-controlled banks, which have made long-term loans available at relatively low interest rates. In addition, the government has provided attractive incentives to foreign private investors and had itself invested heavily in improvement of public transportation and utilities. The marked economic expansion can also be attributed in large part to the flourishing export trade, which has been energetically promoted by the government.

The natural resources of the country are limited. Arable land has been intensively cultivated and family-owned farms for many generations have comprised the dominant sector of the economy, with rice the major crop. The long coastline and numerous islands provide excellent fishing grounds and this industry, too, has been highly developed. Mineral deposits are widely scattered, and while many different kinds of minerals are produced, the typical min-

4

ing enterprise is small and inefficient. The government is moving to develop and modernize this industry. Power generation remains a problem: Hydroelectric power is not abundant, coal reserves are being depleted, and the country has no petroleum deposits. These deficiencies are being overcome by development of refineries to process imported crude oil and by construction of thermal and hydroelectric plants where possible. Plans for a nuclear power plant are now being completed by the government, and it is hoped that construction will be begun within the next few years.

Much of the expanding export trade (for example, the export of plywood items) continues to depend on importation of raw materials for fabrication and resale abroad. This sector of the economy relies heavily on one of the country's most important resources, an ample and industrious labor force noted for the ability to attain high degrees of skill. Traditional attitudes—for example, the Confucianist reverence for classical education and the concomitant disdain for engaging in business or "blue-collar" employment—have to some extent impeded the effort to train and utilize this talented working force. However, it is gradually becoming apparent to all that industrialization is important for the survival of the economy. Conservative views are slowly giving way to the forces of change: Labor unions, trade and business organizations are gaining strength and popularity, and the status of the business entrepreneur and workingman is improving.

The foreign policies of both the Rhee and Park governments have been shaped in part by economic and military necessity and in part by a growing sense of nationhood and a desire to enhance national prestige. During the prolonged hostilities with the Communist north, there was heavy reliance on United Nations military aid, particularly that of United States forces. After the Korean conflict, the reconstruction effort was paramount, and close ties developed with industrialized nations that were in a position to assist with this program. Grants-in-aid and loans from the United Nations, the United States and other governments have been important to the recovery effort, though dependence on such assistance is declining as the economy expands. A significant achievement was the signing of a trade agreement with Japan in 1965, normalizing relations between the two countries. Cordial trade relations have also been established with many other countries, but the major markets for exports continue to be Japan and the United States.

In the last half of the decade, the country has increasingly asserted its independence as a sovereign nation (both major political parties advocate a policy of "independent diplomacy"). Though not yet a member, the country adheres to the principles of the United Nations charter and to agreed concepts of international law. Close relationships have been maintained with nations of the Free World and, more recently, with the neutral nations. By 1967, diplomatic relations had been established with 81 countries and special missions were being maintained at the United Nations and in Geneva.

Since the early 1960's the country has made substantial progress in strengthening the economy and solidifying the democratic way of life. Despite these gains, the standard of living for many people remained low in 1968, particularly in rural areas. There traditionalism has bred a certain degree of resistance to change, and even those changes that would be welcomed cannot yet be fully implemented—such as the long-range programs to develop industry and to improve sanitation, electrification, housing, and transport. About half of the population, then, continues to live at a near-subsistence level. And for these same people, the shifting patterns of society, and the confrontation with new ideas that undermine the traditional Confucianist ethic, are still a source of unease.

By far the greatest change has taken place among people in the cities, where the dynamic elements of the society are found. The large urban student population has long been an active, vocal political force; and their numbers continue to increase as educational centers in the cities are expanded and upgraded. Opportunities for better employment have attracted hundreds of thousands from rural areas, particularly young people and women (traditionally home-bound but now beginning to assert their independence). Most industry is concentrated in the urban centers, particularly manufacturing and foreign trade, the most vigorous sectors of the economy.

A general improvement in conditions is beginning to be evident throughout the land, albeit to a lesser extent in rural areas. With inflation in check, wages are slowly rising in relation to costs. More and better jobs are available; increased educational opportunities and more extensive public facilities and services are being provided. By the late 1960's, after several years of political stability, the people could be characterized as gradually developing into an industrialized, democratic society, still struggling, but with increasing success, to accommodate great changes in their historic way of life.

CHAPTER 2

PHYSICAL ENVIRONMENT

Some aspects of the physical environment of the Republic of Korea are highly favorable for the Korean people. The rugged topography provides the people with a very diverse and scenic landscape. An abundance of fish in the coastal waters has provided a major source of food, and the highly indented coast has afforded many excellent seaports. Additionally, ample rainfall has favored agricultural production.

The physical environment of the Republic of Korea is not, however, without its adverse side. Mountains and hills occupy a large amount of the country's territory, leaving only relatively small patches of level area. Also, the rugged terrain causes local areas to be physically isolated from one another, and integrating them by land transport is costly and difficult. West coast ports, while numerous, are seriously handicapped by an extremely high tidal range, which thus limits the effectiveness of coastal water transport. Minerals are not plentiful in the Republic of Korea, and forest resources have been largely lost through excessive cutting and war damage.

Notwithstanding the limitations of the environment, the Korean people have adapted themselves remarkably well. Arable lands are intensively utilized, and new agricultural land is being reclaimed. To allow the forests to develop to their former abundance, other sources of energy and timber are being increasingly utilized. Such resources as fish and other marine products are being developed energetically.

Since a high percentage of the population is engaged in agriculture and agricultural resources are widely scattered, the settlement pattern is one of wide dispersion. The people have occupied virtually all of the land that is reasonably level, and those plains areas that are capable of supporting relatively large populations are densely settled. At strategic points where principal transportation routes intersect, large cities have developed, such as Seoul on the west coast and Pusan in the southeast.

GENERAL SETTING

The Korean peninsula thrusts from the northeast Asian mainland to within 120 miles of the principal Japanese islands of Honshu and Kyushu on the southeast (see fig. 2). North Korea borders a section of the northeastern provinces of Communist China over a distance of about 500 miles and borders the Soviet Union for about 11 miles some 75 miles south of Vladivostok. Elongated and irregular in shape, the Korean peninsula sepa-

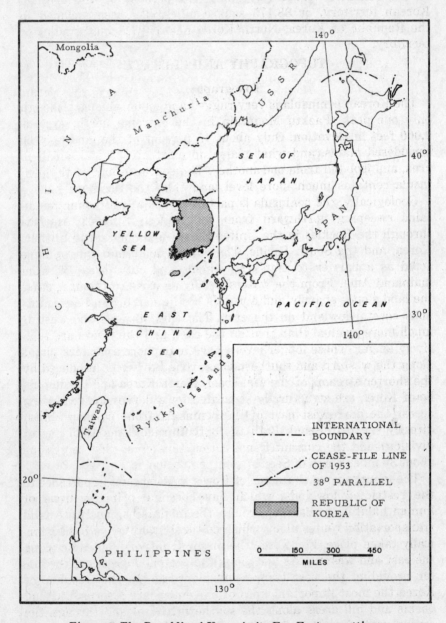

Figure 2. The Republic of Korea in its Far Eastern setting.

rates the Sea of Japan from the Yellow Sea. The peninsula has a north-south extent of about 600 miles and occupies latitudes (43° to 33°) comparable to those from New England to South Carolina. It is broadest at its northern border and narrowest (about 135 miles) in its center where the Demarcation Line divides it into North Korea and the Republic of Korea. As a result of the armistice agreement, about 45 percent of the original Korean territory, or 38,175 square miles, has been included in the Republic of Korea. North Korea has 47,071 square miles of territory.

TOPOGRAPHY AND CLIMATE

Topography

The Korean peninsula is very rugged and mountainous, although only one peak, Paektu Mountain in the extreme north, exceeds 9,000 feet in elevation. Only about 15 percent of the land may be considered plains, and what plains do exist are coastal, small in area, and isolated from one another. The southern half of the peninsula contains much more level land than the northern half.

Geologically, the peninsula is part of a vast belt of young mountains sweeping northward from the Andes of South America through the Rockies in the United States and then on to Siberia, Korea, and the South Pacific. The rugged mountain ranges have acted as a barrier to man's movement and cut Korea off from mainland Asia. From the watershed divide close to the east coast the land slopes sharply and abruptly to the narrow and discontinuous coastal lowland on the east. The slope toward the west is much more gradual than that on the east, and the rivers are relatively longer. These longer rivers have built more extensive plains along the western and southern coast than have been produced by the shorter streams of the east coast. North Korea and the Republic of Korea are structurally separated by a depression extending across the narrowest part of the peninsula from Wonsan almost directly south to Seoul. Both the 38th Parallel (the 1945 line of division) and the current Demarcation Line cross this depression about 30 miles north of Seoul.

The mountainous character of Korea lends special importance to the restricted lowlands, which have become primary areas of human habitation. Passes through the mountains constitute vital transportation routes along which cultural interchange has historically taken place. For Korea the major transport routes lie along the east and west coasts and along the central depression, the latter providing the best trans-peninsula route. In the Republic of Korea the most important lines of movement are a series of small basins and hill areas along the southern littoral and through the central part of the Sobeck Range.

There are five major topographic regions in the Republic of Korea. These are the Central Region, the Eastern Littoral, the Southern Mountain and Valley Region, the Naktong River Basin and the Southern Littoral (see fig. 3).

The Central Region is an upraised area sloping westward from the T'aebeck Range, parallel to and a short distance from the Sea of Japan. The eastern part of this region is rugged and scenically spectacular, with steep slopes and swift flowing streams. Closer to the west coast the topography is more subdued, being less mountainous and more hilly, and the rivers have built fairly extensive alluvial plains. Among the larger of these plains are those of the Han River near Seoul and of the Kum River near Kunsan and Chongju. The rest of the area is a coastal lowland comprised of smaller river plains extending south of Seoul and from 10 to 50 miles inland from the Yellow Sea. The lowland is interspersed with hilly tracts extending from the interior mountains to the sea. The coast is extremely indented, with flooded lower courses of streams alternating with rocky headlands degenerating into offshore islands. The shoreline itself is indefinite; a tidal range of up to 30 feet alternately covers and exposes mudflats, shoals and low-lying islands. Many shallow arms of the sea have been diked off and land reclaimed for agricultural use. The lower courses of the rivers are suitable for limited navigation, and there are many small coastal ports, despite the dangers and navigational difficulties posed by the rocky coast and very high tidal range. Some of the more extensive agricultural areas of the Republic of Korea lie in this western coastal lowland.

The Eastern Littoral is an elongated strip of steep foothills about 20 to 25 miles wide along the eastern flank of the T'aebeck Range. Short streams flowing in narrow, steep valleys have formed a succession of tiny plains at their mouths, separated from one another by extensions of the hills to the coast. The entire coast is rather isolated, with a relatively low population density, a restricted amount of level land available for agriculture, and a number of small fishing ports. In contrast to the situation along the western coast, the water is deep immediately offshore and the tidal range is low.

The Southern Mountain and Valley region is relatively small consisting primarily of the Sobeck Mountains extending southwestward from the southern end of the T'aebeck Mountains. The Sobeck Mountains separate into a series of parallel ridges and valleys, which extend to a complex of coastal indentations and offshore islands at the southwestern tip of Korea (southern Littoral Region). The mountains act as a barrier between the lowlands of the west coast and lowlands of the southeast.

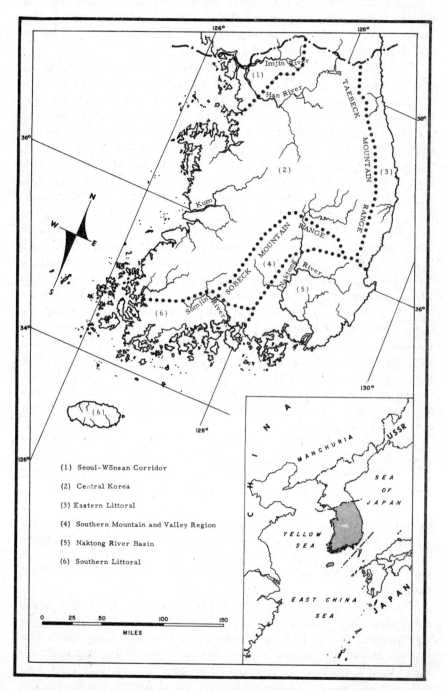

Figure 3. *Physiographic regions of the Republic of Korea.*

(1) Seoul-Wŏnsan Corridor

(2) Central Korea

(3) Eastern Littoral

(4) Southern Mountain and Valley Region

(5) Naktong River Basin

(6) Southern Littoral

The Naktong River Basin in southeast Korea is a complex of structural basins and river flood plains separated from one another by low hills. The Naktong River forms an extensive delta where it reaches the sea a few miles west of Pusan, Korea's major port. The coastline of the Naktong basin may be divided at the river mouth near Pusan. To the north of this point the coast is relatively smooth and, like that of the Eastern Littoral consists of alternating headlands and bays; the latter have small lowlands at their heads, but they are not as isolated from the interior as their counterparts farther north. To the west of the Naktong mouth the coast has the complexity of the Southern Littoral.

In the Southern Littoral, where the various arms of the Sobeck Mountains reach the sea, a number of small structural basins are to be found. Offshore the basins contain deep water and create an extremely intricate coastline of extensive, highly irregular peninsulas flanked by abruptly rising islands. At times the peninsulas almost enclose equally irregular bays deeply penetrating the land. Inland, alluvium replaces the water, and the plains are fertile and agriculturally productive. The hills rise abruptly from the plains, many of which are extremely small. Jeju, a volcanic island with an area of about 700 square miles, lies about 50 miles off the southern coast.

In summary, most of the Republic of Korea is hilly and mountainous, although not of high elevation. The most extensive areas of relatively level land are along the western coast and in the Naktong Basin, these two areas being separated by the Sobeck Mountains. With few exceptions the coasts are mountainous with a low tidal range on the east, or very complex with a moderate tidal range in the south, or moderately complex with a high tidal range in the west.

The Republic of Korea has few natural lakes of significant size; none of these lakes exceeds several square miles in area. Rivers are all short (only one over 200 miles), and only a few are navigable, most river navigation being impeded by either sandbars or rapids. The principal rivers are the Han, Naktong, Kum, and Somjin (see table 1).

The Climate

The climate of the Republic of Korea, like that of eastern Asia, primarily results from the Asiatic monsoon. Korea lies in the path of cold, dry air moving outward in the winter from the central Asiatic high pressure area centered over Lake Baikal. In the summer the reverse flow takes place, and warm, moist air moves inland to a low-pressure area in central Asia. However, Korea extends as a peninsula far enough south that it reaches into the warmer waters of the Kuro Siwo current—the Pacific Ocean equivalent of the

Table 1. Principal Rivers in the Republic of Korea

River	Length (in miles)	Basin (in square miles)	Navigable Length* (in miles)
Han	292	12,871	186
Naktong	326	9,251	210
Kum	149	3,871	80
Somjin	132	1,891	n.a.

n.a.—Not available.
*Sail and motor boats.
Source: Adapted from Chae Kyung Oh, *Handbook of Korea*, 1957, pp. 30–34.

Gulf Stream in the Atlantic. Consequently, in winter the cold and dry monsoon air blowing southeastward out of central Asia is somewhat moderated by its passage over the Yellow Sea before striking the Republic of Korea, and winters are neither as cold nor as dry in the Republic of Korea as they are in North Korea or on the nearby Chinese mainland. Even within the Republic of Korea there is considerable contrast from south to north in the winter. Greater uniformity prevails in the summer when the warm and moist air of the inblowing monsoon covers the entire country. Occasional cyclonic storms pass over the Republic of Korea and contribute to the rainfall, especially in the spring months. Typhoons are relatively infrequent. At least one can be expected each year, though rarely more than three in a single year. They usually occur in late summer, especially in August, and affect primarily the south, causing extensive damage to crops and homes.

The Republic of Korea has a warm summer and a cool-to-cold winter. While summer temperatures are everywhere relatively the same, winter temperatures decrease from south to north and from the coast inland. Thus, a greater annual range exists farther north and inland. The frost-free period—an important measure of agricultural potential—varies from about 175 days near the Demarcation Line to 220 days in the extreme South.

From the point of view of agriculture, no area of the Republic of Korea is deficient in precipitation. Rarely does an amount less than 30 inches fall in any given year, and for the most part the fall is over 40 inches. About one-half of the precipitation occurs during the summer months of June, July, and August during the height of the growing season. Winters tend to be generally dry but less so in the far South. During the winter a few inches of snow may cover the ground.

There are differences in climate among the various regions of the Republic of Korea. These are suggested by the climatic conditions at several selected stations or cities (see table 2).

At Seoul, winter is relatively cold, whereas the summer is warm. There are three months with mean monthly temperatures below freezing and four months above 68°F. Maximum precipitation oc-

13

curs in late summer while the winter is dry. Seoul is located in one of the more important agricultural areas of the Republic of Korea.

The city of Taegu has only one cold month averaging below freezing. The winter season is relatively long but not severe, so that two crops can be grown in the general area; winters are dry, and summer precipitation is heavy. The area surrounding this city includes the most intensive agriculture and the highest population densities of the Republic of Korea.

The climate at Gangneung is more moderate than farther west, since the area is protected from the cold of the outblowing monsoon by the T'aebaek mountains. Precipitation is concentrated in the summer, but the fall and spring bring moderate rain from cyclonic storms. Although the winter is not long, it is sufficiently cold to restrict winter crops.

The south coastal city of Yosu has a mild winter without sub-

Table 2. Average Temperature and Precipitation at Selected Stations in the Republic of Korea

	Seoul	Yosu	Taegu	Gangneung
Average temperature [1]				
January	24.3	34.2	28.6	30.2
February	29.7	36.5	33.3	32.9
March	36.9	42.6	41.4	40.1
April	50.4	52.3	52.5	49.6
May	63.1	63.0	65.5	64.4
June	71.8	69.4	72.7	70.2
July	75.4	73.9	76.3	72.5
August	75.9	77.7	79.5	75.9
September	69.4	71.1	69.3	69.1
October	58.6	62.8	59.5	58.8
November	44.6	52.7	47.8	48.9
December	28.4	38.1	32.7	35.6
Year	52.3	56.1	54.9	54.0
Average precipitation [2]				
January	0.76	1.24	1.08	0.98
February	0.10	0.88	0.56	0.32
March	0.67	0.93	1.16	4.24
April	0.42	4.90	1.73	0.60
May	0.46	5.31	2.58	3.64
June	0.95	1.81	1.08	0.95
July	25.26	17.87	21.32	18.82
August	12.78	6.77	5.80	2.81
September	1.08	0.13	0.12	1.83
October	2.55	2.46	0.74	4.70
November	3.40	5.10	3.83	5.91
December	0.22	1.32	0.57	0.90
Year	48.65	48.76	40.58	45.68

[1] In degrees Fahrenheit.
[2] In inches.

Source: Adapted from Republic of Korea, Economic Planning Board, *Korea Statistical Yearbook, 1966,* pp. 6–14.

freezing weather. The climate is almost subtropical, a result of the protection offered against the outflowing monsoon by the mountains and the relatively warm water offshore. With moderate to heavy precipitation most of the year and a cool winter and a long, hot summer, double cropping is characteristic, and the surrounding area supports a dense population.

In general, climatic conditions do not vary over a wide range within the Republic of Korea. This range, however, does encompass the temperature point which largely precludes double cropping except in favored areas. Obscured within regional generalizations are, of course, the many specific local variations to be found in any mountainous, mid-latitude country. Among these variations are contrasts in soil temperature (critical for crop growing) between north-facing and south-facing slopes; variation in temperature with altitude; valleys either exposed to, or protected from, the cold winds of the out-blowing monsoon; and differences in rainfall between the windward and leeward slopes of mountains.

NATURAL RESOURCES

Vegetation

The Republic of Korea at one time was a heavily wooded country, but much of the natural forest cover has been destroyed during recent decades. In 1964, approximately 68 percent of its total area was classified as "forest land". However, only 82 percent of this so-called "forest land" was actually wooded; the remainder was either bare, cut over, or otherwise devoid of its normal cover. Private owners controlled 73 percent of the forest land. The forests are extensively exploited, largely for fuel and timber. In the more heavily populated parts of the Republic of Korea deforestation is characteristic; intensive restorative efforts are being undertaken.

The forest lands in the west central area are extensive, especially toward the south and in the mountains away from the more habitable lowlands. The species include fir and spruce at the higher elevations, ranging through mixed forests including elms, beech, poplar and maple at the intermediate elevations and scrub oak and pines in the lower foothills. The mixed forests are the most important commercial producers.

In the southwestern region dense population has resulted in extensive deforestation, and attempts are being made to reestablish pine and scrub oak forests on the lower slopes. At the higher elevations inland, some stands of trees remain in areas more remote from habitation.

Generally, in the extreme south, only locally planted and maintained small woodlands, decorative trees, and poplar and bamboos remain in the lowlands, these along the roads and irrigation canals. A dense population and extensive agriculture restrict natural forests to remote mountainous areas. The subtropical climate of the southern littoral could support a broad-leaved evergreen forest. Except for maintained trees, however, only bamboo thrives, planted largely on the lowlands because of its remarkable utility. The higher slopes have been extensively reforested with pine.

Systematic cutting of saw timber is only a minor part of forest utilization. More important is the exploitation of the forest by individual farmers and others to obtain firewood, or clear land for farming or for other purposes. The use of green vegetation as a mulch, for which even young saplings are suitable, is particularly frequent in agricultural areas and places heavy regenerative burdens on natural vegetation.

Soils

Little is known about the soils of the Republic of Korea. The mountainous soils are thin and not particularly fertile. "Firefield" cultivation is relatively common in the more remote areas. Here, clearings are made by burning, both to remove the tree cover and to fertilize the slopes with the ashes. Several years of cultivation deplete the soil and the land is abandoned. Accelerated erosion results from this practice. In the lower hills near cultivated areas, forest stripping for fuel and mulch also accelerates erosion and leaves the ground bare. The cultivated soils are largely artificial after hundreds of years of application of natural fertilizers and, more recently, chemical fertilizers. In the rice fields particularly, the settling of silt from irrigation water or occasional flooding of rivers changes the soil composition from its original character to a uniform silty loam unrelated to the natural soils of the vicinity.

Fisheries Resources

The coastal waters surrounding the Republic of Korea provide the country with excellent fish resources. Numerous inlets, islands, and reefs along the extensive coastline provide favorable conditions for fish and other marine life. In addition, the convergence of the cold ocean current from the north and the warm ocean current from the south favors marine life.

Many varieties of fish are found in Korean coastal waters, including cuttlefish, anchovy, yellow corvina, hairtail, and saury. Various types of seaweed are also important marine resources. Agar-agar, a white viscous substance made from seaweed, is a significant export commodity.

In recent years considerable attention has been directed toward the development of beds for cultivation of shellfish. Conditions along the west coast are very advantageous for propagation of shellfish, including oysters and clams.

Water Power

The swift-flowing streams of the Republic of Korea's hilly interior provide opportunities for the development of hydroelectric power, although the concentration of rainfall into a few months in the summer places a premium on sites where adequate storage of water for year-round operation can be provided. The Republic of Korea has been actively seeking to exploit available sites for power projects. The greatest developments have occurred on the tributaries of the Soyang River upstream of its confluence with the Han. This group of installations lies between 20 and 50 miles to the northeast of the industrial area that surrounds Seoul. Other hydroelectric plants have been constructed in the center of the Republic of Korea in the upper part of the Naktong Basin and in the southwest on the Somjin River.

Mineral Resources

The peninsula of Korea is one of the more highly mineralized areas of Eastern Asia. It is particularly rich in iron and coal. However, most of the mineral resources and actual production lie in North Korea.

In the Republic of Korea, coal fields are found in three widely separated locations: in the mountainous complex in the east where the Sobeck Range joins the T'aebeck, which is the major producing area; and in two less important areas along the central west coast north of Kunsan and in the southwest between Kwangju and the coast. Very little of this is bituminous and is therefore not suitable for coking purposes, being almost all either anthracite or lignite. Thermal-electric power plants have been established either on or near all of the major coal fields. Other thermal plants are located in Pusan and Seoul, both cities being major consumers of electric power.

The major deposits of iron ore on the Korean Peninsula are in North Korea between Pyongyang and Haeju. Only scattered, small deposits are worked in the Republic of Korea. The Republic of Korea has large reserves of graphite but mostly of poor quality. The largest deposits are near Sangju in the Sobeck Mountains.

Gold is found in both lode and placer deposits. Relatively little is mined, and most of this production is along the west coast. Placer mining has all but disappeared. Copper, lead, zinc, tungsten, molybdenum, and manganese are mined in a triangle extending inland from the central east coast to the center of the Republic of Korea, with scattered production elsewhere. Of these, tungsten is the most important and has become a major export item.

BOUNDARIES AND POLITICAL SUBDIVISIONS

As an aftermath of World War II, Korea was divided at the 38th

Parallel into two zones of occupation, with the Soviet Union assuming jurisdiction over the North and the United States over the South. At the conclusion of the Korean conflict in 1953, a Demarcation Line was established. In general, it lay roughly parallel to, and about 25 miles north of, the former line of division along the 38th Parallel. At the western end it was turned south to the Han River estuary; the eastern end was turned north to the coast near Kosong. The Demilitarized Zone is 4,000 meters wide.

Prior to World War II, Korea was divided into 13 provinces. Since then some changes have been made in provincial boundaries within the Republic of Korea. Also, some duplication exists between North Korea and the Republic of Korea since the Demarcation Line splits several of the former provinces. In the Republic of Korea, Jeju-do, the province constituting the large island south of Korea, was given provincial status shortly after the end of the war, and the capital city of Seoul was made independent of the province in which it was located. Similarly, the city of Pusan was given special status on January 1, 1963. The Republic of Korea is thus divided into eleven administrative units (see fig. 4 and table 3).

SETTLEMENT PATTERNS

In 1965, slightly over one-half of the households of the Republic of Korea were classified as "farm" or agricultural households. For the most part, farm people live in small villages of 10 to 40 houses, usually situated on the higher ground adjacent to rice fields in the river valleys, or dispersed rather uniformly across the cultivated plains. In the village the houses typically are relatively close together, forming distinctly definable residential areas. On the other hand, there is little of the crowding of houses that characterizes the Chinese agricultural village. Most of the smaller villages are accessible only by foot path or trails, although there usually is no great distance to a cart track. Larger villages have grown up along roads of the rural areas, especially at road junctions or at junctions with cart tracks. There is thus a hierarchy of village size related to transportation routes.

Larger towns are related in their location to more important transport routes and are to be found particularly where all-weather roads intersect railways. The larger cities of the Republic of Korea are focal points of both rail and road systems in their areas. In 1966, Seoul had 3,805,261 people. The only other city with over a million inhabitants was Pusan with 1,419,808. There were twelve other cities with over 100,000 inhabitants.

Seoul (with a 1966 population of 3,805,261) was the site of the Government-General during the Japanese regime, the capital of the Yi Dynasty, the capital of the Republic of Korea in 1968, and

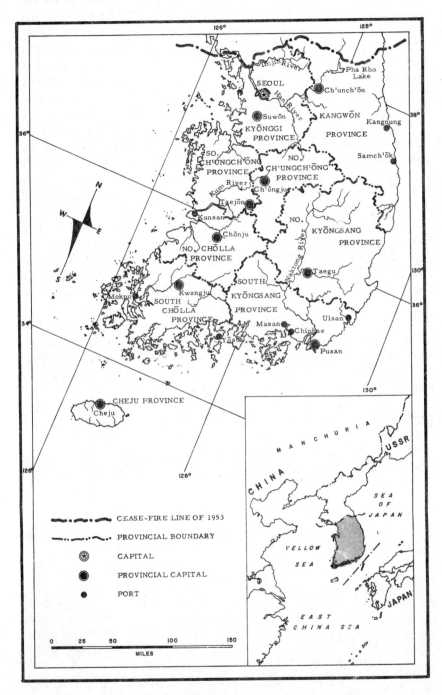

Figure 4. Political subdivisions of the Republic of Korea.

Table 3. The Republic of Korea—Administrative Divisions
(as of 1965)

	Area[1]	Percent of Total	Population Density[2]
City of Seoul	613.04	0.6	4,866
City of Pusan	360.25	0.4	3,527
Gyŏnggi-do			
(Kyŏnggi Province)	10,957.71	11.1	249
Gangwŏn-do			
(Kangwŏn Province)	16,618.20	16.9	96
Ch'ungch'ŏng-buk-do			
(North Ch'ungch'ŏng Province)	7,432.88	7.6	190
Ch'ungch'ŏng-nam-do			
(South Ch'ungch'ŏng Province)	8,710.14	8.8	314
Jŏlia-buk-do			
(North Chŏlla Province)	8,035.28	8.2	293
Jŏlla-nam-do			
(South Chŏlla Province)	12,047.93	12.2	309
Gyŏngsang-buk-do			
(North Kyŏngsang Province) ..	19,959.13	20.3	207
Gyŏngsang-nam-do			
(South Kyŏngsang Province) ..	11,944.35	12.1	255
Jeju-do			
(Cheju Province)	1,811.91	1.8	162
Republic of Korea	98,490.82	100.0	267

[1] In square kilometers.

[2] Per square kilometer.

Source: Adapted from Republic of Korea, Economic Planning Board, *Korea Statistical Yearbook, 1966*, p. 17.

this city is situated on the western plain a few miles upstream from the mouth of the Han River. This location places it at the southern end of the central trans-peninsula depression of Korea and at a strategic location on the west coast. It lies across the Yellow Sea from the Shantung Peninsula of China. Prior to the partition of Korea, Seoul's proximity to raw materials led to the establishment of primary industries, including iron and steel. With the bulk of the raw materials now north of the Demarcation Line, textiles have achieved a more important position. The processing of agricultural products is also important. Seoul is at the heart of a major industrialized area that includes some of the Republic of Korea's larger cities. Within the limits of the special city of Seoul are urban centers in addition to the main center of Seoul itself.

Pusan (1966 population of 1,929,726) is on the southeast coast several miles to the east of the delta of the Naktong River. Pusan is the southern terminus of the central trunk railway of Korea, which leads north to Seoul. The city has an excellent natural harbor, which was developed by the Japanese as the main gateway into their Korean possessions. Pusan is the chief port of the Republic of Korea and is the site of shipbuilding and repair facilities.

Taegu (with a population of 847,949 in 1966) is a regional center of some importance in the upper Naktong Basin of southeast Korea. It lies on the Seoul-Pusan rail line. In addition to being a textile center it is a primary collection and distribution center for a large producing area, which provides copper and tungsten as well as a variety of agricultural products.

Inch'ŏn (with a population of 528,579 in 1966) is the major port for the Seoul area, situated on the coast some 20 miles west of the capital. As a port it suffers from restrictions imposed by a tidal range of 30 feet, which makes some of its docks unapproachable at low water. Inch'ŏn is the western anchor of the Seoul industrial district and possesses iron, steel, and chemical industries.

Suwon (1966 population, 128,352) lies about 20 miles south of Seoul at the edge of the industrial area. It is a rail and highway center. Chunchon is a smaller city 50 miles northeast of Seoul.

Kwangju is the major city of the southwest, lying about 30 miles inland. Other cities on the western lowland are all inland on the coastal lowland and focal points of transportation routes—Taejon, Chŏnju, and Ch'ŏngju. The residents of these cities are primarily engaged in collection and distribution functions and other services performed for the surrounding agricultural areas.

Mokpo and Kunsan are the most important of the many ports located along the west coast south of Inch'ŏn-Seoul. Masan and Jinju are major population centers in the fertile agricultural countryside of southeastern Korea. Masan is an important port on the coast west of Pusan, and Jinju is an agricultural center.

IRRIGATION AND LAND RECLAMATION

The chief grain crop of the Republic of Korea is rice, grown almost without exception under wet (flooded) conditions. Growing wet rice requires a continuous admission of water to the fields. Neither stagnation, which promotes deoxidation of the water, nor rapid flow, which erodes the mud of the rice field, can be permitted. Although the water can be, and usually is, passed sequentially from field to field, the number of fields in a series is limited by the erosive potential of the required water volume and velocity of flow in the first field. Consequently, Korean rice landscapes have as one of their features a multiplicity of ditches and channels ranging in width from one or two up to a hundred or more feet in width. To assure a continuous flow through the fields, both supply and drainage ditches are provided, although the distinction is not always clear; the drainage ditches of one growing area commonly become the supply ditches for another.

The nature and degree to which irrigation facilities are provided are extremely complex and regionally variable, being responsive to such factors as the extent of the local area in wet rice; the drainage area and volume of flow of the streams from which the irrigation water can be taken; the rainfall during the months when the rice is actively growing; and the degree to which the growing season, as determined by temperature, commences before the onset of heavy rains or to which it extends after the summer rains have diminished. In general, irrigation water must be supplied early in the cropping season, following which drainage of excess rainfall becomes more important (during mid-season); irrigation again becomes important toward the end of the season to offset rainfall deficiencies. Although there is great variation in detail, the northern part of the Republic of Korea has a shorter growing season, during which only one crop can be produced, but the area has a single peak of summer rainfall, which occurs at the height of the growing season. Farther south the longer growing season, which permits two crops per year, is matched by spring and fall rains that reduce the early and late season need for irrigation water.

Literally thousands of small, shallow reservoirs dot the rice-growing areas of the Republic of Korea. Some are as small as a hundred yards across; others are several miles long. For the most part they are to be found in the plains areas, especially near the coast. These reservoirs provide temporary water storage, accumulating drainage from fields during heavy rain and releasing it after a storm has passed. Farther inland, where the streams leaving the mountainous areas provide water in abundance, storage is not required, and reservoirs are largely confined to small tributary valleys with catchment areas too small to provide a steady stream flow. Even so, over 40 percent of the rice lands are not under fully controlled irrigation.

In the bays along the western and southern coasts, silt-laden streams are actively deposting alluvium, which the rapidly ebbing and flowing tides have reworked into hundreds of square miles of mud flats exposed at low tide. Where feasible, these mud flats have been diked off from the sea, and the land has been reclaimed for agricultural use. Levees confine the streams to their courses and conduct them to the sea. In these areas, rice fields below river level can be readily irrigated, but drainage presents a special problem, especially at the height of the rainy season. The fields are divided into large blocks, each of about 100 acres and separated by large drainage ditches from which the excess water can be pumped. The Government of the Republic of Korea has seen the tidal lands along the coast to be one of the best sources of new cultivable land and is very actively pursuing policies of reclamation. The availability of more efficient techniques of dike construction, employed along with adequate supplies of electric power to serve the necessary pumps, opens the possibility of adding hundreds of square miles to the total cultivated area of the Republic of Korea. Another possibility for adding to the cultivated land is the bench-terracing of hills not now cultivated. Considerable effort is being made in this direction.

TRANSPORTATION SYSTEMS

Railroads occupy a particularly important position in the overall transport system of the Republic of Korea. In 1965, they handled about four-fifths of all freight carried, while highways and coastal water transports shared the remaining freight traffic equally. In passenger transport the railways were also the dominant intercity carrier.

Railroads and Roads

The railways and the main roads are essentially similar in basic pattern in that they generally parallel one another and are therefore competitive rather than complementary. As a result of this competitive relationship, the quality of the road system has suffered.

Principal transportation routes radiate in all directions from Seoul. The most important one extends south from Seoul to Taejon as a double-tracked main rail line. At Taejon it turns eastward to cross the Sobeck Range to Taegu and then continues southward to Pusan. Other rail routes lead south from Seoul along the western coast to the port of Mokpo and east from Seoul into Kwangwon Province, then through the mountains to the Samchok industrial area on the east coast and to the port of Ulsan near Pusan. The cross connections between the several major routes provide alternative means of movement.

The quality of the highway system of Korea is very low, a reflection in large part of the economic development policy under the Japanese regime, which emphasized the integration of industrial areas and port cities, the latter handling large exports to Japan. As a result, the rural areas remained largely self-sufficient without adequate integration into the general transportation network. In the late 1960's 94 percent of all road mileage in the Republic of Korea was unpaved, there being only about 1,130 miles of paved roads, essentially within cities and where local traffic is heavy, as between Seoul and Inch'ŏn. Since, in 1965, 40 percent of the motor vehicles in the Republic of Korea were in Seoul, the lack of paved highways outside of the cities is not surprising.

The economic development under the first Five Year Plan was based largely on the development of resources readily accessible via the existing rail net or transportable through the construction of short branch lines. As a result, there was a very rapid increase in the demands placed on the existing system. To increase the transportation capability heavy investment was made in refurbishing the roadbed, laying heavier rail, and double-tracking the Seoul-Pusan line, a project which was completed in 1965. The railroad also embarked on a program of dieselizing its railroad motive power and of converting the remaining steam locomotives from coal to fuel oil.

Development under the Second Five Year Plan, 1967–1971, is less oriented toward the rail system than it was under the First Five Year Plan. As a result, there is expected to be a dramatic rise in short-haul road transport, much of it feeder service to the rail system. The Second Five Year Plan includes an extensive paving program on most of the main intercity highways, many of which already possess a stone foundation several feet thick. Plans for a superhighway from Seoul to Pusan are also well advanced.

Ports and Airports

The major ports are Pusan, Inch'ŏn, Ulsan, Mokpo, and Chinhae. In addition, there is some commercial activity in close to 80 smaller ports, and there are about 150 fishing ports along the Republic of Korea's extensive coast. The major port of Inch'ŏn is part of the Seoul complex and serves as an outlet for industrial and agricultural products of that area. Mokpo lies near the southwestern tip of the country and largely serves local needs. Pusan, the chief port, is in the southeast and well situated for trade with Japan. Ulsan, on the east coast 30 miles north of Pusan, is undergoing rapid development as an industrial complex involving oil refining and chemical industries. Chinhae, also undergoing improvement, is about 20 miles west of Pusan. This center is being developed as a deep-water port and, in 1966, was accessible to vessels of 20,000 tons. Thus, three of the five major ports are in the Pusan area at the southern anchor of the main rail line to Seoul and Inch'ŏn. Probably the most serious port inadequacies are in the Samchok industrial and mining district along the central east coast, an area with somewhat tenuous rail connections with both Pusan and Seoul areas.

The principal airport is Kimpo International Airport near Seoul, a focal point for both domestic and international air service. The Korea Air Line has frequent service between Seoul and other principal cities, such as Pusan, Taegu, and Samchok. Relatively frequent service is also available between Seoul and Jeju Island. Kimpo International Airport is served by several foreign carriers as well, among them, Japan Air Lines, Northwest Orient, Cathay Pacific, China Airlines, and Thai Airways.

CHAPTER 3
HISTORICAL SETTING

Korea has undergone much political, economic, and social change during the past few decades. Political division of the peninsula continued into 1968; the Republic of Korea considered that it embraced the entire peninsula. From an economic point of view, Korea suffered major losses during the Korean conflict, which was followed by a period of reconstruction and significant development. The social structure during the period 1945–1968 also changed as a result of the disturbances of war, the process of urbanization, the departure of the Japanese, and subsequent increased contact with the West.

Established in 1945 originally for the military purpose of effecting the surrender of the Japanese forces in Korea — southern zone to American forces and northern zone to Soviet forces—the border at the 38th parallel soon gave solidity to the political and ideological differences between the two zones.

Traditionally, Koreans have viewed the nation's fate as being shaped largely by happenings outside the country rather than by indigenous forces. From the beginning of their recorded history some 2,000 years ago, events on this peninsula have been affected, directly or indirectly, by the dynamics of foreign powers: dynastic changes on the Chinese mainland; repeated tribal incursions southward across Yalu; the Mongolian, Japanese and Manchu invasions; imperialist machinations of Tsarist Russia and Japan; and, more recently, the rivalries between the Great Powers.

Koreans call attention to the fact that their country has had a "glorious tradition and history from time immemorial," which is sustained by a strong sense of unity nurtured by common origin, language, and cultural heritage. Despite their pride in antiquity, a feeling of distinct identity did not assume a political character until the turn of this century. Until then history was written in Chinese characters and its knowledge was mostly confined to the narrowly based upper classes. An overwhelming majority of the people had only a limited knowledge, if any, of their political and cultural heritage. Stimulated largely by the Japanese annexation in 1910 and Japan's subsequent attempts to extinguish the culture of the peninsula, popular interest in history increased despite repression. As a result, a 35-year period of Japanese domination (1910–45) produced a reservoir of patriotic feeling among all segments of the population, which was ready to be tapped after liberation in 1945.

Today there is no uniformity in viewing the country's past; there are many versions of history, though differences among them are marginal and inconsequential. In August 1963 the government decided to use a standardized history for teaching purposes. Historians, however, are free to expound their own views.

HISTORIC ORIGINS

Knowledge of ancient Korea, known as Chosŏn, is derived largely from several ancient Chinese sources. Forms of writing did not exist until Chinese characters were introduced during the latter part of the second century B.C., and the Korean dynastic chronicles said to have been recorded before the 10th century are not preserved. The name Chosŏn first mentioned in a Chinese chronicle recorded sometime during the third or second century B.C., is derived from the name of a native tribe living along the Taedong River basin in the northwestern part of the peninsula. According to a popular legend, which has been orally handed down from generation to generation, Korea was founded in 2333 B.C. by Tan'gun, the legendary offspring of a union between the son of the divine creator and a bear which had been transformed into a maiden.

The earliest Korean peoples are believed to have been migrants or invaders from Manchuria or northern China, of either Tungusic or Mongoloid origin, whose language probably was related to Ural-Altaic. Neolithic remains, found in all parts of the country, indicate that early settlers of diverse tribal origins moved into northwestern and northeastern sections of the peninsula, probably by the third millennium B.C.

Living by hunting, fishing and pastoral pursuits, the early Koreans seem to have worshiped nature deities and ancestral spirits, a phenomenon which was common to all the tribal peoples of Northeast Asia at the time. Unaffected by intermingling with Buddhism, Confucianism and, more recently, Christianity, this shamanistic spirit worship persisted through the centuries and still retains a powerful hold on both the rural and, to the lesser extent, the urban population.

From around the third century B.C., Korean history becomes much less ambiguous. In 194 B.C., General Wiman (Wei-man in Chinese), of either Korean or Chinese origin, founded along the Taedong River basin what came to be known as Wiman Chosŏn. In 108 B.C. the emperor Wu Ti of the Chinese Han dynasty destroyed this tribal kingdom and established in its place four Chinese colonies in the northern half of Korea. One of these, Lolang (Nangnang in Korean) flourished for nearly four centuries, and was predominant as a transmitter of Chinese civilization and as a trading center between China, Korea, and Japan. The other three colonies were shorter lived, and resistance by local inhabitants had thrown off foreign rule by 75 B.C.

Through Lolang the Chinese colonists introduced metal and bronze culture, Chinese characters and Confucian scriptures. The brilliance of what is known as "Lolang culture" is graphically illustrated by a large number of material remains excavated in the vicinity of modern Pyŏngyang in the northern part of the peninsula.

THE THREE KINGDOMS

From the second century B.C. to the mid-seventh century A.D., Korea was divided, aside from Lolang, into three warring native kingdoms; Koguryŏ in the north, Paekche in the southwest, and Silla in the southeast.

Koguryŏ was the first to appear along the Yalu basin. Founded by a group of tribes originating from the Tungusic Puyo tribes of northern Manchuria, Koguryŏ wiped out Lolang in A.D. 313, thus bringing an end to the four centuries of direct Chinese rule in the country. Because of their proximity to a number of aggressive tribes to the north of the Yalu and in China to the northwest, the people of Koguryŏ were much occupied fighting off hostile foreigners.

Koguryŏ authorities ruled much of the area north of the Han River and a substantial portion of southern Manchuria. The Koguryŏ people were highly militaristic, but after A.D. 313 they played an important role in diffusing Chinese culture southward through absorbing the Sinicized population of Lolang.

In the late third century, Paekche was founded, also by a branch of the Puyo tribes along the Han River basin—an area then under strong Chinese cultural influence because of its continguity to Lolang and Taifang (Taebang in Korean), a Chinese colony which was added in the third century, but eliminated shortly after the fall of Lolang. Heavily populated and rich in agricultural resources as it was, Paekche was rent with frequent tribal dissension and often had to ally with its eastern neighbor, Silla, and sometimes with Japan to counter warlike Koguryŏ's southward thrusts.

Silla emerged in the fourth century A.D. in the southeastern corner of the peninsula. Despite its backward status (because of its lack of contact with advanced Chinese culture and because of its continual harassment by Japanese pirates, by Koguryŏ, and sometimes by its on-and-off ally Paekche) Silla, with the aid of the T'ang dynasty in China, succeeded in overthrowing the two rival kingdoms: Paekche in 660 and Koguryŏ in 668.

Shortly after the overthrow of Koguryŏ, however, it became obvious to Silla that the Chinese intention had been to incorporate the entire peninsula into its empire. During the next 8 years, the Silla and T'ang armies frequently clashed, and eventually the Chinese were forced to withdraw from the Han River basin and accept Silla as a "tributary but autonomous state." This arrangement cost Silla much of the area north of the Taedong River, including southern Manchuria.

The success of Silla apparently stemmed from the solidarity and effective leadership provided by its tribal groups and by an elite circle of 500 to 1,000 youths called *hwarang*, or "Flower Boys." Recruited exclusively from the nobility, the *hwarang* emphasized chivalry, moral excellence and loyalty to the king, and played a pivotal role as able ministers and generals during Silla's wars of unification in the latter part of the seventh century. *Hwarang* ideals, seemingly a mixture of both Confucian and Buddhist teachings, stressed the so-called secular five commandments, namely, loyalty to the king, filial piety, friendship through sincerity, no retreat in battles, and no killing without necessity. The "spirit of hwarang" was revived during the Korean conflict of 1950–53 as a guiding symbol of patriotism and bravery. The term *"hwarang"* appears on one of the four distinguished military service medals of the Republic of Korea.

Buddhism

The society and culture of the Three Kingdoms were influenced largely by China, whose higher form of civilization was inherited by Koguryŏ through Lolang. The Chinese culture was imported and spread through the medium of Buddhism.

The Mahayana form of Buddhism, which was to dominate the country until the end of the 14th century, was first introduced to Koguryŏ in 372, to Paekche in 383, and via Koguryŏ to Silla in 528. Confucianism, a Chinese philosophy developed by Confucius (c. 551–479 B.C.), also was introduced to Koguryŏ in 372 and spread through a Chinese-type college founded in that year to teach Chinese classics and Confucian scriptures.

Through royal patronage, Buddhism spread rapidly throughout the Three Kingdoms, presumably because from the fourth to the eighth century it enjoyed great prestige in China as a "spiritual guardian" to the state, and, hence, Korean kings may have wished to derive benefit from its supposed protective powers. With an emphasis on tolerance, social harmony, and secular matters rather than on the transcendental and speculative aspects which had characterized the religion in its initial form as passed on from India, Buddhism was able to win over many people by means of beautiful paintings, colorful ceremonies, music and dancing, awe-inspiring temples, easily comprehensible sermons and scriptures, and finally through the alluring promise of personal salvation in this or the next world; most of these features were lacking in the traditional spirit-worshiping cults. Confucianism, still weak in China in those days, was not popularly appreciated because of its close association with the educated upper classes (see ch. 11, Religion).

UNIFIED SILLA (676–935)

After unification in the seventh century, the country was not divided again until 1945, nearly 1,300 years later. With the perennial threat of invasions from the north temporarily removed, the Silla peoples turned from military exploits to cultural achievements. As a result, the century following unification, often described as the golden age of artistic and cultural achievement for Korea, is still a major source of pride to the Koreans (see ch. 10, Artistic and Intellectual Expression). Scholars from the peninsula traveled widely throughout China and continued to bring home advanced Chinese culture.

The administrative structure was reorganized and its functions greatly expanded, largely on the Chinese model. The country was divided into nine provinces, and each provincial lord was required to send a "hostage" to Kyŏngju, the capital of Silla, as a means of enforcing loyalty to the central authority. At the apex of the society there were the king and hereditary nobles, whose status and function were determined solely by birth and legitimatized by a stratification system applicable exclusively to the self-contained ruling classes, among which only the Kim families of first rank were entitled to the throne.

The century following unification also marked the beginning of disintegration. The old cohesiveness of Silla society, knit together by family ties, soon gave way to a three-cornered conflict involving discord between the king and the aristocracy, a power struggle within the aristocratic families themselves, and disputes between the ruling classes on one hand and the masses of the people on the other. The situation took a dramatic turn in 780 when the king died without issue; thereafter, kings were selected from among a large number of rival aspirants within the royal families. The king as the symbol of national unity was soon degraded and came to represent the supremacy of merely one clan or faction over the others. Until the Silla society was supplanted by the Koryŏ dy-

29

nasty in 935, a kaleidoscopic pattern of coups and countercoups produced no fewer than 20 kings, an average tenure of 8 years per king.

The decline of the king's authority was caused largely by the lack of centralized control over landholding and tax collection. While in theory all land belonged to the king, it was in effect no more than the private domain of local lords who had built up powerful private armies to protect their tax-exempt holdings, or to contend for the throne or lesser positions of power.

Therefore, in 788 the royal court, in an apparent attempt to encourage loyalty to existing authority and to eliminate the traditional practice of competing for power on the basis of family prestige, connection, or brute force, adopted a Chinese civil service examination system based on a Confucian curriculum. By the eighth century this system had fully blossomed in China, providing the court with new talent and able leaders theoretically from all walks of life. The system was, however, coolly received by the Korean ruling class, whose status and function were contingent upon the perpetuation of the old order.

The attitude of the populace toward the government and ruling class was one of extreme dissatisfaction and hostility as evidenced after the mid-ninth century by increasing instances of peasant rebellion, banditry, and piracy. Progressively impoverished by forced labor and by high taxes, many peasants had to seek assistance each spring, in the form of "grain loans," from the usurious aristocrat-landlords; persons unable to pay off their debts became serfs and frequently indigent peasants sold themselves voluntarily into serfdom to escape unbearable government obligations.

Society of the Silla period was in the broadest sense a two-tiered structure consisting of the ruling class and the commoners. The former was made up of the kings, aristocrats, and government officials; the latter included the peasants, merchants, craftsmen, serfs, and so-called "lowborn" or "despised," people—slaves and their offspring, prisoners of war, criminals and their families, and persons convicted of treason or charged with rebellion. In some instances, a whole village or a group of villages was branded as "disaffected" and downgraded to the lowest rung in the ladder of society. The "despised" people were required to maintain separate residential areas apart from the commoners. This basic stratification, inherited by the Koryŏ kingdom (935–1392), grew more rigid under the Yi dynasty (1392–1910) (see ch. 6, Social Structure).'

Culturally, the Silla period was the golden age of Buddhism. A prolonged period of peace, combined with the leisure and wealth of the aristocracy, were conducive to cultural achievements. The royal court patronized temples and monasteries with generous gifts of land, built temples and pagodas, and encouraged painting and sculpture, presumably to enhance the prestige of the monarchs and to bring together every segment of society through the medium of Buddhism.

Buddhism and official sanction of Confucianism in 682 also stimulated interest in the study of Chinese classics. This in turn led to the invention of a script called *idu*, which was designed to aid persons unfamiliar with the syntax of classical Chinese sentences. Devised in the late seventh century by Sŏlch'ong, one of the most honored Confucian-Buddhist scholars in the literary history of Korea, the *idu* script used Chinese characters only for their approximate phonetic value to indicate participles and verbal endings in the spoken Korean language. Used mainly by monks, *idu* contributed to the development of a native literature called *hyangga* (folklore), whose dominant theme was Buddhist. *Idu* also served to inspire the invention of a phonetic alphabet many centuries later. Some Chinese classics were also translated into Korean by this system (see ch. 5, Ethnic Groups and Languages).

The foreign relations of Silla were predominantly cultural and commercial; each year several hundred monks and lay students studied in China and some traveled as far as India. Silla traders carried on a prosperous maritime trade with China and Japan and maintained a number of settlements along the eastern coast of the mainland.

KORYŎ DYNASTY (935–1392)

The salient features of this dynasty, founded by Wang Kon, a leading general during the last days of the unified Silla period, included: the brief appearance of a government under civil supremacy and its replacement by army generals, followed by a series of coups and countercoups; devastating Mongol invasions accompanied by nearly a century of subservience to the Mongols; and the deterioration of Buddhism. The dynasty's name, a shortened version of Koguryŏ, was later transformed into Korea.

The Koryŏ dynasty, based upon a centrally controlled bureaucracy, was, in its formative stage, characterized by the primacy of civil officials. Recalling the disruptive forces of the later days of the Silla kingdom, the founders of the Koryŏ dynasty built a strong institution of kingship. They carefully curbed the power of aristocrats and local strongmen by disbanding private armies not in the service of the state. Moreover, they established centralized control over landholding and taxation, enforced a hostage system, reduced the number of serfs and slaves illegally owned by aristocratic families, and excluded the military from important positions of power in the central government.

The structure of government continued along Chinese lines, and its officials were selected through the Confucian-oriented examination system. This merit system, theoretically open to the commoners (but not to the "despised" persons), attracted aspirants almost exclusively from the aristocracy, partly because of deeply entrenched social prejudices against nonaristocratic classes and partly because most of the commoners were unable, for economic reasons, to master Confucian scriptures and other classics.

The Koryŏ bureaucracy was divided into civil and military wings whose ranking officials had formed the backbone of the upper classes. The two wings formed what was then known as *yangban*, literally, "two groups," the military and civilian. Inherited later by the Yi dynasty, the *yangban* system came to denote "nobility," or ruling class, as distinguished from the commoner class. Under the Koryŏ dynasty the status of military officials was inferior to that of civil officials because many of the military officials, coming from the commoner class, lacked the scholarly qualifications which were particularly regarded as a prerequisite for implementing the Confucian concept of "enlightened rule." Hence, important military positions were often held by civilians.

The Koryŏ economy, like its predecessor, was predominantly agrarian and, accordingly, land was the principal source of revenue to the state. All land was owned by the state, as before, and was divided into public and private domains. While public land yielded revenue to the state, private land was allocated to government officials, civil and military, according to rank; upon the landlord's death or removal from government, lands reverted to the state. On the other hand, lands allocated to temples and monasteries, government agencies, the royal household, and to certain officials for "meritorious" service to the royal house, were tax-exempt and hereditary. Peasants, serfs, slaves, craftsmen, merchants, and actors were excluded from landownership. Peasants were bound to the land by hereditary ties and had to pay taxes in kind and labor.

Political stability, traditionally contingent upon an orderly landholding system, was again disrupted by the gradual ascendancy of aristocrats who, by means of intermarriage with the royal line, had gained access to the innermost circle of the governing elite. Through shifting matrimonial alliances they not only undermined the authority of kingship, but also precipitated incessant court intrigue and internecine warfare. In 1123, for example, an aristocrat named Yi Chi-kyŏm, related by marriage to the king, seized *de facto* control of the government. The resulting political chaos at the court led, in 1170, to the military seizure of power.

Military Rule

The military takeover was engineered by General Chŏng Chung-bu, who had been biding his time after undergoing the humiliation of having his whiskers burned off by a civil official at a social function. Under the system of civil supremacy, the General could demand no apology. During and after his assumption of power, he ordered a wholesale massacre of civil officials.

The reason for the military revolt, however, went much beyond what appeared to have been the personal vengeance of General Chŏng. As early as 1014 a group of army officers had revolted against the government to vent their dissatisfaction with the social and political prejudices against the military. The leaders of the 1170 revolt skillfully capitalized on this reservoir of ill-will.

After the coup there was a momentary breakdown of the old order. Army officers reduced the monarch to the position of a puppet, and many enterprising lowborn persons managed to rise to high positions in government. Until some semblance of public order was restored by General Ch'oe Ch'ung-hŏn in 1196, the country had experienced two decades of revolts by peasants, serfs, and slaves. Ensuing political anarchy hastened a breakdown of the landholding system, resulting in the steady, illegal transfer of public domain into privately owned estates. Wherever possible, power aspirants built up private armies. State revenues declined progressively, and the government found itself defenseless against foreign invasions.

Mongol Invasions and Domination

The collapse of the T'ang dynasty in China early in the 10th century immediately affected the security of Koryŏ, which was forced to contend with powerful tribes from the north without any Chinese assistance. The last 160 years of the kingdom were especially turbulent, punctuated by a series of Mongol invasions which laid waste large areas of the country. With the capitulation of Koryŏ in 1259, the country became virtually a vassal state.

At first the Koryŏ king, then a puppet of the military regime controlled by General Ch'oe's family, had refused to surrender to the Mongols and had fled to the island of Kanghwa in the mouth of the Han River. But with the assassination of the last Ch'oe rulers in 1258, the king, prompted largely by the rapidly dwindling supply of manpower and logistical supplies from the peninsula, was forced to yield to the Mongols.

After 1259, the northern part of the country was incorporated into the Mongol Empire, which was to be known as Yüan (1271–1368); the Koryŏ royal line became a branch of the Mongol ruling family through intermarriage of its kings to Mongol princesses. The crown princes of Koryŏ were obliged to reside in

Peking, capital of Yüan, as hostages, and in time the customs and language of the Mongols came to be patronized by the Koryŏ court. The government, watched closely by Mongol officials stationed in the country, was reorganized along Mongolian lines. Meanwhile, Koryŏ tributes to the Mongol court included large numbers of virgins.

Koryŏ regained national freedom in 1368, when the Yüan dynasty collapsed and was succeeded by the Chinese Ming dynasty, which ruled until 1644. For a while the fate of the country hung in the balance because its ruling class split into two warring factions, conservatives favoring continued vassal ties with the Mongols and the less affluent elements advocating a pro-Ming policy. The issue was resolved in 1388 when the pro-Ming group, headed by General Yi Sŏng-gye, seized control of the government. While the last of the Koryŏ kings was still on the throne, he instituted a new landholding system by confiscating all estates and by burning land records of the Koryŏ kingdom. In 1392, General Yi ascended the throne, and shortly thereafter his capital was moved from Songdo (modern Kaesŏng) to Hanyang (Seoul). The ancient name of Chosŏn was adopted for the new kingdom.

Culture

The dominant theme of culture during the Koryŏ dynasty continued to be Buddhism, which flourished through royal patronage. A considerable number of monks, besides being richly endowed with tax-exempt land and liberal returns from ventures into usury and brewery businesses, served as high-ranking advisers to the court. Thus the institution of Buddhism came to acquire tremendous economic and political power. Some monasteries went so far as to build up strong private armies to protect their mundane interests and in some instances provided support to aspirants for power at the court. In the process, the spiritual and moral aspect of Buddhist values was noticeably eroded with the result that a substantial number of scholar-officials turned to Confucianism for the restoration of order and regeneration of society.

An outstanding cultural relic of this kingdom was a collection of 81,240 wooden printing plates of Tripitaka, a Buddhist scripture, compiled and engraved by a coterie of monks on the island of Kanghwa. Completed during the period of Mongol invasions to solicit the supposed protective powers of Buddha in repelling the invaders, the wooden blocks are preserved intact today at Haein-sa, a temple situated about 28 miles west of Taegu. They are regarded by some scholars as a significant landmark in the history of Buddhism.

The Koryŏ dynasty was noted also for a number of historical works which included among others *Samguk Sagi* (Annals of the

Three Kingdoms), compiled by a 12th century scholar-statesman-general named Kim Pu-shik. This is the earliest and the most important source of the history of the Three Kingdoms. The legendary founding of Korea by Tan'gun some 4,300 years ago was first recorded in this work as well as in a history written in the third quarter of the 13th century, presumably as an exhortation for national unity in the face of continuing threats from the north.

YI DYNASTY (1392–1910)

The Yi dynasty, named after its founder, General Yi Sŏng-gye, who assumed the title of T'aejo ("Grand Progenitor"), remained unswervingly loyal and subservient to China, but it supported the Ming dynasty rather than the Mongols as the legitimate rulers of China. The Yi dynasty adopted Confucianism as the official doctrine of the government, replacing Buddhism; it also initiated a series of reforms to strengthen the central government, and for the first time since the latter half of the seventh century the northwestern and northeastern fringes of the peninsula were brought under the authority of a Korean government. Other significant events of the dynasty included the development of vicious factionalism beginning in the early 16th century, devastating invasions by the Japanese and Manchus, and the forced opening of the country to foreign powers in the second half of the 19th century. Strategically located but militarily weak, Korea was unable to meet the foreign powers on equal terms and was ultimately annexed by Japan in 1910.

Like its predecessor, the Yi dynasty was founded upon a new landholding system whereby its monarchs had secured the support of meritorious and loyal subjects by generous assignments of hereditary but taxable lands. All private armies were disbanded. In time, however, the ever-increasing number of meritorious officials and the steady growth of their large private estates forced the government to limit the size of "reward" lands. As a result, a group of disgruntled junior bureaucrats began to demand reforms in government and in the landholding system, but they were frustrated by a well-established group of conservative, senior-class civil servants. This friction between the senior- and junior-class officials heralded the beginning of ferocious political factionalism—a pattern of political behavior which was to dominate the politics of subsequent centuries.

The government was organized into a state council, a royal secretariat, and seven executive ministries, namely, personnel, finance, protocol-foreign affairs, education-examination, defense, justice, and public works. In addition, there were two judicial bodies known as "censoring organs." Despite their low rank in the bureaucratic hierarchy, the censoring organs became the focal points of factional rivalries because of their direct or indirect powers to dismiss officials from the government. Hence, whoever controlled these organs usually succeeded in removing political opponents from all positions of power. The country was divided into 8 provinces: Kyŏnggi, Ch'ungch'ŏng, Chŏlla, Kyŏngsang, Kangwăn, Hwanghae, P'yŏngang, and Hamgyong.

The social structure was much more rigid than that of Koryŏ. At the top of society were the royal family and the *yangban*, which was composed of the high-ranking landowning civil officials and army officers. The general status of the military officers, however, was lower than that of the civil officials. Immediately below the *yangban* was a class known as *chungin*, literally, "middle people"—a hereditary professional group of petty civil and military officials, accountants, geographers, interpreters, copymen, and law enforcement officials. The term "middle people" was derived from the location of the residential quarters for the *chungin*, which was in the central part of Seoul. The *yangban* normally maintained their quarters in the northern, southern, and a portion of the western sections of the capital. Military personnel lived in the eastern section.

The overwhelming majority of the people were known as *sangin*, or commoners, made up of peasants, fishermen, and merchants; at the lowest rung were *ch'ŏnmin*, known as "despised" or "lowborn" people, consisting of serfs, public and private slaves, actors, shamans, *kisaeng* (female entertainers), butchers, and monks, who were allowed to sink into this position because of the pro-Confucian policy of the Yi government. The Buddhist monks were, for example, forbidden to enter Seoul in 1456 for fear of what was then considered as their subversive potential; this restriction was lifted only in 1895 (see ch. 6, Social Structure).

The most notable intellectual achievement of this dynasty was the invention in 1443 of a Korean phonetic vernacular writing system, known in modern times as *han'gul* ("Korean letters"). Public acceptance of the new writing system was slow at first because the upper class, continuing to patronize the Chinese written language, ridiculed the vernacular system as fit only for the persons of little education, women, and the commoner class. A compromise between the two writing systems began to appear in the 1890's when a mixed use of both Chinese characters and native alphabet was adopted by some scholars.

Confucianism

The Yi dynasty became known as the Golden Age of Confucianism, especially of the so-called "neo-Confucianism" perfected by Chu Hsi, a renowned Chinese philosopher (768–824). Confucianism took deep roots in the social and political institutions through the Confucian-oriented examination system, which produced an elite class of scholar-officials deeply imbued with Confucian political and ethical ideals. Under the Yi dynasty this class molded a social value system designed to perpetuate the existing social structures (see ch. 6, Social Structure; ch. 11, Religion; ch. 12, Social Values; ch. 17, Political Values and Attitudes).

Confucian ethical concepts centered around five human relationships, namely, between king and subject, father and son, husband and wife, elder brother and younger brother, and between friend and friend. Essentially, these concepts extolled the virtues of loyalty to authority and to one's kinship group. Frequent conflicts between the two patterns of loyalty occurred, especially during periods when the monarchy was enfeebled and the integrity of the governing elite discredited. In times of stresses and tensions, as during the later years of the Yi dynasty, loyalty to the kinship group was valued more than loyalty to the state because of the essentially family-centered Confucian orientation. A partial reason for failure to develop strong law-abiding tendencies and concepts of civic duty in Korea during this dynasty may be attributed to a forced emphasis on kinship loyalty adopted as a protective measure against corrupt and oppressive governmental practices. In time, such a trend further served to reinforce loyalty to primary groups as the foci of political, social, and economic activities. The people developed the habit of evading laws and rebelling against the authorities wherever possible (see ch. 7, Family; ch. 12, Social Values; ch. 17, Political Values and Attitudes; ch. 26, Public Order and Safety).

Another feature of Confucianism was the supreme importance attached to education in the humanities as the key to power and wealth and, in rare instances, to upward mobility. Since only those earning degrees in the humanities were allowed into positions of importance, studies in technical and professional subjects such as engineering, agriculture, medicine, and military science were generally neglected, with the result that the sole purpose of education was to secure an appointment to a government position. In time, the failure of the Chu Hsi school of Confucianism to solve the society's growing problems arising from internal and external tensions led to its being challenged, beginning early in the 17th century, by another school of Confucianism which sought social and political reforms through more practical and empirical approaches (see ch. 10, Artistic and Intellectual Expression).

Factionalism
One of the most disruptive forces of the Yi dynasty had been factional strife in the central government. Unlike the Silla and

Koryŏ periods, factional differences were resolved not by military showdowns but by the manipulations of like-minded scholar-officials bound together by ties of blood, region, common school background, or by teacher-disciple relationships. Factionalism among those in power, and struggles between those in and out of power, usually developed from doctrinal controversies over such wide-ranging issues as dynastic succession, the role of censoring organs in the government, and the relative merits of different schools of Confucian ideology as the official doctrine of government. In general the controversies were accompanied by partisan accusations of incompetence in office and disloyalty to the kings.

Triumph of one faction over the other inevitably led to sweeping purges of political opponents—in the form of execution, dismissal, or banishment to outlying regions. Between 1498 and 1545 alone, nearly 200 leading governmental personages were executed in at least four major instances of purges and counterpurges.

Furthermore, the families of purged officials were usually subjected to political disadvantage for several decades. Personal and family antagonisms were given added significance because of the Confucian virtues of stressing filial piety, of according deference to immediate superiors, and of upholding the family name. Factionalism thus acquired the characteristics of a self-perpetuating institution.

Factionalism was also fostered by the more or less constant number of official positions available for a rapidly increasing number of degree holders. This situation created a substantial number of discontented and unemployed scholars within the *yangban* class. Since the only honorable profession for them was politics, their only recourse was to indulge in the pastime of criticizing those in power or retire to their country estates for purely scholarly pursuits or for the purpose of lining up colleagues and followers for court intrigue.

Thus factionalism developed along educational and regional lines. Many of the private academies (*sowon*), founded by ex-officials or scholars on their country estates, were really centers of political activity in academic disguise; by the mid-19th century there were nearly 600 academies, but in 1864, the government abolished all but 40 of them. The intellectuals who were associated with an academy or a group of academies normally shared the political fortunes of their leaders. If their leaders were purged, a whole region might be affected, and indeed might suffer from political discrimination for several generations. Areas most affected traditionally were the northwestern, northeastern, and southwestern parts of the peninsula. The rebellions led by Myonch'ŏng in 1135, Yi Shi-ae in 1467, Chŏng Yŏ-rip in 1589, and Hon Kyŏngnae in 1811 were all inspired, at least in part, by such regional discrimination.

Eventually almost all members of the *yangban* class were involved in factional strife, and even during the period of the Japanese invasions they were unable to form a political consensus across factional lines, despite a substantial abatement in their differences. Another consequence was the increasing practice of appointing officials through favoritism and nepotism rather than by the competitive examination system.

Japanese and Manchu Invasions

With its leadership divided and weakened by internal disunity, and the morale of its military force deteriorated because of corrupt civil leadership, Korea was virtually defenseless against the Japanese invasions of 1592 and 1598. Both invasions, directed by the Japanese general, Toyotomi Hideyoshi, were first steps in his efforts to conquer China. The latter invasion ended because of the General's death in 1598 and because of the dispatch of Chinese troops from Manchuria by the Ming dynasty. The military operations laid waste nearly the whole peninsula and were followed by a series of famines, epidemics, peasant revolts, and a full-scale renewal of factionalism within officialdom.

The war, however, provided Korea with one of its most celebrated national heroes, Admiral Yi Sun-sin, inventor of the world's first iron-plated vessel—the "turtle ships"—which enabled him to destroy in 1592 much of the Japanese fleet and cut off its supply lines. He was credited with having sunk or damaged at least 250 Japanese vessels. Admiral Yi was posthumously awarded an honorary title of *Ch'ungmu*, literally, "Loyalty-Chivalry." One of the military service medals of the Republic of Korea is named after this title.

The war also hastened the decline of the Yi dynasty as well as that of the Chinese Ming dynasty, since the withdrawal of its garrison troops from Manchuria for deployment in Korea permitted the rise of Manchu power. Korea had scarcely begun to recover when the Manchus, moving to overthrow the Ming dynasty, overran Korea in 1627 and 1637, causing further depletion of manpower and economic resources. In 1644 the Manchus conquered the Ming and founded the Ch'ing dynasty (1644–1911).

THE OPENING OF KOREA

In the face of gradual penetration by Christianity early in the 17th century and of the increasing appearance of foreign ships in Korean waters early in the 19th century, Korea adopted a policy of isolation from the non-Chinese world. But the integrity and stability of China became endangered by increasing Occidental pressures at a time when Korea itself had neither the power to resist external pressure nor the strength to institute needed internal reforms, and the country became a pawn of the conflicting world powers.

Social and Economic Condition

The peninsula never fully recovered from the devastations inflicted by the Japanese and Manchus. Nearly 130 years after the first Japanese attack, the amount of taxable land under effective state control was still less than half of the preinvasion level. A number of powerful landowning officials, taking advantage of chaotic war-year administrative practices and the loss of land records during the invasions, usurped public property. The consequent decline in state revenue had to be made up through the levying of harsh taxes; the difficulties in meeting adequate salary payments to officials spawned corruption and maladministration.

Popular dissatisfactions with the government continued to mount. In 1812 and 1813, nearly 5 million peasants were said to have been on the verge of starvation, and many of them left their lands, some taking to the hills for "slash-and-burn" farming as *hwajŏnmin* ("fire-field people"), others trekking into Manchuria and still others joining gangs of bandits. The government's ineptness in mitigating the grievances of the people resulted in frequent local riots.

The general situation prevented an accumulation of domestic capital. Artisans and businessmen, catering traditionally to the needs of the upper classes, were unable to earn a decent livelihood. Exchange of goods was carried on by peddlers in the countryside on a barter basis. Hindered further by technological backwardness, the country was woefully ill-prepared to resist foreign economic penetration.

This social background fostered the development, early in the 17th century, of an intellectual and social movement known as Sirhak ("Practical Learning"), a school of Confucian thought. This new movement was inspired by the "School of Han Learning," developed by the Ch'ing scholars of China who had insisted that "search for evidence" should constitute the basis of true scholarship. The Sirhak concepts were championed by a group of discontented scholars who were chafing at their long subjection to governmental discriminations. The new thought was influenced also by what was then known as Sohak ("Western Learning"), which Koreans equated with Christianity and Western scientific knowledge. The Sirhak followers advocated that the entire range of human problems be approached from a practical angle. The new movement was, in effect, a revolt against the Chu Hsi school of Confucianism and was supported by officials of lower ranks, ex-officials, and commoners. Without official sponsorship, however, the Sirhak failed to bring about any political or social reform. Nonetheless, the movement helped to sow the seeds of intellectual awakening and contributed a number of pioneering studies in medicine, geography, mineralogy, agriculture, botany, and mapmaking. Several encyclopedias dealing with these subjects were also written at the time (see ch. 10, Artistic and Intellectual Expression).

In the early 17th century, Catholicism also reached the country by way of the Jesuit mission in China and spread slowly through to reform-minded Sirhak scholars and the socially oppressed commoner and despised classes. In a Confucian-oriented society, however, Catholicism was regarded by those in power as heretical and even dangerous. They believed that the acceptance of this "Western Learning" would at once endanger the whole fabric of Confucianism because of the Christian refusal to sanction the Confucian customs of ancestor worship. In 1786 a government ban of the Christian movement was followed by ruthless and systematic persecutions. Fear of Catholicism apparently was accentuated by association of "Western Learning" with the Occidental powers which had begun to threaten Korea as well as China.

Power Politics and Resistance

Beginning in the first decade of the 19th century, an increasing number of foreign vessels seeking trade appeared in Korean waters. But Korea, as a dependent state of China, was unprepared to conduct foreign relations independently. Furthermore, Korea was greatly alarmed because China, regarded as the traditional protector, fountainhead of order, and symbol of honor and civilization, had been harassed by "Western barbarians," especially after the Opium War of 1839–42. As a result, Korea sought refuge in a policy of seclusion. Internal affairs were marked by a vigorous persecution of Christians. In 1866 alone, upwards of 13,000 Catholic converts were executed.

Japan was the first to break down the seclusion barriers. Seizing upon the traditional Chinese attitude of noninterference in Korean internal affairs, and insisting that Korea was independent, Japan made skillful use of the Western concept of sovereign statehood to break the historical bond between China and Korea.

In 1875, a Japanese warship, while cruising in Korean waters, reportedly on a provocative mission, was fired upon by the Koreans. The Japanese Government, supported by force, demanded reparations and a treaty of amity and commerce, which was signed on February 26, 1876. The most important clause of the treaty was a declaration that "Korea, being an independent state, enjoys the same sovereign rights as Japan."

Quick to recognize the imminent danger of losing her vassal

41

state to Japan, China then attempted to counter Japanese influence in Korea by widening the country's external contacts. In 1882, Korea signed a treaty with the United States, negotiated through China's good offices, giving the United States trade privileges. Similar treaties were concluded with Great Britain and Germany (1883), Italy and Russia (1884), and France (1886). Each treaty was accompanied by a letter from the Korean king enunciating his dependency on China.

Internally, the Korean court was divided into a conservative faction and a group of young reformists favoring modernization along Occidental lines. In time, these factions aligned themselves into conservative pro-Chinese and progressive pro-Japanese groups, later joined by a third, pro-Russian faction. Meanwhile, the outside powers attempted to exploit the internal schism to their respective advantages and, likewise, the domestic factions allied themselves with outsiders for selfish ends. This situation was most pronounced during the period from 1876 to 1910, marked by frequent shifts in Korean cabinets, each with different foreign orientations.

In this context, the German Consul-General to Seoul in 1885 proposed a scheme for permanent neutrality for the country, but he was rebuffed by the Korean court, apparently because of adverse reactions from other foreign powers concerned.

A popular antiforeign rebellion in 1894 had far-reaching consequences for the nation. Spearheaded by a new indigenous religious movement called Tonghak (literally, "Eastern Learning") as distinguished from Sŏhak (Western Learning) and Catholicism, the Tonghak movement was essentially nationalistic and supported major social and political reforms. Founded in 1860 by Ch'oe Che-u, a scholar of a formerly wealthy noble family, the new sect had been inspired by certain acceptable features from Buddhism, Confucianism, Taoism, and Catholicism itself. The movement was supported largely by peasants, despised classes, discontented scholars and ex-officials (see ch. 11, Religion; ch. 14, Political Dynamics).

The government, apparently unable to cope with the widespread Tonghak rebellion of 1894, requested aid from China. Japan immediately countered by sending a large detachment of troops to Seoul on the pretext of protecting Japanese interests. The result was the Sino-Japanese War of 1894–95, which ended in easy victory for the Japanese. China was then forced to renounce its claim to Korean suzerainty once and for all; the independence of Korea was then "guaranteed" by Japan. Thereafter, rivalry for influence in Korea was reduced to two contestants, Japan and Russia.

Reform of 1894

The Reform of July 1894, prompted in part by the Tonghak rebellion, represents one of the most significant events in the modernizing of Korea. Some of the reform measures struck at the very fabric of Korean society, and, despite vigorous conservative opposition at the outset, they helped to bring about important changes in the country's political, economic, and social life.

The Reform was masterminded by Japanese authorities who readily secured collaboration from a pro-Japanese cabinet. Salient features of the Reform included: (1) Renunciation of Korea's Confucian dependency on China and assertion of sovereign independence; (2) separation of the Royal Household from the affairs of state; (3) reorganization of executive functions into various departments, namely, home affairs, foreign affairs, finance, military affairs, justice, education, industry and agriculture-commerce; (4) elimination of discriminatory practices against the military; (5) outlawing of all forms of discrimination against the non-noble classes; (6) further social measures such as emancipation of public and private slaves, legalization of widow remarriage, ban on early marriage, and prohibition of traffic in human beings; (7) discontinuation of extending punitive practices to the family and relatives of a convicted criminal; (8) separation of judicial functions from the executive departments, the institution of an independent court system, and the creation of a police bureau as an adjunct of the Department of Home Affairs; (9) removal of occupational restrictions imposed on former officials; (10) abolition of the Confucian-oriented examination system and the adoption of a merit-recruitment system irrespective of social status; (11) adoption of a silver standard for currency and the metric system for measurements; (12) organization of banks and business corporations; and (13) institution of a new taxation system based on cash payment rather than in kind. The Reform also called for "modernization" of the army under Japanese supervision, but there were no provisions for strengthening the nation's military potential.

These sweeping changes were immediately followed by the institution of a new school system, the opening of postal services, adoption of a solar calendar system, and expansion of the number of provinces from 8 to 13. In December 1894, a 14-point constitution, Korea's first, which embodied the spirit of the Reform, was promulgated by the king mainly as a code of official conduct in government (see ch. 13, The Governmental System).

The immediate beneficiary of these changes, aside from the pro-Japanese reformists, was the Japanese government itself. The Reform, in effect, helped to pave the way for a slow disintegration of the powerful conservative forces, which had turned to the Russians in an effort to counter the growing Japanese influence.

Russo-Japanese Rivalry

Since the acquisition of Manchurian coastal areas known as the Maritime Province from a weak and troubled China in 1860, Russian territory had adjoined the northeastern tip of Korea for 11 miles along the Tumen River (see ch. 2, Physical Environment). With the dominance of the pro-Russian faction between 1896 and 1904, Russia secured valuable timber concessions along the south bank of the Yalu River and on the Island of Ullŭng in the Sea of Japan. Other concessions included mining rights in the northeastern corner of North Hamgyŏng province and rights to link the Seoul-Wŏnsan telegraph line with that of Siberia. In addition, Russia prevailed upon the Korean Government to reorganize its army along Russian lines with weapons and military advisers sent from Moscow. A Russian named K. Alekseyev was appointed as "financial adviser" to the court, and in time he became the *de facto* Minister of Finance. A Russo-Korean bank was also established.

The Russian example quickly set off a chain reaction among foreign concession seekers representing Japan, Great Britain, Germany, France, and the United States. Moving quickly, Japan, late in the 1890's, in alliance with Great Britain (which was then on hostile terms with Russia over Persia, Afghanistan, and Tibet), foiled the Russian attempt to secure Mokp'o and Masan on the Korea Strait as the naval bases for its Far Eastern fleet, thus successfully blocking further Russian penetration. In 1903 Russia unsuccessfully attempted to divide Korea at the 39th parallel, offering to recognize the preeminent position of Japan in the southern half of the peninsula in return for Japanese consent to transform the northern half into a "buffer zone."

This rivalry contributed to the outbreak of the Russo-Japanese War of 1904 which ended with Russia's defeat in 1905. The Treaty of Portsmouth (New Hampshire), signed on September 5, obliged Russia to accept Japan's "paramount political, military, and economic interests" in Korea, and thus paved the way for Japan's formal annexation of Korea as a colony in August 1910. The Treaty of Annexation, signed by Korea with Japan on August 22, 1910, also awarded titles of nobility to important pro-Japanese collaborators. Yi Wan-yong, then Prime Minister, who had signed the Treaty, has since been regarded as a symbol of treason.

National Awakening

Beginning in the last quarter of the 19th century, large numbers of political, cultural, and religious groups emerged, mainly to awaken the "voiceless masses" to the country's imminent danger of dismemberment by foreign powers.

Most prominent politically was the activity of an Independence Club (1896–99), led by a group of Western-oriented intellectuals.

Inspired largely by Protestant missions from the United States and Canada, the Independence Club published Korea's first newspaper in English and Korean. It clamored for the assertion of national dignity and was, in fact, the prime mover behind the events which led to the abolition of the Russo-Korean bank and the withdrawal of Russian military and financial advisers.

In addition, many nationalist leaders founded schools and, wherever possible, formed quasi-educational societies along regional lines. All of these institutions encouraged the study of national history and culture and introduced Western history, dealing especially with the nationalist movement of other peoples. The Tan'gun myth of the legendary founder of Korea was revived in the form of Taejonggyo, literally, "Great Tan'gun Teaching." In addition, the antiforeign aspect of the Tonghak (Eastern Learning) movement was given added stress in 1906, when it was renamed Ch'ŏndogyo.

Meanwhile, the Christian missions vigorously pressed for a social reform movement. Through social work and their private hospitals, they attempted to reform the people by calling for such measures as an improvement in the status of women, the prohibition of alcoholic drinks, the adoption of monogamy, and the elimination of superstitious practices.

JAPANESE RULE (1910–45)

Korea was subjected by the Japanese colonial administration to systematic economic exploitation and political as well as cultural oppression. While the material condition of the country was substantially improved during the period, many of the resentful Korean people benefited little from the new political order. Under the colonial Government-General of Chosŏn (Chōsen Sōtokufu in Japanese), headed by a governor-general responsible directly to the Japanese emperor in Tokyo, the despotic behavior of the police and gendarmerie was especially pronounced.

Freedom of the press, political activities, and Korean cultural institutions were vigorously suppressed. An increasing number of Japanese immigrants (178,000 in 1910 increasing to 347,000 in 1919)—fishermen, farmers, officials, merchants, businessmen, and usurers—were brought in to take over the colonizing functions of the new administration. Most of the important administrative and managerial positions were given to Japanese immigrants. Health measures, harbors, roads, railroads, and communication facilities were improved, and a modern banking system was instituted. The Japanese administrators also carried out a systematic land survey program whereby much of the public and private land was taken over by the Japanese Government or sold to Japanese settlers.

Consequently, a large proportion of the farm population was severed from the lands they had tilled for generations; furthermore, the newly introduced system of paying taxes in cash subjected the farmers to the fluctuations of money economy, and many were forced to leave their lands. Some joined the "slash-and-burn" farmers, whose numbers increased from 246,000 in 1916 to nearly 700,000 in 1927. By 1921, over 600,000 farmers had moved into Manchuria and 158,000 to the Russian Far East. Between 1915 and 1925, some 126,000 Koreans migrated to Japan as wage earners. About 6,000 enterprising persons sought better fortunes in Hawaii and the United States. The new landholding system also affected some of the traditional landowners, who forfeited lands because of tax delinquency, but on the whole they were allowed to retain much of their old economic (though not political) status in return for their moral and political support of the Japanese colonial policy (see ch. 21, Labor Relations and Organization).

Independence Movement of 1919

Inspired largely by the enunciation of the doctrine of self-determination by President Woodrow Wilson in January 1918, the Korean people began to voice their demand for independence. Zealous Korean college students in Japan drafted a "Declaration of Independence," which was proclaimed in Seoul on March 1, 1919, by a group of 33 religious leaders (16 Christians, 15 Ch'ŏndogyo followers, and 2 Buddhists). This precipitated spontaneous, peaceful, nationwide demonstrations in which about 370,000 persons participated.

Although caught by complete surprise, the Japanese police and gendarmerie reacted quickly and ruthlessly suppressed the movement. According to Korean sources, the total casualties amounted to 6,670 killed, 16,000 wounded, and 19,525 arrested. Property damages included 75 Christian churches set on fire by the Japanese. In commemoration of this event, symbolic of the Korean struggle for independence, March 1 is celebrated each year as "Samil Undong II" (March 1, Independence Day).

The demonstrations had two major consequences: a modification of Japan's colonial policy and activation of an independence movement by Korean exiles abroad. The colonial administration ruled by the military since 1910 was reorganized in 1919, becoming somewhat more liberal under civilian leadership. A step toward local self-government on a limited scale was made. The Japanese encouraged the modernization of agricultural methods and the development of trade and industry. Consequently, the living standards of some Koreans benefited despite the general orientation of the economy to Japanese needs. In some instances, lower-class Koreans found that, with proper educational qualifications, the new developments had opened entirely new opportunities for advancement.

Nevertheless, the Japanese continued to deny the Koreans the advantage of association and experience with political and economic management and also subjected them to a policy of eradicating their cultural identity. Japanese Shintoism was introduced in schools; Confucianism was encouraged to exploit its traditional stress on loyalty to existing authority. The Korean language was forbidden in schools and there was an attempt to force Japanese surnames upon the people. Korean publications were banned, and the study of Korean history was actively discouraged.

This assimilation by force was especially evident after 1937 when the Sino-Japanese War broke out. Japan then stepped up its policy of imperialist expansion and began to gear the unified Korean economy to its war economy. Placing main emphasis on industrial development in the northern part of the country because of its rich hydroelectric power resources and its proximity to the growing industrial complex in southern Manchuria, Japan literally transformed the country into what they called a "continental logistical base." In time the peninsula became economically interdependent not only between the predominantly industrial northern half and the agricultural southern half but also between the peninsula as a single economic unit and Japan (see ch. 18, Character and Structure of the Economy).

In addition, Japan attempted to tap the country's manpower resources for war efforts by instituting a so-called "voluntary enlistment" system for the Koreans in 1937; in 1942, this system was changed to a conscription basis. Many Koreans who had served in the Japanese Army became the leadership core in the police and army after 1945 (see ch. 26, Public Order and Safety; ch. 27, The Armed Forces).

The second consequence of the 1919 demonstrations was the increase in the number of Koreans in exile who continued to champion the cause of Korean independence abroad. A "Korean Provisional Government" was organized at Shanghai in April 1919 with Syngman Rhee, who was then in the United States, as president. Emigrants were scattered in China, Manchuria, the United States, Japan, and in the Russian Far East. They carried on resistance and independence propaganda campaigns wherever they lived; in America some groups worked independently; in the Far East some were supported by Mao Tse-tung's Communist group at Yenan, or by Chiang Kai-shek's Nationalist Chinese Government at Chungking, while others operated as anti-Japanese partisans in southern Manchuria and in the Russian Far East, supported by the Bolshevik Russian Government.

Apart from the physical distance between these scattered Korean groups, they were also widely separated ideologically as to means of attaining independence. The age-old problem of factionalism, based mainly on regional and personal lines, continued to trouble their cause. Without a central clearing house for their activities, they held to diverse and irreconcilable ideas and political techniques as they confronted each other after World War II (see ch. 14, Political Dynamics).

At home, the resistance movement was carried on by all segments of the population. Students and intellectuals were particularly active. The first labor union movement was started in the early 1920's. The Korean Communist Party was formed in April 1925 in Seoul, but on Moscow's order it was disbanded in 1928 because of factional difficulties. A student uprising in 1929 reinforced the role of youth in the country's political scene. Lasting nearly 5 months and participated in by 54,000 students, the uprising was a manifestation of popular disaffection toward the Japanese (see ch. 14, Political Dynamics).

Cairo Declaration

The Korean question, formally closed with the annexation of the country by Japan in 1910, was reopened by the Cairo Declaration on December 1, 1943, when the United States, Great Britain, and China affirmed their determination to bring Japan, once defeated, back into its territorial limits existing prior to the Sino-Japanese War of 1894–95. The Declaration stated that the three signatory governments, "mindful of the enslavement of the people of Korea, are determined that in due course Korea shall become free and independent." At the Potsdam Conference of July 1945, the three powers reaffirmed the Cairo Declaration and further declared that "Japanese sovereignty shall be limited to the islands of Honshū, Hokkaidō, Kyūshu, and Shikoku and such minor islands as we shall determine." The Soviet Union announced its formal adherence to the Potsdam Declaration on August 8, 1945, in its declaration of war on Japan, thus raising to four the number of powers who had an interest in Korea's future.

POSTWAR OCCUPATION

By the time of the Japanese surrender on August 15, 1945, the only effective military powers in the Far East were the United States and the Soviet Union. At the initiative of the United States, these two agreed on a division of Korea at the 38th parallel as a temporary expedient for the sole purpose of accepting the surrender of Japanese forces then in the country. It was soon apparent, however, that the artificial division would be interpreted by the Soviet occupation authorities as creating a permanent delineation between two military zones.

48

The cessation of hostilities in 1945 found the Korean economy depleted. The Japanese had systematically exploited the country's material resources after hostilities began in 1941. During the last stages of the war, economic controls had broken down, currency was greatly inflated, and production had collapsed. The need for instituting orderly governmental processes was immediate.

After V-J Day a multitude of Korean exiles began to swarm back into the country—from China, Manchuria, the Russian Far East, Japan, and the United States. The Soviet Union was quick to make use of the returning exiles, particularly those who had settled in the Russian Far East and had become Soviet citizens. Korean Communists, in many cases trained to assume control in place of the Japanese, were introduced into the Soviet zone of occupation north of the 38th parallel. On August 25, 1945, the Soviet Command transferred the administrative powers of the Japanese government in its zone to provisional political committees, which were later consolidated into a central government bureau having jurisdiction over the five northern provinces.

On February 8, 1946, this bureau was replaced by a Provisional People's Committee, which served as an interim government. A veteran Korean Communist, Kim Il-sung, who had returned to P'yŏngyang with the Soviet occupation forces, headed an all-Korean "cabinet," which was dominated by the Communists. Those who expressed dissatisfaction with Communist dominance were purged. By mid-1946 a governmental structure had been created in northern Korea which would readily respond to Russian direction, even after the withdrawal of Soviet troops. In March 1946 the Provisional People's Committee expropriated all lands and "distributed" them to the peasantry. This seizure was followed by the nationalization of all but 10 percent of the industries in August 1946.

In the south, the primary mission of the United States Military Government, established in 1945, was to replace Japanese authority and to maintain order. While investigating the qualifications of Koreans for administrative work and political reliability, however, the Military Government temporarily retained the existing Japanese administration to facilitate the occupation.

In February 1947, in response to adverse Korean reactions, Koreans were placed in charge of governmental administration, with Americans in advisory capacities. The interim arrangement came to be known as the South Korean Interim Government.

The source of the greatest disappointment to the people was the announcement of the Moscow Agreement of December 27, 1945. The Agreement, worked out by representatives of the Soviet Union, Great Britain, and the United States, provided for a four-power (including China) trusteeship for a period of up to 5 years

49

"with a view to the reestablishment of Korea as an independent state." A Joint Commission, composed of representatives of the United States command in the south and the Soviet command in the north, was to be established to assist in forming a "provisional Korean democratic government," that would have jurisdiction over all of Korea.

Korean political leaders in the south launched a nationwide "anti-trusteeship movement," protesting the postponement of their independence. Only the Communist element in the country supported the plan—on Moscow's order—though initially they, too, opposed it. Thereafter, the political schism between right-wing and left-wing groups progressively widened.

The first main conference of the Joint Commission was held on March 20, 1946; on May 8, it adjourned indefinitely, unable to reach agreement on the components of the provisional government. The Soviet Union insisted that only those "Korean democratic parties and social organizations" which supported the Moscow declaration should be allowed to participate. This was unacceptable to the right-wing political groups, since it would have eliminated most of them and would have put the Communist faction in control in the south as well as in the north. The breakdown of negotiations for an agreement was used as pretext for waves of Communist-inspired strikes, riots, and demonstrations approaching open rebellion. The militant tactics of the Communists were countered by right-wing terrorism and suppressive action by the police.

To check further deterioration of internecine strife, the Commission met again on May 21, 1947, but failed to agree on any major issues. Meanwhile, repeated efforts, under American initiative, to develop a middle-of-the-road or coalition group as the basis for a strong, moderate political movement also proved unsuccessful. On September 17, 1947, the United States submitted the Korean problem to the United Nations.

On November 14, 1947, the General Assembly of the United Nations adopted, over the opposition of the Soviet Union, a resolution to the effect that elected representatives of the Korean people should establish the conditions of unification and determine their own form of government. A United Nations Temporary Commission on Korea (UNTCOK) was established to observe the elections. The Commission was not admitted to the northern zone. Elections were held on May 10, 1948, only in the southern zone, to fill 200 seats in a constituent assembly. One hundred additional seats were reserved for northern delegates until such time as free elections could be held there.

Following the adoption of a constitution on July 12, 1948, Syngman Rhee was elected as the first president. The establishment of the Republic of Korea was formally proclaimed on August 15, 1948, and by 1967, the new republic had been recognized by 81 countries. Theoretically, the authority of the government embraced the entire Korean peninsula (see ch. 13, The Governmental System).

The partition of a mutually complementary economic system into an industrial north and an agricultural south immediately created obstacles for speedy economic recovery and prosperity, especially in the Republic of Korea (see ch. 18, Character and Structure of the Economy). Moreover, the institution of two alien and mutually exclusive political systems quickly led to a multitude of problems for the Republic resulting mainly from lack of experience in government administration (for a complete history of the political state see ch. 14, Political Dynamics).

The new government was soon beset with internal disorders of major proportions. As early as April 1948 a large-scale Communist-inspired rebellion broke out on Cheju, an inland province situated about 50 miles off the southwestern trip of the peninsula. Beginning on October 19, 1948, a contingent of government troops at Yosu and Sunch'on, 80 miles west of Pusan, rebelled against the government while heading for counterinsurgency operations on that island.

THE KOREAN CONFLICT

Shortly after the elections of May 10, 1948, in the Republic of Korea, the United States began to prepare plans to withdraw American forces. In April 1949 the United States, believing that the capability of the Korean defense force warranted the withdrawal of United States troops in a matter of months, ordered a withdrawal, to begin in May, 1949. The last contingent departed on June 29, 1949. Before this contingent left arrangements were made to establish a Military Advisory Group of 500 officers and men. Two formal military agreements were signed and brought into force by the United States and the Republic of Korea on January 26, 1950. One was a military defense agreement. The other, retroactive to July 1, 1949, made provision for the Military Advisory Group mentioned above.

In the early morning of June 25, 1950 (Korean time), North Korean forces launched a sudden unprovoked full-scale attack against the Republic of Korea.

On that date, at the request of the United States, the United Nations Security Council was called into immediate session. At the time of aggression, the Soviet Union was boycotting the meetings of the Security Council—apparently assuming that the Council would not be able to function without Soviet representation. The Security Council called for an immediate cessation of hostilities and the withdrawal of Communist forces to positions north of the 38th parallel.

When this directive was ignored, the Council on June 27 asked the members of the United Nations to furnish military assistance to the Republic of Korea. In response to this request the United States and 15 other member nations (Australia, Belgium, Great Britain, Canada, Colombia, Ethiopia, France, Greece, Luxembourg, Netherlands, New Zealand, Philippines, Thailand, Turkey, and Union of South Africa) responded with military force of varying size. By September 5, 1950, Communist forces held most of the Korean peninsula, except for Pusan in the southeast. United Nations Forces counterattacked and by the end of the month had reached the 38th parallel. A request for the surrender of Communist forces was ignored.

On July 7, 1950, the Security Council asked the United States to designate a commander of all United Nations forces in Korea. On October 7, 1950, the United Nations General Assembly adopted a resolution recommending that all necessary acts be taken "for the establishment of a unified independent democratic government in the sovereign state of Korea." On October 9, acting on the implicit authority of the United Nations General Assembly, the Commanding General of the United Nations forces in Korea ordered the crossing of the 38th parallel. Within three weeks the United Nations forces approached the Manchurian border, reaching the Yalu River at several points. Subsequently, substantial Chinese forces, who had allegedly volunteered to defend the Yalu region, intervened in November, and by the end of June 1951, both sides had settled down roughly along the 38th parallel.

Negotiations, without a cease-fire, were instituted in the summer of 1951 to bring about agreement on the conditions of an armistice; they continued intermittently until July 27, 1953, when an armistice agreement was signed. The armistice, however, was not formally accepted by the government of the Republic of Korea. President Syngman Rhee had repeatedly refused a settlement which he claimed would not facilitate the unification of Korea under his government. On August 15, 1953, he once more expressed his goverment's "wish and determination to march north at the earliest possible time to save our North Korean brethren."

To reassure the government of the Republic of Korea and to deter any future Communist aggression, the United States concluded a Mutual Security Treaty with the Republic in October 1953. The treaty entered into force on November 1, 1954. It provided, among other things, for consultation and aid in case either was threatened with external armed attack.

The armistice agreement of July 1953 recommended that the

peaceful settlement of the Korean question be taken up at a high-level political conference. Subsequent conferences between the major powers, as well as discussions in the United Nations, have failed to produce an agreement.

With respect to the problem of Korean reunification, the position of the Republic of Korea is that reunification should be achieved by general elections in accordance with UN resolutions and under UN supervision. In a press conference in 1966 President Park said that it was inconceivable that any ROK government would think of discussing unification with the present North Korean leadership. He did not believe that there could be full-fledged debate on the subject before the late 1970s, when the current North Korean regime would probably have been replaced. In another statement made later in 1966 the President also emphasized that discussions would not take place for another decade and emphasized the need for economic self-sufficiency and modernization to prepare for meaningful consideration of unification.

The North Korean regime refuses to recognize either the competence or the authority of the United Nations in the Korean question. The regime's declared aim is to reunite the peninsula under Communist rule and to this end it encourages subversive activities against the government of the Republic of Korea.

The unwillingness of the Communist side to accept the United Nations as the responsible agency of supervision in any steps toward unification, particularly its insistence on the right of veto over the unification process, proved to be the major obstacle to an acceptable settlement of the Korean problem. The Communists not only refused to recognize the role of the United Nations in bringing about a settlement, but branded the United Nations itself a belligerent.

In the course of the fighting, the peninsula suffered unprecedented devastation and misery. Beyond the problem of recovery lay the prospect of indefinite division of the country; a prospect which few Koreans were prepared to accept.

THE REPUBLIC OF KOREA SINCE THE ARMISTICE

The history of the Republic of Korea since the end of the Korean conflict can be divided into two periods, a period of political unrest and reconstruction, which lasted into the early 1960's, and a period of relative political stability and rapid economic development thereafter, continuing into 1968.

After the end of the Korean conflict, the tasks facing the Republic of Korea were overpowering. The country had suffered major economic and human losses presenting a huge task of reconstruction. The southern area, already densely populated, was flooded with refugees from the north. Economic misery was widespread. During this period, large United Nations and United States foreign aid programs provided assistance for relief and reconstruction.

Following the Korean conflict the government was under the control of Syngman Rhee and his Liberal Party. Rhee lost the confidence of the people in this period. In 1960, he was returned to office by an 87.5 percent majority, but it was later established that the election had not been fairly conducted. A revolution then occurred, sparked by student demonstrations throughout the country and passively supported by military leaders. Rhee was forced to resign. This revolt is now referred to as the April 19 "Students' Revolution." A caretaker government assumed power and new elections were set for late in 1960. Chang Myŏn (Dr. John Chang) was elected president. While Chang promised sweeping reforms, his administration was handicapped by many of the shortcomings of the Rhee regime. Recognizing these problems, a small group of military leaders led by Major General Park Chung Hee initiated a successful *coup d'état* in May 1961. This group, which later called itself the Supreme Council for National Reconstruction (SCNR), suspended democratic processes but promised a return to constitutional government in 1963. In the interim, the SCNR attempted to eliminate malpractice in the government, and conducted a wholesale removal of government officials. Elections were held in 1963, and Park Chung Hee, who had retired from the military to be eligible for election, was a candidate for the presidency. He was elected, although by a close margin. However, President Park was reelected in 1967 by a solid majority.

Since the early 1960's, the Republic of Korea has experienced remarkable economic growth and political stability despite serious problems of inflation, lagging production of foodstuffs, occasional student unrest, and Communist provocations from the north. The country's reliance on direct foreign economic support is gradually decreasing as foreign investors avail themselves of opportunities to develop manufacturing activities. By means of long-term borrowing from international development agencies, the government has been able to make substantial progress in upgrading and expanding the country's transportation, communication, power, and irrigation systems. Notable progress has also been made in improving living conditions for many through public health and education programs, which have had the participation of a large number of private foreign relief organizations. Problems of inadequate housing, malnutrition, and unemployment resist quick solution, however, because of the rapid rates of population growth and migration of rural people to urban centers.

CHAPTER 4

POPULATION AND LABOR FORCE

The Republic of Korea supports a large population in a land of limited resources. The average population density is 768 per square mile. With only 23 percent of the total area under cultivation, the population density per square mile of cultivated land is 3,803.

Between 1944 and 1966, there was a net increase of over 13 million people, or almost 84 percent. In 1966, when the last complete census was taken, the population stood at 29,207,856 and was increasing at the rate of about 2.8 percent per year. Since then, however, the rate of natural increase has been declining steadily and rapidly to about 2.4 percent. Growth has been uneven and includes significant effects of migrations: Koreans returning from Japan afer World War II and refugees from the north crossing the 38th parallel or the Demarcation Line.

A large proportion of the population is engaged in agriculture, and the work required in this activity is highly seasonal. To a limited extent the agricultural labor force engages in handicraft production during the period of seasonal inactivity in agriculture. The nonagricultural labor force represents a small but increasing proportion of the total as manufacturing and other nonagricultural sectors progress.

POPULATION STRUCTURE

The population in the late 1960's was essentially homogeneous, with only 33,666 non-Koreans reported in the 1966 census. Although there was a large Japanese population in Korea for a time, almost all of these people have been repatriated.

The population has always been concentrated in the more fertile lowlands, especially on the western and southern coastal plains and on the narrow strips of land along the streams. The largest province, North Kyŏngsang Province, is the most heavily populated, having over 15 percent of the national population, but the other southern and western provinces are also heavily populated (see table 4). The population is almost evenly divided between the sexes, there being slightly more males than females. In the "special cities" of Seoul and Pusan there are more females than males,

Table 4. Population of the Republic of Korea,
by Major Political Subdivisions, 1966

	Population	Percentage Distribution
City of Seoul	3,805,261	13.0
City of Pusan	1,429,726	4.9
Kyŏnggi Province	3,107,228	10.6
Kangwŏn Province	1,832,432	6.3
North Ch'ungch'ŏng Province	1,550,475	5.3
South Ch'ungch'ŏng Province	2,913,348	10.0
North Chŏlla Province	2,523,708	8.6
South Chŏlla Province	4,052,429	13.9
North Kyŏngsang Province	4,479,004	15.3
South Kyŏngsang Province	3,177,551	10.9
Cheju Province	336,694	1.2
Total	29,207,856	100.0

Source: Adapted from Republic of Korea, Economic Planning Board, Bureau of
Research and Statistics, *Preliminary Population Count of the Simplified Census*, 1966, pp. 8, 9.

but only in Cheju Province, the island province south of the mainland, is there a serious disproportion, with about 10 percent more
females than males (see ch. 13, The Governmental System).

The population includes a high proportion of young persons. In
1965, persons under 20 years of age made up 52 percent of the
total; those between 21 and 40 years of age made up an additional
28 percent, and those over 40 constituted the remainder. The cities
have a slightly higher proportion of people in the working age group
of 20 to 40 and somewhat fewer numbers among the young and
the old.

POPULATION DYNAMICS

Growth of the Population

The growth of population in the Republic of Korea while rapid,
has proceeded at an erratic rate (see table 5). Prior to 1944,
growth rates for all of Korea ranged around 1.5 percent per year.
The low rate is explained by relatively high mortality rates and
much emigration during the Japanese occupation. With the conclusion of World War II there was an extensive repatriation of Koreans living abroad, as well as of Japanese living in Korea. At the
same time there occurred a considerable influx of refugees from
the north. Most of the explosive growth in the Republic of Korea
between 1944 and 1949 is attributable to migrations of peoples.
Natural growth rates are estimated at around 2 percent per year.
During the period 1949–1955, perhaps 1,000,000 casualties resulted from the Korean conflict, a loss which was largely offset by
the number of refugees moving south. The more peaceful conditions prevailing since 1955 have resulted in a rapid increase in

Table 5. *Population Increase in the Republic of Korea, 1944–1966*

Census year	Population	Increase over previous census year	Average annual rate of increase (in percent)
1944	15,879,110	—	—
1949	20,188,641	4,309,531	5.43
1955	21,526,374	1,337,733	1.11
1960	24,989,241	3,462,867	3.22
1966	29,207,856	4,218,615	2.81

Source: Adapted from Bank of Korea, *Economic Statistics Yearbook, 1968*, p. 6.

population. With growth rates approximately 2.8 percent per year prevailing in the mid-1960's, projections of the Republic's 1980 population have ranged upward from the 40 million level. Such growth in population indicates that any increase in industrial or agricultural productivity is immediately absorbed and contributes little toward raising the standard of living or reducing unemployment. An abrupt reversal of the rising rate of natural increase appears to have taken place in the late 1960's as a result of intensive and extensive programs to limit the number of children born.

Mobility Among Koreans

Remarkable internal and external migrations have occurred during the 20th Century. Millions of people have moved about within the country and to and from foreign lands in response to changing economic and political pressures. Migrants have been primarily young men, and the impact of their movements has been felt in almost all aspects of Korean life.

Throughout the history of Korea, the population has been concentrated in the south, and the distribution of population has reflected the opportunities available to a predominantly agricultural people. During the period of Japanese rule the creation of economic opportunities in the growing industrial cities led to a movement of people into these cities from the surrounding rural areas. The accelerated exploitation of the power, fuel, and mineral resources of what is now North Korea intensified the rural-urban movements during the later years of Japanese control. By 1944, somewhat more than a third of Korea's population lived in the north, the result of a widespread movement of southerners into the growing heavy industrial complex that had arisen in the north.

After the partition of 1945, this northward trend was abruptly reversed. Official Republic of Korea estimates of the north-to-south migration between 1945 and 1950 range from 657,000 to 829,886, but other sources have estimated the numbers as high as 2 million, reflecting estimates of the many refugees who crossed the 38th parallel at points where they could not be registered. The population movement to the south increased when the Korean conflict broke out in 1950; during the course of hostilities millions of Koreans were pushed back and forth before the advancing and retreating armies. Perhaps a million former northern residents have remained in the south in the aftermath of that war. The precise number of refugees from the north will probably never be determined, but in conjunction with the natural increase, and repatriation from abroad, the net effect was to increase the population concentration in the south. By 1966, the Republic of Korea had 70 percent of the total population of the Korean peninsula.

Emigration and Repatriation

Large-scale emigration from the Korea peninsula began around 1904 and continued until the flow was reversed at the end of World War II. During the years of Japanese domination many Koreans left their homeland to escape Japanese rule (see ch. 3, Historical Setting). Migrants from the north tended to go to Manchuria, China, or Soviet Siberia, while those from the south were more apt to go to Hawaii or the continental United States.

Increasing population pressure and decreasing economic opportunities led many Koreans, especially from the south, to emigrate to Japan. Many others moved to Japan as conscripted unskilled labor for use in Japanese industry. In the early 1940's, there was a net outward movement of Koreans amounting to 140,000 per year. In 1944, it was estimated that there were 1.5 million Koreans in Japan, almost as many in Manchuria, and about 170,000 in Soviet Siberia.

Between the end of World War II and the spring of 1948, a million or more Koreans were reported to have returned from Japan. The great majority of them settled in south Korea, particularly in South Kyŏngsang Province and North Kyŏngsang Province, many in the cities. Perhaps as many as 351,000 returnees went to north Korea.

Urbanism

When Japan took control in 1910, only 11 cities had more than 14,000 inhabitants, and only 4.4 percent of the population was classed as urban. The small cities were primarily administrative centers inhabited chiefly by political leaders, government administrators and their staffs and a few tradesmen and professional people. Since 1910, most of these cities, notably Seoul, have grown enormously, and new cities have appeared at rail junctions and harbors and at mine and industrial sites. By 1966, the Republic of Korea had 14 cities with more than 100,000 population and an additional 18 cities with populations in excess of 50,000. Almost one-third of the people lived in these 32 cities. Pusan was approaching 1.5 million in 1966 and has since exceeded that figure. Seoul, which

Table 6. Major Cities of the Republic of Korea,
Population as of October 1966

City	Population
Seoul	3,805,261
Pusan	1,429,726
Taegu	847,949
Inch'ŏn	528,949
Kwangju	404,459
Taejŏn	315,830
Chŏnju	220,944
Mokpo	162,491
Masan	155,103
Suwŏn	128,352
Ch'ŏngju	124,091
Chinju	107,253
Kunsan	102,829
Ch'unch'ŏn	100,294

Source: Adapted from Republic of Korea, Economic Planning Board, Bureau
of Research and Statistics, *Preliminary Population Count of the
Simplified Census,* 1966, pp. 8, 9.

was growing rapidly in 1966 when its population was 3.8 million,
had an estimated population of 4.1 million in October of 1966 (see
table 6).

During the 1950's and 1960's the Republic of Korea experienced
very rapid urban growth. The major reasons for this migration to
the cities lie in the economic problems of an overpopulated rural
environment, although the expanding opportunities of the growing
cities have been a powerful attraction. For the vast bulk of the
farming people the harvest period signals the end of productive
employment during the year, and supplementary employment is
grossly inadequate. This lack of opportunity during a portion of
the year encourages many people to leave the farming areas.

In an overpopulated rural environment the opportunities for the
landless are particularly restricted. Consequently, the destruction
of property and the social disintegration of the rural community
during the Korean conflict coupled with the political insecurity
that followed, forced many people out of the rural areas. For similar reasons the bulk of the returnees from abroad and the refugees
from north Korea settled in the cities, to a large extent in Seoul.
Much of the migration into the cities was from the immediately
surrounding agricultural areas. People living close to the city can
seek employment there during the agricultural slack period without severing their ties to the security of a farm-based family. If
steady employment is found, permanent city residence often results.

Those who are skilled or well educated find their opportunities
much better in the cities than outside of them. This was certainly

a factor which led the returnees to reside in the cities, including men discharged from the Korean Armed Forces. Advanced and technical education is almost exclusively available in the cities and has become a powerful attraction in a society which traditionally has viewed education as the primary way out of a lifetime of manual labor.

POPULATION PROBLEMS AND ATTITUDES

The Republic of Korea emerged from the Japanese occupation and the Korean conflict as an overpopulated country. With peaceful conditions restored, the combination of a dropping death rate and a continuing high birth rate has engendered a rapidly rising level of population, which is in excess of the support capability of Korean resources (see table 7). Agricultural output is being increased by improved methods of farming and by bringing new land under cultivation. Industrial development is being vigorously attempted, and the rapidly growing cities are absorbing some of the excess rural population. Large-scale efforts to limit fertility began in 1962.

There are many traditional aspects of Korean culture which lead to high birth rates. The awareness of lineage and ties with the past commonly related to ancestor worship combine to produce large families to assure continuation of the lineage. The Confucian ethic and the precise recognition of obligations which permeate a Korean society reinforce these duties toward the preservation of family lines. The equation of adulthood with marriage promotes early engagements, and after marriage a woman's status, particularly within the household, improves markedly when she becomes a mother. In the context of a static, parochial, and highly localized village culture, the masses of Koreans have traditionally seen their greatest significance in life in terms of the family, and they tend to equate happiness with the oft quoted "marriage and many children".

Table 7. Vital Statistics in the Republic of Korea
(per thousand)

Year	Birth	Death	Natural Increase
1910–1914	24.0	14.6	9.4
1915–1919	31.5	24.3	7.2
1920–1924	34.2	21.3	12.9
1925–1929	37.5	21.9	15.6
1930–1934	32.8	20.1	12.7
1935–1939	32.1	18.7	13.4
1940–1944	34.7	18.9	15.8
1960–1965	40.6	12.2	28.4
1966	35.0	10.0	25.0

Source: Adapted from Republic of Korea, Manpower Development Research Institute, *Handbook of Manpower Statistics*, 1968, p. 34.

Information on contraception is widely available. Clinical records quoted in early 1965 indicated that 25 to 30 percent of the women of Seoul were aware of contraceptive techniques but that only 7 percent of the rural women were so informed. Rural isolation is a strong factor in retarding the spread of ideas, in reenforcing conservative attitudes, and in lack of access to modern medical facilities. Attitudes are, however, changing. A study published in 1963 indicated that, while people in Seoul married at ages several years beyond those being married in farming communities, parents in both rural and urban communities felt that their children should delay their marriages for several years beyond the age at which they themselves married.

The rate of natural increase in 1962 was a record 2.9 percent but since then has been declining steadily and rapidly. The family planning program is meeting with remarkable success, and the target is a rate of increase under 2 percent in the early 1970's.

STRUCTURE AND DYNAMICS OF THE LABOR FORCE

The dominance of agriculture and a seasonal fluctuation in employment characterize the Korean labor force. Employment reaches its peak in late spring and early summer when the fields are prepared and planted. Once these tasks have been accomplished, the need for women in agriculture drops sharply; and most women simply remove themselves from the labor force and seek no further work. Men, on the other hand, continue to be employed in agriculture until the harvest—although at a slightly lower level than during the early summer. Although a relative few accept idleness during the summer, most of those no longer needed in agriculture obtain employment in nonagricultural activities. During the winter increased employment outside of agriculture absorbs a small part of the surplus labor, but the bulk of it, both male and female, is idle. Technically, these people are not unemployed (seeking work) but are temporarily removed from the active labor force.

The seasonality of employment varies among the several occupational and industrial classes, with the largest seasonal fluctuation occurring among farmers (see table 8). To a considerable extent these people turn to handicraft production in the winter. In 1964, the last year in which agricultural handicraft employment was officially reported separately from all agricultural employment, the number of people engaged in handicraft increased from 20,000 in June to 1,233,000 in December. In all of the nonagricultural industries and virtually all occupational categories, employment is at its highest in the winter—off-peak season for agricultural employment.

During 1967, the number of people engaged in agriculture ranged from a high of 6.6 million at the June survey period to a low of 2.6 million in December. Although it might seem that a large pool of labor would be available during the off-season for other employment, mobility is low, especially for women with obligations in the home. Many of the men have off-season chores in farm operations that require their occasional presence, and alternative employment must be seasonal so that the peak labor demands of agriculture can be met.

The nonagricultural labor force, which is seasonally much more stable than the agricultural, averaged 4 million people during 1967. There were 2.4 million wage and salary earners and 1.6 million others, mainly self-employed. Many of the latter were engaged in marginal activities, such as street vending or minor personal services, in the absence of more suitable employment opportunities. The reservoir of manpower to supply the growing industrialization consists of these marginally employed people, the unemployed (the 1967 average was 590,000, or 6.2 percent of the average labor force), and rural people moving to the cities and industrial areas. The Economic Planning Board of Korea has estimated the net annual increase in the labor force to be 286,000 workers.

Men outnumber women in the labor force at nearly all age levels and in both farm and nonfarm households. There is a preponder-

Table 8. Labor Force of the Republic of Korea, by Economic Sector, 1967
(in thousands)

	March	June	September	December
Employed	8,294	10,397	9,733	7,233
Unemployed	704	557	545	555
Economically active	8,998	10,954	10,278	7,788
Economically inactive	8,142	6,195	6,910	9,413
Total population 14 years and over	17,140	17,149	17,188	17,201
Sector*				
Agriculture, forestry, and logging	4,259	6,612	5,342	2,614
Hunting and fishing	202	139	237	293
Mining and quarrying	89	94	99	100
Manufacturing	960	903	1,116	1,191
Construction	267	234	274	281
Public utilities	19	26	32	34
Commerce	1,059	970	1,165	1,208
Transport, storage, and communication	170	181	205	211
Government service	331	318	264	278
Other service	938	920	999	1,023

*Breakdown of employed persons.

Source: Adapted from Republic of Korea, *Economic Statistical Yearbook, 1968,* pp. 242, 243.

ance of men in the 25-to-44-year age groups, more so among non-farm households, where the concentration exceeds 60 percent of the total, than among farm households. Non-farm women in their childbearing and child-raising years are not in the labor force in very large numbers, unlike women in farm households who tend to work despite their family obligations.

In 1967, agricultural activities in general occupied over 50 percent, on the average, of all the employed persons in the Republic of Korea. Almost 90 percent of the employed persons living in farm households were thus engaged. Most of the others were employed in manufacturing, commerce, and services. In non-farm households, services, and commerce and, to a lesser extent, manufacturing accounted for most of the employed persons. Males dominated all of the industries, but a relatively higher proportion of females was employed in agricultural activities of all kinds and in manufacturing, commerce, and services than in other industries. Women found little employment in government service, which was 93 percent staffed by men.

The labor force has been characterized as having a capacity for sustained work, a receptivity to training and new methods, and an attainment of high levels of skill. Education and training facilities are extensive. In recent years increasing stress has been placed on vocational training, and higher education has begun to shift away from its traditional emphasis on the liberal arts in favor of science and engineering (see ch. 9, Education). In addition to the graduates of vocational and technical schools and institutes, there are roughly 175,000 to 200,000 servicemen discharged annually from the armed forces, many of whom have received training in skills applicable to industrial employment. Since 1966, the United Nations Development Fund has assisted the Office of Labor Affairs of the Ministry of Health and Social Affairs in an expanded program of institutional and in-plant skill training.

CHAPTER 5

ETHNIC GROUPS AND LANGUAGES

ETHNIC GROUPS

Koreans

Koreans form a single ethnic group, with common physical characteristics, language, culture, and feeling of unity. Regional variations exist in culture, for example, dialects. There are also physical characteristics; for example, people in the extreme south, including Cheju Island, tend to be slightly darker and shorter than their northern counterparts. These differences are insignificant, however, in light of the overwhelming similarities among Koreans and their feeling that they are one people. Such homogeneity has spared Koreans from various problems traditionally arising from a multiplicity of ethnic groups and physical types.

A study of the blood types of Asians reveals that the Korean people form a group separate from other Asian ethnic groups but that they have a blood type similar to that of such northern Asian groups as the Tunguses, Manchurians, Mongolians, and Japanese. In terms of length and width of skull, the Korean is closely related to the Japanese, Chinese, Manchurians, Mongolians, and Indonesians. In general, there are no great physical dissimilarities among the Chinese, Japanese, or Korean nationalities. Korean males are usually said to be slightly taller than Japanese males and slightly shorter than northern Chinese, and they have strong physiques and constitutions. Also, Koreans have lighter skin and hair than either the Chinese or Japanese.

Other Groups

When Korea was liberated from Japan in 1945, it was estimated that about 80,000 Chinese, three-fourths of whom were males, were scattered throughout the country. Most were small-businessmen (shopkeepers, restauranteurs, merchants, tradesmen) who dealt with the Koreans only for business purposes and maintained separate residential areas, schools, and clubs. As of 1968, 90 percent of the 33,845 non-Korean residents in the Republic of Korea were Chinese.

At the end of World War II, there were about 900,000 Japanese living in Korea, primarily in the large cities where they held the more important positions in government and business. By the end of 1945, however, almost all Japanese had been repatriated.

LANGUAGE

Korean

The Korean language, indigenous to the entire peninsula, is spoken by all Koreans. It is generally considered to be unrelated to any particular language family. Many Korean linguists believe it belongs to one of the group of tongues originating in the Altaic Mountain region of Central Asia, along with Turkish, Mongolian, and Tungu of Siberia, but some Western scholars link Korean to the Japanese language. It is estimated that, as a result of long-continued Chinese cultural influence, approximately 52 percent of the Korean vocabulary has been borrowed from the Chinese and 3 percent is made up of foreign words other than Chinese.

Korean Dialects

Six main dialects are spoken on the peninsula: Kyŏngsang, Chŏlla, Cheju, Hamgyŏng, P'yŏngyang, and the Central Region dialect; within the Central Region there are four subdialects: Kyŏnggi, Ch'unch'ŏng, Hwanghae, and Kangwŏn. Of these the P'yŏngyang and Hamgyŏng dialects are spoken in the north. The Kyŏnggi and Kangwŏn subdialects are spoken by the people in the areas immediately north and south of the 38th parallel. Names correspond to the provinces in which they represent the principal tongue, and provincial accents can have a socially stigmatizing effect (see ch. 17, Political Values and Attitudes).

The Cheju Island dialect presents the only real difficulty in mutual understanding; the origin of the dialect has not been conclusively established. Now as in the past, the highest prestige has been accorded the pronunciation characteristic of the Kyŏnggi subdialect, particularly of Seoul.

Foreign Languages

Between 1910 and 1945, the Japanese colonial government attempted the total Japanization of the Koreans. Among the first tasks was a program to encourage Koreans to learn and speak Japanese. After 1938, only Japanese was used in the schools, and the teaching of Korean was gradually prohibited. In 1964 an estimated 10 to 15 percent of the total population spoke Japanese fluently; because of geographic proximity, Kyŏngsang province had the greatest proportion of those who could speak Japanese. The impact of Japanese educational influence over Koreans was revealed by the fact that, among males over 35 years of age, the percentage of persons speaking Japanese was perhaps as high as 50 to 60 percent in 1964.

Although the compulsory education system under the Japanese in general was not rejected by the Koreans, the enforced use of the Japanese language was greatly resented, and Japanese was rarely used outside of the classroom. With the liberation of Korea in 1945 and repatriation of the Japanese, use of the Japanese language ended; hence, most persons who began their formal education since 1945 do not understand Japanese.

After 1945, Korean was made the official language in the entire peninsula. English became the secondary language in the south; during the late 1960's virtually all middle and high school students were learning the language (see ch. 9, Education). English language instruction was poor initially, but it is improving under the impetus of such organizations as the Foreign Language Institute, which was established in 1953 by the United Nations Korean Reconstruction Agency (UNKRA) and taken over in 1960 by the United Nations Educational, Scientific, and Cultural Organization (UNESCO). This Institute is preparing students to study abroad and is attempting to improve the teaching materials and techniques in the schools. In addition, a great number of private institutes are engaged in teaching English.

Writing and Literacy

About the middle of the 15th century, a phonetic alphabet, originally called *hunminjŏngŏŏm*—literally, the right sounds to teach the people—but now referred to as *han'gŭl*, was developed at the instigation of King Sejong. Two principles were applied in devising the form of vowels and consonants: consonants symbolize the organs of speech and vowels symbolize heaven, earth, and man—the three elements in the oriental philosophical view of the universe.

Because *han'gŭl* has been used by Koreans since its inception, it has been adopted as the official alphabet. The alphabet consists of 14 consonants and 10 vowels, originally written in the combination of phonetic diagram, symbolic descriptions of the organs of speech, structural principles of man, earth, and heaven, addition of strokes to other consonants, and modification of other vowels. It is written in a square box system of syllables and is arranged in columns from left to right and /or horizontally from top to bottom as in the English language.

Theoretically, the *han'gŭl* alphabet should be easy to teach and therefore should afford rapid mass literacy. Until recently, however, there was no standardized Korean dictionary and, since scholars disregarded the usage of *han'gŭl*, both dialectal and individual spelling differences have occurred. In the Republic of Korea the Korean Language Association formulated rules to standardize the spelling of Korean and, with the help of a grant from the

Rockefeller Foundation, published a six-volume Korean dictionary, the *Han'gŭl Ha'hoe Kŭn Sajŏn*, in 1957. A horizontal writing system has been recommended by American and Korean linguists, but it has not been widely adopted except in textbooks.

Like other Asian languages, such as Chinese and Japanese, Korean lacks vocabularies expressing political and scientific concepts in specific terms. Lacks in these areas are supplemented by English and other European languages. Koreans write Japanese terms, as well as personal nouns and honorifics, in Chinese ideographs, and it is estimated that a minimum of 1,000 Chinese characters must be mastered to read newspapers. On December 6, 1967, the government of the Republic of Korea approved a series of measures instituting exclusive use of *han'gŭl*. Hence, as a result of teaching the language in the schools and of an adult literacy campaign, the government estimated in mid-1964 that some 95 percent of persons over 12 years of age were literate, although some speculate that the number of persons actually able to read *han'gŭl* would be somewhat smaller. Moreover, since most publications present a combination of Chinese characters, some high school and college graduates have difficulty reading academic journals or even daily newspapers (see ch. 16, Public Information).

Social Connotations of the Language

The Korean language is a highly flexible instrument for indicating social distinctions. Choice of pronoun and grammatical form indicates the social relation between two people, such as between superior and inferior or between close friends. Apparently, it is sometimes difficult for Koreans to decide just what form to use, and conventions can, of course, be adapted to humor or to insult through deliberate misuse.

Use of slang has traditionally been associated with low-class status, as has display of strong emotion through gestures, facial expressions, or loud tones, but slang is coming into increasing usage among educated young persons. Personal names of parents are never used in direct address or in the presence of their children unless the speaker is a generation older than the person referred to. However, it is permissible to use personal names between two or more persons of the same age if the motive is to reveal an intimate interpersonal relationship. Otherwise, application of a personal name is indicative of low-class status.

Name

One of the most stable elements within Korean society is perpetuation of the patrilineal family system that persisted throughout the long Confucian tradition. This is continued by the practice of passing the father's surname on to his children. There is an old saying in Korea, "If you throw a stone from the top of Namsan (a mountain in Seoul), it will hit a Kim or Lee," indicating which family names are most common in Korea. In the entire peninsula, there are approximately 411 family names, among the most common of which are Kim, Yi, Pak, Ch'oe, Chŏng, Cho, Kang, Chang, Han, and Yun in that order. With the coming of the United States military forces in 1945, pronunciation and arrangement of Korean names have been anglicized (for example, Yi to Li, Leigh, Lee, and Rhee) ; and also by placing the surname last (it occurs first in Korean names).

The family (and clan) surname usually includes the traditional place of origin of the clan; although this is not used in direct address, it is important in determining whether two families having the same family-clan name are members of the same patrilineal clan.

Upon the birth of a child, much attention is paid to selecting a proper name, especially for a male child. Usually a boy's name has three Chinese characters: one that is his family or surname after his father's; another, shared by his brothers; and still another, which is his distinctive personal name. A further illustration of the complexity of Korean names is exemplified by the process of anglicizing names; the first name (the surname) becomes the last name; the middle name, the first; and the last name, the middle.

CHAPTER 6

SOCIAL STRUCTURE

Traditional social stratification remained strongly in evidence in the Republic of Korea as of 1968, but the structure of society was gradually changing as a result of increasing Western influences. In rural areas the traditional structure remained relatively stable, while urban centers experienced a greater degree of social change.

When Western influences first penetrated Korea in the early 17th century, the country had a rigid class structure sanctioned and supported by Confucian precepts. Government officials, including the military and landowners, were members of the upper class (or *yangban*), which was distinguished from the rest of the population by prestige, power, wealth, dress, education, and social behavior. Members of the upper class were educated primarily in Confucian classics and etiquette. The commoners, who formed the overwhelming majority of the population, were small farmers, agricultural laborers, merchants, craftsmen, and serfs. The lowest position on the social scale was occupied by the so-called "low-born" or "despised" peoples, made up of slaves, monks, nuns, *kisaeng* girls and others.

Social mobility was, in general, extremely restricted. In rare instances, however, a commoner moved upward into the ruling class by winning high honors in the national examination system and thereby obtaining a government post, which provided him with the means to improve his economic position. Since social status was not an individual but a family matter, his family moved up the social scale along with him. Positions of political and economic power carried with them the responsibility of distributing patronage to relatives and friends—a circumstance which has contributed to the persistence of certain phenomena of political life. Thus, all the members of such a circle were kept on roughly the same economic plane. Downward mobility occurred through loss of land, the possession of which was almost essential to the maintenance of upper-class status.

The most important official unit in the traditional social organization was the extended family. Households composed of several conjugal families related through the male line were the basic economic, political, social, and religious units of this traditional society; on various occasions, the larger extended family operated as a collective unit (see ch. 7, Family). Households were generally smaller than the full extended family but often included grandparents, parents, one or more married sons, and minor children. These households were usually grouped into villages; in some of the villages all the members belonged to the same large extended family, but in many a number of unrelated families were gathered together. On an informal basis, the most respected elders of the village acted as a restraining influence in maintaining order and served as a buffer between the people and official government representatives. The village was the most common unit of economic cooperation and social contact outside the family. The only associations based on common interests other than family ties were the guilds into which most merchants and handicraft workers were organized.

Transformation of the traditional social structure began in the late 19th century with the introduction of Western ideas, increasing after the beginning of Japanese control in 1910, and becoming much more rapid and intensified after 1945. During the early decades of the 20th century, a class of urban workers began to develop, the size and functions of the family became more circumscribed, and mobility between classes became more commonplace. *Yangban*, in many though not all cases, were forced to give up their land and were removed from government positions.

In the south, the Korean conflict erased the last open remnant of the basic distinction made by the old order between *yangban* and commoners, although *yangban* origin was still claimed in order to achieve higher status. By mid-1964 the ruling elite included some but not all of the members of the traditional ruling class and was made up of the wealthiest landowners, high-ranking bureaucrats and military and police officers, of whom a number had amassed considerable fortunes.

The increasing number of small entrepreneurs, skilled workers, and unskilled urban proletariat who make a tenuous living does not fit into the traditional system. These growing numbers of people evidently aspire, however, to government or other white-collar posts for themselves or their children in keeping with the traditional pattern. Theoretically, the expanded educational system has provided greater chances for social mobility, but schooling, especially beyond the primary level, is available only to a limited number of children (see ch. 9, Education). Students have tended to prefer liberal arts courses over those in science and technology, but this attitude is beginning to change. The government is continuing to stress the need for technicians and is encouraging scientists who have been trained elsewhere to return to the Republic of Korea.

TRADITIONAL SOCIAL CLASSES

The Yangban

The *yangban* (literally, two groups), originally made up of the *soban* (civil officials and scholars) and the *tongban* (military), included the wealthy and all those holding influential government positions. The most essential formal qualifications for being a member of this class, however, were that the males should be well educated in the Chinese classics, that the family should be one of good standing, and that the elaborate system of etiquette associated with Confucianism be observed. All employment other than that of government office or land ownership was beneath their dignity, and manual labor in particular was felt to be demeaning.

While holding office, most of the higher ranks of nobility—those who had had titles and positions of authority in the family for generations—lived in the capital city of Seoul. Families of these high nobles, provincial officials, and retired nobility lived on country estates. Although at one time the nobility was rigidly exclusive, by the 19th century admission could be achieved in one or two generations. The son of a commoner who excelled in the National Examinations could obtain government office, thereby elevating his own and his family's social position (see ch. 9, Education). Often, however, high office was purchased.

There was also the possibility of downward movement if a branch of a noble family lost its landholdings. The conditions of upper-class status required considerable landed wealth to perpetuate essential patterns of extended family living, hospitality, and education. As a result of these upward and downward movements, one branch of an extended family or clan might belong to the *yangban* and another to the class of commoners. There were gradations within the upper class, but the most significant distance lay between nobles and commoners.

Marriage rarely crossed class lines. Upper-class males, however, often took commoners as secondary wives or concubines. The offspring of one noble and one commoner parent suffered some social discrimination, but was considered to be a member of the *yangban* class.

The houses of nobility, while not differing greatly in basic design from those of common people, were usually larger and had whitewashed walls and tile roofs. So that the women could be kept secluded from the eyes of outsiders, it was essential that there be a special room in which male members of the household could entertain their friends. In addition to the primary structure, which took the form of a hollow square with a central court, the home might include additional courtyards for each of the resident conjugal family units, servants, and retainers; the number of courts was indicative of the wealth and position of the family.

The diet of the upper-class families also differed from that of commoners and was more closely correlated with wealth than some of the other class differences. Rice was highly prized and could be afforded by the peasantry only when it was plentiful. Meat appeared only on the tables of persons of considerable wealth. Another sign of upper-class status was extensive hospitality, which included lavish feasts for male friends and relatives of the households.

Dress also distinguished the nobility from the common people. In earlier periods, the fine gradations of rank were indicated by the type and cut of dress and ornamentation, which were fixed by law. Although these minute prescriptions had disappeared by the end of the 19th century, members of the upper class could still be distinguished by their flowing robes and the use of silk and other fine materials. Even if a gentleman's family was poor, great attention was given to cleanliness and neatness of the clothes and the person. Only the *yangban* were permitted to wear a distinctive style of hat made of horsehair woven in the form of a truncated cone, with a broad brim and an inner hat. This inner hat originally signified that its wearer had passed the National Examinations and was entitled to appointment in government office, but gradually its use became more widespread.

Many men of the *yangban* class had considerable leisure, which they spent in such characteristic pursuits as archery, hunting with hawks, and games similar to chess and checkers. Ceremonious dining itself became leisure-time activity for those who could afford it, and it was for this class that the *kisaeng*, or female entertainers, performed.

Male members of the nobility spent many years learning the Chinese classics and Confucian philosophy. Ideally, they learned to appreciate and compose Chinese poetry, showed great restraint in their social relationships, and accepted responsibility for those dependent upon them. They were addressed in a special honorific form of speech but used "low" language to all others including the female members of their family. A common man might not sit or smoke a pipe in the presence of a nobleman without permission. Other class distinctions appeared in the extent to which family ties were maintained and in the elaborateness of weddings, funerals, and other ceremonies (see ch. 7, Family). The upper class enjoyed exemption from taxation and military duty and received special privileges by law. No despised person could institute legal proceedings against a member of the nobility.

Upper-class women occupied an anomalous position. Although subordinate to the male members of the class, they were held in such respect that they were extremely restricted in their activities and movements and actually had less power and influence among their social equals than lower-class women had among theirs. Like the men of their class, noble women received training in the traditional etiquette, in certain arts and handicrafts, and sometimes in reading the Korean script, *han'gŭl*. But all training was carried on entirely within the home. In addition to learning to show subservience to the dominant males in the household, women were kept secluded from all males except relatives from the time they reached 7 or 8 years of age and had the right to privacy, even from relatives, in their own sections of the house. During the day, upper-class women could only leave the house to visit other women of their class and had to make such trips with heads covered and in closed chairs.

The few suitable occupations for these women consisted of teaching girls in other noble families, practicing acupuncture, raising silkworms, beekeeping, and making straw sandals. They also might do sewing and embroidery, and many learned to play musical instruments.

The rules with respect to the inheritance and management of property were very strict for the upper-class woman, and, even if she earned any money, she was forced to turn it over to a husband or male relative. Her main power lay in her family's social position, through which she could usually force her husband's family to treat her well, and she was seldom sent away from his household.

Commoners

The class of commoners actually was a very diverse group, characterized originally only by their lack of wealth or title and their association with agriculture. They ranged, however, from comfortable, small landholders to tenant farmers who were frequently on the border of starvation. Variations within the agricultural families of common status, who comprised the great bulk of the society, depended primarily on the amount of their wealth, which made possible the extent to which the signs of respectability could be indulged.

Few common families obtained an education for their children before the opening of Christian missionary schools and, later, Japanese schools in the 20th century. Since traditional education stressed the assimilation of the Chinese classics and Confucian philosophy, knowledge of these subjects was an important mark of distinction between the two major classes. Not only did the private academies, which were the only schools, have to be supported by the families of those attending, but the acquisition of this type of education was only possible through many years of nothing but study; in almost all of the common families, sons and daughters both had to start to work in the fields at an early age.

The housing facilities of the common people were naturally smaller than those of the nobles; this fact, and the need for women to work outside the home, made impossible the almost complete seclusion of women found in the *yangban* families. Women in respectable city families, however, covered their heads when walking on the streets, and there was some avoidance of the opposite sex —although not complete seclusion from them—in country areas.

The clothing of the lower-class people, while similar in cut to that of the nobility, was distinguished by the use of coarser materials and the absence of silk. Respectable families tried to maintain high standards of cleanliness. They subsisted generally on the cheaper grains and seldom tasted meat except on special occasions.

Commoners, being untrained in the Confucian doctrine, were not expected to show the stoicism, lack of emotional expression, and philosophic view of life which were the marks of a gentleman. Men expressed themselves in colorful language.

The women of this class, although formally held in low regard, were actually considerably more free in their actions and had a greater control over property than upper-class women. They could engage in many more activities, and whereas an upper-class wife would invariably turn over the proceeds of her work to her husband, the lower-class women might or might not do so. Similarly, in cases of inheritance, some women of common families might control the family property if there were no proper male heir, and, even if a son were adopted, they might continue to control the estate.

On the other hand, the lower-class woman had less control over her treatment in her husband's family; her treatment seems to have been related primarily to the respect in which her own family was held and the desire of the husband's family to maintain a good relationship with it. Many more lower-class than upper-class women were sent away from the house if they did not please their husbands, and, although divorce was seldom resorted to, marriages tended to be much less stable than among the upper classes.

Outcastes

In addition to the commoners, who, though extremely poor in many instances, were considered respectable members of the society, there were a number of categories of people—the so-called "despised persons"—who made their living in ways considered disreputable by most Koreans. As in the other classes, some held higher positions than others, and the ranking seems to have varied in different times and places; but monks, nuns, boatmen, *mudangs* (female sorcerers), *kisaeng* girls, meat sellers, butchers, traveling peddlers, basketmakers, actors, criminals, and slaves almost always fell under this category. Some of these individuals might be quite prosperous, and some of the functions performed by them were essential to the society as a whole; nevertheless they were held in low regard by even the poorest members of the common class.

The *kisaeng* in some instances were among the best educated women in Korea and frequently lived in considerable luxury. Some became the concubines or second wives of nobles. The *mudangs*, though feared and despised, often made a good living from their calling because of the great faith placed in their ability to cure. Monks allegedly were held in low esteem because of their celibacy and consequent failure to comply with the first obligation of filial piety—continuation of the family. Peddlers lived a nomadic life, traveling about with their families. They had a well-defined code of morality for their own members, however, and hundreds might assemble to adjudicate an important controversy.

A number of these occupations required almost constant travel, and this mobility within a predominantly stable, agricultural society may have contributed to their low social position. Further, land ownership was the most important sign of status, and none of these occupations entailed such ownership. Women of this class were free from most of the restrictions placed upon respectable members of their sex.

Slaves were, in general, not badly treated, and some actually received more regular subsistence than did free persons. They were encouraged to marry so that they would have children. Female slaves usually found husbands among the day laborers. The family lived in housing provided by the owner, who also supplied food. Women did all the heavier housework—washing, bringing water from the well, going to market, cooking—and heavier field work; they were seldom personal servants.

WESTERN INFLUENCE ON SOCIAL CLASSES

In the last decade of the 19th century, Western influences began to modify the traditional class structure. Christian schools, for example, founded primarily by American, German, and English missionaries, admitted individuals of any background. In July 1894, the distinction between *yangban* and commoner was legally ended, and examinations for government posts no longer were based on the Confucian classics. When the Japanese (considered "Western" by the Koreans) took over in 1910, they replaced the bulk of top government officials—the elite of the society—with their own nationals, began acquiring land and creating industrial wealth, and started schools which some commoners were able to attend. The examinations they established for the lower ranks of government service were difficult but fair—at least when a choice between Koreans only was involved. The examination score alone was likely to be the criterion for getting a job with the Japanese government. Members of the advisory councils were chosen from the old nobility, however, and even those families who lost their official positions were still regarded as socially superior by other Koreans.

Japanese economic policy worked its greatest hardship on the rural peasantry. Persons willing to work under and with the Japanese and ready to adapt to the new ways of industry and international trade grew prosperous. The body of small agriculturists owning their own land or the greater part of it, however, declined, and tenantry increased. In the 1930's, four out of five Korean farmers were full or partial tenants. Their lot also worsened as the paternalistic aspects of the landlord-tenant relationship weakened with the growth of absentee landlordism. Many younger sons were forced to leave the ancestral farms and move into the expanding cities.

Thus a small, urban middle class began to emerge; its members came mainly from respectable agricultural families and maintained the traditions of the common rural class to a large extent. Some adopted Western ways and probably felt considerable superiority over those who remained behind. Those who were successful in the cities seldom returned to farming in their villages.

In the 1920's and 1930's, many Korean students began to go abroad. A few who had money or who were supported by funds from Christian societies went to America or France; meanwhile, there developed a new type of student who did manual labor to support himself while studying in China and Japan. Previously, no Korean scholar had ever dreamed of working with his hands. The aversion to manual labor is still so prevalent among well-to-do Koreans that students coming to the United States are reluctant to be employed at any except white-collar jobs. The new intellectual elite found, upon their return to Korea, that few could hope to make a living there. Some joined the Korean independence movement; many, especially those in Japan, became strongly influenced by Communist doctrines; and many students in Korea became leaders in political agitations (see ch. 3, Historical Setting).

With the weakening of the old class structure, many of the customs associated with the old concepts of nobility and commoners also declined. Western dress became quite common among urban dwellers, and differences in living habits generally became much more a reflection of wealth than they had been previously.

Members of the old upper class still strongly felt their position, however, and even the gradations within this class were retained. When the Japanese began drafting Korean students for their labor battalions in the South Pacific during World War II, thousands of upper-class Koreans married hastily in order to assure that a child would be left to continue the family. Many made what they considered to be tragic marriages since they could not find a bride of equal status willing to marry a husband who might never return.

The traditional structure of Korean society, weakened by the removal of the *yangban* from positions of political influence in the period of Japanese rule, underwent further and more rapid change after 1945. New means of access to political power, once the exclusive prerogative of the *yangban* and more recently of the Japanese overlords, opened the way into the ruling class for some persons of low social origins. The political scene was infused with new blood upon the repatriation of Korean exiles, many of whom had been active in the Korean independence movement, working from bases in China, Manchuria, Siberia, and the United States. Experience in the independence movement, or connections with persons who had participated in it, proved a valuable achievement, in particular the ability to speak English, a skill which was much in demand during the United States military occupation (1945–1948) and later occupation by the United Nations forces during the Korean conflict.

Between 1945 and 1948, the rate of sociocultural change was accelerated not only by the return of exiles from abroad and the influx of millions of refugees from the north, but by the economic consequences of the Japanese withdrawal. Success in real estate speculations and commercial and industrial ventures permitted a number of entrepreneurs to amass large fortunes. At the same time expanded industrial development paved the way for the emergence of a new class of managers and skilled laborers. In contrast to the small number who profited in the competitive economic situation, however, there were thousands who continued to live in poverty.

The land reform program, initiated by the United States Military Government and carried through by the Government of the Republic of Korea in 1949 and 1951, further weakened the traditional social order by shaking the foundations of the economic power of the old *yangban* families. Some large landowners were able to retain at least part of their wealth, either by selling out in advance of possible confiscation or, as was apparently done in frequent instances, by making private arrangements with their tenants or hired workers, which enabled them to continue to reap profits from holdings which were actually no longer theirs. Other large landowners, however, lost much or all of their wealth and sank to the level of destitute farmers.

The Korean conflict, in the course of which multitudes of persons were again uprooted and deprived of their economic resources, erased the last traces of any clearly delineated class structure and precipitated the decline of old attitudes and values (see ch. 12, Social Values).

In the 1960's, positions in the government continued to go mainly, but not exclusively, to persons affiliated with wealthy families, but their wealth might be derived from industry as well as from land. To qualify for a top-level political post, it is still essential for a man to have a university education. Beyond that, connections with particular schools are important. To have attended Seoul National University, Yonsei University or Korea University is an asset to a political career.

Although the conditions which formed and supported the nobility have been changed and although the ideal is of a society in which all persons are entitled to be treated as equals, the attitudes and social behavior engendered by a long tradition of superior-inferior relations have by no means entirely disappeared (see ch. 13, The Governmental System). The persistence of class distinctions is especially apparent in the attitude toward marriage, where great care is maintained to marry into a family of equal or complementary social status.

Education and academic scholarship remain important criteria of social status. The extension of public education has rendered them less distinctive as markers of social rank, however, and the nature of the education has completely changed in the 20th century. Associated with these changes is the decline of the Confucian ethic as either a consciously held guide to personal conduct or a sanction of class differences in the social order (see ch. 7, Family).

Remnants of old behavior patterns between inferiors and superiors persist. It is still customary, for example, for members of the government to pay social calls on New Year's Day at the homes of their immediate superior officers. Traditionally, the same custom has been observed with respect to family elders, but this aspect of the custom is no longer so scrupulously practiced.

To some extent, status distinctions are implicit in religious affiliation. Although many basic Confucian tenets were accepted by the common people, Confucianism as a consciously held philosophy has been more characteristic of upper-class males than of other members of society. Shamanism and Buddhism are now largely confined to lower-class males, but women of all classes are adherents of both. Christianity has followers on all social levels. It carries certain upper-class connotations, however, because many of the country's political leaders were educated in missionary schools from which they went on to join the independence movement.

In 1968, the distribution of wealth—if wealth alone were used as a measure of social status—indicated a social structure in which the population could be considered predominantly composed of people living at subsistence level (70 percent of the population); the middle class was narrowly constituted (25 percent of the total); and the upper class, in which most of the national wealth was concentrated, was quite small (5 percent of the population).

REGIONAL AND URBAN-RURAL VARIATIONS

Aside from urban-rural distinctions, the class structure, community organization, and general social patterns are fairly consistent throughout the country. At the same time, there are distinct differences in Korean attitudes towards the different provincial areas. Koreans historically have considered Seoul as the political, cultural, and economic center of the country, and residence there imparts status. Also, Kyŏnggi Province, in which Seoul is located, is a preferred residence. Prejudice against some provinces is great; students from these areas attending school in Seoul adopt local customs, manners, and accent. Some provincial accents actually constitute a barrier to graduates seeking worthwhile employment. Provincialism is a historically ingrained trait among Koreans, and its influence remains strong in spite of expanding literacy, increased geographical mobility, and the more widespread influence and authority of the central government.

Probably the most notable change in the social structure of the Republic of Korea since its foundation in 1948 has been the continuing urbanization of the country. While the Republic remains predominantly rural, the number of persons living in urban areas has increased rapidly, and in 1967 represented almost one-half of the population (see ch. 4, Population and Labor Force). Although the implications of this trend for the social structure of the country are not as yet clear-cut, certainly urban living offers greater opportunities for education, greater availability of jobs, and more contact with other than traditional influences—for example, much of the urban population has adopted Western dress. The pace of social change is rapid. Many persons from rural areas, especially younger people, have moved to the cities to take advantage of the greater opportunities. The effects of urbanization on the Korean extended family, the traditional basic social unit, were not yet documented in late 1968.

Despite the population shift, however, the country remains to a large extent an agrarian society. Slightly more than one-half of the population still lives in rural areas and retains much of traditional Korean family and village ways of life. In these rural areas, poverty is more in evidence. As a result of urbanization, a large economic and cultural imbalance has developed within the country. The government has recognized this discrepancy and is attempting to bring the rural areas closer to the economic and cultural norms of the urban areas through education and economic advances.

CHAPTER 7

FAMILY

As in the distant past, the family system in the 1960's underlies and affects all aspects of Korean life. Up to very recent times, a typical family was a large, extended, patriarchal unit, economically self-sufficient and integrally related to the Confucian ethics system (see ch. 11, Religion).

Since the beginning of Korean history, the basic unit of the society has been the family and not the individual. The family unit was structured around the kinship or clan system, which had its nucleus in the conjugal and extended family. Throughout the centuries, an individual's position within his family became the major criterion for his social position.

To westerners, the ancient traditions—respect for elders, elaborate weddings and funerals, family responsibility for the welfare of their members—still appear to characterize the Korean family. Those families living within the framework of modern urban society, however, no longer conform to this stereotyped traditional pattern. The decline of the Hermit Kingdom during the late 19th century marked the beginning of subtle changes that weakened certain aspects of the traditional family system. These changes have been accelerated by subsequent events, such as Japanese colonization, World War II, and the Korean conflict.

In the modern period the conjugal family is gradually replacing the traditional, extended family as the basic dwelling and economic entity. Except on family-owned farms, the family is no longer the producing unit. This fact is well evidenced by the fact that the once-larger family of eight to 12 children has shrunk: The size of an average family at present is 5.04 persons in urban areas and 5.37 persons in rural areas. In Seoul, the most modern city, the size of an average family is only 4.97 persons.

Although the desire to look after distant kin in time of need still persists, the family no longer considers their protection to be a strict obligation. As in other Asian countries, the Korean family system faces serious tensions, partly derived from an ever-widening gap between the older generation's belief in traditional values and the younger generation's tendency toward modernism. Furthermore, conflicts develop when strongly entrenched values, such as the importance of assisting close relatives or accepting the advice of elders, become difficult to accept. The marked increase in what some Koreans see as self-centered, amoral behavior may also be ascribed to the rapid change in the family system in recent years.

TRADITIONAL CLAN ORGANIZATION

Until recently, the Dongnae or Dongni (village-clan organization) was as ubiquitous as rice paddies in the rural landscape. It was originally composed of a "clan"—an aggregation of one or more consanguineous, extended patrilineal families banded together for economic and social cooperation. This relatively permanent clan group consisted of all the men and women related to one another through the males of the family and was headed by the *kabujang* (the father or the head), whose authority was the rule of the clan and was unchallenged by any members of the clan. With the establishment of primogeniture, following the introduction of Confucianism, the functioning segment of the clan was confined to firstborn of the *kabujang* within the extended group of the related males, since the women usually moved to a different village upon their marriage.

Usually, where the members of the clan were living close to one another in a village, clan cooperative activities had considerable social significance. Occasionally, however, clan members lived in widely separated areas; and in such cases the functions of the clan were limited to honoring the clan ancestors and to regulating marriage. The clan practiced exogamy and matrimonial ties between persons of the same clan were prohibited. Because of this practice and the attendant difficulties of identifying distant relatives, clan records were strictly kept.

Buddhism, in conjunction with Confucianism, served as the centripetal force within the clan society. Confucian ethics had an especially strong influence on the shaping of the Korean family (see ch. 11, Religion). The ethical system advocated conformity and unchangeability as major virtues, and any observable deviation from tradition was regarded as taboo and even impious.

The profound effect of Confucian ethics on the social life of rural Korea was well preserved through Dongnae. Even today, the thatched roof of a peasant house symbolizes the unchanging character of rural life in the clan. For more than two thousand years the thatched roof has represented the humility of the commoners and their subordination to the gentry (*yangban*).

The land tenure system was the basis for the clan's socioeconomic structure. Typical ways of securing and maintaining land included (1) the common ownership of certain land to be cultivated and harvested by all members of the clan organization and stored for the needy in time of natural calamities, and (2) the bestowing of certain tracts of fertile land to government officials by the king in return for their service. Furthermore, the gentry selected good land and bought it while they were in power. Lastly, some families moved near the graveyard for convenience of ancestor worship and then settled down there permanently, thereby establishing a new clan organization.

With some variations, determined partly by region and social class, the traditional family-based clan system described above prevailed throughout the country until the turn of the century.

Structure and Function of the Family

The kinship system in the prehistoric society of Korea was not based on a conjugal family, nor on a patriarchal family composed of core families, but was a more primitive tribal system. From the time of recorded history, Korean society has been feudalistic, static, persistent, and conservative; its tradition-oriented, large "extended" family system has continued with relatively little change in its basic structures. From the time Confucianism was introduced into Korea (1122 B.C.) through the fourth century when Buddhism appeared, the primitive pattern of the clan evolved into the patriarchal family system. Traditionally, a complete household consisted of the grandparental generation, their sons and sons' wives, and children of these couples. In case of economic difficulties caused by insufficiency of land to support all household members, younger sons, upon their marriage, usually moved out. From the beginning of the Yi dynasty in A.D. 1392, social status was related to the size of families. Usually, many households contained widows and offspring of male relatives whose parents had died or who required someone to care for them. In the upper classes, many households included concubines and their offspring. The first wife was from the same social class as her husband and had the dominant voice in household affairs. Secondary wives or concubines usually came from the lower classes and in some cases were entertainers, but in general they enjoyed privileges similar to those of the first wife.

In case the head of a family did not have a natural son, a male child of a distant remote relative or even a non-relative was often adopted to become the potential successor and head of the family.

Familism in Korea was either consciously or unconsciously embodied in the five cardinal Confucian virtues of moral-ethical human relationships, namely, the relationships between father and son, between husband and wife, between the older person and his junior, between friends, and between lord and subject.

Based on these ethical relationships, the most important function of the family was the perpetuation of family lines. Thus, early marriage and many children became ideals that most families strove to attain, regardless of economic consequences. Since only males carried the family line, primary value was placed on them; females were considered as means for procreating male members. Bearing daughters was almost as unfortunate as having no children. Traditionally, woman's role in the family was subordinate, and woman's status in society generally was likewise very low. Because of the high value placed on the permanence of the family, divorce was almost unknown.

In Korea, as in other agrarian societies, the basic economic unit was the family. Land cultivation and harvest were shared by members of the household, in which the eldest brother or father was responsible for the supervision of all those under his authority— sons or younger brothers, their wives and children. In many cases, even remote relatives were supervised and cared for by the head of one such extended family.

Three events—birth, marriage, and death—constituted the most important affairs of an individual's life. An elaborate and costly marriage ceremony, regardless of its financial consequence, was a must for the poorest to the richest families. Traditionally, incest and even marriage within the clan at large were some of the strictest social taboos, and to guard against them the marriage was prearranged by the parents or by the hired professional matchmakers (*chungmae* or *chungsin*), whose responsibilities included making thorough inquiries regarding the young persons' ancestors and birthplace. Until very recently, civil law prevented a marriage between fourth cousins, even though they had different family names.

There was little or no opposition when marriage arrangements were made among royal and aristocratic families, including those of the gentry, and marriage across these lines, within the social upper classes, was common during the Yi dynasty. In the lower classes, marriage between artisan families and peasant families took place freely. Butchers, who were considered outcastes (as were beggars, prostitutes, and criminals) intermarried within their own class. Since 1960, in the cities western-style dating practices among young adults and college students have become fashionable. Although modern couples at times marry by free choice, go-betweens still arrange most marriages as a contract between families.

Marriages were traditionally arranged early. During the Yi dynasty the bridegroom was often younger than the bride, the former being about 12 years old and the bride 15 to 18 years old.

Polygamy was a fairly common practice at one time in Korea.

The urgent need for producing a male heir was perhaps the prime reason, for when the first wife proved sterile, the concubine who had a child, especially a son, was formally recognized as being the legal wife. Also, the practice of polygamy symbolized higher social status, wealth and prestige. Regardless of class, women in traditional Korean society had a very low status. This, many scholars think, stems from a tradition decreeing that females were unwanted and sinful. Hence, female infanticide was not uncommon. At the age of six or seven a girl was confined to a separate bedroom dissociated from her brothers and other male relatives. She was subservient to a succession of three masters: first to her parents, then to her husband, and, finally, to her own eldest son in her old age. When she was given away to her bridegroom, she had to learn thoroughly what her husband expected of her, based on the threefold virtues: "three years dumb, another three years deaf, and finally, three years blind."

Family Relationships

Proper conduct of an individual, according to his position within his family, was established over many generations resulting in certain patterns that are unique to Koreans. It is believed that the harmonious relationships that developed between husband and wife, parents and children, brother and sister, cousins, grandparents, mother and father-in-laws, and wives and brothers, can be attributed to the coming of Buddhism and Confucianism into Korea. In a patriarchal society such as that in Korea, the relationship between father and son was particularly important, especially between the father and the eldest son, upon whom heavy responsibilities fell when the father died. In that event the family farm or business, as well as the welfare of family members, became his responsibility. Among the siblings, filial piety and chastity were the supreme virtues in family life.

The influence of Confucianism upon family structure was so strong that behavior patterns formed within the family carried over to social relations outside of the family. The father was not only the authoritarian figure but also the model of good behavior for sons to follow. Consequently, joking, intimate conversation on certain subjects, and games between father and sons (also between mother and daughter) were not possible. Also, sons were not allowed to exhibit certain types of behavior in the presence of the father—for example, drinking and playing games. The father's prerogatives as the head of the family were absolutely respected by all members of the family. Hence, tension or conflict did not have a chance to erupt and create serious problems within the household. Nevertheless, favoritism toward particular offspring did exist. Usually, special parental attention was bestowed upon the firstborn son, and particular affection was directed toward the lastborn child by all members of the family. An impersonal relationship prevailed between the father and his daughter and between him and his daughter-in-law, all important communication being conducted through his wife.

Rules of etiquette dictated by Confucian ethics not only stressed formal behavior between age groups but also between sexes; hence, husband and wife, no matter how intimate they may have been in private, manifested unpretentious formal behavior when other members of the family were present. In accordance with age-old custom, parents made their children's marriage arrangements. Primary considerations in these arrangements were the couple's family background and accomplishments. The participation of the parents was based on the belief that the young were too immature and foolish to make such a decision. Not until the birth of their first child, who brought out a strong common interest for both parents, did the husband and wife feel a bond of marriage. Until then, the couple spent most of their time with the rest of the family rather than as a separate family unit. Thus, child-bearing was emphasized early in married life and especially from the woman's point of view. The subsequent addition of children not only enhanced common interests of husband and wife but solidified the wife's role as an important member of the household. Thus, when the mother voiced her opinion, especially on the subject of rearing her own children, it was duly respected. Traditionally, a woman's emancipation as a respected human being came about only as a result of marrying and bearing a male child.

The relationship between mother and children, especially when they were young, was close and warm. Usually, children under stress ran to either mother or grandmother for comfort. While father was the authoritarian figure, mother represented affection and sympathy. Both parents shared the duties of disciplinarian and educator; however, the mother's relationship with a child continued on a more affectionate basis. When a son married, "mother-in-law trouble" often resulted, and fear of such difficulty was felt by almost every young bride as she reached marriageable age. The daugher-in-law, who owed respect to her husband's mother, was forced to accept almost complete domination in her conduct of household affairs and could not reply to frequent criticism of how she executed the tasks delegated to her. There was often great antagonism between the two women, particularly in the early period of the relationship; on rare occasions a husband might intercede for his young wife.

Although a daughter was treated as a temporary member of the household, the relationship between her and her mother was intimate. By the time she was ready for marriage, what she had learned of life was almost wholly derived from her mother. A dutiful daughter tried her best to become a complete image of her own mother in every way possible. In a society where the male was such a dominant figure, this solidarity between mother and daughter was especially cherished. This close relationship was very evident on the daughter's wedding day when the bride and her mother bade each other farewell, crying openly and unashamedly, until they were forcibly separated by other members of the family.

Since brothers, especially the older ones, were considered from early childhood to be the permanent members of the household, they were encouraged to assist in performing all kinds of tasks. After reaching puberty the oldest one was called *kŏnhyŏngnim* by his younger brother and *kŏn oppa* by all his sisters. This name was indicative of both respect and affection and the fact that now he was ready to learn to assume the family responsibilities. Parents spent whatever they could afford to give him the best kind of education and other privileges.

In comparison, sisters tended to have closer relationships. They shared household chores, and usually the older sisters were second mothers to their younger brothers and sisters. They cleaned, mended, and did other chores required to help the mother. In return, the girls in the family were protected and regarded affectionately by their younger brothers and sisters.

Cousins of members of a given family were treated nearly the same as the younger members of the household. While the oldest son was a permanent fixture in the household, younger sons (especially in the peasant class) tended to move out of their parents' homes at the time of their marriage and establish their own homes.

A close tie generally existed between a younger brother and his oldest brother's wife. The wife of the oldest brother had to be very circumspect with her father-in-law and was under the constant, and usually not very sympathetic, supervision of her mother-in-law. The wife was an alien, and not always welcome, family member in her first years. Although her relationship with her husband's brothers was generally quite formal, she often became almost a second mother to a young brother-in-law. Sisters of the husband were more likely to reflect the mother-in-law's antagonism to the newcomer.

Deference to elders in the Korean family was well demonstrated during the Lunar New Year celebration. At this time children were expected to return to their parents' homes and offer new year's obeisance, *sebae*, before their parents, bowing their heads to the ground ceremonially.

Grandparents of either sex were persons to be greatly respected by their grandchildren. Because of their age they had the right to break some of the forms of etiquette insisted upon for others in the family. Partially because of the great importance their granchildren had for them (particularly males) as leaders in their worship after death, they tended to be much less strict than parents. They frequently spent much time in their grandchildren's company, carrying them about as babies, and generally catering to their wishes in a way that a parent, especially the father, could never do. The caring for and training of children were often undertaken as much by the paternal grandmother as by the children's own mother.

The Life Cycle

Having many sons was generally regarded as a symbol of happiness. Until they reached seven years of age, both girls and boys were very much free to be with anyone's company within the family. However, after the age of seven the separation of the sexes was emphasized. Girls at this age started to learn to help with household chores. The mother took complete charge of the preparation of her daughter for marriage but was occasionally aided by other older female members of the household. Matters of sex were not discussed at all. Without any formal initiation, boys after seven were encouraged to spend their time with male friends and relatives; they were, on some occasions, ridiculed if found in the company of the opposite sex too frequently. Among the upper classes, boys usually received at least a primary education, and if one showed great enthusiasm for study, he was assisted in acquiring higher education in the hope that he would become a dedicated scholar or eventually even obtain an important position in government. In contrast, boys in the peasant class were forced at an early age to work in the fields with little exposure to education.

It is worthwhile to note that the basic patterns of the Confucian ethic were learned by children primarily through observation of the behavior of older members of the family and through reprimand for improper behavior. In these ways girls learned to defer to male relatives and develop appreciation of the importance of childbearing and the maintenance of smooth family relationships. A boy learned that his principal duty would be to arrange for the welfare of those dependent upon him. An upper-class boy learned that a gentlemen must control his emotions and develop a knowledge of Chinese classics. The function of the patriarchal male head of the household prevailed in all strata of society, and women held a subordinate role.

The maintenance of smooth interpersonal relations with other members of the family was the main contribution of the Confucian ethics to the Korean family over the centuries. Other influences of the Confucian ethics were development of a sense of honesty in dealing with one's fellow man and a responsibility toward governmental affairs. Any deviation from basic ethical rules resulted in the loss of face on an individual level, as well as in the whole family.

Marriage was an extravagant affair as arranged by most families. Even under the pressure of very limited means, a costly wedding was considered important. A typical wedding was a formal ceremony and took place at the bride's home. It began with the bride and groom sipping rice wine and exchanging bows. The bride then was carried on a sedan chair to her groom's home where the female members of the groom's household carefully investigated the dowry. In major cities the traditional sedan chair has given way to a flower-decorated bus to carry the bride to her new home.

Upon arrival at her new home, the bride was introduced to her new mother-in-law and father-in-law, either by the hired professional matchmaker (chungmae) or by one of her close uncles. In older times she was even introduced to the deceased members of the groom's family in front of the ancestral tablets. Both bride and groom kept silent throughout the day-long celebration and the bride especially was neither to smile nor converse. Participants in the celebration included the bride's male relatives, the groom's relatives and the villagers. At the end of the affair, the couple for the first time was left alone. It was customary for the husband to take his new wife back to her home for a few days soon after the wedding. After a few more such short visits she finally settled in her husband's home permanently.

While marriage formally marked an abrupt change from childhood to adulthood, particularly for the bride, the groom's family relationship changed slowly. However, gradually he proved his abilities to father many children and make decisions regarding their care, and thus he gained respect as an adult. Then he was permitted to move, if he so desired, from his father's house. Once independently established, he was free to enjoy his leisure time with the company of his choice, that is, persons of his own age and similar interests; also he could joke and drink with them with fewer inhibitions.

In a society where a woman's role was so focused on bearing and caring for children, most girls wanted to marry, but the first years in a new household were frequently unhappy and difficult. Gradually, however, with the arrival of children, the improvement in status, and the establishment of some rapport with her husband, the woman acquired a degree of influence over those aspects of family life related to her children. As her mother-in-law grew older, the younger woman took over more and more of the responsibility of the household; and by the time she was an old woman with grandchildren of her own, she could openly assert her authority.

Another milestone in life was the age of 60. This was called *han-'gab,* an occasion when the family had another costly celebration. Because it was assumed that one was entering his second life cycle at 60, his wisdom was to be revered and his wishes were to be fulfilled.

Among the tradition-minded Koreans, it was a common belief that death is merely a change of state, not a final separation. Also, because of the ancient presumption that a living person embodies one of his family's dead spirits who could influence family affairs, ancestor worship has long been of prime importance.

For the death of a man or woman who had lived to a ripe old age and who had had many grandchildren, little regret was shown. Also, the death of anyone under seven years of age was not a matter for much grieving, since until that age he was not considered a permanent member of the family. If death came to a young man before reaching adulthood, he was thought to be very unfortunate, but he was mourned less for the death itself than for not having been married. The burial ceremony for a woman or man who had children was always a big event. The degree of elaborateness and cost of the services varied a great deal, depending on the individual's position in society and the status of the family. Because Korean families strained their resources to give the best possible funeral, sadness was compounded—it was partly for loss of life, partly for the loss of wealth. For a man, especially if he was the head of the family and of some social standing and wealth, the funeral service was nearly a community affair; participants included relatives from near and far, hired professional mourners, and villagers.

The body was placed in the *sarangbang,* the main room of the house, bathed, and then dressed in new silk clothing or special garments before being placed in a pine coffin. A geomancer (see ch. 11, Religion) was hired to locate a favorable grave site and choose a propitious day for the funeral procession. In the case of a prominent person, because of the elaborate preparations, the funeral might not take place for several months; in most instances, however, burial followed a few days after death.

Incense was kept burning throughout the entire period preceding the funeral day. Along the route of the funeral procession wine, fruits, and cakes were placed to placate evil spirits. A funeral procession, led by torchbearers, included a master of ceremonies, a spirit chair to carry the ancestral tablet in which the soul of the deceased was thought to reside, the bier itself, the chief mourners dressed in special costume, other relatives, and villagers—their number depending upon the importance of the dead man. In case of an eminent person's death, many of the mourners carried lanterns and banners indicating the dead person's achievements. For commoners, usually a *shaman* or *mudang* was brought to lead the funeral procession. The individuals in this procession were the new head of the family, the immediate family, relatives, and friends, in that order.

At the grave site, usually located on a hillside facing the east, a grave was dug, its size indicating the importance of the person being buried. After simple or elaborate rituals, depending again on the deceased's social and family position, the coffin was laid in the grave and covered. For common people a plain stone was used as a grave marker on which were placed offerings of food. In the case of a prominent man, the grave was marked by a stone sculpture of either a man or an animal.

At one time the more important clans owned entire mountainsides for the burial of their dead. The grave sites were maintained with great care by the clans, relatives, or even the immediate families. On special occasions, particularly on *sanso* in the middle of September, family members visited the grave and made offerings of food. These occasions, in contrast with the funeral itself, were festive and gay.

FOREIGN INFLUENCES ON FAMILY TRADITIONS

The impact of the West has altered and weakened essential parts of the traditional family system, giving rise to new attitudes toward authority, filial obligation, and the relationship between the sexes. In this process, new attitudes and values have emerged, first in the urban sector of the society and later and more slowly in rural areas.

Western influences, which ultimately resulted in modification of family traditions in Korea, began when Korea was forced to open its ports to the western trade in the late 19th century. Of the many specific factors that affected Korean culture, perhaps Christianity had the greatest influence. To the early Christian missionaries the practice of ancestor worship was unacceptable and in conflict with their own religious beliefs; therefore, they directly attacked Confucianism.

Because Confucian ethics underlie the family structure, this attack on Confucianism was in effect an attack on basic family traditions. Missionaries also exercised a significant influence in the reform of women's education. Conversion to Christianity encouraged women to emerge from their seclusion in the home and attend churches and schools, to work outside the home, and to participate with men in social affairs.

Education for both sexes resulted, to some extent, in economic independence; and this, together with ideas of the importance of the individual, led to an increase in marriage by choice rather than by traditional parental arrangement. These influences were intensified during 36 years of Japanese reign. During this period, changes in civil laws were especially significant. Compulsory coeducational elementary education was set up by the government and enforced upon Koreans (see ch. 9, Education). For the first time, periodicals and books dealing with the outside world were made available to the public. Private ownership of property was permitted by law. Also, legal changes placed full responsibility for the family in the male parent of the conjugal family instead of in the oldest male head of the extended family. Legalized prostitution, recognition of the rights of illegitimate children, and release of the children of concubines from family duties are some of the radical changes attributed to western influence. Among the most westernized Koreans, even divorce became relatively common practice, although some measures were taken to curb the rate of divorce. Some of the responsibility for punishment of criminals has been removed from the male heads of the households and assumed by the government, and this also weakened the traditional power of the family.

Western influences also caused broad structural change within Korean society, and this had important effects on family life. As a part of the Japanese Colonial Empire (1910–1945) Korea went through drastic socioeconomic changes—industrialization, impoverishment of small, peasant landowners, and a sharp population increase. Mobility of the population within the country increased as people migrated from southern farming communities to industrial cities in the northern part of the peninsula. Also, there was substantial emigration to Japan, Manchuria, Russia, China and other countries.

Such changes weakened the traditionally stable patriarchal family structure that served as the centripetal force for the landholding, agrarian society of Korea. In many extreme cases, as alternatives to near starvation, as the younger sons of small farming households became poorer, they fled to Japan and Manchuria in search of jobs. Once they were financially successful they seldom returned home. Although they sent money home, the ties with their families gradually weakened. And with the advent of industrialization and development of a market system, the family became less and less economically self-sufficient.

By the 1920's and 1930's there were striking differences between urban and rural Korea. These can be attributed partly to the greater contact in the cities with westernizing influences through international trade, higher education and other means of international exchange. As many women and young people became financially independent, particularly in the cities, they were more individualistic and less prone to accept the guidance of elders, thus weakening the extended family ties.

MODERN TRENDS IN FAMILY LIFE

World War II and the Korean conflict resulted in great economic imbalance and shifting of population in Korea. Large numbers of refugees, displaced persons, and Koreans returning from Japan concentrated in the southern part of the peninsula. This created a diverse pattern of behavior throughout the society—especially among urban dwellers. The rapid changes have brought rising conflicts, as new behavior patterns were found to be inadequate replacements for the old, and much disillusionment has resulted (see ch. 12, Social Values).

The simple conjugal family rather than the traditional large, extended family typifies the general structure of modern family life. In a modern family the attitude of respect toward the household, identification of the individual's role within his family, and deference to older generations still remain significant values of the culture for a large segment of the population.

The present Korean family averaging about five persons, is much smaller than the family of 8 to 12 children that was characteristic some decades ago. This decline in family size is attributable to two important factors: an increase in the number of persons living in cities and a rise in the number of people working outside the home. A typical household in the cities consists of the parents, their unmarried children, and perhaps a grandparent. In rural areas, households of two or more such families are not uncommon.

The self-sufficient economic unit that was identified with the traditional Korean family has ceased to exist. This change has occurred, in part, as a result of an increase in the number of women working outside the home.

Although old attitudes are still respected, women of almost all classes are frequently seen in public with a male companion and wearing western dress. Women have voting rights and, among the well-educated, they participate in affairs of government and are involved in various social activities. The divorce rate is comparatively low, but recent statistics indicate that it is on the increase.

Young people generally still show great respect for their elders; however, attitudes and perspectives on social values tend to differ greatly from those of the older generation. Accordingly, the younger people have become insistent that they should make their own decisions on matters such as education, jobs, and marriage.

The attitude toward young persons assuming positions of responsibility and authority is gradually changing as more and more young people seek opportunities, increase their income and rise in business and government. A significant number of men under the age of 30 hold high ranks in the army or governmental positions.

The problem of providing relief for the refugees, unemployed, aged, infirm, and orphaned is so great that, even if the old attitudes toward the support of the family members prevailed, families would be unable to care for all their needy relatives (see ch. 8, Living Conditions). In urban areas this is an especially difficult problem, causing tension within the family, and contributing further to deterioration of the traditional family system.

There also is evidence that the old ethical system associated with and perpetuated by the traditional family unit is being undermined. In poor families where both parents work outside the home, in incomplete families, and among individuals detached from all family groups, the traditional value system seems to have lost its hold. Rural areas and middle- and lower-class families able to maintain stable ties are less affected.

CHAPTER 8

. LIVING CONDITIONS

Living conditions in the Republic of Korea, although generally not up to United States standards, are adequate for most of the Korean people. They are decidedly better than during the mid-1950's when the devastation and dislocations of the Korean conflict were still largely unremedied. Improvements in public health have been significant, as indicated by the reduction in epidemics over the past decade. Agencies of the United Nations, the United States Government and private relief organizations have undertaken most of the work in constructing and rehabilitating water and sewer systems and hospitals, as well as providing medical supplies; however, the government of the Republic of Korea has been expanding its activities in disease control (immunization, pest control, and inspection of food handling), medical training, care of indigents and the disabled, and disaster relief.

HEALTH

Koreans have long been subject to a variety of diseases as a result of overcrowding, inferior nutrition, sanitary facilities, and hygiene. Government efforts to upgrade public health conditions in recent years have produced gradual improvement. Low wages and high unemployment limit the ability of many persons to improve their environmental conditions. Most of the burden of welfare improvement falls upon the government.

Life expectancy rates have been rising over the past decade. The average in 1967 was estimated 63.25 years, compared to 59.75 years in 1957. The improvement is attributed to reduction in deaths resulting from epidemics. Infant mortality is still high, however. In 1961, the rate was 67.9 infant deaths per thousand live births. The principal cause was gastrointestinal ailments. The gross death rate was estimated 9.7 per thousand.

The most prevalent diseases are tuberculosis, typhoid fever, encephalitis, leprosy, and digestive ailments. Statistics on incidence and mortality are unreliable, because of the unwillingness or inability of many Koreans to seek conventional medical attention, and the custom of bringing the dying to their homes so that expiration will not occur in a strange place. Accordingly, it is difficult to determine which diseases are the leading causes of death. In 1960, for example, it was reported that gastrointestinal diseases were the primary causes of death. More recent figures for gastrointestinal diseases are not available. There is reason, however, to believe that the leading cause may now be tuberculosis: Between 1960 and 1966 tuberculosis cases rose from at least an estimated 800,000 to 1,430,000, with fatalities running at 45,000 annually by the latter year.

Encephalitis is the third largest cause of death from disease. Epidemics appear to occur in a generally biannual pattern, with the number of cases rising during the first half of the 1960's. Since 1966, however, mosquito abatement programs apparently have had some success in controlling the disease. During 1966 there were 3,563 cases resulting in 965 deaths; in 1967 the figures were reduced to 2,678 cases and 786 deaths. The disease is most common in the southern provinces of North Chŏlla and South Chŏlla and occurs mainly between August and October.

Typhoid fever is endemic, with 3,000 to 4,000 cases reported each year; fatalities seem to occur in about one percent of the cases. This represents a considerable reduction in incidence over the past two decades. (In 1951, for instance, there were 82,000 cases and 14,000 fatalities.) Preventive measures and improved sanitary conditions are responsible for the improved situation in recent years.

Leprosy appears to be declining. In 1960 the number of lepers was estimated to be at least 45,000. By 1967, however, the number of reported cases was in the neighborhood of 35,000: 7,488 were committed to the nation's five leprosariums, while another 27,079 were being treated in their homes.

Another health problem for Koreans is parasitic infection. According to a study published in August 1967 by the Ministry of Health and Social Affairs, 80 percent of the total population carried one or more types of parasites. Fifty-two types of parasites occurring in the country were reported to the World Health Organization; of these the roundworm was the most prevalent. Fluke infections of all types are widespread, and all are associated with the custom of eating raw fish and crustaceans. Such extensive parasitism causes anemia and contributes to the incidence of other diseases; however, continued improvements in sanitation and food-processing methods apparently are reducing the number of persons afflicted with parasites.

Other common diseases include dysentery, typhus, diphtheria, whooping cough, poliomyelitis, measles, mumps and venereal diseases. The incidence of communicable diseases and the number of fatalities resulting from them have been generally declining because of immunization programs and the development and use of antibiotics and insecticides.

There has been substantial progress in the provision of potable water and the development of waste disposal systems in recent years. Between 1960 and 1967 the percentage of the population served by municipal water systems rose from 14 to 22. The higher figure represents only about half of the urban population, however; and the bulk of the rural population remains dependent upon rivers, creeks, wells, and springs, many of which are contaminated because of the use of night soil for fertilizer.

It is reported that by 1967 there were 1,762 kilometers of sewer line in 64 cities, but that this was far short of the minimum requirement of 16,500 kilometers. A majority of urban, as well as virtually all rural, inhabitants do not have flushing toilets; instead, privies and pails are used, and the contents are collected and used for fertilizer.

Traditionally, medical care has been the concern of the family in Korea, and spirit beliefs have provided the basis of an understanding of disease (see ch. 11, Religion). Such beliefs and practices are still prevalent in the rural areas, where it is thought that problems of health and disease can be solved by establishing a proper relationship with the world of spirits. Some spirits—especially those of persons who died away from home or by violence—are believed to be the cause of serious diseases.

The first reaction of most Koreans when faced with the onset of disease is to seek out a practitioner of the ancient system of medicine, *hanyak*. *Hanyak* is based on Confucian concepts and entails the use of herbs and acupuncture—the application of hot needles to various parts of the body. *Hanyak* practitioners are licensed to practice medicine with the same government recognition accorded to graduates of modern medical schools.

According to the *hanyak* system, disease results from an imbalance between the positive (*yang*) and negative (*ŏm*) forces acting on the five major and six minor organs controlling the body. Twelve great lines of force, or nerves, carry impulses from 360 spots on the surface of the body to the various organs. Application of acupuncture to these spots or the use of herbs, or both, is believed to correct the disorder in the related organs.

In addition to orthodox *hanyak* practitioners, there are "peoples' remedies" and sorceresses (*mudang*) who employ bizarre rituals and prescriptions to cure disease. The cure is often damaging, and many patients subsequently require hospitalization for infections. There are also pharmacists who are allowed to diagnose and treat patients without a doctor's prescription or examination. Often the results of such treatment is unsatisfactory.

Overall responsibility for public health rests with the Ministry of Health and Social Affairs. It consists of five bureaus: Public Health, Medical Administration, Pharmaceutical Affairs, Social Welfare, and Women and Children. The Ministry also controls the National Public Health Institute, the National Rehabilitation Center, the National Medical Center, and the Office of Labor, as well as a number of specialized hospitals and clinics. Further, the Ministry is responsible for administering the state welfare activities. These have been concentrated on the immediate relief of social ills and include such programs as the distribution of free grain rations, relief to flood and fire victims, placement of orphans in institutions or adoptive homes, housing construction, and aid to disabled veterans. The Ministry also handles programs such as promotion of family planning.

A number of foreign and international organizations are engaged in public health activities. Official agencies of the United Nations and the United States Government are engaged in providing medical facilities, rehabilitating and expanding sanitary facilities and water systems, and supplying technical assistance and medical supplies. Some private volunteer agencies train Koreans in hygiene and home economics and distribute surplus food under the United States Public Law 480 program.

The availability of medical services has been increasing, but the country's needs are far from being met. As of the end of 1966 there were 18 government-owned general hospitals, 203 private hospitals, 5,012 clinics, 1,829 dental hospitals and clinics, 2,316 herbalist clinics, 83 medical offices attached to public institutions and industrial facilities, 900 midwifery houses, and 189 health centers. Most of the hospitals are located in Seoul. In general, they are short on beds, and sanitary conditions are below standard; furthermore, their charges are beyond the reach of most persons. Accordingly most of their service is to outpatients.

Medical personnel likewise are inadequate for the country's needs—although their numbers, too, are gradually increasing. In 1966, there were 11,456 physicians, 1,810 dentists, 2,838 herb doctors, 5,811 midwives, 9,851 nurses, and 9,726 licensed pharmacists. They are concentrated in Seoul, Pusan, and the provincial capitals. There is a chronic shortage of nurses.

At the end of 1966, there were 19 schools offering graduate study in the following fields: medicine (9), dentistry (1), public health (1), and pharmacy (8). Most were located in Seoul, including Seoul National University, Chungang University, Ewha Women's University, Kyŏnghui University, Sŏnggyŏnggwan University, Sungmyŏng Women's University, Tongguk University, Usŏk University, Yŏnsei University, and Catholic Medical University. Outlying schools included Chŏnnam National University and Chosŏn University in Kwangju, Pusan National University in Pusan, and Kyŏngbuk National University in Taegu. No evaluation of the present training is available.

Considering the circumstances prevailing at the end of the Korean conflict, the country has made substantial progress in improving public health conditions. Such diseases as smallpox, typhus, and cholera have practically disappeared, and the number of cases annually of whooping cough and poliomyelitis has been dramatically reduced. Continued progress is reported in insect and rodent control, water supply purification, the repair and construction of waste removal facilities, the inspection of public gathering places, regulation of food processing and distribution activities, and crop dusting. Foreign assistance programs sponsored by the United Nations, the United States, and private organizations have made major contributions.

FOOD, CLOTHING, AND HOUSING

The average Korean's diet is high in starch and low in animal protein, fats, calcium, and vitamins, particularly vitamins A, B_1, B_2. The bulk of the protein and nutrient fats is provided by soybeans and fish; fats are also supplied by sesame, pine seeds, and peanut oils. A large part of the vitamin and mineral intake is supplied by a variety of fruits and vegetables consumed fresh in season and pickled during the winter.

Grains, particularly rice, are the basis of the diet. Rice, in addition to being a staple food, is a symbol of good living—to have eaten rice is to have eaten well. When other grains are consumed, they are mixed with rice whenever possible. When there is not enough rice to go around in a household, it is given only to the men or to the head of the family. Women of poorer families may taste rice only on New Year's Day and on their birthdays. Barley is also a social symbol: a well-to-do man mixes no more than one third of barley with his rice; others try to avoid eating barley alone by mixing it with white potatoes. Other grains used are wheat, millet, and buckwheat.

Among the vegetables, white potatoes, cabbage, *daikon* (Japanese radish), turnips, hot peppers, leeks, and beans are universally eaten; cucumbers, sweet potaoes, pumpkins, onions, sorghum, and spices are less important; and corn and carrots are occasionally used. Fruits are prized in season, the commonest being persimmons, peaches, pears, melons, apples, and berries of several kinds. Native nuts such as chestnuts and walnuts are also used. *Kimch'i* —a highly spiced dish made from varying combinations of vegetables, fruits, nuts, fish, red pepper, garlic and ginger—accompanies every meal.

Fish—fresh, salted, dried, cooked, or raw— is eaten throughout the country but especially near the seas and rivers. Meat, which is too expensive to be widely consumed, includes beef, pork, and fowl. Oxen are not killed for food; not only are they too valuable as draft animals, but they are considered almost part of the family. Eggs, though said to be less expensive than meat, are a delicacy enjoyed by the average Korean only on holidays and very special occasions.

Water is the main beverage, and well water is considered superior to all but spring water. Sungyong, rice tea made from cold water and burned rice from the bottom of the cooking pot, is taken after all regular meals. Tea is used only as a special treat in tea-and-cake shops. Coffee, introduced by United States civilian and military personnel, is now used to some extent. Alcoholic beverages made from wheat and rice mash usually are taken as appetizers. The large number of wineshops and the quantity of homemade brews testify to the popularity of liquor. Most drinking is done by men; women will sip a little but ideally never become intoxicated. Festivals are the chief occasions for serving alcoholic beverages.

Quantity and diversity of food consumption vary from class to class and also from season to season. For many years domestic production of foodstuffs has not satisfied domestic requirements. Foreign assistance programs, in particular, the Public Law 480 program of the United States, have provided large amounts of foods. Since 1956, tens of millions of dollars' worth of wheat and other agricultural commodities have been imported each year, either to be distributed and sold by the government or to be donated to private relief organizations operating in the country. There has been a noticeable increase in domestic agricultural production in recent years, however, which has narrowed the gap between domestic supply and demand.

Modes of dress have undergone some change since the advent of the United States forces and the Korean conflict. In the larger cities, western dress is common, although many women continue to wear the traditional long pleated skirt, tight inner jacket, and short long-sleeved bolero. This dress is universal among rural women. Most men wear loose cotton tousers and jackets, but on ceremonial occasions they wear long flowing white coats called *turumagi*. The elderly also wear tall, back hats made of horsehair and silk. During the winter, quilted cotton garments are worn.

Dwellings are simple. Except in the higher-income districts of the larger cities, where multiple-story houses are increasingly seen, the typical house is a one-story structure built of home-fired bricks or stones plastered with a clay-straw mixture. Roofs are thatched with rice stalks and floors are stone. The house is heated by the smoke of fires which is channeled through flues under the stone floor. The floor plan usually forms an "L" or "U," opening into a courtyard. The structure is oriented to the south to capture as much sunlight and warmth as possible. The house is measured by the standard unit of *kan*, roughly about 8 to 9 feet square (about 64 to 81 square feet). Depending on the prosperity of the owner, each room is one to four *kan* in size. Traditionally, both rural and urban houses consist of three basic rooms—kitchen, bedroom, and living room—to which others are added as the need arises.

Household furnishings, though they vary with the means of the family, are few and simple. Earthenware jars, pots, bowls, and a few metal utensils suffice for the kitchen; a chest or two to hold clothing, and the quilts and bedding (rolled up during the day) furnish the bedroom; a cabinet, perhaps a low dining table, a straw mat with occasional pillows and other accessories furnish the living room. Decorative items consist of wall hangings and perhaps ancestral tablets.

There is a substantial and increasing housing shortage. According to the Ministry of Construction, the country had about 3.9 million houses at the end of 1966 and additional requirements for nearly 1.3 million. The situation is particularly severe in the cities, where the number of families is nearly double the number of living units. It is estimated that the housing deficit is increasing by 100,000 units per year, and government efforts to meet the problem have been thwarted by lack of funds. Complicating the situation is the rapid increase in land prices.

Private construction accounted for nearly 90 percent of new houses built during the period 1962–1966. Little of this new construction, however, benefited low-income families. In order to assist families desiring to build, the government in 1967 instituted the Korea Housing Bank, which in 1968 was planning to float a large bond issue to secure funds for lending to homebuilders. High costs of land and high interest rates, however, are expected to deter the average person from undertaking a loan. Other government programs to provide housing include constructing high-rise apartment buildings in the major cities and promoting the development of construction material manufacturing.

CONSUMPTION PATTERNS

Families currently spend about half of their incomes on food and beverage. Between 1961 and 1964 the share stood close to 60 percent; but price controls, increased production of grains, and some improvement in real wages subsequently improved the situation (see table 9). In 1967, expenditures on food and beverages were estimated to have dropped to 48.6 percent of total private consumption spending, but it is not known whether that relatively low figure persisted in 1968.

Urban-rural differences in levels and patterns of consumption are not well documented. During 1966, it was reported that the average rural family spent 9,157 wŏn per month out of an average monthly income of about 10,850 wŏn (100 wŏn equals U.S. $0.36). The average urban family earned and spent more, but incurred a slight dissaving, which apparently has been a common occurrence in recent years. The average urban family's monthly income in 1966 was 13,520 wŏn and expenditures amounted to · 13,560 wŏn. Some segments of the urban population have been able to put aside savings in recent years, however, as indicated by the pronounced rise in savings deposits in the banking system since 1965.

It is significant to note that farmers have been able to save out of current income despite the fact that since 1964 the prices they pay for their purchases of manufactured goods have been rising more rapidly than the prices they receive for their surplus food production. Apparently this saving is being effected by restraining the expansion of consumption. The reduction in the share of expenditures on food since 1964 has permitted urban families to increase their consumption of clothing and of less immediately essential goods and services. The "miscellaneous" category consists of health expenses, transportation, education, recreation and entertainment, and other services. Increased urban consumption of manufactured consumer goods is indicated by a strong upward trend since 1965 in retail sales of such items as beverages and cigarettes, textile products, chemical products (including drugs and cosmetics), and printed materials. The use of electrical appliances

Table 9. Composition of Private Consumption Expenditures
in the Republic of Korea, 1961–1966
(in percent)

Item	1961*	1962	1963*	1964	1965*	1966
Food and beverages	59.7	55.5	57.8	62.3	58.4	56.6
Housing	10.5	10.6	9.8	8.3	8.3	8.5
Fuel and light	4.4	4.5	5.7	3.9	4.3	4.8
Clothing	9.4	11.4	9.8	9.7	11.3	11.0
Miscellaneous	18.0	18.0	17.9	15.8	17.9	19.1
Total	100.0	100.0	100.0	100.0	100.0	100.0

*Percents do not total 100 because of rounding.

Source: Adapted from Republic of Korea, Economic Planning Board, *Economic Survey, 1967,* p. 143.

has increased as a result of efforts by the government to provide additional generating facilities and to promote the domestic manufacture of import substitutes and exports (see ch. 20, Industry).

The relative tranquillity that most of the people have demonstrated in recent years suggests that there is not a great deal of discontent with the low level of living conditions and their slow rate of improvement. This stability is notable in light of the high levels of urban unemployment, continued price inflation, and a government policy favoring curtailment of increases in wages and agricultural prices and the diversion of resources to production of capital goods and exports. Since 1963, when the consumer price index for the city of Seoul rose during the year by nearly 30 percent, price increases have moderated. During 1966 the index rose by about 12 percent. Wage increases have barely kept pace, however, and it is doubtful that the proportional increase in consumption expenditures on recreation, clothing, and health care has appreciably improved the quality of life for most Koreans.

PATTERNS OF LIVING AND LEISURE

Korea officially follows the Gregorian calendar, as do the United States and Europe. Many holidays originated centuries ago when a lunar calendar was used, and the names of the lunar holidays can be misleading—for example, Lunar New Year's Day, which falls in late January or early February. The principal holidays are New Year's Day, 1 January; Lunar New Year's Day; Samil, or Independence Day, 1 March; Soil Conservation Day, 21 March; the Birthday of Buddha, 8th day of 4th lunar month (late May); the Tano Festival, 5th day of 5th lunar month (mid-June); Constitution Day, 17 July; Liberation Day, 15 August; the Harvest Moon Festival (Ch'usŏk), 15th day of 8th month (late September); Armed Forces Day, 1 October; National Foundation Day, 3 October; Han'gŭl or Alphabet Day, 9 October; United Nations Day, 24 October; and Christmas, 25 December. The lunar holidays are occasions for festivities and mark high points in the social life of many, particularly the rural folk. The Tano and Ch'usŏk holidays mark, respectively, the end of plowing and the end of harvest. Tano is noted for its swinging contests (girls in old-fashioned board-and-rope swings vie with each other to see who can swing highest). Ch'usŏk, Tano, and the Lunar New Year are occasions for feasting, drinking, and visiting friends for traditional games such as kite flying, tug-of-war, and wrestling, and for enjoying traditional music.

For the average Korean there is little leisure time; most energies must be devoted to earning a livelihood. People rely largely on their own resourcefulness for entertainment; visiting, storytelling, singing, and playing traditional games constitute the major pastimes. Such western games as baseball and soccer have become popular with the spread of public education and the presence of many foreigners.

WELFARE ACTIVITIES

World War II and the Korean conflict brought about a significant change in popular attitudes regarding welfare. Traditionally, the family took care of its own and the government did not, nor was it expected to, assist the needy. The dislocations caused by the wars made millions of persons destitute and broke up thousands of families, forcing them to look to the government for relief.

Most welfare work has been undertaken by United Nations agencies, civilian and military agencies of the United States Government, and private volunteer organizations. Beginning with the emergency measures instituted by the United States Military Government soon after the Japanese surrender, the program of outside assistance to the Republic of Korea has included long-range plans for reconstruction of the total economy as well as for continuing emergency relief. Generally administered by the United Nations Office of the Economic Coordinator (OEC) with participation of Korean authorities, the program first included a large number of United Nations and United States agencies and was supported by a large number of foreign governments and nongovernmental organizations. In 1956, 31 member nations of the United Nations and 8 nonmember nations were contributing to the United Nations Korean Reconstruction Agency (UNKRA), and 28 members and 3 nonmembers were providing funds for the emergency relief program. Just under 50 nongovernmental "voluntary" agencies were actively engaged in a variety of activities for relief and rehabilitation. UNKRA completed its program in August 1958.

Numerous religious groups, social organizations, and voluntary foreign aid agencies have continued to aid the country. Among them are the United States Agency for International Development (US/AID) ; the United Nations Children's Fund (UNICEF) ; the United Nations Educational, Scientific, and Cultural Organization (UNESCO) ; Cooperative for American Remittances to Everywhere (CARE) ; the National Catholic Welfare Conference; the Salvation Army; the Young Women's Christian Association (YWCA) ; and various missionary societies.

In addition, direct assistance also has been provided by United Nations forces stationed in the Republic of Korea, particularly for children. Many orphans have been adopted by military units, and orphanages and children's hospitals have been supported by personal contributions of servicemen.

The bulk of the official agencies' funds have been spent on reconstruction and rehabilitation of the war-damaged social and economic infrastructure. Since the late 1950's, however, food relief provided by US/AID under the Public Law 480 program has constituted a large part of the total United States assistance effort. Private relief agencies, of which there are at least 40 operating currently, have provided more than one million tons of food, clothing, medicine, and other relief supplies since 1953. These agencies are involved in a wide range of activities, including reconstruction, care of orphans, agricultural technical assistance, religion, education, and medical care.

The government of the Republic of Korea administers its welfare programs through the Ministry of Health and Social Affairs. These programs include care of disabled war veterans; operation of relief centers for the aged, homeless, disabled, war widows and orphans and victims of fire and flood; and provision of facilities for the vocational training of women, the rehabilitation of juvenile delinquents, and the day-care of children.

The effect of these organizations on the welfare of the Koreans has been profound; the improvement is remarkable in view of the fact that the country was devastated at the end of 1952. Despite the serious economic and social problems that persist, living conditions continue to improve slowly, and the country shows an increasing ability to assume a larger share of the development effort.

CHAPTER 9

EDUCATION

Since the latter part of the 19th century, the goals, methods, and content of Korean education have been undergoing change resulting from introduction of educational systems from outside the country. All systems whether introduced by the Christian missionaries, the Japanese, or the Americans, have militated in whole or in part against the traditional educational pattern based on Confucianism.

Under the influence of Confucian thought, which had a strong impact on the feudal aristocracy of the Koryŏ period (935–1392) and which dominated Korea during the Yi dynasty (1392–1910), rote memorization of Confucian ethics and the ability to write Chinese characters was stressed. The goal of education was to develop a small class of learned men able to find the proper ethical form and apply it to a specific social problem, and from this group the wise men and rulers of the country would be drawn. Little value was placed on the kind of critical examination which forms the basis of Western scientific, philosophical, or political thinking.

With the arrival of Christian missionaries and the establishment of mission schools toward the end of the 19th century, a new influence was felt in Korean education. Like Confucian scholars, missionaries sought to indoctrinate the people with an ethical system. They also spread literacy to the common people, men and women alike, and introduced Western ideas and values. Mission schools, serving as a source of dissident political ideas until the late 1930's, continued to play an important role during the Japanese domination of Korea.

Shortly after the turn of the century, still another education system was impressed on the Korean people. The invading Japanese adopted a system of public education designed to help incorporate Koreans into the Japanese cultural sphere and to make them useful citizens of an industrializing society. Also as part of their own training pattern, the Japanese also maintained the emphasis on uncritical learning by rote, which is part of Confucian tradition. Through Japanese influence, elementary education and some technical skills were disseminated to a larger proportion of the population. The Japanese population of Korea, however, was much better educated than the Korean segment and held most of the administrative positions. This situation reinforced both Korean resentment of the Japanese and the traditional view of education as a training ground for scholars and administrative officers.

Since 1945, the Republic of Korea has been faced with the problem of building educational systems geared to a modern industrialized society, a task which has been made extremely difficult by the dislocations and destruction resulting from the Korean conflict, by unsettled economic, social, and political conditions, and by conflicts in aims, purposes, and values in a society undergoing rapid change. The government has clearly recognized the need for greater development of technical schools and for greater emphasis on technical programs in existing schools to supply the manpower needs in an industrial society.

Realization of an educational system attuned to the requirements of a modern society has been hampered, however, by the persistence of traditional teaching techniques and of the popular belief that the goal of education is accession to the ranks of the country's governing elite. A chronic scarcity of financial resources for modernization and expansion of teaching facilities is largely responsible for the slow rate of progress in updating the character of Korean education. The failure of the people to take advantage of an education oriented to life in an industrializing society appears to be partly the product of an awareness that the society is unable to put vocational skills to rewarding use. Equally, if not more, detracting is the tradition of according great prestige to a classical education.

CLASSICAL EDUCATION

Although a few schools patterned after those in China existed in Korea as early as the fourth century, it was not until the adoption of Confucian ideals during the Koryŏ dynasty that any significant system of education existed in Korea. Under the Confucian system, government posts were filled by the educated class—theoretically by those who performed best in the periodic examinations held by the government. After the Yi dynasty replaced the Koryŏ dynasty in 1392, the full commitment to Confucianism, which characterized the Yi dynasty, was accompanied by an elaboration of the educational system to provide the cadre needed to staff government posts.

Classical Confucian education was almost solely pursued by the upper class of society, and education in schools was limited to males. Sons of nobles attended small, private elementary schools called *sodang*, where they spent hours learning to read and write the Chinese characters and memorizing selected passages from the works of Confucius. The schools were small, and no attempt was made to keep all the students at the same level of advancement, so that it was possible for the especially talented or diligent to move ahead rapidly.

Following work at the *sodang*, study might be continued at one of the provincial colleges or at the Four Institutes at Seoul, which were intended to prepare students for degrees. Alternatively, the student could attend one of the academies, which were somewhat like political or literary clubs established in honor of a local scholar and at which prominent men were invited to teach. These institutions gradually replaced the provincial colleges; they developed into centers for academic gatherings and debates and, in the later Yi period, became the centers of dissident political thought. The highest school during the Yi period was the Confucian College in Seoul.

Higher education consisted of interpretive study of the Confucian texts learned in the elementary schools. Passages were expounded by the teacher, and the commentaries by other scholars were consulted. Essays on literary themes were composed by the student, who strove for elegant style in prose and verse. These abilities, as well as an understanding of Confucian philosophy, were necssary to achieve good performance in the government examinations.

Government examinations were given on three levels—district, provincial, and national. They were not completely successive, in that one could apply for the second or for the highest examination without having passed the first. The subjects selected for examination varied from time to time, but usually included problems in the classics, studies of famous men of olden times, consideration of the best system of morality to correct bad customs, and suggestions as to what kind of military organization was best to defend and control the country. Performance in the examination on poetry was believed to reveal the candidate's nature; the examination in the classics and lives of famous men, his knowledge; and other subjects, his judgment and mental ability. Students specialized in military science, literature, language, law, medicine, cosmography, and courses qualifying them for government service.

The attitude of students toward their teachers was marked by great deference, and the scholar held a highly respected position in society. The educational situation was one of unquestioning transfer of knowledge from teacher to student. On the other hand, as the examination system reveals, memorization of the classics was not an end in itself but was generally accepted as a method of developing men wise in those areas of knowledge that had relevance to living a good life and helping others to do so.

There were two major motivations for getting an education under this system. Ideally, education was valued as a means of enjoying the finer things of life and as a source of self-improvement. The operation of this ideal alone is found in the lives of some of the scholars who, although highly regarded, received no financial reward for their teaching. The most common motivation for obtaining an education, however, was receipt of a government appointment and entree into a life of relative leisure, wealth, and position. Theoretically, these position were filled solely through the examination system. Actually, nepotism and cheating on examinatins were not unknown, and at some periods they were the most important basis for government appointment. However, even for those procuring a position through personal favoritism, years of study were still essential, and for the son of a family of moderate means and no powerful friends in the government, competence in the classics was the only road to social advancement.

MODERN EDUCATION

Mission Schools

During the closing decades of the Yi dynasty, the increasing impact of the West, reaching Korea through China and other contacts, gradually overcame the isolationist policies of the essentially feudalistic government. After 1882 the state-operated schools were no longer restricted to children of the upper class.

The educational reforms of 1885 led to the abolition in 1894 of *kwango*, the public service examination based on the Confucian classics. The first mission high school was opened in 1885 and the first girl's school, the Ewha Haktang—now Ewha Women's University—was established in 1886. By 1926, there were 766 elementary schools with 37,767 pupils; 48 secondary schools with 5,107 students; and a number of colleges—Chosŏn Christian College and Severance Medical College in Seoul and Union Christian College in P'yongyang.

The mission schools introduced several revolutionary innovations to Korean schooling: education for common people, which in volved some subsidizing of students; education of women as well as men; popularization of the Korean phonetic script, *han'gŭl*, as opposed to the Chinese calligraphy of traditional education. The mission schools also dealt with such subjects as geography, history, arithmetic, and science, as well as with Christian religious thought and the ideals of Western society. Although both Catholic and Protestant missionaries were present in Korea, those of the Protestant denominations played a particularly active role in education because of the value they attached to literacy in order to make possible reading of the Bible.

The mission schools provided a large percentage of the private education, particularly the medical training, available to Koreans during the period of Japanese domination. Generally, these schools were considered to have high scholastic standards and, particularly when they were subsidized by the missions, were very popular. In fact, they have contributed to much of the pro-Western feeling in the Republic of Korea in the late 1960's. The mission schools were able to maintain considerable independence under the Japanese, at least until the educational reforms of 1938. After that date they were forced to conform to Japanese regulations in order to have their student degrees granted government accreditation—almost a requirement for obtaining a position after graduation.

Although the government maintained a strong Confucian tradition in part of the existing school system, new public schools tended to reflect more modern educational methodology. In the late 1890's, a number of elementary schools were opened in Seoul and in the provinces. A teacher-training high school was established in 1895, and language institutes specializing in Japanese, English, Chinese, German, and Russian were in operation by 1900. Other schools specialized in medicine, commerce and industry, law, mining, communication, postal service, and military training.

Japanese Education

When the Japanese occupied Korea in 1910, they instituted a program of limited public education. The basic aims of Japanese educational policy were to promote knowledge of and respect for things Japanese and to increase Korean technical skills and competence in such basic subjects as reading and arithmetic. The major emphasis was thus placed on primary and technical schools, and less attention was paid to secondary and higher education.

A system of common (elementary), higher common (secondary), industrial, and special schools was instituted for Koreans shortly after annexation in 1910. Gradually, more of these schools, as well as normal schools and a university, were established. An educational bureau in the Department of Home Affairs regulated all schools, both public and private, and public school teachers held civil service rank. The number of elementary schools increased from 100 at the time of annexation to 2,358 in 1935; the number of pupils (including Japanese) increased from 110,800 in 1910 to 1,211,400 in 1937. Superior Korean students were sent to Japan for training.

In the elementary schools, the children were taught Japanese language and culture, Chinese literature, arithmetic, and ethics. Japanese was the language of instruction but the Korean language was also taught as a subject. After 1938, Korean language lessons were abolished and Japanese became the exclusive medium of instruction in the school system, even at the elementary level. The industrial schools provided low-level technical training and were designed to equip workers for nonadministrative positions in industry and agriculture. Special schools prepared Koreans for lower government posts.

Teacher-student relations in these schools were even more authoritarian than in the Confucian schools, and the basic teaching method was rote memorization. Even though some of the subjects presented embodied the results of scientific inquiry, no attempt was made to develop an attitude of independent inquiry in Korean students.

The Koreans had great pride in their culture and resented the deliberate attempt to submerge and disparage it. They particularly resented the 1938 ban on using the Korean language in the schools and the institution of exclusive use of Japanese in all public communication. Further, Korean and Japanese students were sent to separate schools during a large part of the occupation period, and because many Korean families could not afford tuition fees and needed the children at home to help with the work, the percentage of Koreans receiving an education, particularly at the higher levels, was much lower than that of the Japanese living in Korea. Almost every Japanese boy or girl of school age was in primary school, in contrast to one out of every three Korean children in the primary grades. There were, of course, greater problems involved in providing adequate schooling for the primarily rural Koreans, as opposed to the more urban Japanese. However, despite allowance for these problems, and despite the great improvement over the years (in 1919 only 4 percent of the Korean children were obtaining schooling as contrasted with 33 percent in 1938,) the disparity that existed was bitterly resented. There were very few Korean teachers; most educators were Japanese, particularly for the higher grades.

Although Korean culture was undeniably suppressed under the Japanese, the base of common education was expanded and there was some introduction to modern ideas in science and technology. The body of educated Koreans (largely in exile) later became a great influence in the resistance movement, and they accounted for a sizable proportion of those who first entered the newly formed government after 1945.

EDUCATION SINCE 1945

Immediately after World War II, under the aegis of the allied military government, the educational system of the Republic of Korea was radically transformed. The new system, modeled on United States lines, was established by the Education Law of 1949 which has as its guiding principle *Hong-Ik-In-Gan*, philanthropic ideals, or the idea of the individual giving the greatest service to humanity. The Constitution guaranteed every citizen equal educational opportunities according to his ability, required at least an elementary education of all children, and provided that compulsory education be free. The Constitution also provided that, although fundamental matters of education policy would be determined by law, the freedom and political neutrality of education would be guaranteed.

Education Structure and Finance

Overall direction of education was vested in the Ministry of Education, which also was responsible for administration of such institutions as the National Science Center, the National Library, the National Museum, and the National Academies of Science and Arts. State educational institutions were of two types, national and public. The national system, which in 1967 comprised 12 national universities and colleges, 14 junior teachers' training colleges, and four vocational schools and colleges, was administered by a National Educational Institutions department within the Ministry and was supported out of the Ministry's budget.

The public system of schools, comprising some 5,400 primary, and 1,000 secondary schools, 25 vocational schools, 18 vocational and technical junior colleges, and two colleges, was administered by the City and Provincial Board of Education, another department of the Ministry of Education. The Board supervised the activities of its 169 counterpart boards which operated at the city, county, and provincial levels, and which directly administered the public elementary schools. These schools received some support in the form of subsidies and grants from the Ministry, but most funds came from provincial government subsidies and school fees assessed to students to cover the cost of transportation and a part of the cost of instructional materials. Government funds have covered almost all elementary education costs but a much smaller share of the costs at higher levels. These costs have risen sharply beyond the elementary level and have exercised a limiting effect on enrollment in the secondary schools and colleges. In 1964, elementary education costs to the student approximated 3 percent of the average family's income; the cost increased to 13 percent in the middle (junior high) schools and 18 percent in the high schools. Private schools derived support from privately endowed foundations, some of which were foreign-supported, and from student fees. Rates at the primary and secondary levels were regulated by the Ministry of Education, but the private junior colleges and colleges were free to set their rates at any level. The curricula of the private primary and secondary schools are believed to have conformed to those of the public schools.

The regular school system consisted of 6-year primary schools for children 6 through 11 years old, 3-year middle schools for 12 to 14 year olds, and 3-year high schools, both liberal arts and vocational, for the 15- to 18-year age group (see fig. 6). Higher education was provided at junior, 4-year, and technical colleges, and at universities and graduate schools. A parallel sequence of technical schools beginning with the seventh grade followed the elementary level. These schools—called civic schools—existed to provide vocational training for adults and an accelerated equivalent of the elementary grades for those who had missed the opportunity to attend the regular schools. The civic schools provided remedial education and the rapid increase in compulsory school attendance has made them unnecessary. Their number was reduced from 15,399 in 1947 to only 114 in 1967. In addition, some 38 miscellaneous training institutions, such as seminaries and nursing schools, existed in 1967. At that time, the school year was approximately the same as in the United States, running from September through June.

Although the organization of the Ministry of Education included a number of staff bureaus designed to formulate educational policy, their effectiveness at times has been reduced by political pressures. Nevertheless, there appears to have been continued progress in identifying the goals of education and adapting the policies and administrative practices of the Ministry to improve the quality of education. The dominant goals of educational policy have been to increase the availability of education, to give greater emphasis to skills, attitudes, and concepts useful in an industrial society, and to inculcate in the youth of the country a strong sense of patriotism and a resistance to Communist propaganda. Although teachers are nominally organized into the Korean Federation of Education Associations, they appear to take little interest as yet in influencing educational policy.

University students may have exerted some influence on policy through their occasional use of mass demonstrations and active participation in student political organizations. The orientation of these movements, however, has been more towards political than educational issues, and it is not possible to identify any resulting specific changes in educational policy.

Elementary Education

The Education Law of 1949 provides for kindergartens with objectives of social adjustment and preschool familiarization similar to those in the United States. Although there were 468 kindergartens in the Republic of Korea in 1967, all but one were private, and enrollment represented a low 22,020 pupils. Schooling for 4- and 5-

year olds is still a novel idea for Koreans and the relatively high fees prohibit widespread attendance.

The constitutional requirement of compulsory and free elementary education was virtually achieved by 1967 when 96.7 percent of the school-age population was enrolled. The number of elementary schools (grades one to six) had nearly doubled since 1945, while the number of pupils had increased fourfold, reaching 5,377,232. This expansion was even more remarkable in view of the fact that half of the school facilities were destroyed in the Korean conflict and the remainder required extensive renovation. There

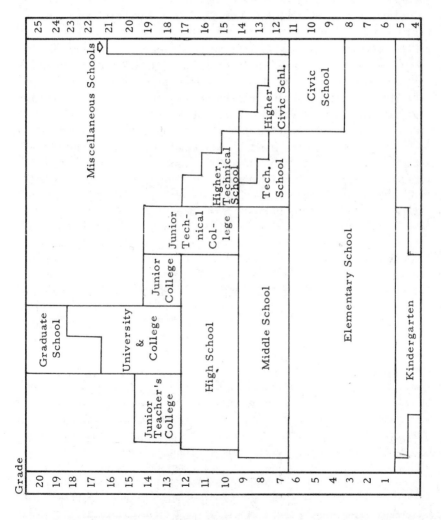

Source: Republic of Korea. Ministry of Education. Education in Korea 1967. Seoul, 1967. p. 2.

Figure 5. Structure of the educational system in the Republic of Korea.

was still severe shortage of classroom space and even minimally trained teachers in 1967; the average class size was 65 pupils and in some crowded urban areas classes reached 100 students. Many schools were operating two- or three-shift systems. Until 1961, graduates of the now-abolished normal schools (grades 10 to 12) were qualified to each at the elementary level. In 1966, graduates of teachers colleges (grades 13 and 14) constituted less than 28 percent of the total number of teachers. However with increasing numbers of graduates of 4-year institutions joining the teaching profession, the average educational level of teachers was being raised.

The curriculum in the elementary schools is generally similar to that of comparable United States institutions. The Korean language, arithmetic, social studies, natural science, music, art, health education, and ethics are taught in grades one to six in all elementary schools and are supplemented by a program of community centered activities. Simple vocational training—gardening, homemaking, and working with tools—is introduced in the fourth, fifth, and sixth grades. Total class hours, including those devoted to student activities, increase from 21 per week in the first grade to 28 in the sixth grade. In accordance with the constitutional provisions for compulsory and free education, the central government meets the bulk of elementary education costs either directly or through subsidy of the local district. Costs to parents are minimal. In 1965, compulsory education accounted for 73.6 percent of total education expenditures and represented 15.9 percent of the national budget.

Secondary Education

A system of middle schools (grades seven to nine) and academic and vocational high schools (grades 10 to 12) provides secondary education in Korea. Attendance at school is not compulsory beyond the sixth grade, and entrance to the seventh grade has been regulated by the administration of stiff competitive examinations. So formidable are these examinations, particularly at the more prestigious schools, that almost intolerable burdens are placed on those 10- and 11-year-olds whose parents hope for their admission. Extracurricular preparatory study of 12 or more hours daily is almost mandatory for those who expect to pass. In an effort to ease the emotional and physical burdens on the children, the Republic of Korea planned to abolish the entrance examinations to the middle school beginning in 1969. The abolition was expected to be gradual and to be coupled with a program of establishing new schools, lessening of quality distinctions between schools, and employment of the neighborhood or district concept with students assigned to particular schools. These changes were part of an overall expansion in secondary education as a result of which the 165

118

schools and 84,572 students of 1945 had increased to 2,096 schools and 1,352,695 students in 1967.

Middle and high schools in the rural areas usually are separate entities, although in urban areas they usually occupy the same campus. Secondary schools are not coeducational except in some rural districts and in experimental schools attached to teachers' colleges. Part of the expense of secondary schools is met by the national and provincial governments and the remainder is derived from fees and tuition charges. Many private schools derive income from school foundations supported by alumni and parents.

Middle school is a bridge between elementary and high school, a status that is reflected in its objectives and curriculum. The middle school attempts to develop work habits needed for success later on in high school; to help students acquire the social, emotional, physical and intellectual maturity necessary to function as responsible citizens; to help them make intelligent choices regarding their future; and to teach basic skills common to all occupations. The basic subjects taught include the Korean language, social studies, mathemathics, natural science, physical education, music, fine arts, a foreign language, and vocational training or, for girls only, home economics. While the foreign language is an elective, almost all students begin the study of English in the first year of middle school.

The aim of education in the high school is to provide advanced general and vocational education based on the foundation laid by the middle school. High school is primarily oriented toward the development of the abilities, attitudes, and skills required for a useful member of society and a responsible citizen. In 1967 there were 782 high schools in the Republic, of which slightly over half were academic and the rest vocational. Boys represented over two-thirds of the student population, and although the sexes were about evenly matched in the academic high schools, only a small fraction of those attending the vocational high schools were girls.

In the academic high schools the curriculum reflects the intention of most students to sit for college entrance examinations. Traditionally, the curriculum has been focused rather directly on preparation for the examination, and the prestige of an institution was directly proportional to the percentage of its students graduating. Now, although the college preparatory function is still important (in the late 1960's close to one-third of the graduates went on to college), increasing emphasis is placed on a well-rounded curriculum with a variety of courses. Required courses include social studies and mathematics, vocational education or homemaking, ethics and morality, physical and biological sciences, physical education, and courses in Korean language, music, arts and history. A variety of elective options provide flexibility in choice of advanced courses in the required fields and include instruction in foreign languages (English, Chinese, French, or German are elective, but in practice, virtually all study English). Laboratory, workshop, and field trip experiences supplement classroom instruction.

In 1967, the Republic had 369 high schools whose objectives were primarily vocational rather than college preparatory. These schools specialized in agriculture (128), technical training (49), commercial training (112), or fisheries and marine activities (11); 32 high schools were comprehensive in their training and 37 had miscellaneous specializations.

Vocational training represents a complete break from the traditional educational values which Koreans have cherished for centuries. For this reason, and despite the pressing need for technically trained manpower, the vocational high schools have not been readily accepted. In an effort to attract more students to these schools, the facilities, financial support, and availability of scholarships has improved in quantity and quality beyond that available in the best of the academic high schools. Even so, students and their parents still seek the prestige of the academic schools, with their orientation toward college and the professions. Other problems arise out of the specialized nature of vocational schools and the physical impracticability of providing a variety of specialized institutions in the smaller communities. Accordingly, in 1956 the comprehensive high school was established to combine in one institution both academic training and a variety of vocationally oriented programs. Although the comprehensive high school has not been readily accepted (only 32 existed in 1967) their establishment has sparked an increasingly widespread introduction of vocational courses among the electives offered at the academic schools.

While the basic problems of vocational education at the high-school level center on prestige, few such considerations affect the technical and higher technical schools. Accepting adults and students who have completed the elementary grades, these schools focus directly on training in skills and trades for immediate occupational utility. The curriculum, taking from 1 to 3 years, leads directly to employment in agriculture, commerce, and industry. Courses are offered in many areas and include mechanics, watchmaking, automobile repair, cosmetics, dressmaking, typing, and spinning. In 1967, 142 technical and higher technical schools had an enrollment of 21,348 students.

Higher Education

Although there have been college-level institutions in Korea since the latter part of the 19th century, the growth of higher education was slow until 1945. At that time there were only 19 such schools; by 1967 the total had increased to 211, including 68 colleges and universities, 49 graduate schools, 23 junior colleges, 14 junior teachers colleges, 19 junior technical colleges, and 38 other specialized institutions. Approximately one-half of these institutions are in Seoul. The junior colleges, colleges, universities, and graduate schools are primarily private institutions supported by tuition and endowments but with some financial assistance from the government. In the late 1960's tuition amounted to between 13,000 and 27,000 wŏn (between $50 and $100) per semester at the national and public institutions. About one-quarter of the students in institutions of higher education were receiving scholarships or other financial assistance, usually in the form of exemptions from tuition fees.

The academic structuring of the educational institutions tends to be patterned on that of the United States. Thus, the student is required to devote about one-third of his total college work to general education courses which include the Korean language, a foreign language, philosophy, cultural history, a broad course in natural science, physical education and elective courses in the humanities and natural and social sciences. Ideally, the student is expected to divide his time remaining after required courses about equally between an area of specialization and elective courses, but in practice the specialization occupies over 50 percent of the average student's time.

The 2-year institutions (junior colleges and junior teachers colleges) allocate somewhat more than half of the total instructional time to vocational courses. The remaining courses are comparable to those of the first 2 years at the colleges and universities. Very few electives are permitted and those available often have a vocational relevance.

An increasing number of students have been studying abroad in recent years. International exchange programs have enabled many to conduct postgraduate studies, mostly in the United States. According to the Ministry of Education, which must grant approval for foreign study, the number of graduate students abroad rose from 1,179 in 1955 to 4,978 in 1966. Fields of study have been divided almost equally between the humanities and social sciences and the natural sciences and engineering. The complaint has frequently been made that students have remained abroad because of the lack of opportunity in the homeland for employment of their advanced skills.

PROBLEMS OF KOREAN EDUCATION

Respect for education and for educated persons is a deeply penetrating and broadly pervasive aspect of Korean culture. After a centuries-old history of denial of educational opportunities under the Yi dynasty, and with educational ideals redirected during several decades of Japanese rule, the average citizen has had new educational vistas opened to him and his children under the constitutional educational guarantees. The Republic's problems lie in satisfying this enormous and increasing demand for education while at the same time channeling training into areas that will be productive for society. The idealized goal of the Korean seeking education still is an entree into the ranks of the country's governing elite; obviously such a goal can be realized by only a few of the student population in a country dedicated to mass education. As a result, much of the curriculum in the school system is not relevant either in terms of the country's needs or in its emphasis on a sequential development from kindergarten through graduate school—a sequence only a few fully realize.

Although almost all children in the appropriate age group are enrolled in elementary schools, in 1967 almost one-half of those who had graduated from these schools terminated their schooling with the sixth grade. The curriculum, patterned on United States practice, seeks to develop social, intellectual, and individual maturity in preparation for the increased specialization of the secondary schools. In the late 1960's, these aims were failing to prepare the terminating students for productive economic life. However, the situation was changing, and with the abolition of entrance examinations to the middle schools, the elementary curriculum should become more meaningful in the future.

The greatest educational need in the late 1960's was for more technically trained workers. Trade school and technical training suffers from the stigma which traditional classical education and the Japanese experience have engendered. Despite the better funding of trade schools and the provision of superior facilities, smaller classes, and a more favorable teacher-student ratio, enrollment pressure is not as great in these institutions as it is in the academically oriented ones.

The expansion of public education since 1945 has been impressive in terms of numbers of institutions, of teachers, and students, especially in view of the widespread destruction resulting from the Korean conflict. This expansion, however, has engendered a reduction of quality. Schools are overcrowded, running two and even three shifts, with extremely large classes and too few teachers. Because of inadequate textbooks, educational materials, libraries, and laboratories, emphasis must still be placed on memorization and group recitation, in line with the long-standing precedent of classical educational tradition. Education thus proceeds largely by statement of principles and elucidation of theoretical considerations rather than by the practical application of theory to concrete situations. Most of the student's attention is directed toward passing examinations.

The goals and objectives of education are conceived of differently by the educators and by the general populace. Opportunities for trade, technical, and vocational education are being made available in some cases faster than demand requires. At the same time, there is gross overcrowding in the academically oriented schools despite efforts to expand this sector. As of the late 1960's, educational policy looks forward to a balance between academic and vocational training, in keeping with the needs of the Korean economy for trained people in all occupations and professions. Achievement of this balance is made difficult by chronic shortages of funds and facilities, both for training teachers and for equipping schools. More importantly, the people apparently have not been persuaded that a vocationally oriented education can provide benefits and status equal to that of the traditional classical type.

CHAPTER 10

ARTISTIC AND INTELLECTUAL EXPRESSION

Korea is rich in artistic and cultural heritage. Though early influenced by Chinese models, Korea's achievements in art and learning have been unique and original. Art and learning have traditionally served both moral and educational functions in Korea as carriers of the values and traditions of the people. Development of formal artistic and intellectual modes of expression has been an upper-class occupation, but all Koreans shared the awareness that these achievements were connected with their daily life and conduct.

The artist and scholar and their abilities have traditionally been held in high regard. They often lived among the village people and imparted to them a respect for learning and artistic creation; thus, the people created a rich folk tradition of their own, reflecting the ideals and principles of conduct taught by the classical scholars.

Today, the poems, songs, and stories handed down from generation to generation in the family and village, together with the tombs, pagodas, temples, and statues scattered throughout the countryside and the relics of ancient skill in handicraft, afford Koreans of all classes a common cultural heritage. This heritage is currently being exploited in schools to stimulate national pride.

Knowledge and appreciation of contemporary Korean artistic and intellectual expression have traditionally been limited to a relatively small number of educated people living in urban centers. The upper classes have become increasingly westernized.

Korean artists and intellectuals are currently trying to cope with the social discord resulting from the mixture of the traditional elements with the modern ideas introduced after World War II. Many feel they are living in a period of cultural decline. However, Korea's rapid industrialization and westernization are stimulating the arts and cultural activities, and Korea's rich cultural background affords potential for a renaissance of intellectual and artistic expression. In the meantime, the majority of the people look to the distant past as the embodiment of their cultural greatness.

THE HERITAGE

Korea has long served as a bridge of cultural transmission from China and India and thence to Japan. Often, however, Korea has herself served as the creative innovator, and both China and Japan have adopted Korean models of artistic achievement, particularly in dance, music, and some genres of painting. From the fifth century on, Korea has produced masterpieces, many of which are still extant, in all the major art forms of the Far East. From the seventh through the 12th centuries the aesthetic-religious impulse of Buddhism gave rise to a Korean Golden Age of artistic and intellectual achievement. The pageantry and ritual of the Buddhist religion and its imaginative and mystical aspects stimulated Korean creativity, and the Buddhist monks' mastery of Chinese cultural achievements provided Koreans with new artistic methods and goals.

Although influenced by Chinese culture, the particular distinctiveness of Korean artistic efforts arises from the reliance on beauty of line and shape rather than upon costly materials. Korean art is thus directed toward strength of expression rather than brilliance, and the artist in Korea created lovely things out of simple materials. Works were marked by elegance and refinement during periods of political stability and were more rustic during periods of war. The strength and attractive honesty of both extremes, however, were admired in China and imitated in Japan.

Although Confucianism was known in Korea before the second century B.C., it did not become a dominant cultural influence until the 13th and 14th centuries A.D. At first, Confucianism also served as an important intellectual stimulus, but gradually its influence came to stultify both the artistic vitality generated by Buddhism and the intellectual energy it itself had engendered.

From the 14th to the 17th centuries, the Korean scholar class established its control over the court, developed a vested interest in the court's power and position, and increasingly favored a conservative, traditionalist attitude toward the search for truth and expression of beauty. A shift in emphasis from imaginative to moral and didactic aspects of art and learning constricted imaginative expression. Dogmatic reliance on the Chinese classics stifled individual expression and curiosity and offered little stimulus for introduction of new ideas. The Chu Hsi school of Confucian philosophy, which placed extreme emphasis upon conformity and orthodoxy, became supreme in Korea and vitiated much of the old vigor of earlier Confucianism. It became more important to live with nature according to established doctrine than to probe its content and mysteries.

By the end of the 17th century, Confucianism in its Chu Hsi

form had begun to have a repressive influence on Korean artistic effort, transforming much of it into repetitive embellishments of past achievement. There was considerable cultural activity during this period, and artists and poets were highly skilled. However, many of their efforts were derivative, drawing not only on their own country's past accomplishments, but also on Chinese (and later, to a lesser extent, Japanese and Western) techniques. With the isolating effects of the Hermit Kingdom policy from the 16th to the 19th centuries and the Japanese suppression of Korean culture from 1910 to 1945, Korea underwent centuries of artistic and intellectual quiescence (see ch. 3, Historical Setting).

Signs of a new artistic and intellectual ferment appeared with the introduction of Western influence at the turn of the 20th century. Western artistic trends exerted strong influence on individual Korean artists, and Western concepts of critical evaluation posed significant challenge to Confucian authoritarianism in intellectual fields.

Much of this new influence, however, has penetrated only the surface. A traditional assimilator of foreign culture, Korea now struggles with the effects of a too-rapid impact of Western culture which it has not yet had time to absorb. Throughout the period between the two world wars, the copying of Western artistic forms and techniques prolonged the stifling of native invention. Within the artistic and intellectual community exist deep rifts between those who wish to emulate past achievements and those searching for a new national expression of modern 20th century Korea.

Visual Arts

Korea was in the mainstream of Far Eastern culture and extensive exchange took place between China and Korea, with subsequent transfer of culture to Japan. Examples of traditional architecture and masterpieces of sculpture reveal the distinguished spiritual and artistic attainment of the Korean people and are among the most beautiful monuments in the Far East and in the world.

The greatest achievement of Korean visual art, in which the Koreans were unequaled after surpassing their Chinese teachers, was ceramics. Gray to black earthenware, often with openwork pedestals in triangular or rectilinear cutouts, was early characteristic. By A.D. 935 the art of glazing had been perfected, and the Koryŏ period (935–1392) is marked by fine, clear green-blue porcelain (celadon) similar to that of contemporary China, though distinctively Korean. Somewhat later this glaze was impressed with designs so delicate that they were almost imperceptible until clear liquid was poured into the bowls. Gradually the patterns were more deeply incised, and by the 12th century they were filled with black or white clays which appeared mistily through the glaze. Delicacy, faultless craftsmanship, and simplicity of design were the distinctive characteristics of Korean ceramics.

The Japanese invasion at the end of the 16th century dealt pottery-making in Korea a severe blow. Many master ceramicists and entire artisan communities found the Korean environment so repressive that they emigrated to Japan, where their influence on Japanese ceramics is still evident. In Korea, however, potterymaking has been unequaled since the 16th century.

Metalwork, lacquerwork, painting and sculpture also flourished under Buddhist influence. Metal casting, in particular bell founding, acquired a distinctive Korean character. Huge bronze bells are one of the major achievements of the Three Kingdoms period (57 B.C.—A.D. 668). Lacquerwork, one of the earliest industrial arts of the Orient, was encouraged by Buddhist monasteries; lacquered articles were inlaid with ivory, jade, coral, or abalone, carved with modeled reliefs or engravings, and decorated in color, usually gold and silver.

Excavations of burial places of early kings or nobles have uncovered bronze, silver, and gold decorations, paintings, iconography, and sculpture reflecting a high order of artistry. Gilt bronze statues, great masterpieces of Korean sculpture, are still preserved at the Great Silla Temple of Pulguksa. Many of the cave and temple sculptures are Buddhas, the most noted of which is found at the Cave Temple near the ancient capital of Silla. The chamber is fashioned of carefully fitted large stone blocks and the dome arches some 30 feet from the floor. The rotunda houses a great Buddha carved from an immense block of granite. Rock chamber walls are carved with life-sized *bodhisattvas* (those who will become Buddhas) and priests carved in low relief on stone slabs.

Under the united Silla Kingdom in the late seventh century, foreign ideas reached Korea, primarily from T'ang China via the Buddhist clergy. Buddhist learning and art flourished, exemplified by numerous pagodas, tombs, bronzes, lanterns, ceramics, and mural paintings of this period. Excellence in painting techniques was transmitted to Japan, where in the ninth century Wu Tao-tzu, a Korean painter working in Japan, was credited as the first to bring landscape to the level of dignified art.

The revival of Confucian scholarship in the 13th and 14th centuries stimulated development of painting through new interest in calligraphy and dexterity in use of the brush. Religious, mythological, and, more rarely, historical subjects were usually chosen for representation. After these, the greatest preference was for subjects from nature. Simplicity of form, dignity, and breadth of execution characterized Korean painting of this era.

Under the Yi dynasty, from the 15th to the 19th century, a Confucian revival replaced Buddhism, and painting was strongly influenced by the techniques of Ming China. For example, An Kyon, one of the foremost landscape painters of the dynasty, rendered his "Spring Dream," an artist's conception of mountains and valleys, in delicate ink and color brushwork on silk scroll. An Kyon's work is often exemplified as combining the "three excellences" of painting, poetry, and calligraphy. Korean painting of this era is far removed from the political turmoil of the times, particularly that of the late 16th century, and the artist's concern was with the inner meaning rather than outward appearance.

The 18th century, the middle of the Hermit Kingdom period, marked Korean consciousness of its own culture, to the point of expression in Korean forms rather than Chinese. All arts—music, dance, painting, drama, architecture and landscaping, and poetry —were productive during this era. Artists repeated old themes with attached hidden, peculiarly Korean, meanings as a reaction to the creative repression of the Confucian influence. Specific Korean innovations that foreshadowed a later period of reawakening and self-consciousness included use of perspective and chiaroscuro in painting. Kyomjae was an early proponent of a distinctively Korean artistic flowering, moving away from the Chinese school and painting landscapes based on actual Korean scenes and subjects.

The 19th century saw a reversal of the cultural flow from China to Korea and on to Japan. After 1850, Japan—a recipient of Western culture—transmitted new techniques and theories to Korea, and Christianity also served as a westernizing influence. Japanese and Western styles and techniques greatly influenced Korean artists, who became acquainted with such trends as impressionism, cubism, and nonrepresentational art. However, Korea had become an ingrown nation, tolerating little change, and though artists experimented with Western methods, the traditional styles still remained dominant. Some artists sought originality of concept by combining traditional Korean elements and modern techniques. An example of blending of styles is Chang Sung-op's painting "Galloping Horses," in which free movement is subtly suggested and implied, in the traditional Oriental manner, but the horses themselves are rendered with Western-style modeling.

One characteristic of Korean artistic expression is traditional conservatism and resistance to change. This may be due in part to past reactions to foreign influence—in order to maintain Korean identity it was necessary to at least feign nonresistance. As an example, the Korean's response to Western painting has been first to grasp, then to master, foreign techniques, and then finally to interpret them in his own way. While critics note Korean adoption of the style of Western artists, it is evident that there are few faithful copies but many interpretations of style.

Another characteristic of Korean expression is a love of nature, evidenced by the exquisite landscape paintings of earlier centuries. Korea is primarily an agricultural nation with a sophisticated elite of educated intellectuals, and basic attachment to the land is strong. Also a distinctive feature of Korean art is the use of silence, or subtle techniques of communication; art forms are loaded with more than ordinary significance as a result of concern with nonverbal communication and highly symbolic inner meanings.

Koreans have been slow to change, despite the flood of Western art styles seen in schools and exhibits. And in the late 1960's as art moves into the industrial era with commercial and other modern applications, the dominant traditions of this rich heritage of symbolic art are still present.

Buddhist temples, stone pagodas, and monasteries of stone or brick reflect the beauty and splendor of Korea's ancient tradition in art. Over 1,000 Buddhist temples and monasteries are in actual use today as centers for learning and contemplation. They are situated in places of great natural beauty and are architecturally well adapted to the surrounding terrain. More modest dwellings, mainly of wood, are usually of one story and are noted for their fine proportions. Lavish decorations—painted, carved, sculpted—are added to temples and palaces, and extensive interior decoration characterizes homes of the wealthy. In ancient times, palaces were surrounded by lakes, terraces, pavilions, and gardens. While many of these have vanished, excavated foundations such as that at the "Moon Terrace" near Kyongju show evidence of beautiful royal gardens.

Gardening was a revered art in Korea, and many famous Japanese gardens were patterned after Korean prototypes. A number of Koryŏ kings were enthusiastic botanists and a royal garden with rare and exotic flora gathered from various parts of the peninsula, as well as from China, was established early in the 12th century and continued until 1419.

Imaginative Literature

As a result of Chinese influence, the imaginative literature of Korea is most often found in poetry, much of it composed in a romantic vein. The faithfulness of two lovers, for example, is a frequent and popular theme. Most poems are lyrical and short; there are no epics. In addition to the formal literature created by the upper classes, there is a substantial body of tales and songs told and sung by the majority of the people.

The religious poem "The Song of Barley," is said to have been composed by King Kija (*c.* 1122 B.C.) and sung by him with the farmers. But the earliest poem of which there is a record is "The Song of the Nightingale," composed by King Yari around the beginning of the Christian era. It is typical of Korean love poems which seek their symbols in nature and express only indirectly the romanticism which inspired them.

Throughout their long history, Koreans have held the scholar in reverence, and he was, among other things, a poet. He was expected to, and did, compose poems for any and all occasions. He took part in poetry contests in the village (a tradition being revived today) and used metaphor and simile extensively. Yi Kyu-po, born in A.D. 1169, was one of Korea's most famous poets.

A distinctive position in traditional Korean literature is occupied by a type of poem known as *sijo*—a poetic form which began to be developed in the 12th century. It is composed of three couplets and characterized by great simplicity and expressiveness. Many of these poems reveal a sensitivity to the beauties of nature, delight in the enjoyments of life, and a tendency toward philosophical contemplation, which together produce a sense of serenity and, sometimes, loneliness:

> I wake up from a nap at the base of a pine
> To open my wine-drowsy eyes.
> Only the seagulls pass at sunset
> Where the river meets the sea.
> They are without a doubt
> The lords of land and water.

The value placed upon individual expression and independence sometimes finds reflection in a desire for proud solitude:

> Chrysanthemum, why do you scorn
> The east wind of spring?
> "I prefer to meet the cold rain beneath
>   a withered hedge,
> And even though it freeze me to the core,
> Would never join the mass of flowers
> That greet the vernal season."

Frequently, the poems disclose a preoccupation with purity, symbolized by whiteness:

> Do not enter, snowy heron,
> In the valley where the crows are quarreling.
> Such angry crows are envious
> Of your whiteness,
> And I fear that they will soil
> That body you have washed in the pure stream.

The ephemeral nature of time, the pleasures of wine, family life, and loyalty to one's sovereign are other common themes.

Prose fiction began in the seventh century when the noted Korean scholar, Ch'oe Chin-wun (called the father of Korean literature), published the novel *Adventures Among the Kuen-lun Mountains*, a fanciful account of ramblings among the great mountains in southern China. Kum Pu-sick, author of the standard history of the Three Kingdoms, considered the greatest of the Koryŏ writers, wrote a historical novel called *The Story of the Long North Wall*. A number of others wrote novels of travel and adventure at home and in foreign lands. Many of these stories, however, were the works of scholars, written in Chinese script and limited to a few readers.

The 15th century development of the Korean phonetic alphabet (*han'gul*) gave rise to a popular literature. Although this alphabet was looked down on by scholars and the literary elite, historical works, poetry, travelogues, biographies, and fiction were written in a mixed script of Chinese and *han'gul* and were widely circulated. Much of the *han'gul* prose fiction was written anonymously, partially because the Confucian scholars regarded anything not written in Chinese as trivial and partially because some of this fiction contained satirical attacks on political conditions under the Yi dynasty.

When Confucianism became the official state philosophy, novels and stories were given themes in the tradition of the Confucian ethic—the blessedness of filial piety, the certainty that good deeds eventually are rewarded by either personal success or gratitude. A voluminous amount of literature was produced in the 18th and 19th centuries—much of it reflecting Confucian themes.

The Confucian tradition continued to control formal Korean literature until the advent of Western influences. The works of Russian, German, French, English, and American authors were read by the more educated Koreans, and Korean writers increasingly adopted Western ideas and literary forms. After 1910, their works were somewhat suppressed by the Japanese; after 1919, however, when control was eased slightly, newspapers and literary magazines began to be published in considerable number, and novels and poems expressing rebellion against oppression began to appear. *The Merciless* by K. S. Yi, *The Muddy Stream* by Ch'ae Man-sik, and *The Heartless* by Yi Kwang-su are outstanding examples of this trend.

There have also been a number of novels which have treated Korean history in times of crises. *Admiral Yi* by K. S. Yi is an example. Two recent works on Korean themes in English have been widely acclaimed by both domestic and foreign readers and critics—*The Living Reed*, a novel on family life by Pearl Buck, published in 1963, and *The Martyred* by Richard Kim, which deals with the presumed martyrdom of twelve Christian missionaries during the Korean conflict, published in 1964.

In general, modernization of Korean literature has lagged behind the main current of postwar world literature. Since the turn of the century, Korean literature has emulated modern European literature and has maintained relatively insignificant ties with Korea's ancient and medieval literary ages. Writers are now trying to establish a national identity and a literary tradition of their own, and the reasons why this is so difficult may, again, be traced to very rapid westernization at the turn of the century.

Modern Korean literature was born under Japanese colonial rule; from the years 1945 to 1950 a new political consciousness arose and a host of younger generation writers moved to the forefront with new techniques. As a result of belatedly adopting the literary techniques of more advanced European nations, early attempts at modernization were imitative and tended toward the melodramatic and the romantic. However, the climate was created for a new modern Korean literature, and during the Korean conflict years there occurred a turning point.

During the war most writers moved south; their set themes at this time were anxiety, a spirit of resistance, and humanitarian social consciousness. Sartre, Camus, and Kafka were widely read during this period, and the hopelessness and discouragement of the Korean intellectual community was embodied in a feeling of rootlessness similar to that of the European "lost generation" between the two world wars. The Korean conflict split a traditionally unified nation and resulted in the literary community's search for a new ideological posture. Schisms arose in this community between the advocates of "pure" and "class" literature. Since 1958, two distinct literary circles have emerged—the older, established authors who describe the existing world with more naturalistic technique, and the younger writers, who delve into the subconscious man and rely heavily on the stream of consciousness technique. Han Musuk's *The Steps of Light*, published in 1960, is an example of this latter school. Concomitant with this is the "new generation" writers' general distrust of the older generation.

Much of the same process has occurred in poetry. Following the Korean conflict, new currents in poetry were evident. Use of the vernacular and more personal insight were expressed, as exemplified by Kim Namjo's poetry, mainly about her personal life. Self-examination and revolt against conventionalism were themes, and the resultant more abstruse nature of poetry widened the gap between audience and poet. This resulted in gradual reduction in space allowed in literary journals and newspapers, thus depriving poets of their traditional media. On the other hand, it has fostered a poetry boom, accompanied by publication of many new poetry magazines and gravitation of writers into groups according to literary allegiance.

The Folk Tradition

The rich and varied folk literature of Korea is more closely related to religion than is the formal literature. There are three main kinds of tales—those derived from spirit worship, those in the Confucian tradition, and those reflecting the influence of Buddhism. Many of the stories are redolent with earthy humor and offer escape from traditional restrictions on individual creativity.

Tales of spirits—more purely Korean than the others—are beyond counting, since everything, animate and inanimate, is thought to have a spirit. Spirits of mountains, streams, rocks, caves, animals, and so forth, most of which are feared, are much a part of Korean tales. The turtle, the symbol of longevity, and the tiger, the awesome king of the beasts, appear most frequently in animal tales.

The Confucian tales, which are known by virtually everyone, are designed to illustrate and teach principles of conduct, and are short, didactic, and unimaginative. Right behavior is shown as necessary for success and is invariably rewarded.

The Buddhist stories, longer and more involved, give much wider range to the imagination and provide opportunity for dramatic effect. Plots are often intricate and contain considerable detail about interplay in human relationships. There is, however, a common core—a monastery that serves as a refuge for the troubled hero; a place where the hero acquires the strength to go back to the world and to conquer; or a monk who intervenes in a miraculous manner to snatch the hero from certain defeat.

Koreans also have a wealth of oft-told myths and legends; tales of wonderful marksmanship, heroic daring, gigantic strength, subtle stratagem, inventive genius, intrepid horsemanship, hairbreadth escape, and the like. There is Yi Yu-song, whose body flattened bullets which fell harmlessly to the ground; and Kwak Chau, "General of the Red Robe," who had the power to wrinkle the ground, make it contract, then expand to normal after he had stepped over. He could fall upon the enemy in Chŏlla one day and breakfast in Kyŏngju on the next. And there is also the myth of the founding of Chosŏn (Korea), "Land of the Morning Calm" by Tan-gun. The classic love story, "Ch'un-hyang," written during the Yi dynasty (A.D. 1392–1910) and recorded in the native alphabet, is known to nearly all Koreans. Taking as its theme the love of a young nobleman and the daugher of a *kisaeng* (dancing girl similar to the Japanese geisha), it was especially popular among those who were critical of the sharp division between the nobility and the common people in the existing social order.

Many tales illustrate the wisdom of magistrates in unraveling problems of law. For example, in one story, a good horse was stolen and a poor, spavined brute was left in its place. The victim of the theft appealed to the prefect, who ordered that the old horse be deprived of water for two days, then set free on the road. When free, it made straight for its former master's house in a distant village, where the stolen horse was found.

Folk stories, whose theme is the winning of fame and success, often center on the great national examinations and illustrate the high status of the scholar. Until very recent times, there was little honor granted business success, and fame that rested upon military success alone was insufficient. In Korean fiction, military glory is thrust upon a man; only literary and scholarly fame are actively sought. Admiral Yi is a national hero because of his success against the Japanese, but he is seen primarily as a scholar and a gentleman who only secondarily filled a naval hero's role when his country needed such service.

These stories have been told and retold through the centuries to the great enjoyment of young and old alike. Any individual could be the storyteller, and often the telling took on aspects of a dramatic production with the narrator freely acting out the parts. In ancient times, professional storytellers would read classical and folk tales to any individual or group that wished to hire them.

Music, Dance, and Drama

Since ancient times music and dancing in Korea have been an intimate part of life. Until the importation of Western classical music and ballet, the formal concert or dance performance was rare except in the palaces or temples. However, a strong folk tradition persists, making music and dance a part of everyday work and life.

Distinctive Korean instruments have been produced for centuries without modification. The *chwage* (sitting drum) and the *hyang p'iri* (tartar pipe) have been known for over 2,000 years, while the *komungo* (harp), *hyang pip'a* (lute), and the *taegum* (bamboo flute) were devised during the Three Kingdoms period. Small orchestras (a few instruments and a drum) have for centuries accompanied folk singing and dancing. Larger orchestras—consisting of stringed instruments such as the zither, harp, flute, a type of clarinet, drum, cymbal, gong, and other percussion instruments—were used in court circles where a special court or "graceful" music evolved.

There are three classes of ancient Korean music. "Graceful" music is the orthodox music, performed at court and at ritual ceremonies. This music is based on Chinese prototypes of the Chou dynasty (1122 B.C.–255 B.C.), and was transferred to Korea during the Kŏryo dynasty (A.D. 918–1392). While this music has gone out of existence in China where it originated, in Korea it has been handed down almost in its entirety, thus preserving an otherwise lost ancient art.

Although instruments of ancient popular Korean music still retain the original Chinese names, musical qualities and character have changed so that they can hardly be said to be Chinese. Native music derived from secular ancient music forms the core of Korean music today.

Korean formal, or classical, music is considered capable of greater variety and complexity than is most Asian music. To the Western ear, it seems to lack definite rhythmic and melodic patterns, but its rules, although allowing considerable freedom, are precise. Musical canons conforming with Chinese conventions were developed under the early Yi kings. Proper music performed a moral function by bringing an individual into greater harmony with the true nature of life, and formal musical theory was bound up with involved ideas on politics, religion, nature, and the universe.

Musical instruments were classified by origin or by materials from which they were made. The Korean classical orchestra instruments are made of the chief elements of nature—wood, stone, and metal—and the full orchestra symbolically represents the sounds of nature in harmony. The Korean court at the turn of the century included several hundred musicians whose traditions have been preserved by students to the present day. However, classical Korean music is appreciated now by only a few.

Korean music, like Chinese, is nonharmonic, based on a 12-tone scale (five basic tones, including two flatted tones, and seven additional tones). Music characteristically begins and ends with a keynote; 12 pieces are played in ancient ritual music, each using one of the 12 tones as its keynote. The basic characteristics of this music lie in its ethical character—the moral, uplifting effect on the audience through melody. The life and spirit of Korean "graceful" music is its message of beauty and goodness, cardinal Confucian virtues.

As with the other arts in Korea, musical expression has undergone considerable change as result of westernization and is currently experiencing much the same problems as those confronting modern art and literature—conflict between new Western styles and ancient traditional forms.

Korean folk music, ignored by court composers in the past, is now very popular with all classes. The song is by far the most important popular musical form; Koreans sing a great deal, at work in the fields, on the road, at feasts, parties and celebrations, or in the home. It is said that when a dozen Koreans gather, it will be only minutes before singing begins. Many of these songs are traditional melodies readily distinguishable by the Western ear. A single, fluid melody, sung to the accompaniment of strong irregular rhythms as women beat their daily wash, is a common sound in the countryside.

Koreans extemporize in song, just as the nobles and scholars once did in poetry. A number of folk songs have been borrowed from the West and have their origin in Christian hymns; Christmas carols with Korean words are also popular. Western, particularly American, popular songs have come in vogue since 1945. Western musical techniques and instruments are frequently adapted in professional performances of traditional songs. Japanese music apparently is also well liked by Koreans.

The subjects of Korean songs are without limit. Romantic love is a very popular theme, and some songs are political in inspiration. One of the most famous is the "Arirang," said to have been composed centuries ago by a political prisoner awaiting execution and sung by him as he trudged up the Hill of Arirang, the place of execution just outside Seoul. The people learned "Arirang," and soon it was the traditional farewell of the condemned man. It has since been given many verses and versions, both as a love song and as an expression of Korean patriotism.

Korea has served as a bridge of cultural transmission from India to China and to Japan. Dance and music forms were part of this exchange, but in these arts Korea also acted as an originator, transmitting to Japan and China techniques and forms of music and dance as early as 285 A.D. For example, in that year, Korean musicians went to teach in Japan. Koguryŏ and Koryŏ dances were imitated and acclaimed in later T'ang China, and the poet Li-po wrote the following description of one dance that particularly moved him:

"Crowned in a golden hat, the dancer,
Like a white colt, turns slowly.
The wide sleeves fluttering against the wind,
Like a bird, from the Eastern Sea."

Korea created its own dance form, particularly folk dance. Folk dances are the oldest dances and are closest to the roots of the people. Informal folk dancing is deeply rooted in the Korean way of life. Korean men sometimes dance with women, but most often the men and women dance separately. As with singing, Koreans dance at almost every possible opportunity—during rest periods in the fields, when entertaining friends, and so on. The ability to extemporize on such occasions is highly prized by Koreans, and guests at parties are expected to perform. The dances are usually accompanied by a drum, sometimes a reed flute or other instruments.

Korean folk dance music exhibits sophisticated rhythmic development similar to that of Afro-Cuban drum rhythms. The dancer's movement takes precedence over the rhythmic accompaniment, however, giving extremely strong emphasis on dance movements. In the Farmers' Dance, for instance, the dancers move slowly and steadily in and out of a triple meter rhythm. The folk musician's training is not formal, and music is learned entirely by rote; he can easily handle complicated syncopated beats and polyrhythms, which often elude notation by the more formally trained musicians educated in the Western classical music tradition.

Originally very creative and subject to much improvisation, folk dances and music are now becoming highly stylized. Much of this transformation is now also occurring in Korean formal dance.

Less spirited and more refined than folk dances are court and ritual dances, influenced by ancient Chinese and Indian models. Korea is rich in dance, the long history of which is revealed by excavated tomb paintings which have inspired the re-creation of ancient dances. Dance reached its apex in Korea during the 14th century, when dance scripts and reference books were written.

Many formal dances are still performed, for example, the Buddhist Drum Dances, Circle Dance, and Scarf Dance. Some, such as the Devil Dance and the Lion Dance, tell a historic story in the manner of ballet; others are a sly commentary on human failings. They are usually executed by one performer, who adheres strictly to traditional patterns and who is accompanied by indigenous instruments, songs, and poetic recitation. Parts of the story not explicit in the dance may be bridged with dialogue. Emphasis on shoulder movement, which governs the slow, graceful arm rhythms, is characteristic of these dances.

In Asian dance the artist is not expected to express his own personal feelings but rather to re-create the traditional form; the spectator's pleasure derives from the genius of the intepreter-performer seen through the familiar form. The ideal of Korean dance is the cultivation of inner beauty rather than demonstration of a technique or dance for its own sake. Dances are highly symbolic; every movement is charged with meaning, every pause or silence carries a message. Formal Korean dance, handed down for centuries, is slow and serene, full of stately movement and harmonious color, blended into an exquisite work of visual art.

Korean dance evolved from ancient religious ceremonies and was linked to agricultural cycles and Confucian and shaman ritual dances. The Yi dynasty, particularly under King Sejong, was most favorable for the flowering of dance and music. In the 19th century, Crown Prince Hyŏmyong composed many dances, and of all extant Korean dances, about 50 are credited to him. One still performed is entitled "Beautiful Persons Picking Peonies." Under the Japanese occupation following the Yi dynasty, traditional court dances and the highly trained *kisaeng* dancers lost their former stature. However, despite modernization, traditional dances are still a symbol to the Korean people of the ancient nobility and beauty of Korea.

After the 1919 Independence Movement, with the introduction of modern Western dancing by the Japanese, folk dance also declined. With the new freedom accompanying the birth of the Republic of Korea in 1948, most performers began creating their own dances rather than looking to the glorious dances of the past. Westernization has radically changed folk art in Korea, and the once-spontaneous improvisation has become rigid and stylized. The modern Korean entertainment seeker wants change and variety as the natural outcome of the increased pace and tempo of modern living.

Closely associated with the folk and formal dance traditions of Korea is the mask drama. This appeared around the ninth century as Buddhist mask drama imported from China and as shamanistic rituals to exorcise evil spirits. Such dramas also served as vehicles for political expression and airing of grievances. Performers were usually men, and the occupation was hereditary, resulting in formation of a theater guild. Plays were held cn makeshift stages or in open-air market places. Performers used highly stylized masks; and broad rustic movements, unsophisticated music, and use of earthly expression were characteristic of this type of popular entertainment.

Aside from poetic recitation, mask dance-dramas, singing, and dancing of stories, Korea has no significant indigenous drama tradition. Confucian scholars generally held the theater in contempt, though an elaborate intellectual play, "The Drama of the Palace Gate," was performed annually at the court to commemorate transfer of the capital to Seoul at the inception of the Yi dynasty.

Korean delight in dramatic performance did, however, lead to the borrowing of *simpa* plays from the Japanese in the 19th century. After the annexation of Korea by Japan, Korean storytellers banded together to present crude stage operettas and farces. These all-male productions acquired considerable popularity throughout the country but had almost disappeared by 1945. Since then, a group of *kisaeng* girls have taken over the repertories of the male companies. In the meantime, Koreans educated abroad have become acquainted with Western theater, which is beginning to achieve some success in the cities today. Thus, Korea's theatrical tradition in the Western sense spans only the past 60 years or so.

Although the arts themselves were valued in the Confucian tradition, the product rather than the individual artist was important. To be a good poet or musician was but one of the attributes of the gentlemen-scholar, and no single talent in itself constituted a particular distinction. Accordingly, professional entertainers, musicians, singers, dancers, and later, actors, traditionally had a relatively low status in Korean society. This is changing today as a result of government sponsorship of the arts, and artists are gaining alliance with the elite. Western music (symphonic and popular), opera, ballet, theater, and movies are becoming increasingly popular in Korean cities, and a developing Korean motion picture industry also is having an impact on the traditional attitude toward entertainers.

Intellectual Expression

Since the 14th century, intellectual expression in Korea has been dominated by an extreme kind of Confucianism unknown in China. (Almost all writings done under Buddhist influence were destroyed.) Its regulating force has tended to suppress intellectual and creative originality, limiting them to the reiteration of ancient concepts (see ch. 11, Religion).

The *Five Classics*—Book of Changes, Book of History, Book of Poetry, Book of Rites, Spring and Autumn Annals—and the *Four Books*—Great Learning, Doctrine of the Mean, Analects, Works of Mencius—have been given a great deal of Korean commentary and interpretation. Of these, the Book of Rites has been most important in Korea, for in a 12th century appendage the Chinese philosopher Chu Hsi recodified the Confucian domestic ritual into a form that Koreans adopted for themselves; also in high favor were the Book of Changes (I Ching) and the Spring and Autumn Annals.

Traditionally, Koreans have classified their formal literature (all written in Chinese characters) into four divisions; Kyŏng (Chinese Classics); Sa (history); Cha (Special Subjects, including religion, war, agriculture, medicine, astronomy and mathematics, geomancy, travel, fine arts, and fiction); and Chip (Collected Writings). The most original Korean contribution to Far Eastern intellectual achievement was made in the writing of history. Usually the focus of Korean histories was on the king and his court rather than on the common people. Yet in addition to the official histories, written by statesmen and scholars and culminating in voluminous dynastic annals like those of China, there also was Yasa, or vulgar history, concentrating on the less formal aspect of events. Among the official histories, the most valuable is a collection known as the

Yicho Sillok (Yi Dynasty Annals), written under unique precautions against bias; at the end of each individual reign, all documents were assembled by a commission of historians protected against interference; copies of the collection were then deposited and guarded for posterity in several widely separated mountain citadels as well as in the capital.

Geographical studies, encyclopedias of history, government, law and culture, and biographies were also included under Sa. Among the most important of the geographical encyclopedias is the *Tongguk Munhon Pigo*; 100 volumes were printed in 1770.

Extensive writings on astonomy and mathematics, geomancy (selection of lucky sites for graves, houses, palaces, and so forth), languages, and music, as well as quantities of essays, biographies, state papers, and letters, also testify to the energy once characteristic of Korean intellectual life. But the weight of Confucianism—at first the stimulus for all this activity—stultified Korean intellectual expression for centuries because of the necessity for extreme conformity to some of its conventions.

The social status of Korean intellectuals is at present unstable, and they are seeking a new political stature. However, the Korean intellectual does not generally think of himself as participating in the creation of new social values.

THE SITUATION IN THE 1960'S

The Republic of Korea is a blend of the old and the new. Major characteristics of intellectual and artistic expression seen in 20th century Korea derive from her traditional heritage—conservatism and resistance to change, love of nature and respect for learning, use of the nonverbal in communication, and the ability to retain identity in response to foreign culture. Awareness of these traditional traits is helpful in understanding the changes now taking place in Korean arts and thought.

The liberation of Korea in 1945 provided new inspiration and opportunity for artistic and intellectual activity. While both parts of the peninsula suffered a loss of artists and thinkers during the Korean conflict, the traumatic experience of war seems to have added impetus to a desire to achieve new and meaningful forms of artistic and intellectual achievement.

Artists and intellectuals of the Republic face a difficult struggle for material security but enjoy a much greater degree of intellectual privacy and freedom of expression than their northern counterparts. While they may at times be prevented from saying certain things considered politically offensive, their thinking and working are not prescribed. Today they are making a serious effort to assimilate the impact of Western culture, to achieve a synthesis of the old and the new, and to develop original forms of imagina-tive expression. This effort holds the promise of a new vitality in the arts. While contemporary artists and writers have a small pub-lic, there are signs of the beginning of a general artistic and intel-lectual revival.

The Contemporary Cultural Scene

Seoul in recent centuries has been the center of artistic and in-tellectual activity in Korea, and it is still the cultural center of the Republic of Korea. The Ministry of Culture and Education has under its supervision a number of functioning libraries, conserva-tories, museums, and other such institutions, most of which were originally established by the Japanese to preserve Korean art. The National Art Museum contains more than 10,000 art objects and a National Music Conservatory (successor to the Yi Academy of Music) has a collection of classical Korean instruments in addition to a small staff of musicians dedicated to the study and develop-ment of Korean classical music. The National Academy of Sciences and Letters and an Academy of Arts were founded in 1954. Most of these and similar institutions, however, are short of funds. Re-pair of long-neglected Buddhist temples and shrines, ranking among Korea's finest art treasures, has been financed largely by the contributions of pilgrims.

The Institute of Koreanology, formerly known as the Social Sci-ence Research Center, was created in Seoul in 1956 for the purpose of collecting documents and sponsoring studies on current Korean history and social problems. By 1964, it had supported some 15 projects in these fields and its library was housed in a permanent center, built in 1958.

Visual Arts

Western influence in contemporary artistic expression is pro-nounced. Painting has been stimulated by frequent exhibitions of both Western and Korean work, and the major schools of painting reflect these differences. The Korea Painting Society, inaugurated in 1967, attracts primarily Oriental painters; the Korea Figurative Painting Society supports the Western-oriented abstractionists and realists. In the early 1960's, many young Korean painters exhib-ited abroad in both Western and Oriental exhibitions, and interna-tional recognition has been give to such Korean artists as Kwan ham, Sung Ja Lee, and sculptor Chong Hyok Lee.

The year 1968 was marked by the controversy and turmoil in Korea's fine arts world. The schism between the traditional Ko-rean and new Western schools continues; in general, critics have been disappointed in national documentary painting projects, some involving the nation's most celebrated painters, and in the

1966–1968 period there was considerable dissension over selection of executors for government-initiated painting and sculpture projects. Since 1945, architecture has broken away from the old styles and by 1968 was following the latest international trends.

Music

Further westernization is taking place in contemporary Korean music, with introduction of electronic music compositions in the late 1960's. The most prominent of the young Western-oriented Korean musicians today is Nam Jun Paik.

Korea has two state-financed symphony orchestras. Recitals and concerts are frequent and include those given by chamber and choral societies and by the municipal symphony orchestras of Pusan, Taegu, and North Chŏlla Province. As evidence of Korea's success at westernization, a number of musicians—primarily violinists— have placed high in international music contests, and the Korean pianist Tong Il Han is world renowned. In 1965, a concert by Byung Ik Hwang, outstanding composer and performer on the *kayakeum*—a traditional Korean stringed instrument—drew attention to Korea's past musical heritage; in 1964 a series of dance tours was undertaken to elevate the reputation of classical dance. Western ballets were also performed, an in 1967 a Japanese company joined a Korean troupe for a joint production of *Carmen*.

Western-oriented musicians are calling for modernization and popularization of the folk arts. In 1967, the first individual folk music composition presentation was held in Korea. Popular songs were mass-produced that year for the first time. Singers and songs are becoming very popular in Korea, deflecting a change in the traditional low status of such performers. Also, the recording industry is booming.

Publishing

Publication on a large scale in Korea started in 1908. By the late 1960's, over 250 magazines were published in the Republic, 113 of these commercial. Most newspapers and magazines not published in Korea are imported from Japan and the United States (see ch. 16, Public Information).

While many literary magazines went out of publication in 1967, other more stable monthly magazines give space to new poems, fiction, and critiques. The Korea Writers Association published no 1967 issues of poems or stories but instead began compiling a 15-volume collection of Korean short stories, representing 150 writers, to commemorate the 50th year of the new literature movement in Korea.

Korean literary circles are generally active, and short stories by

Korean authors have fostered the modern Korean literary school. Many such works use the Korean conflict as a theme, for example, Richard Kim's *The Martyred*. Indeed, the war marked a turning point in Korean literature. Broader opportunities now exist for publication of novels as well as essays and criticisms.

Book publishing was relatively stagnant in 1967. Ten hardbound books were published, while paperbacks flourished (see ch. 16, Public Information). Best-selling books were historical novels and some serials, including *History of the Three Kingdoms* and *A Collection of Dostoevsky*. Also printed are "working libraries" for secondary school students and books for housewives. The more popular literature is aimed at all classes. Best-sellers again reflect the influence of Western writers and include Korean authors as well as Herman Hesse (*Demian*), André Malraux (*Memoirs*), and Svetlana Alliluyeva (*Twenty Letters to a Friend*).

Drama

Development of the dramatic arts was greatly stimulated in the early 1960's by construction of a drama center, financed by contributions from a number of foreign foundations. This center specializes in the production of translated works, while a national theater specialized in the production of works by Koreans. In 1962, both an academic theater and a children's theater were established, and high school drama clubs held a national competition.

As of 1967 Korea had 14 registered stage troupes and 30 minor ones. The Korean stage grew rapidly in 1966 and is expected to continue, though in July 1967, broadcasting and television firms prohibited their performers from working on the stage. Nevertheless, troupe performances presented Korean-directed Western dramas and some dramas written by Koreans. As part of this revival of stage drama, "Underground Shack," a play written by Yu Chi-jin in commemoration of the 60th anniversary of introduction of modern culture into Korea, was presented in 1968.

Plays by Western authors are popular, from Shakespeare to such modern writers as O'Neill. In 1964, a Shakespeare festival was held, and Korean dramatic groups, such as Sin Hyop, now perform original Korean plays as well as foreign translations. There are also revivals of classical dramatic pieces.

Motion Pictures

One of the fastest growing of Korean arts is motion pictures. This is developing partly through foreign assistance, and Korean specialists have been sent to the United States for study. New motion picture laboratories are being constructed to serve several independent studios, and in response to the demand for qualified performers and technical personnel, Korean universities and colleges now have departments of drama and motion pictures.

The movie industry has made great strides since 1957. More than 100 feature-length films are produced annually, of quality equaling the international cultural level (see ch. 16, Public Information). At the Ninth Asian Film Festival held in Seoul in 1962, Korean films captured nearly all prizes offered.

Movies are the most popular form of mass entertainment. Foreign films are well liked, particularly those from Britain, France, and Germany. A move to curtail foreign film imports was made in 1967 in order to foster the domestic motion picture industry. However, foreign films are still much in demand.

Government organization of movie producers into the Korea Motion Picture Producers Association in 1967 reduced the number of producers from 23 to 12. However, stimulated by the government quota on foreign picture imports, box office records were attained by a number of domestic films. Among these were literary films (based on short novels), revival films (based on past best-sellers), and Korean versions of westerns.

The Artist, the Scholar and Society

The general intellectual climate today is one of renewed life and active government encouragement. Under government auspices, nationwide music and theatrical contests are held, and government-controlled schools are placing increased emphasis on the fine arts (see ch. 9, Education). A number of awards and prizes to encourage literature and other arts have been established, some by the government, some by private publishing houses, and one by the United States-sponsored Asia Foundation. For example, the Ministry of Public Information sponsors a nationwide folk art festival. In this annual event, selected groups of folk artists representing Seoul and various provinces compete in such fields as mask dance plays, farmers' bands, folk dancing, and opera.

There is considerable controversy among modern Korean intellectuals, and in 1967–1968, debate revolved around political trends associated with the domestic political situation, exemplified by the irregular parliamentary elections of June 1967 (see ch. 14, Political Dynamics).

There is much agitation in and around the academic community on the subject of "purification" of college education. Qualitative stagnation of graduate schools is discussed, along with problems of mass production of college graduates and unwholesome growth in size of some universities. Public anger has been aroused over increases in tuition at private universities, and in 1968 vocational educational development plans were effected to increase the number of vocational schools in relation to liberal arts colleges (see ch. 9, Education).

There are conflicting, shifting schools of expression in Korea. As an example, the talented *kisaeng* dancers and musicians have all but been driven out of business by recorded stylized Korean folk music or by Western music ranging from classics to jazz to rock. At the same time, however, Korea is experiencing a revival of the old Korean forms of music and dance. In 1967 and 1968, for example, worldwide tours were undertaken by dance troupes performing the traditional dances of ancient Korea.

In general, there is evidence of a growing awareness in Korea of its place in world intellectual society and the international community of scholars. Korea sent 18 scholars to the Oriental Studies Conference held in the United States in 1967, and 10 Korean scientists represented Korea at the Biochemistry Conference held in Tokyo.

A general modernization of religious dogma and reform of rule is being carried out amidst heated controversy between conservative and progressive forces. Controversy also exists in the philosophic circles in Korea. On the other hand, there is activity in the research field in almost every area of inquiry, ranging from research on Korean culture by the East Asia Cultural Institute to pharmacological research on ginseng as a cancer retardant. There are a number of academies of science and research organizations in Korea. Research programs are conducted in agriculture, medical science, meteorology, chemistry, biology, mathematics, atomic physics, and oceanography, and extensive archeological excavation and research activity is being undertaken by college museums. Scientific research is primarily linked with industrial application. For example, the first Korean technical team to go abroad went to Venezuela in 1967 to survey manganese mines.

While academic research funds were scarce in 1967, Seoul National University initiated a research professor system and the Education Ministry granted extensive research allowances to professors and college institutes in natural sciences, social sciences, and the arts. Much research is being done on Korea itself—tomb excavation, folk song and folklore collecting, and symposiums on the influence of American culture, held by the Asiatic Research Center of Korea University. There is also a move toward codifying "cultural property" as national treasures; these include art objects, historic sites, music, dance, and other intangible cultural property.

There is considerable government interest in promotion of more academic science, evidenced by the founding of the Science-Technology Research Center and attempts to bring back prominent Korean scientists from abroad. In general, these fields are hampered by lack of funds. Most advanced degrees awarded in science are obtained abroad, primarily in the United States.

Other evidences of government support and encouragement of scientific and artistic endeavor include inauguration of the Science-Technology Ministry in April 1967. Also, many awards are offered in recognition of outstanding work in scientific or cultural fields. For example, the Academy of Arts and Sciences gives recognition to outstanding examples of art, motion pictures, and various other fields of culture from literature to choreography and handicraft. Finally, Order of Cultural Merit awards are made to promote Korean national culture or welfare.

CHAPTER 11

RELIGION

Several religious systems or ethical systems with a religious base have helped shape the course of Korea's cultural development. The first was spirit worship (shamanism) of a type commonly found in northern Siberia. Buddhism in its Mahayana form and Confucianism—an ethical system rather than a religion—both appeared in parts of the area in the fourth century. The former, however, was dominant until the end of the 14th century when, under the Yi dynasty, Confucianism replaced it as the official doctrine. Christianity was permanently established in the latter part of the 19th century, as was an indigenous religious movement called Tonghak (Eastern Learning) which later split into two groups, Ch'ŏndogyo and Sich'ŏngyo. Obeisance to Shintoism was enforced during the latter part of the Japanese occupation, but has left little mark.

In the early 1960's, all Koreans continued to be more or less influenced in varying degrees by Confucian ethics. In the south, where the Constitution provided for complete religious freedom, Buddhism, Christianity, and other religions which had helped shape the country's cultural and political development retained a substantial number of followers (see ch. 13, The Governmental System). In addition, a number of adherents had been attracted to Pak Chang No Kyo (lit., the teachings of Elder Pak) and others of the so-called new religions which had emerged since 1945 as a result of the confrontation between Korean tradition and the alien, in many respects, moral systems and cultural patterns of the industrialized West.

CONFUCIANISM

The framework of Korean culture is based almost solely on Confucian thought. Although this cult probably did not become influential until the fourth century A.D., the original date for the introduction of Confucianism into Korea is often given as 1122 B.C. (Confucius, himself, was not born until c. 551 B.C.; however, the actual advent of the philosophical system known as Confucianism is usually considered to have been much earlier because it is based on his compilation and editing of ancient writings.) From the Yalu basin area Confucianism spread into the rest of the country, but it was not until the 14th century that it was adopted as the state religion and became deeply interwoven in the social and political institutions of the society.

In some periods of Confucian history in Korea, either the king or the president of the Confucian college performed priestly functions. The Confucianists, however, do not form a church and have no religious leaders or formal educational institutions (see ch. 9, Education). Unlike conversion to many other formal religious sects, becoming a Confucianist is relatively simple in the sense that acceptance of the doctrine makes one a Confucian and does not preclude other forms of belief as long as they are not directly contradictory. Because of these circumstances, statistics on the number of professed Confucianists must be understood in terms of the persistence of the social structure and the cultural values associated with it. The continuing influence of Confucian teaching in Korean cultural and social life is nowhere more evident than in the prestige of Songgyangwan University at Seoul, one of the country's leading institutions of higher learning.

Although Korea adopted rules of conduct quite different from those Confucius and his followers taught, the fundamentals were originally very similar, in that Koreans—like classical Confucianists—viewed the world as a simple unit, natural in organization, with a set of hierarchical relationships. According to Confucian ethics, the society of man must be based on the natural hierarchical order, and on proper conduct, varying according to the sex, age, and social position of the individual. These elements were the foundation of the harmonious social order which Confucianists sternly advocated. Society, according to the five cardinal virtues of Confucianism, is based on five social relationships: between lord and subject, between father and son, between husband and wife, between older and younger brother, and between friends.

The corresponding standards of conduct, or *li*, for these pairs are righteous behavior in the husband, obedience in the wife; love in the father, filial piety in the son; benevolence in rulers, loyalty in subjects; gentility in the elder brother, humility in the younger; humane consideration in elders, deference in juniors.

In China and in Korea, Confucianism was accompanied by certain beliefs in spirits and deities and in the ritual practices associated with them. For many years the spirit of the site on which Confucian shrines stood was given recognition; in some places yearly sacrifices were offered to heaven and earth, and Confucian government officials conducted rain ceremonies. All over Korea there were shrines to the mythical dragons of the Confucianist cult. The neo-Confucianism of Chu Hsi, that varient of the sage's philosophy which had the greatest influence in Korea, incorporated many Buddhist ideas as well.

For centuries the Confucian ethic operated to preserve order within the society by encouraging certain modes of behavior between individuals, reinforcing kinship ties, and securing for the individual a sense of continuity with the past and a link with the future through ancestor worship (see ch. 7, Family). The Confucian emphasis on the pragmatic approach to both family and social functions, however, did not foster the development of ideas of absolute good and evil.

Many of the precepts of Confucianism were almost impossible for poorer households to follow. The pattern of filial obedience, for example, required a complex system of etiquette which could neither be learned nor conveniently practiced without a great deal of leisure. It was especially difficult for women (on whose labor the maintenance of the household often depended) to find the time to observe the prescribed rules of conduct; and for common people the preserving of the family line and the keeping of ancestral tablets were infeasible. Therefore, although their lives were shaped by the official doctrine of Confucianism and although they shared many of its values, the bulk of the Korean population was in no position either to learn fully or to carry out the Confucian doctrine.

Certain areas of Korea were less affected than others by the Confucian penetration. Although they profess to be Confucianists, people in northern Korea in particular have more consistently practiced traditional spirit worship, produced fewer Confucian scholars, and permitted more freedom to women. They have not developed the elaborate class distinctions (so characteristic of Confucian teaching) that are common to other parts of the country. This difference presumably resulted both from their greater distance from the centers of Confucian learning and government and from the fact that their mountainous country did not permit the development of relatively large, permanent villages with a fairly stable subsistence economy.

BUDDHISM

The influence of Buddhism upon the daily lives of the Korean people is not as obvious or as formal as that of Confucianism, yet it too is pervasive. Buddhism, which was introduced to Korea by way of northern China during the latter half of the fourth century, had spread throughout the Korean peninsula by the first half of the sixth century. The Silla Kingdom of Southeastern Korea (A.D. 673–935), which attained the highest civilization, established Buddhism as the state religion; at that time Buddhism enjoyed a golden age, winning large numbers of adherents and stimulating great artistic accomplishments. It continued as a powerful force during the Koryŏ dynasty (A.D. 935–1392) ; during this period a number of Buddhist monasteries monopolized national wealth and political power. Toward the end of the dynasty, however, Buddhism became, through its close association with the corruption and decadence of the ruling elite, more a political and economic power and declined in spiritual vigor. As a result, many leading intellectuals began to turn to Confucianism.

Buddhism was somewhat revived by the Japanese following their takeover of Korea in 1910. The Japanese government gave official encouragement by providing better religious training for the monks, sending some to Japan for religious education. Since the end of the Japanese occupation, the chief significance of Buddhism has lain in its influence on concepts of the supernatural and life after death held by Koreans of other religions and sects whose doctrines do not extend into those areas.

Buddhist doctrines have also had an important effect on social values. For example, two Chinese characters, Pyŏng Dŏng, meaning equality, were originally a Buddhist term, embodying the concept of equality among classes and races, and between men and women. This has strong attraction for women, since they have never been educated or accepted on an equal basis under Confucianism. Like other religions, Buddhism was not as strongly practiced in the north as in the south; furthermore, since the communist regime, profession and practice of the faith have become difficult.

The basic belief of Buddhism is that all living beings go through cycles of birth and death, gradually reaching higher forms through good behavior. The concept of good behavior is derived from the belief that the passions of the flesh cause desires which one must learn to control. Buddha's program for regeneration was called the Middle Way—between asceticism and self-indulgence—and is succinctly expressed in the Four Noble Truths and the Noble Eightfold Path. The Four Noble Truths are that suffering is universal, that the cause of suffering is craving or selfish desire, that the cure for suffering is the elimination of craving, and that the way to eliminate craving is to follow the Noble Eightfold Path in one's behavior. This path consists of right knowledge, right intention, right speech, right conducts, right means of livelihood, right effort, rightmindedness, and right concentration.

The varient of Buddhism which reached Korea is that generally characteristic of northern Asia and is called by its adherents Mahayana, or the Greater Vehicle. Buddha, himself, has come to be worshipped as an eternal deity; and salvation may be attained through the intercession of *bodhisattvas*—virtuous men who voluntarily defer their own elevation to assist others—as well as through individual contemplation. A whole series of heavens and hells and their guardians are explicitly pictured. Salvation is consciously thought of in terms of reaching one of these heavens rather than nirvana, the state of essential perfection and identification with Buddha himself.

Supernatural powers are created and worshipped in many different forms in Korea. Korean Buddhism is unique in that it has absorbed many of the native beliefs about the supernatural from the folk culture of both China and Korea, and both magic and the use of charms are practiced by Buddhist monks. The priests are often appealed to for protection against evil spirits, for ensurance of domestic tranquility, or for the birth of sons.

The various sects of Korean Buddhism all originally come from China, and pilgrims have traditionally journeyed there to study and to bring back the tenets and the religious literature. However, in the early 1960's it is reported that Buddhists of the Republic of Korea divided into numerous sects, differing on various points of doctrine. One issue on which there was perennial controversy was the question whether or not monks should remain celibate.

Buddhist contributions are outstanding, especially in the field of education and welfare work. Buddhists maintain, besides Tongguk University in Seoul, a large number of schools, orphanages, homes for the aged, and workers' rest homes, which are supported by the proceeds of various Buddhist-owned commercial enterprises.

CHRISTIANITY

Christianity first became known to Koreans in its Roman Catholic form. It was between 1592 and 1598 that Catholicism began to make its way to Korea, then under Japanese occupation. At that time, some 50,000 Koreans, including children, were taken to Japan to be sold to other nations as slaves. At Nagasaki, a port on the Japanese island of Kyushu, about 2,000 persons were fortunate enough to be saved by foreign missionaries; they became Catholics in 2 years. However, it was not until the 17th century that Catholicism was formally introduced by the Korean diplomats returning from China. The first foreign missionary in Korea—a Chinese Catholic monk—arrived about 100 years later.

Because the new doctrine was accompanied by intellectual and scientific concepts current in the Western world, it became known as the Sohak (Western Learning) movement and was embraced by a number of eminent scholars who saw it as a solution to the deepening social problems of the day.

From the start, the Korean Catholic church was exposed to government persecutions. The persecutions continued until 1886, when a friendship, navigation, and commerce treaty was signed between the governments of France and Korea.

Periodic persecutions of Korea's growing number of Catholics took place in the 19th century, the last of which, occurring between 1865 and 1868, resulted in the death of about 8,000 persons, or about half the total number of adherents.

It was not until 1882, the year Korea signed its first treaty of friendship and commerce with a Christian country—the United States—that full-fledged missionary work began. This opened the door for the propagation of the Christian faith in the country, and Methodists and Presbyterians came in large numbers.

In the late 19th and early 20th centuries, Christianity had a great appeal for many Koreans and generally met less resistance than it did in other Asian countries. Christian schools and missionaries first introduced Western concepts of science, democracy, and individualism to Korea. Christian missionary activity was responsible for a considerable increase in literacy in the phonetic alphabet and for a noticeable change in women's position in the Christian households. It also stressed the development of educated native leaders and self-supporting churches. No foreign missionary has been moderator of the Korean Presbyterian Church for almost 50 years, and the same is true of other Christian bodies.

During the first several years under Japanese occupation (1910–1945), both Catholic and Protestant groups continued to operate in relative freedom. However, later, when their support of the underground nationalist cause and the participation of some church leaders in the independence movement were revealed, the Japanese government became totally antagonistic toward the churches and took strong retaliatory measures (see ch. 3, Historical Setting). Increased supervision of Christian activities eventually led to the recall of almost all Catholic and Protestant missionaries during World War II.

Having been instrumental in preparing Korea for its entrance into the modern world, Christianity in the post-World War II period found itself increasingly divorced from the main currents of Korean life. Although the country had been a field of intense missionary activity for over half a century, Christians in the early 1960's represented only a small fraction of the population. More importantly, statements made by church authorities at a conference in Seoul in mid-1964 suggested that they shared a common concern that the church itself had lost touch with its popular base.

CH'ŎNDOGYO

Opposition to Catholicism, or Sohak (Western Learning), centered chiefly in the indigenous religious movement known originally as Tonghak (Eastern Learning). Founded in 1860 by Ch'oe Che-u, a Korean nobleman, the movement developed during a period of social ferment and awakening nationalist sentiment, and from the beginning had a specifically political and nationalist orientation. Its doctrine, borrowing heavily from other major faiths, stressed the dignity of man and egalitarian ideals, committing its adherents to work to end prevailing forms of social injustice in Korea and to liberate the country from foreign oppression. While acknowledging his debt to Catholicism and other religious traditions, Ch'oe Che-u stressed his conviction that differences between religious concepts formed in the East and those of the West were inevitable and that the Tonghak was the right way to faith for the Korean people because it was born out of their own unique experience.

Ch'oe Che-u was arrested by the government in 1864 and executed as a heretic, an act which served to strengthen the Tonghak movement by giving its adherents a martyr around whom to rally. Although the Tanghak was forced underground, it spread rapidly thereafter among the peasantry. In the final quarter of the 19th century, several Tonghak-inspired popular insurrections broke out, the last of which, in 1894, was crushed only after Chinese and Japanese troops had come in to assist Korean authorities. Some 400,000 Tonghak adherents, including the movement's two leading spokesmen, were massacred in the course of suppressing the revolt.

In opposition to the government, leading Tonghak members in 1904 formed a political organization known as the Progressive Society; but a factional dispute, which resulted in the merger of the party with a pro-Japanese political organization, brought an end to Tonghak political activity. The leader of one faction, Son Pyŏnghui, reorganized the Tonghak as the Ch'ŏndogyo movement, setting up a network of places of worship throughout the country; some adherents, however, followed the leader of the second faction, who organized a new sect, Sich'ŏngyo.

Under the Japanese occupation, Ch'ŏndogyo was tolerated by the authorities until 1919, when Son Pyŏnghui and 14 of his followers, along with 18 religious leaders from the Christian and Buddhist communities, organized nationwide demonstrations on behalf of the independence movement (see ch. 3, Historical Setting). The Japanese imprisoned Son Pyŏnghui together with thousands of other participants and closed more than 30 Ch'ŏndogyo schools which had been centers of revolutionary sentiment. The Ch'ŏndogyo had been dealt a severe blow, but its surviving members rallied to continue efforts in the cause of independence.

The position of Ch'ŏndogyo, weakened by the Japanese occupation, was further impaired in 1945 by the division of Korea into two military zones. In the north, where the majority of its adherents were to be found, it was grudgingly tolerated by the Communist authorities, who exploited certain of its doctrines for political purposes. In the south, Ch'ŏndogyo continued to attract a moderate number of followers, its strength considerably expanded by the arrival of refugees from the north before and during the Korean conflict. With central headquarters in Seoul, it reportedly had several hundred thousand members in the early 1960's. Substantial numbers of other persons belonged to one or another of the sects which traced their origin to the Tonghak as well. A Tonghak Association was formed in 1957 to spread the faith in areas outside Korea.

Ch'ŏndogyo is a monotheistic religion stressing the unity of man and the universe. Man is the summit of the evolutionary process, and his nature reveals the perfection of the universe, of which he is the ruler. Man and God are one, and there would be perfection here on earth if the unity were properly realized. Between men there should be no gradations.

Perfection of the world is to be sought first through a change in man's character, primarily through a widening of his interests to include the whole world. Then civil changes must be made. When these have occurred, there will be everlasting peace within Korean society and good will towards those outside it.

Ch'ŏndogyo places of worship closely resemble Christian churches. They usually contain tablets of the founder of the religion. The chief rituals are the saying of the formula; the setting out of clean water (which is a symbol of the shedding of blood of the great teacher, Ch'oe Che-u) ; the attending of services on Sunday for the study of the doctrine; and the setting aside of a spoonful of rice daily for the church. In their services, worshippers sing hymns derived largely from Chinese poems written by the founder and other leaders and sung to such Christian melodies as that of "Bringing in the Sheaves."

Special ceremonies are held on the fifth day of the fourth lunar month—called Heaven Day—in memory of Ch'oe's receiving the formula. The 14th day of the eighth month is celebrated in memory of another leader and is called Earth Day. The 24th of the 12th lunar month is Man Day, and the Korean New Year's Day is also a special occasion.

SPIRIT WORSHIP

Before Korea's contacts with other areas led to the introduction of more evolved religious systems, Korean religion consisted of unorganized beliefs about the supernatural world, a kind of animism. This animism (also called shamanism) is the oldest of Korean religious patterns and has remained the underlying religion of all Korean areas. As such, it is still accorded some deferential recognition by the farming populace and also persists as the only religious belief for many uneducated people despite discouragement by the Japanese government and, more recently, by the government of the Republic of Korea. Particularly in time of trouble—frequently illness—the *mudang*, or curer of diseases caused by malevolent spirits, is still called upon. Even in Christian or Confucian households, the *mudang* may be brought in to supplement other forms of help.

Beliefs

The Koreans believe in a large number of spirits, which vary from place to place and from time to time. There are spirits of the earth and the air, spirits of the waters and mountains, spirits of the living and the dead, and spirits which reside in rocks and trees. Most are malevolent and, therefore, are to be placated or ritually protected against; some, however, are helpful to man or are merely mischievous like the *tokkaebi* who spend their time playing pranks on mortals.

The spirits with the greatest power are those of the heavens or the air. At the head of them stands Hananim, who is thought of as being far above the other spirits, although his relation to them is not clear. It has sometimes been suggested that belief in Hananim involves a monotheistic concept. In recent years his name was used by the Protestant missionaries to stand for the concept of a single, all-powerful god. In earlier times, Koreans of many different religious inclinations accepted him as the sender of harvests and rain and as the force by which people lived. Few forms of worship are addressed directly to him. He was the god worshipped by the legendary founder of Korea, Tan'gun, to whom most ritual worship is directed.

Below Hananim are the gods of the four directions and the zenith. Each is master of his domain, and each has a host of lesser spirits under his control. Rudely carved posts, still seen occasionally in Korean villages, represent these gods who are thought to protect the village from the lesser spirits. Below them are spirits of mountains, mountain passes, and valleys. On the top of most hills is a sacred grove with a shrine to the mountain spirit, pictured as an old man seated on a tiger. He is offered animal sacrifices by hunters, miners, and medicine dealers. Travelers offer sacrifices to the guardians of mountain passes—usually a piece of cloth or a stone is added to a pile near the shrine. The spirits of valleys are especially worshipped by the farmers who throw them a spoonful of their noonday meal before starting to eat.

Each house has its own particular spirit, and when a new house is built, a special ceremony is held to appease the spirit so that all will go well with the household. On all important occasions and when things go wrong, food is spread before this spirit and prayer is offered.

Even such animals as snakes are propitiated to ward off evil—especially a variety of black snake about five feet long that the people consider the embodiment of both the ridgepole and garden wall spirits. Should this snake enter a house, the occupants treat it with respect and under no circumstances may this species of reptile be killed.

Spirits of ancient trees are widely respected throughout Korea, and it is believed that anyone cutting into a tree that is over 300 years old will die. The spirit which so protects the venerable growth is not in itself a source of good or evil, and one has the feeling that the people's attitude is a carry-over from their general Confucian admiration of things deep-rooted in the past. Trees of great age are more characteristic of monastery grounds than of villages, so they are generally removed from the immediate purview of the farmers.

The spirits of people, particularly those who have died a violent death, are very much feared. The spirits of persons who died before marriage are especially likely to be malevolent since such persons do not receive regular burial ceremonies.

There are numerous precautions taken to avoid the influence of these spirits. Roads are made crooked because spirits travel in straight lines only; the front door is blocked off at times to keep out illness; a little straw man is thrown into the road to get the disease in place of the householders; children are given names which include the character for "dragon" in order that lesser spirits may bring no harm to them. Many of the ceremonies associated with death are practiced to placate or circumvent the actions of these spirits.

Specialists

No organized system of beliefs or hierarchy of religious practitioners developed out of these folk customs; but there are certain individuals, believed to possess special influence over certain spirits, who are called upon when intercession is necessary. The most important types of practitioners are shamans, diviners, and geomancers. The male shaman is called a *paksu*; the females, who predominate as the most powerful shamans, are the *mudangs*.

Shamans become members of the profession through a psychic experience during which they establish contact with the spirit of a dead shaman. They cultivate the friendship of evil spirits in order to coax them to do their bidding. In addition to curing sickness by exorcising the spirit causing it, they quiet the ghosts of those who have drowned and drive away spirits molesting a house. They also make charms to be worn by children or placed in the house.

The most distinctive ceremony of the shamans, however, is that used for curing. A special attire is worn—male dress for women and female dress for men. The performance takes place at night and starts with the sacrifice of a chicken, pig, or god as a feast for the spirit. The shaman then dances to the sound of drums, pipe, and rattle, gradually working herself into a state of trance-like ecstasy. She teases, jokes, and pleads with the spirits to come to her, speaking in unrecognizable tones. The performance may last for a night or more, and once the spirit has eaten, it can be persuaded to leave and the sick person recovers.

The diviners also do some curing, but give more of their time to telling fortunes and giving advice on the basis of their reputed ability to see into the unknown. In order to get their information, they use little bars of metal which are cast out of dice boxes, and books of spells and incantations which they memorize. When they are curing, they depend on their divining ability to determine where the evil spirit is located; after it is located, the spirit can be exorcised. The geomancer was primarily a specialist in locating propitious grave sites, but there are few practitioners left and they are little used today (see ch. 7, Family).

TRENDS

The Constitution of the Republic of Korea guarantees religious freedom; and, in fact, considerable freedom is permitted to all religious groups. Spirit worship is not officially favored, however, and persists primarily in rural areas.

There are few Buddhists in the country, and as a group they have little influence on the society. There are, however, a few fairly prominent Buddhists in the government. In 1945 there were 1,524 Buddhist temples in the whole peninsula. Many were destroyed during the Korean conflict, and there are now 688 temples in the Republic. The number of practicing Buddhists is unofficially estimated at 200,000. Buddhism is controlled by a strong central organization, the Buddhist Central Association. No transfers of land or forest rights—the main source of revenue for the temples—can be made without its approval.

Confucianism has no formal organization or way of numbering its adherents. It remains, however, an influential force; and a return to strict observance of Confucian ethics is regarded by many Koreans as the best solution to the problems of social disorganization and lack of idealism (see ch. 12, Social Values). The Confucian ethic was not designed for an industrialized society. Yet the ideals associated with Confucianism still command greater respect and

159

offer more support to the individual and the society than does any other religious or ethical system.

Estimates of the number of Christians in the Republic of Korea, the majority of whom are Protestants, vary widely, some ranging as high as two million. Since 1945 a great increase in missionary activity has produced sectarian rivalries in the Protestant community, but Protestants still comprise about half the Christians. Charges of corruption against Protestant government officials have hurt Protestantism and have contributed to an increase in respect for Catholicism.

Another development in the religious field has been the growing strength of the so-called new religions, which have achieved popularity among a substantial section of the population. The Japanese-based Ch'angga Hakhoe (Value Creation Learning Society) (in Japanese, Soka Gakkai), for example, introduced into Korea only in 1963, had, by early 1964, an estimated 10,000 to 20,000 followers, and branches in at least eight major cities. Organized in Tokyo in the early 1930's, the Ch'angga Kakkoe is a militant society of followers of a 14th century Japanese Buddhist priest, Nichiren, who taught that Buddha was genuinely revealed in only one of the sacred scriptures—the Lotus Scripture—and that all others were false and dangerous. His assertion that salvation would come to Japan and, ultimately the world, only by understanding and practicing this doctrine has been taken by Ch'angga Hakhoe leaders as sanction for the group's confessed political ambitions. In the Republic of Korea, the government, though neither approving nor condemning the Ch'angga Hakhoe as a religion, has labeled it antistate and anti-Korean and restricted its propagation activities.

Considerably larger was the Pak Chang No Kyo, a new religious movement which originated in Korea in the mid-1950's, and which by 1964 had an estimated 800,000 to 1 million or more adherents, including a high proportion of refugees from the north. Also called the Olive Tree movement, the sect was founded by Pak T'ae Sŏn, a Korean who spent his youth in Japan, leaving there in 1944 for Seoul, where he established permanent residence, opened a business, and became active in the Presbyterian church. By 1955, having become increasingly disillusioned with the church and its leaders, he began to hold religious services himself, offering his own interpretation of the gospel. At these services, conducted much like revival meetings, Pak was an immediate success, preaching and performing his own brand of faith healing. He soon developed a loyal following, and within a short time began to refer to himself as "the one and only prophet and interpreter of the 'true' law." In 1956 he was expelled by the Presbyterians, but continued to profess Christianity.

Pak, who had been a controversial figure, was jailed on various charges by both the Syngman Rhee and Chang Myŏn governments, but the Park government has demonstrated a more tolerant attitude toward him. In the meantime, the sect he founded has continued to flourish. By mid-1964, some 20,000 of his followers were congregated in their own community development near Seoul, called Sinang Ch'on (lit., The Village of Faith), where they were housed in comfortable, modern dwellings, earned a small but steady income in an array of commercial and industrial ventures sponsored by the movement, and were provided with educational and social services. A second community has been developed at Inch'on. With its growing resources, Zion Foundation, as the business arm of the movement was called, is becoming a modest force on the economic scene.

CHAPTER 12

SOCIAL VALUES

Korean social values are based primarily on the Confucian system of ethics introduced to the peninsula from China during the Three Kingdoms Period (57 B.C. to A.D. 668). During the following seven centuries, Confucianism alternated with Buddhism as the official order (Buddhism had been introduced in A.D. 372), but gained permanent ascendancy with the advent of the Yi dynasty (1392–1910).

Confucianism made itself evident in countless areas of thought and action and provided moral sanction for characteristic modes of behavior in every facet of life. Influencing but not dominating the tradition were Buddhism and ancient indigenous religious beliefs, such as the pantheistic shamanism and, of more recent impact (19th century), Christianity and Ch'ŏndogyo, a locally originated doctrine combining elements of the other Eastern beliefs with strong nationalistic overtones (see ch. 11, Religion).

From an early date, the cohesiveness of the society reflected to a greater or lesser extent the unifying force of the Confucian principle of filial piety, which established reverence for authority and the demonstration of an abiding loyalty to the family as the highest demands to which an individual was subject. At times, when the monarchy was benevolent and the economy stable, the force of this appeal in unifying Koreans was somewhat like the impact of the emperor tradition on the Japanese.

Under Japanese rule (1910–1945), the moral unity and clearly defined pattern of authority inherent in this traditional system were badly shaken. A new landholding system that resulted in the forfeiture of certain holdings for delinquent taxes somewhat weakened the economic position of the *yangban* ruling class and precipitated the decline of the clan as a dominant influence on individual, social, economic and political behavior. Moreover, the position of the *yangban*, whom other Koreans had regarded as the source of moral and intellectual guidance as well as of political authority, was further undermined by their enforced removal from the political scene (see ch. 3, Historical Setting).

The Japanese encouraged Confucianism, reasoning that the dual principle of loyalty to high authority and to the family would work to the benefit of their own administration, since respect for high authority would be transferred from the displaced Korean officials to their own administrators. The Koreans themselves, however, had less respect for the conquerors than they had had for their own ruling class, with the result that loyalty to the state was deemphasized while loyalty to the family was greatly reinforced. The feelings of obligation and responsibility extended at first to all members of the clan; but as the economic situation deteriorated, loyalty tended to focus increasingly on the immediate family rather than on a large kinship group.

Since liberation in 1945 and particularly since the Korean conflict, the Koreans have been confronted with fundamental changes in their environment. The government has attempted to inculcate democratic concepts of social justice, individual freedom and the dignity of man—concepts that are alien to the Confucian system of social order. At the same time, sweeping changes in the economy have been effected through the development of industry and the ongoing displacement of agriculture as the main source of employment. For millions of Koreans, the bonds of kinship and tradition have been broken by war, and in their stead have been imperfectly substituted the impersonal institutions of urban life, industrial employment, and the government welfare programs. For many, problems of poverty, poor health, and hunger have outweighed the Confucian obligations regarding proper behavior; the breakdown of the old codes was evidenced in the early 1960's by rising crime rates (see ch. 26, Public Order and Safety).

Insufficient time has passed for the new social, economic, and political forces to alter many of the basic attitudes of the people. For the rural society, which still accounts for about one-half of the total population, the code of social relationships apparently has undergone little change. The traditional structure of family relationships that governs each member's role remains relatively intact. Urban society, on the other hand, displays increasing diversity, with social attitudes ranging from the traditional through the democratic to anarchic. The university students in particular appear to be increasingly disenchanted with the Confucian standard of social organization and behavior, but their own ideas regarding alternate ways of life are still amorphous.

The fundamental dilemma is the apparent irreconcilability of a system of social values based on a structure of kinship relationships with a political and economic system requiring the cooperative interaction of autonomous individuals. Independent action and social relationships based on function rather than kinship are alien

concepts to the average person; and individuals are finding it difficult to adapt to the changing character of life.

VALUE SYSTEMS

Korean attitudes and behavior reflect a system of values that
has evolved as a result of many influences. The values governing
family and social relationships are predominantly Confucian in origin, but to some extent Buddhist and indigenous religious beliefs
have moderated the asceticism of the Confucian ethic with mystical and naturalistic concepts. Thus Koreans may live in a highly
structured system of interpersonal relationships based on an agnostic concept of human existence while at the same time maintaining a belief in supernatural powers, transmigration of souls,
and life after death (see ch. 11, Religion.)

Confucianism, weakened but still influential, conceives of the
universe as a single reality in which all things, including man, take
their places in a hierarchically arranged natural order. Human society reflects this reality in its own division into high and low, superior and inferior, rulers and ruled. For the individual, proper behavior is determined by his position in the social hierarchy. An
elaborate code of etiquette prescribes the forms of appropriate
conduct, which vary with occupation, education, sex, and age; and
it was through the observance of these prescriptions by each member of the society that the ideal Confucian harmony was to be realized.

Focused on the practical problems of social existence, Confucianism has been concerned with human relationships rather than spiritual phenomena. The Confucianists undertook to order the social
system in terms of five paired human relationships: king-subject,
father-son, husband-wife, elder brother, younger brother, and
friend-friend (see ch. 11, Religion). *Li*, the ideal standard of conduct in each of these relationships, called for love in the father,
filial piety in the son; gentility in the elder brother, humility and
respect in the younger; righteous behavior in the husband, obedience in the wife; humane consideration in elders, deference in juniors; benevolence in rulers, loyalty in subjects. Most important
was implicit that loyalty to authority as well as to one's kinship
group was a compelling obligation.

"Righteousness" in the abstract is not defined in Confucianism,
which teaches that the traditional forms of behavior are important
in themselves and embody lasting values for society. If, in a particular instance, it is impossible to accord with these forms—as on
the receipt of a command that cannot be carried out—they are
more often circumvented than openly flouted. Lying, for example,
is evil only when it violates other canons of behavior required by

the social situation, such as obedience to one's father or to any superior. Lying to preserve a proper relationship is sanctioned in many instances—although certainly not always—for it maintains order and harmony. Similarly, legal theory and practice do not assume an absolute standard but take into account the social status of the participants.

In traditional Korean ethics, family honor, or *kamyŏng*, depended upon the judgment of the community that every member of the family was conforming to *li*. The individual shared the *kamyŏng* of his family, and it formed an important part of his own self-image. Individual or personal honor was termed *che'myŏn* (face), and it was a measure—perceived inwardly and recognized by others—of an individual's success in behaving according to Confucian precepts. Loss of *che'myŏn* involved shame with an admixture of guilt feelings. The submergence of the individual in the family meant that individual loss of *che'myŏn* struck directly at the *kamyŏng*. In the modern period, these concepts retain some importance, but for most persons they operate mainly on an unconscious level—much more in the manner of the Western concept of morality than the traditional Confucian concept of *li*.

Although the basic approach of Confucianism is agnostic, belief in spirits and in the persistence of the individual after death existed side by side with Confucianism in Korea (see ch. 11, Religion). Many spirit beliefs were indigenous, whereas others were Chinese, and a stimulus was given to metaphysical thought and mysticism by the neo-Confucianism of the Chinese philosopher Chu Hsi (A.D. 1130–1200). The supernatural world, for most Koreans, is peopled by various types of spirits. They are both benevolent and malevolent.

One of the most important influences of Buddhism was the concept of a supernatural reality and of the transmigration of souls. Koreans seemed to find no conflict between accepting these ideas and at the same time conforming to the basic Confucian view of proper social relationships and a natural order and harmony in the world. Similarly, at a later date, Christianity won many converts in Korea without the development of any general sense of contradiction between the new faith and existing beliefs.

Most Confucian families treated the souls of deceased ancestors as though they were spirits which could still influence family life. The ancestral spirits were to be fed, visited, and remembered on the ancestral tablets. The funeral was a mark of respect to the dead, and its elaborateness was symbolic of the status of the family in society. Through the persistence of the family line, a sort of immortality was achieved. There was, in effect, no hard and fast line between the natural and the supernatural, the living and the dead, the spirit and the flesh—they formed a continuum with the natural order, a bridge between the present, past, and future—hence the wish of all individuals to have at least two sons and a daughter.

Thirty-five years of Japanese occupation, division of the peninsula, war, and the penetration of Western concepts and methods have all contributed to a conflict of values—a contrast between the old and the new, between the ideal and the actual—which is creating confusion for the individual and instability in the society. Observers in the later 19th and early 20th centuries reported social alterations which deeply concerned many Koreans. Changes were then occurring in the structure and values of Korean society; and, whereas some recent developments have set into motion entirely new processes, others have only continued or intensified internal changes which have been taking place for a long time.

The Korean conflict and the economic and political confusion following it have accelerated the rate of social change. The increasing entrance of young people, and particularly women, into universities, into the labor force and into political activities increases their independence and undercuts the patriarchal system. Despite the increasing availability of education, the lack of opportunity for many in the younger generation has engendered disillusionment with the old system of moral values and social organization. A good many have ceased to find the Confucian view of life relevant to their needs. Some see the answer in Christianity, but to many Christianity also represents an alien philosophy, and they are seeking something more specifically Korean. Evidence of this dissatisfaction with the traditional can be seen in the adoption by youth of less formal and less polite language, Western dress, and increased informality of relationships between the sexes.

Only at the village level are the old social patterns being maintained in anything like their traditional form, but the outside urban world is also influencing village ideals. Younger, and even elder, sons are leaving home to earn a livelihood in the city, to obtain an education or to serve in the army. In the army they are exposed to new attitudes and values and often return home impressed and changed by their experiences.

Education is still highly valued, but for somewhat different reasons than in the past. Formerly, education, the appreciation of beauty, and proper behavior were important in themselves, and the acquisition of wealth was a concomitant of these attainments. Today, Koreans value education chiefly as a prerequisite for obtaining high government positions (see ch. 9, Education). Many students experience disillusionment because of the limited capacity of the government sector to absorb them.

THE INDIVIDUAL

To a considerable extent, the traditional life goals of the individual Korean were simple: caring for the parents, supporting the clan, and raising at least two sons and a daughter. If an education was possible, the culminating achievement in life was to become a Confucian scholar, to whom accrued the society's highest material and psychic rewards.

For the woman, life's main goal was to bear children—preferably sons—and to care for her husband and master. Considerations of love and affection between husband and wife were of little consequence, since the families arranged the marriage. For all members of the society, proper manners required a stoical acceptance of life, and relief from the responsibility of observing and preserving the proprieties could be obtained only through death or by reaching 60 years of age. If one lived so long, he was, in the Chinese tradition, considered to be reborn and free to pursue an existence of leisure, contemplation, and the enjoyment of being venerated by his descendants.

The place of the individual in the social hierarchy was largely determined by his family. In theory, with the exception of persons in certain despised occupations, the individual was supposed to be free to rise above or fall below the circumstances of his birth and in rare instances actually did so. With few exceptions, however, the Confucian ideal of the peasant boy who rises to high official position through success in the civil service examinations remained only a dream. Loyalty to family superseded personal ambition, and the demands of family loyalty frequently blocked the individual's hopes for advancement. Any man who achieved fame, position, or wealth was subject to the claims of members of the extended family which he could not honorably reject. The extended family system assured that almost all persons would have relatives on whom they could depend for moral support and financial cooperation; thus everyone was given a well-defined place in society.

Ideally, the Confucian system spelled out appropriate behavior for all social situations. Actually, however, individuals held several social positions, and in particular situations it was by no means clear which status should dominate. For example, although a government official might find no difficulty in dealing with a stranger in a purely official way, in the case of a member of his own family, a person from his native place, or a high-ranking noble, the same official often found himself caught in a conflict of obligations and motives which the Confucian code gave him little help in resolving.

The rapid pace of industrialization and urban growth since the early 1950's has imposed increasing strains on the Confucian system of behavior. The bonds of kinship, upon which the Confucian ethic is based, have been broken for millions of Koreans. In place of family ties there have risen functional relationships based on the impersonal forces of a market economy and a large government sector providing many of the goods and services hitherto supplied by the family and clan. Whereas in times past the behavior of an individual was largely determined by the ability of his family to exercise sanctions, now many persons have been cut loose from these stabilizing influences, and their cultural heritage has left them ill-equipped to deal constructively with strangers. The environment contrasts sharply with the Western situation where individuals tacitly acknowledge their reliance upon strangers who supply many of their needs and where the accepted norm is to cooperate on the basis of functional interdependence rather than social relationship.

RELATIONSHIPS BETWEEN PEOPLE

Interpersonal relationships among Koreans, as noted earlier, traditionally have been determined by the Confucian concept of *li*, or proper manners. Proper behavior entailed observance of a prescribed attitude depending upon one's place on the vertical scale of relationships *vis-á-vis* the other person. Except for friends or between student and teacher, the code largely restricted the extension of trust to members of one's own family and clan.

Occupational differences affected one's relationships with others. The traditional order of social rank listed the scholar at top, followed by the student, the government official, the farmer, the artisan, the merchant, the soldier, and lastly, the outcastes: the *kisaeng*, musicians, dancers, and butchers. Little concern was given to the feelings, rights, or comfort of these despised persons (including beggars, prostitutes, criminals, and others) and to a certain extent, foreigners. To a superior, one did and does express selfless humility, self-negation, and self-effacement. An inferior one could treat with a superior attitude or even with disdain if the social gap were large. Of paramount importance was the preservation of "face," one's own as well as that of the other person (unless the latter were an inferior). Great effort would be made to avoid any unpleasantness or conflict, for to do otherwise would be to risk making an implacable enemy. Korean history is replete with generations-long family feuds.

This structure of attitudes is still important in Korea, although the introduction of Western ideas over the past few decades has reduced the rigidity of the system, particularly in the cities. A factor tending to preserve the observation of strict protocol in interpersonal relationships is the pressure of overcrowding and lack of privacy or space. In such circumstances a ritualistic approach to social relationships reduces the chances for conflicts from which escape is difficult. Although this technique is conducive to smoother relationships, it often prevents taking action which over the longer term may be necessary to overcome deep-seated problems.

Honesty and good faith are relative values to the extent that they impinge upon the higher motives of family loyalty and obligation or the strictures against losing or causing the loss of "face." The individual usually places great importance on preserving the mood of the moment.

LOYALTY AND COMMITMENT

Under the Confucian tradition the hierarchy of interperson relationships was based on the following code: The king is the mainstay of the state; the father is the mainstay of the son; and the husband is the mainstay of the wife. Between friends there was to be trust; between elder and younger brothers, respect; between husband and wife, distinction in position; between father and son, intimacy; and between king and minister, loyalty. This hierarchy of relationships forms the basis for extension of loyalties, for each position within the structure involved not only the receiving of honors from subordinates, but also the exercise of authority over—hence responsibility for—those subordinates.

The Confucian system placed its greatest stress on the proper manners of the members of the family, the basic social unit. Loyalty to the family was the prime responsibility of the individual, and his behavior and activities were directly determined by their expected effect on the family's welfare.

Within the family, the father received unquestioned loyalty from the other members, over whose lives he exercised complete dominion. Under the father, the eldest son ranked next, for it was his responsibility to carry on the family name and heritage. Thus the first son's primary loyalty was to his parents, then to his brothers in order of their ages, then to his sons, and finally to his wife and daughters. The welfare of the family was and is paramount, and the personal wants and needs of many are subordinated to that end. In present-day life, for instance, it is only in modern urban areas where a son or daughter might marry against the desires of the parents, in contradiction of the age-old tradition that the parents arrange marriages.

Before the first third of the 20th century, when the Japanese occupation resulted in the gradual breaking down of some of the Confucian traditions—e.g., the position of authority of the *yangban* aristocracy—relationships of trust extended beyond the immediate family to the village and to the clan. The dislocations resulting from foreign occupation and war destroyed the basis for these extended familial relationships. The razing of farms and villages disunited countless clans and families, and forced many persons to move to new locations.

The lack of employment opportunities in rural areas since the early 1950's has also contributed to the breaking up of clans, as people have migrated to cities in search of work.

Relationships of trust have tended to develop frequently with close relatives; and increasingly, as a protective measure, individuals think in terms of providing first for their immediate families. Some organizations tend to be overstaffed because of feelings of responsibility to those employed or the need to help friends and close relatives.

Despite the tendency of youth in the cities to act independently, the contravention of family authority is still cause for disgrace and feelings of guilt for many young people. Threats to the integrity of the family name are sufficient reason for extraordinary efforts to obtain vindication. On the other hand, the welfare of strangers is of little concern, and few involve themselves in defending a stranger against some misfortune. The Confucian tradition has done little to instill a general sense of social consciousness. For the majority of Koreans, the struggle for survival precludes the luxury of entertaining such concept. The meagerness of daily existence and the intensity of effort expended in securing the bare necessities of life tend to limit the individual's loyalty to those who directly depend on him and on whom he is most dependent, such as relatives, teachers, leaders, and patrons.

AUTHORITY AND RESPONSIBILITY

Confucian scholars have disagreed as to whether the basic nature of man is good or evil, but they have all accepted that human beings, in the course of their lives, do not develop equally. The superior man, who cultivates his mind and lives according to the tenets of Confucian virtue, should be placed in a position of authority so that he may guide those less developed. Within the limits of native ability, the course that men take depends upon whether they are guided by the precepts and examples of superiors who know how to rule and who in their own lives conform to the natural order. In theory, official rank was open to any adult male (except butchers, barbers, and others in despised occupations) who passed the prescribed examinations in the Confucian classics. As it is a means to so high a goal, education was and still is greatly valued.

The exercise of both formal and informal authority in Korea has been characteristically harsh, but the wielder of authority in most cases also has obligations to others above him. Responsibility was first to one's family; and, when official positions were to be dispensed, those already in power, the *yangban*, gave preference to their relatives. The relatives, as members of the small social class which could afford a higher education, could usually meet the minimum requirements for official positions. Within the family, the father or grandfather assumed major responsibility for all in his household, but in his stead the eldest son might serve. Within the village, power and responsibility were vested in a small group of elders whose status was derived from their position as family heads. Thus there existed traditionally a concentration of rank, power, and responsibility in relatively few individuals.

Responsibility and power were most often involuntarily achieved. Family heads and village elders owed their positions to their heritage, and even those who obtained official positions through the examination system were most often pushed by their families. Although there were variations between classes, the younger sons led a relatively carefree life in comparison with the responsibilities and work devolving upon the father and the eldest son.

Within the larger society, there was a hierarchy of loyalties so that the individual's responsibility was to the extended family, the clan, the village, and ultimately to his sovereign. There was a reciprocal aspect of this scheme of responsibility, for though the interests of the group transcended the individual interests of its members, each of the members could also expect to be helped and protected throughout life by the group.

Responsibility, being equated with power, was total and indivisible. The individual saw himself primarily as others saw him—in terms of rank, power, and responsibility. To delegate power or responsibility was in effect to decrease oneself, to take away from one's stature as an individual. Thus, power was rarely divided or delegated. The manner in which authority is exercised has changed only slowly over the years. Power is guarded and preserved as well as exercised by those who hold it.

Authority is not impartially administered. Family connections, friendships, superior rank, and gifts at times elicit more from an office-holder than conformance to formal procedures. The rank of an official in the government hierarchy entails a structure of informal but nonetheless real obligations to his superiors, to indicate respect, and from his subordinates, who must also tangibly indicate their respect.

STATUS AND PRESTIGE

In the Confucian tradition, the highest achievement of man was to become a Confucian scholar. Only persons attaining such a rank were deserving of positions of leadership, and to them, as noted earlier, society bestowed its highest honors and material rewards.

The teacher is still the most respected individual in the present-day Republic; material affluence as such is not the primary criterion of success and prestige.

Outward symbols of social rank have undergone considerable modification since the turn of the 20th century. Traditionally, the *yangban* aristocracy displayed many symbols of their position: rich and varied foods, elaborate dress (some forms of which were forbidden to commoners), tile roofs and elegant furnishings and appointments in their houses (although, interestingly, the basic structure of their houses did not vary substantially from those of commoners) and lavish funerals. Since the downfall of the nobility and the *yangban* and the impoverishment of the country by war, fewer persons have been able to display material symbols of social distinction. The educated continue to use higher forms of language, and the Korean tongue is rich in forms of verb endings that permit the speaker to indicate social distinctions. Modes of dress are fairly uniform, with principal differences appearing in quality, according to the prosperity of the wearer. A significant status symbol that persists is the avoidance of eating barley, which is considered a very inferior food. Rice is universally regarded as the ideal food and people go to great lengths to secure it (see ch. 8, Living Conditions).

In traditional times, the use of a person's name in direct conversation was an affront; instead one was addressed by his title, position, trade, profession, or scholastic rank. Titles, accordingly, were of supreme importance. In present-day Korea, the standard is less rigid, particularly in the larger cities; but the custom persists, and the use of names is still not considered a part of polite social intercourse.

As has been noted, the highest status is attached to the scholar, hence the frequent use by Koreans of the honorific terms of *paksa* (doctor) and *sŏnsaeng* (senior, or teacher) in addressing one another. Men in certain high levels of government or at a certain age and station in life are addressed as *Yŏng-gain* (Honorable Sir). It is interesting to note that Korean politicians apparently are making increasing use of their surnames along with their titles and proper honorifics for the purpose of better identifying themselves to the voting public.

THE SOCIAL ORDER

Confucius conceived of an ideal society whose members were bound by ties of blood and loyalty to a feudalistic system of reciprocal obligations and responsibilities guaranteeing a peaceful productive existence for all under the benevolent guidance of a highly educated elite. So long as the principal occupation of the people was subsistence agriculture and population growth was slow, the system worked admirably. The introduction of Western notions of democratic equality and Western industrial technology, however, upset the traditional order (whose decline was hastened by the Japanese during their occupation from 1910 to 1945). The system of authority of the Confucian ethic—control by the family elders of the individual through the use of shame and material sanctions in order to promote the family's interests—has induced an attitude in most Koreans that is not compatible with a social system based on individual initiative and the determination of economic activities by the impersonal forces of the market place. Many of those millions who have been freed from the traditional system of familial control because of dislocation by war and migration to the cities have not been able to assimilate new values that are essential to meaningful life in an industrialized society. The conflict of values has not been resolved despite impressive industrial development in recent years.

To a considerable extent, the difficulty that the Korean people are experiencing in their transition to a modern society is attributable to a lack of accepted national goals. The acute problems of political and economic instability since the early 1950's have prevented national leaders from identifying and defining goals and standards that will enlist the concerted efforts of the people. Little effective effort has yet been made to identify where the best aspects of the traditional ethic can be combined with those necessary to industrial development in a democratic milieu. The Korean people display a sometimes contradictory set of attitudes reflecting their search for a value system that can accommodate the rapidly changing reality.

SECTION II. POLITICAL BACKGROUND

CHAPTER 13

THE GOVERNMENTAL SYSTEM

The history of constitutional development of the Republic of Korea can be divided into three separate periods or republics. The First Republic came into being as a presidential system (headed by Syngman Rhee) in 1948 and ended in April 1960. It was replaced by a parliamentary system, which was in existence from August 1960 to May 1961 (the government of Chang Myŏn) which was supplanted by a provisional arrangement based on the rule of the military. This latter system lasted until December 1963 when the present republic, known as the Third Republic and embodying once again a presidential system (headed presently by Park Chung-hee) came into being.

In mid-1968 the Government of the Republic of Korea, patterned mainly after the presidential system of the United States, was organized on the theory of the separation of powers. The executive, legislative, and judicial establishments are set up as independent of one another so that no one will dominate the others. In practice, however, the executive branch, and especially the office of the President, has developed into the focal point of the Korean political system. The trend is toward a strong presidency. One important factor is the process of the President's being elected by a majority of the voters. He therefore becomes not only the chief executive of the nation but also the representative of the "national will." Whereas other politicians may reflect the interests and aspirations of local constituencies, the President's constituency is the nation.

Under the Third Republic, Korea's governmental system is highly centralized with authority centered in the President. A system of checks and balances obtains among the executive, judicial, and legislative branches of the government.

To the Koreans, who have lived for a long time under the Confucian doctrine with its stress upon "rule of wise men" rather than "rule of law," a constitution with its regularized checks upon the rulers was a novel idea. However, the growing habit of justifying actions on constitutional grounds has combined with slowly increasing literacy and political consciousness among the people to make the Constitution a strong force in Korea.

BACKGROUND OF THE CONSTITUTIONAL SYSTEM

Traditional Concepts of Government

Traditional Korean concepts of government are based on the Confucian doctrine, which was the official social and political philosophy of the Yi Dynasty (1392–1910). In the Confucian philosophy the government is not viewed as a contractual arrangement between the rulers and the people but rather as a natural institution designed to maintain a proper relationship among people in a hierarchical social order. The Confucian "code of conduct" teaches that the hierarchical but benevolent relationship between the ruler and his subjects constitutes one of the five natural relationships in the human community.

It was not in the Confucian tradition that government was based on "rule of law." Rather, government was regarded essentially as a "government of men"—ideally, virtuous men—namely rulers, to be respected and followed as models of wise conduct. The ideal ruler was primarily a teacher and a preceptor able to indoctrinate his subjects with the Confucian rules of proper conduct. He was to exercise his punitive powers only when his subjects could not be swayed by reason and instruction. The so-called "Mandate of Heaven," which the ruler assumed upon becoming king, had it that he regard the welfare of his subject as a father would and that he cultivate virtue within himself and live up to the Confucian principles of "royal" behavior.

The Mandate of Heaven implied the right of the subject to rebel against the existing political authority. Since the Confucian doctrine viewed government as "rule of men," man, namely the ruler, was held responsible if the country suffered natural calamities or social disorder. Natural catastrophe or social unrest was considered to be a sign of Heaven's displeasure with rulers who deviated from their responsibilities and from the prescribed order of the world. Thus, in the political history of the Yi Dynasty, natural calamities were often followed by a wave of popular revolts, aimed at the overthrow of the existing regime.

In Yi Korea governing was exclusively the function of the small aristocratic gentry. The ruling class was composed of scholar-officials (*Yangban kanryo*) who obtained their position of prominence by passing highly rigorous, competitive examinations conducted by the central government. In theory these examinations (*kwako*) were open to all applicants from most social classes, and this particular institution was used by commoners as a means of upward social mobility. In practice, however, the commoners passing the examinations were very few in number. Commoners found it very difficult to go through the long, rigorous process of preparation, mainly because of the financial burden.

The governmental structure which Yi established was patterned after that of the Koryŏ Dynasty which he had toppled. Although the governmental structure underwent numerous changes in the course of the Yi Dynasty, the essence remained unchanged. Basically, the king was responsible for making and executing major decisions of the state, assisted by six ministries: Personnel, Revenue, Rites, War, Justice, and Public Works. Although there existed a coordinating body (*Uijŏngbu*) immediately below the king, these ministries were allowed direct access to the king, thus bypassing the *Uijŏngbu*, and this practice gradually led to the decline of the office, and the *Uijŏngbu* remained more or less as a nominal organ. There was no separate judiciary system, and legislative, administrative and judiciary functions were ultimately concentrated in the hands of the monarch; provincial governors and local magistrates, appointed by the monarch, were judges as well as administrators.

It was not until 1894 that the traditional Korean government structure was officially abandoned in favor of a system similar to the Meiji system of Japan. In that year a group of progressive Koreans successfully carried out the so-called Reform of 1894. One of the prominent features of this reform provided for a separation of judicial functions from the executive departments, the institution of an independent court system, the separation of the Royal Household from the affairs of state, and the reorganization of executive functions along Japanese lines.

The Reform of 1894 was soon followed by the Japanese annexation of Korea. Between this time and 1942, Korea was administered by Japan as a colony and was thus placed under the supervision of the Overseas Ministry of the Japanese government. In 1942, the Japanese government made Korea an integral part of Japan and put her under the supervision of the Home Ministry. The Japanese administrative machinery in Korea was known as the Government-General of Korea. At the top of this structure was the Japanese Governor-General, who was appointed by the Emperor of Japan on the recommendation of Japan's Premier. The Governor-General exercised wide powers over administration, appointment of lower officials, justice, and public safety. Although he was governed in general by the laws of Japan, he had the power to issue decrees on a wide range of matters affecting the Koreans. He was assisted by a Civil Administrator, who functioned as the chief administrative assistant to the Governor-General and, as assisted by a secretariat, supervised the various government bureaus. There was also an advisory organ, composed of Koreans, whose function it was to advise the Governor-General on Korean matters. Members were drawn from the wealthy, aristocratic Koreans, and the advisory body "could offer advice only at the request of the Governor and then upon a specific subject."

Korea was divided administratively into 13 provinces (*do*), which were in turn subdivided into counties, municipalities, towns, townships, and villages. The total number of Japanese and Korean officials who staffed the Government-General and its subordinate bodies at the end of 1943 totaled 160, 569, of which 80,589 (50.2 percent) were Koreans. Sixty-three percent of the Koreans, however, held positions in the lower echelons of government, mostly in local government. Japanese colonial policy called for near monopoly by Japanese citizens of administrative positions on the higher levels. Not only were Koreans denied important government positions, but the Korean people as a whole did not take part in government affairs.

Japan's rule in Korea was in essence a police rule resting on police and the gendarmerie. The Governor-General had the right to call upon the commander of the Japanese armed forces in Korea for troops whenever he felt that an emergency situation existed. Japanese troops were strategically stationed throughout the country for prompt action upon call.

It was during the period of the Japanese rule that many young Korean intellectuals, at home or in exile, were influenced by a variety of political theories. Koreans who had emigrated to China and to the Soviet Far East became acquainted with Marxist and Leninist doctrines, and those who established themselves in the United States were strongly attracted to American democratic ideals. Furthermore, even though the policies of the Japanese were strict and authoritarian and generated great bitterness, Japanese rule did much to create a growing respect for law as a substitute for the arbitrary power of individuals.

When Korea was liberated in August 1945, there was general popular agreement on the broad issue of immediate national independence, but few could come to an agreement on a constitutional framework which could implement this desire. The majority of the people hardly thought in terms of constitutional principles. The small group of intellectuals that did subscribe to some set of constitutional concepts were influenced by diverse currents of political theories and techniques such as traditional Confucian ideals, the Japanese example, Communist ideology, or Western democratic ideals.

Development of the Constitution of 1948

The Republic of Korea's first constitution (*hŏnpŏp*) was promulgated on July 17, 1948, a date which is officially celebrated each year as "Constitution-Making Day." It was amended in 1952 and 1954 during the First Republic, in 1960 during the Second Republic, and finally on December 17, 1962, through popular referendum. While promulgated on December 26, 1962, the Constitution in force today did not become effective until December 17, 1963, when the first National Assembly, elected under the provisions of the amended Constitution, convened. This 1962 version is often known as the Constitution of the Third Republic.

The first steps in writing a constitution for the Republic of Korea were taken in 1945 by the American Military Government after it replaced the Japanese rulers of Korea. Under its direction, a joint United States-Korean committee, headed by an American, reviewed foreign constitutions in order to fashion a model. Further positive steps toward the making of the Constitution were made on May 10, 1948, when a national election was held under the supervision of the United Nations Temporary Commission on Korea. The election selected members of a Constituent Assembly, which met on May 31, 1948 and appointed a Constitution Drafting Committee composed of Assemblymen and constitutional experts. The drafting committee adopted as its basis for discussion the draft constitution worked out by Yu Chin-o. The prominent feature of the Yu draft was its inclination toward a parliamentary form of government and a bicameral legislature—a structure embodied in the Weimar Constitution.

In the initial stage of constitution-making the views of Dr. Yu prevailed among the members of the drafting committee, which generally concurred with his position that a cabinet system was needed to resolve any constitutional conflict between the executive and the legislature. However, strong opposition to the adoption of the parliamentary system was raised by Syngman Rhee, then the speaker of the Constituent Assembly. Rhee favored a presidential system for several reasons: he considered, first, that the country needed a stable government under viable leadership to achieve the vital task of nation-building; and, second, that a strong government was an absolute requisite in waging a successful struggle against communism in Korea, and that a parliamentary system was likely to promote factional strife in national politics, a situation to be avoided, especially in light of the factionalism that had long been a characteristic of Korean politics and had contributed to the Japanese takeover of Korea.

Rhee, being regarded as a great national hero and virtually the sole presidential candidate at the time, voiced views that carried much weight. Furthermore, Rhee stated before the drafting committee that if the draft of Dr. Yu should be adopted without revision, he would wage a nationwide campaign to oppose the draft. Rhee even went so far as to threaten the constitution-makers by saying that he would decline an offer of any position under the proposed cabinet system.

The solution to the conflict between the Yu draft and Rhee's views was a compromise plan in which the constitution-makers attempted to combine two systems of representative government—presidential and parliamentary. As a result, a constant and intense struggle took place between the President and the Assembly under the new system, each competing for recognition of what each had sought as its share of power and authority under the Constitution.

Constitutional Amendment

Following two amendments aimed at ameliorating these problems, a third major constitutional change was effected in 1960 in the wake of the student uprisings which had toppled the Rhee regime. The 1960 amendments are commonly known as the Constitution of the Second Republic. After the fall of the Rhee government, members of the Democratic Party assumed control of the government, and they proceeded to institute a parliamentary system in Korea. The 1960 amendments replaced the presidential system with a parliamentary system similar to the British model. The power of the President was drastically reduced, and he was made the titular head of the state, to be elected to a five-year term by a joint session of the two house legislature. Functions assigned to the president were strictly of ceremonial nature. Unlike the provisions of the Constitution of the First Republic, the new document denied the president veto power over the bills passed by the legislature and the power to issue orders having the effect of law in times of national crisis. Under the new system, as in Great Britian, the executive power was vested in the Cabinet, which was headed by a prime minister.

As leader of the dominant party in the lower house, the prime minister was empowered to appoint heads of ministries to make up the Cabinet, and the Cabinet was collectively responsible to the lower house. It was soon learned, however, that the new system was not very effective in insuring political stability and governmental efficiency under the prevailing political conditions in Korea. Parties were extremely fragmented, and no single party was able to obtain control of a dependable majority in the lower house.

As a result of a military revolution the Second Republic fell in May 1961. The Constitution was thereafter for all practical purposes suspended by the revolutionary junta and superseded by the

Law Concerning the Extraordinary Measures for National Reconstruction of June 6, 1961. Consisting of 24 articles, the emergency law provided that the fundamental rights of the people would be honored insofar as they did not conflict with the fulfillment of revolutionary tasks. The Supreme Council for National Reconstruction, the governing body of the junta, established by the Law, took over the legislative, executive, and judicial functions of the government. The Law also suspended the functions of the Constitutional Court. Furthermore, the emergency Law prevailed over any provision of the Constitution which conflicted with it.

In anticipation of the restoration of political activities in 1963 and the transfer of governmental power from the military to the civilians, the military junta, aided by a contingent of constitutional scholars and lawyers, proposed a substantial change in the Constitution.

Although members of the military junta's Supreme Council participated actively in the work of the 30-man Constitution Deliberation Committee, and the Chairman of the Council made his preferences known publicly, the proposed amendments were not based solely on the desires for the military junta. For one thing, the Constitution Deliberation Committee consisted largely of leading constitutional scholars, political scientists, and economists of the country. Furthermore, in the amendment-making process, the Supreme Council made efforts to insure reflection of the people's wishes in the new amendments. For example, public hearings were conducted throughout the country to solicit views of local representatives. It was the first time in Korea's history that the country had opportunities to express views in the constitution-making. Finally, the proposed amendments were approved through a popular referendum on December 17, 1962, with 6,339,330 favoring and 2,008,800 rejecting. Thus, an overwhelming majority of the voters supported the adoption of the proposed constitution of the Third Republic.

In the process of amendment-making, the dominant political philosophy favored by the military junta and the Constitution Deliberation Committee urged a return to a presidential system. This view was clearly dictated by the political lesson under the Second Republic that a parliamentary system is likely to cause political instability in a country where political fragmentation is common.

THE CONSTITUTION OF THE THIRD REPUBLIC

The Constitution consists of a preamble, one hundred and twenty-one articles, and nine supplementary rules. The main part of the basic document is divided into five chapters: General Provisions, Rights and Duties of the Citizens, Organs for the Government,

Economy, and Amendments to the Constitution. There is no separate provision for a constitutional court, and the constitutionality or legality of a law or administrative ordinances is to be contested in ordinary courts of law.

Basic Principles

The basic principles on which the Constitution rests are enunciated in the Preamble and in Chapter I. The Constitution proclaims that the people of Korea, who possess "a glorious tradition and history from time immemorial," are now in the process of establishing a "new democratic Republic on the basis of ideals as manifested in the April 19th Righteous Uprising and the May 16th Revolution. . ." Specifically, it pledges to achieve national unity, to modernize the country, to establish democratic institutions, to afford equal opportunities to every person, to provide for the fullest development of the capacity of each individual in all fields of endeavor, to promote the welfare of the people at home, to strive toward the maintenance of international peace, and to ensure the security, liberty, and happiness of the people.

The Constitution declares that sovereignty is vested in the people, and the nature of the Third Republic is defined as "democratic." The territory of the Republic is to consist of "the Korean peninsula and its accessory islands," which means that North Korea is also an integral part of the Republic of Korea.

In regard to international obligations, the Constitution declares in Article 5 that "treaties duly ratified and promulgated in accordance with this Constitution and the generally recognized rules of international law shall have the same effect as that of the domestic law of the Republic." The new Constitution reminds public officials that they are "servants of the entire people and shall be responsible to the people." Therefore, they are forbidden to join a political party.

Civil Rights

The Constitution recognizes the principle of guaranteeing the basic rights and freedoms of the individual. Chapter II of the Constitution, entitled, "Rights and Duties of the Citizens," contains a long list of civil rights and privileges, thus setting limits on the exercise of governmental powers and stating that the liberties and rights of the people may be restricted "by law only in cases deemed necessary for the maintenance of order and public welfare." Political rights include: equality before the law, regardless of sex, religion, or social status; freedom from arbitrary arrest; the right to elect public officials and to hold elective office; and the right of the accused to have the prompt assistance of counsel and a speedy trial. No citizen may be prosecuted for a criminal offense by means of retroactive legislation, nor may he be placed in double jeopardy. The Constitution also sets forth the inadmissibility of a confession, as evidence in court, if the confession is obtained by means of torture, threat, deceit, etc.

Among the guarantees are those providing for the privacy of correspondence and for freedom of religion, speech, press, assembly, and association. The government is, however, empowered to prescribe by law the standard for publication facilities of newspapers in order to "prevent disorderly establishment of newspaper or press service." The government may also regulate the time and place of public assembly so as to curb street demonstrations injurious to public order. The freedom of the press is restricted by an article stipulating that "the press or publication shall not impugn the personal honor or rights of an individual, nor shall it infringe upon public morality." The government may, in addition, censor films and theatrical plays to "insure good public order and social ethics."

Economic rights include the right to own property, but the exercise of property rights shall conform to public welfare; the rights as well as the duty to work; freedom of choice of occupation; and the right to bargain collectively. In case of expropriation, or the use or restriction of private property for "public purposes," due compensation shall be paid in accordance with the provisions of law. The economic rights are circumscribed by Article 111 which allows the state to "regulate and coordinate economic affairs within the limits" necessary in the public interest. Under Article 117 private enterprises may be transferred to and controlled by the state "in cases determined by law to meet an urgent necessity of national defense or the national economy."

In social and cultural fields the Constitution guarantees the freedom of science and art, compulsory and free elementary education, welfare benefits for persons incapable of earning a living, and protection for working women and children. The sanctity of marriage and health of the family are to be specially protected by the state.

Special Provisions

Perhaps the most unusual feature of the Third Republic Constitution is its provisions governing political parties. In this sense, the Constitution is very similar to that of the Fifth Republic of France in that parties are regulated by constitutional provisions and differs sharply from the American Constitution. The Constitution amplifies the importance of laying a firm foundation for the establishment of a sound political party system as a matter of basic principle. The constitutional provisions governing the parties are designed to achieve two basic objectives: first, to prevent the rise of one-party domination as was the case under the Government of Rhee, and secondly, to discourage the development of a multi-party system, which was very common in the immediate post-World War II years and shortly after the fall of the Rhee regime. Paragraph 1 of Article 7 states that the establishment of parties shall be "free and the plural party system shall be guaranteed." Paragraph 2 of the same article is intended to prevent multiplication of parties by stipulating that "political parties shall have necessary organizational arrangements" (see ch. 14, Political Dynamics).

Another distinct feature of the provisions pertaining to parties is the constitutional disapprobation of "anti-democratic" parties. Paragraph 3 of Article 7 empowers that, in case "the purposes or activities of a political party are contrary to the basic democratic order," the executive establishment may bring an action for dissolution of the party before the Supreme Court.

In addition to the provisions on political parties, the new Constitution contains special provisions on the management of elections. Article 107 empowers the Central Election Management Committee, a neutral body, and its subordinate committees to manage elections.

The section Supplementary Rules of the Constitution stipulates that the law, orders, and treaties pursuant to the Law Regarding the Extraordinary Measures for National Reconstruction shall remain in force unless incompatible with the Constitution. Specifically, it provides that the Law Concerning the Purification of Political Activities, the Law Regarding Disposition of Illicit Profiteering, and other laws related thereto shall not be "amended or abolished" (see ch. 14, Political Dynamics).

Amendment Procedure

A motion to amend the basic law may be introduced either by one-third or more of the National Assembly members or by the concurrence of at least 500,000 electors who are qualified to vote in general elections. Proposed changes in the Constitution must be made public by the President for more than 30 days. The National Assembly, then, is required to act on the amendment bill within 60 days of this public notice.

An amendment requires consent of two-thirds or more of the National Assembly members "duly elected and seated." It is then submitted to a national referendum within 60 days and must be affirmed by a majority of the votes cast representing more than half of all eligible voters. When approved through popular referendum, the amended constitution must be promulgated by the President. Thus, the procedure devised to amend the Constitution is an

184

onerous one, and would make it difficult for a political leader to augment his power by constitutional manipulation or amendment.

THE LEGAL SYSTEM

In Korea, as in China, the development of law has been very slow. The most significant factor impeding development has been the Confucian ethics. The Chinese *li*, or Korean *ye*, the Confucian ethical rules governing the five main human relationships, were regarded as the route to harmonious conduct and had therefore the force of law. The *ye*, may have been effective in the pre-industrialized periods of Korea, but there began to develop inherent conflicts between the need for an institutionalized system of justice to handle human problems accompanying modernization and the traditional commitment to Confucian ethics. It was the Japanese rulers that brought the most profound change in this field by introducing their own laws based largely on European Continental laws Further modernization in this area has been made by the Koreans by borrowing many features of the Anglo-American legal system. Thus, today Korean law represents a mixture of unwritten customary law reflecting Confucian teachings, of Japanese law, and of more modern law.

When independence came in 1945, the American Military Government ordered that the existing Japanese laws—criminal, civil, commercial, and others—should remain in force. When the new Constitution was adopted in 1948, it carried the provision that all current laws were valid to the extent that they were not in conflict with any of the Constitutional provisions. Shortly after the Republic came into being, the government launched the gigantic task of writing up new laws to replace all Japanese laws. The Criminal Code was promulgated in 1953; the Criminal Procedure code in 1954, the Civil Code in 1958, and the Code of Civil Procedure in 1960, after its draft had been considered by the National Assembly Committee on Legislation and Justice for almost 7 years. The Commercial Code was proclaimed in 1962. In addition, other laws affecting such special segments of society as labor were also codified.

The civil laws are strongly patterned after the Japanese equivalents. The new criminal laws have incorporated many features of both the Japanese criminal laws and of the Anglo-American counterparts. The civil and criminal laws, quite elaborate, are to cover situations arising from civil conflicts and criminal cases, respectively. The Constitution of the Third Republic grants constitutional sanctity to the basic principles of the criminal codes. When there develop civil situations not covered by the civil laws, customary law shall be applicable, and if they cannot be dealt with by customary law, "sound reasoning shall apply to them." For a commercial situation which cannot be handled by the Commercial Code, commercial customary law shall apply, and "if there is no such law, the provisions of the Civil Code shall apply."

The Criminal Code contains general provisions applicable to all crimes and specific provisions defining more than 200 crimes. It also contains a minor offenses law defining some 45 petty crimes, and provides penalties for violations of various administrative laws, including the customs law, tax laws, and laws on foreign exchange controls. The Code also defines in great detail the various crimes against the state, as well as penalties for crimes. In addition to the Criminal Code, two other laws—the National Security Law and the Anti-Communism Law—govern matters involving national security. The Code on Criminal Procedure defines the principles of criminal proceedings, including the requirement of warrants for detention, defense counsel, system of bail, the writ of habeas corpus, and a few other Anglo-American principles.

These various constitutional guarantees protecting civil rights are embodiments relatively new to Korea, and the Koreans have not yet fully cast off the traditional Confucian tradition that society is to be ruled by "wise" men, not "rule of law." Thus, despite these provisions, the arbitrary use of power by prosecuting agencies has not yet been eliminated.

The Civil Code defines civil or private rights, obligations, contracts, relationships, and succession. One unique feature of the present code is its provisions which signify the Republic's gradual departure from the traditional emphasis on the paternal family system, for the new code has considerably modified the paternal system and permits a female to become the head of a family in case of the death of her husband. Furthermore, now a daughter, whether married or not, is entitled to a part of an inheritance; formerly, only the male members of a family shared it. The Japanese code established the husband's control over the wife's property, but under the new Korean code a married couple is required to "submit a contract giving notification of the separate management of each other's property."

The Code of Civil Procedures is one of the many laws governing civil cases. Others include the Domestic Litigation Law and Law on Domestic Relations. These procedural laws again reflect South Korea's growing disenchantment with traditions and move toward regularization of private relationships. Domestic matters which have traditionally been handled through highly informal channels can now be subject to more institutionalized proceedings. The Law on Domestic Relations enacted in 1963, for example, is "intended to take into account the special nature of problems involving do-

186

mestic relations and to permit the solving of such problems without a lawsuit, if possible." Most cases of this nature are first referred to mediators with psychological, sociological or educational backgrounds. Cases that cannot be settled in this manner are taken up by the system of family court. The first of such courts was recently established in Seoul.

STRUCTURE AND FUNCTIONS OF THE CENTRAL GOVERNMENT

The Executive Establishment

Under the third Republic Constitution and the Amended Government Organization Law of December 14, 1963, executive functions are vested in the President, the State Council as the highest "deliberative" body on major governmental policies, and a varying number of advisory organs and executive agencies.

The President

At the apex of the executive establishment stands the President. Under the Constitution he is elected by a universal, equal, direct, and secret ballot. Candidates for the presidency must be endorsed by a political party and must be at least 40 years of age. The President is elected for a 4-year term and may serve a maximum of two terms. Since the post of the vice-president is not provided for in the Constitution, in case of presidential disability or departure, an election is to be held immediately. If the remaining tenure is less than 2 years, the National Assembly is to elect his successor. Until the elected successor assumes office, the Prime Minister may temporarily act as the President. To remove the possibility of conflict of interest, the President is forbidden to hold concurrently any other official or private position as determined by law or to engage in private business. He is independent from and not answerable to the National Assembly. He is responsible only to the electorate and the constitution.

In the present Korean political system the President plays six major roles. First, the President is chief of state, and in that capacity he symbolizes and represents the whole nation. The duties of the President are many and include ceremonial and pardoning functions. He receives foreign ambassadors accredited to the Republic of Korea, awards decorations and other honors, grants "amnesty, commutation and rehabilitation." Second, the President is chief administrator. Thus, he takes care that laws passed in the legislature are faithfully carried out, and he can issue orders and decrees for the enforcement of laws. He is authorized to appoint public officials, including the Prime Minister and heads of executive agencies. Third, the President exercises supreme command of the Republic's armed forces and has the power to declare war. Fourth, the President is the leader of a major political party with nation-wide organizations. Fifth, the President plays the role of chief diplomat and foreign policymaker. He is empowered to conclude and ratify treaties, accredit, receive or dispatch diplomatic envoys, and conclude peace with foreign nations.

Finally, the President plays the role of chief policymaker or chief lawmaker. He is empowered to propose a legislative bill to the National Assembly, and he has the veto power over bills passed by that body, although his veto can be overriden. The President enjoys the rights to address the National Assembly or make his policy views known to the legislators by written message. The President has no right to dissolve the legislature. Conversely, the National Assembly cannot dismiss the President, but it can hold him ultimately responsible to the Constitution, juridically speaking, by means of the impeachment process.

In addition the President is vested with broad powers to meet national emergencies arising from civil war, natural calamity, economic and financial crisis, or war with foreign countries, including the power to issue emergency decrees having the effect of law and to take necessary financial and economic measures. The use of such emergency powers, however, is subject to the approval of the National Assembly. He is also empowered to proclaim state of siege in accordance with the provisions of the law.

State Council and Executive Agencies

The President directs the work of the executive branch through the State Council (*Kukmu hoeui*), which is made up of 10 to 20 members and is presided over by the President, who is solely responsible for deciding all important executive matters. At the end of 1967 the State Council was composed of the President (chairman); Prime Minister (vice chairman); vice-prime minister, who was concurrently the Minister of Economic Planning; 15 heads of executive ministries; and one minister without portfolio. Heads of executive ministries are selected by the President from among the members of the State Council.

The purpose of the State Council is to provide a forum for deliberation on major government policies and on issues among its members and to advise the president accordingly. Constitutionally speaking, unlike its predecessor under the regimes of Syngman Rhee and Chang Myŏn, the present State Council functions in a consultative capacity and has no decisionmaking power. Unlike the British Cabinet, for example, the State Council does not constitute a significant check upon the President. Under the Constitution, however, all presidential acts must be countersigned by the

Prime Minister and a competent member of the Council so as to "forestall and preclude the dictatorship or tyranny of the President."

The Prime Minister is appointed by the President without recourse to the National Assembly. Thus, he is the President's personal appointee. As the chief executive assistant to the President, the Prime Minister supervises the executive ministries under the direction of the President. Members of the State Council are also appointed by the President upon the recommendation of the prime minister. Military personnel on active duty are excluded from the Council to maintain the "political neutrality and fidelity of the Armed Forces." Council members are not allowed to hold concurrent membership in the National Assembly and vice versa. They are collectively and individually responsible to the President only, and hence the National Assembly cannot pass a non-confidence resolution against the State Council. The President is, however, obliged to remove the Prime Minister or a Council member if strongly urged by the National Assembly "unless there is a special reason to do otherwise."

The matters to be referred to the State Council for deliberation include: basic plans on state affairs; important matters pertaining to foreign relations (proposed treaties, declarations of war, conclusions of peace) ; proposed budgets and fiscal matters; proposed legislative bills and ordinances of the president; important military affairs; proclamation and termination of a state of siege; and appointment of justices of the Supreme Court, the prosecutor general, the presidents of national universities, ambassadors and ministers to foreign states, the chiefs of staff of each armed service and Marine Corps commandant and other public officials and the managers of important state-operated enterprises; proposals for the dissolution of a political party; formulation and coordination of important policies of each executive ministry; and the delegation or allocation of powers within the executive establishment.

The State Council meets regularly on Tuesday and Friday of every week, and when necessary it can convene any time on the call of the President. Normally, matters referred to the Council for deliberation are already discussed at a vice-ministerial meeting held a few days prior to the Council meeting. In addition to executive ministers, the Director of the Office of Legislation, the Director of the Office of Veterans Administration, the Director of the Office of Planning and Control, the Director of Central Intelligence Agency, the Secretary to the President, the Secretary to the Prime Minister, and other public officials determined by law may attend meetings of the Council and state their opinions.

In addition to the State Council, there are four agencies and councils under the direct control of the President, designed to assist and advise the President in making policies and in carrying out his duties. They are: the National Security Council, Economic and Scientific Council, Board of Audit, and Central Intelligence Agency. The National Security Council, chaired by the President, is made up of Prime Minister, the Ministers of Foreign Affairs, Home Affairs, National Defense, and Finance, Ministers Without Portfolio, Director of the Central Intelligence Agency, and other officials designated by the President. The NSC advises the President on matters of foreign, military, and domestic policies insofar as they affect the national security before the matters are referred to the State Council. The ESC, also headed by the President, is composed of public officials and specialists appointed by the President, and this agency advises and makes recommendations to the President on major policies and projects pertaining to national economy and science.

The Board of Audit, a constitutional body, is an organ under the President acting independently of the executive ministries. It is designed to serve as a watchdog organ over the administrative branch. It audits the accounts of national and local government agencies as specified by law, inspects the administrative functions of the executive agencies, and investigates the conduct of public officials. The results of its investigations are reported to the President and the National Assembly. The Board is composed of nine members, including a chairman appointed by the President, but to ensure independence of the Board, the presidential appointment requires the concurrence of the National Assembly. Other members of the Board are appointed by the President but upon recommendation of the Board chairman. The chairman and members of the Board serve for four years and cannot be removed from the office except for specified reasons.

The Central Intelligence Agency was established in June 1961. It is authorized to collect strategic information of internal as well as external origin. It coordinates and supervises the activities of all intelligence and investigative agencies of the government, engages in anti-Communist activities, and conducts political investigations.

Heads of the executive ministries are selected by the President from among the members of the State Council. In mid-1968, there were 15 ministries which were subordinate to and supervised by the Prime Minister. They were: Foreign Affairs, Home Affairs, Finance, Justice, National Defense, Education, Agriculture and Forestry, Commerce and Industry, Construction, Health and Social Welfare, Transportation, Communications, Public Information, Science and Technology, and Government Administration. Other agencies of ministerial rank were the Economic Planning Board, the Office of Legislation, the Office of Veterans Administration, and the Office of Atomic Energy.

Managerial functions in such nationalized industries as ship-building and electricity and other governmental concerns are carried out by state-operated "autonomous" organizations. Chief officers of these organizations are appointed by the President on the recommendation of their respective executive minister. Some of the more important bodies were: the Bank of Korea, Korean Reconstruction Bank, Korea Electric Power Company, Korea Shipping Corporation, Korea Shipbuilding Corporation, Korea Coal Corporation, Korean Tungsten Mining Company, National Council of Agricultural Cooperatives, Korean Heavy Industries Corporation, Korea Housing Corporation, Trade Promotion Corporation, Korean National Airlines, and National Council of Fishery Cooperatives. The purpose of such bodies is to manage important sectors of the national economy independently of the executive ministries and free from political pressures.

The members of the President's Secretariat in the Republic of Korea have come to perform very important functions. Both formal and informal functions performed by the Secretariat make it an important organ in the Republic's policy process. It serves as the major channel of communication between the President and the rest of the governmental establishment, and a representative of the Secretariat sits in every meeting attended by the President, and keeps the records of the proceedings. The Secretariat is headed by a Director who is at the same time the Chief Secretary to the President. Under the Director the Secretariat is divided into 6 sections: General, Political, Information, Civil, Protocol, and Intelligence. Of these sections the Political Section is the largest, made up of 8 secretaries including a Section Chief. Functions within the Secretariat are subdivided among secretaries in parallel with functional divisions in the executive branch.

The Legislature

Legislative power is exercised by the National Assembly—a unicameral body. The number of Assemblymen is determined by law within the constitutionally prescribed range of no less than 150 and no more than 200. At the end of 1967 there were 175 Assemblymen. The members are elected for a four-year term by universal, equal, and secret vote. The electoral system for the National Assembly is based on both single-member constituency principle and proportional representation (see the section on electoral system below). In the 1967 Assemblymen elections 131 members were elected from single-member constituencies, and the remaining 44 were elected on the basis of proportional representation.

To be eligible for election, a candidate must be recommended by a political party to which he belongs and must be at least 25 years of age. The provision barring an independent from running was clearly designed to ensure the development of party politics. An elected member loses his membership if he leaves his party or joins another or if his party is dissolved. This provision does not apply in case of a merger of parties or expulsion from a party.

An Assemblyman is entitled to the usual privileges as a legislator. He is not held responsible outside the Assembly for any opinions expressed or votes cast in the legislative chamber. During the sessions of the Assembly, no Assemblyman may be arrested or detained without the consent of the Assembly except in cases of *flagrante delicto*. Aside from the privileges, an Assemblyman is subject to certain limitations. The Constitution prohibits him from seeking "any rights or interest in property or position from facilitating the securing of the same in behalf of others by means of contract with, or disposition of, a State of public agency or any enterprise determined by law." In contrast to the parliamentary system, the present Constitution does not recognize the principle of concurrent assumption of legislative and executive responsibilities. The basic document bars an Assemblyman from concurrently assuming the position of President, Premier, or a State Council member or taking other government posts. The legislator is also banned from establishing formal affiliation with any profit-making private organizations, including commercial firms.

Two types of legislative sessions are provided for: regular and extraordinary. A regular session convenes on September 1 every year. The period of a regular session is limited to 120 days. An extraordinary session may convene at the call of the President or at the request of one-fourth or more of the representatives of the Assembly and cannot exceed 30 days in duration. A quorum is constituted by the attendance of more than half of the Assembly members "duly elected and seated." Legislative sessions are open to the public, but this rule can be waived when so decided with the approval of more than one-half of the members present. Members of the State Council, if requested, are required to attend any meetings of the Assembly and to answer questions. The President is thus shielded from direct legislative accusation and questioning, this function being delegated to Cabinet members, who are the President's personal appointees.

Functions

In the political system of the Republic of Korea the members of the National Assembly perform individually or collectively several functions. The foremost constitutional function assigned to the legislature is in the area of lawmaking. The Assembly has the power to deliberate and vote on all legislative bills introduced by members of the Assembly or by the administration. In practice, however, this lawmaking function is exercised not so much in the form of initiation of legislation as in legitimation or revision of bills formulated in the executive branch.

A second function given to the Assembly pertains to budget-making. The Assembly has the power to deliberate upon and approve the annual budget formulated by the executive. The legislature is required to act on the budget at least 30 days before the beginning of a new fiscal year. However, the Assembly cannot be assertive in the budgetary process largely because of the presidential party's control of the Assembly. Constitutionally, any legislative attempt to make changes in the proposed budget involving additional expenditure cannot be undertaken without the consent of the executive. The result has been that virtually all budget-bills have been approved by the legislature as originally proposed.

A third function of the legislature is in the area of foreign policymaking. All treaties are subject to legislative ratification. A fourth function is related to the warmaking power. The declaration of war, the dispatch of armed forces abroad, or the stationing of alien forces within the country all require legislative approval.

A fifth function of the Assembly is that of checking on and exercising control over the administrative agencies that carry out the laws of the country, as expressed in legislation. Each Assembly committee has the responsibility to oversee the activities of agencies subject to its legislative jurisdiction. And the Assembly reserves the right to establish special investigating committees to highlight administrative practices called into question. The legislature is also empowered to demand, if necessary, the submission of necessary documents and appearances of witnesses. If the Assembly concludes that the improper administrative practices they find in the course of investigations are attributed to the Prime Minister or any Cabinet member, the legislature has the power to adopt a resolution recommending to the President the removal of the individuals concerned, but this resolution is not binding upon the executive.

A sixth function of the legislature, related very closely to the fifth function, is that of informing the public. A seventh function of the National Assembly is impeachment. Article 61 of the Constitution stipulates that in case the President, the Prime Minister, State Council members, executive ministers, and any other public officials designated by law have violated the Constitution or other laws in the exercise of their duties, the Assembly has the right to pass motions for their impeachment. When impeachment is instituted against an individual, he must be suspended from his duties until the impeachment has been tried by an Impeachment Council.

Internal Structure

The Assembly elects one Speaker and two vice-speakers, who serve for two years. The Speaker is empowered to maintain order in the chamber, regulate legislative proceedings, supervise its business, and represent the legislature. He may participate in meetings of any committees but does not have the voting right. The vice-speakers assist the Speaker in performing his functions and, in the absence of the Speaker, one of the vice-speakers designated by the Speaker performs the Speaker's duties.

The Speaker has often been identified as a legislative agent of the majority party, whose main concern is to pass bills coming from the Administration. Speakership is not an institution with an independent source of power.

The Assembly is divided into 12 standing committees with the following functional designations: Legislative and Judiciary; Foreign Affairs; Home Affairs; Appropriations, Finance, and Banking; National Defense; Education and Public Information; Agriculture and Forestry; Commerce and Industry; Public Health and Welfare; Transport and Communications; Public Works; and Steering.

Chairmen of the standing committees are elected by the Assembly from among members of the respective committees. In addition, special committees may be established whenever necessary. The number of members of a standing committee is determined by the National Assembly Law. Members serve for two years, and concurrent membership in more than one standing committee is prohibited. The committee chairman is authorized to control the proceedings, maintain order, and represent the committee. He is also empowered to decide the order of business and time and date of the opening of committee meetings, but he must convene a meeting when so requested by more than one-third of committee members.

Bills and petitions are referred to the standing committee for examination. The committee constitutes the chief forum for clashes between the ruling political party and the opposition party. In this respect the Assembly is quite similar to the United States Congress, but the parallel stops there, because in the Republic the ruling political party also controls the committees through its majority position and the straight party voting in committee. The primary function of the standing committees has largely become that of recommending Administration bills to the plenary session for approval.

Under the present National Assembly Law, each political party having more than 10 members in the Assembly forms a negotiating group. It acts as a unit in inter-party negotiations in the Assembly. "Unaffiliated" Assemblymen can also form a separate negotiating group, if they number more than 10. The negotiating groups name their floor leaders and whips, who are responsible for negotiations with other groups. The floor leaders meet to discuss matters pertaining to the operation of the Assembly and to time-tables and debating order of the bills, both for the floor and for committees.

The administrative matters of the Assembly are handled by the National Assembly Secretariat headed by a secretary-general. He and other members of the Secretariat are appointed by the Speaker with the Assembly's approval.

Legislative Process

A bill may be introduced either by an Assemblyman, if it is endorsed by more than 10 Assemblymen, or by the Administration, and is then referred to the pertinent committee for consideration. If the bill requires extensive examination involving the use of a subcommittee, the committee may create such a subcommittee. Before initiating its deliberation on the bill, the committee hears the explanation of the bill usually given by the Vice-Minister of the ministry concerned, in the case of Administration bills, or by the sponsor in the case of a private member's bill. According to the National Assembly Law, a committee man may speak on the bill as many times as he wishes. On important bills, including budget bills and revenue bills, or any other controversial bills, a public hearing may be conducted with the approval of the Speaker, and opinions can be heard from witnesses and other interested parties.

Once a bill is acted upon, the committee's actions are reported out to the Assembly floor. The chairman submits both majority and minority reports in case there were members dissenting from majority action. A bill voted down by the committee may not be taken up on the floor, unless a request has been made by more than 30 Assemblymen to deal with it in the plenary session. On the floor the bill is voted upon, may be amended, rejected, approved, or sent back to the committee.

A bill passed by the Assembly, by majority vote, is sent to the President and must be promulgated within 15 days or returned with his veto and explanatory statement to the legislature for reconsideration. The Assembly can, however, override the veto by a two-thirds majority, and the bill in question becomes law.

The Judiciary

The court system, as provided for under the Constitution of 1963 and the Court Organization Law of September 26, 1949 (amended more than ten times, most recently on March 9, 1966) functions on three levels. The highest court of the state is the Supreme Court, followed in order by 3 appellate courts, 10 district court, 1 family court, and 36 branch courts.

The Supreme Court, located in Seoul, is empowered to establish procedures for judicial proceedings and the internal regulations of the courts. The qualification of judges is to be determined by law. Judges may be dismissed or have their salaries reduced only through impeachment proceedings or in the case of criminal or disciplinary punishment. The Supreme Court is to have fewer than 16 justices (1 Chief Justice and 11 justices in mid-1968.) The Chief Justice is appointed by the President with the consent of the National Assembly upon the nomination of a Judges Recommendation Council. (The council is composed of the Chief Justice, three Supreme Court justices, the president of the Korean Bar Association, a law professor appointed by the President, the Justice Minister, and the Attorney General.) His term of office is 6 years and cannot be renewed. Supreme Court justices are also appointed by the President but upon the proposal of the Chief Justice after he has secured the consent of the Judges Recommendation Council. Justices are appointed for a 10-year term and may be reappointed. Judges of lower courts are appointed for a term of 10 years by the Chief Justice on the basis of the decision of the Council of the Supreme Court Justices. Compulsory retirement age for all judges is 65.

The Supreme Court has the power to pass upon the constitutionality or legality of any law and administrative order or regulation. In this capacity, it serves as the guardian of the fundamental rights of the citizens. It may also hear appeals against the decision of appellate courts in civil and criminal cases. Supreme Court decisions are final and form judicial precedents which are binding on all lower courts.

The Supreme Court also has the constitutional power to decide on the dissolution of a political party provided three-fifths or more of its justices agree. Such action may be initiated by the executive branch of government. Military trials are handled by courts-martial established as special courts, but the Supreme Court has the final appellate jurisdiction over them.

An appellate court consists of a presiding judge and usually of three associate judges, all of whom are appointed by the chief justice in accordance with the decision of the Council of Supreme Court Justices. The Seoul Appellate Court hears appeals from the rulings of the district courts sitting at Seoul, Ch'unch'ŏn, Ch'ŏngju, and Taejŏn. The Taegu Appellate Court is responsible for the Taegu and Pusan district courts, and the Kwangju Appellate Court exercises jurisdiction over the Kwangju, Chŏnju and Cheju district courts. It is stipulated in the Court Organization Law that only appellate courts can administer justice on all litigations filed by private individuals or organizations against any government decision, order, or disposition.

A district court, which has original jurisdiction over most cases, is provided for Seoul and eight other provincial capitals. In Seoul the District Court is divided into two separate courts: Seoul Civil District Court and Seoul Criminal District Court. Usually, a District court trial is conducted by a single judge except in serious cases in which a three-judge trial is mandatory. A district court is assisted by one or more branch courts with single judges.

The newly amended Court Law provides for a Family Court in Seoul which is empowered to hear all cases involving matrimonial, juvenile, and other domestic matters. Court sessions are closed to the public to insure the privacy of the individuals concerned. In places other than Seoul, family disputes are handled by the appropriate District Court. Today, the independent status of the court system in the Republic of Korea is assured, and the judiciary as a whole enjoys a high reputation in terms of its integrity and competence.

In parallel with the judicial structure, there is the system of prosecutors' offices. The prosecutors are empowered to conduct investigations into violations of law and to institute legal suits against suspected law-breakers. According to the Prosecutor's Office Law, at the top of the prosecutors' structure stands the Supreme Prosecutors' Office, headed by an Attorney General, which is the state's highest prosecuting agency. The Supreme Prosecutors' Office is charged with responsibility for the supervision and control of all subordinate offices: the High Prosecutors' Offices, District Prosecutors' Offices, and Branch Prosecutors' Offices. The high and district prosecutors' offices are located in the cities where the judicial counterparts sit.

All these offices, including the Supreme Prosecutors' Office, are under the direction of the Minister of Justice. Article 14 of the Prosecutors' Office Law states that "the Minister of Justice, in the capacity of the highest official directing prosecuting matters, shall exercise general control and supervision over prosecutors" but he is not authorized to assume control over administrative matters pertaining to prosecution. This function is assigned to the Attorney-General. The Attorney-General, the Deputy Attorney-General, and the Directors of the High Prosecutors' Office are appointed by the President from among experienced prosecutors, judges, or lawyers who have been practicing law for more than 10 years. Other officials are appointed by the Minister of Justice.

LOCAL GOVERNMENT

The principle of local self-government is an ideal novel to Korea introduced in the Constitution of 1948. Traditionally, the country was ruled by strong central government, and all the affairs of localities were administered by officials sent by the central government. Thus, traditionally the people were denied opportunities to participate in local self-governing.

Legal Basis

Following the promulgation of the Constitution, a Local Autonomy Law was enacted in July 1949 to provide each local governmental unit with a representative assembly. These legal provisions on local self-government, however, were utterly meaningless during the regime of Syngman Rhee when the central government held firm control over the local units. The Local Autonomy Law has been amended several times. The local government, as existing in mid-1968, operates under the so-called Law Concerning Temporary Measures for Local Autonomy, adopted by the supreme military council in September 1, 1961, and as amended on March 21, 1962.

Under the temporary law, the functions of all local assemblies were suspended, and executive heads of local units were made appointive. The Constitution of the Third Republic states that the time of the establishment of the first local councils or assemblies is to be determined by law. The local assembly, as stipulated in the law, is a legislative organ whose chief functions are to make, revise, or abolish local laws and to determine budgets for the local government. Since 1961, however, these functions have been performed by the Minister of Home Affairs and the proper Provincial Governor, virtually suspending the self-governing activities of local units despite the constitutional provisions in favor of local autonomy.

Structure

Adminstratively, the country is divided into 9 provinces and two special cities (Seoul and Pusan) which enjoy provincial status. Each province (*do*) is in turn divided into cities (*si*) having populations of more than 50,000 and into counties (*kun*). Cities are not included within counties but are under the direct administration of provinces, as are counties. Counties are further subdivided into towns (*ŭp*) with populations of no less than 20,000 and into townships (*myŏn*) which are in charge of rural areas. Although by the 1961 law *kun* was made the basic local unit of the central government (which means that units below *kun* are subordinated to, and under the control of, the *kun* government), such units as *ŭp* and *myŏn* still can and do perform functions of the central government. For the rural population, *myŏn* is usually the first and frequently the last point of contact with governmental authorities. Each *myŏn* is composed of a varying number of *ri* (villages) and each *ri* is in charge of approximately 5 *burak* or hamlets. Seoul and Pusan are each partitioned into *ku* (wards). Each *ku* is in turn subdivided into *tong* (block), and *tong* into *t'ong* (sub-blocks). *Si* and *ŭp* are usually subdivided into *tong*. *Tong*, *t'ong* and *ri* are not headed by government employees but by influential community leaders. These posts are, therefore, more or less honorific ones. As of December 31, 1965, there were 30 *si*, 139 *kun*, 91 *ŭp*, 1,376 *myŏn*, and 18,447 *tong* and *ri*.

At the end of 1966, there were 63,000 local government employees. Of this number, 19 percent were appointed by the central government, and the remainder, by local government units. This means that 19 percent of public officials employed by local governments are subject to the provisions of the National Public Servant Law.

The most important duty of local government units has been to perform functions assigned to them by the central government. This trend was largely the result of the tradition of bureaucratic, unitary central government in which the affairs of the state were the concern exclusively of an educated minority at the apex of the social hierarchy. The ruling elite had traditionally been separated from the great bulk of the population by a wide social gap. As a result, the political and social climate was least conducive to the evolution of a self-governing spirit or practices at the grassroots level. Other problems confronting the local government since 1949 include chronic financial difficulties and a lack of trained capable administrators, most of whom are invariably attracted to positions in the central government.

Financially, the central government normally allocates about 15 to 16 percent of its annual budget for local government in the form of grants-in-aid. This amount is sufficient to cover 76 percent of all local government expenditure. The remaining portion is raised by local units themselves through taxation. The degree of financial dependency on the central government varies with each province. For example, 90.1 percent of Kangwŏn-do's 1960 revenue came from the central government, whereas the comparable figure for the Special City of Seoul amounted only to 45.3 percent. To correct this inequity, the government has introduced numerous reforms. The *kun* has been made the primary unit of local government rather than the *myŏn* and *ŭp*. Also, the local taxation system has been revised to improve the financial status of local governments. The tax reforms undertaken in 1967 are reported to have resulted in a substantial increase in local revenue, but much of the increased revenue is spent in performing the delegated functions of the central government.

The provincial governor and mayors of Seoul and Pusan are appointed directly by the President. Heads of *ku* in the special cities are also appointed by him but on the recommendation of the mayors of Seoul and Pusan. Executive chiefs of *kun* and *si* are recommended by provincial governors for presidential appointment. The recommendation for mayor or governor is channeled through the Ministry of Home Affairs. Thus, the President has virtually complete control over appointments for local government chiefs.

Administratively, provincial governors and the mayors of Seoul and Pusan are directly responsible to and supervised by the Ministry of Home Affairs. *Kunsu* (county chief) and *sijang* (mayor) are responsible primarily to provincial governors and secondarily to the Minister of Home Affairs; heads of *myŏn* and *ŭp* are answerable to the chiefs of the *kun*, the provincial governor, and the Minister of Home Affairs in that order. *Tong* and *ri* are supervised by *si* and *myŏn* heads, respectively.

A typical provincial government consists of 1 public information office and 6 bureaus, namely Home Affairs, Education, Health and Welfare, Industry, Public Works, and Police. Some provinces maintain a separate Office of Agriculture. The bureaus may supervise a varying number of sections, usually around 29. The province of Cheju-do has, however, 2 offices (*wŏn*), 3 bureaus, and 15 sections. Seoul Special City has 11 bureaus and 47 sections.

THE ELECTORAL SYSTEM

In the Republic of Korea elections perform the function of determining who will be the official policymakers of the national government. Today, the presidency and the 175 seats in the National Assembly are the only elected offices. As demonstrated in the 1961 military coup, however, elections cannot be said to be the only means of political alternation; since the Third Republic came into being, however, the feeling is stronger than ever among the South Korean people that elections are to be the only legitimate determinant of political competition. In addition, elections, and specifically the presidential elections, have been the primary means by which the Koreans have voiced a collective opinion.

The electoral process provides an important means of political education and participation, which will contribute to the political development of the Republic. Presidential contests nationally fought out arouse much interest on the part of the voters and focus much public attention on the salient issues of the time. Elections in the past were focused mainly on personality and ideology issues. For example, in 1963, the two main issues were the so-called "guided democracy" doctrine and the personality of Park Chung-hee, but in the 1967 election the issues were centered largely on matters of policy, and, as one observer noted, "the initial attempt of the DRP to attack the personality of Yun Po-sŏn (the major opposition candidate) aroused such immediate and vehement criticism from news media that both the DRP and the NDP (National Democratic Party) changed their tactics and the personality issue was greatly toned down." Electoral contests conducted in this manner are bound to play the role of educating the voters on important issues of the day.

In order to be a candidate a person must obtain party nomination, and persons without party affiliation are not allowed to seek elective office. Presidential candidates must be at least 40 years of age and must have been in continuous residence in the country for more than 5 years prior to election day. Civil servants or members of election management committees, if seeking the office of President, must resign from their post 180 days before the term of the incumbent President expires. The President is elected for a 4-year term and can succeed himself for a second term only.

Candidates running for Assembly seats must be at least 25 years of age. Most of them are chosen by plurality vote in single-member constituencies, which in 1968 numbered 131. The remaining 44 seats for the 175-member Assembly are filled through proportional representation. Under the present system of proportional representation, parties obtaining more than 50 percent of the popular vote or winning the minimum of 3 or more seats are entitled to elect members to seats without constituencies, the number being proportionate to the number of popular votes received. In the elections held on June 8, 1967, however, only two out of 11 parties could qualify for seats under the system of proportional representation. The Democratic-Republican Party obtained 102 single-member constituency seats by receiving 50.61 percent of the votes cast. The New Democratic Party won 28 single-member constituency seats by receiving 32.73 percent of the votes cast. Thus, the 44 proportional representation seats were divided between these two parties in proportion to the popular votes received. The Central Election Management Committee determines the number of winning seats for each party.

In the case of presidential elections, voting day must be proclaimed by the President, not later than 40 days before the announced date, and the comparable time limit for Assembly elections is 30 days. Polling stations are set up in each *ku* (ward in Seoul and Pusan), in each *ŭp* (usually county seat), and in each *myŏon* (township). Voting lists are prepared by the heads of each *ku, ŭp,* and *myŏn* office. A presidential candidate must file his candidacy with the Central Election Management Committee within ten days following the proclamation of the voting day, and an Assembly candidate is required to file his candidacy with his district election management committee within 7 days after the voting day has been announced. Candidates are allowed to launch their campaigns following the filing of their candidacy. Polls open at 7 a.m. and close at 5 p.m. Ballots are counted at *ku* and *kun* offices only.

Since 1963 elections have been managed by the government through its constitutional organ, the Central Election Management Committee. The committee's function is to ensure fair election management. Election committees, subordinate to the central organ are set up in Seoul, in Pusan, in each province, and in each electoral constituency. The central committee is composed of 2 members appointed by the President, 2 members elected by the National Assembly, and 5 members elected by the Council of the Supreme Court Justices. Membership of subordinate committees is to be made up of those with educational or legal background and other persons of "learning and experience." Committee members serve a 5-year term which may be renewed. To ensure impartiality, all election committee members are barred from joining parties or participating in any political activities. They cannot be removed except through impeachment or criminal conviction. Since membership in these committees is largely honorific, remuneration is limited to travel and other official expenses. In case of electoral disputes, parties concerned may bring a suit before the Supreme Court against the Central Election Management Committee.

Expenses incident to the management of elections are borne by the government. Campaign expenses, however, are to be paid by candidates themselves within the ceiling established by the Central Election Management Committee. Ever since the electoral process was introduced into South Korea, an unusually large percent of the eligible voters go to the polls which indicates their interest in elections as the only legitimate means of political competition. Citizens attaining the age of 20 are given the right to choose public officials in universal, direct, and secret elections, irrespective of their sex, religion, or social status. Certain persons are, however, disfranchised by reason of criminal convictions or by court ruling. In June 1967 eligible voters numbered 14,717,354, or 50.3 percent of the total population.

PUBLIC SERVICE

Traditionally, the civil service had the greatest prestige and was regarded as the only honorable profession; it embodied the highest social and political aspirations of an individual because it usually ensured wealth, power, and social status (see ch. 2, Historical Setting). After 1945, however, the civil service was no longer the only socially acceptable occupation, and the traditional deference accorded officialdom by the people substantially diminished. In a "monistic" society such as Korea, however, where the government is the principal employer and regulates and controls economic activity to a considerable degree, and where the so-called *kwanjon-minpi* (officialdom exalted and people downgraded) attitude is still very much a part of the culture, the civil service continues to provide one of the most desired and expedient avenues to prestige, influence, and wealth.

The civil service system familiar in western nations was introduced into Korea in August 1949 when the National Assembly enacted the Civil Service Law. It was amended in 1950, 1961 and 1962. In 1963 a new law known as National Civil Service Law, was promulgated. This law continues to govern the national civil service today.

Size and Structure

The civil service (Kongmuwŭn) is made up of national and local government employees who are recruited, selected, and appointed by competent executive agencies of the central and local government. Officials of the central government generally have more prestige than their local counterparts, mainly because local officials perform functions delegated to them by the central government and are thus subject to subordinate status.

The national civil service is also divided into two types — "special" category (*byŏljŏng-jik*) and "general" category (*ilban-jik*) — according to official function. The special category is not regulated by the National Civil Service Law and is subject to presidential decrees, thus making it relatively easy for the President to maintain effective control over most officials in this category. The special category includes virtually all the top-ranking positions in the government. Some of the more important ones are: all elective officers; members of the State Council, vice ministers of executive ministries, directors of other Cabinet-level offices, ambassadors and ministers, judges, secretaries to political appointees, military personnel, mayors of Seoul and Pusan, civilian employees of defense establishments, and provincial governors. Presidents, deans, and faculty members in the national universities, and teachers in all secondary and elementary schools are collectively known as "educational civil servants" and are thus subject to a separate law called the Educational Civil Servant Law (Kyoyuk kong-muwŏn-boŏp). But they are still regarded as "special" civil servants.

The general category is divided into five grades; most of the central government officials, that is, those excluding the officials in the special category, come under this classification. Officials of Grade 3 and above are appointed by the President on the recommendation of the ministers concerned. Ministerial recommendations must first go through the Minister of Government Administration (Chongmu-chŏ); those in Grades 4 and 5 are appointed by the proper ministers. The President's appointment power is further enhanced by the fact that he, unlike the President of the United States, is not required to submit his appointments to the legislature for confirmation.

Ordinarily, the positions immediately below the "special" category officials are entitled to Grade 1. Grade 2 is given to the directors of bureaus in executive ministries; heads of sections and subsections in the central government, second and third secretaries in the foreign service, or police chiefs in cities are usually holders of Grade 3. Police lieutenants or administrative assistants in executive ministries are given Grade 4. Clerks, police sergeants, or patrolmen are given the ranking of Grade 5. Except for Grade 1, each of these grades is subdivided into A and B, with Subgrade A being the higher of the two.

The civil service is under the authority of the Ministry of Governmental Administration, headed by a presidential appointee of Cabinet rank. This office handles recruitment of candidates through open, competitive examination.

Basis of Selection and Promotion

Prior to 1963 the office held two basic examinations every year: "high" civil service examination (kodŏng koshi) for Grade 3, and "ordinary" examination (botong koshi) for Grade 4. These were qualifying examinations, and success in these examinations did not automatically insure appointment to an administrative post, and the Ministry of Government Administration only prepared a list of those who had successfully passed the examinations for selection and appointment by individual executive agencies. The high civil service examinations were so rigorous that in the 1949–1962 period only two percent of the applicants successfully passed the examinations. The ordinary examinations were equally difficult.

Thus, these examinations produced only a very small fraction of new Grade 3 and Grade 4 recruits. The rest were hired through competitive examinations held as the occasion arose. Today, under the 1963 National Civil Service Law, most new recruits for each grade are hired by means of open, competitive examinations conducted by the Ministry of Governmental Administration. In addition to the hiring examinations, qualifying examinations are often held to select competent candidates for governmental jobs. In 1967, such examinations were held four times, and 507 candidates were selected out of 7,914 applicants, or 6.4 percent. In the same year 16 open, competitive hiring examinations were conducted, and 10,631 out of 112,635, or 8.9 percent of the applicants, were hired. These figures show that the civil service is still one of the most competitive occupations in Korea.

Promotions are, according to the civil service law, based on efficiency ratings, experience, merit and competitive examinations. The Central Officials Training Institute of the Ministry of Governmental Administration offers short-term, intensive, technical instruction to civil servants, including judges and prosecutors. Special training is also provided by the Graduate School of Public Administration, Seoul National University, to familiarize public officials with the "higher aspects of the administrative sciences." Ministries themselves sponsor their own training programs. Appointees are required to serve a prescribed "conditional" period before being assigned to "regular" status. A civil servant may not be discharged against his will without cause as provided in the basic statute. Aggrieved parties may appeal to the Board of Appeals. Compulsory retirement age varies for each grade: 50 for Grade 5; 55 for Grade 4; and 61 for Grade 3 and above.

Officials in local government are classified also into "general" and "special" categories. The conditions and procedures of recruitment, selection, appointment, job classification, promotion, discipline, compensation, and other matters are governed by the Local Civil Service Act promulgated in 1963. In general, the law is similar to that of the national civil service.

The South Korean civil service is youthful, with the average age being in the 31–35 bracket (as of 1962) and, despite strong emphasis on college education for Grade 4 and above, the educational level is rather low. As of 1962, only 15.8 percent of the entire civil service had a college background.

As of 1966 there were 275,731 national civil servants and 54,021 local civil servants. No single particular group dominates the civil service, although graduates from Seoul National University Law School occupy many of the high-ranking posts in the central ministries. All social classes are represented. The incumbent government has an ambitious program of gradual pay hikes designed to guarantee the minimum living costs for every civil servant by 1971, and this plan has been closely followed in the past three years.

CHAPTER 14

POLITICAL DYNAMICS

In mid-1968, the locus of political power appeared to be in the hands of President Park Chung-hee and his close associates in the government and in the ruling Democratic Republican Party. There were indications, however, that the political leadership operated under various restraints of both constitutional and political nature. The political awareness of the population as a whole appeared to have heightened, and the farmers appeared to be increasingly discriminating and to consult their "self-interest" when they cast their ballots. Many of them voted for the opposition party in the 1963 and 1967 elections. Such political forces as the students and the press appeared to exert active restraints on the government; and the military, although much divorced from politics, remained as a potential check upon the governmental leadership. Indications were that power was much more openly and freely contested than in the past.

In 1968 economic and military factors — specifically, economic modernization aimed at creating a self-sustaining economy and an increase in the living standards of the people and improvement in the country's preparedness against the Communists in the north — dominated the policy goals. A majority of the citizens appeared to concur in these policy goals, although there was some disagreement on the means to achieve them.

In mid-1968, the party system was controlled by the Democratic Republican Party, which had more than a two-thirds majority of seats in the legislature. This party appeared to resort often to its absolute majority position in legitimating policies coming from the executive branch, headed by President Park Chung-hee. Members of the opposition New Democratic Party appeared to be very much outside the arena of parliamentary policymaking, and there appeared to be little political communication between the two parties. Although there were interest groups representing almost every walk of national life, most of these did not appear to be effective in the governmental policymaking process. Although competition for political power took the form of election, the parliamentary elections of 1967 were marred by a variety of irregularities that undermined the growing confidence of the public in the electoral process. Some segments of the population — specifically those committed to liberal democratic ideals — appeared to lack confidence in either party. Both parties were loose coalitions of different factions, and there was mounting evidence of factional strife within them over the question of power and office.

HISTORICAL BACKGROUND

The First Republic (1948–1960)

The Japanese surrender of 1945 brought liberation and hope of immediate independence to the Koreans. This hope, however, was soon diminished by the division of the country into two halves, the attempt of the three powers (the United States, Great Britain, and the Soviet Union) to place Korea under trusteeship, growing polarization of domestic political forces into two hostile camps, and deteriorating economic conditions (see ch. 3, Historical Setting).

The United States troops set up a military government to replace the Japanese colonial administration. This military government was faced with a series of internal political and economic confusions. The division of the country left the south with limited national resources, and waves of refugees from the north, repatriates from Japan, and returnees from overseas contributed to housing and food shortages and to widespread unemployment. The lack of skilled manpower, coupled with the shortage of electric power, brought about a slowdown of economic and administrative activities. Vehement political competition between rightist and leftist political forces further complicated the already difficult situation. The left-wing forces, discontented with the slowness of the military government to cope with these difficulties and prompted by the politically motivated agitation from the north, waged a series of antigovernment demonstrations. Syngman Rhee, by gaining the confidence of the Americans in Korea, rapidly established his position as the country's leader. He advocated immediate unification of the two halves of the country and Korean independence of all foreign influence. Stating that he stood above partisan struggles among various political groups, he urged all groups to join his newly organized Central Committee for the Rapid Realization of Independence. This action served to identify him personally with the national aspiration of the Koreans.

In 1947, the United States submitted the Korean question to the United Nations, which had recommended (despite the Soviet veto) elections throughout Korea under the supervision of a United Nations commission. The commission, however, was not allowed into the northern half of the peninsula, and elections were held only in

208

as much of the country as the commission could supervise. Because of his popularity, Rhee encountered no difficulty in becoming President. The constitution was adopted, and the Government of the Republic of Korea came into being on August 15, 1948, the day celebrated as Korea's Independence Day (see ch. 13, The Governmental System).

The Rhee government inherited a host of unsolved problems, especially in the economic field, with which it found itself unable to cope. Another difficulty was the acute and immediate need for building up security forces to encounter widespread Communist insurgent activities. As resources for this purpose were diverted from economic needs at the same time that American troops were withdrawn from the south (June 1949), public morale deteriorated. This trend was reflected in part in the May 1950 general elections, for pro-Rhee candidates for the National Assembly received only 26 percent of the seats, a resounding defeat for the President in terms of public approval. Despite this clear indication of the public's dissatisfaction with the Rhee government and popular demand for a change in leadership, Rhee tended to identify his own destiny with that of Korea. Apparently convinced that he alone could unify the country and engage in the task of nation-building, he began to regard any opponents — however legitimate — as "Communist agents" who were obstructing his anti-Communist policies and plans for unification and development of the country. As anti-Rhee feeling was most obvious in the reorganized National Assembly, that institution became the focus of his attacks.

As Rhee's support dwindled in the National Assembly, the organ entrusted with the constitutional responsibility of electing the President, he began to feel that the population as a whole was more likely than the Assembly to reelect him. For this purpose he needed a nationwide organization that could fulfill the function of building support for this candidacy. Therefore, in December 1951, at the height of the Korean war, he created a state party called the Liberal Party (*chayu-dang*), which was a heterogeneously organized group, lacking any measure of cohesiveness and unified only in its members' devotion and deference to Rhee. Also, in an attempt to appeal to wider segments of the populace, Rhee brought under the party's umbrella several auxiliary organizations, including the Korean Youth Corps headed by Yi Pom-sok, a former premier under Rhee, the Korean Federation of Trade Unions, and the Korean Women's Association.

The next step Rhee took to ensure his reelection was to attempt to amend the Constitution to deprive the Assembly of its power to elect the President and make the people choose the President in direct elections. The amendment bill met with strong opposition in the Assembly; but he obtained passage of the bill by proclaiming martial law. This was justified as a necessary countermeasure against alleged communist guerrilla activities near Pusan, the wartime capital, but was actually used to limit the political activities of assemblymen who opposed the measure. Once the amendment had been pushed through, Rhee's 1956 reelection for a second term came easily, as many rural voters responded to the urging of the Liberal Party to give their popular mandate to Rhee. When general elections were held in May 1954 to elect members of the legislature, the Liberal Party received 72 percent of the popular vote.

After these successes, Rhee set out to eliminate a constitutional barrier to his continued rule by abolishing the two-term limit on presidential office. The proposed amendment would allow an unlimited number of terms for a President permitting Rhee to run for office as long as he lived. In the crucial showdown voting of November 27, 1954, however, Rhee's party, by a single vote, failed to muster the required two-thirds majority (136 out of 203), and the presiding officer declared the bill rejected. When the legislature convened two days later, however, the speaker announced that a different method would be used to compute two-thirds of the vote: Fractional votes would be rounded off to the preceding whole number. Since the Assembly had 203 members, only 135 votes were required to pass the controversial bill and, the speaker declared, the bill had received this required majority. In the midst of great confusion, the bill was then declared to have been passed. The opposition's challenge of this computation was not supported by the Supreme Court.

Some influential Liberal Party assemblymen bolted from the party in protest against Rhee's methods and joined with leading members of the Democratic-National Party to form a new conservative party called the Democratic Party. The new party, founded in September 1955, contained most of the leading figures who opposed the Liberal Party, including such well-known persons as Shin Ik-hi (Patrick Henry Shinicky), Cho Pyŏng-ok, Chang Myŏn, and Pak Sun-ch'ŏn. Without the support of such leaders as Cho Bong-am, however, the party, though united in its opposition to Rhee and his political machine, was inherently a weak political grouping, and it failed to establish itself as a unit of opposition. In December 1955, Cho Bong-am organized his own party, the Progressive Party, left of the conservative Liberal and Democratic parties.

Growing anti-Rhee feeling among the people was reflected in the May 1956 presidential elections. He was reelected for the third term, but his share of the vote was only 55 percent as compared with the 1952 figure of 70 percent. Moreover, his running mate,

210

Lee Ki-pung, Rhee's heir-apparent, was defeated by Chang Myŏn, the Democratic Party's vice-presidential candidate. The Democratic Party's presidential candidate, Shin Ik-hi, died suddenly 10 days before the election at the peak of his popularity, yet received protest votes of more than 1.8 million, or almost 20 percent of the total votes cast. In Seoul alone the deceased candidate received 280,000 votes, compared with Rhee's 205,000 votes. The Progressive Party's presidential candidate, Cho Bong-am, polled 2,163,000 votes, or 23.5 percent of the total.

The 1956 elections clearly demonstrated that Rhee was rapidly losing popularity among the people. Uncertain about his chances of reelection in 1960, Rhee and his Liberal Party supporters proposed another constitutional amendment. This amendment would reverse the earlier one, permitting election of the President by the National Assembly rather than by popular vote. The reasoning behind this scheme was that the Assembly, then controlled by the Liberals, could more readily be manipulated into electing Rhee for a fourth term. The amendment also proposed nullification of an article under which Vice President Chang Myŏn would automatically succeed to the presidency in the event of Rhee's disability or death. This scheme failed because the Liberal Party was unable to obtain the needed two-thirds majority in the general elections of May 1958. On the contrary, its seats were reduced from 131 to 126, or only 54 percent of the total. The opposition won 79 seats (an increase of 35 over 1956), including 14 out of the 16 seats contested in Seoul.

When Rhee failed, he decided to revise statutory laws. He first proposed, in August 1958, to revise the National Security Law of 1949 for the purpose of indicting, as Communists or subversives, those who opposed him. Confronted with vehement opposition in the Assembly, the Liberals directed policemen to remove the opponents and lock them up in the basement of the Assembly building. Thus unopposed, the Liberals passed some 25 bills, including the new security law and the Local Autonomy Law. Under the revised law on local autonomy, all elective offices in cities and townships were made appointive.

The first victim of the National Security Law was Cho Bong-am, leader of the Progressive Party, which had been outlawed on charges of antistate conspiracy. Cho was tried on charges of subversive activities and executed on July 31, 1959. Rhee's next move was to suspend for several months *Tong-A Ilbo*, the largest daily newspaper, which was critical of him. *Kyŏnghyang Sinmum*, another paper hostile to Rhee, was shut down in 1959. Despite these measures against the press, critics did not subside, and other periodical publications, especially *Sasanggye*, a leading monthly, greatly widened and deepened opposition attack.

In the midst of growing antigovernment feeling, the presidential elections of March 1960 were held. In view of Rhee's age, the choice of vice-president was crucial, and many Liberals doubted that Rhee's running mate, Lee Ki-pung, could be elected. With complete control over governmental instruments, including police, and aided by the new National Security Law, the Liberal Party pushed for the election of Lee. Rhee was unopposed in the elections because of the unexpected death of Democratic Party candidate Cho Byong-ok one month before election day. The Liberal ticket won, but only after a series of maneuvers which included election rigging and proclamation of emergency martial law on the grounds that special measures were required to ensure maintenance of peace and order during the election campaign. In protest, the Democrats declared the election illegal and void and sought a court injunction to nullify the results.

The April Student Revolt and the Fall of the Rhee Regime

The Rhee government, seemingly unassailable, was overthrown in April 1960 after massive student demonstrations. The events surrounding the elections had pushed the urban and intellectual elements of society to a point of consensus. The students' anger at the government's political machinations againt the opposition was first evidenced on February 28, 1960, when about a thousand students clashed with police at Taegu. This demonstration was followed by similar incidents on a smaller scale in other cities. On March 15, disturbances of major proportion took place at Masan, a port city about 45 miles west of Pusan; several thousand students and adults clashed with police, who fired into the crowd, and scores of casualties resulted.

The situation became even more explosive four weeks later, when fishermen in Masan harbor accidentally discovered the disfigured body of a student missing since election day. This incident provoked intense antipolice hostility among the people and eventually touched off waves of student demonstrations elsewhere, climaxing on April 19, when almost 100,000 students clashed with policemen in major cities. On this day alone, 130 students were killed (109 in Seoul) and some 800 were reportedly wounded, again as the result of police firing into the crowds. On April 25, college professors in the Seoul area, who, although critical of the regime, had avoided taking active part in antigovernment activities, waged protest marches.

When Rhee reacted by proclaiming martial law, the military contingents that had been brought into the capital city adopted an attitude of sympathetic neutrality toward the demonstrating students. Faced with rapidly mounting antigovernment sentiments and declining political and military support, Rhee resigned on April 27, 1960, ending his 12-year rule.

The Caretaker Government

Following the fall of the Rhee regime, a caretaker government was formed under Hŏ Chŏng, then Minister of Foreign Affairs. Promising to rid the country of long-accumulated illegalities, injustices, and corruption, the interim government implemented several reforms. The much resented Anti-Communist Youth League, an arm of the Liberal Party, was disbanded, and legal proceedings were instituted against some 30 former cabinet members and politicians on charges of fraud in the March 1960 election. On June 15, the governmental form was changed to a parliamentary one by a constitutional amendment. Under its provisions the President was to be elected by the National Assembly and his activities would be limited mainly to ceremonial functions. The center of power was shifted to the Prime Minister, who was responsible to the legislature (see ch. 13, The Governmental System). Despite these actions, the Hŏ government was widely criticized for letting Rhee slip out of the country in late May.

In July, a general election was held to select members of the new legislature; as predicted, the Democrats won a decisive victory. The Assembly elected Yun Po-sŏn to the presidency and Chang Myŏn to the premiership. The Cabinet was formed on August 23, 1960, which marked the beginning of the Second Republic.

The Second Republic (1960–1961)

The Second Republic was short-lived. It restored constitutional rights suppressed by the former government and continued the task of prosecuting Rhee's principal political aides. It exposed many big businessmen who had amassed illicit fortunes by providing the Rhee regime with political funds in return for favors. It prosecuted police officials responsible for firing at the student demonstrators and neutralized the police and the military. It also instituted a series of measures to combat poverty and corruption. Besides expressing hope for an early normalization of relations with Japan, it set forth a vaguely defined formula for national unification.

Initial popular response was markedly enthusiastic and optimistic, but this optimism began to wane as factional feuds developed within the ruling party as soon as the single most important factor binding it together — opposition to the Rhee regime — was gone. Chang Myŏn's faction, known as the "New Faction," quickly established itself as the stronger of the two major groups. The strength was reflected in the makeup of the new government. Although the presidency was given to Yun Po-sŏn, leader of the Old Guard faction, Chang Myŏn asssumed the office of Prime Minister, the real locus of power under the amended constitution. The factions wrangled over patronage and power. In the course of dispute, fragmentation rapidly took place. Yun's Old Guard faction was subdivided into moderate and hard-line cliques, and Chang's faction into "old," "youth," and "centrist" cliques. In October 1961, the Old Guard faction broke away and formed the New Democratic Party.

The economic situation continued to deteriorate. Unemployment rose, and, as a result of poor crops in 1960, in the spring of 1961 nearly 27 percent of the population was in need of relief. The government attempted to alleviate tension by diverting defense expenditures to relief needs, but a projected 100,000-man reduction of the armed forces did not materialize because of military opposition.

The frequently irresponsible activities of the press compounded the government's difficulties. The hundreds of newspapers that had sprung up during the Chang regime had little sympathy for the problems this regime was struggling to solve within a democratic framework.

The immediate post-1960 years were also marked by the rise of numerous political parties. This fragmentation, coupled with the split of the Democratic Party into two separate parties, added instability and confusion.

As the popularity of the Chang government waned, it was the students who voiced most active opposition to the government. Once again they took to the streets. During the 9-month period of the Chang regime, at least 726 student demonstrations were recorded. In addition, nonstudent urban groups were active in attempting to influence the government by means of protest demonstrations. In all, 1,109 such demonstrations were reported. The high point of student protest against the regime occurred on October 11, 1960, when students forced their way into the Assembly floor and occupied it, demanding severe punishment of antirevolutionary elements and calling for immediate end to factional strife.

The issue of peaceful unification also had an unsettling effect on the Chang government. In an obvious attempt to capitalize on confusion in the south, on August 14, 1960, P'yŏngyang proposed a plan to unify the nation through a so-called "confederation" of the northern and southern regions as a transition step. A governing committee made up of representatives of the two governments would administer such matters as foreign relations, postal service, and currency. During this period, however, each regime would retain its own governmental system. As an alternative to the confederation proposal, P'yŏngyang suggested a joint economic committee, composed of businessmen from both sides, to coordinate economic activities.

While the Seoul government rejected the overtures of the Communists, some college students, trade union members, and several progressive parties endorsed the Py'ŏngyang proposal. Even some conservative politicians and newspapers expressed qualified support. Furthermore, in the last months of the Chang regime, apprehension mounted because of indications of some leftist infiltration into a few universities and the formation of a leftist group called the National Students Federation for National Unification. The group advocated peaceful unification and tried to arrange a joint north-south student conference at P'anmunjŏm. The group, although small and organized in only a few universities, was vocal and appeared to be growing.

With the police discredited, the government appeared unable to cope with the unification movement. Its attempt to enact two special laws designed to curb demonstrations and all Communist-inspired activities failed largely because of vigorous protest demonstrations by student and leftist sympathizers. It was against this background that a group of military officers headed by Major General Park Chung-hee and Lieutenant Colonel Kim Chong-p'il concluded that the country, already chaotic and possibly drifting slowly toward communism, had to be saved.

Military Coup d'Etat

The Chang government was overthrown in a bloodless coup d'état on May 16, 1961. The coup was a reaction to what its leaders considered the incompetence and chaos of the Chang regime, which in their view was no better than the Rhee regime — a view shared by a large segment of the population.

The military coup was conceived as early as February 1960 by Park Chung-hee and his colleagues. A leading role was played by the handful of survivors of the seventh (1948) and eighth (1949) graduating classes of the Korean Constabulary Officers Training School (the fore-runner of the 4-year military academy established later), which had suffered heavy casualties during the Korean conflict. According to initial plans, the coup was to take place on May 8, 1960, but it was rendered unnecessary because of the April student uprising. The officers shifted their strategy to promote a "military purification movement" — a peaceful movement aimed at ousting from the military what they considered incompetent and corrupt elements. They also advocated political neutrality of the military and the elimination of factionalism within the military establishment. However, the movement met with heavy opposition from above, and the officers involved were severely reprimanded and court-martialed on charges of revolting against their superiors. One was sentenced to a prison term; while others were acquitted, most of them were later placed on reserve status. As a result, the purification produced little result.

In the meantime, without the knowledge of the Army group, elements in the Marine Corps had been planning their own coup; upon learning of the Army plan, however, they dropped their scheme in favor of a joint Army-Marine operation. The new plan called for a strike on April 19, 1961, the first anniversary of the student uprising. Since the military was under standing orders to quell anticipated student riots, coup plotters planned to act under the guise of riot control. The student demonstration on April 19 was peaceful, however, and the military was left with no pretext for troop mobilization. The successful coup was finally carried out on May 16, 1961, by a group of 62 officers with the backing of 5,000 troops. They occupied major government buildings, and when government leadership went into hiding, coup leaders announced they had taken over all government functions.

The victorious officers immediately formed a Military Revolutionary Committee, proclaimed martial law, dissolved the National Assembly and local councils, suspended political party activities, and took over the executive, legislative, and judicial functions of the government. On May 19, the Committee was renamed the Supreme Council for National Reconstruction. Until December 16, 1963, the military leaders, headed by Park Chung-hee, ran the government, initially aided by college professors, in the name of the Supreme Council.

The Council carried out extreme reform measures. It arrested 4,200 hoodlums who had been active ever since the Rhee years. It promulgated a law intended to nullify usurious loan contracts binding upon farmers and fishermen, the poorest segment of society. To curb Communist activities, the Supreme Council arrested 2,100 suspected Communist sympathizers and promulgated a new Anti-Communism Act. In the economic sphere, a tentative 5-year development plan was announced in July. Steps were also taken to prosecute certain leaders under Rhee, who had been implicated in the March 1960 election frauds, and plans were announced to confiscate some 12 billion wŏn ($44 million) from 59 illicit fortune makers. By the end of August, 35,000 government employees had been dismissed on charges of corruption or incompetence, making room for government service by discharged or retired military personnel.

Park Chung-hee announced his intention of restoring civilian government by mid-1963. In an attempt to remove what they considered unfavorable elements, in March 1962 the military leaders enacted a law concerning the purification of political activities, whereby a blacklist of some 4,300 politicians was made public. Later, most of these individuals were screened and declared fit for participation in political activities. On December 17, 1962 the Constitution was amended to change the parliamentary system of government back to the presidential form. On December 31, 1962, a Political Party Act was promulgated, and early in 1963, new election laws for the National Assembly and for the presidency were announced.

These reforms and innovations were greeted by the public with restrained enthusiasm and some skepticism, which was due largely to the traditional popular concept that statecraft should be the function of civilian rather than military authorities (see ch. 3, Historical Setting). This attitude soon developed into a feeling of disenchantment with the Supreme Council. Civilian politicians denounced the Political Purification Law as unduly harsh and criticized certain provisions of the amended constitution and the Political Party Act as unfair to opposition forces. By mid-1962, charges of incompetence were being leveled against the military government. It was widely asserted in Seoul that the officers' mechanistic approach to the complex problems of government and politics had been partly responsible for such allegations.

The popular disenchantment with the military also derived from factional conflicts within the military leadership, which were soon revealed to the public. Power and patronage rather than policy differences appeared to have been the primary point at issue. General Song Yo-chan, premier in the military cabinet, charged that the faction headed by Kim Chong-p'il (director of the Central Intelligence Agency and nephew-in-law of General Park) was attempting to perpetuate itself in power. Shortly afterwards, General Yu Won-sik, another member of the Council, made similar accusations. These were followed by the accusation of Kim Tong-ha, also a member of the military government, that it was failing to uphold its pledges to the public.

Against this background, on February 27, 1963, General Park Chung-hee candidly admitted partial failure of the revolutionary regime and declared that he would turn over the government to civilians by summer and would not participate if they would abide by certain conditions to ensure political stability. Kim Chon-p'il himself, yielding to opposition as well as internal pressures, withdrew from hs public posts and went into exile abroad. The civilian politicians were jubilant over Park's proposal and wasted no time in accepting it.

Within two weeks, however, in a sudden reversal of his earlier position, Park Chung-hee proposed 4 more years of military rule. The reasons behind this sudden change are not fully known, but following his announcement, Park reportedly encountered heavy opposition to civilian rule from a segment of the military. A group of young army officers staged a demonstration in front of the Council building, demanding extended military rule.

Park's reversal immediately provoked antigovernment demonstrations and denunciations by civilian politicians and students. He announced that an election would be held later in the year.

In the meantime, while the military government's ban on political activities was still in effect, the colonels around Kim Chong-p'il proceeded in early 1962 to organize a political party that would carry on the military government's program after military rule was terminated.

The party thus organized came into being as the Democratic Republican Party on February 2, 1963, soon after Park lifted the ban on political activities. On August 31, the party's national convention elected Park, then on reserve status, to enter politics as party president and nominated him as the party's presidential candidate to compete against the civilian politicians in the election schedule for late 1963. The party upheld the revolutionary pledges of the military government and promised to usher in the so-called "new democratic order" and provide the country with national leadership.

The civilians, however, though now freed of the official ban on their activities, were not able to counter the military leaders with any measure of solidarity. Even their common opposition to civilians-turned-politician could not serve as a common rallying point, and the populace remained fragmented. The most active civilian party was a splinter group from Chang Myŏn's Democratic Party. This party was able to solicit the support of some of the former members of the Democratic Party and Rhee's Liberal Party to form a new party known as the Civil Rule Party.

The new party nominated Yun Po-sŏn as its presidential candidate. The Democratic Party, however, lost its former vigor, largely because of the loss of its leader, Chang Myŏon, who had been convicted of activities against the military government. Some of the members of the party joined either the Civil Rule Party or the New Politics Party, organized under the leadership of Hŏ Chŏng, head of the caretaker government. The remaining Democrats formed a new party, retaining their old name, with Madame Pak Sun-ch'ŏn as party president. The Liberal Party, discredited after the 1960 student uprising, attempted to revive, and Yi Pŏm-sŏk, one of its leading members, formed the People's Friends Party.

But the party remained small, largely because many former Liberals felt more comfortable with the ruling Democratic Republican party. There was also the Liberal Democratic Party, which included some of the anti-Kim Chong-p'il members of the junta. The party nominated as its presidential candidate Song Yo-ch'an, who was later arrested by the junta on various charges. In addition, a few other groups nominated their own presidential candidates. As a result, a total of seven candidates, each representing a separate party, filed their presidential candidacy with the Central Election Management Committee.

Although the civilian politicians, operating under the various party labels, were in agreement on the end for a single civilian candidate to fight against General Park Chung-hee, they were badly divided when it came to nominating such a candidate and working out a united-front formula. Later, the situation for the civilian parties somewhat improved, when two of the candidates, Hŏ Chŏng and Song Yo-ch'an, withdrew shortly before the voting to throw their support behind Yun Po-sŏn, the strongest civilian candidate against Park.

In addition to the fragmentation of their potential strength, the civilian politicians were subject to numerous other disadvantages. Most of them were on the military government's blacklist and therefore had to undergo screening. For more than two years after the coup, the military government kept them from political activities. They were even uncertain as to the election date until the public announcement was made on August 15, and they were then allowed only 30 days for campaigning. By this time the government party, under the protective umbrella of the political activity ban, had almost completed the task of its organization throughout the country.

The main issue in the election campaign was the nature of the regime to replace the military government. The opposition parties contended that democracy could not be created unless the military turned over the intricate art of politics to the civilians. The military leaders countered by arguing that civilian rule would invite political instability and a cycle of revolutions and that General Park's objective was to create a liberal democracy on the basis of strong nationalism. Policy matters were significantly played down by the candidates during the entire course of the campaign, as each side sought to emphasize the other's weakness and past failures.

The election of October 15 was recorded as the most honest ever held in Korea. Park Chung-hee won the presidency — but by only a minority of the votes cast, because the majority was divided among Yun and three other civilian candidates. Yun won in Seoul and four northern provinces, while Park carried southern provinces. In the urban areas, Park received only 27 percent of the votes as against Yun's 63 percent. But in rural areas Park fared well, receiving 59 percent of the votes as against Yun's 41 percent. In Kangwŏn Province, where troops were heavily concentrated, Park received less than 40 percent of the votes cast, while Yun carried the province by obtaining about 49 percent of the votes.

The parliamentary elections were held on November 26. These elections were reported to have been quite fair, although there were some charges of irregularities. Again, Park's party failed to receive a majority of the votes cast, but it was able to capture 110 seats for the 175-man Assembly, even with its mediocre showing (polling only 32 percent of the votes cast) because the opposition parties were unable to unite behind a single candidate. Altogether, 12 parties took part in the elections. The party that exhibited the best showing was Yun's Civil Rule Party, which won 41 seats. The old Democratic Party (of Chang Myŏn) attained 13 seats, with the remainder divided between two minor parties.

After the elections were over, the Constitution of the Third Republic, which had been approved in the 1962 national referendum, was officially promulgated on December 17, 1963. President Park Chung-hee formed his first postelection cabinet with Ch'oe Tu-sŏn, a nonpartisan intellectual, as premier. This marked the beginning of the Third Republic.

The Third Republic

The new regime soon faced numerous problems in attempting to move forward. Normalization of relations with Japan had been one of the basic goals, but for a long time Seoul and Tokyo had failed to find a formula acceptable to both sides. For diplomatic, military, and, most important, economic reasons, the Park government intended to bring about normalization on equitable terms. Park dispatched his right-hand man, Kim Chŏng-p'il, to oversee Seoul's official delegation to the negotiations. In April 1964, the terms of a tentative agreement between Kim and his Japanese counterpart were informally revealed. However, opponents and students felt that Washington was exerting pressure on the Park government to bring about speedy rapprochement between Tokyo and Seoul, even on terms favorable to the former (see ch. 23, Foreign Economic Relations). As a result, the news of the proposed agreement was not received well. Yun's Civil Rule Party and other opposition parties immediately launched joint efforts to oppose the terms of the government. There was a flurry of anti-American feeling, and demonstrating students demanded the recall of Kim from Tokyo and immediate cessation of the negotiations.

Park retreated in a tactical move by recalling his emissary, who left on his second exile to the United States, and negotiations were hastily suspended. But Park let it be known that he would try to bring about an early treaty. This attitude provoked students to further protest. Park reacted by declaring martial law in Seoul. Schools were closed, news media were censored, and all gatherings were forbidden. Furthermore, student leaders and a number of prominent persons in news media were arrested.

As the student protest movement subsided, negotiations with Japan were quietly resumed in Tokyo toward the end of 1964. The talks were followed in early 1965 by a visit of the Japanese Foreign Minister to Seoul, where he and the Seoul government reached agreement on some of the fundamental issues. In April, Korean Foreign Minister Lee Tong-won visited Tokyo, and the two foreign ministers signed a draft agreement on such outstanding issues as fishery restrictions, property claims, and the legal status of Korean residents in Japan. In June in Tokyo, the two ministers formally signed the treaty restoring diplomatic relations between the countries (see ch. 23, Foreign Economic Relations).

In the Republic of Korea, however, a sizable segment of the population — specifically, students, opposition parties, Christian leaders, various civic organizations, and even retired generals who had served in Park's government — considered the treaty unfair and felt that the government was selling out the country to the Japanese. Public anger against the treaty was vented in acts of violence similar to those that led to the 1960 ousting of Syngman Rhee. A state of emergency was declared on August 25 when over 10,000 students and other protesters battled with the police. Combat-ready troops were on hand in Seoul, and punitive measures were carried out against students and professors active in the anti-treaty demonstrations.

The treaty issue brought the two major opposition parties — the Civil Rule Party and the Democratic Party — together into a single party on June 14, 8 days before the treaty was signed in Tokyo. However, the new party, known as the People's Party, made up of two distinct factions, was never able to agree on how best to oppose the Park government and block the treaty. Madame Pak Sun-ch'ŏn's faction, representing the Democratic Party, favored parliamentary opposition, while Yun Po-sŏn's group (the former Civil Rule Party) insisted on more radical, extraparliamentary approaches.

The ruling Democratic Republican Party, equally determined to ratify the treaty, tried to push the treaty hurriedly through the Assembly. The People's Party members resigned from their seats, and during their absence the Democratic Republicans ratified the treaty — a move that the opposition party termed null and void.

As for the opposition party, the members of the Pak faction returned later to the Assembly, while Yun's members stayed out. Intraparty differences were also manifested in the form of struggle for leadership, which endangered the precarious alliance between the two warring factions.

In the course of factional fights, Madame Pak emerged as party president, while Yun was relegated to the role of political advisor. While Madame Pak, devoted to a moderate approach, was seeking some sort of accommodation with the ruling party on the treaty issue, Yun and six others seceded from the party late in July to form a new party called the New Korea Party.

Even before the dust had settled over the Japanese-Korean normalization issue, a series of political crises flared up. One crisis was precipitated by President Park's request for 25,000 additional troops to be sent to South Vietnam and by the manner in which the request was pushed through the Assembly. A majority of the members of the opposition parties exhibited outright opposition; others indicated lack of enthusiasm for the proposal (see ch. 15, Foreign Relations). Some felt that the dispatch of additional troops would adversely affect Seoul's diplomatic position; others felt that Park was trying to send troops without first obtaining guarantees from Washington as to what voice the government of the Republic of Korea would have in the conduct of the war and the future settlement of the conflict; still others simply argued that the dispatch was unconstitutional.

In the face of stiff opposition, the Democratic Republicans, resorting to their majority power, pushed the bill through the Assembly on March 20, 1966. Although opposition members were critical of the Republic's expanded involvement in the Vietnam conflict, most Koreans accepted the increase in their country's strength in Vietnam.

The turmoil over the troop dispatch had hardly subsided when the government again became the focus of bitter criticism over alleged smuggling activities (in which high-level official collusion was charged) of the huge Samsŏng industrial combine, headed by Korea's richest man, Yi Pyŏng-ch'ol. The opposition members charged that the government was unusually lenient toward, and in fact was shielding, the Samsŏng, as it was let off with a light fine. The opposition demanded that stern measures be taken against the individuals of the Korean Fertilizer Company (a Samsŏng subsidiary) involved in the smuggling.

The crisis reached its peak when Assemblyman Kim Tu-han, long known for his strong-willed personality, publicly insulted the Prime Minister and other Cabinet members during an Assembly interpellation on the smuggling issue on September 22. The entire

Cabinet immediately resigned *en bloc*, but Park announced that only two portfolios — Finance and Justice — would be replaced and that other ministers would remain in office. Park proclaimed martial law, but the situation eased somewhat when Kim resigned from the Assembly, thus subjecting himself to arrest for charges of contempt of the Assembly.

The opposition members of the Assembly were not appeased either by the official investigation into the smuggling case or by Yi Pyŏng-ch'ol's readiness to relinquish part of the fertilizer company's stocks. They demanded more thorough investigations. Many of the country's intellectuals — students and journalists — sided with the opposition assemblymen in reprimanding the government for its laxity toward the Samsŏng. Again the students held protest rallies, and it was against this background that both the government and opposition parties began to make preparations for the forthcoming 1967 presidential (April) and parliamentary (June) elections.

On October 20, 1966, the People's Party nominated as its presidential candidate a total outsider to professional politics, Yu Chin-o, over Madame Pak, the head of the party. A former university president, hitherto not active in partisan politics, Yu was well known for his role in the making of the Constitution of 1948 and in negotiations with Japan during the Rhee regime.

Yu and other leaders in the opposition were of the opinion that the only way to defeat President Park was to unite all opposition elements behind a single candidate, and with the aid of two prominent figures in Korean politics, Paek Nak-chon and Yi Pom-sok, they approached Yun Po-sŏn, leader of the New Korea Party. After a series of consultations, Yu and Yun agreed on highly makeshift arrangements solely for the purpose of winning the election. Yu was made chairman of the new party, known as the New Democratic Party, and Yun was offered the party's presidential nomination. The organizational principle adopted was that of dual leadership or representation, which tended to keep the new party from functioning efficiently. Both parties were given equal representation in each party organ. In a functional sense, therefore, the New Democratic Party was nothing more than a loose alliance of the two parties.

Despite the merger of the two opposition parties, it was still impossible to bring about complete antigovernment electoral solidarity, since four other nongovernment party candidates remained on the presidential ballot as contenders. The party system, already badly fragmented, saw the emergence of two socialist or progressive parties in 1966: The United Socialist Party, headed by Kim Song-suk, and the Democratic Socialist Party, led by Sŏ Min-ho.

Sŏ who spent many years in prison under Rhee, was soon jailed — later released on bail — on charges that he had expressed willingness to talk directly with Premier Kim Il-sŏng, head of the Communist regime in the north, about unification and had accepted political funds from pro-Communist sources in Japan. Sŏ originally ran for the presidency as his party's candidate but withdrew from the race in support of Yun a few days before the voting.

The April 1967 election is generally believed to have been fair and honest. Election results show that, despite several crises that jeopardized the popularity of the government, Park fared much better in this race than in 1963 when he won by a very narrow margin. In 1967, Park received 51.4 percent of the valid votes cast, whereas Yun received 41 percent. Park's impressive showing boosted his already undisputed position within the Democratic Republican Party.

The Democratic Republican Party won an impressive victory in the June 1967 parliamentary elections by obtaining more than a two-thirds majority of seats in the legislature. Despite this decisive victory, the image of the party was seriously tarnished in the course of election campaigns.

The opposition parties demanded an immediate nullification of the elections, and there were student demonstrations against election rigging. President Park, while taking stern measures against student protests, promised to take disciplinary action against irregularities uncovered. As a result, one Democratic Republican Party seat was relinquished to a New Democratic candidate. The Democratic Republican Party also expelled seven other candidates-elect. This reduced the Democratic Republican Party strength from its original 130 to 122 seats.

Both the opposition parties and the students continued with their protest marches, demanding Park's resignation and new elections. Shortly before the opening of the 61st Assembly session, the New Democratic Party announced that it would boycott the session unless new elections were held and refused to register its elected members with the Assembly Secretariat.

The session opened on July 10, while the boycotting New Democrats staged protest demonstrations outside the Assembly building. This situation lasted for five months until the New Democrats agreed to return late in November. The Democratic Republican Party tried to establish a dialogue with the opposition party in an attempt to break this political impasse, but the New Democratic Party remained adamant in demanding Park's personal apology to the public for election rigging; promise of new elections; disciplinary measures against four high-ranking officials (including Kim Chong-p'il and Prime Minister Chong Il-kwon), allegedly involved in election rigging; and adoption of measures to prevent future irregularities.

The prestige of the legislature, already at a low ebb, was seriously impaired by the continued deadlock between the two parties, which resulted in complete paralysis of legislative functions of the Assembly. The Democratic Republican Party, despite its control over a two-thirds majority of seats, at first refrained from unilaterally handling legislative matters lest it should be charged with one-party rule, although there were pressing problems (especially allocation of additional funds for the governmental programs) that required the legislature's consent. After a period of inactivity during which the Democratic Republican Party made serious efforts to find some sort of accommodation with the New Democratic Party, the Democratic Republican Party began to handle government bills without the presence of the New Democratic Party members — an action that became the target of severe criticism from the New Democratic Party.

It soon became obvious that the New Democratic Party was split into two groups over strategy and tactics in dealing with the political impasse. One group, the defeated members, was reluctant to retreat even one step from the so-called "four demands," whereas the elected members were willing to find a compromise with the Democratic Republican Party.

Although they were in agreement on three of the four demands, the two groups found themselves in sharp disagreement on the fourth, because the elected members demanded new elections only in areas where voting irregularities were uncovered. Thus, the 1967 parliamentary election had a divisive effect, not only on the Democratic Republican Party but also on the opposition party.

The intraparty conflict became acute when a New Democratic Party assemblyman registered his election with the Assembly in defiance of the party's official stand. Indications are that the group of those elected won out in the course of the conflict, for the New Democratic Party became much more conciliatory as the year end approached. After a series of meetings with the Democratic Republican Party, the New Democratic Party members agreed to return to the Assembly on the condition that their new demands, far less drastic than their original four demands, be met. The agreement, signed by leaders of both parties, called for, among other things, extensive changes in the election laws; neutrality of police and public officials in future elections; more strict controls on political funds; creation of a special investigating committee composed of both assemblymen and outsiders to look into election rigging; and changes in the Political Party Law.

This spirit of detente was, however, soon shattered by subsequent developments. The Democratic Republican Party unilaterally passed a new tax law shortly before the New Democratic Party's return to the Assembly. In the Assembly both parties encountered many problems in the process of implementing the provisions of the bipartisan agreement. Frustrated partly by the failure to solve these problems and partly by their feeling of a lack of sincerity on the part of the Democratic Republican Party members, the New Democratic Party accused the Democratic Republican Party of failing to live up to the agreement. The situation reached its climax when the New Democratic Party members went on a 10-day long hunger strike after the Democratic Republican Party unilaterally decided to skip part of committee deliberations on the 1968 budget bill. The Democratic Republican Party subsequently passed the budget bill in the midst of great confusion and open violence. This confrontation, known as the Crisis of December 28, seriously impaired the already poor relationship between the two parties, thus jeopardizing the Assembly's ability to adjust conflicting interest.

The New Democratic Party members considered that the Democratic Republican Party's subsequent behavior would not help alleviate the fear — shared by a sizable segment of the intellectual community — that the ruling party had made excessive use of its majority position, thus endangering the role of the opposition minority, which received support of one-third of the voters in 1967. The opposition party, in the absence of other means of influencing the Democratic Republican Party in the legislative process, has often resorted to such approaches as walkouts, hunger strikes, protest demonstrations, and even violence. Some opposition members appeared to fear that the Democratic Republican Party might go as far as to amend the constitutional provision against three terms for a president.

POLITICAL AWARENESS AND SOCIALIZATION

Political awareness and socialization have been very much affected by the country's political heritage. The unusually high literacy rate (about 85 percent) and many other factors — national awakening during the period of Japanese rule, territorial division in 1945, social and economic dislocations precipitated by the Korean conflict, holding of electoral contests, a series of political crises during the past 20 years, absence of traditional social barriers, and the hyperactive press — have contributed to a high degree of awareness of issues and events among the population and have affected the nature of the political attitudes of the people.

This heightened political awareness is especially evident in the urban areas. Partly because of the lack of exposure to the channels of political communication and partly because of traditional indifference to politics, the rural population has been less conscious of political issues and events than the urbanites. However, a recent opinion survey suggests that the gap in political awareness between the rural and the urban sectors has significantly narrowed and that the rural people are becoming increasingly interested in local and national politics, particularly as these matters affect their basic farm, social, and economic problems. The growing level of political astuteness on the part of the rural people is largely attributable to such factors as improvements in communication, increase in the numbers of educated persons in rural communities, and the government's policy of eradicating illiteracy.

The high degree of political consciousness may also be explained by a wide gap between the level of popular expectation and the actual performance of the government. Both the 1960 student uprising and the military coup of 1961 may have stemmed at least in part from the people's general dissatisfaction with existing conditions and with what they regarded as the poor performance of governmental authorities.

The people — especially such politically articulate elements as teachers, professors, students, and professionals — believe that the political processes of the country are still underdeveloped. Political parties are frequently viewed as groupings fighting solely over power and patronage. The National Assembly is depicted as an institution characterized by repeated political confrontations.

In political attitudes the least educated segment of the rural population still tends to be tradition-bound. Many persons in this group tend to believe that officeholders are working first for national improvement and second for personal gain. Among these persons the deferential view is still widespread that the government officials are always well versed in all aspects of their work and that one "ought to do as he is told." This attitude may partly explain why the rural people have been more readily subject to political pressures from the governing party of the time.

SOURCES AND AGGREGATIONS OF POLITICAL POWER

As of mid-1968, the leadership core appeared to be made up predominantly of former military elements. Many of the original members of the military government occupied leadership positions both in the government and the Democratic Republican Party organization. This group, although united in their devotion to President Park Chung-hee, has been far from being a cohesive elite. Closely allied with this military group are civilian politicians and statesmen who cooperate with the government of Park Chung-hee and the ruling Democratic Republican Party. Members of this group occupy important posts in the administration.

Members of the old political elite, especially members of the Democratic Party, now affiliated with the various factions of the New Democratic Party, appeared to be outside the arena of decision-making. As members of the main opposition party, the so-called old politicians are now found in the National Assembly. Important bills are often pushed through the Assembly by the Democratic Republican Party, which controls a two-thirds majority, and the significance of the legislature has diminished.

Since 1960, one of the popular political axioms has been that a government cannot be expected to endure for long without support from the military, the students, and the press. Political events tend to bear out such a view. The peasants also received much attention in the 1967 elections, and the importance of the farm group may continue to increase in the future electoral contests. In addition the business elite appears to be influential in policymaking. Industrial workers make up only a fraction of the total population and, since the trade union movement is weak and divided, their political power is inconsequential at the present time (see ch. 21, Labor Relations and Organization).

The Military

Despite the long tradition of civilian rule, the military emerged as the major political force, as a result of the failure of civilian party politics and the absence of an effective nonmilitary counterbalancing force. In 1961 the military successfully asserted itself as the dominant power on the basis of its strength and discipline and the conviction among its leaders of the country's need for modernization through a more dynamic and efficient leadership.

Upon the assumption of power, the military promoted administrative efficiency. Both domestic and foreign pressures worked against the continuation of the military in power, and many military leaders responded by casting off their military uniforms and entering civilian politics.

After civilian rule was restored, the military was very much depoliticized and in 1968 the traditional political neutrality of the military was restored. The newly emerging leadership within the military centers around the elite core of graduates from the Military Academy, who are committed to such values as honesty and to resisting such conditions in government as corruption, favoritism, and factionalism.

The Students

Student involvement with politics has been motivated by varying factors at different times. Before 1945, national independence was their objective. After independence, political and socioeconomic matters of immediate concern became the focus of their attention.

The social origin of the student groups in the late 1960's was no limited to any single segment of the society, as it was in earlier times. All social groups, urban and rural, were represented. Because of this diversity, student reaction to political issues may be regarded as generally reflecting the prevailing mood of the public.

The students do not have a national organization to guide and direct their activities, nor do they have a unifying political platform. Yet on many occasions, they have successfully demonstrated their ability to function as a cohesive force, at least for a limited time. Their political potential is enhanced by their numbers, their common-value orientation (molded by a uniform pattern of education), their sense of social justice, their inclination toward action, and their penchant for criticism of the government and of existing conditions. These attributes are given impetus by their pride in their predecessors' role in the independence movement of 1919 and in the 1929 nationwide anti-Japanese demonstrations, which were touched off in South Chŏlla Province.

After Rhee resigned, the students became overconfident of their power. As a result of their activities, the government of Chang Myŏn was often described, with some justification, as a government of demonstrators. Under the Park government, students continued to be politically active as advocators of honest politics.

Students remain a potent force, although there is evidence that many disapprove of their political involvement. This attitude is generally believed to be a popular reaction to the excessive activism demonstrated by the students during the Chang regime and the early years of the Park government. It is also based on a suspicion that the students were often exploited as tools of opposition forces and ambitious politicians or of the Communist-agitated unification movement. Nevertheless, to many people the students appear to represent one of the more important checks on the government. The practical wisdom of making peace with the students was underscored by the government itself in early August 1964 when the Democratic Republican Party was forced to yield to student pressures and withdraw a controversial "campus protection bill" which was intended to outlaw student political activities. The students' influence in politics was also demonstrated in 1967 when the Democratic Republican Party, as a result of joint pressure from the New Democratic Party and the students, ousted several of its candidates from the party for their irregular electioneering.

The Press

Newspapermen play a significant role in politics, out of proportion to their numbers. They are vocal and, at times, irresponsible critics of the government. Many journalists tend to regard any pro-governmental editorial policy or reporting as unprofessional. Their criticism frequently has been harsh and rigid. At times, it has proved a source of irritation and embarrassment to the government. As a result, the relationship between the press and the government has been less than cordial.

The influential role of the press in politics is partly due to its heavy political coverage. All the major dailies are published in Seoul and are geared to the urban, educated readership. Accordingly, in a society where politics is still largely an urban and intellectual concern, the attitude of the press is a matter of serious concern for the authorities (see ch. 16, Public Information). The important role of the press in shaping the political climate was demonstrated in the 1967 elections when both the Democratic Republican Party and the New Democratic Party felt compelled by the attitudes of the press to emphasize the policy issues and tone down personality issues. The defeat of big names running on small party tickets in the elections was also largely attributable to the lack of press coverage of their campaign activities. Furthermore, the press provided strong impetus for the formation of the two major opposition parties into the New Democratic Party.

The press derives its strength from its long-standing tradition of outspokenness. Under Rhee, it was one of the few remaining active antigovernment forces, despite Rhee's restrictive policies. Post-Rhee administrations have refrained from antagonizing the press for fear of being labeled dictatorial. In August 1964, however, the Park administration, believing that political confusion was compounded by the agitation of certain journalists, whom they regarded as irresponsible, enacted a new press bill intended to encourage self-discipline (see ch. 16, Public Information). Faced with intense protest from the press, however, the application of the press act had to be postponed indefinitely. Again in November 1966, the government had to bow to pressures from the news media and shelve a new press regulation bill.

Peasants

The horizons of the peasants, who make up about 60 percent of the electorate, are being broadened by the educational impact of frequent election campaigns, the rising level of education, the influence of ex-servicemen in their home communities, and improvement in communications facilities. The Korean conflict has also had much to do with the political awakening of the peasants, as have President Park's active interest in and frequent visits to rural communities.

Rhee and his aides took the farmers' support for granted in electoral contests, relying upon their traditional rural conservatism. In the post-1960 years, the peasants have become more discriminating in their voting behavior, as evidenced in the presidential elections of 1963 and 1967 in which they received much attention from both the Democratic Republican Party and the New Democratic Party.

Businessmen and Financiers

Wealthy businessmen and financiers contribute to the funds of the ruling party and constitute an influential factor in the country's policymaking, especially in economic areas. Their views and recommendations are often sought by the executive and legislative branches, and their control over the mass media is growing. The so-called Samsŏng Combine, for example, owns a daily newspaper, *Chungang Ilbo*; a monthly newspaper, *Chungang*; and a television and radio network. Through such means, influential businessmen participate as opinion shapers. During the Samsŏng smuggling episode, all the mass media owned by the Samsŏng were reported to have made joint efforts to defend the Korean Fertilizer Company, the Samsŏng subsidiary involved. This overt attempt to mold public opinion was very much resented by the public, especially the intellectual segment and the press corps, which demanded enactment of a law that would prevent an individual from gaining excessive control over the mass media (see ch. 16, Public Information).

POLITICAL PARTIES

Party politics was introduced into the country for the first time in August 1945. Until then there was no organized, legal party appealing to popular sentiments. The party system since then has been characterized by: predominance of conservative parties and the weakness of left-wing parties; overwhelming importance of personalities rather than issues as the focus of party activities; lack of clear alternatives in terms of platforms among competing parties as a result of their uniformly conservative orientation; high rate of partisan realignment under different labels; internal party fragmentation or factionalism; absence of grass-roots support and organization; and lack of adequate political dialogue between the ruling party and the opposition parties.

The political structure has been a multiple party system with a trend toward a two-party system. By mid-1947 there were some 40 political parties of varying political shades and sizes, including the South Korean Workers Party, a descendant of the pre-1945 Korean Communist Party, and the Korean Democratic Party, a forerunner of the present New Democratic Party. Until the end of 1951, because of unfamiliarity with organized party activities, however, the role of political organizations was little appreciated either in or outside the political arena. Parties were little more than political clubs of a few aspirants to power, each with an insignificant number of followers, attracted mainly by regional, kinship, or personal ties. In the 1950 assembly elections, for example, 66 percent of all candidates ran as independents, accounting for 51 percent of the total number of elected representatives.

The turning point for the development of the party system was Syngman Rhee's December 1951 attempt to perpetuate his personal rule under the guise of popularly based party support. Creation of the Liberal Party in that month and Rhee's subsequent practice of using it as a means of acquiring personal power stimulated the formation of an opposition Democratic Party. This group was a conglomeration of diverse factions united by a common determination to challenge Rhee and his party. Accordingly, when the Liberal regime collapsed in 1960, serious factional wrangling erupted among the members, largely over the question of patronage and power. The immediate post-Rhee years were marked by the emergence of numerous parties, including several vocal but weak leftist-oriented parties.

After the military coup of 1961, party politics were temporarily banned, allegedly because of corruption and lack of discipline among party politicians. In January 1963, however, after stringent rules governing political parties had been adopted, the military government lifted the ban, thus restoring partisan activities. Parties are subject to several constitutional provisions as well as to the Political Party Act of December 1962. To prevent the multiplication of parties and splinter groups, the Constitution in effect in 1968 stipulates that parties must have "necessary organizational arrangements" as elaborated in the party law. The government is constitutionally empowered to bring an action before the Supreme Court for a party's dissolution in case the party's purposes or activities are deemed contrary to the basic democratic order. This provision is intended to discourage the rise of leftist or other parties deemed irresponsible.

The Political Party Act recognizes the legitimacy of a party only after it is registered with the Central Election Management Committee. A party may be initiated by 30 or more signatories, with chapters in at least one-third of 131 electoral districts. Each chapter is required to have a membership of 50 or more. Membership is open only to citizens of the Republic of Korea. Persons barred from party membership or political activities include civil servants, military servicemen, employees of state-operated enterprises, officials of any enterprise wherein the government holds a controlling share of the stock, and persons disqualified by law. No one can be regarded as a legitimate party member unless he is on the party's membership list. In an attempt to facilitate the development of a sound two-party system, party law puts the leader of the major opposition party on stipend, and parties are tax exempt. Parties are also required to file an annual statement with the Central Election Management Committee on their properties, income, expenditures, and general activities. Parties are prohibited from soliciting or accepting donations or contributions from foreigners residing outside the country, or from any government-operated enterprise, financial institution, labor union, educational foundation, or religious group. The law forbids the officials of an outlawed party from establishing another party based on platforms identical with or similar to those of the previous party.

By virtue of the political fund law enacted in 1965, all contributions to parties are channeled through the Central Election Management Committee. Funds thus collected are distributed to parties in proportion to their parliamentary strength. In 1968, there were nine parties registered with the Central Election Management Committee, but only two — the Democratic Republican Party and the New Democratic Party — were actively involved in political competition.

Democratic Republican Party

The Democratic Republican Party was founded in February 1963 by Kim Chong-p'il and his military colleagues. At the end of 1967, the party reportedly had over 1.5 million members, with chapters in all 131 electoral districts. The party held 114 seats in the National Assembly in 1968. Its ideology is creation of national identity and liberal democracy, based on the ideals of the 1919 independence uprising, the anti-Communist spirit shown during the Korean conflict, and ideals of the 1960 and 1961 revolutions. The party also supports speedy unification of the country and champions the cause of rapid modernization.

Financially, the Democratic Republican Party is far better off than any other party. Portions of the funds for the Democratic Republican Party came from various economic associations through the Central Election Management Committee, but the amount has been far from meeting the party needs. Other funds were obtained from membership dues and from so-called unspecified sources, which appeared to constitute a substantial portion. The party's monthly operational expenditure was estimated to be around 20 million wŏn ($74,000).

The party membership represents almost every major segment of the population. Retired military officers, former bureaucrats, and former members of the Liberal Party constitute a large percentage of the leadership element of the party. As shown in the recent voting results, the party appears to appeal significantly to farming and rural segments of the population, while such politically articulate elements as intellectuals and students and many urbanites appear to be unfavorably disposed.

Theoretically, the party's supreme policymaking body is its national convention, called together annually by its president, Park Chung-hee. In actuality, the party is governed by its 11-member Executive Council appointed and supervised by the president. The Executive Council is empowered to designate the party's presidential candidate and party president. The endorsement of the Executive Council's choice by the national convention appears to be perfunctory. The party president is elected for a 2-year period and is empowered to appoint the party chairman, who is his immediate deputy, and to name the secretary-general, who heads the party's Central Secretariat. Appointment of the party chairman is for a 2-year term and is subject to endorsement by the national convention. The Executive Council prepares the list of candidates for election. Despite the seemingly all-pervasive influence of the council, effective power appears to be exercised by the party president. Much power was also exercised by the party chairman while the post was held by Kim Chong-p'il, largely because he was an influential party member in his own right. The party's organizational principle itself strongly encourages the exercise of effective power by the party president.

In mid-1968 the party's leading figures included Park Chung-hee (president), Kil Chae-ho (secretary-general), Kim Song-jin (Chairman of the Central Committee), Paek Nam–ok (Chairman of the Policy Committee), Kim Sŏng-kŏn (member of the Executive Council), Yi Hyo-sang (Speaker of the National Assembly), and Kim Tong-whan (former secretary-general and now member of the Executive Council). Kim Chong-p'il, who had been the party chairman until May 1968, suddenly bolted from the party on May 30, 1968 as a result of factional dispute, but he still had a large following within the party.

Ever since its formation, the party has been plagued by intense factional activities. Alignments have been subject to such constant changes that they defy any systematic analysis. Two major factions could be identified: the so-called main current or militant faction centering around Kim Chong-p'il, and the anti-Kim or moderate faction, led by Chang Kyong-sun (a leading participant in the military revolution), Kim Sŏng-kŏn, and Yi Hyo-sang. The militant faction included a large number of civilian politicians drawn from the southern and northern Kyŏngsang provinces; hence the faction is often known as the Kyŏngsang faction. The moderate faction was composed of many civilian politicans, with their power base in the southern and northern Chŏlla provinces and several cliques built around personalities and previous political associations.

The cause of factional formation and wranglings appeared to be largely personal, having to do with competition for party hegemony. Policy and strategy matters appeared to be less important, although at times they have had the effect of seriously disrupting the party or aggravating the already acute factional fights.

One issue that played a significant role pertained to the party's organizational structure. The disagreement centered around whether the party's parliamentary members or its extraparliamentary organizers should take precedence in making party policies. The main faction, led by Kim Chong-p'il, proposed to subordinate the parliamentary wing of the party to the organizational wing. The apparent purpose of the scheme was to make the parliamentary group more responsive to popular aspirations and needs which could be channeled through the regional party organizations to the Central Secretariat. The moderate faction rebelled against this proposal, fearing that the whole party machinery under Kim's scheme might come to be dominated by him. Instead, the moderate faction pushed for an amendment to the party constitution which would weaken the powers of the party's secretariat apparatus, the bastion of the mainstream faction, in an attempt to block Kim's alleged drive at one-man rule. In March 1965 the two factions agreed on a compromise, as a result of which the party constitution was amended. Although the basic structure of the secretariat machinery remained intact, its former control over party finances was now transferred to a financial committee independent of the Central Secretariat.

Another major divisive issue has been the attitude toward those elements opposed to the Democratic Republican Party. During the 1964 crisis over the Japanese-Korean treaty, the moderate faction favored peace with the student demonstrators and more compromises with opposition parties. Many of the moderate faction members felt so strongly about these issues that they voted for the opposition parties' motion of nonconfidence against three cabinet members. By contrast, the mainstream group tended to feel that compromises with the opposition might subvert the party's rationally formulated policies and that concessions to the students would cause them to make more trouble for the government.

Neither of the two major factions enjoyed any significant measure of cohesiveness, and each was subdivided into several cliques. The main current or militant faction, for example, was divided into two major cliques: the more militant led by Kim Yong-tae and the more moderate, headed by Kil Chae-ho. Indications are that Kim Chong-p'il has tended to identify himself with the more militant clique. Kim Yong-tae is regarded as Kim Chong-p'il's closest follower. Recently, Kil's less militant clique has collaborated with many members of the moderate current faction under the leadership of Kim Song-kon. Some political observers have begun to refer to this new group — the coalition of the more moderate clique of the main faction and the moderate faction — as a "new main faction."

In mid-1968, the party leadership both in and outside the National Assembly appeared to be in the hands of the group which was identified as the "new main faction." Support for such militant members as Kim Yong-tae appeared to be on the decline. He and two other militant members, who were Kim Chong-p'il's loyal followers, were reportedly "purged" in May 1968 for their alleged factional activities to push Kim Chong-p'il for the presidency in 1971. Their removal was immediately followed by Kim Chong-p'il's withdrawal from the Democratic Republican Party.

Although both governmental control and partisan leadership are merged in the hands of President Park, relations between the administration and the party apparatus have at times been strained. There have been open rebellions by some Democratic Republican Party assemblymen against some of Park's chief executive aides, accused of failing to take into adequate consideration their views in governmental policymaking. To correct this situation, in August 1967 the party and the administration created a number of coordinating organs. The Party Policy Consultation Council, composed of cabinet members and top party personnel, meets twice a month to coordinate policy differences between the executive and the party apparatus. In addition, there are a few other coordinating institutions, both formal and informal, made up of leading party and government persons.

New Democratic Party

The New Democratic Party came into being in 1967 as a result of the merger of two opposition parties — Yu's People's Party and Yun's New Korea Party. In mid-1968 the party held a membership of about 820,000 and 44 seats in the 175-man assembly. The leading members of the party — the parliamentary members — represent most of the civilian politicians who were opposed to the Democratic Republican Party regime. Although the party membership is drawn from all segments of the population, the party, like the Democratic Republican Party, appeared to lack solid ties with any specific segments. Electorally, however, the party candidates tended to fare well in urban areas. In 1967, for example, all but three of the party candidates were elected from large urban districts such as Seoul, Pusan, Kwangju, Inch'on and Taegu. The New Democratic Party has also been the beneficiary of the protest vote cast by many intellectuals and students against the Democratic Republican Party. But the New Democratic Party did not appear to be popular outside the urban centers, for it lost virtually all of the rural constituencies.

In basic objectives the party differs very little from the Democratic Republican Party. It champions modernization of the country, economic improvement, national unification, meaningful democracy, and related goals. In specifics, however, this party differs from the ruling party. It advocates a strengthened assembly and a weakened presidency, abolition of the Central Intelligence Agency, repeal of the Political Party Act, revision of the Japanese-Korean treaty, and further democratic guarantees. Party funds were made up largely of contributions collected through the Central Election Management Committee, donations from the party's national constituency candidates, parliamentary membership fees from the party's assemblymen, funds collected by influential members of the party, and funds raised by local chapters.

Of these, the donations from the party's national candidates constituted the most important source. The party's monthly expenditure was reported to amount to about 2 million wŏn (about $7,400) one-tenth of the Democratic Republican Party equivalent.

Theoretically, the national convention is the supreme policy-making organ of the party, but in practice the central standing committee appears to act as the real decisionmaking organ. The party chairman (Yu Chin-o since 1966) exercises much power and appoints important officials of the party. But his appointments are subject to the standing committee's approval. Influential members of the party included Yu Chin-o, Yun Po-sŏn (1967 presidential candidate and now party advisor), Madame Pak Sun-ch'ŏn (party advisor), Yu Chin-san (member of the standing committee), Sŏ Pom-sŏk; and Chang Chun-ha.

Like the Democratic Republican Party, the New Democratic Party has been seriously plagued by factional feuds. Disputes have revolved largely around power and patronage rather than policy issues. The party is divided into two major factions — the Minjung group, composed of members of Yu's People's Party, and the Shinhan faction, composed of former New Korea Party members led by Yun. Each faction is subdivided into several cliques. Conflicts between these groups appear to be one factor adversely affecting the party's potential strength as the major opposition party.

Small Parties

A total of nine small parties contended for political power in the 1967 elections. Though they collectively received 16 percent of the valid votes cast in the 1967 parliamentary elections, only one party, the Masses' Party led by Sŏ Min-ho, was able to obtain a seat in the Assembly. These parties were small political groupings, each centered around a notable personality, and lacking an organization comparable to those of the two major parties. They also suffered from inadequate political funds. Ideologically they ranged from progressive (socialist) to conservative. At the end of 1967, the future of the small parties was highly precarious, as the two major parties attempted to amend the Political Party Act in a manner unfavorable to small parties. One of the proposals tentatively agreed on by the Democratic Republican Party and the New Democratic Party in November 1967 stipulated that any party failing to receive at least 10 percent of the total valid votes cast would automatically lose its legal status as a political party.

SPECIAL INTEREST GROUPS

During the regime of Syngman Rhee, most special interest groups were organized as subsidiary groups of the ruling party and therefore they tended to function as agents of the party. In 1968, with the economic differentiation of society, there were many groups representing nearly all walks of national life. Most were loosely controlled and weak organizations. Many were headed by former assemblymen or high-ranking ex-governmental officials. Under the constitution and laws, elective as well as appointive officers of the government were barred from any position in an interest group.

Agriculture

Farmers constitute an important voting bloc, but their group activities in governmental policymaking appear to be almost negligible despite their large numbers. This lack of influence is primarily due to the low level of political awareness among the farmers and their general reluctance to get involved in politics. The Federation of Agricultural Cooperatives is composed of about 93 percent of the entire farming population. It is organized from above and in the functional sense appears to be a subsidiary organization of the governmental establishment. The Federation caters to the financial and banking needs of farmers. Chairman of the Federation's Central Committee (Shin Myŏng-soon as of 1967) is appointed by the President.

Labor

Labor union activities are governed by the Labor Union Law. Unions are not allowed to engage in any activities in support of a specific political party or a person running for an office. Unions are also prohibited from collecting political funds from their members or from using union funds for political purposes (see ch. 21, Labor Relations and Organization).

Prior to 1960, there was a national federation of trade unions, but it was part of Rhee's Liberal Party. In May 1961, the unions were affected by the military government's ban on political activities and were disbanded. In August 1961, the Federation of Korean Trade Unions was authorized by the military government. In 1968 it was the sole nationwide labor organization and represented 16 major trade unions, comprising 366,973 members as of mid-1967. The Federation was headed by Yi Ch'an-hyok, who had long been affiliated with labor movements. A Central Committee composed of chairmen of constituent unions appeared to be the policymaking organ of the Federation. The 16 constituent unions were divided into branches and chapters to represent workers in their respective industrial jurisdictions at the regional and enterprise levels. The Federation's activities centered mainly around matters affecting its immediate interests.

Business

Two leading business organizations were the Korean Chamber of Commerce and the Federation of Korean Industries. The former, created in 1952, had a membership of 299,531 as of 1967. It had branch organizations in major cities, and was headed by Pak Doo-byŏng, a leading businessman. A general meeting committee and a standing committee were the policymaking organs. The Federation of Korean Industries, also composed of leading businessmen, was a much smaller organization. It came into being in 1961, and in 1968 was headed by Hong Joe-son. It held a regular general meeting of its members and a board of directors meeting, which made policies along with six standing functional committees.

The Korean Chamber of Commerce and the Federation of Korean Industries had similar economic goals. Both were believed to wield much influence in the governmental policymaking. Their views and recommendations were often sought by the government. Their influence appeared to be derived from the high level of political awareness of the membership, expertise in economic areas, and financial resources, among other factors.

Others

The Korean conflict produced a number of veteran organizations representing wounded servicemen and police or the families of those killed in action. These organizations demanded better governmental protection for those affected by the war, but the government has found it increasingly difficult to deal with these problems because of limited resources. Under President Park Chung-hee, an Office of Veterans Affairs was created to handle grievances, and more employment opportunities have been made available for veterans. Veterans organizations have presented petitions to the government, often accompanied by sit-in demonstrations, although of limited scope.

The Korean Education Federation is the sole organ representing the interests of teachers. Lawyers are organized in the Korean Bar Association. Newspaper editors have formed the Korean Newspaper Editors Association, which is an influential group. There are many women's organizations, most of which are members of a consultative organ called the National Council of Korean Women's Organizations.

COMPETITION FOR POLITICAL POWER

In the late 1960's, competition for political power took the form of intensely fought elections, although extralegal methods were not unknown. The National Security Act, adopted in 1960 and amended in 1962, imposed penalties including death on those persons convicted of anti-North Korean activities. The Park administration has taken precautions against attempts at forceful overthrow of the government, the primary instrument of political surveillance appearing to be the Korean Central Intelligence Agency. In 1960 and 1961 the people tolerated extraconstitutional methods of political takeover partly because the student uprising of 1960 and the military coup of 1961 came at a time when the population felt aggrieved at the performance of the existing government. The popular tolerance of the military takeover may also be explained by the traditional Confucian recognition of the right on the part of the subjects to rise against the ruler whose "mandate of heaven" is revoked.

ANALYSIS OF 1967 ELECTIONS

The presidential election of May 3, 1967 was reported as fair and honest. There were six candidates, but the election boiled down to contests between two major contestants, Park Chung-hee of the Democratic Republican Party and Yun Po-sŏn of the New Democratic Party. The press focused its attention on these two candidates, virtually ignoring the others. The election differed significantly from the previous ones. Whereas in the 1963 presidential election the dominant issues were the so-called guided democracy and the personality of Park Chung-hee, in 1967 the principal issues raised by the opposition were those of corruption in the government and the alleged failure of the government's agricultural policies.

Park and his well-organized political machine defended achievements under the First Five-Year Plan. The party depicted Park as the only leader equipped with determination strong enough to carry out the Second Five-Year Plan and emphasized the necessity of having political stability for plan implementation. Park tried to appeal to every segment of the electorate by making campaign promises. Farmers were promised a reduction in the price of fertilizer; consumers, an annual increase of less than 7 percent in consumer prices; civil servants and servicemen, pay hikes; and the nation as a whole, an average annual increase of 8.5 percent in economic growth rate, as well as self-sufficiency of the food supply by 1971. To fishermen, Park promised modernized equipment and governmental assistance; to the intellectual and scholarly community, he pledged further academic freedom and greater governmental aid for scientific activities. In foreign relations, Park said the government would work for the enhancement of the country's international prestige, and he promised to achieve national unification by late 1970's. In domestic politics the Democratic Republican Party would guarantee a balanced order. Local political autonomy, guaranteed in the Constitution, Park said would come only after local financial independence had been established.

The New Democratic Party, on the other hand, charging that the country lived under a political order imposed by a military government, advocated establishment of a liberal, democratic political order. Yun and his party promised meaningful freedom of speech, expansion of human rights, curbing of presidential power, neutrality of the police, repeal of the Political Party Act, and the realization of local autonomy. Also, in an attempt to appeal to the major segments of the population, the New Democratic Party made specific promises which differed little from those of the Democratic Republican Party. However, it was not able to provide an alternative to the Democratic Republican Party's Second Five-Year Plan.

The major issue for both parties seemed to have been the welfare of the farmers who constituted the largest occupational segment of the population. For this reason the Democratic Republican Party promoted the image of Park as the son of a farmer who was determined to bring about agricultural modernization of the country along with industrial development. The New Democratic Party countered this by arguing that the Democratic Republican Party's agricultural policies were in fact anti-agricultural policies. The concentration of both parties on economic issues was a natural reaction to the electorate's serious concern with their economic welfare. According to one recent study, an overwhelming majority of the respondents both in Seoul and other localities indicated that their major concerns were economic—rising prices, employment, food, housing, and clothing.

In many ways the New Democratic Party was placed at a disadvantage during the 1967 elections. As the ruling party the Democratic Republican Party enjoyed certain advantages, including the services of cabinet members. In addition, the party had a very extensive nationwide organization far superior to that of the New Democratic Party, and was relatively free from financial worries.

On May 3, 83.57 percent of eligible voters went to the polls—the lowest turnout ever among presidential elections. Of total valid votes 51.4 percent went to Park, 41 percent to Yun, with the remaining 8 percent divided among the other four candidates. The margin between Park and Yun (over 10 percent of the total valid votes) was considerably higher than in the 1963 election, when Park won by only 1.55 percent of the total votes.

In several ways these results differed from those of previous presidential elections. In 1963 Park won the southern half of the Republic, but in 1967 he carried the provinces in the eastern region of the country. The new alignment of support may have resulted from much government investment in the eastern provinces. In Seoul, Park fared better in 1967 than he did in 1963, but he still lost the city to Yun by a 3 percent margin. This increase in support could mean that his policy of modernization was well received by the urban population. On the other hand, in Seoul, there was a drop of 11 percent in voting, from 77.5 percent in 1963 to 66.6. percent in 1967.

As in the presidential elections, the Democratic Republican Party and the New Democratic Party were the only major contenders in the Assembly elections of June 8. Although nine other parties took part, only these two were able to put up candidates in all 131 constituencies. The Democratic Republican Party candidates defended the government's record under Park's leadership and boasted of their ability to bring government projects into their districts. They further advocated that, since the people had given Park another 4-year term, he should be given a stable majority in the Assembly so that he could continue with the government's modernization programs and complete the Second Five-Year Plan.

The Democratic Republican Party won a decisive victory by obtaining 130 seats, 13 more than a two-thirds majority—the number required to amend the Constitution. No political party in Korean history has occupied such a healthy majority in the legislature. The New Democratic Party won 44 seats and the Masses' Party, one seat.

The opposition parties, protesting the alleged irregularities, demanded an immediate nullification of the Assembly elections. There were student demonstrations. President Park promised to take disciplinary action against irregularities uncovered. One Democratic Republican seat was relinquished to a New Democratic Party candidate. The Democratic Republican Party also expelled seven other elected candidates, reducing its original strength to 122 seats.

CHAPTER 15

FOREIGN RELATIONS

Foreign policies under the government of Park Chung-hee have been shaped primarily by the need for economic modernization of the country, maintenance of military preparedness against the danger from Communists in the north in alliance with Communist China and the Soviet Union, emerging nationalism, and the desire to enhance national prestige on the international scene.

The government has maintained close ties with nations having common interests. Especially close are its relations with the United States, on whose support it has depended to a considerable degree for economic development of the nation and strengthening of its military posture, although at times the two nations have been subject to strains arising from conflicts of interests. One significant diplomatic event under the Park government was establishment of relations with Japan, thereby normalizing relations between two ancient enemies. The government also has vigorously pursued a policy of fostering relations with other industrialized nations which are in a position to contribute to her programs of modernization.

At the same time, largely in keeping with the newly emerging nationalism, the country has increasingly asserted its independence as a sovereign nation, and sought international respect as such, among nations of Asia, Africa, and Latin America. It has also cultivated amicable relations with some of the uncommitted nations in an attempt to counteract the Communists' diplomatic moves to win friends. Diplomatic expansion into these regions was also prompted by the growing strength of uncommitted nations within the United Nations which pursue a neutralistic foreign policy. The government continued to attempt to gain support among these nations for its position on national unification.

Despite considerable opposition to its policy of seeking rapprochement with Japan in 1963–65 and to its Vietnam policy, the government appeared to enjoy a general consensus in support of its basic external objectives. Differences between the two major parties centered around techniques rather than principles of objectives. In mid-1968 main lines of foreign policy were established by the President, who had the final word in policy-planning and major decisions. In policymaking he was assisted by the Prime Minister, the Foreign Minister, and other responsible ministers. He was subject to constitutional restrictions but the National Assembly, dominated by the Democratic Republic Party, in practice tended to defer to his decisions.

MOTIVATION AND GOALS

The Republic of Korea's motivations and goals in her external relations are shaped to a significant degree by her historical past and geography. Her geographical proximity and her historical subordination to the three East Asian powers—China, Russia, and Japan—have largely contributed to her apprehensions regarding the intentions of these nations. From this insecurity arises a recognition of the need for the maintenance of strong national power. This desire for national survival also appears to form the basis of her policy of maintaining close ties with the Free World nations, including the United States.

The country's foreign economic policies have been constructed to strengthen national power which she feels is necessary to deter the Communists in the north from embarking on an aggressive course of action or to meet such aggression if it comes. Friendly relations with the United States have partly been dictated by the continued need for her economic assistance to carry out rapid industrialization of the country.

The Korean peninsula has a considerable variety of mineral deposits, though in most cases not in great abundance nor in ores of very high grade, and there is a relative paucity of natural resources vital to industrialization. The country is wholly lacking in petroleum and is deficient in timber, iron and steel. For these items it is dependent on foreign sources. This factor underlies the policy of friendship toward foreign nations.

Growing nationalism appears to be a significant motivating force in the Republic of Korea's foreign policies. In recent years an increasing number of persons—many of them intellectuals, students, bureaucrats, and military officers—have argued that foreign policies should be constructed to elevate the country to a position of international power and prestige as an independent nation state. Many appear to believe that continued dependence on the United States is not consonant with the national dignity. Growing nationalistic sentiments are reflected in the platforms of the two major parties—the Democratic Republican Party and the New Democratic Party—both of which advocate an "independent diplomacy." The government of Park Chung-hee has put forward a new political slogan called nationalistic democracy, or democracy

246

founded on nationalism, which would be attuned to the country's own desires and needs. The government's active diplomatic activities in much of the neutralist world appear to be largely in keeping with the policy of enhancing her international prestige.

TECHNIQUES AND CAPABILITIES

The means of implementing policy appear to be somewhat limited, as is often the case with small powers. National resources are channeled toward maintaining the large standing army and developing the industrial state. As its external objectives are primarily of a peaceful nature, geared mainly to the goal of national reconstruction, the means employed are within the proper realm of peaceful diplomacy, and use of belligerent means had not been advocated in recent years. Although the government under Syngman Rhee frequently asserted that national unification could be attained only by military means, subsequent governments (including the Park regime) have depended upon the communications media to win over their northern counterparts, as well as upon diplomacy to gain international support for their unification proposals.

The country has declared adherence to principles of international law as well as to the United Nations Charter, although she is not a member of that body, and has also become a signatory to various multilateral conventions. Seeking wide international support, she feels morally committed to these international rules rather than be pressed by temporary expediency. Treaties of friendship, official visits, and goodwill missions are most frequently relied upon by the government. Being committed to national unification primarily within the peaceful framework of the United Nations, the country has assigned much importance to the United Nations and other multilateral bodies in its diplomacy.

Heavily dependent upon foreign aid and loans for her rapid modernization programs, the country lacks economic potential that larger powers often utilize to attain a given external objective. In recent years, however, the government of Park Chung-hee has depended, on a limited scale, on technical aid to cultivate friendship among African nations.

RELATIONS WITH SELECTED COUNTRIES

Shortly after the Republic of Korea came into being in 1948, the United States, Great Britain, and Nationalist China extended diplomatic recognition, and by January 1950 some 30 other nations (none Communist-controlled) had followed.

Although recognized by a large number of states, the country remained relatively isolated internationally until after 1960. A shortage of foreign exchange, a lack of trained personnel, and doubt about the policies of former President Syngman Rhee combined to prevent the establishment of diplomatic relations on a wider scale. Since the overthrow of Rhee, the government has undertaken to explain its position in various areas of the world and to broaden the range of its diplomatic contacts. Various special delegations and goodwill missions have been sent to Europe, the Middle East, Southeast Asia, Latin America, and Africa.

By 1967 diplomatic and consular relations had been established with 81 countries, and special missions were being maintained at the United Nations and in Geneva. The Park government has widely expanded its diplomatic relations in order to carry out its stated policies: "to obtain international understanding and support; to strengthen ties with friendly free nations; to promote cooperation with the United Nations and international organizations; to strengthen economic cooperation with foreign countries; to resolve problems pending between the Republic of Korea and Japan; and to strengthen protection of nationals living in other countries and cultural dissemination and public information activities."

At the end of 1967 ambassadors were accredited to Argentina, Australia, Austria, Belgium, Bolivia, Botswana, Brazil, Cameroon, Canada, Chad, Chile, Republic of China, Colombia, Congo, Costa Rica, Dahomey, Denmark, Dominican Republic, Ecuador, El Salvador, Ethiopia, the European Economic Community, France, Gabon, Gambia, Federal Republic of Germany, Greece, Guatemala, Honduras, Iceland, Iran, Italy, Ivory Coast, Jamaica, Japan, Jordan, Kenya, Liberia, Luxembourg, Madagascar, Malawi, Malaysia, Malta, Mexico, Morocco, Netherlands, New Zealand, Nicaragua, Nigeria, Norway, Panama, Paraguay, Peru, Philippines, Portugal, Saudi Arabia, Senegal, Sierra Leone, Spain, Sweden, Switzerland, Thailand, Togo, Turkey, Uganda, United Kingdom, United States, Upper Volta, Uruguay, Vatican City, Venezuela, and the Republic of Vietnam. In addition, consulates or special missions had been established in Burma, Egypt, the Geneva Disarmament Conference, Hong Kong, India, Indonesia, Pakistan and the United Nations, as well as several consulates in Japan and the United States.

Relations with the United States

The United States was one of the first major powers to extend recognition when the Republic of Korea was established in 1948. With the conclusion of an agreement for economic aid in December 1948 and the signing of two military agreements in January 1950, the Unites States assumed a major share of the economic and military burdens of the government. The economic aid agreement stipulated that the United States would supply "financial, material, and technical assistance to avert economic crisis, promote national recovery, and insure domestic tranquility." The military agreements provided, among other things, that a United States Military Advisory Group be established to help train Korean military personnel. The United States furnished an overwhelmingly large proportion of the United Nations military support in the conflict which followed the invasion from the north in June 1950. Shortly after the armistice which ended the hostilities, the Republic of Korea and the United States signed on October 1, 1953, a mutual defense treaty "to secure the Republic of Korea against future Communist aggression." In the treaty each nation recognized that "an armed attack in the Pacific area on either of the Parties in territories now under their respective administrative control . . . would be dangerous to its own peace and safety" and declared that "it would act to meet the common danger in accordance with its constitutional processes."

Nevertheless, relations between the two governments have frequently been subject at times to severe strains. President Rhee, aiming primarily at the creation of a united, independent Korea under his control and believing passionately that the obstacle to its achievement was communism, insisted that the United States should provide unqualified economic, military, and political support for his government.

Rhee contended that any nation which failed to take an unequivocal, aggressive anti-Communist position, or which established either trade relations with Communist China or diplomatic relations with the Soviet Union, was giving "aid and comfort to the enemy."

Rhee apparently was convinced that negotiations could not stop Communist expansion and that only military action would liberate the north from the Communists. He tried, therefore, to force the United States into an openly militant position. In June 1953 the Rhee government attempted to disrupt the truce negotiations by releasing the north Korean and Chinese prisoners of war who had declared against repatriation to their homelands, thus giving dramatic emphasis to its opposition to any settlement short of unification of the peninsula under its control. Tensions between the United States and the Republic of Korea then arose over disagreements about the size and strength of the armed forces of the Republic. President Rhee, for his part, continued to denounce the armistice agreements, which his government refused to sign; he called for the "march to the north" to liberate that area by force. A major factor contributing to his position was his fear of a decrease in United States interest in his country's problem and a feeling that every available means must be used to keep the issue alive. Such problems as the unrealistic exchange rate insisted on by the Rhee government and the taxation of foreign business establishments were resolved, but the government's intransigent economic policy continued to plague relations between the two countries (see ch. 23, Foreign Economic Relations).

Relations with the United States under the Rhee government were further strained by public disturbances that followed the election of March 15, 1960, during which governmental election irregularities on an unprecedented scale were reported. The United States government expressed its displeasure by indicating that "the demonstrations in Seoul were reflection of popular dissatisfaction regarding the conduct of the elections and repressive measures unsuited to a free democracy."

After the Rhee government collapsed in the wake of student demonstrations in April 1960, the United States reaffirmed its policy toward the Republic of Korea. After the election of the new government of Chang Myŏn and the dissolution of Ho Chong's caretaker government, the United States announced its support of the government. However, when a group of military officers led by Park Chung-hee overthrew the Chang regime, the United States at first continued to support the ousted government, thus evidencing disapproval of the unconstitutional means of political takeover. Relations between Seoul and Washington were somewhat strained for a time; however, they were later again placed on a most friendly footing after assurances were given that the new government was determined to root out corruption, to create a new atmosphere for national reconstruction, and to provide a firmer economic base.

The Park administration has in general pursued moderate polcies, and relations with the United States are friendly. Unification has not been abandoned as a major goal of foreign policy, but the government maintains that it should be won within the peaceful framework provided by the United Nations and that the campaign against communism is to be waged first at home by creating a new social order based on a sound economy.

Relations with the United States were further strengthened on July 9, 1966, when, after nearly 14 years of intermittent negotiations, the two governments signed a Status of Forces agreement governing the status of United States troops in the Republic of Korea. The new pact replaced the so-called Taejon Agreement of July 12, 1950, by which United States troops in the country were placed under American jurisdiction. The Status of Forces agreement made the provision, among others, that primary jurisdiction over certain designated offenses committed by off-duty United States servicemen be granted to the Republic of Korea government.

Relations with the United States under the Park government,

though based firmly on a principle of mutual amity, have frequently been subject to strains and stresses arising from conflicts of interests. One factor contributing to the strain seems to be the fear on the part of the government and the public that the United States may lose interest in the country's cause. There was a suspicion, shared by both the government and leading citizens, that, once relations between that country and Japan were normalized, the United States might drastically reduce its aid and commitments in the hope that Japan would contribute significantly to the country's economic development and become her strong ally.

North Korean Communists continue to seek to undermine the Park government through various means including terrorist and subversive activities. Such activities have sharply increased since 1966 and reached a peak when a group of commandos from the north attempted to assassinate President Park in January 1968. Of the 31 infiltrators, one was captured alive and 27 were shot to death in the course of escape. Immediately after the assassination attempt, the *USS Pueblo* was seized by North Korean naval forces. The Park government maintained that these activities were designed "to upset and obstruct the political stability and economic progress in the Republic of Korea and to apply braking pressure on Korea in her assistance to the Republic of Vietnam." Therefore, the Seoul government insisted, such aggressive actions should be met with "firmness and resoluteness," and "any sign of appeasement or irresolution" on the part of the Republic of Korea or the United States would only encourage further aggression.

Relations with the United States were adversely affected when the United States, on February 2, 1968, began negotiations with P'yongyang in an attempt to have the ship and her crew returned. Cyrus R. Vance, as President Johnson's personal envoy, met with President Park in Seoul to explain the United States position. Furthermore, plans were worked out to facilitate greater consultation between the United States and the Republic of Korea on matters affecting the security of the latter. Park and Vance also agreed that the two countries should undertake an immediate joint study of what measures they might take under the mutual defense treaty if aggression continued.

Relations with Japan

An agreement of friendship, commerce, and navigation between the Republic of Korea and the Supreme Commander for the Allied Powers, acting for Japan, was signed in April 1949. It provided for the export of grain to Japan and for the establishment of a consular mission in Tokyo. Relations between the two states became tense, however, after Japan's resumption of sovereignty in April

1952. The official attitude toward Japan was hostile, at least until the end of the Rhee regime in 1960, and the two countries did not establish normal diplomatic relations until 1965.

Normalization of relations was a basic foreign policy objective both for the government of Syngman Rhee and for the Japanese government under the conservative Liberal-Democratic Party. The two countries, however, were unable to reach satisfactory agreements on such outstanding issues as the size of the Republic of Korea property claims, the so-called "Rhee line" declaring Japanese fishing illegal in waters within 60 miles from the Korean coast, and the legal status of some 600,000 Korean residents in Japan. The normalization talks between the two states, begun in February 1952, were broken off a number of times. Memories of Japanese oppression shaped the views of many Koreans. The government and the press emphasized Japan's pre-World War II aggressive acts in Asia and warned against Japanese rearmament and political dominance. At the same time, many Japanese assumed an attitude of arrogance and contempt toward Koreans.

The emotional undertone of the matter was most dramatically demonstrated in the so-called "Kubota" controversy. In October 1953 Kubota Kanichiro, chief Japanese delegate to the talks, stated that Japanese rule in Korea had been beneficial to the Koreans and that Korea had no legal status as an independent state. As a result, the talks were abruptly broken off. Despite official Japanese statements repudiating the Kubota statement and despite offers of compromise, the Rhee government remained suspicious of Japanese motives.

After the military coup of 1961, however, the Park government made vigorous efforts to normalize relations with Japan. These efforts were motivated partly by Park's program of economic modernization which called for large-scale investment and partly by the general economic stimuli which Japan could provide. A factor was the consideration that Japan's payment of property claims could contribute significantly to the Park government's program of economic reconstruction.

Normalization talks were hampered by domestic opposition in both countries. In the Republic of Korea, both the students and members of the opposition parties adamantly opposed the talks, since they regarded the terms of the unofficially announced Seoul-Tokyo agreement on normalization as another "sellout" of the country to the Japanese. This issue caused a major government crisis.

In the midst of this domestic turmoil the two states agreed in 1965 to exchange ambassadors for the first time in more than half a century. The two governments had also reached agreement on the major outstanding issues. The normalization treaty recognizes the Republic as "the only lawful government in Korea, as specified in the resolution of the United Nations," but makes no reference to the extent of that government's territorial jurisdiction.

The treaty was accompanied by a series of bilateral agreements on the major outstanding issues. Japan consented to pay $300 million in property claims and to extend $200 million in long-term low-interest governmental loans, and an additional $300 million or more in commercial credits. On the legal status of Korean residents in Japan (estimated at two million at the end of World War II in 1945), the Japanese government agreed to grant permanent residence to those registered as nationals of the Republic of Korea. Most of these had been brought to Japan after 1938 as forced laborers to be used in war industries. Some 1.3 million returned to Korea by the end of March 1946, but approximately 600,000 refused repatriation and remained in Japan. Most of them are uneducated and poor and are often victims of discrimination; many are also under Communist influence. This combination of circumstances explains why only 230,000 Korean residents of Japan, or about 37 percent of the Korean population in that country, registered themselves as nationals of the Republic of Korea by the end of 1966. A majority of Koreans resident there are registered as nationals of North Korea; these argue that their legal status in Japan must be settled through a separate treaty between Japan and the North Korean regime. Finally, the Republic of Korea government agreed to accept a 12-mile limit as its fishing line. Both states also agreed to undertake a series of joint programs of maritime conservation.

Although the normalization treaty greatly strengthened Republic of Korea-Japanese relations by settling some of the thorny issues, there are several potential sources of ill-feeling that often strain relationships between the two states. The Republic's opposition to the so-called "two-Korea" policy is one such factor. During the normalization negotiations, the Park government feared that Japan's reluctance to extend Seoul's jurisdiction beyond the demilitarized zone stemmed from Japan's desire to improve relations with North Korea. In 1966 Seoul-Tokyo relations were threatened by a crisis over Japanese economic negotiations with the North (connected with the proposed entry of three North Korean technicians into Japan in preparation for the export of a textile plant to North Korea). But the crisis was averted when the Japanese firm cancelled negotiations for the plant export. In return, the Park government promised to purchase a similar plant from Japan. More recently, relations between the two states were somewhat strained when the Socialist governor of Tokyo granted accreditation to Communist-operated Chōsen University in Tokyo in April 1968.

The issue on repatriation of Korean residents to North Korea also subjected Seoul-Tokyo relations to strain. In accordance with the Calcutta agreement of 1959 between the Japanese and North Korean Red Cross societies, Japan had repatriated 88,360 Koreans to the North by November 12, 1967, the date on which the agreement expired. After that date, the two Red Cross societies met to find ways to repatriate those Koreans desiring to return to the North; and when they agreed on the continued application of the Calcutta agreement through July 1968, the Park government lodged a strong protest with the Japanese government. Repatriation of 251 Koreans to the North in December 1967 further exacerbated relations between the two states.

Relations with Other Asian Countries

Seoul has maintained amicable relations with the Republic of China, Malaysia, the Philippines, Thailand, the Republic of Vietman, Australia, and New Zealand, which are all closely allied with the United States. The government took the initiative in forming the Asian and Pacific Council (ASPAC) in 1966 to provide a forum for regional cooperation and to strenghten ties among the countries friendly to the Republic of Korea. The first ministerial meeting of ASPAC convened in Seoul June 14–16, 1966. It was attended by foreign ministers from Japan, the Republic of China, Australia, Malaysia, New Zealand, the Philippines, Thailand, the Republic of Vietnam, and the host nation.

The delegates agreed to create a standing committee of ASPAC, to be located in Bangkok and composed of member nations' ambassadors accredited to Thailand. It was also decided that a second ministerial conference would be held in Bangkok in 1967. Although such anti-Communist states as the Republics of Korea, China, and Vietnam were deeply conscious of Communist threats and hoped that the conference would take a strong anti-Communist position, the member nations limited their joint communique to recognizing "the acute need for more active and effective cooperation, in economic, technical, cultural, social, and informational fields, for their mutual benefit," and made no reference to Communist threat.

Again during the second ministerial conference of ASPAC, Seoul joined with the Republic of China, Thailand, the Republic of Vietnam, and the Philippines in an attempt to transform ASPAC into a system dealing with political matters common to the member nations, but such moves were rejected by Japan and New Zealand. In cultural, social, and economic areas, however, the conference made substantial progress. The delegates agreed to facilitate cooperative efforts to exterminate poverty, ignorance, and disease in the region, to set up a technical service center in Australia to aid countries in need of technical information, to create a sociocultural center in the Republic of Korea, and to study ways to liberalize trade restrictions and other economic problems common to the member nations.

In addition to her efforts at multinational regional cooperation, the Republic of Korea has vigorously sought to strengthen ties with Asian countries faced with the common threat from the Communists. In February 1966, President Park made state visits to Malaysia, Thailand, and the Republic of China during which their joint struggle against communism was discussed at length. Believing that its country's security is closely tied with that of the Republic of Vietnam, the Park government has played an increasingly important role in the Vietnam conflict since 1965 when it sent its first military contingents composed of noncombat troops. As of mid-1968 it maintained some 50,000 elite troops in that country.

Relations with African Nations

The Park government has acted vigorously to establish rapport with the developing countries in Africa. To seek friendly allies among these nations has been an important objective of the government, and in this the Park government appears to have made significant progress. Policy toward the so-called uncommitted nations has been governed by the doctrine that relations with any state which recognizes the North Korean regime will be terminated. The Republic of Korea government accordingly suspended its relations with the Congo (Brazzaville) in 1964 and Mauritania in 1965 when these countries extended diplomatic recognition to P'yongyang.

At the same time, the government continues to maintain consular relations with Burma, Pakistan, and India, which established similar relations with North Korea. The flexible application of the doctrine was deemed necessary in view of the intensive diplomatic drive the North Korean government has been waging to establish diplomatic relations with Afro-Asian countries, including even those that have recognized the Seoul government. Furthermore, in an attempt to block P'yongyang's diplomatic moves, the Park government decided to send its delegates to international conferences attended by their northern counterparts.

Interest in Africa stemmed also from the changed character of membership in the United Nations since 1960. Prior to 1960 the predominant sentiment among the members of the General Assembly was in favor of Rhee's position on unification. With the large-scale entry of newly-independent nations into the international body in 1960, however, the voting strength of the so-called Afro-Asian bloc has increased. Many of these nations tend to pursue a policy of nonalignment on controversial cold war issues, including the Korean question. Thus, many African member nations have abstained from voting on the question in the General Assembly. In 1967, for example, of 38 African member nations, 16 voted for the Republic of Korea; for North Korea; the rest either abstained from voting or were absent. Countries taking a "neutral" position included Sudan, Nigeria, Mali, Algeria, and some other African nations. Unqualified support has been given to the Republic by such members as Gabon, Madagascar, and the Ivory Coast. A significant aspect of the Park government's African policy has been to win support of "neutral" members for its position on unification.

Activities in pursuit of this policy included several high-level goodwill missions to Africa. Envoys sought, with a considerable degree of success, assurances from the countries visited that they would support Seoul's position in the United Nations. Cultural pacts were signed with some, and others were promised teams of technical experts and medical doctors. Diplomatic ties have been established with several newly independent nations including Malawi and Ghana. A sizable number of students from African nations have received technical training in the Republic of Korea. Furthermore, the Park government authorized $100,000 (27,200,000 wŏn) for technical aid to African nations for 1968.

INTERNATIONAL ORGANIZATIONS

Although the country is not a member of the United Nations, she has maintained close ties with that international body, is a member of, and has taken active part in the activities of various subsidiary and specialized agencies of the United Nations and other multinational organizations. International cooperation with the basic framework provided by the United Nations is one of the basic foreign policy principles of the government.

The relationship with the United Nations dates back to 1947. On November 14, 1947, the United Nations General Assembly adopted a resolution calling for the establishment of a Korean government through general elections in the northern and southern parts of the peninsula. An *ad hoc* United Nations Commission was sent to supervise the elections. However, P'yongyang refused to concur with the United Nations decision, and the elections were held only in the south, on May 10, 1948. On December 12, 1948, the General Assembly adopted a resolution declaring that "there has been established a lawful government having effective control and jurisdiction over that part of Korea where the Temporary Commission was able to observe." The resolution further recognized the validity of the elections as an "expression of the free will" of that part of Korea observed by the Commission. The newly established Republic of Korea applied on January 19, 1949, for membership in the United Nations but was rebuffed by a Soviet veto on April 8, 1949, in the Security Council. Vetoes on December 13, 1955, September 9, 1957, and December 9, 1958, and subsequently the threat of veto on the part of the Soviet delegate have served to bar the country from membership in the international organization.

Though denied formal United Nations membership, the government has sent its observational delegations to the annual sessions of the United Nations General Assembly and sought support from member nations for its membership in the international body. The country is represented in the United Nations by a permanent observer of ambassadorial rank. Prior to 1960 when 22 new members (largely "uncommitted" Afro-Asian countries) were admitted, resolutions favoring the Republic of Korea's entry into the United Nations and favoring the country's national unification received support of an overwhelming majority of the member states— usually more than a two-thirds majority. After 1960, however, the number of member states supporting the Republic of Korea dwindled to a simple majoriy. Under the circumstances the government has launched vigorous campaigns to solicit support from Afro-Asian members of the United Nations.

Ever since its independence in 1948, the country has sought to bring about unification primarily within the peaceful framework of the United Nations. The Korean armistice signed in 1953 between the United Nations Command and the Communists provided for a conference to settle the Korean question by peaceful, political means.

On February 18, 1954, in the course of a Foreign Ministers Conference at Berlin on German and Austrian problems, the United States, the United Kingdom, France, and the Soviet Union agreed to the holding of a conference at Geneva beginning April 26 for the purpose of reaching a peaceful settlement of the Korean question. Participating in the Korean phase of the Geneva Conference on one side were delegations from the Republic of Korea and from all the countries, except South Africa, that had contributed military contingents to the United Nations Command in the Korean conflict. The Communist side was represented by delegations from North Korea, Communist China, and the Soviet Union. The delegations from the countries making up the United Nations side shared a common viewpoint on the essential requirements for a Korean settlement. The Republic of Korea at first proposed that, in effecting unification, elections be held only in North Korea, since they had already taken place in the south. After the Communists expressed their dissatisfaction with the proposal, and at the suggestion of several allied delegations, the Republic of Korea agreed to the holding of elections throughout the peninsula if necessary. The Seoul government also recommended the taking of a census with a view to apportioning representatives in a new National Assembly in proportion to the population. Both the census and the elections would take place under United Nations supervision. The Republic of Korea proposal also provided for (1) the maintenance of the Constitution of the Republic of Korea subject to amendment by the all-Korea legislature to be convened after the elections, (2) withdrawal of Chinese Communist troops one month before the elections, and (3) withdrawal of United Nations forces after a unified government was certified by the United Nations.

The delegations representing the United Nations side endorsed the 14-point proposal of the Republic of Korea but it never became a matter of serious negotiation with the Communists, who remained adamantly opposed to the basic Allied demand—democratic elections under United Nations supervision.

The Communists presented proposals of their own which called for the creation of an All-Korea Commission, composed of an equal number of representatives from north and south, to draft an election law for all-Korea elections. Although the south had more than two-thirds of the Korean population, the Communists equated the two regions and by giving each area equal voice in the commission, they proposed in effect to provide the North with the power to paralyze the work of this important body. Furthermore, there was no mention of a role for the United Nations in the Communist proposal.

The United Nations side and the Communists failed to agree on a mutually acceptable plan for Korean unification, and the primary responsibility for resolving the Korean question automatically reverted to the United Nations General Assembly. However, the Communists' intransigent rejection of United Nations proposals has continued to thwart all subsequent attempts at peaceful settlement of the Korean problem.

In parallel with the policy of seeking a political settlement of the Korean question, however, the government under Syngman Rhee frequently advocated the use of force to bring about unification of the peninsula. For example, in the course of the Korean conflict there developed considerable differences between the Republic of Korea government and the United Nations Command. Rhee maintained the position that the hostilities should be brought to a successful end—namely, unification of the peninsula—and was inflexibly opposed to United Nations attempts to seek a cease-fire. Rhee's opposition perhaps reached its peak when he unilaterally released Communist prisoners in an attempt to sabotage armistice negotiations then under way. His attitude appeared to have produced strain in the relationship with the United Nations. However, the Government of Chang Myŏn, Rhee's successor, quickly rescinded Rhee's policy, announced that "its basic position on the unification question was to seek a peaceful solution within the framework of the United Nations," and officially renounced the use of force. This policy has been upheld by the present government of Park Chung-hee. An official Republic of Korea letter circulated among all United Nations members on October 5, 1967, fully recognized the competency and authority of the United Nations on the Korean question, and reaffirmed the United Nations formula that the peninsula be unified through general elections under United Nations supervision.

Except for the organs of the United Nations, admission to which is obstructed by Soviet vetoes, the Republic has joined as a full-fledged member almost all the major specialized and subsidiary agencies of the United Nations as well as virtually every major international organization (18 specialized and subsidiary agencies of the United Nations; 18 intergovernmental organizations; and 188 nongovernmental organizations). Major international organizations to which the country has been admitted include: Food and Agriculture Organization (1949); United Nations Educational, Scientific, and Cultural Organization (1950); World Health Organization (1949); International Monetary Fund (1955); International Telecommunication Union (1952); Universal Postal Union (1949); United Nations Children's Fund (1950); Economic Commission for Asia and the Far East (1954); the United Nations Conference on Trade and Development (1965); and the General Agreement on Tariffs and Trade (1967).

DOMESTIC REACTIONS TO FOREIGN RELATIONS

There is broad consensus in favor of the basic external objectives of the Park government. The country's foreign policy has been constructed to elevate her international role and status, to assure the security and well-being of the people, and to bring about unification of the peninsula. To reach these objectives, the government of Park Chung-hee has attempted: (1) to promote friendly ties with, and form a regional collective security system among, non-Communist nations; (2) to expand economic cooperation with friendly states; (3) to strengthen the national defense force; (4) to gain support among members of the United Nations for the unification proposal—originally endorsed by a two-thirds majority of the member nations—that called for a nationwide election under United Nations supervision; and (5) to uphold the principle of national self-determination. The major political forces, including the ruling Democratic Republican Party and the opposition New Democratic Party, concur in these general policies.

In recent years, however, some of the specific foreign policies implemented have engendered bitter controversy among the people. The absence of general consensus on specific issues is apparent in the policy pronouncements of the two major parties—Democratic Republican Party and New Democratic Party. While agreeing on the need for strengthening ties with non-Communist nations, including the so-called "neutral" nations, the two parties appear to have somewhat differing views on such issues as the conflict in Vietnam, relations with Japan, and national unification.

During election campaigns in 1967, the ruling Democratic Republican Party advocated continued support of the Vietnamese struggle against Communist aggression and at the same time advocated an "honorable" settlement of the conflict. The opposition New Democratic Party proposed that while support be given to the allied attempt to end the conflict by negotiation, every effort should be made to withdraw troops from Vietnam "in an honorable way." The party opposed the dispatch of troops to Vietnam in 1965 and the increase in 1966. Both parties, however, take pride in the performance of Korean troops and believe that dispatch of these troops has increased the Republic of Korea's international stature. On Japanese relations the government and the opposition have disagreed. While the Democratic Republican Party supports the 1965 treaty of normalization with Japan, the New Democratic Party has advocated a substantial revision of the treaty on the grounds that it is inequitable. On the unification issue, the ruling party proposes the strengthening of national power and the promotion of conditions favorable to unification in the United Nations, that is, the gaining of further international support for the unification proposal calling for a United Nations-supervised election. The opposition party advocates less reliance on the United Nations, and has favored the inauguration of postal services and exchange of correspondents between the north and south in an attempt to promote an atmosphere conducive to national unification.

Available evidence indicates that the policies of the Park government in these areas generally meet with approval by the nation as a whole. A recent public opinion survey taken by the *Dong-a Ilbo*, the leading opposition paper, showed considerable public support for the government's foreign policies. On the Seoul-Tokyo rapprochement issue, 45 percent of the respondents favored normalization of relations with Japan, while 28 percent were opposed. The remainder expressed no opinions on the normalization talks between the two states. On the Vietnam issue, specifically on the dispatch of troops to Vietnam, a substantial majority of the respondents, according to two surveys taken in 1966, "accepted the appropriateness of what had been done." On the unification issue, a recent government survey demonstrated the largest percent of the respondents (approximately 25 percent) supported the long-standing policy of the government—all-Korea United Nations-supervised elections proportional to population—and the next largest group (about 17 percent) favored direct negotiations between the north and south. Approximately 15 percent endorsed unification by military means.

Despite general public endorsement, indications are that an appreciable segment of the population—specifically, students, many intellectuals, and the press—disagree with some of the policies implemented by the Park government. Perhaps the most controversial foreign policy issue in recent years pertained to the treaty with Japan. The government was intent on speedily normalizing relations between the two countries, whereas the opposition party leaders, including Yun Pko-sŏn, warned against the conclusion of a normalization treaty at that time or any excessive concessions to Japan. The opposition also demanded a nonpartisan Japan policy based on broad consensus among the major political forces of the country (see ch. 14, Political Dynamics). The negotiations leading to the signing of the agreement were conducted amidst shouts of protest from the opposition parties, students, and a sizable segment of the press corps.

When the treaty was up for ratification, all 111 of the Democratic Republican Party members of the Assembly were present and voted unanimously for it. No opposition party members were present, as they had previously turned in their resignation to the Assembly as a protest against the treaty. It was observed by political commentators that normalization of relations with Tokyo had been achieved while the government followed policies of "repressing the dissident student and intellectual elements." The opposition's attack was focused mainly upon what it regarded as "underhanded methods" in normalizing relations. It entertained considerable apprehension toward a government which was able to bring 14 years of negotiations to a final conclusion "with speed" and "military efficiency." It also feared Japan's possible economic exploitation. The opposition further felt that the Park government had made excessive concessions in the treaty, and it is for this reason that a substantial revision of the treaty is insisted on by the New Democratic Party.

A 1964 survey among college students on the normalization

issue was generally indicative of the feelings of those opposed to the treaty. Asked to give reasons for the anti-normalization student demonstrations of March 23, 1964, 31 percent of the 1,468 respondents indicated that their protest demonstrations were motivated by fear that the country would again be subject to Japan's economic and political exploitation; 20 percent cited their distrust of the incumbent government; 15 percent referred to the "underhanded" method of negotiations; 13 percent felt that the government's concession on the so-called Peace Line (concerning territorial waters) was the primary cause for their demonstrations.

The government decision to send noncombatant troops to Vietnam in 1965 was the target of criticism for the opposition parties. In defense of its decision, the government of Park Chung-hee announced that the outcome of the Vietnam conflict had direct bearing on the security of the country and that the government was morally obliged to repay the assistance given to it by the United States during the Korean conflict. The government bill providing for the dispatch of 2,000 noncombatant troops was approved by the Democratic Republican Party-dominated National Assembly while protesting members of the opposition parties walked out of the legislative chamber. Members of the opposition parties refused to endorse the government bill for a variety of reasons. Some cited the absence of bilateral agreements with the Republic of Vietnam that would permit the government to send troops. Some stated that the diversion of troops might endanger security at home. Others argued that "the people of South Vietnam lacked the determination to defend their freedom" and that Republic of Korea aid was therefore meaningless.

While government proposals to increase the contingents in Vietnam were debated in the legislature in 1966, the government met with greater censure from the opposition parties as well as criticism from the press. The opposition argued that "there was no reason why the Republic of Korea should carry the heaviest burden in containing communism" while other Asian allies were extending only token assistance. Much resentment was also expressed concerning the secret negotiations between Seoul and the United States government that led to the decision to increase Republic of Korea troops in Vietnam. Some opposition members feared that the government's growing military involvement in the Southeast Asian conflict might result in the decline of her prestige among the so-called "uncommitted" nations whose support was vigorously sought to counter P'yongyang's aggressive diplomacy. Furthermore, opposition to the proposed increases sometimes took the form of resentment against the United States which was reported to have repeatedly urged the government to send additional troops to Vietnam. These arguments also underlay the growing press criticism of Park's Vietnam policy.

Partly in response to the opposition's arguments, the Park government, on its part, vigorously sought from the United States improved benefits for Republic of Korea troops in Vietnam as well as additional United States military aid to modernize the armed forces and to activate three divisions on reserve to make up for the troops to be sent to Southeast Asia.

POPULAR ATTITUDES
TOWARD FOREIGN PEOPLES AND NATIONS

Contacts with foreign peoples, other than Chinese and Japanese, are largely post-World War II phenomena, and their attitudes toward foreign nations appear to undergo a process of crystallization. Although individual foreigners have been treated cordially, until quite recently there has been relatively little interest in foreign affairs among the masses. As can be expected of a small nation surrounded by large, powerful ones, many people are inclined to regard foreign intervention as the source of most of their ills, and the underlying attitude toward foreign national states is generally one of distrust.

Attitudes toward foreign states have also been shaped by the rivalry between Communist and non-Communist states. The government has often asserted that it stands in the front lines of the Free World's struggle with Communist tyranny, and according to a recent opinion survey as well as abundant additional evidence, the people demonstrated an intense dislike for communism and countries associated with the Communist system.

Traditionally, Japan as a national power has been an enemy to be feared. Few Koreans, however, harbor intense antagonism toward individual Japanese. It is the Japanese state which is distrusted. The negative attitude toward Japan has been shaped principally by the Koreans' experiences under the Japanese rule. Syngman Rhee's anti-Japanese policies have reinforced this attitude, and most of the present generation, who had no personal experiences under the Japanese, express bitter animosity toward the Japanese nation. It was this attitude, among other factors, which prompted students to react unfavorably to the rapprochement of the two governments in 1964 and 1965. While many continue to see Japan as a political antagonist, there is also widespread admiration of such things as Japanese education and technical training.

China for centuries was regarded by many Koreans as an "elder brother," and their relations, until recently, were rarely characterized by open hostility. Educated people, in particular, recognize the cultural affinity between the Koreans and Chinese. Clear attitudes toward modern China, however, have not yet evolved. Mainland China is intensely disliked and is considered dangerous because it is a Communist power, which is now equipped with nuclear capabilities, and which during the Korean conflict fought the people and their allies. In general, the Chinese Communist Government, and not the people, is blamed for bad relations. The government has often indicated that it regards the Chinese Communist Government as an aggressive power intent upon an imperialistic course involving the whole of Asia.

The people have had little direct experience with their third neighbor, Russia. Russian imperialism in the latter part of the 19th century aroused the distrust of educated Koreans, but throughout the 20th century Russian opposition to Japan was welcomed. Today, most people hold the Soviet Union largely responsible for the sorrows of the Korean conflict, and point to the Soviet Union as the source of the Communist threat. The government has repeatedly stated that it regards the P'yongyang government as a Soviet puppet regime which "has blindly followed the expansion policy" of its "superiors in the Soviet Union . . . totally disregarding the rights and benefits of the people" under its rule.

Of the distant nations, the people have had extensive experience with the United States only. American missionaries and businessmen have generally managed to generate goodwill. People today, on the whole, look upon the United States as a friend and an ally. They greatly admire the economic and scientific advances of the United States; most students regard the United States as a land of educational achievement and ardently seek opportunities to study there. American military action during the Korean conflict, on the whole, appears to have had favorable effect on popular attitudes toward the United States, but there is the feeling among many educated people that national interests, not altruistic considerations, dictated the American intervention in the war.

The favorable feeling toward the United States is modified, however, by a sense of strain and tension resulting from policy differences between the two states, by the dependence upon American support, and by occasional friction that arises between American servicemen and the local population.

The popular attitude toward other nations cannot be ascertained, but polls taken in mid-1963 among college students indicated that they like the Germans, Americans, British, Swiss, French, Japanese, Chinese, Turks, Indians, and Russians in that order. They regarded Germans as diligent, creative, practical, and frugal, although they also considered them to be selfish, dictatorial, and exclusive. Americans were regarded as gay, independent, active, pragmatic, progressive, and creative, but carried these characteristics to extremes, putting too much emphasis on practicality, mechanics, and money. The English were thought of as cultured, gentlemanly, diligent, frugal, utilitarian, but also arrogant and "colonialist." The Swiss were regarded as peaceful, meticulous, sincere, and diligent, but retiring and lacking in vigor. The French were considered artistic, emotional, romantic, courteous, and sociable, but also radicals who were oversensitive to politics. The Japanese, although they were regarded as gay, kind, diligent, aggressive, patriotic, and imbued with a strong team spirit, nonetheless were considered too arrogant, imitative, cunning, and shallow-minded. The Chinese, a resilient and enduring people, patient, hard-working, who operated on a large scale, spurning details and trivialities, were also regarded as slovenly, selfish, secretive, and foolhardy.

ORGANIZATION AND OPERATION

The Constitution of the Republic of Korea vests the conduct of foreign affairs in the President and the State Council, subject to the approval of the National Assembly. The President and the State Council, specifically the Prime Minister and the Minister of Foreign Affairs, make periodic reports on foreign relations to the legislature; and members of the National Assembly under the general right of interpellation may question members of the State Council (but not the President) on matters pertaining to foreign relations. The state is represented by the President, who has the power to conclude treaties and appoint ambassadors. The President's ambassadorial appointments are not subject to legislative confirmation; however, treaties must receive legislative consent before they are domestically binding. Declaration of war, the dispatch of troops overseas, and the stationing of foreign soldiers within the national borders are also subject to legislative approval. The Assembly has a standing foreign affairs committee which reports its deliberations to plenary sessions of the house. The Assembly may also establish *ad hoc* committees to consider questions of special importance to the state.

Although the formal constitutional powers given to the National Assembly bar the President from conducting foreign relations in an arbitrary manner, main lines of foreign policy are established by the President, constitutionally and traditionally the dominant figure in the nation. He has the final word in policy planning and major decisions. Constitutionally, however, such matters as declaration or cessation of war and other important matters pertaining to the nation's foreign relations are expected to be submitted to the State Council for deliberation and advice (Art. 86). Chief foreign policy advisers in the State Council are the Prime Minister, who heads the Cabinet, and the Minister of Foreign Affairs, who is assisted by a Vice-Minister of Foreign Affairs in the conduct of foreign relations. The major advisory body for the President in foreign policymaking appears to be the National Security Council. Composed of the President, the Prime Minister, ministers of foreign affairs, home affairs, national defense, and finance, ministers without portfolio, the Director of the Central Intelligence Agency, and other officials designated by the President, the National Security Council advises the President in the formation of policies involving national security. The United Nations Measures Committee, originally created in 1966, is empowered to examine major issues before the United Nations and to suggest policies for the government to pursue. It is made up of representatives from the Foreign Affairs Ministry, the National Assembly, and major political parties, as well as academicians.

Missions abroad function as a major source of information in

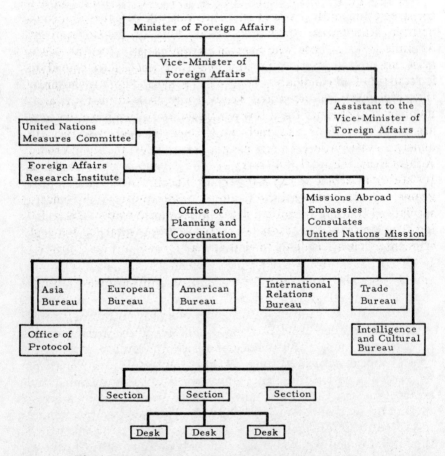

Figure 6. Organization of the Ministry of Foreign Affairs in the Republic of Korea, 1968.

the making of foreign policy. The Central Intelligence Agency also plays an important role in the gathering of information pertaining to the security of the nation. Each of the military service branches also maintains its own intelligence system.

The organization of the Ministry of Foreign Affairs is on functional and area lines (see fig. 6). It includes an Office of Planning and Coordination, which comprises an Office of Protocol; Asian, European, American, and International Relations Bureaus; a Trade Bureau and an Intelligence and Cultural Bureau. Policymaking power within the Ministry rests with the Minister. He is advised by his vice-minister, Director of the Office of Planning and coordination, and chiefs of bureaus who periodically meet in conference. Recommendations of the conferences of bureau-chiefs are first examined by the planning and coordination office before being submitted to the Minister.

The foreign ministry staff consists of a career foreign service corps, selected on the basis of education and performance in a competitive examination supervised by the Ministry of Government Administration. Those who pass the examination, given as needs arise, are offered positions in the foreign service. College education is required of all candidates. Long a profession of high social prestige, diplomacy has attracted bright individuals. Due to a large number of applicants for a few openings, recruiting examinations are considered to be extremely stiff. Once selected, new recruits undergo systematic training programs provided by the Foreign Affairs Research Institute (formerly the Foreign Service Training Institute) attached to the Ministry of Foreign Affairs. The programs include a general curriculum in international diplomacy, specialized training in subject areas, and intensive language training. The Institute also conducts special programs intended for government officials scheduled to visit abroad.

CHAPTER 16

PUBLIC INFORMATION

In the Republic of Korea there has been a great development of mass communications media since 1945. These developments include a sharp rise in the number of newspapers and periodicals in circulation, the appearance of student newspapers published at various universities, an increase in the number of books published, and the production of a growing number of motion pictures. Radio broadcasting, which had been only moderately developed under the Japanese, has expanded so greatly that in mid-1968 five broadcasting companies were in operation and an estimated 2.7 million radios and receiving devices in use. Television was introduced in 1956 and an estimated 68,497 sets were in use.

The government was actively engaged in propaganda activities in mid-1968, emphasizing in its messages the need for self-discipline and vigorous efforts in the interests of the country's future and stressing the unfavorable aspects of the Communist system. Radio broadcasting and government-subsidized newspapers were the principal channels of government informational activities. Like radio, most newspapers, publishing houses, and motion picture companies were privately owned.

Privately owned mass media operated largely under a system of self-restraint and self-control, being accorded much discretion in their coverage, but they were expected to conform to minimal standards in facilities set by the government. They were also constitutionally required not to "impugn the personal honor or rights of an individual" or to "infringe upon public morality and social ethics." Activities and materials detrimental to national security were also prohibited.

Communications media, perhaps with the exception of motion pictures and television devoted primarily to public entertainment, appeared to play an increasingly important role in the dissemination of public information, and radio and newspapers especially were influential factors in shaping the political climate.

269

CHANNELS OF DISTRIBUTION

Newspapers

At the end of 1967, 44 daily newspapers were being published in the Republic of Korea, of which 20, including all the leading dailies, were published in Seoul (see table 10). Each provincial capital had at least one daily, and Taegu had as many as four dailies. Seoul was nonetheless the press center, and no provincial newspapers had more than local significance. A number of weekly newspapers were also published in Seoul and other cities.

The most influential Korean language daily was *Dong-A Ilbo,* an outspoken opposition paper. It had the largest circulation (over 600,000 at the end of 1967) in the country and was the most popular paper among the educated people of the country. Other influential dailies included three normally independent but sometimes opposition papers. *Choson Ilbo, Kyŏnghyang Sinmun,* and *Han'guk Ilbo,* which had the second largest circulation in the country. *Seoul, Sinmun,* a government-subsidized paper, followed a pro-governmental editorial policy and had a relatively small circulation among the intellectuals. The independent *Jungang Ilbo,* which began publication in September 1966, became increasingly influential. *Seoul Kyŏngje Sinmun* and *Sanŏp Kyŏngje Sinmun* were two prominent dailies covering economic news.

There were two English-language papers, both published in Seoul: *The Korea Times* and *The Korea Herald.* The latter, a government-supported paper, had the larger circulation. These papers had little domestic importance as their readership was predominantly foreign.

A number of foreign newspapers were read by a small educated group of Koreans, principally for scholarly and journalistic purposes—the *New York Times, Christian Science Monitor,* and such influential Japanese dailies as *Asahi Shimbun* and *Mainichi Shimbun.* The Japanese newspapers accounted for the largest percentage of foreign newspapers in circulation in the country.

The typical Korean newspaper consists of four pages and is illustrated. The front page is usually devoted to political news: governmental activities, the public and private activities of political figures, changes in government appointments, and so on. The second page is commonly reserved for editorials, economic matters, and foreign news. Social affairs, human interest stories, articles on artistic events, and a serial appear on the following pages. All the newspapers use Chinese as well as *han'gŭl* characters; some, however, print certain features or even entire pages exclusively in *han'gŭl* (see ch. 5, Ethnic Groups and Languages).

The regular newspaper-reading public remains small, and the

Table 10. *National and Local Newspapers in the Republic of Korea*

Name	Location	Publisher	Circulation
NATIONAL			
Choson Ilbo	Taepyŏng-no, Seoul	Pang U-yong	150,000
Chungang Ilbo	Sosŏmun-dong, Seoul	Wŏn Chong-hun	n.a.
Han'guk Ilbo	Chunghak-dong, Seoul	Chang Ki-yŏng	240,000
Han-Hua Jih Pao (Chinese)	Chungmu-ro, Seoul	Chu Kyŏp	n.a.
Hyŏndae Kyŏngje Ilbo	Taepyŏng-no, Seoul	Sŏk Chong-sŏn	n.a.
Ilyo Sinmun	—do—	—do—	n.a.
Korea Herald (English)	—do—	Kim Pong-gi	n.a.
Korea Times (English)	Chunghak-dong, Seoul	Chang Ki-yong	10,000
Kyŏnghyang Sinmun.	Sŏgong-dong, Seoul	Park Chan-hyŏn	120,000
Sanŏp Kyŏngje Sinmun	Hoehyŏn-dong, Seoul	Paek Sŏng-jin	15,000
Seoul Kyŏngje Sinmun	Chunghak-dong, Seoul	Chang Ki-yŏng	20,000
Seoul Sinmun	Taepyŏng-no, Seoul	Chang Tae-hwa	80,000
Shin-A Ilbo	Sosŏmun-dong, Seoul	Chang Ki-bong	n.a.
Taihan Ilbo	Taepyŏng-no, Seoul	Kim Yong-jun	n.a.
Tong-A Ilbo	Sejong-no, Seoul	Ko Chae-uk	300,000
LOCAL			
Cheju Sinmun	Itoil-dong, Cheju	Kim Son-hui	3,000
Chŏnbuk Ilbo	Kosa-dong, Chŏnju	Pak Yong-sang	20,000
Chŏnnam Ilbo	Kumnam-no, Kwangju	Kim Nam-jung	25,000
Chŏnnam Meil Sinmun	Kwangsan-dong, Kwangju	Pak Chol	10,000
Ch'ungch'ŏng Ilbo ...	Nammun-no, Ch'ŏngju	Yi To-yong	5,000
Chungdo Ilbo	Sonhwa-dong, Taejŏn	Yi Ung-nyol	10,000
Honam Ilbo	Chungang-no, Kunsan	Won Sang-sik	2,000
Honam Meil	Sangnak-tong, Mokpo	Kim Pyong-sam	n.a.
Inchŏn Sinmun	Sa-dong, Inch'ŏn	Ho Hap	5,000
Kangwŏn Ilbo	Chungang-no, Ch'unch'ŏn	Ham Chae-hun	10,000
Kukche Sinbo	Taegyo-dong, Pusan	Yi Hung-bae	30,000
Kyŏnggi Ilbo	Sinpo-dong, Inch'ŏn	Hwang Kwang-su	n.a.
Kyŏnggi Meil Sinmun	Chungang-dong, Inch'ŏn	Song Su-an	7,000
Kyŏngnam Ilbo	Ponsong-dong, Chinju	Pak Se-je	2,000
Masan Ilbo	Chungang-dong, Masan	Kim Hyong-yun	2,000
Meil Sinmun	Namil-dong, Taegu	Kim Yong-ho	30,000
Pusan Ilbo	Chungang-dong, Pusan	Choe Se-gyong	40,000
Samnam Ilbo	Kyŏngwŏn-dong, Chonju	Yi Ung-u	5,000
Taegu Ilbo	Tongin-dong, Taegu	Yo Sang-son	15,000
Taegu Kyŏngje Sinmun	Taepyŏng-no, Taegu	Cho Yak-suk	5,000
Taejŏn Ilbo	Unhaeng-dong, Taejŏn	Nam Chong-sop	40,000
Yongham Ilbo	Somun-no, Taegu	Yi Sun-hui	5,000

n.a.—Not available.

Source: Adapted from Hapdong News Agency, *Korea Annual, 1968.*

papers as a whole have a small circulation despite impressive increases in recent years. As of mid-1967, the total circulation was estimated at 2,052,747 as compared with 1,257,000 for mid-1964. This increasing trend is expected to continue. As of July 1967, approximately 71 copies of daily papers were in circulation for every 1,000 persons. Circulation remains limited, both because most families cannot afford to subscribe to a newspaper and because of the difficulty that reading Chinese characters presents to most high school graduates and even to some college graduates. This difficulty was somewhat alleviated in 1967 when the newspaper publishers agreed to limit the use of Chinese characters to 2,000. Formerly, 3,000 to 5,000 were used. The leading newspapers are made up to appeal mainly to an urban, educated readership, with few concessions made to popular tastes or the local interests of the small number of less educated readers.

The newspapers play important roles in politics as information providers and opinion shapers for the attentive segment of the public. The papers devote more space to political-diplomatic news than to any other subject. One recent survey showed that seven Seoul dailies devoted 48 percent of their space to political-diplomatic news. According to another study, a large majority (almost 78 percent) of those with higher education relied on the daily newspapers for their information.

With the exception of a few government-subsidized dailies, papers are privately owned. Most of the influential national and local papers are owned by wealthy individuals. The close ties between the press and powerful economic groups were demonstrated in 1966 when *Jungang Ilbo* owned by the Sansong Combine, defended the much-publicized Samsong smuggling case while all other papers severely reprimanded the company. The influential papers attract bright young recruits from among college graduates, and many journalists affiliated with these papers are men of ability and sound training. However, the newspapers in the mid-1960's were generally unable to pay adequate salaries to their reporters and lacked the services of a sufficient number of experienced and highly qualified personnel. Most young recruits in the past majored in either social science or humanities, and the institutionalized journalistic training programs were inadequate. To alleviate this situation, several universities have added journalism programs to their curriculum, and a Graduate School of Journalism was created at Seoul National University.

News Agencies

At the end of 1967 there were 16 news agencies operating in the country, all located in Seoul. Eight were owned by Koreans. Others were mostly Korean branches of foreign news agencies including

Associated Press, United Press International, Reuters, and Kyodo Agency of Japan. The three largest Korean agencies were the Hapdong T'ongsin, the Tongyang T'ongsin, and the Tongwha T'ongsin. Each had a network of offices and local correspondents throughout the country as well as its own foreign correspondents stationed abroad. The Hapdong, under an exclusive contract, received foreign news bulletins from Agence France Press and distributed them to domestic newspapers and other subscribers. The Tongyang had similar arrangements with United Press International, and the Tongwha with Associated Press and Reuters. The news agencies constituted the most important source of foreign news for the Korean newspapers. Only the major dailies could afford to maintain a small number of their own foreign correspondents abroad.

Periodicals

At the end of 1967 a total of 250 periodicals were registered with the Ministry of Public Information. Of these, 137 were specialized journals published by academic institutions, professional associations, banks, and governmental agencies. A total of 2,137,000 issues were published during the first nine months of 1967, but about 70 of the magazines were running in the red because of poor facilities, a limited market, insufficient funds, and paper shortages.

The major magazines included: *Hyŏndae munhak*, a literary monthly; *Sasanggye*, a leading intellectual journal; *Sindong-a*, another intellectual magazine; and *Yŏwŏn*, the leading woman's magazine. The intellectual magazines such as *Sasanggye* and *Sindong-a*, which tend to be critical of the government, appeared to play an important role in shaping the political climate, but on the whole magazines were of far less importance than newspapers.

The proportion of Chinese characters used in periodicals was higher in the intellectual and specialized periodicals than in those designed primarily as entertainment for the general public. Many modern technical and theoretical concepts were expressed in Japanese, English, or German terms which were not easily translated into Korean. Stories, historical tales, and humor in the popular magazines followed traditional patterns of popular entertainments, which could be easily expressed in Korean terms and written in *han'gul*. Such popular magazines as *Yŏwŏn*, *Arirang*, and *Myŏnrang* carried many articles on Western culture and ways of life.

A very limited number of educated Koreans read Western popular magazines and professional journals. The primary factor responsible for limited readership was the lack of language fluency even among those with college educations. The major Western periodicals were largely American publications and included *Newsweek, Time, U.S. News and World Report,* and *Readers' Digest.* On the other hand, Japanese periodicals, especially popular magazines, were widely read by those over the age of 35 who had studied Japanese before 1945. But the government's stringent import policy limited the circulation of Japanese journals.

Books

In the mid-1960's book-publishing was relatively stagnant as compared with that in the early 1960's. Although the demand for paperbacks appeared to be great, not more than 10 new titles were published in hardbound editions during the first 9 months of 1967. During 1966 a total of 8,655 titles were published, and 5 percent of these were reprints. Books intended for children and teenagers (cartoon books and secondary school reference books) accounted for more than 70 percent of the total. Stories, both fictional and nonfictional, were very much in demand, and most of the 1967 bestsellers were either historical or fictional stories. Especially popular were translations of foreign novels and biographies, and 10 of the 21 bestsellers for 1967 were such translations.

With the exception of several established publishing houses, most firms were inexperienced and suffered from inadequate credit facilities, poor wholesale and retail trade outlets, paper shortages, and a scarcity of qualified authors. Many such firms turned to the publication of cheap pornographic books, mostly translations of Japanese works. However, the more stable publishing companies, including Minjung and Ulyu companies, relied on their college textbook lists. Translations of foreign scholarly books were favored items for the established firms.

A limited quantity of foreign books was annually imported into the country. Since 1966 Korean book importers collectively spent approximately $700,000 annually on foreign books. Books from Japan accounted for about 80 percent, followed by American books. Like other printed materials of foreign origin, foreign books were intended primarily for academic use and thus their readership was very limited.

Radio

In the 1950's under the government of Syngman Rhee broadcasting was largely a governmental function. In the late 1960's, however, private broadcasting became increasingly important. Whereas in the 1950's there was only one private broadcasting company, in mid-1968 four private companies were in operation (see table 11).

The government-owned Korean Broadcasting System (KBS), operating under the direct supervision of the Ministry of Public

Table 11. Radio Stations in the Republic of Korea

Name of station	Call sign	Frequency (in kilocycles)	Location
Korea Broadcasting System (KBS):			
First National Network ..	HLKA	710	Yejang-dong, Seoul
Second National Network	HLCA	970	—do—
International Network ...	HLSA	600	—do—
		710	
		860	
		890	
		970	
		6.015*	
		9.64*	
		11.925*	
KBS Local Network:			
Pusan	HLKB	890	Taechŏn-dong, Pusan
Taegu	HLKG	740	Wŏndae-dong, Taegu
Chŏnju	HLKF	570	Kosa-dong, Chŏnju
Taejŏn	HLKI	880	Mok-dong, Taejŏn
Kwangju	HLKH	750	Sa-dong, Hwangju
Ch'ŏngju	HLKQ	920	Nammun-no, Ch'ŏngju
Ch'unch'ŏn	HLKM	659	Okchon-dong, Ch'unch'ŏn
Cheju	HLKS	940	Cheju
Kangnung	HLKR	860	Yonggang-dong, Kangnung
Masan	HLKD	570	Wanwol-dong, Masan
Mokpo	HLKN	860	Sanghyŏng-dong, Mokpo
Namwŏn	HLKL	1030	Namwŏn, North Cholla Province
Yŏsu	HLCY	1340	Sogyo-dong, Yŏsu
Sokcho	HLCS	1030	Sokcho, Kangwŏn Province
Pohang	HLCP	1420	Tongbin-no, Pohang
Wŏnju	HLCW	1190	Wŏnju, Kangwŏn Province
Christian Broadcasting System (CBS):			
Seoul	HLKY	840	Chongno-gu, Seoul
Taegu	HLKT	1000	Taemyŏng-dong, Taegu
Pusan	HLKP	1400	Yonson-dong, Pusan
Kwangju	HLCL	1000	Yangnim-dong, Kwangju
Iri	HLCM	1400	Hwasu-dong, Iri
Korean Munhwa Broadcasting Corporation (MBC):			
Seoul	HLKV	900	Insa-dong, Seoul
Taegu	HLCT	810	Chon-dong, Taegu
Kwangju	HLCN	820	Chungjang-no, Kwangju
Taejŏn	HLCQ	580	Taehung-dong, Taejŏn
Chŏnju	HLCX	1140	Kosa-dong, Chŏnju
Pusan	HLKU	1035	Chungang-dong, Pusan
Evangelical Alliance Mission (EBS)	HLKX	1068	Puksong-dong, Inch'ŏn
Tong-A Broadcasting System (DBS)	HLKJ	780	Sejong-no, Seoul
Tongyang Broadcasting Company (TBC)	HLKC	640	Sosŏmun-dong, Seoul
Tongyang FM	HLCD	89.1*	—do—

*Megacycles.

Source: Adapted from Hapdong News Agency, *Korea Annual, 1968.*

Information, was the major domestic radio service. It had three principal stations, two broadcasting to domestic audiences, the third to listeners abroad. The domestic stations, HLKA and its affiliate HLCA, are located in Seoul and broadcast on 710 and 970 kilocycles, respectively, each using a 100-kilowatt transmitter. Kilocycles for the international service, HLSA, ranged from 600 to 970, depending on the nature of audiences to which the broadcast was directed. HLSA, also located in Seoul, used a 500-kilowatt transmitter. The KBS also included a number of provincial stations (16 in 1967) which relayed most of the programs originating in Seoul.

HLKA broadcast 154 hours per week. Sixteen percent of the time was devoted to news report, 40 percent to educational programs, 25 percent to entertainment, and the rest to other programs. HLCA, which broadcast 126 hours per week, was heavily devoted to educational and anti-Communist programs. The international system known as the Voice of Free Korea broadcasts a total of 19 hours in seven languages, and more than half of the total hours were devoted to English and Japanese language programs.

Besides the government-owned KBS, there are a number of private broadcasting systems. The Christian Central Broadcasting System (HLKY), located in Seoul, broadcast 129.5 hours per week and featured musical and religious programs. It broadcast on 840 kilocycles and had four local stations which relayed most of the programs originating in Seoul. The Korean Munwha Broadcasting Corporation (HKLA) was on the air for 140 hours per week, and devoted most of its time to entertainment and educational programs. It had five local stations. The Tongyang Broadcasting Company (HLKJ), owned by Yi Byŏng-ch'ol, was a newcomer in the field. HLKJ which was on the air for 147 hours broadcast on 640 kilocycles. It had no local relaying stations and thus its audience was limited to the Seoul area. The Tongyang was heavily devoted to music and other entertainment programs. The Tong-A Broadcasting System, affiliated with the *Tong-A-Ilbo* and using the call letters HLKJ, opened in 1963. It broadcast on 780 kilocycles and had no relaying stations. In addition to these networks, Team radio (HLKX) has been operated by the Evangelical Alliance Mission in Inch'ŏn since 1957. Also, both the United Nations Command and the United States Armed Forces broadcast over their own services to listeners in the area.

The number of radio receivers in use has been rising rapidly, in part because of domestic production increases. In mid-1967, according to the Ministry of Public Information, there were approximately 1,464,000 sets in the country (about one for every four households) as compared with only 300,000 in 1953. The ratio of radios to the number of households was highest in Seoul, lowest in North Kyŏngsang province. Multiple listening was a common pattern, and a large number of sets were located in public gathering places, placed there either by private persons, such as restaurant owners, or by the government. In addition, there were more than 1.2 million extension speakers, installed mainly by the government, in farming and fishing communities.

In 1967 the five major radio networks devoted approximately 13 percent of their time on the air to news reporting. A recent survey showed that the radio was the most important medium of public information for the average Korean. More than 35 percent of the respondents indicated that they relied on radio as their primary source of information. For the respondents with college education, however, the neswpapers ranked first.

Television

Television was not a common household item in 1967 with a total of only 68,497 sets available for 5,118,000 households (1 set for every 74 households). Viewers were limited to Seoul and other urban areas, and a fee was charged for viewing the programs. As a source of public information, television had little significance.

In mid-1967 two television networks were in operation: the government-owned KBS-Television and the Tongyang Television owned by Yi Byŏng-ch'ol. Seoul-based KBS-TV, using the call letters HLCK and a 2,000-watt transmitter, operated on Channel 9. In 1967, it was on the air for approximately 12 hours daily and educational, cultural, and entertainment programs were given much emphasis. News reporting received about 12 percent of the total hours on the air. The Tongyang, though a newcomer, was far ahead of KBS–TV in ratings as of July 1967. It had studios in Seoul and Pusan. In Seoul the Tongyang, using the call letters HLCE, operated on Channel 7. It telecast approximately 11 hours daily and devoted much of its time to educational and entertainment programs. About 12 percent of its time was reserved for news reporting.

Films

The National Film Production Center of the Public Information Ministry was engaged in the making of a small number of newsreel and documentary films every year. The role of newsreels in the dissemination of public information, however, was practically negligible; only a very small percentage (less than 1 percent) of the public was believed to rely on newsreels for public information. In addition, a number of commercial motion picture firms (12 in mid-1967) were engaged in film-making, but the government appeared to play an important role in the film-making through its subsidies and other forms of assistance to the industry.

Motion pictures were the most popular forms of mass entertainment in 1967, and the popular demand for movies appeared to be great. The industry produced more than 100 feature-length films annually, and the quality of films is believed to have risen over the years. Foreign movies, especially American movies, were well received by Koreans, and for the first 10 months of 1967 a total of 51 new foreign movies were shown.

Despite increases made in the number of motion picture theaters in recent years, the film industry appeared to suffer from inadequate permanent facilities for showing films, especially in rural communities. Schools and other public auditoriums were often used for film showings. Outdoor showings were also common, and the government used mobile equipment to carry films to rural areas.

Face-to-Face Contact

Direct, face-to-face contact continued to play a vital part in the dissemination of public information for Koreans. This form of communication appeared to be much more effective than radio and newspapers for the rural people, as the latter media offer abstractions that sometimes are not understood by many villagers. A recent government survey showed that word-of-mouth communication was the major media of information, while the comparable figure for urbanites was significantly lower (7 percent for Seoul). Particularly important in the person-to-person encounters were village elders, local government officials, visitors from cities, and public meeting places such as markets and local inns. Another traditional method still in common use was the public bulletin board, on which announcements and copies of newspapers were posted. Mobile loudspeakers were also an important means of spreading news, ideas, and opinions.

CONTROLS, RESTRAINTS, AND CENSORSHIP

Under the Rhee government a vigorous journalism was much frowned upon by the government, as it was critical of the government as well as of Rhee's Liberal Party. Stringent limitations were imposed by the government on the press and other communication media. Newspapers were often confiscated or suspended. At times, direct physical violence was resorted to against editors and publishers who did not conform to official directions. The Office of Public Information controlled the licensing and censorship of newspapers, magazines, motion pictures, and radio broadcasting. Prepublication copies of newspapers, magazines, and books were supposed to be submitted to the Office for approval, but most newspapers did not wait for this. The Minister of Education controlled copyrights, regulated the importation of books and the licensing of importers, and supervised conformity to the standards of the code for public performances.

In the liberal atmosphere which prevailed immediately after Rhee's fall in April 1960, the stringent controls previously exerted over the press were abolished. In July, Ho's caretaker government passed a law providing for freedom of publication and assembly. Publishers were obliged to register with the government, but the newspaper licensing system which had prevailed under the previous regime was discontinued and censorship was abolished.

In the absence of government regulation, however, standards of journalistic ethics declined. Inaccuracies, distortion, and exaggeration became commonplace, and the practice of criticizing the government in order to attract broader readership grew increasingly prevalent. Moreover, the legitimate press came into disrepute as a result of the infiltration of its ranks by profit-seekers. During the first week alone after the abolition of the press licensing system, some 700 newspapers and news agencies were established.

The assumption of power by the military junta in May 1961 brought an abrupt change in the press situation. The military leaders put into effect a number of emergency measures, including press censorship, and closed down 1,200 newspapers and agencies, virtually all of which had been established since the fall of the Rhee government. Some 700 journalists associated with these newspapers were arrested; 13 of them—all staff members of the pro-Communist news organ *Minjok Ilbo*—were prosecuted, 8 convicted, and 1 executed. Press censorship was ended within two weeks of the military takeover, but publication of material "detrimental to national security" was prohibited. Also, the press licensing system was reinstituted.

The military leaders sought by various means to raise journalistic standards and to improve their relations with the press. The Supreme Council for National Reconstruction reduced tariff rates on imported newsprint, arranged bank loans for a number of publishers, and built a press center where journalists could meet and discuss topics of interest to them. It also encouraged the formation in 1961 of a Korea Newspaper Ethics Commission through which journalists would regulate their own conduct in accordance with a code of ethics drafted by the nation's editors and later ratified by the publishers and news agencies.

The principle of press freedom was upheld in the new constitution, which stipulated that "All citizens shall enjoy freedom of speech and press . . ." and that "licensing or censorship in regard to speech and press . . . shall not be recognized." The constitution further stated, however, that the government reserved the right "to prescribe minimal standards for publications plants and facilities."

Nevertheless, within a little over six months of the promulgation of the new constitution, the administration and the newspapermen were locked in a bitter dispute over the enactment in August 1964 of a new press law, which most journalists regarded as a gross infringement on freedom of the press. Known as the Press Ethics Commission Law, the decree called for the creation of a new Press Ethics Commission to investigate alleged instances of violation of a new code of ethics and to impose punishments prescribed by law. In September President Park decided to "defer" its application indefinitely. At the same time, the nation's publishers and editors decided to create a Deliberation Office which had the power to scrutinize any articles published in the newspaper and to examine printed materials against which complaints had been lodged. It also had the right to demand corrective actions from the newspaper charged with violation of the ethics code. Violations of the code were reported to have decreased markedly following the creation of the Deliberation Office.

In the wake of the so-called Samsŏng smuggling case of 1966 (see ch. 64, Political Dynamics) the administration attempted to enact a mass media ownership control bill designed to curb the growing control by wealthy individuals over communication media. According to the bill, no company was allowed to engage in more than one medium, and anyone on the staff of a communication media company was prohibited from concurrently holding a governmental post. The bill further stipulated that companies and individuals engaged in mass media activities should act "in the best of public interest" and not for interests of any specific individuals or groups. The administration, however, had to shelve the bill because of the strong opposition of the newspaper editors.

In mid-1968 nongovernmental radio and television was under governmental regulation. A broadcaster or telecaster could not operate without a license from the Communications Ministry. Those granted such license were obliged to use the designated airwaves and to conduct their operations in a manner not "detrimental to national security." Nongovernmental radio broadcasting was subject to the broadcasters' own system of censorship. The Broadcasters' Ethics Commission was designed to ensure that broadcasting operations were conducted in the public interest and that minimal standards were maintained. The Commission was empowered to take punitive measures against broadcasters not complying with its rulings. However, the constitution stipulated that "censorship over motion pictures and dramatic plays may be authorized for the maintenance of public morality and social ethics." Television was also subject to this provision. A Film Control Law specified government censorship over films and television. Live television coverage, however, was excluded. The law also required producers of films (including television commercials) to meet certain minimum standards in facilities and equipment.

The government also controlled copyrights. Magazines were subject to a code of ethics prepared by the magazine publishers, and a Magazine Ethics Committee functioned as a nongovernmental censorship organ. The Committee was empowered to take corrective and punitive measures against the magazine publishers not complying with the ethics code. Book publishers were also expected to abide by their own code of ethics formulated in 1965. The Code specified that the primary duty of publishers was to "contribute to the development of arts and sciences, to the educational enlightenment of society, and the enhancement of the people's well being." For this purpose, the publishers were expected to refrain from abusing the constitutional guarantees on freedom of the press and speech, as well as from harming "public interests" in pursuit of private gains. As of 1967, however, the publishers' compliance with the ethics code remained purely voluntary, as no enforcement organ similar to the Magazine Ethics Committee was in existence.

ATTITUDES AND EFFECTIVENESS

A 1965 survey conducted by the Ministry of Public Information suggested that a large majority (over 60 percent) of Koreans regarded the spoken word—specifically, radio and person-to-person contact—as their favored medium of public information. The next largest proportion (approximately 32 percent) felt that the printed word—the newspaper—was their primary medium of information. This finding was corroborated by other similar studies. Television, limited to the wealthy, urban segment of the population, played an insignificant role in the dissemination of public information.

A closer examination of the relative effectiveness of communication media shows that the degree of dependency on the spoken word among Koreans was significantly correlated to the degree of urbanization. The radio as well as communication media based on direct face-to-face contacts appeared to be much more effective in rural communities (towns and subordinate administrative units), with most of the rural population dependent on the spoken word. Less than 25 percent of the rural respondents regarded newspapers and periodicals as their primary information source.

The pattern in the urban areas of the country provided a striking contrast to the rural pattern. In Seoul the newspaper was the most effective medium of information. As of mid-1967 in Seoul there were 151 copies of newspapers for every 1,000 persons, as compared with only 42 copies for Kyŏngsang province. A government survey indicated that approximately 63 percent of the Seoul respondents viewed the newspaper as their main source of information, while about 27 percent relied on the radio. Furthermore, the Seoul respondents' reliance on person-to-person communication media was very small (7 percent). A pattern remarkably similar to the Seoul pattern prevailed in large cities such as Pusan, Taegu, Taejŏn, and Inch'ŏn.

The relative effectiveness of information channels among Koreans varied not only in terms of the level of urbanization but also in terms of sex, educational background, and occupation. The newspaper appeared to be more effective with the male segment of the population than with the female. As for the educational factor, the major channel of communication for Koreans with elementary education (6 years) was the spoken word via community elders, travellers, radio, and local government officials, while most of the college-educated persons regarded the newspaper as their major source of information, and only a small percentage of the educated category relied on the radio. Occupationally, the spoken word—radio and face-to-face contacts—appeared to be the most important media among those engaged in farming and fisheries, while the newspaper was the most effective medium in the category of occupations requiring higher education. The newspaper was popular, particularly among students, doctors, journalists, civil servants, teachers, and white-collar workers.

Although there has been a trend on the part of the newspapers to popularize their editorial contents to appeal to a greater segment of the population, primary emphasis was still placed on the educated, politically alert elements of the populace. Largely because of this, the press failed to reach the majority of the population who found abstract and sophisticated expressions used in the papers difficult to comprehend or who were simply unable to read Chinese characters. On the other hand, the educated Koreans were attracted by the analytical commentaries provided by the press which the radio could not offer. Another factor responsible for the relative ineffectiveness of the radio among the educated public appeared to be the traditional attitude toward the radio. Under Rhee, radio broadcasting was a governmental monopoly and was used by the government as a major means of political indoctrination and persuasion. Accordingly, the radio was not favorably received by the intellectuals. Still in mid-1968, when broadcasting was no longer a governmental monopoly, a significant portion of Koreans shared the traditionally negative view of the radio as an information medium.

GOVERNMENT ACTIVITIES

Agencies

In the Republic of Korea in mid-1968, government information activities rested largely with the Ministry of Public Information. Its function included supervision of dissemination of publications, management of the government-owned radio and educational films, censorship of motion pictures and television programs, dissemination of information on government activities, assessment of national and international opinions, and handling of overseas public relations activities.

The Ministry was headed by a cabinet-rank minister appointed by the President. The minister was assisted by a vice-minister and an Office of Planning and Management. The Ministry was divided into the bureaus of Public Information, Research, Culture and Public Relations, and Radio Management. The Ministry maintained regional information centers throughout the country as well as overseas information offices in several foreign countries. The Ministry also managed a National Film Production Center, a National theater, and a National Classical Music Institute.

Activities

The government subsidized publication of several newspapers and itself published and distributed an array of periodicals, reports, collections of speeches, and other informational materials intended to promote popular understanding of government policy, add support to its anti-Communist position, and promote friendly relations with foreign nations. The government was extensively involved in radio and television broadcasting, operating the country's major network, which had both a domestic and an international service. It distributed a large number of radio loudspeakers and transitor—or battery—operated receivers in rural areas so as to enlarge the listening audience. The government also produced more than 30 different newsreels and other educational-informational films, which were shown throughout the nation.

The basic themes which the Park government has sought to spread among the population through the use of these media have been those of anticommunism, national loyalty and pride, and the need for self-discipline and hard work in the interest of the country's future. To counteract the Communist "peaceful unification" campaign, major emphasis has been placed on stressing the unfavorable features of the Communist system.

Anti-Communist programs reportedly have been stepped up under the Park administration, largely in response to increased espionage activities from the north. During 1967 the government sponsored in 230 different locations anti-Communist lectures by North Vietnamese or Viet Cong defectors in which Communist atrocities were exposed. To strengthen the anti-Communist posture among the students, the government conducted a series of anti-Communist seminars and sponsored a nationwide essay contest on the theme of how to best counteract communism. The Ministry of Public Information authored and distributed anti-Communist educational materials to elementary and middle schools.

Propaganda programs abroad reportedly have also been accelerated under President Park. Important agencies for disseminating information were the overseas information offices established in Japan, the United States, France, and Vietnam, as well as information officers attached to Korean embassies. The Korean Information Office in Washington, D.C., for example, conducted a comprehensive program including maintenance of a library from which requests for information on Korean affairs could be filled, showing motion pictures on various aspects of Korean life, and publication of pamphlets and periodicals generally of an educational nature.

The international service of the Korean Broadcasting System was another arm of the government's foreign information program. Communist elements in the north were the principal target group. Other programs were beamed to North America, Hawaii, Southeast Asia, Europe, Japan, Communist and Republican China, and Soviet Russia.

MATERIALS FROM ABROAD

In mid-1968, the principal non-Communist effort was that supported by the United States, which was carried on chiefly by the United States Information Service (USIS) and its affiliate, the Voice of America (VOA). USIS in South Korea had its headquarters in Seoul and regional offices in Kwangju, Pusan, and Taegu. The information offices maintained collections of books and other visual materials on American history and culture and conducted English language classes for Korean Students. The USIS also sponsored exhibits throughout the country. Over 35 exhibits were seen by an estimated 2 million persons. USIS published and distributed 8,000 copies of Wikuri Rebyu (*Weekly Review*), a Korean-language periodical which dealt mainly with political developments in the non-Communist world, and over 15,000 copies of *Chayu Sege*, the Korean version of *Free World*. It also sponsored a citizenship education campaign and administered an educational exchange program. USIS-prepared newsreels and documentary-educational films were shown at many Korean theaters and school auditoriums.

The government-operated KBS broadcast two 30-minute Korean

language programs daily from its studios in Seoul, which were relayed from the Voice of America in Washington. It also relayed other VOA programs, as did two privately owned stations. VOA broadcasts were believed to be heard by approximately 1.3 million listeners each day, and a large number of other radio programs prepared locally by USIS also were used on various stations.

Communist propaganda appeared to originate largely from the north and from Korean Communist organizations in Japan and consisted principally of radio broadcasts, which the government of the Republic of Korea attempted to block out with its own transmitters. Communist publications from the northern part of the peninsula were banned, but some pamphlets advocating Communist lines were printed clandestinely and others were dropped from balloons launched in the Communist-held territory to the north. Both Radio Moscow and Radio Peking also had Korean language programs. Radio Peking, for example, broadcast a program beamed at Koreans for 14 hours weekly in the mid-1960's.

In the Republic of Korea itself, Communist front organizations were engaged in clandestine distribution of Communist propaganda. According to a recent report, for example, one Communist underground establishment composed of two corporations, a publishing firm and a book store, was uncovered in July 1968. Operating under directives from the Communist government in the north, the organization had been engaged for the past seven years in the clandestine distribution of Communist propaganda in the south through various left-wing oriented organizations and through its own publishing activities. *Chongmaek* was a monthly published by this organization.

CHAPTER 17

POLITICAL VALUES AND ATTITUDES

Traditional authoritarian values are subject to numerous erosive influences. Growing urbanization and industrialization, the high literacy rate, increasing contact with Western nations, and the existence of groups committed to essentially Western values have exerted much impact. As a result, high value is placed on such political principles as individual rights and freedom, popular sovereignty, free elections, and majority rule.

Confucianism, which stresses a hierarchic social order and group values, has been the dominant influence on traditional political values. In Confucian teachings, the relationship between ruler and subjects represents one of the five natural hierarchic relationships and there was little room for Western-type individualism and egalitarianism in past Confucian tradition. Subjects were counted on to defer to the actions and judgments of their ruler, who was not expected to rule benevolently. As a result, the central government was generally viewed with distrust, with most rural people regarding it as a distant, taxing enemy.

Some of these traditional attitudes still prevail, reinforced by the 12-year rule of the Syngman Rhee government. The people's acquiescence in unpopular government policies within reasonable limits contrasts with most Koreans' pride in the nation as a whole; they possess a strong sense of cultural unity and are conscious of belonging to one race, of having one language, of sharing a proud past.

Political values have been shaped principally by the historical past, Confucian legacy, and the nature of the contemporary political environment. In Confucian teachings, government is viewed not as a contractual arrangement between the ruler and ruled, but as a natural institution designed to maintain the proper relationship among men in a hierarchic social order (see ch. 11, Religion; ch. 12, Social Values). Furthermore, government is not based upon law but is regarded essentially as a government of "wise men." The ideal ruler is primarily a teacher able to indoctrinate subjects with the rules of proper conduct. He is also considered a father who looks to the welfare of his people.

The traditional rule during the Yi Dynasty was never absolute, but the role of the individual was not recognized and group needs and values were promoted instead. An individual possessed intense loyalties to the family, clan, and local community. This also was largely in accordance with Confucian teachings, in which respect for individual freedom and Western-type egalitarianism had no place.

Koreans generally tend to defer to their ruler and acquiesce in his policies, even if unpopular. However, when policies go beyond the popular expectation, segments of the population that are adversely affected may rebel. As an example, Syngman Rhee, attempting to rule in the Confucian tradition, engaged in numerous unpopular practices, which were largely accepted until Rhee was overthrown in the wake of the 1960 student uprisings.

During the 36-year Japanese rule, Koreans were excluded from important responsibilities in government; as a result, there was a long intermission in political responsibility and administrative experience.

The Japanese rule did little to inculcate Western liberal values in the Korean people, for it rested on police rule permeating every aspect of an individual's life. The regime of Syngman Rhee, characterized by one-man rule and the subordination of individual values to state needs, also reinforced traditional authoritarian, deferential attitudes. Moreover, the family, the most important shaper of social and political values, has been so strongly entrenched in the Confucian tradition that the head of a family still enjoys an undisputed position of leadership in accordance with Confucian "father-son" subjugation rules. Also, Koreans traditionally tended to equate responsibility with power and regarded it as total and indivisible. The individual saw himself mainly as others saw him—in terms of rank, power, and responsibility. To delegate power or responsibility was in effect to degrade oneself, to take away one's stature as an individual. Thus, traditionally, power was rarely divided or delegated.

This historical legacy and the authoritarian tradition largely explain why many people feel ill-prepared for effective emulation of liberal political principles, even though they are intensely admired. Such Western principles as popular sovereignty, free elections, political rights and freedoms, equality, and separation of governing powers are incorporated into the constitution of the Republic, and most people have demonstrated preference for these principles. A recent government study showed that more than 80 percent of respondents prefer democracy to any other political system, and dislike for communism is intense.

Despite their preference for a democratic system, many people, especially intellectuals and students, entertain serious doubts about the suitability of Western democracy at this time. For example, results of a poll among 377 social science majors indicated that 86 percent thought Western democracy not suitable for Korea because the country was not socially and culturally prepared for such a system. However, there are influential groups strongly committed to liberal values who demonstrated a considerable measure of resilience in opposing some of Rhee's actions.

News media, college professors, students, opposition parties, church organizations, and other institutions of political participation function as important domestic agencies through which liberal political values are inculcated in the people. Even the rural population, still imbued with traditional values, is participating in public politics on a larger scale and with more vigor and intelligence than at any time in their history. Such participation is marked by the growing exercise of individual free will. Furthermore, most people appear to be increasingly optimistic about the prospects for democracy in their country in the foreseeable future.

The Park government has a set of values which it has attempted to implant in the people through control over elementary and secondary schools and government-operated information media. It has increasingly called upon the people for loyalty to the state and to a set of unifying national ideals. Being committed to programs of modernization and to the maintenance of military preparedness against North Korea, the government has accentuated the economic programs and interests of the nation. The Park administration, many of whose members are former military officers, places much emphasis on speedy actions. The opposition, New Democratic Party, regards this practice as running counter to compromise and accommodation and believes that the emphasis of the citizen's civic duties and obligations to the state adversely affects his political freedom and rights.

A considerable discrepancy in political values exists between the politically articulate and liberal urban segment of the population and the rest, especially the rural population, which represents the most tradition-bound segment of the population. However, the Korean conflict and the subsequent social-political upheavals have accelerated the rate of change in the value system. Young and even older sons leave home to earn a living in the city, to obtain an education, or to serve in the army. The increasing entrance of young people into the urban labor force and political activities appears to have enhanced their disenchantment with traditional authoritarian political values, and a good many consider the Confucian value system irrelevant to their contemporary needs.

NATIONAL PRIDE AND POLITICAL IDENTIFICATION

Koreans as a whole take pride in their nation, their landscape, their contributions to the arts and sciences, martial traditions, and national character. Sources of national pride include the phonetic alphabet (*han'gŭ*) invented under the auspices of King Sejong during the Yi Dynasty; movable metal type developed at least 50 years before Gutenberg; celadon pottery perfected during the Koryŏ Dynasty (955–1392); the cultural accomplishments of the Silla Dynasty; Kwangk'aet'o the Great, a martial king of the Koguryŏ Dynasty who repelled invading nomads from the north; Admiral Yi Sun-sin, inventor of the iron-clad turtleship, who fought off Japanese invaders in the 1590's; and, more recently, economic achievements under the Park administration. These accomplishments significantly reinforce Koreans' loyalty to their nation.

There is less pride in the political system. Acceptance of the formal governmental structure as embodied in the constitution is more widespread, and there is less dissatisfaction with it now than at any time since the formation of the Korean Republic in 1948. Great political debates are couched in constitutional terms, and no one seriously suggests that the constitution be ignored or drastically modified. However, the actual practice of politics in the post-independence years has negatively affected feelings about the political system. The major political parties profess support of the constitution, but their actual behavior inside and outside the National Assembly raises some doubts.

Rulers during the latter part of the Yi Dynasty and under the Rhee government rarely governed in a manner expected of a benevolent ruler. The political leaders and the bureaucracy were generally perceived as lacking the necessary caliber, integrity, and sincerity. Furthermore, the manner in which past electoral contests were conducted appears to be responsible, at least in part, for the lack of pride in the political system (see ch. 14, Political Dynamics).

There was also lack of pride in the economic system under the government of Syngman Rhee because of accusations of misuse of foreign aid funds, of malpractice by wealthy individuals, and collusion with government officials. The country's economic progress was seriously retarded (see ch. 18, Character and Structure of the Economy). The lack of opportunity for many younger generation members engendered dissatisfaction with the economic system. Many young people left the country, despite stringent governmental emigration limitations, to seek better opportunities elsewhere. Many students abroad preferred to stay in their host countries upon completing their studies, particularly in the United States.

Koreans, however, increasingly pride themselves on the impressive economic gains and achievements made since 1961 under the Park government. With growing opportunity for young people, there is greater willingness on the part of students to return to their country. At the same time, in an attempt to ease difficulty arising from the discrepancy between large manpower increases and still limited economic opportunity, the Park government has relaxed government restrictions on emigration. Under the new policy, many have emigrated to Colombia, Brazil, and Canada.

Traditionally, the great bulk of the people had little conception of themselves as citizens of a national state, and virtually all formulated their political values mainly on the basis of family, clan, and village identifications. Within the larger society, there was a hierarchy of loyalties so that the individual's responsibility and identification was first to the extended family, the clan, the village, the province, and finally the nation. Loyalty to the extended family and sometimes even to the entire clan superseded personal ambition, and the demands of family loyalty frequently blocked hopes for advancement. The intense identification with the extended family appears to have had profound impact on political styles. An individual who achieved political fame or powerful position in the government was subject to the claims of members of his family, which he could not honorably reject. This situation has frequently led to favoritism in government.

An essentially Western pattern of allegiance to the state is relatively new in Korean experience. The growing identification with the nation appears to have been aided by such factors as the Japanese rule, which in many cases resulted in the breakup of the traditional familial or clan ties, the Korean conflict, and a greater interregional mobility arising from urbanization and industrialization. Also, the political leadership has increasingly called upon the people to identify themselves with the nation and the state and has attempted to implant a set of unifying national political ideals.

ATTITUDES TOWARD THE NATION

Most Koreans possess a strong sense of cultural unity and pride in their nation. Major segments of the population demonstrate much more keen interest in their nation than in their regional community or village. The pride shared by most Koreans in their antiquity and culture is coupled with an abiding attachment to their land, which they consider beautiful, unchanging, and sustaining. Loyalty to the nation, however, is not easily transferred to a central government. Koreans view the division of their country under two mutually inimical governments as unnatural and intolerable; their essential cultural unity overrides whatever diversity may have been created among the Koreans by historical, political, and geographic factors.

At the same time, differences among various regions of the country are reflected in the popular attitudes of the inhabitants. The capital, Seoul, is considered to be the center of all political, social, economic, educational, and cultural activities. Seoul has served as the capital of Korea ever since the latter half of the 14th century. Japanese influence in Korea was strongest in the urban centers of the country, particularly in Seoul and Pusan. Thus, Seoul is also viewed as a Westernized city and is sometimes looked down upon by inhabitants of more traditional towns such as Chŏnju, capital of North Chŏlla Province, which regards itself as more aristocratic.

During the Korean conflict, Seoul changed hands several times. Despite its proximity to the demilitarized zone, it has been kept as the seat of the government, except for a brief period, and has become a symbol of aspiration for unity. The Communist regime in the north also regards Seoul as its true capital, considering P'yongyang to be only a provisional political center. The native inhabitants of Kyŏnggi Province are to be "like a beauty looking in a mirror." People from Ch'ungch'ŏng Province are regarded as courteous and gentle.

Regional prejudices and provincialism were so great that factional political groupings during the Yi Dynasty were formed principally along geographic lines. However, the large-scale migration during the Korean conflict and in subsequent years, maintenance of a large standing army representing all geographical groups of the country, improved transportation and communication facilities, and interregional marriages appear to have had an integrating effect on regional feelings and ancient prejudices.

The government relies on both old and new national symbols to evoke the loyalty of its citizens. Certain national holidays are celebrated with either official or customary sanction. October 3 is celebrated as Tan'gun Day, in memory of the legendary Tan'gun who founded Korea as a nation nearly 2,400 years before the birth of Christ. Widely observed is March 1 (Samil), anniversary of the 1919 declaration of independence from Japan and one of the most important Korean holidays. The most significant holiday is August 15, Liberation and Independence Day, a celebration which honors the 36 years of resistance against, and final independence from, Japanese domination. This day is also celebrated in commemoration of the founding of the Republic in 1948.

Other holidays, especially those of more recent origin, are also observed but they do not evoke the nationalistic feeling associated with traditional holidays. On June 25 the government commemorates the 1950 Communist invasion from the north, and June 6 is set aside as Memorial Day, when tribute is paid to the war dead. July 17 is Constitution Day, commemorating proclamation of the Republic's constitution in 1948. On May 16 the government also celebrates the military coup of 1961.

A host of national heroes are widely honored. Among them are Admiral Yi Sun-sin and An Jun-don, a Korean patriot who assassinated Japanese statesman Ito Hirobumi in 1909 and was executed by the Japanese. Additional national symbols include a national anthem, written by the late composer An Ik-t'ae, and other songs of both ancient and recent origin, including "Arirang" and "Bŏngsŏnwha" (balsam), appear to arouse much emotion on the part of Koreans.

The flag of the Republic of Korea, red and blue on a white background, utilizes ancient symbols borrowed from China. The circle of red and blue in the center, according to Korean interpretation, represents the absolute, the essential unity of everything in nature. The divisions within the circle, the *um* and the *yang*, corresponding to the Chinese *yin* and *yang*, represent the eternal duality within nature—good and evil, male and female, night and day, being and not being. Duality within absolute unity is seen as the paradox of life that forever escapes human comprehension.

The symbolism of the flag is not intended to express any one specific meaning but rather to embrace all the contradictory and varied meanings of the universe and to stimulate the mind in contemplation. The bar designs in the corner, for example, are given many meanings: They are the four points of the compass; the four elements—earth, air, fire, water; the father, mother, sons, and daughters in a family. That there are only two kinds of bars—long and short—arranged in a variety of combinations illustrates the diversity that can issue from basic simplicity. Thus these symbols are capable of endless interpretation.

Educated and politically conscious Koreans frequently think of their country in political terms—as a "shrimp between two whales." They lament that their nation has always been a stepping stone from Japan to China and back again and from Siberia to the south. They complain that their long-civilized country, for centuries a center of culture, repeatedly had to suffer invasions. At the same time, they are very proud that, despite foreign conquests and devastation, the nation has retained its identity and is now only waiting to rise again.

There appears to be a general feeling that the country has not yet come into its own. The defeat of Japan in 1945 aroused great hope and optimism; the Koreans felt that Japan would no longer press hard on Korea and that the country would witness a revival in culture and civilization. This hope was quickly followed by deep disillusionment. Most of the people see the partitioning of the land and the suffering that has followed upon it as having been caused once again by outside interference; it is felt that Korea has again been victimized by foreign powers.

An increasing number of persons, many of them intellectuals, young bureaucrats, military officers, and journalists, believe that continued dependence on the United States is not consonant with national dignity. At the same time, however, those who entertain aspirations of total independence appear to realize that it is in conflict with the country's present condition. They have become apprehensive about the decrease in United States aid because of the fear that cutoff or any drastic reduction of this aid might create a situation conducive to a Communist takeover from the north.

In an attempt to enhance self-respect for the nation, the Park government put forward a new political slogan called "national democracy." It has taken various steps to the attainment of *charip kyŏngje* (self-supporting economy) and the conduct of *chaju woekyo* (independent diplomacy) as prerequisites to the achievement of a national renaissance. The government, for example, has carried on national economic construction and modernization in accordance with developmental plans and has also indicated a desire for a greater voice in the settlement of the Vietnam conflict. As part of the national renaissance movement, it has stepped up its campaigns to revive Korea's classical arts by actively supporting classical musical festivals and encouraging studies of classical arts (see ch. 10, Artistic and Intellectual Expression). Although the national democracy program has not yet captured the popular imagination, the government's efforts to enhance the nation's prestige enjoy wide support among the population.

ATTITUDES TOWARD THE GOVERNMENT

Traditionally, the central government has been regarded by the average Korean as a "distant, taxing enemy," thought to exist largely for the benefit of the rulers. People tend to feel that, ideally, a government should be concerned with the welfare of the people but should not interfere greatly in local and private affairs. Few Koreans, however, appear to expect that those in power will actually govern in a benevolent manner. Most Koreans expect government officials to use their positions for their own advantage.

The negative attitude toward government has been shaped to a significant degree by popular awareness of malpractices in the government, especially before 1961, and to a lesser extent by the individual citizen's unfavorable encounters with petty officials, particularly the police. The traditional slowness with which the private citizen's affairs were handled by bureaucrats also molded the popular view of the government. The new official title of public servants and the decline of authoritarian attitudes have tended to mitigate the bureaucratic practices in recent years, but open expression of criticism by the public has grown and reflects the greater demand for service to the public.

While the institutions of government are viewed with a blend of cynicism, distrust, and fear, most Koreans traditionally expect the government to be the responsible father of the people. It was widely assumed that, if a natural calamity occurred, heaven was laying a curse on the corrupt governing group which was delinquent in looking after the welfare of the people. Thus, in case of a calamity, some official was expected to bear moral responsibility for it and offer his resignation, even though he may have been far removed from the actual incident. This attitude still appears to prevail to a considerable degree.

To the extent that the government has taken concrete steps to improve the general welfare of the people, it has met with approval. As the 1967 presidential and parliamentary elections demonstrated, the desire of the Park government to modernize the country through industrialization, technical training, and resource development finds wide popular support, and members of the opposition New Democratic Party appear to concur with these basic policy goals.

The impressive economic strides of the government are generally regarded by the people as objects of new national pride. However, a number of citizens do not feel that the government's modernization programs are equally beneficial to all segments of the population. For example, a recent study showed that a majority of college professors and journalists surveyed felt that the present governing elite and wealthy businessmen were the primary beneficiaries of the various governmental programs.

To provide for the military defense of the country is another of the important tasks of the government. There appears to be general consensus of opinion on the need for maintenance of adequate military preparedness against a Communist invasion from the north. In mid-1968, however, there was considerable disagreement about approaches to be employed to achieve this objective. The so-called Homeland Reserve Force was one issue on which popular opinion was divided (see ch. 27, The Armed Forces). The ruling Democratic-Republicans supported the government-sponsored Homeland Reserve Force, while opposition was voiced by the New Democratic Party on the grounds that maintaining a 2.5-million-man Homeland Reserve Force would constitute a serious drain on the national economy and that such a force might be used by the ruling party as a political weapon. A government survey indicated that approximately 37 percent of the respondents expressed opposition to the present Homeland Reserve Force for various reasons.

The Confucian deference to rulers and the traditional *kwanjon minpi* (the officialdom exalted and the people downgraded) attitude have long characterized the Korean people, and there appears to be a long-standing tendency for the people to acquiesce in unpopular government actions and policies. Most of the citizens do not feel that they have effective legal recourse. However, many urbanites, the spirited press, the students, and the opposition parties voice vociferous opposition to unpopular policies of the government. Furthermore, even the rural population, whose political significance has increased in recent years, undergoes changes in their traditional political attitudes and is more discriminative in its acceptance of, or acquiescence in, government policies (see ch. 14, Political Dynamics).

SECTION III. ECONOMIC BACKGROUND

CHAPTER 18

CHARACTER AND STRUCTURE OF THE ECONOMY

The Republic of Korea's economy may be generally characterized as a mixed economic system involving both government enterprise and private enterprise. Agriculture is the dominant sector of the economy. In recent years, however, significant structural changes have occurred as a result of comparatively rapid development in manufacturing, mining, transport and electric power while the growth of the agricultural sector has lagged. Also, the relative importance of private enterprise has been enhanced as a consequence of a strong government policy favoring private development.

The economy of the Republic of Korea was adversely affected by the partition of the peninsula into North Korea and the Republic of Korea and the consequent interruption of trade between the two areas. Moreover, the Korean conflict and subsequent tense relations in the area have required that the Republic of Korea maintain very large armed forces, imposing an extremely heavy burden on the economy.

Economic progress in recent years has been substantial. The average annual rate of growth of the gross national product from 1962 to 1967 was over 9 percent. Few countries of the world have experienced such a high growth rate. Among the factors responsible for this rapid economic growth were political stability, stabilization of prices, large inflow of foreign capital, availability of large export markets and, with the exception of 1967, good weather conditions for agriculture.

Notwithstanding this remarkable economic progress, per capita income is still relatively low. Although it has increased somewhat in recent years, the high rate of population increase holds down the growth in per capita income levels, the 1968 level being about $139. Indications of a reduction in the rate of population increase during the 1960's give encouragement that per capita income may rise more rapidly in the future, assuming the high growth rate in gross national product continues.

ECONOMIC DEVELOPMENT UNDER JAPANESE DOMINATION

Starting from an almost exclusively agricultural and handicraft base, the Korean economy underwent considerable industrialization during the period of Japanese domination. Between 1910 and 1930, Japan exploited Korea as a source of raw materials and rice. After 1931, however, Korea became Japan's principal base for expansion on the Asiatic mainland and a producer of significant quantities of industrial goods for home consumption. Communications and transport facilities, hydroelectric stations, and heavy and light industries were rapidly developed. An efficient monetary system was introduced, linked closely with that of Japan and integrated with a financial and banking structure appropriate to Korea's economic development.

Before 1931, agriculture accounted for substantially more than half the gross value of national output. By 1938, it accounted for slightly less than one-half the gross national product—then valued at 3 billion yen (about $855 million). Industry had reached 38 percent; mining and forestry, 5 percent each, and fisheries, about 6 percent. The upward trend continued until 1941, when industrial output exceeded that of agriculture. Even in 1941, however, an estimated 75 percent of the Korean labor force of about 8.9 million still was engaged in agriculture and related activities. None of the other activities, including industry, engaged more than 5 percent of the labor force.

With the exception of the large Japanese estates, where production was primarily destined for export, Korean agriculture was essentially carried on by small farmers. In 1938, there were over 3 million farms, each averaging little over 3 acres. Comprising only about 20 percent of the total land, these farms had to provide most of the food for a rapidly growing population. Methods of cultivation were primitive by Western standards, and the principal component was cheap and plentiful hand labor. One-third of the cultivated area—most of it in what is now The Republic of Korea—usually was double cropped: rice in summer and fall; barley, wheat, or rye in winter and spring.

Rice consistently accounted for more than one-half of the total value of agricultural production, averaging in the 1930's about 150 million bushels annually and accounting for approximately one-third of the total value of Korean exports. Over 40 percent of the rice crop was exported to Japan. To increase the supply of rice available for export, the Japanese consolidated landholdings and rigidly enforced crop collections. As a result, farm tenancy increased from less than 40 percent of all farm households in 1910 to about 75 percent in 1945. During this period land rentals were usually paid in rice; the amount paid averaged about 60 percent of the individual tenant's annual crop. As rice exports increased and the population grew, per capita rice consumption and overall dietary standards declined (see ch. 8, Living Conditions). After 1931, the Japanese imported cheaper and less desirable millet and soybeans from Manchuria, partially to replace declining imports of those products from Korea.

Most of the large industrial plants, including chemical and heavy industry, were concentrated in the north to take advantage of the excellent sources of hydroelectric power and raw materials. The chemical fertilizer plants at Hungnam (in Hamgyong-namdo) were larger than any comparable units in Japan. Industrial plants in the south were generally smaller than those in the north and produced mainly consumer goods. The bulk of the textile industry, however, was located in the south. Before World War II, the textile industry produced less than half of the domestic requirements.

With its long coastline and numerous islands, Korea is favorably situated for a fishing industry. Under the Japanese, this industry reached considerable development. But, beginning in 1939, sardines, which comprised the greater part of the catch, virtually disappeared off the east coast. Although more than 75 percent of the prewar catch was exported, fish and marine products were and still are almost the only source of animal protein for Koreans. Because of inadequate transportation and refrigeration facilities and the great volume of exports, however, consumption of fish and fish products in 1938 was less than one-fifth of the per capita production of over 200 pounds of marine products.

Korean mineral resources, especially iron ore, tungsten, graphite, and coal, were of vital importance to Japan during World War II, but exploitation was pushed beyond economic peacetime limits; mining of marginal ores was heavily subsidized, and mineral production reached heights only possible under wartime conditions.

About 95 percent of Korea's foreign trade was conducted with the Japanese Empire, including that part of China under Japanese domination. The principal Korean exports to Japan were foodstuffs, minerals, and raw silk; Japan shipped textiles, metals, machinery, and metal manufactures to Korea. Throughout most of the period 1910 to 1945, Korean imports from Japan exceeded exports to Japan, chiefly because of capital imports required to develop Korea's resources.

This persistent import surplus was largely offset by the acquisition of Japanese interests in Korean industry and agriculture.

Non-Japanese investment in Korea was insignificant. Nine-tenths of Korean industry was Japanese-owned and Japanese-managed. This circumstance and the requirements of the Japanese war economy did not allow the increasing value of total output to be reflected in any improvement of the economic position of the Korean worker and farmer.

The Japanese also barred Koreans from full participation in the industrial development of their country by reserving managerial and technical posts largely to their own nationals. At the end of Japanese rule, the Korean labor force was made up of a relatively small group of unskilled workers and an overwhelming proportion of peasant farmers and farm laborers but no managers or technicians (see ch. 4, Population and Labor Force). However, a small Korean commercial and professional class had developed, largely trained in Japan and usually oriented toward Japanese ideas.

At the outbreak of World War II, Korea had a sizable capital structure of relatively modern design, including an excellent railroad system, a communications network, chemical and metallurgical industries, and textile factories. The Korean labor force, however, was relatively inefficient; the economy still lacked such basic fuels as bituminous coal and petroleum, and mineral resources and forest reserves were seriously depleted. Agriculture had not kept pace with that of industry in rate of development, and a growing population was exerting increasing pressure on relatively limited food resources.

ECONOMIC CHANGE 1945–1960

Along with making Korea's economy complementary to their own, the Japanese developed north and south into interlocking units. In 1945, the partition—the north under Soviet military occupation and the south under the United States—not only severed the economic and social bonds between Korea and Japan but also tore apart the two complementary parts of the Korean economy. The area north of the 38th parallel retained two-thirds of all Korean industry, 90 percent of the hydroelectric power, and practically all major coal, iron, and mineral deposits, as well as forests. The Republic of Korea was left with two-thirds of the population, 75 percent of the agriculture, and only light industries.

For 3 years after partition economic cooperation between the two regions was essentially limited to the sale of electric power from the north to the south; it was completely shut off by the north in May 1948. In June 1950, the Republic of Korea suffered direct military aggression, and whatever economic gains had been made since 1945 were quickly erased. From 1950 to 1953, a large proportion of the working population was taken into the armed forces. Of the 95 cities with a population of 20,000 or more, 58 suffered major war damage. Throughout the country, 400,000 homes were completely destroyed, and 200,000 were partially demolished. Over 40 percent of all industrial facilities and power-generating stations were damaged. Production declined, and government expenditures, financed chiefly by advances from the Bank of Korea, rose steeply. Total damages amounted to the equivalent of about $1.8 billion, which was roughly equal to the Republic of Korea's gross national product for the year preceding the invasion (1949). Aggravating these dislocations are the approximately 3 million refugees that, from 1945 on, have entered the Republic of Korea.

Inflation was a serious problem not only during the Korean conflict but also for many years after that war. Attempts to control inflation were generally unsuccessful until about 1963. Thereafter, prices rose slightly, but inflation was essentially under control.

Reconstruction was the primary emphasis in the economy during the period 1953 to 1960. Rehabilitation of the railway and other transport facilities and of mining was accomplished. These efforts were greatly strengthened by heavy economic aid from the United States. Despite this assistance the country faced serious economic problems in 1960, including substantial unemployment, a huge trade deficit, large shortages of electric power, and continuing inflation.

RECENT ECONOMIC DEVELOPMENT

Conditions in the Republic of Korea during the period 1963 to 1968 favored relatively rapid economic development. First, the government achieved marked success in bringing a halt to serious inflation (see ch. 25, Banking and Currency). Also, the political situation was stabilized and government leaders adopted certain policies that stimulated development. The government provided attractive incentives for foreign private capital and vigorously promoted export trade (see ch. 23, Foreign Economic Relations). Another basic factor explaining the relatively rapid growth after 1963 is that foreign economic assistance to the Republic of Korea over a period of many years helped the Republic of Korea reach a position by 1963 that enabled the country to move ahead more easily.

The rate of economic progress increased sharply in the period 1963 to 1968. Particularly high growth rates were evidenced in the manufacturing sector (see ch. 20, Industry). A major stimulus for the development of industry was the curtailment of trade with North Korea, since the southern area had historically depended on industrial products of the north. In 1968, chemical fertilizers, formerly obtained from North Korea, were being produced in plants that had been developed in the Republic of Korea, and the country was producing a substantial part of its needs for these vital products. Cement production capacity has been greatly expanded and iron and steel production has risen sharply. A major petroleum refinery using imported crude oil was constructed in 1964, and this facility has since supplied much of the nation's needs for refined products. Other major developments have occurred in the electronics, transportation equipment, and textile industries.

The mining industry has experienced rapid growth in recent years despite the somewhat limited mineral resources base. Production of anthracite coal is the primary mining activity. There is a small production of metallic minerals including tungsten, iron ore, copper, lead and zinc. Production of limestone and kaolin has increased substantially in recent years. Electricity production has greatly expanded during the past few years. A number of new hydro and thermal facilities have been developed substantially augmenting electric power generating capacity.

Transportation is another sector of the economy that has grown relatively rapidly (see ch. 22, Domestic Trade). Rail and highway transport has experienced a particularly high rate of growth.

Agriculture has developed at a much slower rate than the overall economy (see ch. 19, Agriculture). Expansion of farm acreage has proved very difficult since nearly all of the available land has been under intensive cultivation for many years. Some land has been reclaimed but increases in farm output have come largely from modest increases in productivity of existing farms. The forests of the Republic of Korea have yielded some products despite serious depletion of forests. In recent years a reforestation program has helped to restore some of the lost forest resources. Considerable timber must be imported.

The fishery resources are being rapidly developed. Not only are the local waters supplying large quantities of fish but also a Republic of Korea deep-sea fishing industry has been created.

The Republic of Korea's export trade expanded an average of about 42 percent per year from 1962 to 1967. An increasing percentage of total exports has been represented by manufactured goods. Imports have also risen sharply during recent years, and the trade deficit has widened. The United States and Japan have been the principal trading partners (see ch. 23, Foreign Economic Relations).

A breakdown of the gross national product shows the predominance of agriculture, forestry, and fisheries (forestry and fisheries contribute relatively small proportions of this sector's product) (see table 12). Manufacturing ranks second while wholesale and retail trade constitute the third major sector.

Agriculture, forestry and fisheries, which accounted for about one-third of the gross national product, employed almost two-thirds of the labor force. By contrast, manufacturing, which contributed 16.4 percent of gross national product, represented only 8.7 percent of total employment.

Table 12. Percentage Breakdown of the Gross National Product in the Republic of Korea, 1967

Sector of product origin	Percent of gross national product
Agriculture, forestry, and fisheries	32.8
Manufacturing	20.5
Wholesale and retail trade	16.4
Services	7.1
Public administration and defense	4.6
Transportation, storage, and communication	4.5
Construction	3.9
Ownership of dwellings	3.0
Rest of the world	2.2
Mining and quarrying	1.8
Electricity, water, and sanitary services	1.6
Banking, insurance, and real estate	1.6
Total	100.0

Source: Adapted from Republic of Korea Government sources.

FOREIGN ECONOMIC ASSISTANCE

The purpose of the economic assistance provided before 1957 was largely for relief and reconstruction. Thereafter, the assistance was primarily directed toward fostering economic development. Accordingly, much of the aid has been channeled into importation of capital goods, development of the mining industry, expansion of electric power plants, development of fertilizer plants, and establishment or enlargement of other productive facilities.

Since 1945, the government of the Republic of Korea has received over $4 billion of economic assistance, very largely from the United States. Most of this assistance has been provided in the form of grants-in-aid, but in recent years increasing proportions of the total have been in the forms of loans. During the 10 years beginning in 1958 the level of the economic assistance from the United States has declined.

In recent years, economic progress in Korea has been substantial. Undoubtedly, the large amount of foreign assistance received over the years was a major factor enabling the country to achieve this progress. It has been suggested that the economy of the Republic of Korea is approaching a "take-off" stage of development. The growing strength of the economy is indicated by the fact that, as foreign assistance in recent years has declined, the economy has moved forward impressively. In this same period a substantial inflow of private capital has occurred, contributing notably to the development of the country.

ECONOMIC DEVELOPMENT PLANS AND POLICIES

A basic objective of the Government of Korea in its development plans and programs is to strengthen the industrial sector of the economy. Through these concentrated efforts the government is attempting to bring about major structural changes in the economy that will reflect a lesser dependence on the agricultural sector.

Fiscal and monetary policies are important factors affecting the ability of the country to achieve substantial economic progress. Maintenance of overall price stability is a major objective of the government. Having recently experienced relatively good economic growth during a period of comparative price stability has no doubt impressed government leaders with the importance of controlling inflation.

Another basic policy adopted by the Republic of Korea's government is encouraging the inflow of private investment capital. Various steps have been taken to improve the climate for foreign investment, including the enactment in 1967 of the Foreign Capital Inducement Law. This law provides no minimum ownership requirements, nor does it limit profit and dividend remittances.

Strong promotion of export trade is another important policy of the government. In various ways export industries are provided governmental assistance. Among these measures are preferential credit rates, exemption from custom duties on imported raw materials and components, and selective subsidies.

The First Five-Year Plan, 1962–1966, incorporated the objective of achieving an average annual growth rate significantly higher than had been attained in previous years. The gross national product was to increase an average of 7.1 percent per year during the five-year period. Actually, the rate realized was 8.3 percent, substantially better than had been expected. The manufacturing segment showed a particularly high rate of growth, and foreign trade rose much more rapidly than had been anticipated under the plan.

The Second Five-Year Plan, 1967–1971, contemplated a 7 percent average rate of increase in gross national product. Particularly high rates of growth were established for the manufacturing sector, notably in chemicals, machinery, and iron and steel. Ambitious export goals were also set in the plan. During the first year of operations under the Second Five-Year Plan, the principal targets were exceeded except in the field of agriculture where adverse weather conditions seriously limited crop harvests.

CHAPTER 19

AGRICULTURE

Agriculture is the largest sector of the economy measured in terms of either the number of people engaged or the contribution to gross national product. While cultivation of crops constitutes the principal activity in the agricultural sector, stock-raising and sericulture are other activities of lesser consequence. Forestry is closely related to agriculture, and fishing is, to a considerable extent, a side occupation of many farmers.

Agriculture, forestry, and fishing represented 32.8 percent of gross national product in 1967, a substantially larger percentage than that for any other sector of the economy. Nearly two-thirds of the persons employed in the country were engaged in these activities.

The Republic of Korea does not produce all of its food requirements, but the proportion of total food consumption that is produced within the country has been increasing. A goal of the First Five-Year Plan, 1962–1966, was for the Republic of Korea to become self-sufficient in foodstuffs, but this target was not achieved. Again in the Second Five-Year Plan, 1967–1971, self-sufficiency in food was established as a major goal. To accomplish this goal, however, sizable wheat imports will have to be eliminated or offset by food exports.

Expansion of production in the agricultural sector has been relatively slow for several reasons. Government policies have emphasized industrialization rather than agricultural development. Through government actions, increases in prices of agricultural products have been minimized and the availability of credit has been limited. At the same time, opportunities for expanding agricultural lands are inherently very restricted.

LAND USE AND DEVELOPMENT

Throughout the country soils have been intensively cultivated for centuries. As a result, continued application of large amounts of fertilizer is essential to maintain satisfactory levels of productivity. Agriculture is widespread in the country but is generally concentrated in the numerous small river valleys and narrow coastal plains. Moderate slopes of the many hills and low mountains are also cultivated.

Regional variations of climatic conditions are very significant for agriculture. The relatively heavy precipitation and high temperatures of the southern and southwestern areas are very advantageous for agriculture, particularly for rice cultivation. Farther north, the lower temperatures, lesser rainfall and shorter growing season make agriculture somewhat less productive.

There are four agricultural regions. First, the west coast, which is the most important agricultural area, consists of basins of varying sizes. Rice is the dominant crop, and the climate permits one rice crop and a winter barley crop. Second, the south coast, which enjoys the mildest climate in Korea, is also a major rice-producing area but, in addition, cotton and other crops requiring a mild climate are produced. Third, the east coast is a narrow coastal strip, where rice is grown in paddy fields: barley, millet, and other crops are grown on the higher land. Here, the growing season permits only one crop per year. Fourth, the central interior, is largely mountainous, and agriculture is restricted to the valleys and lower slopes. Farmers live on isolated farms rather than in villages, as in the rest of the country. Fast-maturing varieties of rice are grown in the valley bottoms, but millet and barley are the most important of the cereal crops.

Approximately 22 percent of the land area is arable, and about 68 percent is forested or suitable for forests, 10 percent for other use. The remainder of the land includes areas used for farm building sites, urban development, and roads, while a small portion is wasteland. Over half of 5.7 million acres of cultivated area is paddy lands and upland. The percentage of total land devoted to agriculture has been increasing slowly, largely through land reclamation projects.

Some uplands and tidelands have been reclaimed under government programs. The Ministry of Agriculture and Forestry has proposed that nearly a million acres of upland and wastelands be brought under cultivation over a 5-year period.

The agricultural benefits of additional land brought into cultivation through these programs will be partially offset, of course, by acreage taken out of cultivation to accommodate space needs for housing, schools, roads, industrial plants, and other developments as the population grows.

Substantial rice paddy areas are irrigated, and the irrigation facilities have been expanded in recent years. Installation of pumping facilities and wiers and the construction of reservoirs have resulted in an increased percentage of rice paddies being irrigated.

LAND TENURE

Since 1945, a number of land reform programs have been instituted in the Republic of Korea. The net effect of these programs has not been great; large holdings have again become concentrated in the hands of relatively few owners, and many of the small farmers have slipped back into tenancy.

In March 1948, the American military governor, General William F. Dean, directed the transfer of a large portion of Japanese landholdings to the newly established National Land Administration, for sale to Korean farmers, with a limit of 2 chungbo (1 chungbo equals 2.45 acres) per purchaser. That phase of the program was completed by the end of United States control in mid-August 1958.

The newly established government of the Republic of Korea then began to take steps to distribute the remaining Japanese holdings and also to break up the large, private Korean landholdings that were being established. Appropriate legislation was not enacted until the end of 1949, however, and the outbreak of the Korean conflict in June 1950 spurred the government to implement the program. It purchased all land not farmed by owners and all holdings in excess of 3 chungbo, but certain exemptions from the law, allowed at the discretion of the government, permitted Republic of Korea landlords to buy additional large tracts. The net effect of the land reform program has been great. Only a few large holdings exit, and few farmers have slipped back into tenancy.

By August 1951, about 1.5 million farmers had received about 1.6 million acres of land, for which they were to pay in farm products over a 5-year period. According to official data, 78.5 percent of the farms in 1953 were under 1 chungbo, 16 percent were between 1 and 2 chungbo and 4.2 percent were 3 or more chungbo. Data for 1965 indicate a decrease in the smaller holdings and an increase in the larger ones.

While average holdings are small, even by Korean standards, it is unlikely that they will be split further, since in Korea, unlike in most other Asian countries, the land is generally inherited intact by the first-born son. But even in the absence of newly rising tenancy, this tradition has had the effect of driving many young men without hope for land to the city and of swelling the ranks of the unemployed there without, however, appreciably relieving overpopulation in the countryside (see ch. 4, Population and Labor Force).

To recompense landlords for land given up, the Government of the Republic of Korea gave preferential treatment to small landlords by paying compensation, consisting of negotiable government bonds, on the principle of progressive diminution—the greater the landholdings, the smaller the compensation. The bonds were redeemable over a 5-year period, and payment was calculated on the current price of the principal crop. In view of the steeply rising price level, the arrangement stimulated inflation. The government, moreover, subsidized land distribution by buying land at 150 percent of the annual value of the principal crop and by distributing it at 125 percent. This imparted another upward push to the price level, especially since legislative efforts to restrict the investing of bond proceeds in industry were defeated. The new owners of former Japanese lands, however, did not have the right to sell until after they had paid for them and until at least 10 years had elapsed since the contract date. The limitation was meant to develop independent new landholders and to prevent indebtedness, which would undo the desirable effects of the land redistribution.

Despite these provisions, strong inflationary pressures on small holders since the end of the Korean conflict have produced a new trend toward centralization of landownership. In the process of making good on their debts, a few small holders again have lost the titles to their land. Apparently, the small farmer in most cases stays on as tenant of the land he formerly owned.

ORGANIZATION AND OPERATION

The structure of farming communities differs among regions of the country. The plains areas support the largest and most closely integrated communities. Farmhouses are typically grouped in a compact village, surrounded by fields and usually close to a stream or river. Irrigation in Korea traditionally entails intervillage cooperation in the use of water.

There are plainslike communities in the river valleys of the uplands, but the quality and quantity of arable soil is less in the mountains, and the villages become smaller, the houses more widely spaced. In the mountainous areas, the houses are scattered about the fields, occupied by single family units, and are not banded together in villages. Some "fire-field" cultivators, or *hwajonmin*, travel in bands of one or two families. They burn forest slopes or trees and underbrush, grow crops as long as the soil remains fertile, and then move on. This type of cultivation is extremely inefficient and creates serious erosion conditions. The Republic of Korea government has estimated the area under "fire-field" cultivation at between 122 and 147 thousand acres.

The village is a cooperative unit in which transplanting, weeding, and harvesting are done collectively. The habit of working in company with other villagers is a major feature of Korean farm life, contrasting with the farm life pattern in China and Japan where the farmer works alone or in a small family group.

Traditionally, each unit of six or seven adjacent families in the village has a chief—the *panjang*. As the rest of the villagers, he is a farmer, but at harvest time he receives from each family a portion of the rice crop for his services of disseminating information from local government units, supervising community activities, collecting "voluntary contributions," and representing his group before the *myon* (township) officials. A *kujang*, or district chief, supervises the distribution of irrigation water and calls out the villagers to clean the ditches several times a year. None of these village officials has a fixed term of office; they are recallable by the community.

Under the Japanese, the *panjang* was required to supply a certain number of "volunteers" for work on roads, construction projects, schools, etc. This type of local organization and the demands made upon it have remained relatively unchanged in the Republic of Korea since 1945.

Farm work is done with simple tools and implements, either handmade or manufactured, and involves a large amount of manual labor in all phases of cultivation. The land is not allowed to lie fallow. There is intensive application of compost and fertilizer, largely of human origin, since there is little dairying. Use of chemical fertilizer has been increasing rapidly in recent years. The cycle of work performed by the farmer is complicated and involves diverse operations. Even the smallest holdings may consist of several types of land—paddy and dry field—so that the tendency is to grow five or more different crops in one season. The land on a farm is subdivided in many tiny plots, near enough to one another to allow the farmer to go from one to the other in the course of a day's work. The amount of manual labor required from early spring to late fall leaves the farmer very little leisure time. During the off season, the farmer devotes his time to cottage production to supplement his income (see ch. 20, Industry).

A substantial part of the farm output is consumed on the farm or is used for bartering purposes. Less than half of the rice production in 1964 entered into commercial channels.

While there remains considerable potential for improving agricultural productivity, some progress has been made. The fact that food production has been increasing at a more rapid rate than population is encouraging.

Among the factors responsible for the increased food production are expanded diffusion of improved seeds, distribution of pesticides, encouragement of double-cropping, and reduction of fertilizer prices, and increase in the cultivated land.

AGRICULTURAL PRODUCTION

Principal Agricultural Products

Rice is the major crop in the Republic of Korea, the production ratio of rice to all other grains being more than two to one (see table 13). Over half the total cultivated acreage is devoted to rice and more than half the rice paddies are provided with controlled irrigation facilities.

Table 13. *Volume of Grain Production in the Republic of Korea, 1960–1966*
(in thousands of metric tons)

Grain	1960	1961	1962	1963	1964	1965	1966
Paddy rice	4,169	4,715	4,105	5,117	5,385	4,767	5,555
Barley	1,054	1,141	1,078	306	1,174	1,424	1,565
Wheat	139	151	145	66	166	162	231
Millet and sorghum..	87	106	108	115	120	100	122
Corn	14	16	18	20	35	40	43
Other	36	37	36	22	34	36	40
Total	5,499	6,166	5,490	5,646	6,914	6,529	7,556

Source: Adapted from U.S. Department of Agriculture, Economic Research Service, *The Far East and Oceania Agricultural Data Book*, May 1967, p. 22.

Except for the roots, the entire plant is used—kernels as food and hulls as fuels, fertilizer, packing material, and as a source of cellulose for rayon. Most farmhouses have roofs thatched with rice straw.

When rice bags, which are made of rice straw, are worn out, they are used mostly for compost. Rice straw is also turned into rope, chopped to mix with livestock feed, and used for making hats, sandals, raincoats, brooms, baskets, and bricks. And, if not usable otherwise, rice straw is used for manuring.

The practice of double cropping—planting a second crop on the rice paddy fields in the fall for harvest before shoots are transplanted from seed beds—has made barley the second most important food crop primarily as a staple food among the poorer classes. It is also used for various cakes and candies.

Wheat competes to some extent with barley as a second crop in rice fields, but its longer period of growth may put harvesting into the rice transplanting season. Wheat has been important in distilling spirits and in the interwar years was exported to Japan for beer brewing.

Millet is an important grain since it takes up less acreage than barley. When Korean farmers can not afford to eat rice or barley, they eat millet.

Aside from grains, the most important crops are vegetables for the Korean national dish, *kimch'i* (see ch. 8, Living Conditions). Almost every farm has its garden of celery, cabbage, radishes, and other ingredients for *kimch'i*. Fruit growing is of relatively lesser importance, but orchards have been developing rapidly in recent years.

Tobacco, ramie, hemp, mulberry trees for sericulture, ginseng, and cotton are grown. A few farmers raise cotton every other year to meet family needs for padding winter clothing. While homespun cotton is still made in some parts of the country, manufactured cotton of finer quality is usually purchased for clothing (see ch. 20, Industry).

Cocoon-raising is an important subsidiary for Korean farmers and is a major source of cash income for many. Before World War II, about 800,000 farm families were engaged in silkworm production, and about two-thirds of the production took place in the Republic of Korea. After a temporary decline in mulberry tree acreage in the post-war years, silk production in the south, judging from increased exports of raw silk and silk waste, appears to be regaining its importance (see ch. 23, Foreign Economic Relations).

Ginseng, used primarily in root form and highly valued as a restorative or aphrodisiac throughout the Far East, grows chiefly in the mountainous areas and constitutes another source of income for farmers.

Several types of livestock are raised in significant numbers, but livestock does not in general play a major role in agriculture. The cattle in the country are used very largely as beasts of burden, although some milk cows are present near major cities. Chickens and rabbits are important among the livestock. Fish rather than livestock provide the major animal protein in the diet of the Korean people.

Production Trends

Agricultural production, which constituted about one-third of the Republic of Korea's gross national product in 1967, has increased moderately since the end of the Korean conflict. Production of rice, representing approximately half of total agricultural production, has increased (see fig. 7). Rice production reached 5.6 million tons in 1966. As indicated in the chart, the years 1956, 1962, and 1965 were comparatively poor years as a result of adverse weather conditions. In addition, 1967 was a relatively poor year for agriculture as a consequence of the worst drought in 70 years.

Barley production increased very little between 1954 and 1964. A substantial drop took place in 1963 as a result of typhoon and disease. Production increases in 1965 and 1966 were relatively

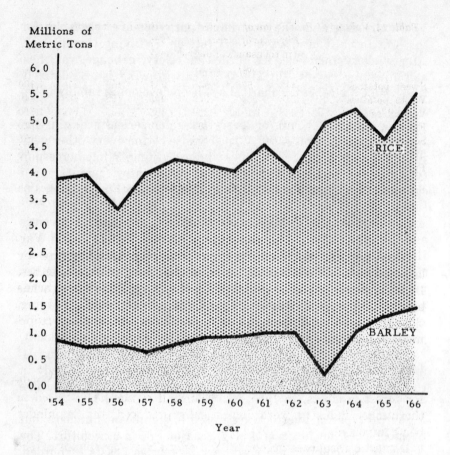

Millions of
Metric Tons

RICE

BARLEY

'54 '55 '56 '57 '58 '59 '60 '61 '62 '63 '64 '65 '66

Year

Source: U.S. Department of Agriculture. Economic Research Services.
The Far East and Oceania Agricultural Data Book, ERS-Foreign
189, Washington: GPO, May 1967, p. 22.

Figure 7. Rice and barley production in the Republic of Korea, 1954–1966.

large, but a decline of about 5 percent occurred in 1967. Other
grains, which together account for much less tonnage than barley,
have increased in production over the past decade.

The volume of production between 1960 and 1966 increased not
only for rice and barley but also other types of grains (see table
14). Wheat is the third leading grain in the Republic of Korea, and
production has increased relatively sharply. Corn, millet, sorghum,
and other grains have also increased in production. Nevertheless,
wheat has been imported in substantial quantities.

Potatoes, particularly sweet potatoes, have increased sharply in
output since 1960. Production of other food products has grown
more modestly. Among the principal non-food products, tobacco
has shown the greatest increase in production.

Table 14. Volume of Production of Selected Agricultural Commodities in the
Republic of Korea, 1960–1966
(in thousands of metric tons)

	1960	1961	1962	1963	1964	1965	1966
Sweet potatoes	443	526	645	787	1,485	1,679	1,700
White potatoes	316	347	309	293	428	436	440
Vegetables	1,088	1,191	1,300	1,187	1,436	1,576	1,600
Fruit	166	155	195	178	229	310	320
Soybeans	130	165	156	156	163	174	175
Tobacco	29	32	35	29	49	56	66
Pulses	20	24	24	24	26	26	26

Source: Adapted from U.S. Department of Agriculture, Economic Research
Service, *The Far East and Oceania Agricultural Data Book*, May 1967,
p. 22.

Domestic production of foodstuffs has been supplemented by
large imports of food grains, principally from the United States.
Dependence on imported grains, with the exception of wheat, has
been declining as agricultural production has improved. However,
the sharply reduced production in 1967 caused by severe drought
made it necessary to import about 680,000 tons of grains.

Forest Products

Forest resources are not sufficient to supply the country's needs
for forest products. In 1965, less than half of the logs utilized in
the lumber industry were domestically produced, the remainder
being imported.

Domestic resources accounted for only about one-fourth of the
pulp consumed by the local populace. In the past, wanton cutting of
the forest for fuel and other purposes greatly reduced the magni-
tude of the forest resources.

In recent years the cutting of the forest has been controlled, and
in 1962 a program of reforestation was initiated. Since that time
many thousands of acres have been reforested. The principal forest tree, *pinus desiflora*, is very hardy and regenerates prolifically
so that, given adequate protection, the forest could be restored at
minimal cost. Reforestation of forests is important not only to provide a basis for supply of forest products but also to prevent flood
damage.

AGRICULTURAL ECONOMICS

Cooperative Associations

In the Korean countryside various types of communal and cooperative associations have a long tradition. Of outstanding importance today is the National Agricultural Cooperatives Federation
and Member Cooperatives, which includes both irrigation and

financial associations. Up to July 1961, this agency was the Agricultural Bank and before that, up to April 1956, the Federation of Financial Associations (FFA) and Member Associations. Generally, the Korean cooperatives have been severely limited by lack of capital and credit and, in addition, often manipulated for private gain. The Park government, however, reorganized the cooperatives in 1961 and greatly increased the budget of the newly established Federation.

In May 1956, the Republic of Korea State Council established the Agricultural Bank to assume the financial functions of the FFA, which was liquidated over a 3-year period. The Agricultural Bank also took over the distribution of fertilizer. The subsidiary financial associations of the FFA were converted into credit associations, and a system of agricultural cooperatives was established. Cooperative associations, part of a new National Cooperative Association of Agricultural Cooperative Associations, were formed as follows: *ri* (commonly consisting of 5 to 10 villages); *tong* (single uplands village); *kun* (county), or *ku* (ward of a city), agricultural cooperative associations; horticultural cooperative associations; livestock cooperative associations; and special cooperative associations.

The *ri* or *tong* associations are to assist in establishing and carrying out individual farm plans or an overall plan for the *ri* or *tong*; purchase materials jointly; market products; utilize community facilities for processing, storage, and medical care; give mutual help in the event of congratulatory ceremonies or funeral services; provide mutual insurance against effects of disasters; and support credit operations involving the collection of deposits, the making of loans, and the mediating necessary in procuring farm loans. The city associations, operating in a wider area, were assigned correspondingly wider responsibilities, including the establishment of rural industries.

In 1961, the government brought about the merger of the Agricultural Bank and the Agricultural Cooperative Association, forming the National Agricultural Cooperatives Federation and Member Cooperatives. Administrative changes included the establishment of 21, 250 *ri* associations designating the leadership and issuing "a clear-cut statement on the line of command." Functions of the associations included the distribution of fertilizer and insecticides to farmers either through sale or on credit. The government has subsidized the associations heavily since the reorganization in 1961, and associations have supplied farmers with over a million tons of fertilizer per year. Prices of chemical fertilizers were reduced from 10 to 15 percent in January 1967 to encourage increased agricultural production.

Agricultural Credit

The National Agricultural Cooperative Federation has been a primary source of agricultural credit. It has obtained its funds primarily from the Bank of Korea, savings deposited in the Federation and purchasers of Federation bonds.

Agricultural credit in the Republic of Korea has been characterized by small sizes of typical loans and short periods for repayment. The limited availability of agricultural loans and the short periods for which loans are provided reflect the government's general economic policy to emphasize development in non-agricultural sectors of the economy.

Irrigation Associations

In the rice bowl area, where large-scale irrigation projects are indispensable, irrigation associations have had formal status since 1906 through a series of laws and decrees. These were reorganized in 1961, and the 695 irrigation associations were reduced to 198 Land Improvement Associations under the principle of one such association for each county.

Considerable importance is attached to the work of these associations in raising the agricultural productivity of the Republic of Korea. At least half of the total area under rice cultivation has already been provided with controlled irrigation facilities, and a sizable increase in such facilities is planned for the next several years.

Marketing of Agricultural Commodities

Traditionally, farm produce has been sold to middlemen who frequently have had a monopolistic position. The farmers are generally forced by circumstances to sell their produce immediately after harvesting and, as a consequence, the prices tend to be low. Moreover, the government has traditionally favored low prices for food products as a means of holding down the cost of living. In 1967, however, the government enacted the Agricultural Price Stabilization Act under which the government would purchase large quantities of grain in the harvest season and release it in the off-season, thereby stabilizing prices through the year.

Agricultural commodities constitute an important part of the export trade of the Republic of Korea. In 1967, agricultural exports accounted for about 20 percent of the total. Silk, rice (in years of good harvest), and live hogs are the major items. While the country exported 40,000 tons of polished rice in 1966, there were no exports in 1967. Imports of rice totaled over 40,000 tons in 1967, while imports of all grains reached over 680,000 tons.

Burden of Interest, Rents, and Taxes

The farmers of the Republic of Korea are heavily burdened by high interest rates, rents, and taxes. Since per capita productivity of farmers is low, the available income to bear these burdens is extremely limited. As a result, the level of the farmers' debts has increased. Between 1956 and 1964, farmers' debts in the Republic of Korea increased nearly fivefold. Some attempt to alleviate this condition was made by the government in 1961, but the level of debt was still rising in 1966.

FISHERIES

The fishing waters adjacent to Korea are among the best in the world. Not only are the fish abundant but there is also a wide variety of species. Fish provide most of the protein in the Korean diet and also constitute the basis for considerable export trade.

The share of the gross national product originating in the fisheries sector is only 1.1 percent, but 4.6 percent of the people obtain income from the industry. Inshore fishing operations are generally small scale, with draft of very limited size being used, few of which are motorized. When the Japanese departed in 1945, they took with them practically all of the offshore fishing fleet. In recent years, the government of Korea has encouraged, through financial assistance, the building of motorized fishing vessels for coastal fishing. The Korean Fishery Cooperatives have taken the lead in the construction of fishing vessels.

The development of improved fishing vessels has been one of the major factors accounting for increased productivity in the fishing industry. Installation of radios in boats and the acquisition of new nets and other fishing gear have also helped to raise productivity in the coastal fisheries. Despite these improvements the coastal fishing industry is greatly in need of modernization. At the beginning of 1953, the fishing fleet consisted of nearly 44,000 vessels with a gross tonnage of 159,000 tons. Only 8 percent of these were power boats, but they accounted for 45,000 tons, or 29 percent, of the total gross tonnage. The size of the fleet has expanded substantially since that time. By the end of 1966, the number of motorized ships had increased to 8,884, representing a gross tonnage of 160,500 and constituting about two-thirds of the total fleet in terms of tonnage.

Deep-sea fishing began in 1957, and has grown rapidly. These operations are organized on a large-scale basis by Korean business concerns. Early in 1967, there were 150 modern fishing vessels engaged in operations in three oceans. The principal fishing grounds are in the vicinity of Samoa, and Santo, in the Pacific; Durban in the Indian Ocean; and Monrovia, Freetown, Las Palmas, Port of Spain and St. Martin in the Atlantic Ocean. All of the deep-sea catch, which consists largely of tuna, is exported.

The government has recognized deep-sea fishing as a promising export industry and has provided considerable financial assistance to aid in its development. Economic assistance from the United States government and foreign private investment capital have been major forces contributing to the rapid growth of the Korean deep-sea fishing industry. The future of the industry depends in large part on ability to obtain additional capital for expansion and on international management of fishing resources.

Total production of the fisheries industries has increased substantially in recent years. During the period 1963–1967, the total fish catch (excluding the deep-sea catch) increased from 25,075 to 440,910 tons, or nearly 20 percent per year. Among the principal types of fish caught are cuttlefish, anchovy, yellow corvina, hairtail and saury.

Approximately 70 percent of the catch is either consumed directly or crushed into fish meal and fish oil. Pressed fish meal is produced by small factories using simple processing methods and is used as fertilizer. Ground fish meal is used for animal fodder. While traditional methods of preserving local marine products, such as drying, salting, and smoking still prevail in the country, a small amount of these products are canned, primarily for export. Virtually all of the catch from deep-sea fishing is canned and exported. In 1966, marine products represented 14.7 percent of total exports.

Prices of fisheries products are subject to wide fluctuations because of seasonality of production and the limitations of fish preservation capabilities. Development of new ice-making plants is helping to alleviate the problem of price instability.

The role of government with regard to fisheries has been important in several respects. The government has made funds available to the Korean Fishery Cooperative to aid in the building of modern fishing boats. Substantial government loans have been made to encourage the expansion of the deep-sea fishing industry.

A basic contribution of the government has been to protect the rights of Koreans to fish in international waters in the vicinity of Korea. After years of controversy over fishing rights in this area, The Republic of Korea and Japan signed an agreement on June 22, 1965, clarifying those rights. This important agreement provided that each nation had the right to establish a fishery zone extending 12 miles from its coastline and over which it would exercise exclusive jurisdiction. In addition, a joint control zone was established, within which nationals of both countries could engage in fishing. Control measures were to be enforced on fishing activities within this latter zone. A Joint Fisheries Commission was created to supervise operations under the agreement.

AGRICULTURE AND SOCIETY

While the agricultural people of the Republic of Korea adhere strongly to traditional farming practices, they nevertheless seek improvements in their economic condition. To some extent economic advancement of the farmer is hindered by a reluctance to change traditional farming practices. A more fundamental deterrent to raising farm income per capita, however, is the limited opportunities for further development of agricultural resources in view of the present intensive utilization of the country's arable land and the very large number of people engaged in agriculture. Recognizing these limitations, many younger people are moving to the cities in search of better opportunities.

The government, through various policies and programs, has concentrated its attention on economic development in non-agricultural sectors. Thus, the government has been responsible to a considerable degree for the relatively slow progress in the agricultural sector. The prevailing attitude toward agriculture as an occupation is one of disdain. Farming involves much hard work and little economic reward. The low social and economic status of farming probably explains in part the tendency for many young people to migrate from the farm to the city.

CHAPTER 20

INDUSTRY

Industrialization in Korea had its beginnings during the Japanese occupation (1910–1945). However, under the Japanese it was directed toward linking Korea's economic capabilities with Japan's needs and not toward creating a balanced and self-sufficient industrial complex in Korea itself. The industrialization process deteriorated when Korea was partitioned after the end of World War II. Most of the heavy industry (including mining, power generation, and the production of steel, cement, and fertilizer) was located in the north, while light industry—in particular, textiles —and agriculture were located in the south. Before the Republic of Korea was able to develop its own balanced industrial capability, the Korean conflict devastated a large part of the country's existing industrial capacity.

After the Korean conflict the economic infrastructure and production facilities of the economy were rebuilt with the help of foreign aid, and during the period of the First and Second Five-Year Plans (1962–1971) industry became the most rapidly expanding sector of the economy. During the First Five-Year Plan, major investments in the manufacture of cement and fertilizer made the country largely self-sufficient in these essential goods; an oil refinery was established for the first time to process imported crude oil for domestic needs; the iron- and steel-making capacity was expanded and the power-generating capability was greatly augmented. Furthermore, there were large increases in both capacity and production of textiles, plywood, chemicals, plate glass and glass products, food processing, machinery, and electric and electronic appliances. The further industrialization of the economy is continuing into the Second Five-Year Plan. Emphasis is being placed on a major expansion of iron- and steel-making capacity, the development of a petrochemical industry, the institution of an aluminum reduction plant, and the further expansion of other industries. Efforts will also be directed to integrating the total industrial complex into a better-functioning whole, and particular attention will be paid to the small and medium-sized industries.

ROLE OF INDUSTRY

For the last several years, industry has been the most dynamic sector of the economy. While the output of industry is still less than that of agriculture, the significance of industrial production in the recent period has expanded considerably. In 1967, industry generated 28 percent of the gross national product, up from 18 percent in 1960. In this same period the relative importance of agriculture declined from 37 percent of the gross national product to 31 percent. In the industrial sector in 1967, the most prominent industry was manufacturing, which contributed 20 percent of the gross national product, followed by construction (4 percent), mining and quarrying (1.7 percent), and electricity and gas (1.4 percent).

A large part of government and private investment during the last several years has been in industry. In 1967, of the 257 billion invested, about one-third was in industry, compared to about 9 percent in agriculture. These figures represent the trend for the last several years (see ch. 24, Public Finance; ch. 25, Banking and Currency). The resulting expansion of industrial capacity has been the major determinant in Korea's recent rapid economic development. From 1960 through 1967, electricity and gas production led all industrial sectors with an average annual real growth rate of over 17 percent. Construction realized a 15 percent average real growth rate in this period; manufacturing, 14 percent; and mining and quarrying, over 11 percent. The average real rate of growth for all industry was over 14 percent, compared to a rate of 6 percent per year in agriculture during this period.

Industry—in particular, manufacturing—is in turn an increasing source of employment. While the agricultural labor force has remained relatively stable for several years, employment in industry increased at an average rate of nearly 16 percent per year; and in 1967, employees in industry represented 15 percent of the labor force, up from 10 percent in 1964.

The products of industry figure importantly in the rapidly expanding export trade. In 1967, industrial products accounted for 88 percent of the Republic's total exports. Of the industrial products exported, the greater part were manufactured goods and the remaining portion, minerals. Earlier, in 1960, industrial products were nearly as important in the export trade, but manufactured goods accounted for somewhat less than 40 percent of the much smaller absolute amount of exports, with minerals representing more than 40 percent (see ch. 23, Foreign Economics Relations). The government has pursued export promotion policies, especially for manufacturing industries, throughout this period.

Because the country is relatively poor in natural resources, much of the recent industrial growth has been dependent on the importation of raw materials (as well as on low labor costs). For example, logs are imported and later exported as plywood; most of the raw materials for textiles must be imported; and since the country has no domestic sources of crude petroleum, it must also be imported (see ch. 2, Physical Environment). At the same time, many raw materials such as iron ore have been exported because of lack of adequate domestic facilities for processing or inadequate domestic demand for finished products.

Availability of capital has been and continues to be a problem facing industry. Because it is an underdeveloped country, domestic savings available for capital formation are quite limited. A great deal of the country's capital formation in the past has been made possible through foreign aid, although in recent years public and private foreign loans and foreign direct investment have assumed large importance. The government is making vigorous efforts both to accelerate the flow of foreign capital into the country and to increase the domestic savings rate. The government directly assists capital formation in industry with investments and loans. The success of these efforts is largely due to the effectiveness of the government's monetary and fiscal policies, which in recent years have been characterized by restraint. The curbing of inflation has done much to produce a climate favorable to economic expansion (see ch. 24, Public Finance; ch. 25, Banking and Currency).

MINING

About 50 different kinds of minerals are produced in the Republic of Korea. Of these, anthracite coal, iron ore, tungsten, gold, graphite, fluorite, and salt predominate in terms of production, exports, and contribution to the gross national product. Other less important minerals are silver, copper, lead, zinc, manganese, molybdenite, kaolin, talc, asbestos, limestone, silica, and feldspar. The deposits of all of the above minerals are dispersed throughout the country with the major concentrations in the northeastern province of Kangwŏn (see fig. 8).

Anthracite coal is an important energy source, and nearly all of the production is consumed domestically. Because the country is very poor in energy resources, the government has pursued a continuing program to increase coal production. As a result of government programs and the substantial domestic demand, coal production more than doubled from 1960 to 1967. Reserves are limited and, because coal production is expected to increase at a rapid pace, the coal supply is expected to be depleted in the not too distant future (see table 15). At that time imported petroleum will probably become the predominant energy source. While only a small

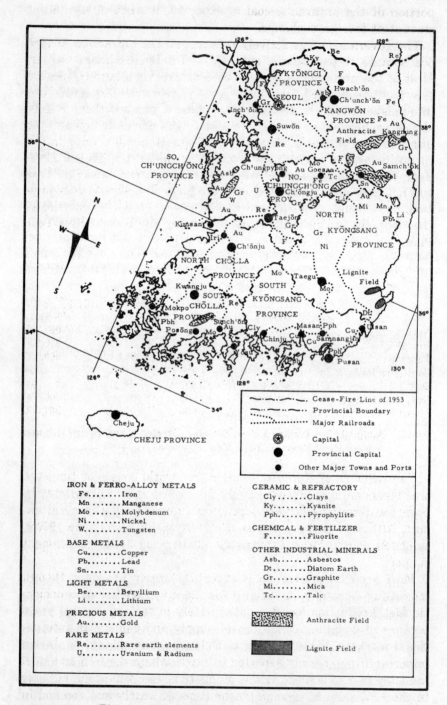

Figure 8. Mineral locations—Republic of Korea.

portion of the anthracite coal is exported, it earns a significant amount of foreign exchange.

The government has actively encouraged the extraction of iron ore because it has been a substantial foreign exchange earner. Most of the iron ore has heretofore been exported, largely because few facilities existed for converting the relatively low-grade ore into finished products. By the same token, it was necessary to rely almost exclusively on imports to satisfy the domestic demand for iron and steel products. However, this situation will change in the future because a major investment program of the Second Five-Year Plan is expansion in iron- and steel-making capacity. This will not only divert most iron ore products to domestic consumption, but will also require imports of additional ore. It is envisioned that iron ore production will double during the Second Five-Year Plan.

Table 15. Annual Production, Export Value, and Reserves of Major Minerals in the Republic of Korea

	Annual production (in metric tons)		1967 Export value (in U.S. dollars)	1966 Estimated reserves (in metric tons)
	1960	1967		
Anthracite coal	5,350,000	12,436,000	1,750,000	540,000,000
Iron Ore	392,000	698,000	6,059,000	80,350,000
Tungsten	4,459	3,693	11,027,000	300,000
Gold (in kilograms) ..	2,097	1,970	—	4,000
Salt	399,000	612,000	—	—
Graphite	92,000	64,000	994,000	32,600,000
Fluorite	19,000	57,000	990,000	967,000

Source: Adapted from Bank of Korea, *Economic Statistics Yearbook, 1968*; and Korean Reconstruction Bank, *Industry in Korea, 1967*.

The Republic of Korea is a major free-world source of tungsten ore. Tungsten is produced entirely for export and has consistently been the country's largest foreign-exchange-earning mineral export. Although production was relatively stable during the 1960's, tungsten mining was extensively modernized with government support.

Most graphite production is exported, largely to Japan, though increasing demand is envisioned for the mineral's use as a domestic fuel. Production has fluctuated widely in the last several years because of changing conditions of supply and demand in international markets. Fluorite, used as a flux in steelmaking, is also an important item, mainly exported to Japan where the iron and steel industry is flourishing. Again, production was somewhat variable in the 1960's due to changing conditions of supply and demand in international markets. Salt, produced from seawater by the solar evaporation method, is sufficient for domestic uses. Gold, a mineral with which the country is fairly well endowed, also is absorbed entirely in domestic markets.

The mining industry is composed of both government-owned and private mines. Government-operated mines produced 38 percent of the country's anthracite coal in 1967, nearly all of its tungsten, and a substantial portion of its iron ore. Government-owned facilities also produced much of the total output of salt. (Iron mines and salterns were turned over to private enterprise in 1967.) The government offers capital and technical aid to mining enterprises through the Korean Mining Corporation.

While several mining firms are quite large and while some use efficient capital-intensive methods, the typical enterprise is small and inefficient. Productivity in Korean mining increased more slowly than any other sector of the economy in the 1960's. In general, the industry is in need of consolidation and modernization. Since the formation of the Republic, the government has made continuing efforts toward this goal, with increasing success. In the early years after World War II, substantial foreign aid funds were channeled into the development of the mining industry. During the 1960's, however, foreign economic assistance declined as the country evidenced growing ability to participate in the general industrialization effort. After 1963, development was encouraged by the (largely government controlled) Korean Reconstruction Bank, which has made long-term loans available for equipment modernization at relatively low interest rates. The government has also provided incentives for foreign private capital investment in mining activities. The industry has benefited from government progress in two other areas: the continuing improvement of transportation facilities, and the expansion of upgraded technical and vocational training opportunities (see ch. 4, Population and Labor Force; ch. 9, Education; ch. 18, Character and Structure of the Economy; ch. 22, Domestic Trade; ch. 25, Banking and Currency).

MANUFACTURING

Since the early 1960's, marked increases in capacity and production in the manufacturing sector of the economy have resulted in a considerable change in the economic structure of the country. Manufacturing has, in fact, been the leading force in the recent rapid economic development. From 1960 to 1967, manufacturing production increased two and one-half times, and manufacturing's share of the gross national product increased from 14 percent to 20 percent, adding close to $900 million in 1967 (see ch. 18, Character and Structure of the Economy).

The country's principal manufacturing asset is an ample and industrious labor force noted for low wage rates, inherent skills, and adaptability (see ch. 4, Population and Labor Force; ch. 21, Labor Relations and Organization). However, the country is capital-poor and has limited natural resources for raw materials. The main thrust in manufacturing since the beginning of the First Five-Year Plan has been expansion in import-substitution industries (for example, cement and fertilizer) and in export-expansion industries (for example, textiles, electronics, and plywood). In this period the Republic has become more self-sufficient in several basic goods which previously were imported, and at the same time, exports of manufactured goods have increased considerably. Because there is not a large domestic market for certain of the country's finished products, a significant part of the growth in the manufacturing sector since the early 1960's has been accomplished through export expansion. In 1967, for example, approximately one-third of the goods produced in the manufacturing sector of the economy were exported (see ch. 23, Foreign Economic Relations). Many of these exported goods have required the importation of raw materials—for example, logs for plywood. A number of manufacturers—taking advantage of the country's low wage rates—have thus become intermediate fabricators using imported raw materials to produce items for sale abroad.

Structure of Manufacturing Industry

Cement and fertilizer plants, mining activities, and many small-scale manufacturing firms are dispersed throughout the country. However, most of the manufacturing firms are concentrated in the Seoul and Pusan areas where adequate transportation and export facilities exist. A large and energetic labor force has also been attracted from rural areas to these urban centers by the hope of better employment and educational opportunities (see ch. 4, Population and Labor Force; ch. 21, Labor Relations and Organization).

Firms are predominantly owned and operated by Korean nationals. While the sole proprietorship and partnership forms of business have been the most widely used, the corporation form is rapidly gaining in popularity. The government owns and operates a number of manufacturing enterprises; it has important production facilities in iron and steel, shipbuilding, oil refining, cement, salt, and fertilizer.

There are also a number of large industrial conglomerates engaged in a wide range of manufacturing, banking, and trading activities; among the more important are the Samsŏng, Lucky, Whashin, Samho, and Kamsung combines. Such syndicates constitute an important factor in the shaping of the country's economic policies (see ch. 14, Political Dynamics). They may be roughly compared to the Japanese zaibatsu—such as the Mitsubishi, Mitsui, and Sumitomo combines—which together "control" about 40 percent of Japan's big business.

In addition there are numerous trade associations, including many producers cooperatives, and a number of prominent and influential business organizations such as the Korean Chamber of Commerce and the Federation of Korean Industries (see ch. 14, Political Dynamics; ch. 22, Domestic Trade).

Because of the scarcity of capital, the typical enterprise is small and uses inefficient methods of production. Capital equipment, generally in short supply, is often technologically outdated. However, as economic development has progressed, more capital-intensive and large-scale enterprises have been established (ch. 24, Public Finance; ch. 25, Banking and Currency).

Manufacturing firms averaged 26 employees in 1966. In that year 4 percent of the total number of firms had 100 or more employees (see table 16), but these generated 63 percent of the total output and employed over 50 percent of the total manufacturing labor force. The average such company had over 300 employees.

Table 16. Number of Firms and Employees in Manufacturing
in the Republic of Korea, 1966

Type of firm	Number of firms	Firms with more than 100 employees	Total Employees
Food	3,191	109	47,018
Beverages	1,751	28	25,588
Tobacco	14	14	8,267
Textiles	2,687	263	167,749
Footwear, wearing apparel, and made-up textile goods	1,807	62	32,170
Wood and cork	1,287	18	21,753
Furniture and fixtures	733	3	9,159
Paper and paper products	525	26	14,538
Printing, publishing, and allied industries	1,362	32	26,657
Leather products	95	11	3,016
Rubber products	185	26	25,847
Chemicals and chemical products	701	62	31,517
Petroleum and coal products	1,280	18	16,879
Clay, glass, and stone products	2,485	81	37,590
Basic metals	381	37	17,926
Metal products	1,469	36	29,931
Machinery	990	22	20,866
Electrical machinery, apparatus, and appliances	618	40	23,312
Transport equipment	979	34	27,747
Miscellaneous	681	60	24,600
Total	23,221	982	612,130

Source: Adapted from Korean Reconstruction Bank, *Report on Sample Survey for Mining and Manufacturing Establishments*, pp. 80–100.

In 1966 the most important manufacturing groups were food, beverages, and tobacco, which together accounted for over 28 percent of the manufacturing output. The textile, clothing and footwear manufacturing groups generated 18 percent of the manufacturing output in that year. The output of heavy industry (chemicals, petroleum, metals, and machinery) saw a marked expansion in the 1960's, increasing from less than 20 percent of the total manufacturing output in the early 1960's to more than 30 percent by mid-decade. This increase reflects the recent rapid pace of industrialization. Together the above manufacturing groups generated over three-fourths of the manufacturing output in 1966. Though light industry, other than food and textiles, is of lesser significance, the most marked change in the 1960's was in the diversity of products manufactured. For example, during this period, goods such as electric appliances, plastics, and plywood became important products of light manufacturing.

Food and Beverages

In terms of output, the food, tobacco, and beverage industries together constitute the most significant segment of the manufacturing industry. Important categories within this group include: food canning, flour milling, sugar refining, refrigerating, agar-agar production, tobacco processing, alcohol production and beer brewing (see tables 16 and 17). The processing of food and beverages expanded in the 1960's, but its growth has been modest compared to manufacturing in general. Domestic consumption of processed foods and beverages is limited by the low level of per capita income. Nevertheless, most of the food and beverage production is domestically consumed. Some goods such as canned seafoods, canned mushrooms, and agar-agar are exported, and the government is attempting to develop additional export markets for food products, especially seafood products.

Textiles

Next to foods, tobacco, and beverages, textiles are the single most important manufactured product, accounting for over 15 percent of the value added by manufacturing. Important products include: raw silk, knitted goods, fishnet and rope, and silk, cotton, woolen, nylon, and rayon fabrics. Cotton textiles are by far the most important product. Textile production increased significantly in the 1960's but not quite as rapidly as manufactured products in general. As a group, textile exports constitute the largest source of foreign exchange, representing more than 13 billion wŏn (nearly $50 million) in 1967. About 90 percent of the raw materials for textiles are imported. Approximately 55 percent of the exported textiles are produced in bonded processing plants.

Table 17. Growth in Representative Manufacturing Industries
in the Republic of Korea

	Unit	1960	1967
Canned Food	M/T	5,811	4,956
Flour	1,000 bags	10,464	25,739
Beer	Kiloliters	17,570	42,177
Raw Silk	1,000 kg	297.1	1,329.1
Cotton Fabrics	1,000 kg	126,121	186,356
Nylon Fabrics	1,000 m^2	3,922	41,864
Kraft Paper	M/T	2,403	28,314
Rubber Shoes	1,000 pr.	40,769	35,455
Car Tires	Each	56,035	197,324
Plastic Products	M/T	6,088	27,308
Urea Fertilizer	M/T	13,361	314,709
Glass Products	M/T	22,510	51,780
Cement	M/T	430,857	2,441,206
Pig-Iron	M/T	13,234	22,393
Steel Ingots	M/T	50,051	320,147
Engines (steam, gas, etc.)	Each	2,167	13,033
Sewing Machines	Each	22,888	162,273
Transformers	Each	3,066	87,930
Radios	Each	40,260	439,908
Wooden Ships (fishing, barges)	S/T	2,605	7,767
Bicycles	Each	38,030	147,623
Plywood	Million sq. ft.	186.9	1,490.4

Source: Bank of Korea, *Economic Statistics Yearbook 1968*, Seoul, 1968,
pp. 225–231.

The textile industry was to a large extent devastated during the
Korean conflict, but factories were later rebuilt and furnished with
more modern equipment. This upgrading, coupled with the low
wage rates, now makes Korean textiles competitive in international markets.

Korea possesses some domestic facilities for the production of
synthetic textiles such as nylon and acrylics. With the increase in
world demand for these textiles, expansion of the existing facilities and installation of new facilities for the production of synthet-
ics are planned for the near future.

Chemical Industry

The chemical industry developed greatly during the 1960's, and
further expansion is envisioned. Important categories of production in chemical manufacturing include basic chemicals, chemical
fertilizers, oils and fats, coating and printing ink, man-made fibers,
pesticides, industrial explosives and synthetic resins. The most dynamic segment of this industry in the 1960's was fertilizer production. For example, production of urea fertilizer increased 23 times
from 1960 to 1967. Until recently, the country had to import most

of its fertilizer, but the growth of domestic productive capacity in this industry has greatly reduced the country's dependence on imports. Of the seven fertilizer plants in operation in 1967, three were constructed in the early 1960's and three began operation in 1967. Three additional plants were also under construction during that year. The chemical fertilizers produced are predominantly the urea and compound types; production capability in potash and phosphate fertilizers is limited.

The production of basic chemicals such as sulphuric acid, caustic soda, and ammonia also increased rapidly in the 1960's. A significant development in the basic chemicals industry occurred in 1967 with the introduction of two sulphuric acid plants (total capacity 300,000 metric tons per year), the doubling of caustic soda capacity, and a tremendous increase in ammonia capacity as a by-product of the newly established fertilizer plants.

In accordance with the Second Five-Year Plan, a major investment program will be the establishment of a petrochemical industry as an intermediate user of the products of the newly established oil refining industry (see ch. 18, Character and Structure of the Economy). The petrochemical industry will have the capability to manufacture such products as naphtha, PVC, polyethylene, polyesterene, caprolactum, and PVA. The products of this industry will, in turn, provide raw materials for the developing plastics and synthetic textile industries which were being developed in 1968.

Ceramics

Important products of the ceramics industry include cement, glass, bricks, pottery, tile, and abrasives with cement and glass production predominating. The index of industrial production for ceramics more than tripled between 1960 and 1967.

Expansion of capacity for cement production has been a major program of the First and Second Five-Year Plans, and production in that period increased substantially. In 1968 the country had six modern cement-producing plants, four of which were constructed after 1960. Total annual capacity of these plants was over 2 million metric tons. Construction of three new facilities with a total annual capacity of nearly 3 million metric tons was in progress in that year; one of these new plants was to have an annual capacity of 2 million metric tons. The Second Five-Year Plan estimates that, as a result of additional facilities, cement production will increase to 6.8 million tons by 1971. The country is well endowed with limestone, the primary ingredient of cement, but other raw materials such as gypsum and bituminous coal must be imported.

Flat glass production was begun in 1957 when a facility with an annual capacity of 130,000 cases was established. By 1967, the capacity of this facility had been increased to 600,000 cases per year. This facility basically supplies domestic demand and allows for some exports. Silica sand, a primary ingredient of glass is abundant, as are limestone and feldspar. Soda ash and many other auxiliary raw materials have been imported. However, a soda ash production facility began operation in 1967, eliminating the necessity for its importation.

Oil Refining

In 1964 an oil refinery capable of processing 35,000 barrels of crude oil per day began operation at Ulsan. The refinery is a joint venture of the government of The Republic of Korea and the Gulf Oil Corporation of the United States. The Republic has no known oil resources and all of the crude oil must be imported. Prior to the establishment of the Ulsan refinery it was necessary to import all refined petroleum products as well. The Ulsan Refinery's capacity was expanded to 55,000 barrels per day, and in 1968 was to be expanded to 110,000 barrels daily. Construction of a second oil refinery at Yosu, with a planned capacity of 60,000 barrels of crude oil per day, was begun in 1967 as the joint venture of a private Korean firm and Caltex of the United States.

Output of petroleum products has increased rapidly since 1967. Major products include gasoline, solvents, kerosene, diesel oil, fuel oil, and bunker C oil. Korean petroleum production basically satisfies domestic needs, although demand has been expanding rapidly.

Iron and Steel

While iron and steel capacity and production expanded markedly in the 1960's, the industry remains small. The industry has been unable to supply rapidly expanding demand for iron and steel products, and substantial imports of finished products are necessary. The Second Five-Year Plan envisions the construction of an integrated iron and steel mill with an initial capacity of 600,000 metric tons of crude steel and an ultimate capacity of 1 million metric tons. Construction of this facility began in 1968. The country possesses some iron ore, most of which is presently exported, but when this facility is in operation not only will domestic iron ore be used, but also large amounts will have to be imported.

Machinery

The machinery industry produces a variety of products including prime movers, agricultural implements, transportation equipment, electrical and electronic equipment, and appliances. The index of industrial production for machinery increased over five times during the years 1960–1967, showing this to be a leading manufacturing sector in terms of the growth rate during that period. Its relative importance had increased to nearly 10 percent of value added in manufacturing in 1967. However, the machinery industry in general is still small in scale; it lacks technological development and requires importation of many of its raw materials, and it cannot satisfy domestic needs.

The general machinery industry saw fairly rapid expansion in the 1960's. The most rapid growth in the light machinery group was in the production of engines and sewing machines. The manufacture of transport equipment was the most rapidly expanding category in the heavy machinery group in the 1960's. Ships, automobiles, and bicycles were also important products.

Prior to the 1960's electrical machinery and appliances and electronics manufacturing had been declining, but production was since expanded rapidly and both the quantity and diversity of products increased. By 1968, products included motors, transformers, switches, radio and television receivers, fans, refrigerators, lamps, telephone and telephone switchboards, and integrated circuits. Many of these products are exported; a significant part of the industry is based on the processing and assembly of imported materials taking advantage of the country's low wage rates and its energetic and competent labor force. The rapid expansion of the industry is partly attributable to government efforts to develop it as an export industry, partly to foreign direct investment, and partly to a rapidly increasing domestic demand based on the further electrification of the country.

Other Manufacturing Industries

The plywood industry in the 1960's had matured rapidly from infant status to become the number one source of foreign exchange; plywood production in 1967 was eight times greater than its 1960 level, and in 1967 plywood exports earned 36.6 million dollars. About 80 percent of the plywood produced domestically is exported. Logs for conversion to plywood are imported.

Paper production has markedly increased since 1960, reducing the country's dependence on imports, which had been 40 percent of requirements. There are over 60 paper plants in the country, but most are small and they use technologically inferior methods of production. Because timber resources are lacking, raw materials must be imported. A small part of the paper production is now exported.

Rubber products include footwear, tires, and belting. While production has generally increased, the industry suffers from overinvestment in production facilities by manufacturers. Both tires and footwear are exported.

HANDICRAFTS AND ARTISANRY

Handicrafts and artisanry, usually significant factors in the economy of underdeveloped countries, have been of great importance. In 1965, the last year statistics were published on the handicrafts industry, 752,000 workers (representing 9 percent of the labor force) were employed in handicrafts. Traditional Korean handicrafts include pottery, lacquerware, and silk, cotton, and hemp textiles. To this list could be added grass-cloth wallpaper, bambooware, artificial flowers, tiles, and *wangul* (fiber) products. These latter products are of relatively recent development and are produced in manufacturing plants as well as by hand. Handicrafts were once a very important export product, but their relative importance among total exports has declined.

Information on the handicraft industry is sketchy. Few figures are available concerning location and structure of shops, sources of raw materials, and marketing of products. There are indications that handicrafts are produced largely by the agricultural labor force in a cottage industry from readily available raw materials. An increasing amount of so-called handicraft products are produced commercially in manufacturing firms.

CONSTRUCTION

Spurred by the Five-Year Plans and the rapid pace of economic development, the construction industry expanded markedly in the 1960's. Construction increased at an average rate of 15 percent per year from 1960 to 1967, and in 1967 accounted for 4.2 percent of the gross national product. The construction industry employed nearly 3 percent of the labor force in that year.

In the 1960's, construction was concentrated on the building of production facilities and public works, reflecting the progress in economic development in the country. Housing construction, however, was lagging. Of the approximately $500 million (approximately 137 billion wŏn) of investment devoted to construction in 1967, 34 percent was for nonresidential buildings, 21 percent for dwellings, and 45 percent for other construction and works. Because the country is capital-poor, construction has been limited by the amount of domestic and foreign savings made available for investment.

Public works construction, an integral part of economic planning, proceeded at a rapid pace throughout the 1960's. Major public works included the construction and improvement of dams, water supply and sewerage facilities, roads, and harbors, and the establishment of industrial estates such as the one at Ulsan.

A chronic shortage of housing has been a continuing problem, and one for which a quick solution is not foreseen. In 1965 the demand for housing exceeded the supply by over 1 million units. The annual construction of 80,000 dwelling units per year falls short of the annual increase in demand by over 20 percent. While the government recognized the problem and planned to construct 833,000 dwelling units by 1971, this will still fall far short of needs.

An analysis of building construction permits in the principal cities indicates that the construction of brick, stone and reinforced concrete buildings increased rapidly in the 1960's. The construction of wooden buildings—which once dominated the construction industry—was generally declining both absolutely and relatively.

POWER RESOURCES

Electric power generation in the country experienced rapid growth in the 1960's. Total power generated in 1967 was 9,911 million kilowatts compared to 2,209 million kilowatts in 1963 and 1,697 million kilowatts in 1960. Of the total power generated in 1967, 82 percent was from thermal as opposed to hydroelectric plants. In 1967, power generation accounted for more than 1 percent of the gross national product and employed more than 10,000 workers.

The availability of electric power has been and will continue to be a problem. This obstacle has been serious since the partition of Korea; at the time of the division of the country, most of the power-generating facilities were in the north. In addition, the Korean conflict devastated a large part of the country's power-generating facilities. As a consequence, the country has had to develop its power resources from an extremely small base. Another aspect of the problem, and the most pressing for the present, is the lack of power resources. The country's potential for hydroelectric power —already largely developed—is inadequate to serve its needs. Consequently, thermal power plants using anthracite coal have become predominant, but the country's anthracite resources are limited and will probably be depleted in the not too distant future. Thermal generating plants using petroleum are being developed, but such development will require substantial imports, as there are no oil resources. In the future, nuclear power plants are envisioned as a possibility.

The growth in the power industry in the 1960's reflected a continuing government program to increase power generation as a basic element of economic development. As a result, in 1964 the government was able for the first time to lift restrictions on power use. However, since that time, demand has increased strongly, and in 1967 the country experienced a power shortage, caused in part by a drought. The government plans to continue its program of electric power development. By 1971, the Second Five-Year Plan calls for a total power-generating capability of 7,797 million kilowatts.

All of the power-generating facilities are owned and operated by the government through the Korea Electric Company (KECO). Generating facilities are widely dispersed throughout the country, and most are tied into a single transmission network. Principal concentrations are around Seoul and Pusan. Major hydroelectric plants are located at Hwachon, Cheunchon, Chongpyong, Samjin-gang, Bosong-gang, Unam, and Goesan; thermal plants are located at Yongwol, Danginri, Masan, Samchok, and Pusan.

ROLE OF GOVERNMENT

The government, which exerts a strong influence on the industrial sector of the economy, has taken the leading role in the industrialization of the country. First, the government owns and operates major industrial facilities, including much of the existing capability for the production of fertilizer, iron and steel, and cement, as well as for shipbuilding, oil refining, power generation, and mining. While the portion of industrial output generated by the government sector of industry is not precisely known, it is substantial. The government-owned enterprises are operated as public corporations. Since 1963 these enterprises have been required to show profits and to operate without government subsidy (see ch. 24, Public Finance).

In the 1960's, the government committed itself to a policy of promoting free enterprise in the economy, reversing the trend of previous periods. While the immediate requirements of development and the general lack of private entrepreneurs have often thwarted this goal, the government has taken steps to establish private enterprise. For example, a second oil refinery using private capital was under construction in 1968, and in 1967 mines formerly owned by the government were turned over to private firms. The government was in 1968 considering a franchise allowing a private firm to build a power-generating plant.

Through its function as a central planning agency, the government has either promoted or established industries which it considered vital to economic development. Predominant in this category during the 1960's were import-substitution industries and export-expansion industries. For such enterprises the government has provided preferential treatment such as aid in obtaining capital, generous depreciation allowances, reduced taxes, and preferential railway freight and electricity rates. The laws contain very generous provisions regarding foreign investment, but the government controls the kinds of foreign investments that can be made.

The government also exercises influence on industry through

implementation of its vocational training programs. Recognizing the need for technical education to supply the manpower needs of an industrial society, the government has provided funding for more and improved trade schools with superior facilities, smaller classes, and a favorable teacher-student ratio to encourage enrollment (see ch. 9, Education).

INDUSTRY AND SOCIETY

To assess Korean attitudes towards industry is difficult because these attitudes have been in flux as a result of economic, social, and political changes. The customary feeling of the people towards business in general has been negative. Influenced by Confucianism, the traditional way of life has dictated acceptance of one's social position, and obedience to authority. Being engaged in business has always been looked upon as socially undesirable, and there has been no great urge to take business risks. Immediate satisfactions have been preferred to more distant pleasures. Labor unions have not had political power nor have they attracted wide membership (see ch. 21, Labor Relations and Organization).

In contrast to this established pattern, recent economic progress has probably encouraged a more enterprising spirit, at least among those associated with the industrialization of the country —industrial workers, the newly emerging managerial class, government officials, and students. The older persons and the rural population cling more closely to tradition. However, there does seem to be an increasing awareness among Koreans generally that industrialization is necessary to increase their economic well-being.

CHAPTER 21

LABOR RELATIONS AND ORGANIZATION

For centuries the relationship between employers and employees in Korea was strongly conditioned by Confucianism, which stresses loyalty to authority, and a labor movement has evolved only in the modern era. In the period of Japanese domination (1910–1945) a labor movement in Korea had its beginnings, but in general it was politically motivated, the main objective being to gain independence from Japan. Since 1945 the labor movement has been dominated by the Han'guk Nodongchohap Ch'ongyonmaeng (the Federation of Korean Trade Unions, known as No Ch'ong). However, prior to 1961, the federation was allied with the government in power and consequently its impact was limited. During the Park regime it became relatively free of direct government manipulation and attempted to pursue economic goals more or less independently. Nevertheless, the labor movement in 1968 remained small in relation to the total work force and the industrial work force, and was still somewhat tarnished by its past political involvement. For these reasons, the government can still exert strong indirect pressures on the movement through the labor laws.

CHARACTERISTICS OF LABOR

Composition

In 1967, the total labor force averaged 9.5 million persons. The number of persons employed in agriculture in that year ranged from a low of 2.9 million in December to a high of 6.7 million in June, the variation being the result of the high degree of seasonality in that sector of the economy. The less volatile nonagricultural labor force averaged 4 million persons: 2.4 million wage and salary earners and 1.6 million self-employed. As industrialization has progressed in recent years, the percentage of the labor force employed in primary industries (agriculture, forestry, fishing and hunting, mining, and quarrying) has declined, while the percentage in other industries has increased. However, employees in primary industries still represent over half of the total labor force (see table 18).

Unemployed persons averaged 590,000, or 6.2 percent of the

labor force, in 1967. A larger problem than unemployment is under-employment, which results from the inclusion of a large number of seasonal and part-time employees in the labor force. Under-employed and unemployed persons together have been variously estimated to constitute 20 to 30 percent of the labor force.

Table 18. Distribution of Persons Employed in the Republic
of Korea, by Occupation, in 1967
(persons 14 years of age and older)

Occupation	Percent of active labor force*
Farmers, wood cutters and related workers	53
Craftsmen, production processers and laborers	15
Sales workers	13
Service workers	6
Clerical workers	5
Professional, technical, and related workers	3
Fishermen, hunters, and related workers	2
Communications and transportation workers	1
Mining, quarrying, and related workers	1
Managers and officials	1
Total	100

* Percents based on average figures for the year.

Source: Adapted from Bank of Korea, *Economic Statistics Yearbook, 1968*, pp. 242, 243.

The organized labor movement in 1967 represented only 4 per-cent of the total labor force and 16 percent of wage and salary earners in the nonagricultural part of the labor force. This low figure is explained by several factors. First, the part of the labor force represented by industrial workers (the segment that, in most countries, provides the principal basis for an organized labor movement) is small, since the country still has a predominantly agrarian economy.

Another factor is the relatively short period that organized labor has been active. The labor movement was generally sup-pressed during the Japanese occupation and had its beginnings es-sentially after World War II.

Still another cause of the limited size of the organized labor force is found in its unfortunate political involvement. After inde-pendence, it became allied with Syngman Rhee's Liberal Party. The political aims of the party took precedence over the economic aims of the movement, and the unions were largely used by the party as an instrument to gain support for the government's eco-nomic policies. Since these policies did not enjoy wide popularity, the No Ch'ong became largely discredited.

The growth of the movement has been further inhibited by Confucian philosophy with which Koreans have been imbued. Confucianism stresses obedience to authority—and employers constitute an important authoritarian group.

A further reason for the slow growth of the movement may be found in the high unemployment rate. When a relatively large number of persons are not gainfully employed, it is extremely difficult to persuade those who are employed of the benefits of union affiliation.

Skills, Training, and Productivity

The labor force is generally recognized for its capacity for sustained work, its receptivity to training and new production methods, and where opportunities exist, its attainment of relatively high skill levels. At least a primary education is becoming common since roughly 97 percent of the primary-school-age children are enrolled in primary schools. Around 58 percent of primary school graduates enter middle school. While 66 percent of the middle school graduates go to high school, only about 30 percent of the high school graduates continue their education in institutes of higher learning (see ch. 9, Education).

The country still has a shortage of skilled workers to support its industrialization and development. In recent years it has placed increasing stress on vocational training, while higher education is beginning to be shifted away from its traditional emphasis on the liberal arts in favor of science and engineering. As of 1967, there were 75 technical schools operating at the middle school level, 368 vocational high schools, 67 higher technical schools, 19 junior technical colleges and 68 colleges and universities. Of 22,338 graduates of colleges and universities in 1967; 3,351 were in fields of engineering, 1,428 were in natural sciences, and 1,945 were in medicine and pharmacy.

In addition to the graduates of vocational and technical training institutes, many of the 175,000 to 200,000 servicemen discharged annually from the armed forces receive training during the course of their military service in skills applicable to industrial employment. Since 1966, the Office of Labor Affairs of the Ministry of Health and Social Affairs has carried on an expanded program of skill training, both in-plant and institutional, with technical and financial assistance from the United Nations Development Fund. In addition, a large number of Koreans have been trained through the foreign aid programs of individual countries and international organizations and through educational exchanges (see ch. 23, Foreign Economic Relations). Since 1967, the Republic of Korea has had a Vocational Training Law, which provides for the training of skilled workers through vocational training programs.

Significant advances in productivity have taken place in recent years. These have been the result of both the improved skills of the labor force and the introduction of more efficient methods of production. One estimate is that the productivity of laborers increased 50 percent from 1960 to 1966.

Labor Force Mobility

There has been a continuing flow of workers, particularly young people, from farms to urban areas. This has been the result of the pressure of population on limited agricultural land, better opportunities for education available in the cities, and universal military conscription, which has tended to draw many young people from the rural areas, to which they are reluctant to return after being discharged. This continuing migration from farms to cities has provided more than an ample labor force for industrialization. With a relatively high rate of urban unemployment and underemployment, labor mobility does not create a problem for employers.

In recent years, a significant number of workers have found employment in foreign countries. In 1967 the country had 13,000 civilian workers in South Vietnam, 3,700 miners and nurses in West Germany, 230 construction workers in Thailand, 100 doctors in Uganda and Malaysia, and 1,900 sailors in various countries. Koreans residing and working in foreign countries have made remittances to their homeland, which have helped alleviate the international balance of payments problems (see ch. 23, Foreign Economic Relations).

CONDITIONS OF EMPLOYMENT

Recruitment

Because of the abundance of labor relative to demand, actual recruitment of employees is not widely practiced. Competition for available jobs is severe. Laborers are hired by companies mainly on the basis of "backing." Personal contact with someone in a shop is important. Dock workers, for example, have a strong tendency to keep the work within families of the existing workers.

Once hired, employees are generally classified as daily, temporary, or permanent workers. Daily workers are paid daily, do only manual labor, and have no assurance of continuing work. Temporary workers are paid monthy, may do skilled or semiskilled work, and are supposed to be promoted to the status of permanent employees after three months. In actuality, a worker may remain on the rolls as a temporary worker for years. To become a permanent worker is a primary goal, since pay is usually higher, fringe benefits are made available, and job security is better. About two-thirds of a typical company's employees are permanent workers.

Wages

Employees may be compensated either in cash or in kind. Base pay is supplemented by cash payments for bonuses, overtime, cost-of-living adjustment, increments for increased skill or length of service, and various types of allowances for recreation, meals, transportation, housing, uniforms, production, profit-sharing, family, and education. In addition, it is the practice of many companies to provide for retirement and severance pay. Payments in kind include provision of meals, transportation, food, uniforms and, in some instances, housing. Dormitory facilities are provided in many industries in which a large number of female workers are employed—for example, in the textile industry. A 1967 survey of 103 firms indicated that base pay accounted for 62 percent of wages paid; bonuses, 16 percent; allowances for meals, 5 percent; overtime allowances and cost-of-living adjustments, 4 percent each; housing, uniforms and duty allowances, 1 percent each; transportation allowance, 0.5 percent; and other miscellaneous allowances, about 5 percent of total pay.

A breakdown of wages paid in "manufacturing" industries, by education level achieved, type of work performed, sex, and worker status indicates that male workers receive more than female workers (but not necessarily for similar work performed), that wages are positively correlated with education, and that clerical, white-collar and managerial workers are more highly paid than production workers. Unskilled workers are at the bottom of the wage scale (see table 19). Korean employees of the United States military forces stationed in the Republic of Korea received higher wages than are generally paid by Korean employers. The compensation of Korean government employees has historically been low compared with wages obtainable in other pursuits, but in 1968 steps were being taken to increase the wages of government employees to more competitive levels.

No minimum wage standards of general applicability have been established by law. However, the Ministry of Health and Social Affairs is authorized—with the concurrence of the Labor Committee, a quasijudicial body responsible for review and enforcement of the labor laws—to set minimum wages in particular industries and occupations.

Generalizations about wage levels are complicated by two factors. First, compilation of accurate data is made difficult by the complexity of the structure of wages and benefits and by the reluctance of employers to reveal this information because of its confidential nature. Second, wage patterns in particular job classifications, even in specific regions, are subject to considerable variation. Differences among employers in total wages and benefits paid have been found to vary as much as 400 percent for similar work performed. The absence of a more or less uniform wage structure is explained by the lack of multi-employer collective bargaining, the prevalence of cash allowances that vary from firm to firm, differing lengths of service of employees, and differences in the wages paid by firms, based on size of the establishment. Regional differences in wages also exist, but data on their relative magnitudes are not available.

The index of nominal wages increased from 100 in 1960, taken as a base year, to 182.1 at the end of 1965. In the same period the wholesale price index increased to 221.2. These figures indicate that, in general, the standard of living of wage earners declined

Table 19. Average Age, Time Worked, and Monthly Earnings of Employees in Manufacturing Industries in the Republic of Korea, Classified by Education, Type of Work, and Status, as of June 1967

	Average age	Average years of service	Average days worked	Average hours worked	Average monthly earnings[1] (in won[2])
All workers	28.8	2.9	25.2	218	8,100
Male workers	31.5	3.3	25.5	218	9,700
Production	30.2	3.0	25.2	217	8,100
Middle school and below	30.2	3.0	25.0	214	7,200
High school and above	30.3	2.9	26.1	227	11,300
Permanent	30.6	3.3	25.5	219	8,600
Middle school and below	30.7	3.3	25.4	216	7,600
High school and above	30.5	3.0	26.2	227	11,700
Temporary	27.5	1.2	23.1	204	5,500
White-collar	35.9	4.2	26.4	221	15,000
Managerial	40.2	5.7	26.4	217	21,700
Clerical	33.3	3.3	26.4	224	11,000
Middle school and below	35.1	3.5	26.4	229	8,900
High school graduates	38.8	3.2	26.6	225	10,900
College graduates	31.9	3.0	26.2	216	12,500
Female workers	22.6	2.0	24.6	217	4,500
Production	22.5	2.0	24.5	216	4,300
Middle school and below	22.5	2.0	24.4	216	4,200
High school and above	23.1	2.0	26.1	227	6,400
Permanent	22.5	2.2	25.0	222	4,500
Temporary	22.6	1.3	21.9	192	3,300
Clerical	23.6	2.3	26.4	227	6,700
Middle school and below	23.0	2.1	26.5	233	4,300
High school and above	23.9	2.4	26.3	225	7,700

[1] Average earnings include all regular monthly cash payments, including base pay and various allowances, plus any overtime or holiday pay recorded during the reporting month. Bonuses and other payments made during the year and the cash value of payments in kind are not reflected in average monthly earnings.

[2] 100 won equal U.S.$ 0.37.

Source: Adapted from Bank of Korea, "Wage Survey," Monthly Statistical Review, March 1968.

over this period. However, real wages have been improving since 1965. Wages from 1965 to 1967 increased 43 percent, while the consumer price index rose only 23 percent, implying a real wage increase of 16 percent. Continuation of this improvement in real wages depends on the government's ability to control inflation while permitting further wage increases.

Working Conditions

Conditions of employment are prescribed by the Labor Law instituted in 1953 and since amended. Included in this law are provisions regarding labor contracts, wages, working hours and recesses, dormitories, employment of females and children, safety and health, apprenticeships, workers' accident compensation, labor inspectors, reporting of employment regulations by firms, and penalties for violations of the law.

Standard hours of work are set at 8 hours per day and 48 hours per week, exclusive of rest periods, which are set at 30 minutes rest for every 4 hours work. Working hours can be extended to 10 hours per day and 60 hours per week by mutual agreement, but work beyond these limits is subject to the approval of the Ministry of Health and Social Affairs. Overtime pay equal to at least 50 percent of regular wages is required for work in excess of 8 hours per day or 48 hours per week. Similar overtime rates must be paid for work performed between 10:00 p.m. and 6:00 a.m. and on holidays. Employment in dangerous work—in particular, underground mining operations—is limited to 6 hours per day and 36 hours per week; minors between 13 and 16 years of age are limited to working 7 hours per day and 42 hours per week. Authorization of the Ministry of Health and Social Affairs is required for employment of females or minors under 18 between 10:00 p.m. and 6:00 a.m. and on holidays. Minors under the age of 13 cannot be employed unless certified by the Ministry of Health and Social Affairs—and only with the approval of the minor's parents or guardians.

Employers must provide 1 day of rest per week with pay for employees who work on all designated work days and an additional day of leave per month with pay to workers who were in attendance during all workdays during the month. Workers with 1 full year's service without absence receive an additional 8 days of leave with pay, and workers with 90 percent attendance in a year receive 3 additional days of annual leave with pay. Employees with over 2 years of service earn 1 additional day of annual leave with pay for each year of service. Females may request an additional day off with pay per month for menstrual leave and are granted 60 days leave with pay for pregnancy.

The Labor Standards Law required that employers institute appropriate measures to protect the safety, health, and morality of employees in their place of employment. In addition, employers are required to provide medical care at their expense for injuries incurred by employees while on the job. If an employee is permanently disabled on the job, the employer is required to provide up to 1,000 days of pay to the employee; and in case of death on the job, the employer is required to pay to the employee's survivors the equivalent of 1,000 days plus 90 days' pay for funeral expenses.

The government seeks compliance with the Labor Standards Law by requiring firms over a minimum size to submit to the Ministry of Health and Social Affairs a statement of actual working conditions as related to the provisions of the Labor Standards Law. Also, labor inspectors are designated by the Ministry and other government bodies to observe actual conditions to see that they comply with the provisions of the law.

LABOR RELATIONS

The Basis of Labor Relations

Attitudes underlying the relationships between working people and the individuals or groups for whom they work have been conditioned in part by Confucianism, which stresses the virtue of loyalty to authority. The prevailing pattern of employer-employee relationships in Korean society under the Yi Dynasty (1392–1910) was for centuries one in which a landlord expected and received loyal service and unquestioning acceptance of his authority from his workers, in return for which he provided them in varying degrees with paternalistic guidance and protection.

Since 1945, a structure of labor laws in the Western tradition has been promulgated in the Republic of Korea. The present laws defining employer-employee relations are: the Korean Labor Standards Law, the Labor Union Law, and the Labor Dispute Adjustment Law. The Korean Labor Standards Law is concerned with wages and conditions of work, as previously discussed. The Labor Union Law guarantees employees the right to organize for purposes of collective bargaining and to seek improvement of their working conditions. The Labor Dispute Adjustment Law sets forth conditions for the settlement of labor disputes. The present pattern of employee-employer relationships is based primarily on these laws; however, traditional influences also remain of significance.

Historical Background

During their occupation of Korea from 1910 to 1945, the Japanese generally suppressed the local labor organizations. The labor movement that did evolve in this period was politically motivated with the goal of obtaining independence from Japan. After the end of World War II in 1945, the first organized labor movement to appear was the General Council of Korean Trade Unions. This organization was formed under the influence of Communist elements. In 1946, with the encouragement of the United States occupation authorities and of leading local politicians, the anti-Communist Federation of Korean Trade Unions (No Ch'ong) was established. When the Republic of Korea was later established in 1948, Communist organizations were outlawed, and the No Ch'ong became the only recognized federation of trade unions. During the period that followed, it became increasingly associated with Syngman Rhee's Liberal Party and was formally included in that party's organization in 1955, thus becoming an arm of the government in power. During the Chang regime of 1960–61, the No Ch'ong purged itself of connections with the previous government; and a new leadership, favorably disposed to the new government in power, evolved.

Following the takeover of government by the military in 1961, the activities of labor unions were suspended, but soon afterward the No Ch'ong was reestablished and reorganized under government supervision into a federation of 16 national unions. The government's approved choices for important positions in the No Ch'ong were in turn elected by the membership. Since this period, the union movement has taken a stance more independent of the government. For example, in the first nationwide election of union officers after the return of civilian rule in 1963, the government's candidate for chairman of the No Ch'ong was defeated. Moreover, the No Ch'ong has in recent years become more active in promoting the welfare of its members, much of the time in opposition to the government's policies. The government has not attempted to reestablish direct control over unions; rather, it has exercised influence through legal constraints and informal consultation with union officials. The union movement is still not entirely independent of the government, though the government's influence has become indirect rather than direct.

Structure of the No Ch'ong

At present the No Ch'ong is composed of 16 affiliated unions with a total membership of 375,000. The unions are generally organized along industry lines (see table 20).

The No Ch'ong itself is headed by a chairman, and has a 19-man central committee composed of the chairman, the vice-chairman, the secretary-general, and the presidents of the 16 member unions. The central committee makes decisions on policy matters. The No

Table 20. Affiliated Unions of the Federation of Korean Trade Unions in the Republic of Korea*

Union	Areas of jurisdiction	Number of members
National Auto Workers	Bus, truck, and taxi transportation companies	40,000
National Bank and Financial Workers	Major commercial banks and insurance firms	11,000
National Chemical Workers	Chemical industry, oil refining, cement, food, paper, rubber products, beverages, etc.	24,000
National Communications Workers	Postal, telegraph, and telephone facilities	14,000
National Dockers	Dockworkers	20,000
National Electrical Workers	Korea Electric Company, electric tramway companies	11,000
Foreign Organization Employees	United States military forces (PX's, commissaries and clubs, etc.), foreign firms registered outside of the Republic of Korea	34,000
National Maritime Workers	Coastal and international shipping firms, Korea Shipbuilding Corporation	25,000
National Metal Workers	Factories, steel manufacturing and fabricating, machinery, auto and bus assembly, and electrical products	14,000
National Mine Workers	Coal and metal mining	32,000
National Monopoly Workers	Cigarettes, ginseng, and salt production	13,000
National Publishing Workers	Publishing companies	3,000
National Railway Workers	Railway system	34,000
National Textile Workers	Textile mills, wearing apparel, and textile products	47,000
National Transportation Workers	Korea Express Company	17,000
National United Workers	Cooks, tailors, bakers, municipal employees, etc.	37,000
Total membership		376,000

*The Federation of Korean Trade Unions (Han'guk Nodongchohap Ch'ongyonmaeng), known as No Ch'ong.

Source: Adapted from U.S. Department of State, Embassy in Seoul, *The Labor Situation in Korea*, pp. 16, 17.

Ch'ong maintains standing committees on minimum wage deliberations, women and juvenile workers, education, official and state-run enterprises, labor-laws research, and wage problems.

Little information is available on the decisionmaking process and leadership of the union movement. The labor union laws prescribe that unions must follow democratic practices, and presumably, therefore, they represent the wishes of the membership. Union officials are elected by the union membership. In the past, top union officials were either appointed by the government or their election was subject to the government's approval. Union officials in general have worked their way up through the ranks of their respective trades or industries.

A worker becomes a union member in the Republic of Korea through voluntary participation. In some cases, the law allows a union shop to exist, and under this arrangement all new employees of the company must join the union. Policymaking seems to emanate largely from the top of the union organization rather than through the initiative of local union members. This practice is related to the comparative youth of the union movement and the lack of sophistication at the local level. High-placed union officials attempt to expand the movement's stature and influence.

The No Ch'ong and its affiliated unions are at present financed from internal sources, though they were in the past partially subsidized by the successive governments. Financing is a troublesome problem, for although trade unions can legally charge membership dues of up to 2 percent of wages, only about 20 percent of the members actually pay dues. This difficulty in funding has had the effect of restricting the No Ch'ong's activities.

The No Ch'ong and its affiliated unions have several international contacts. Since 1949 the No Ch'ong has been a member of the International Confederation of Free Trade Unions (ICFTU), and since 1965, it has maintained an exchange agreement with the Japan Federation of Labor (DOMEI). In addition, 13 of the country's 16 trade unions are affiliated with international organizations in their respective industries. The Republic of Korea is not a member of the International Labor Organization (ILO) of the United Nations, but has taken steps toward obtaining membership. Because a two-thirds majority of the United Nations is required to obtain ILO membership, the country has hesitated to apply for membership until could be certain of mustering the necessary votes.

Besides the No Ch'ong, there are two organizations which are not registered as trade unions, but which have as their primary goal the economic betterment of their members. They are the Korean Federation of Education Associations with 94,000 members, and the Journalists' Association of Korea with 2,500 members.

Legal Framework

The rights and obligations of labor unions are detailed in the Labor Union Law. This law guarantees the rights of workers to freedom of association, collective bargaining and collective action to improve their working conditions, but excludes from its protection organizations financed and/or controlled by employers, and organizations formed to hamper existing unions. By the provisions of another law, government employees are prohibited from forming unions with the exception of those employees engaged in labor work as designated by presidential decree. This restriction has created some problems for labor unions in the past in their attempts to organize government-owned or -operated enterprises, but as of 1968 the government had eased the restrictions applying to these enterprises and many had become unionized. Unions themselves are forbidden to engage in any political activities. The establishment of a national union must be reported to the Office of Labor Affairs; and internal activities such as charters, finances, holding of conferences, and elections are also regulated.

Aims and Policies

It is difficult to state categorically what the goals of the organized labor movement are, because it is only recently that these goals have been formulated independent of outside influences. The goals of the No Ch'ong include the economic betterment of union members, and the expansion and strengthening of the union movement itself. By law, unions are not allowed to be involved in political activities, and therefore they cannot and do not pursue political ends.

Achievement of union goals is made difficult by several factors. First, organized labor represents an insignificant portion of the total labor force, and only about 10 percent of the industrial labor force. Labor unions have never had the active support of the working people, partly because of corruption and manipulation in an earlier period which alienated the unions from the workers. There is also evidence of factionalism within the union movement, a characteristic tending to discredit it in the eyes of workers. Second, the government in 1968 was committed to an economic development program calling for restraint on consumption and wage increases and the encouragement of saving; the government could thus be expected to resist union demands. Third, substantial unemployment and underemployment continue to have a weakening influence on the labor movement.

In recent years, the No Ch'ong has attempted to expand the scope of its activities as it achieved greater independence. Present activities include the holding of conferences on different aspects of the labor movement, organizational drives, education and training, cultural and public information activities, legislative efforts, involvement in collective bargaining and labor disputes, campaigns to increase wages, and international activities.

Labor-Management Relations

The regulations applying to relations between employers and employees—other than labor standards—are based on the Labor Union Law, the Labor Dispute Adjustments Law, and the Labor Committee Law. The Labor Union Law guarantees the constitutional right of workers to organize for purposes of collective bargaining in order to improve their working conditions. It prohibits employers from certain unfair labor practices such as dismissal of, or discrimination against, workers involved in labor union activities. Furthermore, employers cannot require their employees to join or not to join a union as a condition of employment, although a union shop is permitted if a union represents two-thirds of the employees in a workshop. As previously mentioned, employers are also forbidden to subsidize the expenses of a union. Collective bargaining agreements cannot exceed 1 year in duration nor can they violate provisions of the Labor Standards Law.

The Labor Committee Law has provisions regarding the establishment of administrative machinery for enforcement and review of various requirements of the labor laws, and for helping to settle labor disputes. Labor committees have been established in the country's nine provinces and in the cities of Seoul and Pusan. A Central Labor Committee handles labor affairs involving more than one province and hears appeals from the provincial labor committees. The Central and Local Labor Committees are selected by a method which attempts to insure that many points of view — from labor, management, public, and government—are represented.

If an employer and a union representing his employees cannot agree in a collective bargaining matter, either party to the negotiations notifies the labor office of the city or province and the appropriate labor committee. The labor committee may, within 5 days of the initial request, dismiss a dispute if it is deemed unlawful, that is, if proper procedures have not been followed or the union requests are not permitted by law. Once a dispute is declared lawful, the chairman of the labor committee may designate a conciliator from among the members of a committee or set up a special commission to help settle the dispute according to provisions of the Labor Disputes Adjustment Law.

This law also provides for the alternate and more formal procedure of mediation. Arbitration of a labor dispute may take place if both parties request it, if the collective bargaining agreement provides for it, or, in the case of public utilities, if the government agency involved requests it. A large number of industries—for example, monopoly enterprises, transport, communications, electric power, and banking—are included in the Labor Disputes Law as public utilities; other industries may, subject to consent of the National Assembly, be declared by the government to be public utilities. In addition, the Minister of Health may render a decision if a labor dispute threatens the economy or endangers the public welfare. A strike by a union may not be called until 20 days after a labor committee has been notified that a dispute exists and has declared it lawful. The cooling-off period is 30 days in the case of public utilities. Unions cannot call strikes unless the majority of union members approve and the appropriate labor office is notified in advance. Violence, sabotage or interference with normal plant safety and maintenance are prohibited. Also, employers are prohibited from strike-breaking activities.

LABOR AND SOCIETY

The labor movement has neither the political power nor the popular backing that labor enjoys in some other countries. This lack of support is related to the excess supply of labor, the relatively small size of the organized labor movement, the labor laws which clearly define union prerogatives and in particular prevent union participation in political activities, and a general mistrust of the union movement on the part of the populace because of the movement's subordination to the governments in power in earlier periods. The government is able to exert strong indirect influence on the labor movement for these reasons. No Ch'ong has made an effort in recent years to influence labor legislation, but has not been completely successful.

In general, the organized labor movement is not at present a dominant economic and political force in the Republic of Korea, and only modest support for it exists among the people generally. While unions do receive some support from the press, the No Ch'ong is not at the center of attention of the public.

Labor disputes commonly arise over wages and conditions of work and they usually occur at an early stage of negotiations, shortly after expiration of the mandatory cooling-off period. Actual work stoppages, however, are quite nominal. Eighteen work stoppages occurred during 1967 as a result of labor disputes involving 2,787 workers and the average duration was only 3.6 days.

Collective bargaining agreements generally define management and union rights, establish rules governing union-management relations at the place of work, specify conditions of employment along lines set forth in the Labor Standards Law, and often set forth procedures for settling labor disputes. Wage agreements are often concluded separately. Collective bargaining contracts in the private sector are generally concluded at the single-company level, although in banking and textiles a form of industry-wide bargaining is practiced.

CHAPTER 22

DOMESTIC TRADE

The domestic trading system of the Republic of Korea is based essentially on the free exchange of goods and services by individuals. Transactions are settled by both money and barter—the former more common in urban areas, and the latter still common in rural areas. Government intervention in the market is extensive, however, in the form of direct and indirect controls and regulations. The main objectives of these controls are to prevent interruptions in the movements of essential commodities, to maintain price stability, and to discourage speculation. Despite the fact that controls on trade have been exercised for many years, the marketing and distribution system retains many imperfections. The movements of goods and services are erratic, prices fluctuate over wide ranges (partly as a result of speculation), and supply shortages develop in local areas even though adequate stocks of goods are often available elsewhere.

A number of structural and institutional factors contribute to this situation. Agricultural production is inhibited by uneconomic small landholdings and parcelization of crop land. Individual farmers are slowly accumulating the resources and economic strength necessary to counteract the power of middlemen. Thus, production of marketable surpluses is discouraged, supplies are limited, and inflationary conditions exist periodically in the urban markets for foodstuffs.

Because of shortages of investment capital, storage, transportation, and processing facilities are not expanding in step with growth in demand. Extensive government controls on production, consumption, finances, and trade, together with frequent changes in policy, distort supply and demand relationships and divert energies into speculative activities. The drive for export production in order to ease pressures on the balance of payments diverts resources from agricultural development. Price relationships are not allowed to reflect the consumption preferences of the public, with the result that improvement in living standards has been deterred.

The government has chosen to intervene extensively in the economy in order to overcome constraints on growth resulting from the country's traditional agricultural orientation. Trade patterns and the economic behavior of individual persons have not changed as rapidly as the productive structure of the economy.

ROLE OF TRADE IN THE ECONOMY

Roughly half of the population is engaged in agriculture (including forestry and fishing), and this sector accounts for one-third of the gross national product. The other half of the population is urban, engaged in a variety of occupations, dominated by manufacturing, commerce, and various services. Domestic trade accounts for a significant share of total economic activity. Since the early 1960's wholesale and retail trade has represented an average 14 percent share of the gross national product. This reflects the trade sector's expansion in step with the rapid growth of the overall economy. The number of workers in commerce (which would include foreign as well as domestic trade activities) has averaged about 10 percent of the economically active population since 1964. In 1967, the overall number of trade workers was slightly over one million.

Investment in trade facilities had fluctuated between 3.5 and 6.6 percent of gross domestic investment in fixed assets since 1957. The government's share of investment in the trade sector is not known, although it may be substantial owing to government participation in trade through its various monopolies (tobacco, salt, and ginseng), nationalized cooperatives, government agencies, and vested properties.

Considerable information is published on agricultural and manufacturing production and on imports and exports, but little on internal commodity movements and the patterns and processes of distribution and consumption. Because of the general character of the economy, trade between the rural and urban sectors tends to be unbalanced. The outflow of foodstuffs and agricultural materials from the rural areas is not balanced by a counterflow of manufactured goods, principally because the average level of rural income is depressed by high taxes, high interest rates on loans, low productivity, and low prices paid the farmer by middlemen. These factors have restrained the initiative of farmers to increase their output, with the result that for many years the urban sector has had to rely to a considerable extent on imports for its foodstuffs and manufacturing inputs.

Much of the recent growth in domestic trade has been due to expansion of urban consumption of manufactured products. An increasing proportion of these products is being manufactured domestically, although imported raw materials and intermediate goods are used extensively in production. Most manufactured products are exchanged or consumed in the urban areas, and a relatively small proportion in rural areas. The factors underlying the high rates of urban consumption are rapid urban population expansion (largely the result of immigration of surplus agricultural workers from the countryside), generally higher levels of urban per capita income, persistent inflation, government policies encouraging private investment, increasing production of export and import substitutes, and government spending on developing transportation, electric power, and communication services.

Government programs to increase agricultural productivity through land and forest reclamation, irrigation projects, and technical assistance to farmers and fishermen may tend to balance rural-urban trade in future years. It is noteworthy that recent increases in domestic production of certain foodstuffs have led to reductions in some food imports. Most agricultural production is in grain, principally rice, although in recent years there has been an increase in the share of total output of various commercial commodities, such as natural fibers, oil seeds, vegetables, fruits, silk, and various marine products (see ch. 19, Agriculture).

An important factor in the imbalance of rural-urban trade is underdevelopment of the country's transportation and storage facilities. Despite government efforts to improve the situation, continuing shortages of railway freight cars, poor roads, insufficient truck fleets, poor warehousing and port facilities, and inadequate means of preserving perishable goods (packing, canning, and refrigeration) hinder the movement of goods, cause local shortages, and depress producer incomes while raising consumer prices. Since the early 1960's freight and passenger movements have been increasing at rates well in excess of gross national product growth. Yet in spite of large annual government investments in the development of transportation, storage, and communication facilities (between one-fifth and one-fourth of total national fixed investment), the supply of transport services has not kept pace with demand. However, elimination of government operating subsidies to the nationalized railroads and continued progress in upgrading the highway and railroad systems are evidence of progress.

THE STRUCTURE OF TRADE

The structure of domestic trade has been greatly affected by government efforts to industrialize the economy. The concentration of resources on development of manufacturing, electric power, and transportation has caused the rural sector to fall behind the urban in terms of growth of income and production. Contributing to the growing disparity have been bottlenecks in transportation and storage, and excessive expansion of currency. The effect of these conditions has been to stimulate inflationary increases in urban market prices but at the same time to depress the level of prices paid to farmers. Opportunities have increased for middlemen to manipulate prices and exploit fluctuations in supply. Government intervention in the distribution system through price control, rationing, and direct distribution of key commodities has had only moderate success in stabilizing prices. The problem of effective urban area demand consistently exceeding supply remains, however, and constraints on the balance of payments have prevented the level of imports from rising enough to completely satisfy consumption requirements at stable prices.

Excessive parcelization of farmland, inadequate rural credit, inadequate transportation and storage facilities, and price controls on foodstuffs have prevented farmers from responding to increasing demand for their products. Recent government efforts to assist farmers in increasing their productivity have had some success, but the individual small farmer is still dependent on grain buyers and creditors. Although manufacturing activities in the urban areas have been expanding, the rate has not been sufficient to absorb all additions to the labor force; and since unemployment is chronic, buying power is generally low. Confronted by such circumstances, the average farmer has few alternatives to pursuing his traditional livelihood.

Marketing of agricultural production is generally characterized by individual producers selling part of their small surpluses to brokers, government-sponsored agricultural cooperatives, or agents of wholesale houses; delivering part to creditors; and turning over the remainder to the government in payment for taxes and fertilizer purchases. Quantities marketed are generally small. The typical farm contains less than one chŏngbo of land (about 2.45 acres), most of which is paddy land and is double-cropped with rice and barley (see ch. 19, Agriculture). Since the average farm household consists of five or six persons, usually about one-half or less of total production is available for marketing after family food requirements are met. Although agricultural output has been increasing at a somewhat faster rate than population growth, food surpluses are not yet sufficient to meet national requirements. Supplemental imports have been necessary for many years.

The government plays a considerable role in the distribution of foodstuffs through its collection of taxes, direct purchase of grains for price stabilization purposes, and acceptance of payment in grain for farmers' purchases of chemical fertilizers and land. In 1966, for instance, the government secured through collection and purchase nearly 20 percent of the total grain harvest not consumed by farm households. Most was used to supply the open market through auctions held by the agricultural cooperatives during the spring months, when shortages generally develop and drive up food prices. In contrast to the 1950's, when the government dominated the distribution of agricultural output, private interests now handle the bulk of distribution of food surpluses produced by farmers and fishermen. Brokers and agents secure stocks from farmers, landlords, and fishermen; haul them by truck and rail to urban centers; and hold the supplies for subsequent resale in the various permanent market places to retailers, food vendors, and industrial consumers. Foodstuffs acquired by the government-sponsored agricultural cooperatives—the National Agricultural Cooperative Federation (NACF)—are sold through their marketing centers operated in several major cities. Farmers both sell and consign foodstuffs to the NACF market centers via the local village member cooperatives. On arrival at the centers, goods are inspected, graded, prepared for sale, and then auctioned.

The practice of partial payment of employee wages in foodstuffs and other goods by firms and the government has been common for several years. The domestic market for manufactured goods is still not sufficiently developed to support the large-scale industrial sector to the extent necessary to attain significant reductions in unit costs and prices and effect rapid increases in industrial employment. The principal factors in this imbalance are low per capita income levels (partially a result of government policies to hold down wages), scarcity of capital, and limited natural resources. The rapid expansion of manufacturing output since the mid-1950's has resulted mainly from development of intermediate goods and export industries, which have received subsidies, preferential exchange and freight rates, and special credit facilities from the government. However, development of these industries, many of which are large-scale capital-intensive operations, has not strongly affected the level of industrial employment and wages. The consumer goods sector, which receives the bulk of domestic demands and is characterized by large numbers of small-scale, labor-intensive operations, has not received equivalent government support and has thus lacked both the incentive and the means to expand output as rapidly as the intermediate and heavy industries. As with farmers, small manufacturers have few alternatives but to submit to the situation and scale output levels to the demand of their immediate local markets. The large numbers of small producers have favored the proliferation of commercial intermediaries, who have been able to take advantage of scarcities of raw materials and fluctuations in the supply of goods.

Distribution of processed and manufactured goods varies somewhat according to the kind of product. Handicraft and artisan products move from the producer directly to the customer or retailer. Consumer goods involving a greater degree of manufacture, such as canned goods, beverages, textiles, and tobacco products, generally move from producer to wholesale distributor to retailer, although the producer will sometimes undertake some of the wholesaling function.

Many of the import-export firms operating in the country act as wholesalers of domestic manufactured goods. Many of these firms handle a broad line of products ranging from imported raw materials, intermediate goods, and consumer durables to such domestic products as processed foodstuffs, beverages, and textile products. Accordingly, their trading operations are likely to have many aspects.

Some departments within the firms may handle a variety of consumer products and deal in small quantities with many small-scale suppliers and customers on the open market. On the other hand, some departments may specialize in related industrial products and commodities and deal in large orders directly with a few large-scale industrial clients. The typical outlet for consumer goods is an open-door stand or stall in an open market or a few feet of space on the street or by the roadside. The larger cities have a considerable number of retail stores, including department stores, but their share of the total volume of trade is small. As a rule, even larger stores operate with very limited selections of goods and a minimum of sales promotion and advertising.

As transportation limitations are overcome through improvement in highways, rural distribution of low unit value consumer products should increase; but at present, most production is scaled for the level of demand generated in the immediate urban markets. The recent rapid increase in urban consumption has probably resulted in part from the improvement in highway and other travel conditions: more rural inhabitants can now purchase their necessities and sell their handicrafts directly in the larger urban markets. During the period 1962–1966, the number of passengers transported by all modes doubled—an annual growth rate of over 17 percent—with the proportion carried by motor vehicles increasing from two-thirds to four-fifths of the total.

Movement of the inputs and outputs of heavy industry—chemicals, minerals, construction materials, paper, metals, and machinery—is generally similar to the patterns encountered in more industrially advanced countries. Depending on the stage of manufacture, a product may move from the manufacturer to an intermediate processor who will subsequently sell his product to a wholesaler or, possibly, directly to retail customers. Paper products and some chemical products and metal manufacturers are examples.

Such products as heavy machinery and construction materials can move either directly from the producer to the user or to consumers via wholesalers. Wholesalers generally are import-export houses specializing in supplying a line of related industrial products and often acting as local representatives for overseas manufacturers. Many manufacturing firms, having obtained import-export licenses, conduct their own wholesaling operations and sell to overseas customers while importing supplies not available domestically. Firms doing business in this manner include those producing such specialized types of machinery as sewing machines, pumps, electrical equipment, and motors. Several such firms also have established factory outlets for direct sale to domestic customers.

Although trade in manufactured consumer goods accounts for the majority of transactions in industrial products and has been expanding faster than growth in the gross national product, the share of such goods in total manufacturing trade has been declining. Based largely on imported inputs, heavy industry increased its share of total manufacturing output from 17.6 percent in 1960 to 28.3 percent in 1966. During the same period, exports increased almost eightfold with the contribution of manufactured products increasing from less than one-fourth to nearly two-thirds of total exports.

The heavy reliance of the manufacturing sector on overseas supplies and customers has given import-export firms a very important position in the economy. These firms have developed the principal sources of industrial supplies as well as the main distribution networks for many manufactured products. The rapid growth of the trading sector is to a large degree due to the increasing proportion of imported goods handled by the private sector. Whereas in the mid-1950's over 90 percent of total imports were brought in under official aid and relief programs, by 1967 this share had dropped to less than 30 percent. Most of the overall growth of imports has been accounted for by commercially financed imports.

Although comprehensive information is not available about consumer services offered in the country, the observer is immediately struck by their numbers and variety in the larger cities. The list of urban service enterprises inspected by the government for compliance with sanitary regulations gives an indication of the range and scope of this sector (see table 21). Many services other than those shown on the table are available, including medical, dental, financial, and legal aid, although outside of Seoul the number of such enterprises in proportion to the local populations is likely to be smaller.

In rural areas, the services utilized are limited to satisfaction of some of the basic requirements of farm households. Required serv-

Table 21. Service Enterprises Subject to Government Inspection
in the Republic of Korea, 1967

Type of enterprise	Number of firms	
Hotels	10,670	
Barber and beauty shops	30,808	
Bathhouses	1,034	
Swimming pools	20	
Recreation places	2,018	
Foodstuff sellers	54,103	
Cabarets		456
Bars		419
Restaurants		1,327
Dining houses		56
Public houses		13,316
Bakeries		2,289
Tearooms		3,496
Not otherwise specified		32,744
Licensed pharmacies	9,726	
Total	108,379	

Source: Adapted from Hapdong News Agency, *Korea Annual, 1968.*

ices are provided partly by village tradesmen and partly by itinerants whose cycle of visits may range from 2 months to a year. Services provided include tool repair, shoe repair, carpentry, umbrella and cooking implement repair, and collecting snakes for medical purposes.

Generally, the trading system satisfies most requirements of the consumer public. Consumers are able to buy the necessities, although supplies and prices tend to fluctuate widely during the year in response to seasonal cycles, interruptions in commodity movements, and price manipulations of commercial intermediaries. Undoubtedly, the distribution system could be considerably more efficient if buyers, sellers, producers, and consumers were better informed of market conditions. However, active government intervention in the system appears to have increased the ability of intermediaries to widen the disparity of prices between producers and consumers: Frequent changes in government policies regarding taxation, price controls, economic support, availability of credit, and designation of which commodities may or may not be freely imported, create confusion in the marketplace and invite speculative activities.

Organization of the Trading Community

The trading community consists mainly of a large number of independent vendors and itinerant merchants operating with a minimum of operating capital, inventory, and fixed assets. In the cities there are many stores and shops, some fairly large, but their share of total trade is not great. Most establishments are owner-operated, but some of the larger ones are joint stock companies.

Underlying the retail sector is a sizable group of intermediary marketing organizations. This group consists of wholesale houses, import-export houses, commission agents and manufacturers' representatives, and various private and government-sponsored cooperatives. As noted, a number of manufacturers compete with the wholesalers and import-export houses. Various textile and light machinery producers, for instance, operate factory outlets to serve consumers, and other producers maintain their own trading contacts with overseas suppliers and customers.

It is estimated that retail establishments may number in the tens of thousands because of the low barriers to entry into the trade. The following figures give some indication of the dimensions of the sector at the wholesale level. The 1967 edition of the *Korean Trade Directory*, published by the Korean Traders Association, lists 998 registered foreign trading companies, 263 commission agents, and 86 trade associations. A number of the foreign trading companies listed are actually manufacturing companies that directly import raw materials. Examples are Chosun Brewery Co., Ltd. (one of the country's two principal breweries), Korea Cement Manufacturing Co., Ltd., and Taesung Lumber Industries Co., Ltd. Many of the 263 commission agents listed also appeared in the registered foreign trade listing. Of the 86 trade associations, 23 of the member organizations were producers cooperatives. These included the government-sponsored National Agricultural Cooperative Federation and National Federation of Medium and Small Industry Cooperatives; the remainder represented private producers cooperatives manufacturing such goods as agricultural chemicals, canned goods, clothing, fish and glass products, machinery, metal products, paper, plastics, rubber goods, soap, and woolen wear.

Virtually all the organizations listed in the three groups were located in Seoul, with the few exceptions located in Pusan, Taegu, and Inch'ŏn. A number of the registered foreign traders listed had overseas branches, mainly in Japan and the United States. Some of the commission agents were overseas branches of foreign companies, such as Connell Bros. Co., Deutsche Maschinen Handelsgesellschaft, Frazar International, and Sterling International. Supporting the trading community were 27 airline and tourist agencies, seven banks dealing in foreign exchange (including the government's Bank of Korea), 28 government-designated inspection agencies for export goods, 13 marine insurance companies, and 44 shipping companies.

Generally, the foreign traders and commission agents handle related lines of merchandise. A firm will specialize in goods relating to, say, the textile or light machinery trade. A sizable number of firms, however, carry a wide range of consumer as well as producer goods. For example, the Samho Trading Co., Ltd., one of the country's principal trading houses, lists more than 100 agricultural, mineral, and manufactured products which it exports and imports. Some of the exports include dried cuttlefish, mushrooms, iron ore, ginseng, silk and synthetic fabrics, Christmas tree bulbs, sewing machines, wigs, and pianos. Imports include wheat, raw sugar, raw wool, industrial acids, pig iron, steel shapes, internal combustion engines, transport equipment, scientific instruments, watches, and optical goods. Samho, like several other trading companies, acts as a commission agent for various foreign firms and maintains several overseas branch offices. Some of the larger houses, such as Young Poong Trading Co., Ltd., and Sammisa Co., Ltd., also operate subsidiary companies in shipping, mining, fishing, textiles, and forest products and produce for the domestic as well as the export market.

Trade Practices

Most retail trade is conducted in open market areas resembling bazaars. Scores of individual tradesmen assemble, each occupying a small stall or a few feet of space, with his goods piled before him. Transactions are strictly in cash. Permanently located shops and department stores are common in the downtown areas of the larger cities. The practice of selling consumer durables, such as stoves, refrigerators, television sets, and automobiles, by installment credit is beginning to be established. Markets in the larger urban areas operate daily, 6 days a week. In rural areas, however, itinerant merchants may visit about every 5 days. In addition to this "market day," every rural town has a number of permanent shops. Depending on the size of the village, the marketplace may have a permanent site and be surrounded by shops or it may be just an open courtyard or wide place in the road.

Retail trade is relatively free of government regulation, and prices to consumers tend to reflect the interaction of supply and demand. As indicated earlier, however, currency expansion and restrictions on the movement of goods—both artificially induced and resulting from natural and physical factors—produce a generally upward trend in prices, marked by wide fluctuations.

The government attempts to influence prices at the wholesale level by licensing traders and setting price ceilings on principal foodstuffs and such essential commodities as chemical fertilizers, cement, coal, coke, petroleum products, electric power, newsprint, and textiles. The government directly controls the prices of foreign aid imports and goods and services produced by its monopolies and state enterprises, including tobacco products, salt, ginseng, rail transport, telephone, telegraph, broadcasting, and ports. Provincial and city governments control prices, rates, and fees for such various services as taxicabs, doctors, dentists, barbers, baths, hotels, and amusement establishments. In most cases the government-controlled price is lower than the free-market price of the given commodity. Where the government directly controls the distribution of goods and services—for example, government-purchased grains, chemical fertilizers, petroleum products, and public utilities—prices are not subject to manipulation by intermediaries. But for the distribution of some government-acquired foodstuffs, private interests are able to intervene.

Qualitative control of goods and services by the government is exercised principally over exports. As previously noted, in 1967 there were 28 government-licensed inspection agencies whose function was to ensure that exports would meet international standards. For goods marketed domestically, some degree of control over quality is exercised; for instance, the government-sponsored National Agricultural Cooperative Federation grades foodstuffs it purchases prior to auctioning them. Establishments serving the public—for example, restaurants, barber shops, hotels, and nightclubs—are required to be licensed to ensure maintenance of sanitary standards. During 1967, several thousand establishments had their licenses withdrawn or temporarily suspended because of sanitation code infractions.

Financing of domestic trade activities does not rely heavily on the country's banking system. At the retail level, as noted earlier, the typical trader employs a minimum of capital. In the 1950's, wholesalers relied on retained earnings for most of their operating capital requirements and it was mainly manufacturers that used bank credit. Since the early 1960's, however, wholesalers and even retailers to some extent have been using increasing amounts of commercial bank credit. Thus, between 1961 and 1967 commercial bank loans and discounts to the commerce sector (principally wholesalers) rose from 2.3 billion wŏn to 23.3 billion wŏn. This represents a tenfold increase, compared with a fourfold increase in the nominal value of the gross national product over the same period. Most domestic credit is still allocated to directly productive activities, but as the economy matures, an increasing share of commercial bank lending operations may be directed toward financing trade activities and consumer credit.

Public Consumer Services

Public utilities in the Republic of Korea are all government owned and operated. These include electric power, municipal water and sewerage systems, telephones, and telegraph service.

Since the country has no petroleum resources, there is no use of natural gas. Coal is extensively used for heating in homes and industry; about half of it is produced by a government-owned mining enterprise. The government also owns and operates one of the country's six radio broadcasting networks and one of the two television systems.

The government has placed high priority on development of the country's consumer service infrastructure, particularly for electric power and transportation. Since the initiation of the First Five-Year Plan in 1962, expansion of public services has been very rapid and increasing numbers of persons have benefited. The gross national product share represented by electric power, sanitary services, and communications amounted to 1.6 percent in 1966, up from 1.3 percent in 1961. The utilities employed about 30,000 workers in 1966, about one-third of whom were in the electric power sector.

Most public utility services are produced and consumed in urban areas. The rural electrification program of the government is progressing, however, as new generating and transmission facilities are constructed. Industrial consumption of electric power accounts for the largest part of total demand, amounting to 83.3 percent in 1966. In 1964, power rationing was terminated for the first time as a result of the rapid expansion of generating capacity, but it was reimposed once during 1966 because drought curtailed the output of the hydroelectric power facilities at a time of peak industrial demand. The government anticipated that to keep abreast of energy requirements by 1971 it will have to nearly triple the 1966 installed generating capacity of 769 megawatts.

Electric power rates are relatively high. Most electric power is generated from coal-fired plants, and coal production costs are high because of the complex geologic characteristics of the country's coal deposits. Hydroelectric potential is not great because of the highly seasonal rainfall; and because coal reserves are limited, the government is seriously considering development of nuclear-powered electricity generation.

According to government figures, 83 cities, with a total population of 6.23 million persons, had water service in 1966, up from 70 cities (4.71 million persons) in 1962. The cities of Seoul, Pusan, Inch'ŏn, Taejŏn, and Taegu were each provided with supply capacities in excess of 10,000 tons of water per day. Thus, slightly more than one-fifth of the population had water service while the remaining population was dependent on local wells and streams.

Communications services are limited, although expansion has been rapid since the early 1960's. At the end of 1966, there were 1,728 post offices across the country. Telephone circuits totaled 313,331, comprising 202,980 city telephone circuits and 110,351 rural circuits, and averaging 11 telephones for 1,000 persons. Long distance telephone circuits numbered 2,355 in 1966 including 18 international circuits, 1,268 intercity circuits, 1,068 intertownship circuits, and one radio broadcasting relay circuit. There were 420 telegraphic circuits in 1966, comprising 20 international circuits and 400 telex circuits. These latter connected with six telex exchanges in the country's major cities.

Transportation and Storage

In recent years the transportation system has undergone considerable expansion and improvement. However, it does not yet adequately serve the needs of the country, as indicated by congested urban traffic, overcrowded public transport facilities, shortages of railcars and storage facilities, poor roads, and fluctuations in supply and price of essential commodities. Much agricultural production is still transported on human backs and most rural travel is accomplished on foot.

The transportation and storage sector contributed 4.7 percent of the gross national product in 1967 and employed about 200,000 workers, or about 2 percent of the economically active population. This sector has been the object of a substantial development effort by the government, as a result of which investments in transportation and storage facilities have averaged about 20 percent of gross domestic fixed capital formation since the early 1960's. All but about 5 percent of the investments have been in transportation, with the railroads and highways receiving most of the outlays.

The government-owned Korean National Railroad provides the principal means of inland transportation. Although the tonnage of freight hauled in recent years has been less than that carried by road transport, railroad freight traffic, measured in ton-kilometers, has averaged about 87 percent of total inland freight transport owing to the greater distances traveled. Highways, on the other hand, account for more passenger traffic—9.3 billion passenger-kilometers in 1966, compared with 8.7 billion on the railroads and 0.4 billion on coastal shipping and domestic air lines.

The national railway system consists of approximately 1,750 miles of main-line standard-gauge track, 77 miles of narrow-gauge track, and 287 miles of siding and station track which serve all the principal industrial areas, ports, and cities. The network is single track with the exception of 276 miles of double track between Seoul and Pusan. Bridges and tunnels are in good repair, and terminal facilities are adequate for normal business. Warehouses, dockside rail service in major ports, and material-handling equipment are available. In 1966, the Korean National Railroad carried 24.1 million tons of freight and 138.3 million passengers.

A large-scale program for equipment modernization and conversion to diesel locomotives was undertaken during the First Five-Year Plan (1961–1966) with substantial assistance from the United States. As of December 1967, the Republic of Korea had 252 diesel locomotives, with an additional 151 to be imported by 1971. As of that date, rolling stock consisted of 1,559 passenger coaches and 12,793 freight cars, and plans exist for expanding these facilities to 2,150 and 15,500, respectively, by 1971.

There are about 20,450 miles of road in the country, most in poor condition. Only 1,200 miles of road are paved and about 800 miles of this are intercity roads. Most roads are narrow with a gravel surface, and year-round maintenance is generally inadequate.

By 1971, the government planned to pave some 1,000 miles of road, improve 1,950 miles, and construct 160 miles of bridges. In late 1967 the government announced plans to build a limited-access toll highway between Seoul and Pusan. Groundbreaking for the first link in the highway took place early in 1968, and highway completion was expected by 1971. A similar road is under construction between Seoul and Inch'ŏn.

At the end of 1966, there were 50,160 registered motor vehicles, including 17,502 passenger cars (of which 7,481 were privately owned), 19,432 trucks, and 10,888 buses. Of total registered motor vehicles, about 60 percent were engaged in commercial operations. The trucks in use carried about 24.5 million tons of freight in 1966. Buses carried a total of 1 billion passengers.

Domestic air service is provided mainly by Korea Air Lines, a government enterprise. In 1966 the Korea Air Lines fleet consisted of two DC–3's, one DC–4, and four F–27's (two leased). One DC–9 has been purchased and is in operation between Korea and Japan. Korea Air Lines links Seoul with Pusan, Taegu, Kwangju, Kangnung, Samch'ŏk, and Cheju Island for domestic service and also connects Seoul with Osaka and Tokyo, and Pusan with Fuku-'oka, on the Japanese mainland.

Although air service has expanded rapidly, it still only accounts for about 1 percent of total passenger and freight transport. In 1966 Korea Air Lines carried 191,607 passengers and 986.8 metric tons of freight and mail on domestic routes. International carriers serving the country, together with Korea Air Lines on its routes to Japan, carried 131,359 passengers and 7.37 thousand metric tons of cargo and mail in 1966.

The Republic of Korea had eight principal airports in 1966, but only three (Kimpo/Seoul, Pusan, and Cheju) could operate at night. Air navigation facilities are being expanded and improved with the assistance of the United States Agency for International Development.

Marine transport is an important element in the national economy because of the country's long shoreline, numerous islands, geographic isolation, and dependence on fish for food. In 1966 there were 12,562 vessels registered, a total gross tonnage of 470,145 tons. Oceangoing vessels numbered 83 ships as of August 1967 (301,000 gross tons). Most vessels are wooden, but because of their small average size (most are fishing boats) they account for only about 40 percent of total gross tonnage. Most smaller vessels are old and poorly equipped. Large-scale shipbuilding facilities are limited, and most oceangoing vessels have to be imported.

Coastal shipping accounted for 4.2 percent of total domestic cargo traffic and 1.1 percent of total domestic passenger traffic in 1966. Since 1961, cargo movements by coastal shipping have been increasing at nearly 20 percent annually. Traffic being diverted from the congested rail lines of the country is contributing to this growth. Most of the country's international commerce is carried by foreign flagships. From 1961 to 1966, an annual average of about 25 percent of the 8.4 million tons of imports and exports moved on the country's vessels.

Port facilities are limited, and ships often must be worked with double shifts and lighters. Fourteen harbors are considered comparatively large, but only three—Pusan, Ulsan, and Mokpo—can accommodate ships larger than 10,000 gross tons. Continuous dredging is required in order to maintain accessibility. Inch'ŏn harbor, serving Seoul, can take ships up to only 4,500 tons. Pusan is the primary port; in 1966 it handled 45 percent of total dry cargo for all ports. Other important ports are located at Kunsan, Mŏkho, Masan, Chinhae, and Yŏsu. All major ports have stevedoring services and commercial warehousing facilities. Port capacities have been expanded gradually, increasing from 9.0 million tons in 1961 to 12.2 million in 1966.

Storage facilities and related activities such as packaging, crating, and freezing, are inadequate. The economy is unable to accommodate seasonal variations in the flow of agricultural products from producers to consumers, as indicated by the fluctuations in food prices, the relatively low per capita consumption of processed foodstuffs, and the need for quarterly government reappraisals of admission of key imports. Inadequate storage and processing facilities are also a major factor contributing to supply and price instability. Most warehousing facilities are located at ports, railroad junctions, and cities, where commodity movements are concentrated.

ROLE OF GOVERNMENT

The government exercises considerable influence over the economy and the movement of goods and services. The aim of the policies of the government agencies regulating commerce is to ensure the flow of resources into national development. Implementation takes the form mainly of controls and regulations that counteract the physical obstacles and market factors tending to disrupt this flow and induce price instability.

During the early 1960's when inflation was dangerously rapid, the government imposed a large number of direct controls on prices, production, and imports in an effort to stabilize the economy while still promoting its growth. By 1966, price increases had moderated substantially as a result of constrained consumer spending and decrease in imports, and the government shifted its policy in favor of reduced direct controls on trade. Devaluation in 1964 and adherence to financial stabilization programs contributed to stabilization. Nevertheless, there remain many indirect as well as several direct controls on trade. The government is further able to influence the economy through fiscal and monetary policies as well as through operation of its various manufacturing, mining, banking, transportation, and communications enterprises.

The principal instrument of government trade regulation is licensing of foreign traders and wholesalers, which is overseen by the Ministry of Commerce and Industry. To qualify for licensing, traders must demonstrate that they are able to conduct a prescribed minimum volume of business. The Ministry of Finance exercises quantitative control over imports and exports, administration of tariffs, national taxes, foreign exchange transactions, and supervision of government enterprise operations and government-sponsored cooperatives. A bureau of this ministry—the Office of Supply—is responsible for administration of the Commodity Budget established by the government in 1966. This budget consists of seven items of construction supplies, 16 items of shipbuilding supplies, 12 items of major industrial raw materials (including chemical fertilizers), and 10 essential consumer commodities—the steady supply of all of which is considered necessary for price stability and economic growth. Each quarter the Office of Supply reviews the supply and demand situation for these items and increases or decreases imports in order to maintain economic balance.

Rates and tariffs for public services are set by various ministries: electric power rates by the Ministry of Commerce and Industry; rail and road transit, aviation, and maritime rates by the Ministry of Transportation; and telephone and telegraph rates by the Ministry of Communications. These agencies establish and implement trade policies in line with the overall development policies determined by the Economic Planning Board, which holds ministerial rank in the government.

DOMESTIC TRADE AND SOCIETY

In the two decades since the departure of the Japanese, people engaged in trading activities have overcome much of the disrepute traditionally attached to their vocation as a holdover from the days when the rigid class structure and the Confucian tradition gave merchants low status. The United States presence and the recent national drive for industrial development have brought changes in attitudes. The Western respect for contracts, for instance, has been accepted to some degree in the commercial community, and is reflected in the growing volume of trade financed by bank credit.

Changes in status and attitudes are most pronounced in the larger urban areas, where the process of westernization is more rapid. Education, mass media, international contacts and influences, the dislocations of war, and the breakdown in family relationships all contribute to an abandonment of traditional attitudes and ways. The process is much slower in rural areas where living conditions change slowly and outside influences are less strong. Also, merchants' practices of usurious lending to farmers reinforce rural attitudes of distrust and disdain for traders.

The role of foreigners in trade is small. Japanese and American trading firms are prominent in the commerce sector, but most employees are Korean nationals. Of considerable importance in the conduct of trade are the social relationships of businessmen with one another and with the government. Family connections are of great importance, and often these may determine, for instance, whether an entrepreneur can secure a license, a contract, or a loan.

CHAPTER 23

FOREIGN ECONOMIC RELATIONS

Much of the recent economic growth of the Republic of Korea can be attributed to a rapid expansion of foreign trade. The Republic's primary asset in developing foreign trade is a highly literate and industrious labor force working for relatively low wages. A policy of vigorous promotion of foreign trade by the government has been a major factor in the growth of export trade. Since the country is relatively poor in natural resources, export trade has tended toward an increasing emphasis on manufactured products. The domestic market for finished products is limited by the low level of income per capita. If recent trends continue, economic growth in the future will depend to a large degree on expansion of export markets. In this regard, the Republic of Korea at present parallels in many respects the Japanese economy at an earlier stage of development.

The foreign trade of the Republic's economy was not, in mid-1964, without continuing problems. Despite an extraordinary expansion of exports over the past decade, imports have increased even more rapidly, and the trade balance has thus shown a growing deficit. The country has traditionally paid for its import surpluses with foreign aid funds, but it appears likely that foreign aid will decline in the future. Pressures are increasing for both expansion of exports and encouragement of capital inflows. Until recently, capital inflows have been negligible, presumably because of the country's precarious politico-geographic situation. A further problem is that international competition for the kinds of goods the Republic of Korea produces is becoming very keen. Moreover, economic growth based largely on export expansion makes the economy even more sensitive to world economic conditions. The government was attempting to solve them through appropriate measures. The general situation of foreign trade was relatively good, especially in comparison with earlier periods. Economic plans indicated that imports would decline relative to exports in the future as the country became more self-sufficient in basic goods and commodities. Also, private capital inflows were increasing.

FOREIGN TRADE PATTERNS

Foreign trade is a large and rapidly growing element of the economy. In 1967, exports amounted to $358.6 million, and imports totaled $679.9 million. Between 1960 and 1967, exports increased over ten times, while imports nearly doubled.

The composition of the export trade in 1967 was as follows: manufactured goods, 70 percent; fisheries products, 14.7 percent; mining products, 10.5 percent; and agricultural products, 4.8 percent. Ten leading products accounted for 54 percent of the exports, namely, plywood, sweaters, wigs, raw silk, clothing, cotton fabric, terrycloth, dried laver (or edible seaweed), tuna, and tungsten. Plywood, by far the most important export, represented close to 12 percent of the total value of the export trade in 1967. Other notable exports in that year were iron ore, tobacco, rubber shoes, fish, tricot and lace, agar-agar, and synthetic fabrics. Principal exports to the United States are plywood, raw silk, textiles, garments, footwear, and handicraft products. Between 1960 and 1967, the relative importance of manufactured goods in the exports of the Republic of Korea increased dramatically from 20 to 70 percent of the total.

Asian countries in 1967 received 43.6 percent, and western hemisphere countries, 43.4 percent of the Republic's exports. Europe was the recipient of 9.5 percent and Africa 2.5 percent of the export total. Among specific countries, the United States and Japan were the major markets, accounting for 41.9 and 26.6 percent of the total, respectively. Other countries that received significant amounts of Korean goods were South Vietnam, Hong Kong, Sweden, England, Thailand, Canada, Nigeria, and West Germany. Between 1960 and 1967 the pattern of exports changed markedly, with the United States becoming more important and Japan declining in relative importance as a destination.

The import trade of the Republic in 1966 breaks down as follows: machinery and transport equipment, 24 percent; crude materials, 21 percent; manufactured goods, 19 percent; chemicals, 19 percent; foodstuffs, 11 percent; and fuels, 6 percent. This distribution of imports has generally continued into 1967. The principal change in the composition of the import trade between 1960 and 1967 has been the increased relative importance of machinery and transport equipment. This change reflects the government policy of concentrating on industrialization programs.

The origin of the Republic of Korea's imports in 1966 reveals that Asian areas supplied 54 percent of the total, while the western hemisphere accounted for 36 percent and Europe for only 8 percent of the imports. Among particular countries, Japan supplied 41 percent of the total in 1966, up sharply from the preceding year when relations between the countries were normalized. The United States provided 35 percent of 1966 imports. Thus, Japan and the United States predominate in the Republic's trade—both as to origin of its imports and destination of its exports.

Trade between the Republic of Korea and the United States has been greatly stimulated by the economic cooperation agreements between the governments of these countries. Much of the import trade had been made possible by the economic assistance provided by the United States under these agreements. Also, the 1965 agreement between the Republic of Korea and Japan, normalizing relations between the governments of those countries, has resulted in expanded trade. The Republic has also negotiated economic cooperation agreements with several countries of western Europe, and trade agreements have been signed with a number of African and Latin American countries. These various agreements reflect the policy of the government to foster the expansion of the country's international trade. The Republic of Korea has no official trade relations with any Communist country.

INVISIBLE TRANSACTIONS

Services as well as merchandise are international transactions of the people of the Republic of Korea. Sale and purchase of such services as transportation and insurance are significant items in these transactions. In 1966, total invisible transactions provided $204.4 million of foreign exchange to the Republic, while payments were $97.8 million. A net inflow of foreign exchange from these transactions has occurred over the past several years, a factor that has helped alleviate the substantial deficit in commodity trade. The major source of foreign exchange in the transactions account is the purchase of goods and services by United Nations forces within the Republic of Korea. The largest outflows of foreign exchange in this category are for transportation and insurance, a situation explained by the country's dependence on foreigners for these services. While travel and tourism have yielded a negligible amount of foreign exchange in the past, foreign exchange earned from these sources has expanded significantly in recent years.

Transfer Payments

Transfer payments have been a significant part of the international transactions. In 1966, they constituted a net credit of $219.6 million to the Republic of Korea. Transfer payments include funds sent to the country from residents living abroad or funds donated by private citizens of other countries. Private transfer payments have expanded considerably in the Republic recently. This is largely a result of the growing numbers of Koreans working in foreign countries, particularly in South Vietnam, Japan, and West

Germany. Government transfer payments include foreign government aid but not capital flows. Foreign government transfers to the country include official foreign aid and grants under U. S. Public Law 480. In 1966, private transfers amounted to $130 million, and government transfers to $124 million. Transfer payments have been the primary means by which the Republic has financed its trade deficits for many years.

Capital Flows

Capital inflows have become of major significance in the Republic's foreign transactions. In the past, most of the capital inflows were foreign government loans. Foreign private loans have become of great significance since 1963, however, and, since 1965, a small but rapidly increasing amount of foreign capital inflow has been in the form of direct investment by foreign firms. The rapid increase in private capital inflows in recent years has been largely the result of continued political and economic stability in the Republic, a rapid rate of economic growth, the availability of investment opportunities, and the provision by the government of incentives to foreign investors.

In mid-1967, foreign loans and investments in the Republic of Korea totaled $780 million. Of this amount, 46 percent consisted of public loans; 47 percent, private loans; and 7 percent, direct investment. More than 70 percent of the loans and investments were from the United States and Japan. Other important contributions were West Germany, France, and England.

Debt servicing does not create a large problem at present because the total external debt is relatively small (though increasing rapidly) ; terms are, in general, generous; and gross national product is growing steadily. Debt servicing is kept at a minimum by borrowing on a long-term basis and by attracting equity investment.

Foreign direct investments in the country are varied but are primarily in labor-intensive industries. As to the origin of the direct investments, 87 percent are from the United States, and nearly all of the remainder are from Japan. Examples of major foreign direct investments are a food processing plant, oil refineries, fertilizer plants, electronics plants, construction of a hotel, and shipbuilding. Other direct investments of lesser significance are, for example, in the manufacture of furniture, integrated circuits, ornaments, and pharmaceuticals.

Public and private loans as well as direct investments in the Republic have expanded considerably in the 1960's. To a large extent this growth in the rate of capital flow reflects a change in U. S. policy in which greater emphasis is placed on more conventional means of financing and a lesser role is accorded foreign aid. Capital flows have become an important balancing item in the balance of payments and, if current trends continue, will likely replace foreign aid as the major means of financing trade deficits.

THE BALANCE OF PAYMENTS

The Republic of Korea's balance of payments for the years from 1960 through 1967 indicates, as previously noted, that exports and imports have expanded sharply during this period (see table 22). Invisible trade, reflected in the services portion of this statement, maintained a positive surplus, and the level of this invisible trade has expanded. The commodity trade balance of current account has consistently shown a deficit. During the 1960–67 period, the level of transfer payments was relatively stable. Though foreign aid (included in government transfer payments) has been declining, private transfers have expanded considerably, especially since 1964. There has also been a considerable inflow of capital, transfer payments, and capital inflows have financed the trade deficit on current account. In addition, capital inflows are becoming the more significant equating entry in the balance of payments.

FOREIGN AID

Since 1947, the Republic of Korea has received over $4 billion in foreign aid. In the years 1947 to 1967 between 85 and 90 percent of the Republic's foreign aid was obtained from the United States (see table 23). It should be noted, however, that much of Civil Relief in Korea (CRIK) and United Nations Korean Reconstruction Agency (UNKRA) funds contributed during that period were of United States origin. The Republic of Korea also received a substantial amount of military aid (see ch. 27, The Armed Forces).

The purposes of nonmilitary foreign aid to the Republic of Korea have been to provide civilian relief, to help reconstruct facilities demolished by war, and to aid in economic development. Foreign aid played a very important role in reconstruction after the Korean conflict, consequently revitalizing a significant part of the infrastructure upon which Korea's recent economic progress is based. While there has been some criticism of the foreign aid program among Koreans and foreign participants alike, the general feeling of Koreans regarding foreign aid seems to be one of appreciation.

United States Foreign Aid

United States aid to the Republic of Korea administered through the Agency for International Development has taken several forms. Supporting assistance is used for purchase, through normal commercial channels, of specific raw materials and essential imports which the Republic cannot finance with its own exchange earnings. For example, importation of commercial ferti-

Table 22. Republic of Korea Balance of Payments
(in millions of U.S. dollars)

	1960 Credit	1960 Debit	1962 Credit	1962 Debit	1964 Credit	1964 Debit	1966 Credit	1966 Debit
GOODS AND SERVICES	116.9	379.2	163.2	455.2	211.0	432.0	454.7	777.7
Merchandise (f.o.b.)	32.8	305.4	54.8	390.1	119.1	364.9	250.3	679.9
Services	84.1	73.8	108.4	65.1	91.9	67.1	204.4	97.8
Net goods and services	—	263.3	—	292.0	—	221.0	—	323.0
TRANSFER PAYMENTS	282.0	6.3	238.7	2.2	198.6	3.7	227.3	7.7
Private	20.6	1.0	37.5	1.0	56.7	2.8	103.3	5.7
Government	261.4	5.3	201.2	1.2	141.9	0.9	124.0	2.0
Net transfer payments	275.7	—	236.5	—	194.9	—	219.6	—
Net total	13.4	—	—	55.5	—	26.1	—	103.4
ERRORS AND OMISSIONS	n.a.	2.1	—	1.6	—	1.1	—	4.4
CAPITAL AND MONETARY GOLD	n.a.	n.a.	30.6	26.5	— 3.1	30.3	107.1	206.1
Private capital	0.6	2.6	7.2	2.8	— 2.6	9.9	1.3	184.9
Central and local government	—	13.0	0.6	5.6	— 0.3	17.5	3.0	37.6
Other	4.2	1.2	38.4	18.1	— 0.2	2.9	102.8	16.4

Source: Adapted from Bank of Korea sources.

Table 23. Foreign Aid Received by the Republic of Korea, 1947–1967[1]

Agency	Amount[2]	Time period
Aid of Government and Relief in Occupied Areas (GARIOA)	447.7	1947–1949
Economic Cooperation Administration (ECA)	109.2	1949–1953
United States Public Law 480	683.7	1956–1967
Agency for International Development (AID)	2,477.4	1953–1967
Civil Relief in Korea (CRIK)	457.4	1950–1956
United Nations Korean Reconstruction Agency (UNKRA)	122.1	1951–1960
Total	4,297.5	

[1] Excluding military aid.
[2] In millions of U.S. dollars.

Source: Adapted from Bank of Korea, *Economic Statistics Yearbook, 1967*, p. 290.

lizer has been the largest item financed through this source. The importer of goods under this program pays the full value in Republic of Korea currency, which is then deposited in the "Counterpart Funds Special Account" of the government's budgetary accounts and becomes a source of governmental revenue (see ch. 24, Public Finance). Technical service, a second form of United States assistance to the Republic of Korea, is directed toward development of human resources and provision of technical and professional advice in important areas of the economy. These funds have been used in projects to improve education, health, housing, and diet and to provide experienced technicians for key development projects and for aid in government policymaking. Aid also has provided development loans to the Republic on very generous terms. Loans have been granted, for example, for construction of cement plants, fertilizer plants, thermal-electric plants, and the purchase of diesel locomotives. Loans have also been made to the Korean Reconstruction Bank and the Medium Industry Bank for re-lending. In recent years, an increasing portion of United States aid to the Republic of Korea has taken the form of loans as opposed to direct grants.

The Republic of Korea also received economic aid from the United States through U. S. Public Law 480, which provides that surplus agricultural commodities may be given to developing countries to help meet local food and fiber needs, to provide direct relief when needed, to handle food requirements resulting from natural calamities, and for self-help economic activities. Funds from this source also enter the "Counterpart Funds Special Account" of the Republic of Korea government accounts. As of June 1966, total United States aid under the different categories of economic assistance was classified as follows: supporting assistance, $1,965.9 million; technical cooperation, $290.0 million; development loan, $230.8 million, and grants under Public Law 480, $752.5 million.

Assistance from Other Countries

While in the past the Republic has received the predominant part of its foreign aid from the United States, other countries have begun to account for increasing shares. Since 1962, West Germany has become an important source of capital for the Republic. German government and commercial loans have financed development of cement, iron works, machinery, mining, and electrical industries. The German government has also provided technical assistance in vocational education. France has provided both technical and capital assistance, including a loan for a hydroelectric plant.

As a result of the Normalization Treaty with Japan in 1965, the Republic of Korea is to receive from Japan $300 million in grants and $200 million in loans over a period of ten years. The government plans to use these funds for investment in agriculture, fisheries, transportation, and industry and for the importation of vital raw materials. In addition, the Republic is to receive a substantial amount of commercial credit from Japan as a result of the treaty.

Through the Colombo Plan, the Republic has received study grants and technical assistance from the United Kingdom, Australia, and Canada. In addition, Scandinavian countries and Israel have provided specialized assistance in the health and agricultural fields.

In addition to the above foreign assistance programs of individual countries, the Republic of Korea also received substantial loans for railway equipment in 1962 and 1967 from an affiliate of the International Bank for Reconstruction and Development. In 1966, the International Consultive Organization for Korea was established, consisting of representatives from Monetary Fund, International Bank for Reconstruction and Development, the United Nations Development Program, and nine participating nations. This organization is expected to considerably enhance the Republic's ability to attract foreign capital in the future.

United Nations Programs

During the period 1950–1960, the United Nations, through the United Nations Korean Reconstruction Agency (UNKRA), expended a total of $122 million on various programs. These funds were subscribed by 31 members of the United Nations and 5 non-member governments. UNKRA gave special attention to technical assistance programs and drew upon the specialized agencies of the United Nations—the Food and Agriculture Organization (FAO); the United Nations Educational, Scientific, and Cultural Organization (UNESCO) ; and others. The limited funds available precluded UNKRA from undertaking major programs on its own. In some cases, programs such as that of an agricultural project recommended by FAO and estimated to cost some $300 million were transferred to the International Cooperation Administration (ICA), now the Agency for International Development (AID). Special programs in education were undertaken by UNKRA in conjunction with the Republic of Korea and other governments. The reconstruction of the Taegu Medical College, for example, was undertaken jointly with the Swiss government.

In addition to UNKRA, other United Nations agencies have conducted programs in the Republic of Korea. The United Nations Children's Fund (UNICEF) has supported a program of providing powdered milk for children between 2 and 10 years of age, as well as a program devoted to training midwives, in cooperation with the Ministry of Health and Social Affairs and private organizations. UNESCO has conducted a primary education project, has assisted in the financing of the Seoul textbook printing plant, and has awarded several scholarships for Koreans to study abroad.

In 1962, the Republic received approval for aid totaling $2 million from the United Nations Special Fund for management development and productivity improvement and for the establishment of a telecommunications training and research center. In addition, the United Nations Expanded Program for Technical Assistance approved the Republic's applications for technical assistance amounting to $133,500. In 1966, the United Nations Development Program approved an application of the Republic of Korea government for $1.25 million to help finance a preliminary survey for the development of the Naktong River Basin.

ORGANIZATION OF FOREIGN TRADE

The foreign trade activities of the Republic of Korea are heavily influenced by the government, and trading interests are subject to a number of government requirements and controls. All firms partaking in foreign trade must be licensed by the Ministry of Commerce and Industry as registered traders. Each trading firm must have paid-in capital of 5 million wŏn ($20,000) and, in addition, a letter of credit from an overseas customer or other evidence of future exports of at least $100,000 in merchandise. No volume requirements are stipulated as far as imports are concerned. In the case of AID-financed goods or goods imported under Public Law 480, a license is not necessary. While there were about 1,000 registered traders at the end of 1966, this number was expected to decline as a result of the government's increasing the minimum export volume in an effort to stimulate the export drive and to weed out small unreliable traders. Trading firms are predominantly owned and operated by Korean nationals. The government's considerable influence on trade is based more on its supervisory, regulatory, financing, and promotional functions than on direct operations.

While the government has substantial ownership of productive facilities in the economy, export trade is largely carried on by private trading firms. In 1966, 86 percent of exports were commercial exports, 11 percent were imports processed in bond and re-exported, and 3 percent were from various other sources. The government accounts for a sizable portion of imports (about 15 percent in 1966).

There are nearly 100 private trade associations in the Republic of Korea. Their general purpose has been to promote export trade in commodities produced in the country. The most important of these associations is the Korean Traders Association, composed of government-licensed traders. This organization offers information services, makes recommendations to the government on trade policy, issues publications, and participates in trade exhibits and missions. The government has taken an active role in trade promotion in the 1960's, and its efforts have overshadowed those of the private trade associations.

THE ROLE OF GOVERNMENT

Government Policy

The government has been very active in the area of foreign economic relations during the 1960's, and its policies in this area largely reflect the country's development needs. Control over foreign trade and exchange transactions by the government conserves foreign exchange reserves and provides protection and encouragement for domestic industry. Generally, the government has committed itself to a policy of free trade, but development needs and balance of payments problems have precluded immediate achievement of this goal. During the last few years there had been an easing of import restrictions, many commodities being added to the "automatic approval lists." The government still maintains control over imports through high duties on luxuries and goods competing with domestically produced items and low customs duties on essential imports.

The government has actively promoted export trade. Special inducements are given to export industries, and the government has actively participated in trade expansion activities with foreign countries. In 1967, the Republic of Korea was accorded membership in the General Agreement on Tariffs and Trade (GATT), culminating an effort by the government to expand trade horizons. To obtain necessary foreign capital as a means of compensating for declining foreign aid, the Republic passed a revised foreign capital inducement law that provides very favorable conditions for foreign loans and investment.

The Government and Foreign Trade

Export Trade Promotion

The government's principal agency for the promotion of foreign trade is the Korea Trade Promotion Corporation (KOTRA). The functions of KOTRA are survey and exploration of overseas markets, promotion of export industries and fostering of new export industries, operation of trade centers and participation in trade fairs, and issuing publications regarding exports. KOTRA has three trade centers in the United States—in New York, Chicago, and Los Angeles—two in Europe, and six in the Far East. In addition to KOTRA, the government established the Korea Exchange Bank in 1967 to help finance foreign trade and to handle foreign transactions (see ch. 25, Banking and Currency).

Measures employed by the government to encourage exports by domestic producers represent a large effort on the part of government to promote exports, and there has been some concern in recent years that this policy was encouraging a misallocation of resources (see table 24). The government plans to rescind special privileges of export industries as they become self-sufficient and to discourage uneconomic export industries. The government also has instituted a system to finance imports of raw materials for processing and re-export and commodities urgently needed for domestic use.

Export Inspection System

To uphold the prestige of the Republic's products abroad, the government requires that a wide range of products be inspected by the government prior to export. Inspection covers quality, packaging, and processing. Firms with products that do not meet requirements are not granted an export license. Failure of a firm to conform to inspection provisions or exportation by irregular means carries the risk of fines or imprisonment.

Foreign Capital Inducement

In 1966, the government passed an amended version of the Foreign Capital Inducement Law. The revised law provides for exemption from income, corporate, and property taxes for five years and exemption from 50 percent of these taxes for three years thereafter. Furthermore, imports of capital goods are exempt from cus-

Table 24. Measures Employed by the Republic of Korea Government
to Promote Export Industry

General type of measure	Specific nature of measure
Taxation	Exemption from business tax
	50 percent reduction in corporation income tax
	Special depreciation allowances for tax purposes
	Exemptions from the customs duties on equipment and machinery imported
Banking and finance	Export loans at 6.5 percent per annum
	(a) to industries with exports of merchandise valued in excess of U.S.$ 50,000
	(b) to industries with established export letters of credit in excess of U.S.$ 100,000
	Payment guarantees on the import of raw materials used in the manufacture of export items for the period from opening of letter of credit to arrival of bill of lading (1.5 percent per annum)
Railway freight charges	30 percent discount on freight charges for exported minerals
Electricity rates	20 percent discount on electricity rates for installations of export industries drawing over 200 kilowatts

Source: Adapted from Republic of Korea, Economic Planning Board, *Economic Survey, 1967*, p. 66.

toms and commodity taxes and, if domestic capital goods account for 50 percent of the investment in a given development, approval is given for capital goods imports on a priority basis and special tax concessions are granted. The purpose of these generous provisions was to attract substantial foreign capital which the Republic requires for its development plans. The government maintains strict control over the kinds of investments that can be made.

Customs Duties

Customs duties were set in the past at relatively moderate rates, with the primary aim of obtaining revenue for the government. The 1967 tariff revision indicates a shift in emphasis with a greater degree of interest in the protection of local industry, curbing luxury consumption, and encouragement of essential imports. The revised law also gives certain government agencies broad discretionary authority to change individual rates. Customs duties in 1967 accounted for over 10 percent of total government revenues. However, the relative importance of customs duties as a source of governmental revenue has been declining in recent years (see ch. 24, Public Finance). Raw materials to be processed by bonded firms and later re-exported are exempt from customs duties. The

Bureau of Customs of the Ministry of Finance is responsible for the administration of the customs laws.

Foreign Exchange

Until the mid-1960's, the Republic was plagued with foreign exchange problems which forced repeated devaluations of the currency. Foreign currency was so scarce that the government often auctioned it to the highest bidders. Since the mid-1960's, however, trade expansion and exchange reforms have produced dramatic improvements in the situation.

The Republic of Korea originally possessed a fixed exchange rate system, but in 1964 a fluctuating exchange rate system was instituted based on the supply of and demand for foreign exchange. The initial rate was established at 255 wŏn to 1 U. S. dollar and was not allowed at first to rise above this basic rate but to depreciate as supply and demand conditions determined. Between 1965 and 1968, the basic exchange rate was relatively stable although it climbed to 275 wŏn per U. S. dollar. The Bank of Korea determined the basic exchange rate on a daily basis.

The Republic's foreign exchange holdings have expanded considerably during the 1960's as a result of continuing conditions of economic growth and inflationary control and rapid expansion of foreign trade. As of January 1968, foreign exchange holdings totaled $387.2 million.

The government at present controls the sale and purchase of foreign exchange. All exports from the Republic of Korea are made against the customer's irrevocable letter of credit, which the exporter must submit to the Korea Exchange Bank. For exportable items in the "restricted" category, an export permit also is required. No permit is necessary for "automatic" export items, as specified under a Semi-Annual Trade Plan formulated and administered by the Ministry of Commerce and Industry. Proceeds from export trade are collected through the Korea Exchange Bank. Import procedures are analogous to those for exports. For the importation of "automatic items" only the confirmation of the Korea Exchange Bank is required, but for items in the "restricted" category, an import license issued by the Ministry of Commerce and Industry is necessary with one exception—only registered traders are allowed to carry on foreign trade. Importers of goods financed by the Agency for International Development need not be registered traders.

CHAPTER 24
PUBLIC FINANCE

Public finance operations have had a profound influence on the rate of economic growth and the distribution of income in the Republic of Korea. Since 1945, the government's effort to undertake necessary public programs while attempting to keep a proper balance between governmental revenues and expenses has been extremely difficult. Extensive public programs were precipitated by two major occurrences, namely, the division of the country and the severe damage caused by the Korean conflict. The division of the country made it necessary for the government of the Republic of Korea to undertake large power development projects and other public programs. The Korean conflict resulted in extensive damage to public facilities, imposing a heavy burden of reconstruction on the government. In addition to these burdens the government has also faced the problem of contributing to the general economic development of the country. Substantial foreign economic assistance has been a major factor enabling the government of the Republic of Korea to handle its heavy financial responsibilities.

Notwithstanding the large receipts of foreign aid, very serious inflation occurred in South Korea between 1945 and the early 1960's. The inflation resulted in a shift in real income away from those least able to bear a loss of income, a trend which in turn contributed to social and political unrest and reduced incentive to work. Inflation also caused a diversion of resources from productive activity into socially less desirable activities involving high speculative profits. Entry of foreign capital was discouraged by inflation, and the balance of payments problem was aggravated in that imports were encouraged and exports discouraged. Inflation also made rational planning and cost calculations extremely difficult for government and business alike.

In the early 1960's, the inflationary trend was greatly moderated as the Park government achieved considerable success in bringing public finance under control. Since 1963, government expenditures have been held more in line with available resources, and deficit financing has been eliminated. Government revenues have been enhanced through tax reform and through more stringent enforcement of tax laws.

GENERAL NATURE OF THE BUDGET

In accordance with the present budget format, adopted in 1959, expenditures are listed under the following general headings: general services, including government administration, defense, justice and police; community services, including roads, waterways, fire protection, water supply, and sanitation; social services, including education, health, social security, war veteran benefits, mother and child care, and housing; economic services, including agriculture, forestry, fuel and power, mining, manufacturing, construction, transport, storage, and communications; and unallocable expenditure, including interest on debts, subsidies to local governments, and government payments abroad. The revenue divisions in current use are tax revenues and stamp duties, revenue from government enterprises and properties, miscellaneous revenues, military support in Vietnam, and transfers from special accounts. The practice of deficit financing, including bond issues and borrowings from the Bank of Korea, has not been used since 1963, when a government monetary stabilization policy went into effect. The government also maintains 23 special accounts, which represent a significant portion of total expenditures. Each special account has its own budget, although there are sizable transfers of funds between the general account and the special accounts.

Expenditures included in the government's budget for the military establishment and for economic development do not reflect the total expenditure involved; they cover only those of the Republic of Korea Government and omit those of the United States and the United Nations. Direct assistance to the Republic of Korea armed forces, for example, does not appear in the military expenditure category. While this military assistance has been large, it is noteworthy that the Republic has relied increasingly on its own resources for defense.

In 1962, significant advance in government budgeting and accounting was made possible through the establishment of a Bureau of Statistics. This bureau has generated a voluminous amount of statistical material useful for budgeting and accounting. This activity has contributed much to improving the quality of budgets and the effectiveness of financial controls.

Government-operated enterprises, presently included among the special accounts, required large government subsidies prior to 1963, and these grants were only partially reflected in the budget. Since the Budgeting and Accounting Law of 1962 was promulgated, the government has required that these enterprises operate

384

on their own funds and show profits. In the official statistics of recent years they have shown substantial profits, which have been transferred to the general account as a revenue source. Apparently, government enterprises no longer receive subsidies.

The Budgetary Process

Until the end of 1962, each ministry or government agency submitted an annual budget request to the Bureau of the Budget, which analyzed and held hearings on these budgets and recommended revisions. In the late 1950's it was usual for budget requests to be reduced at this stage by as much as 50 percent. The combined, revised requests were transmitted to the State Council (Cabinet), for review, then passed on to the President, who submitted the budget to the National Assembly. There, committees studied segments of the budget and recommended revisions to the Finance and Economic Committee, which considered the draft in plenary session.

The Budget and Accounting Law of 1962 initiated a new system whereby the chairman of the Economic Planning Board issues instructions for drawing up draft budgets to the heads of all government agencies and enterprises. Each, in accordance with these instructions, formulates for the following fiscal year a budget of expenditures and revenues, which he submits to the chairman of the Economic Planning Board. The chairman thereupon compiles a draft budget based on the budget requests he has received from all government agencies and enterprises. This he presents for approval to the Cabinet, which has wide powers to effect changes in the budget. After being approved by the Cabinet, the budget is submitted by the president to the National Assembly.

An additional feature of the budgeting process has been the frequent need for supplementary budgets. In some years as many as three supplements to original budgets have been required because of substantial inflation, unforeseen expenditures, and underestimation of expenditures.

Budgets of the provincial governments, after approval by the governor, are submitted to the Ministries of Home Affairs and Education and to the other government agencies concerned for review of those features that will require contributions from the ministries. Provinces and smaller government units have the right to tax for their own purposes and also to collect taxes for the central government, even though a portion of their funds is supplied by the central government. Approved budgets are returned to the provinces, and budgetary and fiscal processes similar to those employed in the central government are used for controlling expenditures. The provincial governments in turn contribute to the county (*kun*), town (*ŭp*), and township (*my'on*) budgets.

The whole budgetary structure is thus largely supervised and coordinated by the national government. Moreover, the national government, in addition to giving budgetary assistance to local governmental entities, either directly or through the provincial offices of its ministries, spends large amounts for local purposes, such as police protection and other services.

GOVERNMENT EXPENDITURES

An analysis of the central government's expenditure plans for 1968 in the general government sector (includes economic development and loan-fund special accounts) reveals that an expenditure of 221.5 billion wŏn (270 wŏn = $1) was planned. Of this total, 34 percent was budgeted for current expenditures, 27 percent for national defense, 24 percent for government investments and loans, and 14 percent for transfer to local governments. This 221.5 billion wŏn expenditure does not constitute total expenditures because it omits most of the special accounts. In 1967, for example, the total government budget called for gross expenditures of 380 billion wŏn in the general and special accounts (including 63 billion wŏn of the inter-account transfers), which would represent about one-fourth of 1967 gross national product.

The government sector makes a relatively large contribution to gross national product in the Republic of Korea. However, the proportion has been declining in recent years as a result of expansion of the economy's private sector. The very sizable nature of government expenditures can be attributed in large part to the heavy requirements of national defense. The political-military situation demands that the country allocate a relatively large amount of its resources to national defense as compared with the defense budgets of most underdeveloped or developing countries. Notwithstanding the size of the government's national defense budget, it should be noted that these allocations do not include the substantial, though at present declining, volume of United States military aid.

Another reason for the large size of the government budget is that the government operates a substantial part of the country's enterprise. In the fields of transport and communications, the government plays a dominant role. Still another significant reason is the sizable public investment in development programs—both in government programs and in loans to private industry. The recent heavy government participation in capital formation reverses a trend of the mid-1960's. In that period the government was attempting to operate on a balanced budget basis, without deficit financing, and it was necessary to adjust the level of expenditures to available revenues. One result of this effort was a reduction in, though not the elimination of, government investment and loan activities. As the stabilization policy became effective in the mid-1960's, the government was able to concentrate more resources on investment programs. According to the Second Five-Year Plan, government investment and loan activities will be substantially raised from 62 billion wŏn in 1966 to 89 billion wŏn in 1971 (at constant 1965 prices).

Even more significant than the large size of the government's recent investments is the improvement achieved in project selection. In the Second Five-Year Plan, the government is making a concerted effort to insure that investment projects are in the economy's best interets.

As previously indicated, the special accounts of the government budget represent a very large portion of the government's total expenditures. In 1967, it was estimated that the special accounts would generate about 60 percent of total government expenditures. These accounts therefore must enter any analysis of the government public finance operations. They cover a wide range of government activities from the administration of counterpart funds and loans for economic development to the operation of the railroads, a hospital, the prison system, and national television. The more important special accounts are: Counterpart Funds, Economic Development, Government Loan Fund, Monopoly Enterprise, Grain Management, Railway Transportation, and Communications. Taken together, these seven special accounts at present generate nearly 90 percent of the expenditures of the 23 special accounts.

An accounting of the public finance activities represented in the government's general and special accounts still underestimates the government's total influence in the economy. While the special accounts do include the government's ownership and operation of railway transportation, communications, and monopoly enterprises (tobacco and ginseng), the government's substantial ownership role in oil refining and its ownership and operation of power-generating facilities and significant parts of banking, mining, shipbuilding, and iron and steel manufacture are not included as part of the government's public finance operations (see ch. 20, Industry; ch. 25, Banking and Currency).

Local Government Expenditures

Local governments, which include Seoul Special City, Pusan Special City, the provinces, cities, and counties, made expenditures on general account totaling 32 billion wŏn in 1966. Of this amount 27 percent was for general expense, 20 percent for construction, 18 percent for economic improvements, and 11 percent for community services. The remaining 25 percent represented transfers. The local governments also expended 43 billion wŏn on special account, largely for education. Total local government expenditures were 75 billion wŏn in 1966.

SOURCES OF REVENUES

Perspective

Before the Japanese occupation, government funds were collected by the provincial governors, with specified quotas sent to the royal court at Seoul. Whatever amounts the provinces collected in excess of the quota they were permitted to retain. Since no one was certain how much could be collected, there were no controls on the amounts filtering upward through the government structure, and many officials helped themselves along the way.

Under the Japanese, Western concepts of taxation were introduced. This included procedures by which the citizen contributes, generally according to his means, to the upkeep of the government. The Japanese also imposed a system of local donations for education and police protection. Nevertheless, the tax burden was considerably lighter during most of the Japanese period than it is today. Less than one-third of the colonial government's total revenue came from taxes; the balance was supplied by government monopolies and foreign trade. Land rents, however, paid primarily to Japanese landlords, were quite high. The Japanese also imposed discriminatorily high taxes on Korean properties they wished to take over.

The Tax System

The tax system that evolved in South Korea after 1945 has not adequately served the goal of economic development nor has it, until recently, been a major source of revenue for the government. Traditionally, it has generated less than half of the total revenue requirements of government. The government has supplemented its tax revenues with revenues from other sources, including deficit financing which was a major factor contributing to inflation until recent years. The inflation itself made the tax system difficult to administer, as values and prices continued to change drastically.

The tax system that developed was and remains very complex. As of 1962, it comprised twenty-two separate taxes. This complexity has placed a heavy burden on the government's tax administration authorities while at the same time making taxpayer compliance most difficult. Koreans have traditionally regarded the central government as a remote instrumentality that oppressed them with heavy taxes and onerous laws. It is the poor who have borne the brunt of taxation in Korea because their incomes have been more stable and thus relatively easy to assess for tax purposes. Also, the poorer people have had less opportunity to influence public officials and to evade taxes. Significantly, those in the lower income groups require most or all of their incomes to support themselves, and the tax system has emphasized indirect taxes which bear most heavily on final consumers.

The tax system that developed neither recognized the need for capital accumulation nor took business risks adequately into account. Tax privileges have been given for new businesses in such vital sectors as mining, oil refining, and fisheries, but these privileges were on an individual basis, much discretion being left to tax assessors and collectors. In the business sector the tax schedule was based on size, with little relation to the profit on investment. Consequently, there was a tendency for business organizations to split up enterprises and operate under multiform guises. Even at present there is no allowance for carrying forward, as deductions, losses from a succeeding year's taxes. This omission unduly penalizes enterprises of high financial risk and discourages the establishment of new firms. Depreciation allowances, greatly understated because they were computed in terms of original rather than current replacement costs, made the tax base appear larger than it actually was.

Taxation in kind, paid by the farmer, was introduced some years ago to give the government a direct means of obtaining the large quantities of grain required for supplementing the wages of its employees, for supplying food for the armed services, and for meeting civilian relief. It was also intended to provide the treasury with a form of insurance against the depreciation of a substantial portion of tax revenues under the prevailing inflationary conditions. Although income from paddy fields and dry fields is theoretically nontaxable, farmers pay a land tax which is no longer a national government tax, but which, since 1962, has been collected by provincial and county authorities.

The practice of levying taxes in kind and making payments in kind on a fairly large scale, commuted to cash in 1961, disguised the real size of the government's financial activities; both revenues and payments were greatly understated. The prices set on grain collected and on aid goods handled by government agencies were generally only a fraction of market prices. Such omissions and inadequacies made it impossible to estimate with any degree of accuracy the total size of the South Korean government's fiscal operations. Again, control of inflation and the keeping of better statistics by the government have essentially corrected the situation.

Most revenues are collected by the Ministry of Finance through its Bureau of Taxation. Tax assessments are made by 69 tax collection offices, subordinate to four tax control centers, one each in Seoul, Pusan, Taejon, and Kwangju, which operate under the Bureau of Taxation. Collections are accomplished both indirectly through the municipalities (land, business, and personal income taxes) and directly by tax collectors. Cash revenues collected by both means are turned over to local branches of the Bank of Korea —or to other banks if no branch office of the Bank of Korea exists in the locality—and are transferred daily to the main office to the credit of the general account. The Bureau of Customs of the Ministry of Finance collects all import and tonnage duties and receives certain excise taxes on such imported commodities as gasoline and textiles.

Recent Tax Reforms

Since 1960, the government has made significant efforts to correct the previous shortcomings of the tax system. Revisions of varying degree in both the content and the administration of the tax laws have taken place in almost every year since 1960. The major objectives of these reforms have been to redesign the tax system to promote savings and investment, to simplify the tax system, to eliminate corruption and tax evasion, to bring about a more equal distribution of the tax burden, and to increase the government's revenues from tax sources. Pursuit of the latter goal has been partially motivated by a decline in revenue from other sources. Another factor has been the government's interest in increasing tax revenues while minimizing current expenditures, thus achieving involuntary saving for the economy as a whole. Through this means resources can be captured and then invested without causing adverse inflationary effects.

Some of the specific measures taken by the present government in recent years are as follows. In 1963, the number of personal income tax brackets was increased from three to four, corporation tax rates were increased, and administrative reforms were made in several other systems. In 1964, a Board of Inspection was established, reporting directly to the President and having more comprehensive powers than did its predecessor agencies. The function of this body is to audit and supervise the activities of all government departments. In 1965, the laws relating to the commodity tax and the petroleum tax were changed. The commodity tax base was expanded, and the rates on some luxury goods were increased. Petroleum tax rates were increased by 10 to 40 percent above their former levels. Customs duties were also raised as a means of increasing revenue from that source. Administrative reforms in the income tax, registration tax, and liquor tax systems substantially increased revenues from these sources.

In 1966, the Office of National Tax Administration (ONTA) was established to uncover hidden tax sources and to maximize tax revenues. It was found that, of those taxpayers subject to self-assessment in 1965, only 29 percent had fully complied. In 1966, the ONTA established a new "green returns system" to encourage voluntary compliance. The new system encouraged individuals and firms to file tax returns on a self-assessment basis rather than under government supervision. Also in 1966, the Foreign Capital Inducement Law was amended to augment special tax concessions to foreign investors. In 1967, the customs laws were amended, the purposes being to protect domestic industry, limit the importation of luxury commodities, reduce the rates on essential raw materials and give individual ministeries broad discretion to change specific rates.

According to the Second Five-Year Plan, tax rates were to be increased on property and non-wage income, especially on speculative real estate holdings. Also, the plan contemplated a modification in the nature of the income tax structure, shifting away from a tax system based on differentiated rates, by source of income, to a system that would consider total income without regard to source. Moreover, under the plan there would be increases in tax rates on luxury items and a shift to emphasis on direct taxes. Furthermore, the plan contemplates increased tax revenues as a result of a vigorous enforcement program. Nearly one-half of the increase in tax revenues will be channeled into public saving. Government saving is projected to increase from 0.5 percent of gross national product in 1965 to nearly 6 percent in 1971.

Sources of Tax Revenues

Customs Duties

Until recently, customs duties have constituted over 20 percent of total tax revenues, but, because of recent reforms in domestic taxes, their relative importance has declined somewhat. In the past, duties were set at relatively moderate ad valorem rates and were in most cases aimed at producing maximum revenue rather than at protection of domestic industry. However, the 1967 amendments to the customs laws, previously mentioned, reveal a shift in emphasis from revenue considerations to protection of domestic industry, restriction of imports of luxuries, and reduction of duties on raw materials. Smuggling has been widely practiced, but it is not possible to estimate its present importance in this context.

Imported commodities are classified for tariff purposes into four categories: domestic products, parts, raw materials not domestically produced, and luxury items. The rates vary from 0 to 250 percent. Tariff rates on several specific imported items, based on the 1967 revision, are: fertilizers—0 percent, automobiles—250 percent, textiles—100 percent, raw cotton—10 percent, liquors—180 percent, and watches—180 percent.

Commodity Tax

The commodity tax is collected from manufacturers and importers at rates varying from 2 to 100 percent; the highest rates apply to such luxury goods as precious stones, cameras, and automobiles. More than two-thirds of the commodity tax revenue is derived from commodities subject to rates from 5 to 10 percent. These commodities include rubber footwear, paper, matches, and leather products. Raw materials and commodities for export are exempt. As previously mentioned, the tax base was extended and the rates on some particular luxury items increased in 1965.

Temporary Land Tax

The land tax, originally levied in kind as well as in currency, was divided into three categories. The first category, cereals production, yielded about 95 percent of total land tax proceeds (during the fiscal year 1955) 20.5 billion hwan out of a total 21.5 billion hwan). The tax was based on the gross yield of the land and calculated at rates progression from 6 to 18 percent. The second category applied to net income on agricultural production other than cereals (chiefly to fruits and vegetables), with rates varying from 25 to 60 percent of net income from these crops. The third category was based on net income from nonfarm property, including rentals, salterns, and the like. Among the tax reforms of 1961, the first category became a local tax collected by the provinces and districts, and the second and third categories became payable under the personal income tax law.

In 1954–55, the first category of the land tax provided an estimated one-sixth of total national revenues. This estimate is probably understated because of the official prices—generally below market prices—at which collection proceeds were valued. No tax was levied when natural calamities or abnormal weather conditions caused a harvest to fall below 30 percent of a farm's rated crop average. As an inducement to greater production, the portion of the crop in excess of the rated average was made tax-exempt. Until 1961, payment in rice was optional, regardless of the type of crop produced. Exemptions from the tax, other than for catastrophes and for farmers paying annual installments on land purchased under the land reform laws, are very low (see ch. 19, Agriculture). No allowances were made for dependents. As in other cases, inequities in taxation were often adjusted through negotiation with the collectors, often involving some form of bribe.

At the local level, the practice of collecting in kind was abolished in 1962. However, it was temporarily reestablished in 1964 as a means of securing grains for government use and as a check on inflation. This practice was to remain in effect only until 1966.

Income subject to this tax is derived from dividends, interest, entrepreneurial undertakings, earnings (salaries and wages), capital gains, and miscellaneous sources. Until the tax reforms of 1961, income from these sources was subject to the personal income tax under three schedules. The highest schedule, with rates from 19 to 57 percent, applied to non-farm real estate; the next highest, with rates from 14 to 52 percent, to interests, dividends, and capital gains; and the lowest, ranging from 4 to 40 percent, applied to earned income.

About two-thirds of annual receipts from personal income tax was originally derived from the net earnings of unincorporated businesses. The tax rate on such operations was substantially higher than the corresponding rate on wages because of the opportunities for tax evasion in such businesses. In practice, however, the higher rates tended to encourage evasion.

Based on the 1963 income tax revision, there are four income tax schedules: one for personal income, which includes real estate income and business income; one for interest and dividends; one for earned income, which includes wages and salaries; and one for miscellaneous income, which includes income from awards, prizes, and similar sources. Interest and dividend income and miscellaneous income are taxed at proportional rates of 12 percent and 7 percent, respectively. The personal income tax and the earned income tax are both progressive taxes. The tax rate schedule applied to personal income is divided into three income brackets, with rates ranging from a 15 percent tax on an income of up to 120,000 wŏn per year to a 30 percent tax on incomes greater than 360,000 wŏn per year. This tax is collected every six months. The tax rate schedule applied to earned income is divided into four brackets, and rates vary from a 7 percent tax on income up to 240,000 wŏn per year to a 35 percent tax on income greater than 720,000 wŏn. This tax is collected either monthly or quarterly. Personal income tax rates have been subject to an upward trend in recent years, which will likely continue, especially if the government continues to emphasize direct taxes.

As of 1961, exemptions included income from real estate of 1,500 wŏn ($5.89) or less per 6-month period, from dividends and interest of 1,000 wŏn ($3.90) or less per 6-month period, wages or salaries of 12 wŏn ($0.05) or less per day or 300 wŏn ($1.17) or less per month, as well as enlisted men's pay, disability allowances, travel allowances, interest on designated corporate debentures, and indemnity for injury. New investment in essential industries is encouraged by exempting income earned from such investments for several years.

Business Tax

The business tax is a gross sales tax rather than an excise tax, with rates ranging from near zero to a few percent. It is similar to the business and occupations tax used by some state governments in the United States. This kind of tax is difficult to shift to customers of a business. Several particular rates are 0.3 percent for insurance and manufacturing, 0.1 percent for retail stores, 0.7 percent for financing, and 2 percent for entertainment services.

Liquor Tax

The liquor tax accounted for approximately 15 percent of total national government tax receipts in April–October 1954 and 10 percent in fiscal 1963, and it was estimated that the tax would account for 7.5 percent of government tax revenue in 1967. This tax is collected from manufacturers and importers and varies according to the alcoholic content of the product. The tax for each class consists of a flat rate per unit, plus a percentage of the selling price. The percentages begin at 20 percent for Korean wine and go as high as 100 percent on Korean beer (a popular beverage in urban areas) and Japanese-type sake. As compared with liquor tax rates in other countries, the rates are low. Bootlegging has been so prevalent, however, that an increase in the liquor taxes probably would not bring in added revenue.

Corporation Tax

The corporation tax is relatively simple administratively. In late 1957 it was levied as a flat rate on corporate net income—32 percent for commercial corporations and 27 percent for special corporations. As of 1963, a net income of 1 million wŏn ($3,922) from all sources was taxed at the rate of 25 percent, regardless of type of corporation, and income over 1 million wŏn, at the rate of 30 percent. While the corporation tax has traditionally produced a very small percentage of the total tax revenues, it has become a substantial revenue producer as a result of further rate increases, administrative reforms, and the continuing rate of growth of the economy. It was estimated that the corporation tax would contribute 13 percent of tax revenue in 1967, surpassed only by the income tax and customs as a tax source.

Petroleum Tax

The petroleum tax is applied to all petroleum products, and has been a substantial revenue producer in the past. For example, it matched the corporation tax in yield in 1962. It continues to be a significant revenue source, especially since the 1965 rate increases. However, its relative importance has declined as tax authorities have concentrated more on other tax sources. In 1967, it was estimated that the petroleum tax would bring 4½ percent of the total tax revenues.

Other Tax Sources

Other taxes levied by the government in 1967 were inheritance tax, electricity and gas tax, admissions tax, travel tax, reassessment tax, stock transactions tax, and stamp duties. Of these, the travel tax, electricity and gas tax, and registration tax were most productive. It was estimated that all of the above taxes together would yield about 12 percent of the government's total tax revenues in 1967.

Local Taxes

The most important formal local tax in years past was the household tax. Provinces, school districts, and municipalities all received a large portion of their revenue from this source. The household tax was levied at graduated rates, according to a schedule which took into account the income, property holdings, and general standard of living of each household. The arrangement left loopholes for individual interpretations and for many abuses. The household tax, as such, was eliminated as one of the revolutionary government tax reforms, and a property tax was substituted.

Other important local taxes are a tax on buildings, assessed according to appraised rental value; a tax on transfer of property; a fishery tax; and special taxes on eating places and amusement establishments. A local school tax, assessed against all taxpayers, was instituted in 1961. Local governments also receive revenues in the form of transfers from the central government. At present transfers provide 20 percent of local government revenues.

Other Revenue Sources

Government Monopolies

Government monopolies, which are at present included among the special accounts in the government budget, have through the years made substantial profits which have been transferred to the general account as a revenue source. In 1967, it was estimated that 9 billion wŏn, representing about 6 percent of total government revenue, would be so transferred.

The products that have been included under monopoly enterprises are salt, tobacco, and ginseng. At present, tobacco generates 99 percent of the revenue of the monopoly enterprises and ginseng, the rest. The government has apparently ceased to monopolize the production of salt since 1964. As profits of the monopoly enterprises are about 50 percent greater than the production costs, it is evident that the government seeks to maximize revenues from this source. A widespread black market in American cigarettes in the past prevented the government from raising tobacco prices. It is not possible to estimate present importance of this influence.

Counterpart Funds

Foreign aid has been a substantial revenue source of the government since 1945. However, the importance of this source has decreased as foreign aid has declined, and as other revenue sources have expanded. Counterpart funds are derived by the government from the local sale of goods provided by the United States Agency for International Development (AID). Surplus foods granted under U. S. Public Law 480 are also sold by the Republic of Korea government and generate substantial funds. It was estimated that counterpart funds would provide about 16 percent of total government revenues in 1967, down from 24 percent in 1962.

Other Non-Tax Sources

The government receives some revenue from its operation of a hospital and of theaters, from licenses and fees, and from similar sources. Also, the government was to receive some net revenue in 1967 from its Vietnam involvement. Taken together, these residual sources were estimated to contribute 7 percent of total government revenues in 1967.

Public Lotteries

A scheme to raise revenues for the national government through public lotteries, instituted in April 1956, was not successful. After deducting payments and expenses, only 24 million hwan was realized, or about one-tenth of the amount hoped for. Koreans evidently felt that the chances of winning in these lotteries were too small; even though the government was prompt in making payments to winners, they were distrustful of lottery operations. In early 1957, certain winners received on-the-spot awards, and this innovation led to some improvement in the sale of lottery tickets; but after 1957, the government-operated lottery was discontinued.

1962–1968 Revenue Trends

As a result of the government's tax reforms, a decline in the volume of foreign aid, and the elimination of deficit financing, the structure of the South Korean government's revenue system has changed significantly in recent years. Revenues from all sources expanded considerably in the period from 1962 to 1967—from 76 billion wŏn to 152 billion wŏn (in 1968 market prices). More significantly revenue from tax sources increased in the same period from 39 percent of total government revenue to 70 percent of total government revenue. Revenues from counterpart funds increased somewhat in 1968 prices but likely declined in real terms. At the same time revenues from monopoly enterprises increased sharply. Government borrowing, which accounted for 29 percent of government revenue in 1962, was completely eliminated by 1964. Most significantly, direct taxes, which were 26 percent of tax revenues in 1962, increased to 37 percent of total tax revenues in 1967, signifying a trend toward direct taxation.

An additional feature of the tax system was that between 1962 and 1967 the number of taxes in use was reduced from 22 to 15 through consolidation, transferral to local governments, or elimination. In this period the national tax burden (relationship of total domestic taxes to gross national product) increased from 5 percent to greater than 10 percent, indicating the success of the government's tax program.

Voluntary Contributions

Regular tax revenues have been supplemented by a variety of "voluntary contributions"—actually, forced payments solicited by representatives of the organizations for whom these "voluntary contributions" are destined. In the fiscal year 1955 such contributions were estimated to amount to 40 billion hwan, in comparison to a total tax revenue of 118.6 billion hwan.

Until the revolutionary government prohibited the practice of collecting voluntary contributions for education and abolished the Parent's Association, the largest share of these contributions was collected by the Association and absorbed by the school system (see ch. 9, Education). Since then, "school supporter's associations" have continued to collect fees and make donations. Other uses include supplements for official's salaries; funds for political parties and organizations; and social services, such as garbage collection, relief, and community projects. Neither the use nor the collection of the funds has a statutory base, but the pressure exerted by the various official and quasi-official organizations making the exactions is difficult to resist. Householders try to negotiate, but in the end they contribute.

In practice, extra-legal contributions actually have had priority over the payment of legal taxes. Aside from enforcement considerations, South Koreans often have felt more closely identified with the purveyors of the services paid for by "voluntary contributions" than with those financed by the more distant and impersonal government.

Local associations in urban areas, known as tong associations, also use this system of voluntary contributions (see ch. 13, The Governmental System). Part of the money collected is used to defray the tong's operating expenses. The sale and distribution of certain foreign aid supplies have often been made contingent upon compulsory donations. The "voluntary contributions" thus take on the aspect of an extra-legal sales tax, the proceeds of which are not subject to auditing requirements. It is not possible to estimate the extent to which the above practices continue. It seems likely that in light of other reforms, the present government would not condone them.

THE BUDGETARY DEFICIT AND PUBLIC DEBT

Government Borrowing

Taxes, a major source of government revenue in Western countries, have never been sufficient to fund government expenditures fully. It is only recently that taxes have become important.

The excess of expenditures over funds produced by the tax system was financed by foreign economic aid, profits of monopoly enterprises, and borrowings. While the former sources are, in general non-inflationary, government borrowing, and, in particular, the specific method of borrowing employed, has been the major source of inflation in Korea. It is important to note that the government has not used borrowing as a source of revenue since 1963, when it successfully halted inflation. The particular forms of borrowing used in the past were bond issues and government overdrafts.

Republic of Korea bonds were sold by the government, through the Bank of Korea, to commercial banks and other financial institutions, which in turn sold them to the public. Most bond sales were compulsory—that is, an applicant for an investment loan, for foreign exchange, or for an import license had to buy a certain number of bonds before his application would be granted. There were also compulsory government bond sales to business enterprises, including nationalized corporations.

Prior to 1963, an average of 80 percent of the budgetary deficit was financed by overdrafts (loans) on the Bank of Korea against the issue of banknotes. Government overdrafts on the Bank of Korea did not create a national debt in the normal sense of the term in that the debt was incurred between two government instrumentalities and was simply a matter of money creation. Furthermore, it was not subject to legislative checks. This operation was a prime inflationary factor in the economy, with overdrafts being substantially repaid in only a few years.

This government-controlled bank is the major source of financing for government-supported investment projects. Before 1963, this bank's loan activities were financed similarly to government overdrafts in that the Korean Reconstruction Bank was granted loans by the Bank of Korea to finance its own loan activities. Since this was money-creation on the part of the Bank of Korea, the financing method was highly inflationary, greatly surpassing the significance of government overdrafts. Since 1963, the government has financed investment from current revenues, a non-inflationary source of investment.

The National Debt

At the end of 1966, the outstanding government debt was 15.3 billion wŏn as compared with a gross national product of 967 billion wŏn. This debt did not include government overdrafts, which amounted to 31 billion wŏn in the same period. Interest payments on this debt were 1.3 billion wŏn. Of the total debt, 89 percent was held by the Bank of Korea, and apparently none was externally held. Since most of the debt was held by the Bank of Korea, outstanding debt and interest payments were relatively small in relation to the level of the gross national product, and since no debt was externally held, the burden of the debt, in terms of character, has not been large. The real burden of the debt is the inflation it originally created. A further characteristic of the national debt is that, since 1963, the government has not issued any new debt and has retired existing debt as it has come due. Therefore, outstanding debt has been declining in the last several years, while gross national product has been rapidly advancing. If the trends continue, management of the government debt in the future would not seem to create any large problems because most of the debt is held by the Bank of Korea—the central banking institution—and because the government is committed to a program of sound financial management to control inflation.

CHAPTER 25

BANKING AND CURRENCY

The banking system in the Republic of Korea, as a government-controlled system, has functioned largely as an instrument of the executive branch of the central government. During the Korean conflict and for several years thereafter, the Bank of Korea—the central bank—aided the national administration in the implementation of fiscal policies that caused very serious inflation. In more recent years, the Bank of Korea and other banking institutions have pursued policies of financial restraint, reflecting the government's basic fiscal policy of monetary stabilization. The government's program has effectively controlled inflation, thereby contributing much to improving the climate for economic development.

While conditions in the Republic of Korea have favored development in recent years, the availability of loans or credit on favorable terms has not been adequate to meet the demands for funds. Loans are generally made on the basis of high interest rates and short repayment periods. The availability of credit is particularly limited in the agricultural sector, industrial needs for loans and credit being somewhat better served. The Korean Reconstruction Bank has been a major institution facilitating industrial development. Thus, the basic economic policy to direct substantial resources into industrialization is reflected in the operations of the banking system.

A significant step taken by the government in 1965 was to raise the general structure of interest rates. This action had the effect of attracting savings into the banks and to curb, to some extent, inflationary pressures. This measure was part of the general financial stabilization program that has achieved a considerable degree of success.

KOREAN BANKING BEFORE 1945

Under Japanese rules, the Bank of Chosen (nationalized and renamed the Bank of Korea in 1948) served as the central financial institution. Its stock was held by Japanese banks and large corporations, and its governors—all Japanese—were appointed by the Japanese government. Within Korea, the bank issued paper money, served as the official clearinghouse, and engaged in ordinary banking business. In the early 1920's, the bank became the spearhead of Japanese economic penetration in Manchuria, the Russian Far East, and China. These activities came to an end as Soviet territory was closed to foreign financial interests, Western banks became more active in the Far East, and Chinese banks, more active in Manchuria. In 1936, Manchuria was closed to the Bank of Chosen, and the bank's foreign activities were limited to China proper.

In 1940, the Korean banking system consisted of three special banks which handled commercial transactions: the Bank of Chosen, with 13 branches; the Industrial Bank, with 67 branches; and the Oriental Development Corporation. In addition, there were six small commercial banks, one savings bank, credit cooperatives, and three Korean branches of Japanese banks. There also were a number of mutual aid companies, or *mujin hoesa*, which collected stipulated monthly installments from members and distributed them as loans. The element of chance in the scheme had great appeal, and well-to-do farmers and merchants apparently profited from the system of reloaning money received through the lottery at much higher rates of interest.

The credit cooperatives developed into strong banking institutions and supplied credit to farmers and to small businessmen in the cities. Their combined membership was nearly 2 million at the end of 1939, but their paid-up capital was minute—only about 7.8 yen per member. The cooperatives worked chiefly with funds borrowed from the Industrial Bank and with capital supplied by depositors, who were chiefly nonmembers attracted by government-guaranteed deposits and high interest rates. In 1939, the cooperatives' deposits and loans, respectively, amounted to 44 percent and 28 percent of those of the banks. Representing a substantial addition to credit facilities available in Korea, cooperative funds nevertheless remained inadequate because of the sharp rise in prices.

Before World War II, the Japanese government pursued a policy of low interest rates, both at home and in Korea. In 1929, Korean banks paid 5.1 percent on savings deposits and charged 9.1 on secured loans. By 1938, these rates had slipped to 3.6 percent and 6.6 percent, respectively. There was a great disparity in rates charged to clients, however, with Koreans as a rule paying about 25 percent higher rates than Japanese, and rural credit cooperatives charged—to a predominantly Korean clientele—much higher interest rates on loans than did the banks. Because of the high rate of interest charged, the farmer was generally behind in his payments, and his debt kept increasing. Heavy rural indebtedness was aggravated by the fact that, since the farmer had to borrow even to buy food, particularly in the springtime, he was unable to borrow to increase his crop output and thus could not break the vicious circle. According to a survey made in 1940, more than three-fourths of the rural loans outstanding at that time were for subsistence, for such ceremonies as weddings and funerals, and for other nonproductive purposes.

GENERAL STRUCTURE
OF THE BANKING SYSTEM

The Republic's government, directly or indirectly, holds the controlling interest in all major banks—thus, the banking system is essentially operated as a financial arm of the government. This control of the banking system began at the end of World War II when the Japanese banks were turned over to the Koreans.

Banking institutions operated by the government include the Bank of Korea (the central bank), the Korea Exchange Bank, the Korean Reconstruction Bank, the Medium Industry Bank, the Citizens National Bank, the National Agriculture Cooperatives Federation, and the Central Federation of Fisheries Cooperatives. With the exception of the Bank of Korea and the Korea Exchange Bank these government banks in 1967 held 28 percent of total bank deposits and accounted for 56 percent of the total outstanding loans and discounts of the banking system.

The Bank of Korea

The Bank of Korea is the central bank and its official functions are issuing currency, establishing credit policies, supervising bank operations, and acting as a central clearing agency. The central bank's authority to control and supervise the banking system and implement monetary policy is governed by the Bank of Korea Act of 1950. Until 1950, the Bank of Korea was directly controlled by the Ministry of Finance. The Bank of Korea Act of 1950 established a seven-man board to set the monetary policy and operational directives of the Bank of Korea. The members of the board are to be appointed by the President of the Republic to represent various sectors of the national economy. Prior to 1962, the Bank of Korea played a major role in the implementation of the government's fiscal policies and thereby contributed to a problem of serious inflation. The present government has instituted a program of financial stabilization, however, and the Bank of Korea has pursued a policy of monetary restraint.

Banks are supervised and examined by the Superintendent of Banks, appointed by the President of the Republic. The superintendent is charged with enforcing the banking laws and monetary board rulings and with maintaining sound and solvent banking institutions; but the superintendent has had only a limited field staff to deal with about 700 head offices and branches (including the 550 branches of the National Agricultural Cooperative Federation) that, legally, should be examined at least once a year. The existence of other bank supervisory and examining authorities, including those of the Ministry of Finance, the Office of Property Custody, and the Board of Inspection, causes duplication and confusion which tend to weaken the authority and effectiveness of the superintendent of banks.

The Korea Exchange Bank

The Korea Exchange Bank was established in January 1967. At that time it took over international banking functions previously handled by the Bank of Korea, thus enabling the latter to concentrate on its central bank functions. The Korea Exchange Bank specializes in financing foreign trade and handling foreign exchange transactions. The avowed purposes of the bank are to maximize the export potential of the economy by facilitating the financing of foreign trade, to assist in attracting foreign capital, and to provide information to potential exporters relating to the development of overseas markets. The Korea Exchange Bank maintains several foreign offices, as well as domestic branches. At the end of September 1967, the bank had assets of nearly 225 billion wŏn, making it the largest Korean banking institution in terms of this measure. The bulk of these assets was in the form of foreign exchange holdings.

The Korean Reconstruction Bank

The Korean Reconstruction Bank was established in 1954, at which time it took over the operations and obligations of the Industrial Bank of Korea, which had been in operation since 1918. The primary function of the Reconstruction Bank was originally to supply loans for industrial rehabilitation. When the reconstruction activity was completed, the bank's function was changed to facilitating economic development. The bank specializes in long-term loans at relatively low interest rates for industrial projects in secondary and tertiary industries. It is the primary mechanism through which the government extends loans to the private sector for basic industrial projects. The scope of the bank's operations includes making loans of more than one-year duration; providing short-term credit for working capital to enterprises that have been extended loans for capital development; subscribing to, underwriting, or guaranteeing the bonds and debentures of corporations involved in important industrial projects; and underwriting or guaranteeing loans extended by other financial institutions. The bank is also the principal agency through which certain aid and loan funds have been channeled, namely, funds from the United Nations Korean Reconstruction Agency (UNKRA), the Agency for International Development (AID), the United States Export-Import Bank, and other sources.

In the past, the lending operations of this bank were a primary factor causing the expansion of the money supply and, consequently, inflation. This activity contributed even more to inflation than did acceptance of government overdrafts by the Bank of Korea. Much of the bank's lending activity was financed through loans from the Bank of Korea, a practice that amounted to money creation. However, this was eliminated in 1963, and in recent years the bank has financed its operations predominantly from counterpart funds and borrowing from government funds for economic development. These latter types of financing operations are non-inflationary in character.

In terms of lending operations, the Korean Reconstruction Bank is the largest institution in the country. In late 1967, its outstanding loans to the private sector were 51 billion wŏn, or about 25 percent of the total loans extended by the government-operated and commercial banking institutions (except the Bank of Korea and the Korea Exchange Bank). This bank had assets of nearly 178 billion wŏn near the end of 1967.

The Korean Reconstruction Bank also engages in a small amount of commercial banking business, including checking and demand deposits and short-term loans. These services are limited to the enterprises or individuals who have received development loans from the bank. The arrangement is designed not so much for the borrower's convenience as for the bank's convenience in supervising their uses of loan funds. Information is not available to permit an evaluation of the effectiveness of this arrangement. The bank maintains branches in Pusan, Taegu, Taejon, Inchon, Kwangju, Chunju, Samchuk, and Chongju, in addition to the headquarters in Seoul.

The Medium Industry Bank

The Medium Industry Bank opened August 1, 1961, under a special law promulgated the previous July by the revolutionary government. The bank's purpose is to provide credit to small-scale and medium-scale industry involving risks too great to be undertaken by commercial banks. Capitalized jointly by the government and private business, it was given government funds previously assigned to other banks for loans to small business. The Medium Industry Bank has 39 branches in addition to its head office in Seoul. At the end of the third quarter 1967, the bank had outstanding loans of 15.5 billion wŏn, or 7.6 percent of the total loans of the government operated and commercial banks (except the Bank of Korea and the Korea Exchange Bank), and total assets of 23.5 billion wŏn.

The Citizens National Bank

The Citizens National Bank was established by a special law of the revolutionary government through the merger of two mutual loan companies, the Hanguk Mutual Loan Company and the Korea Mutual Loan Company. The bank started business on February 1, 1962. Its purpose is to provide banking services to people by handling mutual loans and receiving deposits. Headquartered in Seoul, it maintains 68 branches. By law, a limit is set on the amount that the bank may loan to any individual. In late 1967, this bank accounted for 2.6 percent of the loans of the government-operated and commercial banking institutions (except the Bank of Korea and the Korea Exchange Bank) and has assets of 22.6 billion wŏn.

National Agricultural Cooperative Federation

In August 1961, the agricultural bank that had been established in 1957 to assume the financial functions of the Federation of Financial Associations was merged with the Agricultural Cooperatives to form the National Agricultural Cooperatives Federation. For many years the financial associations and their branches were the primary organized sources of credit for farmers. Established under the Japanese, the financial associations were essentially small cooperative banks, widely spread over Korea and organized into a federation of financial associations, which acted as their central coordinating agency and banker.

The system was able to satisfy only a fraction of the legitimate agricultural credit needs. The remainder had to be met by private money lenders. Between 1945 and 1956, the federation increasingly became a government agency, carrying out on its behalf a wide range of functions of public character, such as collecting, purchasing, and distributing rice, grains, fertilizers, and other related products. These operations were financed by loans from the central bank. As a result, the federation was diverted from the agricultural credit business and tended to become a political instrument. The transformation impaired efficient management of the federation's functions and caused its former members to lose confidence in it. The same allegations were leveled at the agricultural bank, which succeeded the federation in 1957, and led to its replacement four years later by the National Agricultural Cooperatives Federation.

In 1967, the National Agricultural Cooperatives Federation made 18.2 percent of the outstanding loans of the government-operated and commercial banking institutions (except the Bank of Korea and the Korea Exchange Bank), had demand deposits of nearly 23 billion wŏn, and had assets of nearly 112 billion wŏn. As have most banking institutions in the Republic of Korea, this bank has experienced a considerable increase in deposits in recent years, but its loans outstanding have increased to a lesser extent. At present, the bank's primary financial activities are the provision of credit for agricultural production and the purchase of farm supplies and other necessities. The National Agricultural Cooperatives are also involved in marketing and processing activities (see ch. 19, Agriculture).

Central Federation of Fisheries Cooperatives

This government-operated banking organization was instituted in 1963 and took over functions previously assigned to the Korean Reconstruction Bank and the National Agricultural Cooperatives Federation. The bank provides credit facilities for the fisheries industry and accepts demand deposits. At present, it is relatively small having assets of 6.5 billion wŏn and loans outstanding of 4.2 billion wŏn.

Other Government-Operated Banks

The government established the Korea Housing Bank in 1967 for the purpose of granting credit for housing construction. The bank took over this particular function from the Korean Reconstruction Bank. Its assets are valued at about 100 billion wŏn, half of which were provided by the government. Data are not available at present on this bank's financial operations.

Commercial Banks

The five commercial banks in the Republic of Korea are Chohung Bank, the Commercial Bank of Korea, the First City Bank of Korea, the Hanil Bank, and the Bank of Seoul. All of these banks have their head offices in Seoul, and they collectively operate 202 domestic branches. As previously mentioned, they are substantially owned by the government. In the past, because their capital was extremely limited and demand deposits small, the commercial business consisted essentially of accepting deposits and making short-term loans to primary producers, to businessmen, and to government agencies. Holdings of securities were relatively small. In the early years of reconstruction, government control of all but one of the commercial banks then in existence tended to subject commercial banks to political pressures and interference not conducive to sound banking policies and practices.

At present, checks are used by the public to only a very limited degree; where use of money is involved, currency notes constitute the medium of exchange in the vast majority of transactions. Interbank transactions are usually made by bank drafts.

Deposits in commercial banks have increased significantly as a result of several factors, namely, the government's inflationary control program begun in 1963, general increases in interest rates in 1965, and the general growth of the economy. Since 1963, deposits have increased eightfold. As a consequence, the commercial banks have become much less dependent on government funds for financing their operations, although they remain undercapitalized. Also since 1963, loans made by these institutions have quadrupled. Nearly all of the loans have been to the private sector. Commercial bank holdings of government securities are at present about 15.5 billion wŏn, representing about 17 percent of their outstanding loans. In the period from 1963 to 1967, commercial bank borrowings from the Bank of Korea doubled, but the relative importance of borrowing from this source has declined significantly. By late 1967, the commercial banks had extended over 44 percent of the outstanding loans of both the government-operated and commercial banks, compared to 28 percent in 1961. In late 1967, the commercial banks collectively had assets of 233 billion wŏn. In short, commercial banks are becoming an important part of the financial sector of the economy of the Republic of Korea.

Foreign banks are showing increased interest in the Republic of Korea. In the last two years several commercial banks in the United States have established foreign branches in Seoul. Specifically, Chase-Manhattan Bank, Bank of America, and First National City Bank of New York have established branches in the Republic of Korea.

INSURANCE

As of 1966, there were six life insurance companies, 10 damage insurance companies, one reinsurance company, one automobile insurance company, and one joint fire insurance company serving all banking institutions, or a total of 19 companies. In late 1967, the insurance companies collectively had outstanding nearly 250,000 contracts, and total assets of these companies amounted to about 15 billion wŏn. Operations of insurance companies are supervised by the insurance commissioner within the Ministry of Finance.

THE SYSTEM OF MONETARY CONTROL

Loan and Rediscount Ceilings

A principal instrument of credit control used by the Bank of Korea, under the direction of the Monetary Board, has been the imposition of loan ceilings, supported by rediscount ceilings (actually loan limits) on its advances to commercial banks. Both sets of ceilings are fixed so as not to limit the aggregate expansion of bank loans and also to influence the distribution of loans between different sections of the economy. Separate ceilings are set for three categories of economic enterprise; public, private, and special. Loan and rediscount ceilings are especially liberal for the special category, which includes purchase of aid goods, the financing of exports, and the provision of working capital for government contractors.

The ceilings for each major category are divided into sixteen, seven, and three sub-ceilings respectively. One major sub-ceiling in the private category is formally allocated among the commercial banks, but all other sub-ceilings in this and the other categories are allocated only on a case-by-case basis, as the individual banks apply to make loans within the overall limits of these ceilings. These complex arrangements are further complicated by an eligibility schedule on private loans for rediscount by the Bank of Korea; differing maturities, interest rates, and other terms are set for the various kinds of discounts, depending upon their purpose. Finally, all ceilings, sub-ceilings, and schedules are frequently changed by the Monetary Board—even within a quarter—to meet specific needs as they arise.

At present, the rediscount rate at the central bank varies from 2 to 28 percent, depending on the purpose of the loan. Similar interest rates are applied to loans and discounts of commercial banks. Rediscount rates were increased significantly in 1965 to their present levels as part of the government's general effort to adjust interest rates to higher levels.

Reserve Requirements

The commercial banks are required to maintain a percentage of their deposits in the Bank of Korea as reserves. Changes in required reserve ratios, then, are a tool of monetary policy available to the Monetary Board. Through 1965, reserve ratios varied from 10 to 20 percent. Reserve requirements were used as a primary measure of monetary control before 1963. Since that time more stringent reserve requirements have been established to control the inflationary potential of the expanding money supply. The present reserve requirement is 35 percent of demand deposits, by United States standards a very high rate. However, this rate reflects the efforts of the government to control the money supply which has recently been greatly expanded.

Purchase and Sales of Government Securities

Only recently has the central bank employed the purchase and sale of government securities as a method of monetary control. At present, the commercial banks are being required to buy Bank of Korea Stabilization Bonds as part of the overall financial stabilization program. In addition, the Bank of Korea has begun a program of selling treasury bills to the commercial banks. The Bank of Korea allows commercial banks to purchase these bills with funds previously frozen in a monetary stabilization account. Both of the above measures help to reduce the present expanding liquidity of the monetary system in the Republic of Korea.

Interest Rates

Until 1965, interest rates were legally limited to an annual rate of 20 percent. In that year the maximum legal annual interest rate was increased to 40 percent. The purpose of this measure was to encourage saving in the commercial banking system by bringing those rates in line with rates charged outside the banking system —that is, by private non-bank lenders. Since 1965, deposits in commercial banks have expanded considerably. This in itself makes the government's efforts at monetary control more effective by putting more of the country's financial resources at government disposal. Also, higher interest rates tend to discourage borrowing, thereby curbing additional pressures on the money supply. Still, the primary means of monetary control employed at present are changes in reserve requirements and sales of government securities to the commercial banks. In the past, a wide difference between the Bank of Korea's rediscount rate to the commercial banks and the interest rate commercial banks could legally charge resulted in borrowing by the latter banks from the central bank. The central bank was a major source of financing for the commercial banks, and the heavy borrowing by these banks reduced the effectiveness of measures of monetary control. Available information indicates that this situation has been corrected. While the amount of borrowings from the central bank has continued to increase in recent years, excess reserves are at present negligible, and net free reserves (excess reserves less central bank borrowings) are increasingly a negative amount. In short, bank funds available for lending have been effectively curtailed.

THE CURRENCY SYSTEM

Korean Currency before 1945

Although iron blanks were used as money as early as the second century A. D., coins—which were of solid iron—were not used until 996. Silver ones were minted in 1101, and the circular copper coin with the square hold appeared about the same time. Rice and cloth, however, were the primary units of trade under the Koryŏ Dynasty (935–1392), and metallic money almost disappeared. Silver "bottle" money and "dollars" are mentioned as being circulated just before the Mongols lost power (see ch. 2, Historical Setting). There was also some arrowhead money, with characters inscribed on both sides, which was issued in 1464; none is known to have survived. Paper money was ordered printed by the first Yi

King in 1392, but became discredited when the Japanese invaded the country in 1592. In 1651, metal money was again minted, and the use of cloth as a medium of exchange was prohibited so that money could be established successfully as the medium of exchange.

Just before Korea's annexation by Japan, monetary circulation consisted of copper, nickel, and gold coins and some notes, issued chiefly by a Japanese bank. According to Japanese sources, the "excessive issue of nickel coins—brought the credit of the coins to the ground, and the stability of commodity prices was destroyed." Beginning in the mid-1920's, the Japanese reformed the system by substituting paper for "the mischievous nickel coins" and large-scale inflation for previous moderate price instability.

By early 1940, the reserves of the Korean central bank (the Bank of Chosen), equal to 42 percent of note circulation, consisted only of Bank of Japan notes. The yen was made the basic unit of currency and was maintained at par with the Japanese yen. Money was printed at such a rate that, between 1936 and 1940, for example, prices of manufactured products more than doubled, but prices of agricultural products lagged far behind. To stop inflation, the government froze all prices in 1940, including those received by the farmer on official grain deliveries. At the same time, however, the issue of notes and the expansion of credit continued unabated. Commodities disappeared from the open market, and black market dealings increased substantially. Credit expansion, brought about by Japanese war preparations and, later, actual warfare, further undermined the stability of Korean money. In August 1945, just before their evacuation from Korea, the Japanese planted an inflationary time bomb by issuing a vast amount of unbacked yen notes.

Currency in Circulation

At the end of World War II, currency circulation consisted of Bank of Chosen notes and smaller amounts of Bank of Japan and Bank of Taiwan notes, as well as other smaller notes and coin of Japanese origin. The American Military Government in 1945 promptly voided all Japanese regular and military currency. A new unit of currency, the wŏn, was issued, but it had no single official rate of exchange in terms of dollars or any other foreign currency. Gradual conversion resulted in the establishment in June 1950 of a note circulation consisting essentially of Bank of Korea notes in denominations of 100, 10, 5, and 1 wŏn. Chon notes (100 chon equals 1 wŏn) were also legal issue, but inflation rapidly devalued these virtually out of existence—and even the small wŏn notes disappeared from circulation.

Before the outbreak of hostilities in 1950, the wŏn-dollar rate

(50 to 1 in 1945) was 1,800 to 1. When the Republic of Korea Government was forced to evacuate Seoul, it was unable to remove currency plates and paper from Bank of Korea vaults. Since the currency and plates fell into the hands of the Communists, it was essential that an immediate currency conversion be made in those areas of south Korea still under control of the Republic of Korea government. The Japanese government cooperated by rapidly printing a new series of Bank of Korea notes, which were shipped by air to Pusan. As the area under Republic of Korea forces expanded, special conversion periods were decreed. By November 1950, conversion was almost complete, but the wŏn-dollar rate had slipped to 2,500 to 1, and, by November of 1951, it had reached 6,000 to 1.

From June 1950 to January 1953, the total notes outstanding increased 16 times. In February 1953, the government replaced the wŏn with a currency of higher nominal value, the hwan, at the rate of 1 hwan for 100 wŏn. Undertaken as a counterinflationary measure, the conversion produced a mild but quickly subsiding panic. At the end of the conversion period, the government had succeeded in collecting a substantial amount of back taxes, and the bulkiness of money in everyday transactions had been reduced.

At the time of original issue, the currency was pegged at 60 hwan to the U. S. dollar but had a much lower value on the free market. In December 1953, the hwan was first devalued to 180 to the dollar, and in August 1955, to 500 to the dollar. This official rate was maintained at Syngman Rhee's insistence until he was up for reelection in 1960, even though effective rates on the free market ranged from 850–900 hwan to the dollar. In January 1960, the hwan was again devalued and the dollar exchange rate set at 650 to 1. After the overthrow of Rhee, the Chang government, in attempts at reform, carried out further devaluation; in January 1961, it pegged the hwan dollar exchange rate at 1,000 to 1, and in February a new rate of 1,300 to 1 was established.

In June 1962, the revolutionary government, which came to power after the coup of May 1961, again reformed the currency with the twofold aim of securing capital for its Five-Year Plan (1962–66) and warding off a rising inflation. The hwan was ordered out of circulation and replaced with the wŏn at the rate of 10 hwan for 1 wŏn. The official exchange rate was established at 130 wŏn to the U.S. dollar, or one-tenth the previous rate of 1,300 hwan per dollar. The wŏn was further devalued in May 1964 to 255 wŏn to the U. S. dollar. In 1965, the government adopted a fluctuating exchange rate system based on the supply and demand for foreign exchange; since then the exchange rate has remained relatively stable. The official basic exchange rate in March 1968 was about 275 wŏn to one U. S. dollar. The notes in circulation at present are 500 wŏn, 100 wŏn, 50 wŏn, 10 wŏn, 5 wŏn, 1 wŏn, and 50 chon (½ wŏn). Coins in circulation are 10 wŏn, 5 wŏn, and 1 wŏn.

Changes in the Money Supply

The money supply has continued to increase, though presently for different reasons than in the past. From 1953 to 1963, the money supply increased over twelve times and, since 1963, has more than doubled. Prior to 1963, the Bank of Korea's policy of accepting overdrafts of the government and granting loans to the Korean Reconstruction Bank were acts of direct money creation that substantially swelled the money supply. Also, the central bank's general policy of monetary ease in lending to the commercial banks accentuated the increases in the money supply. Since about 1963, the money supply has been considerably expanded as a result of the increased level of economic activity in the Republic of Korea. However, the increase in foreign exchange holdings that have been converted into local currency by Korean nationals has been the primary factor causing an expanded money supply. The government has taken several measures, previously discussed, to control the inflationary impact of the expanding money supply. In late 1967, the money supply was about 80 billion wŏn compared with 37 billion wŏn in 1963 and 3 billion wŏn in 1953.

METHODS OF FINANCING

Available information on methods of finance is incomplete and sketchy. It is evident that the government attempts to provide favorable financing for the various sectors of the economy through its ownership and operation of several banking institutions, such as the Korean Reconstruction Bank and the National Agricultural Cooperatives Federation. It is also apparent that the commercial banks are playing an increasingly important role in financing the private sector of the economy, and the Korea Exchange Bank was recently set up to aid in financing of foreign trade. A sharp influx of foreign capital to Korea in recent years has provided valuable external capital resources for development.

A flow of funds analysis in 1965 indicated that corporate sources of funds were 41 percent from savings, 27 percent from special and commercial bank loans, 16 percent from Bank of Korea loans, 15 percent from security issues. Sources of funds for individuals were as follows: 61 percent from savings, 19 percent from special and commercial bank loans, 5 percent from trade credit, and 15 percent from unknown sources.

The unorganized or non-banking sources of funds have in the past served the private sector to a substantial extent. It was indicated in a 1963 study that 66 percent of manufacturers used non-banking sources of funds, and that 62 percent of rural debt was held outside the banking system. Interest rates in the unorganized financial market were estimated to be double the legal ceiling rates. It was furthermore estimated that, in terms of outstanding loans, the unorganized financial market was as large or larger than the banking system. The role of non-bank lenders has likely declined in recent years as a result of structural changes in banking. Nevertheless, a great deal of financing has taken place through unorganized financial channels.

SECTION IV. NATIONAL SECURITY

CHAPTER 26

PUBLIC ORDER AND SAFETY

There is a renewed determination in the Republic of Korea to continue the improvements in the maintenance of public order and safety. The problems of the past, caused principally by an absence of a traditional respect for codified law and order, are rapidly being overcome. There is a better appreciation of the need for a totally independent judiciary system to fight crime and subversion. The task is threefold: overcoming the historical attitudes of distrust, and resentment toward the police and other law enforcement agencies; reducing the crime rate and juvenile delinquency; and developing a strong capability to deal with threats to internal security. The solutions to the three problem areas often work at cross-purposes; they are not simple, nor can the problems be overcome quickly. The ingredients for achieving a secure and tranquil national environment are present. The people now have the desire, the constitutional framework, and the resources to design and implement a viable system for public order and safety.

Law enforcement is vested in a constitutionally established judiciary and a national police force under the Ministry of Home Affairs. Judicial power is exercised in the various courts, including the Supreme Court, appellate courts, district courts, and a family court. A prosecutor's office acts in the national and public interest by conducting investigations of law violations, directing the judicial police under its control, and instituting legal action against suspected law breakers. The Korean National Police numbered 40,622 at the end of 1967, a considerable increase over the previous year. The maritime police (coast guard) and the firefighting division also come within the administrative and operational control of the National Police.

The United States Agency for International Development has had a continuing program to assist the Korean National Police since 1954. Technical advice; commodity support; and participant training to improve their organization and administration, training, criminal investigation, patrol, and firefighting capabilities have been provided. In 1967, United States assistance was increased and expanded to help upgrade all facets of the police force, with particular focus on communications, transport, training, and operations, to improve the capability of the National Police to maintain national security. The National Police is now organizing and training, from within current strengths, a paramilitary component called the Combat Police, which has the primary mission of countering infiltrations and subversion. A projected strength of 4,000 is planned for this combat force. In addition, the recently organized Homeland Reserve Force (see ch. 27, The Armed Forces) will also include a limited auxiliary police force. Since 1962, the police have evolved into a more democratic service-type organization and have worked hard to encourage and develop better public relations, so that now the public holds the police in high esteem, trusts them, and has confidence in their ability to uphold the law.

PERSPECTIVE

Historical Attitudes Toward Law

The present system of law represents a mixture of unwritten common law reflecting Confucian teachings, Japanese law, and modern law (see ch. 13, The Governmental System). During the middle of the monarchial rule, a small national police force was created, but it served mainly to maintain public order and safety in the capital. In practice, the family, clan, and village combined to exert heavy pressures on individuals to conform to traditional ways. Criminal acts or, indeed, any deviations from accepted behavior reflected on the individual's family, clan and village. The application of collective legal responsibility, especially in civil disputes, reinforced the social controls. The head of a household, for example, was responsible for the debts of sons and younger brothers.

The military held jurisdiction in major criminal cases. Civil disputes and violations, as well as minor criminal offenses, were under the jurisdiction of local magistrates appointed by the central government.

Standard legal codes as known in the West did not exist in pre-20th century Korea. Arrests and punishments were at the discretion of the local officials. Crimes against the state, treason, sedition, and the like were handled at the national level. There were no lawyers; the parties faced each other before the local magistrate who conducted the case in his own fashion. Claimants told their stories and brought their own witnesses with them. All were questioned by the judge. There was little formal procedure connected with the court process, and at times chaos was approached as tempers became heated. Social status, family connections, and wealth were major elements influencing decisions. Members of the "despised" or "low-born" classes were prohibited from initiating court proceedings against the nobility. Torture was freely applied to both defendants and witnesses in civil and criminal cases.

The concept of collective guilt was accepted in varying degrees. Persons convicted of treason, sedition, or other activities against the state jeopardized their entire families. In lesser cases, both civil and criminal, punishments involved fine, imprisonment, and beating. Relatives might be arrested and held in the event that the accused could not be found.

Prisons consisted primarily of unheated mud huts which lacked sanitary facilities. Food and clothing were provided by the families of the prisoners, or not at all.

Theft, extortion, and disputes over property rights and debts were the major types of criminal and civil cases. Few persons expected to receive impartial justice from the courts or administrative officials. Whenever possible the formal system was avoided. Disputes were settled by direct bargaining, or the village elders and other local leaders of opinion were called upon.

As contacts with the West increased during the latter part of the 19th century, the government attempted to reform the administration of justice and to establish a police system. To this end, in 1894, the services of a Japanese mission were engaged. A new legal system was adopted. It was patterned after the Japanese system, which in turn was strongly influenced by the German codes of 1871. Projected reforms included the separation of judicial from executive functions and the creation of a police bureau. Appreciable improvements, however, were not effected because of the caliber and training of the personnel involved in police work and in the administration of justice. The reform program was given new impetus by the arrival of a second Japanese mission in 1904 and by the establishment of the Japanese protectorate in the following year.

The Japanese Period

The Japanese occupation of Korea in 1910 resulted in the introduction of the Japanese police system, legal codes, court procedures, and penal system—all based on European models. Under the Japanese governor general there were two separate offices which dealt with public order—Police and Justice. Both functioned in an authoritarian fashion in support of the Japanese program in Korea, which aimed at the suppression of Korean resistance.

Japanese control also produced major changes in the relation of the populace to the agencies of public order. The Japanese administration enlarged the area of governmental concern, and officials of the central government dealt with the population on a scale previously unknown in Korea. Local police stations were established throughout the country. The social change attendant on the Japanese imperial program contributed to weakening the traditional institutional factors for the maintenance of public order and safety. Urbanization and impoverishment of the farmers helped to weaken the power of the extended family and its concept of collective responsibility (see ch. 7, Family). The increasing mobility of the population, the implementation of the Japanese educational system, and the development of a major industrial-commercial sector in the economy introduced new values (see ch. 12, Social Values).

Japanese were placed in all positions of authority in the police system and accounted for more than 60 percent of the total police force, which numbered some 60,000 in 1941. The Koreans in the Japanese police system operated almost entirely at the lowest echelons, and it was with them that the bulk of the population had most contact.

No effective limits were set for the exercise of police power in Korea under the Japanese. Police authority extended to economic crimes, sanitation, fire fighting, and thought control. Police methods involved heavy reliance on physical duress, especially in regard to the interrogation of suspects. The Korean members of the police force were noted for their brutality.

The basis of the legal system in Korea between 1910 and 1945 was Japanese law code (principally German in origin) taken over either entirely or with some minor modifications in favor of Korean customs. Most judges, prosecutors, and police officials were Japanese. Legal procedures, moreover, were conducted in the Japanese language. A small number of Koreans were able, however, to receive legal training and experience, both as practicing attorneys and as judges.

The police functioned also in a judicial capacity. Local police officials were empowered to exercise summary jurisdiction. The number of such cases tried by police officers each year has been estimated at 100,000. Gambling, simple assault, and traffic violations made up the bulk of the cases. Almost all of the cases heard by police officials resulted in conviction.

The effective barring of the bulk of the population from recourse to the courts—as a result of the language problem as well as the cost—reinforced the pre-Japanese tendency to seek solutions to disputes outside the formal system. Experiences encountered at the hands of police also reinforced the traditional attitude. The police continued to be despised and feared.

United States Military Government

The occupation authorities, expecting an early evacuation following the establishment of a representative government for all of Korea, were in no hurry to replace the Japanese police with inexperienced and untrained Koreans. Within two months after the surrender on August 15, 1945, however, the idea of retaining the Japanese police was abandoned. Popular resistance against them was often expressed by physical violence against both the Japanese and Korean members of the Japanese police system.

An all-Korean police force was organized by the end of 1945, under auspices of the Military Government, with an initial strength of 10,000 men. The force was recruited and trained by United States Army officers. Efforts to develop a police system along United States lines were frustrated by the general turmoil which prevailed in Korea in the post-1945 period. Popular unrest and the threat of Communist subversion required the full utilization of available forces to maintain order. Moreover, the new police force soon became involved in quasimilitary actions against Communist guerrillas and later against Communist invaders from the north. Thus, the patterns established by the Japanese continued to characterize police functions (see ch. 14, Political Dynamics).

THE LEGAL SYSTEM OF THE REPUBLIC OF KOREA

With the establishment of the Republic of Korea on August 15, 1948, the police force was officially designated as the National Police of the Republic of Korea. The Constitution also established the Judiciary as an independent branch of the government with judicial powers vested in the various courts. The Criminal Code was promulgated in 1953 and the Criminal Procedure Code in 1954. From 1948 to 1960, President Syngman Rhee maintained close control of the police force and strong influence over the judiciary system; this did little to encourage popular support and faith in the police and judiciary. It took the military coup of 1961 to begin the needed reforms and build the respect and professionalism that the legal system enjoys today.

Criminal Codes

Because of popular opposition the old Japanese code was superseded in September 1953 by the new criminal code, a compromise document that retains some of the classical Chinese legal concepts and reflects the influence of German and United States criminal laws. Features of Chinese origin include the recognition of Confucian status levels by prescribing more severe penalties for high officials than for ordinary persons committing comparable offenses. Moreover, because of Confucian concepts of filial duty, aggravated penalties are imposed for crimes against lineal ascendants, and certain criminal charges against lineal ascendants are prohibited.

German influence is evident in parts of the code which emphasize protection of the state, and United States influence is reflected in the protection of individual rights pertaining to police searches, arrests, charges, bail arraignments, and trials. The code is applicable to nationals, wherever they are, and to aliens who commit crimes within the Republic of Korea's territory or on the country's vessels or aircraft.

The code lists nine types of punishments: death, penal servitude, imprisonment, deprivation of qualifications, suspension of qualifications, ordinary fine, detention, minor fine, and confiscation. The death penalty is inflicted in prison by hanging. Penal servitude is for life or for a "limited term" (1 to 15 years). In aggravated cases the limited term of penal servitude may be extended up to 25 years. Deprivation or suspension of qualification may include qualifications to vote, to practice law, to become a public official, or to become the director, auditor, or custodian of a corporation. Detention may be from 1 to 30 days. A person sentenced to penal servitude or to imprisonment automatically forfeits the above-mentioned qualifications until released from custody. As of late 1964, the minimum ordinary fine was 500 wŏn (100 wŏn=U. S. $0.37), and minor fines ranged from 500 to 50 wŏn. Confiscation is applicable to property illegally in possession of a person or to anything which constitutes evidence in a crime.

Persons under 14 years of age are not punishable for criminal conduct. The punishment for a repeated crime (one committed within 3 years after the completion or remission of a sentence) is twice the maximum penalty that can be imposed upon a first offender.

Heavy sentences are authorized for crimes which threaten national security, incur damage or destruction of public property, or endanger the health or life of the general public. Otherwise, the punishments are comparable to those incorporated in United States law.

Sentences by summary courts for minor offenses are mostly fines. This policy seems to be favored by the judicial authorities because it provides income for the state and prevents overcrowding of detention facilities. Fines collected by the Seoul District Court in 1965 reportedly amounted to almost 150 million wŏn. If fines cannot be paid, a substitutive term of penal servitude is imposed. The number of days in custody before imposition of sentence may be deducted, in whole or in part, from the period of imprisonment or penal servitude.

Sentences may be reduced or suspended under mitigating circumstances, and prisoners may be paroled for good behavior. There is a statute of limitations, which prescribes the statutory period after which the offender cannot be brought to trial for his offense, unless the offender in the meantime has been beyond the reach of the law.

The Status-of-Forces Agreement between the Republic of Korea and the United Staes was signed by Korean Foreign Minister Yi Tong-won and Secretary of State Dean Rusk on July 9, 1966, and became effective on February 9, 1967. The agreement is composed of a preamble and 31 articles. It provides that the United States has primary jurisdiction over offenses occurring during the performance of official duty or those solely concerning its personnel or property. The Republic of Korea's jurisdiction extends to all other offenses committed by United States servicemen in the country and covers mainly criminal acts, labor laws, and civil claims. As of December 1967, Korean authorities had exercised jurisdiction in only 10 out of 1,710 criminal cases involving 2,029 United States military personnel and their dependents. The Ministry of Justice has reported that whenever government waived its right to exercise jurisdiction, it did so in recognition of punishments by United States courts-martial or other disciplinary actions for the United States military offenders.

The claims provision of the Status-of-Forces Agreement went into effect on a nation wide basis on February 9, 1968 (a year after the initial agreement was signed). Previously, the claims provisions were effective only for the Seoul metropolitan area.

The Police System

National Police

The Korean National Police is a centralized civil police force employing approximately 40,000 officers and men and functions as a part of the Ministry of Home Affairs. The authority of the police is derived from that inherent in the power of the state in the enforcement of edicts, but is not defined specifically by the Constitution, by law, or by decree. The present organization of the National Police was established by the Organization Rule for the Minister of Home Affairs (Cabinet Decree No. 116, October 2, 1961, amended to Presidential Decree No. 1824 on May 27, 1964). The functional responsibilities of the police are:

1. Enforcement of law and ordinances;
2. Maintenance of public order;
3. Protection of life and property;
4. Prevention of smuggling (primary responsibility of the Minister of Finance, Customs Bureau);
5. Prevention of enemy agent infiltration and in-country activ-

ities (shared with the Korean Counter-Intelligence Corps, as well as the Korean Army and Navy, and the United States Central Intelligence Agency);

6. Protection of the fisheries fleet (shared with the Ministry of Agriculture);
7. Protection of forests (primary responsibility of the Ministry of Agriculture).

A Vice Minister, within the Home Affairs Ministry, has the sole duty of administration and funding of the police force. Reporting to the Vice Minister is the National Police Commander, who is also the Director of the Police Bureau. The Bureau, with a personnel strength of 511, is organized into nine main divisions: administration, planning, public safety, guard, fire protection, investigation, intelligence, communications, and foreign affairs. The Director is also responsible for eleven police bureaus—nine provincial bureaus and the metropolitan police bureaus of Seoul and Pusan. In addition, the Police College, the Scientific Investigation Laboratory, the Police Hospital, and the Marine Police (coast guard) are also within the jurisdiction of the Director.

Each provincial bureau has an academy for basic training of policemen and policewomen. An increasing number of applicants are college students or graduates, and the police force is successfully being upgraded into a well-educated public safety organization. Specialists and officers are trained at the National Police Academy in Seoul. All applicants for officer training must take the 12-week training course for recruits as well as advanced training before being appointed officers. The officer candidate program is a 1-year, intensive course in modern police sciences. Refresher courses lasting 6 to 8 weeks are given regularly to both patrolmen and officers.

National Police pay schedules conform in general to those of the civil service system. The government has attempted to keep pace with the rising cost of living and has voted periodic pay and allowance increases. The pay scale is geared to the six ranks for public personnel: Colonel, Major, Captain, Lieutenant, Sergeant, and Patrolman.

Women constitute a small but important part of the police force. They are employed mainly for traffic control, investigation of female security suspects, care of abandoned infants and children, juvenile problems, and for vice control duties. They are generally a part of the Public Safety Section in each of the police bureaus. A Women's Police Bureau was established as early as July 1946 and was subsequently merged with other public safety activities through reorganizations.

The National Police has over 1,500 vehicles, including jeeps, sedans, light and heavy trucks, buses, and motorcycles. Also available to the police are light aircraft, such as four Cessna-180's, one L-19, two twin-engine Beech Barons, four C-45's, and two helicopters. In addition, the police are equipped with walkie-talkies, teletype sets, and phototransmission equipment. A national communications network using ultra-high frequencies is capable of reaching all police units in the country.

The police are distributed throughout each area in units and stations varying in size according to local requirements. In early 1968 there were 165 police stations, 1,394 substations, and about 1,000 smaller units, including detachments. In addition, the National Police has 24 combat companies that are trained in special military tactics for counterinsurgency activities, and nearly all policemen have had extensive training in guerrilla warfare.

The National Police, in addition to using modern scientific methods in crime detection and investigation, has launched programs of education and prevention. In an effort to curb the previously increasing traffic accident rate, juvenile delinquency, and crime in urban areas, it has formed civilian committees and conducted extensive nationwide campaigns with emphasis on preventive measures and guidance. In addition, police officials conduct public relations campaigns stressing their role as public servants sworn to protect the entire community. Crime rates took a dramatic turn downward in 1966; juvenile delinquency appears to be responding to the new programs, and traffic accidents, while still a serious problem, appear to be within the probability of control.

The National Police is a disciplined, well-equipped organization, able to cope effectively with sizable riots, major crimes, and other civil disturbances. It is centrally controlled, with adequate mobility to permit rapid concentration in areas of disorder. The practices that plagued the police system of the 1950's are virtually nonexistent. The government appears to have successfully developed a spirit of cooperation between the police and the people. The populace in turn has a new respect for law and order and in the ability of the National Police to enforce them justly.

Maritime Police

The Maritime Police is under the direct jurisdiction of the Director, National Police Bureau, within the Ministry of Home Affairs. Although not an integral part of the National Police organization, it has a police function and operates in close cooperation with the other police divisions. The force has 64 patrol ships, nine high-speed boats, and the necessary ancillary equipment. The Maritime Police, headquartered in Pusan, patrols the principal harbors and the national coastal waters. It protects fishing vessels from harassment by vessels of other nations, captures smugglers, intercepts illegal entries, enforces maritime laws and regulations, and helps boats in distress.

The Courts and Legal Personnel

The first constitution of the Republic of Korea, proclaimed on July 12, 1948, provided for a court system to act independently from the other branches of the government. The court system, as provided for under the new constitution of 1963 and the Court Organization Law of 1949 (most recently amended in March 1966) functions on four levels. The highest court of the state is the Supreme Court, followed by three appellate courts, 10 district courts, 36 branch courts and one family court.

The Supreme Court, by law, must have fewer than 16 judges (one Chief Justice and 11 justices as of mid 1968). The Chief Justice is appointed by the President with the consent of the National Assembly upon the nomination of the Council for Recommendation of Judges. Judges may be dismissed by impeachment only, and in the case of criminal or disciplinary offenses, a reduction in salary can be imposed. The Chief Justice's term of office is 6 years and cannot be renewed. Supreme Court justices are also appointed by the President upon the recommendation of the Chief Justice and with the consent of the Council for Recommendations for Judges. The council is composed of four judges, two lawyers, one professor of law nominated by the President, the Minister of Justice, and the Procurator General. These procedures have been established to insure the independence of the Supreme Court from political pressures. Justices are appointed for a 10-year term and may be reappointed.

The Supreme Court has the power to pass upon the constitutionality of any law, administrative order, or regulation. It may also hear appeals of decisions of the appellate courts in civil and criminal cases. Supreme Court decisions are final and form judicial precedents that are binding on all lower courts. Although military trials are handled by courts-martial within the armed forces jurisdiction, the Supreme Court has the final appellate jurisdiction over them.

Each appellate court is composed of a presiding judge and usually three associate judges, all of whom are appointed by the Chief Justice upon recommendation of the Council of Supreme Court Judges and approval of the Council for Recommendation of Judges. There are three appellate courts—one each at Seoul, Taegu, and Kwangju—and their primary function is to hear appeals from the decisions and judgments of lower courts.

District courts have been established in each of the nine provincial capitals. In Seoul the district court is divided into separate courts—Seoul Civil District Court and Seoul Criminal District Court. Normally, the court is administered by a single judge, but in serious cases three judges are required. A district court may establish branch courts, with single judges, to hear cases in outlying areas. Circuit judges may also be appointed to try minor offenses in areas where there are no permanent courts.

The newly amended Court Organization Law provides for family courts which are designed to hear all cases involving matrimonial, juvenile, and other domestic matters. The first such court was established in Seoul in 1963. Court sessions are closed to the public to insure the privacy of the individuals involved.

The office of Minister of Justice is responsible for the administration of the nation's judicial affairs. Its organization consists of three bureaus: Legal Affairs, Prosecution, and Penal Administration. The ministry has, for example, drafted and initiated legislature bills dealing with important national legal questions. It also grants exit permits and resident permits for aliens.

Within the Ministry of Justice a system of prosecutors has been established. The prosecutors are empowered to conduct investigations into violations of law and to initiate legal action against suspected lawbreakers. The Supreme Prosecutor's office (headed by the Prosecutor General), is the government's highest prosecution agency. This office is responsible for the supervision and control of all the appellate, district, and branch prosecutors' offices. The Minister of Justice is not permitted to prosecute cases, this being the sole domain of the Supreme Prosecutor's office. The Prosecutor General, his deputy, and the directors of the appellate prosecutors' offices are appointed by the President from among experienced prosecutors, judges, or lawyers who have been practicing law for more than 10 years. Other prosecutors are appointed by the Ministry of Justice.

The availability of legal personnel has been a problem. With the increasing acceptance of the courts as a means of redress for civil suits and the demands of criminal cases, the need for competent lawyers and judges is increasing rapidly. Although the law schools are training larger classes each year, the difficult bar examination permits only a small percentage to pass, further aggravating the legal personnel shortage. Too, the country's relatively short experience as a full participant in the judiciary system, which required the staffing of a national organization in the short period of 20 years, has contributed to the shortage of personnel.

A current problem faced by the judiciary has been to maintain an adequate number of judges to cope with the increasing number of cases at hand. For example, in early 1968, the judiciary system required 468 judges for its courts, but only 388 were available (a shortage of about 25 percent in the appellate courts and 17 percent in the district courts). The average number of cases, both criminal and civil, handled by an individual judge usually exceeds 130 per month, a heavy work load. A partial reason for the shortages appears to be the modest government salaries compared to income from private law practice. Also a factor, however, is the reluctance of young lawyers to expose themselves to possible political involvement, which characterized the judiciary in the past. The continued progress toward a totally independent, nonpolitical judiciary is doing much to overcome this barrier.

Criminal Procedure

The Korean Criminal Code was promulgated on September 18, 1953 (Law No. 293); the Code of Criminal Procedure (Law No. 341) became effective on September 23, 1954 and was amended in December 1963. Under the Constitution of the Republic of Korea all citizens are equal before the law. Personal freedoms are protected in a variety of ways. For example, a warrant issued by a judge must be presented in case of arrest, detention, search, or seizure. In serious criminal offenses, however, the warrant may be obtained after arrest. All persons arrested or detained have the right to the prompt assistance of counsel, and when the defendant is unable to secure counsel by his own efforts, the state will assign one to the defendant. Persons arrested or detained also have a right to request the court for a review of the legality of the arrest or detention. Confessions are inadmissible if made against the will of the accused or if the confession is the only evidence against the accused. Trial is not by jury but by a system of judges, and decisions are made on the basis of oral proceedings.

The district courts (courts of first instance), in general, have jurisdiction over offenses committed within their territorial boundaries as determined by the place of the offense, residence of the accused, or the place where accused was at the time of the offense. In a case of urgency, a court may take the necessary steps to investigate a case even when it has no jurisdiction. Transfer of cases between courts of the same level is permitted when it is deemed to be in the best interest of all concerned. In cases of jurisdictional dispute, the next higher court can designate the court that shall have jurisdiction.

The criminal codes provide a statute of limitations, for example, 15 years for a crime punishable with death penalty; 10 years for a crime punishable with penal servitude or imprisonment for an undetermined term—and progressively less with less severe penalties.

Court Procedures

The public prosecutor begins the criminal trial procedure by investigating the suspect and the circumstances surrounding the offense. Members of the National Police or appointed judicial police officials are usually assigned to assist the public prosecutor in his investigation. All aspects of the investigation are accomplished as discreetly as possible so as not to violate the personal rights of the accused or others in the course of investigation.

Summons are issued by the court when there is reasonable evidence that a criminal offense has been committed. The accused may be detained if he has no fixed dwelling, if there are reasonable grounds for suspicion that he may destroy evidence, or if the court feels he may try to escape. Before detention, the accused must be informed of the nature of the offense and of his right to counsel. If the court determines that it is unnecessary to detain him, he must be released within 24 hours after such determination. The warrants for detention are executed by a judicial police official under the direction of a public prosecutor. When an accused is detained, his defense counsel or a person designated by him must be informed of the detention within three days. The period of detention may not exceed two months, except in the case of a continuance, when the detention may be renewed twice by a ruling. Release from detention may be requested by use of bail and is normally granted; the amount of the bail money is determined by the severity of the offense and the accused's ability to pay. A person arrested and subsequently released cannot be rearrested in connection with the same crime without another warrant. Flagrant violators, however, may be arrested by any citizen without a warrant.

Before interrogation of a suspect, his true identity must be ascertained and the facts and conditions of the offense made clear to the suspect. The suspect, in turn, must be given an opportunity to state facts favorable to him. The entire interrogation takes place in the presence of a third party from the police or prosecutor's office. Statements made by the suspect become a part of the protocol after he has inspected the protocol document and signed and sealed it.

When the prosecutor deems it necessary for the gathering of evidence, he can request search-and-seizure warrants. These are issued by the courts and are executed by a judicial police official during daylight hours. Special permission must be granted by the court for night searches and seizures. The prosecutor may also request the court to direct such action as physical examination of witnesses, dissection of corpses, or the opening of graves.

Documents that may relate to a case to be tried are not made public prior to the opening of the trial except when necessary in

427

the public interest or for other valid reasons. Statements or depositions by persons examined for the purpose of the trial must be read aloud or inspected and signed by them.

After the investigation the public prosecutor decides whether there was, in fact, a crime committed and if there is sufficient evidence to try for a conviction. Once the prosecutor decides to proceed, public action is instituted by his filing a written indictment with a competent court. He must do this within three months after the complaint or accusation has been made. Notice not to prosecute must be made to the suspect promptly by the prosecutor. In the event the person lodging the complaint or accusation disagrees with the prosecutor's decision not to take public action, he may reassert his demand to a higher court.

When a case is committed to court for trial, the court appoints a prosecutor from among the advocates available who applied for public trials. The advocate so appointed assumes the official duties of a public prosecutor and is paid by the government. The accused must be served a copy of the indictment no later than 5 days prior to the date of the trial. Both sides may submit documents, articles, or other evidence prior to trial date, and each may examine the evidence.

Trial judges may be challenged for cause by the prosecutor or the accused; however, peremptory challenges are not permitted. A judge may also be excluded from duties of a case when he himself is the injured party, a relative of the accused, a witness in the case, or if he is or has acted as a legal representative of the accused.

The trial takes place in a courtroom and is convened in the presence of the judge, a clerical official and a public prosecutor. The accused sits in front of the presiding judge and is subject to no physical restraints; guards are normally stationed within the courtroom to prevent violent action or escape. A defense counsel must also be present where the offense charged is punishable with death, penal servitude, or imprisonment for three years or more.

The trial opens with the judge confirming that the accused is the same person cited in the indictment. The prosecutor proceeds by making his opening remarks stating the essentials of prosecution in accordance with the indictment. The accused (or defense counsel) is then accorded time to state facts which may be favorable to his case. Both the prosecutor and the defense counsel may in turn directly question the defendant concerning the alleged offense. The judge may also make inquiries of the accused, if he so desires. Documentary evidence is examined after the questioning of the defendant is completed. The accused is asked his opinion regarding the articles of evidence and is advised of his right to question the validity of such evidence. Objections regarding the evidence may be made by the prosecutor, the defense counsel, or the accused and are ruled upon by the judge.

The courts may examine any person as a witness by issuing a summons at the request of prosecutor, defense counsel, or accused. A written oath is read aloud by the witnesses, then signed and sealed. A witness is examined first by the party (prosecutor, defense counsel, or defendant) who requested his appearance; next the judge may also examine the witness. Expert witnesses may be used to give testimony upon issuance of a court order. Each witness is afforded the right to avoid self-incrimination.

The public prosecutor may, with the permission of the court, add, delete, or change the facts of the accusation or the applicable provisions of the law in the indictment. Such change will be permitted by the judge if it does not modify the offense charged. If the changes appear to prejudice the defense of the accused, a recess is granted so that the accused and his counsel may prepare a proper defense. The prosecutor and defense counsel may raise objections to any rulings by a presiding judge. The court, in turn, renders a ruling on the objections raised.

Before the trial ends, the presiding judge must afford an opportunity to the accused and his counsel to make a final plea after hearing the closing arguments of the prosecutor. A court can, if necessary, reopen oral proceedings which had been concluded, by means of a ruling, upon request of the prosecutor, accused, or his defense counsel.

A record of the trial proceedings is normally published within 5 days of the trial. The testimony given during the trial may be recorded in whole or in part by the court and obtained by the defendant at his own cost. The cost of trial, in whole or in part, is charged to the accused when a penalty has been pronounced. Even when no penalty is given, the costs which have arisen from a cause imputable to the accused may be charged.

Court Sentencing

When there is proof of guilt, the judge pronounces the penalty, based on the nature of the offense, the gist of the evidence, and the applicable laws and ordinances. At the same time the judge will announce any suspension of punishment, the number of days of detention prior to trial, or days in arrest status. In cases where sentence is pronounced, the presiding judge will advise the accused regarding the time for appeal and the court to which the appeal can be made.

A finding of "not guilty" results if it is determined that the actions of the accused do not constitute an offense, or if the evidence of a criminal act is insufficient. An acquittal is pronounced in cases when a previous binding judgment has been made, an amnesty has been proclaimed, the statute of limitations is in effect, or the applicable law or ordinance has been abolished subsequent to the commission of the offense. Cases may also be dismissed when such action is proper according to law.

Appeals

Judgments rendered by a lower court may be appealed to another or higher court by the prosecutor, the accused (or defense counsel in his behalf), spouse, lineal relatives, sisters, brothers, or proxy on behalf of the accused. The appeal may be filed against the whole or part of the decision and must be made within the period announced in the original sentencing. Waiver of appeal must be in writing, except when stated orally in court.

Appeals made to an appellate court may be lodged in cases where the finding of the court of second instance is not satisfactory, or from the collegiate court of the district courts. The period allowed for appeal to the higher court is 7 days and is made by lodging a petition for appeal to the original court.

Appeal to the Supreme Court is also available to the defendant. Appeal, for example, may be made when the finding of the court of second instance is not satisfactory. Appeals may also be lodged after action by the appellate court. Appeals to the Supreme Court are filed by petition within 7 days of the last judgment. Defense counsels in Supreme Court cases must be advocates, and only the defense counsel will argue on behalf of the accused.

An extraordinary appeal may be made to the Supreme Court when it is discovered, after a judgment has become binding, that trial or judgment of a case was in violation of a law or an ordinance.

The Penal System

The United States Military Government took over the Japanese penal system in Korea south of the 38th parallel after the end of World War II, and it was turned back to the Republic of Korea in 1948 when it attained independence. Prison facilities soon were overcrowded as thousands of Communist agents and sympathizers were incarcerated. This condition was aggravated by a sharply increased crime rate and by the destruction of most of the detention installations during the Korean Conflict. After the fighting ceased, the government appointed the Committee for the Reconstruction of Correctional Institutions to make recommendations and arrangements for restoring facilities and improving the penal system. Teams were sent abroad to study foreign methods and, as a result or their reports, many advanced features were incorporated into a rehabilitation program. The term "prison" was replaced by "reformatory." Educational and vocational training courses were set up to supplement regularly scheduled work. An intermediate correctional institution was established and separate detention facilities were provided for unconvicted prisoners. Subsequent reform measures have included medical and dental services, improved rations, and provision for recreation.

The penal system is administered by the Bureau of Reformatories, an agency in the Ministry of Justice. The system employs about 3,000 persons who operate 21 reformatories and a school for guards and specialists. Reformatories are of three types: for adults, for juveniles, and one for each of four special categories of prisoners: lepers, tubercular cases, "leftists," and those who are mentally deficient or physically deformed.

The Ministry of Justice reported that as of August 31, 1966, its reformatory population was 31,277, of which 21,108 were convicted inmates; the remainder were unconvicted prisoners in detention facilities. During the same period the Juvenile Reformatory Center accommodated about 3,000 minors from all provinces.

Incidence of Crime

Since 1966, the incidence of crime has been decreasing (see table 25). Despite the general decrease, however, certain criminal of-

Table 25. Changes in Population, Criminal Offenses, and Police Manpower, Republic of Korea, 1961–1968

Year[1]	Population	Numerical index	Criminal offenses	Numerical index	Police manpower	Numerical index
1961	25,694,108	100	473,522	100	29,315	100
1962	26,277,635	102	723,985	153	29,910	102
1963	27,489,848	107	710,780	150	33,879	115.5
1964	28,181,096	109.7	858,818	181.4	33,882	115.6
1965	28,647,176	112	967,594	204.3	34,572	118
1966	29,207,856	113.7	852,795	180	39,352	134
1967	30,067,000[2]	117	772,600[2]	163	38,600	131.7
1968	30,789,000[3]	120	695,340[3]	146.8	40,622	138.6

[1] As of January 1, based on latest figures for preceding year.
[2] Preliminary count.
[3] Estimated.

Source: Adapted from U.S. Government sources.

fenses increased in numbers. In the first 8 months of 1967, for example, increases were noted in felonious cases: murder by 5.4 percent; rape, 19.4 percent; arson, 26.5 percent; thefts, 1.4 percent; and fraud, 6 percent. During the same time span, a total of 515,410 cases of criminal offenses were reported, or a decrease of 11.5 percent from a like period in 1966.

Most of the crimes, such as assault, robbery, and theft, were concentrated in the urban areas. At the same time there was a substantial increase in robbery in the rural areas. The most frequent offenses are those having an economic basis, such as robbery, theft, and smuggling, followed by fraud, embezzlement and bribery. Previous statistics, although incomplete, occasionally mentioned sex crimes, giving the impression they were not a major problem. However, as noted above, the first 8 months of 1967 showed almost a 20 percent increase in rape offenses. The explanation may lie in the evolving traditions of Korean life, which previously reflected a rigid disdain of exposing family problems to the public eye. This is to say, more rapes are being reported to authorities than previously. A rash of child kidnappings in 1966–67 drew the wrath of the public because in most cases the victims were killed by their kidnappers.

The typical citizen is becoming more aware of the seriousness of crime and its attendant corrosion of national moral health. As corruption disappears from government, the judiciary becomes more independent from government influences, and the police become more efficient and impartial, the citizenry appears to be responding as a concerned partner in combatting crime and injustices.

Crime prevention committees are working with the police in the urban areas to plan and implement methods to fight crime. The program appears to be succeeding, as reflected by a decreasing crime rate.

ORDER, SECURITY, AND SOCIETY

Respect for constituted authority has not been traditional in Korean society. Rather, it has been the family, the clan, and the village who joined to implement the traditional ways (see ch. 7, Family). The Japanese occupation, through repressive rule, further contributed to the development of fear, distrust, and resentment of police and law enforcement agencies. Noncompliance with Japanese regulations, harassment of police, and evasion of controls were regarded as commendable behavior. This national attitude has been changing, although the evolution during the past 20 years in developing an appreciation for public order and safety has been a difficult one (see ch. 12, Social Values; ch. 14, Political Dynamics). The public attitude toward the police has fluctuated over the years, usually in response to the use of police and judiciary powers.

The need and desire for public order and safety have only recently been based on a national popular attitude. This change in attitude can be partially attributed to the spread of communications media, particularly the thousands of radio amplifiers installed throughout the nation through the National Reconstruction

Movement and the National Education System, as well as to banking and cooperative groups that encourage the need for unity. The resulting tendency toward a homogeneity has evolved into a public concern over abnormal social behavior even beyond the citizen's own neighborhood or village. However, attempts at reform and improvements by individual citizens have been, in the main, fragmentary.

The groups that tend to have a stabilizing influence on society and encourage the maintenance of order and security are those that are nonpolitical. The large urban areas of Seoul and Pusan have groupings of this type which display a definite and cohesive character: churches, not only as centers of worship, but as agencies for handling social and employment problems; the Young Men's Christian Association (YMCA); the Young Women's Christian Association (YWCA); and the innumerable schools and colleges. In addition, the press has frequently launched campaigns to promote law and order. These efforts are often joined by local civic groups for such activities as anti-accident rallies. Student groups are attempting to demonstrate a sense of maturity and national purpose. The New Tide Movement, for example, is a student campaign designed to create a responsible academic atmosphere on college campuses. It was developed by the student council of the United Nations Educational, Scientific, and Cultural Organization (UNESCO) Korean Chapter under the slogan "Dialogue, Understanding, and Cooperation."

Juvenile delinquency has received added attention. The police estimate that there are about 500,000 boys and girls who are in need of some kind of assistance and guidance. These include criminal offenders, beggars, runaways, and other delinquents. In response to this need, such organizations as The Big Brothers and Sisters Movement, Boy Scouts, Girl Scouts, and the Korean Youth Hostel Association are combatting the problem. In 1966, a total of 6,576 orphans were adopted through the efforts of these organizations. Another step toward alleviating the juvenile delinquency problem was the assignment of 83 college graduate policewomen to juvenile affairs. The use of college graduates for police work is another example of the high standards and calibre of the law enforcement personnel being established in the Republic of Korea to encourage respect and cooperation with the police and judiciary.

CHAPTER 27
THE ARMED FORCES

The Republic of Korea military establishment is a well organized, disciplined, fighting force of significant strength. The army is considered to be the fourth largest in the world, surpassed only by those of Communist China, the Soviet Union, and the United States, and built on a tradition of antimilitarism and a nonindustrial base (see ch. 18, Structure of Economy; ch. 20, Industry). The United States has been an influencing partner in the growth and shaping of the military establishment of the Republic of Korea since the initial days of the National Defense Constabulary in January 1946, an organization created to support the National Police in maintaining internal security and to provide a nucleus for expansion into a force capable of eventually assuming its own defense responsibilities.

Financial, industrial, and technical limitations initially made the Republic of Korea largely dependent on external logistical support and advice in training and organization. By 1968, however, this was changing, and industry was burgeoning. The south Koreans were taking to modern technology with such enthusiasm that Korean engineers were found in many cities of Asia. Agriculture was being modernized, and output was rising. The efficiency and morale of the armed forces reflected the growing national health.

The estimated total strength of the regular armed forces in mid-1968, based on published accounts, exceed 600,000. The military establishment includes the Army of 550,000; the Navy of 50,000, including a Marine Corps of 30,000; and the Air Force of 30,000.

A milestone in contemporary military history is the celebration of the Republic's third anniversary of participation in the military conflict in Vietnam. It was on September 25, 1965, that the Republic of Korea Forces, Vietnam Command, was formally activated. An initial Korean force of 2,000 men had expanded to approximately 48,000 by 1968 and had established an excellent combat record.

MILITARY TRADITION IN NATIONAL LIFE

History

Korea's history is devoid of militarism, particularly as an instrument of national policy (see ch. 3, Historical Setting). Imbued with the Confucian ethic which rejects military service as a degrading form of human endeavor, the Koreans carried this concept into the field of foreign affairs and for centuries showed antipathy toward war and military conquest. The soldier usually ranked low on the social scale.

The country, however, has not been free of war. It has suffered the consequences of conflicts between internal factions or those brought on by invasions of hostile neighbors. Military adventures between rival kingdoms for domination of the peninsula occurred at various times during Korea's 20 centuries of recorded history. Externally, the major invasions included those of the Chinese in the 2nd century B.C., the Mongols in the 13th century A.D., and the Japanese at the end of the 16th century. Wars over dynastic successions, however, were largely confined to sporadic engagements between small, privately organized military forces and were of little consequence in establishing national military traditions, although several military heroes have emerged from past invasions.

In A.D. 612, a Chinese emperor of the Sui Dynasty, with "a million men," attacked the ancient Korean Kingdom of Koguryŏ, defended by an army of 300,000 under the courageous leadership of General Ulchimundŏk. By a combination of diplomacy and skillful tactics, he defeated and drove out the Chinese hordes. General Ulchimundŏk is generally regarded as a great military hero and his memory is preserved in the "Ulchi" Medal, the second highest ranking Distinguished Military Service Medal in the Republic of Korea.

Another Korean military hero is Admiral Yi Sun-sin, whose brilliant naval operations during the Japanese invasion of 1592–1598 were instrumental in forcing the Japanese from the Korean peninsula. The Japanese general, Toyotomi Hideyoshi, sought to conquer the Ming Dynasty and bring China into the Japanese Empire. The quickest and easiest route to Peking, China's capital, was through the Korean peninsula. This required the transportation, by sea, of large quantities of men and supplies to Pusan, the Japanese base camp. With only 80 ships against an 800-ship invading force, Admiral Yi faced enormous odds. Among the Korean armada, however, were the "kŏbuksŏn", or turtleships, the first ironclads in history. These unlikely looking warships, were destined to greatly reduce the odds. During the six years of naval engagements, Admiral Yi was able to consistently defeat significant numbers of Japanese warships. These naval losses denied the Japanese the needed men and supplies to carry out their 500-mile march to Peking.

In addition to the "turtleships" Admiral Yi utilized other innovations to naval warfare. He employed a smoke generator in which sulphur and saltpeter were burned, emitting great clouds of smoke. Psychologically, this first recorded smokescreen struck terror into the hearts of the superstitious enemy sailors and, more practically, it masked the movements of Yi's ships. An example of his tactical brilliance was his defeat of a large enemy convoy by utilizing a formation described as a fish trap or inverted V. His smaller patrol craft were at the open end of the V and the heavy ships grouped at the vortex. As the enemy ships were forced inside the V they were trapped and destroyed by Yi's heavy ships.

Admiral Yi also utilized salvo fire against a large force of Japanese warships, an early, if not the first, use of such fire power. He also used a new Korean weapon, a type of flame thrower, a small cannon with a shell shaped like an arrow in which the head contained an incendiary charge. It was successfully used to set hundreds of enemy ships afire. As a result of these exploits, Admiral Yi Sun-sin remains to this day one of the few military heroes of Korea. His honorary posthumous title, Ch'ungmu, has been given to the third-ranking Distinguished Military Service Medal. A further tribute was paid when, in April 1968, a 55-foot statue of Admiral Yi Sun-sin (reportedly the tallest in the Orient) was unveiled in Seoul. Except for General Ulchimundŏk, Admiral Yi, and a few less notable examples, Korean history had comparatively few military heroes, and military heroism never seemed to form a very significant part of the people's pride in their past traditions.

The Japanese occupation of 1920–45 gave Korea its first exposure to modern warfare. Many Koreans served in the Japanese military and police force while others escaped Japanese control and fought with other foreign forces. A small number of present officers of the Republic of Korea forces served with Japanese units during the years of Japanese control, although they were generally restricted to positions of field grade and below. Other Koreans escaped to China or the Soviet Union and served in the Communist military forces of those countries. Some of these Korean Communists become expert military leaders as a result of Communist Military Academy training in Peking or Moscow and extensive experience in combat. This group formed the leadership in the North Korean armed forces after 1945. A respect for military action could be seen developing as a result of the sporadic armed resistance movement against the Japanese occupation forces in Korea, Manchuria, and China. Although the resistance was of guerrilla character, it was viewed with great favor by the Korean populace, especially in North Korea, and served to strengthen a growing spirit of militant nationalism.

Contemporary

Gratitude for liberation from the Japanese military control and optimistic hopes for peace ushered in the United States 7th Army Division as it landed at Inch'ŏn in September 1945. The Korean's distrust of foreign military forces on Korean soil and the traditional antipathy toward military solutions of political problems were seemingly put aside. In January 1946, the United States military government established the National Defense Constabulary of the Republic of Korea which became the nucleus of a modern army. The Armed Forces of the Republic of Korea, consisting of the Army, Navy, Air Force, and Marine Corps, were created in 1948 with the independence of the country. Thus, the Republic of Korea became a partner and a full-fledged participant in modern military preparedness.

The armed forces were heavily dependent on external support—principally that of the United States. As a result, much of the military organizational structure, training programs, and strategy and tactics, are similar to those of United States forces. The initial stages of development were difficult, principally because of the absence of a living military tradition, the Republic's former colonial status, and its internal sources of disunity. War, however, forced a belated application of training and discipline to overcome these disadvantages. Through overcoming them, the Korean Army became the first Korean organization that eliminated most of the sources of fluidity and disunity within Korea's mass society. Postwar emphasis on advanced courses, such as those taught at the Command and General Staff School at Chinhae, laid great emphasis not only on modern management procedures but on concepts of patriotism, spirit of service, loyalty to service, and avoidance of politics. In addition, courses of the National Defense College introduced officers to economics, political science, national development, and the broader terms of the Army's role in world strategy and national defense.

In the Republic today, the armed forces have gained the esteem of many persons because of their restraint during the revolt of April 1960, which was instrumental in overthrowing the regime of President Syngman Rhee. A similar reaction was seen in the popular acquiescence to the military coup of May 16, 1961. Koreans take great pride in the contributions which their troops have made in the Republic of Korea and the high praise which has been bestowed on their combat effectiveness.

In September 1964, in response to a request for assistance from South Vietnam, the Republic of Korea sent a noncombatant group called the "Dove Unit." This unit consisted of a mobile Army surgical hospital, a group of karate instructors, and 2,200 noncombat engineers and security troops. A year later, South Vietnam formally requested military combat assistance from the Republic and authorized the Koreans to establish a military command on its soil. With the approval of the National Assembly, an Army combat unit, called the "Tiger Division," and the "Blue Dragon" Marine Corps Brigade were dispatched to South Vietnam. In October 1967 the Korean commitment was increased to nearly 50,000 men by the addition of a second Army Division, called the "White Horse Division," a Navy transport unit, a logistics command, and two Air Force support squadrons.

The combat record of the Korean soldier in Vietnam is impressive. In addition to his high state of combat readiness, he exhibits the feeling of national and personal commitment to a cause that stems from a situation both Koreans and Vietnamese have faced. Both nations have been divided by international agreement and a confrontation with communism—Korea at the 38th parallel and Vietnam at the 17th. The Communist world, particularly the North Koreans, respect the Republic's military readiness and combat effectiveness as an effective deterrent.

THE ARMED FORCES AND THE GOVERNMENT

The Constitution of the Republic of Korea provides for the creation of an army, navy, air force and marine corps as the only military organizations authorized to defend the country. The Armed Forces Organizational Act, in turn, describes the organizational structure and mission of each military service. Under the Constitution the President is designated as Commander in Chief of the National Defense Forces. He is empowered, by Article 71 to declare war and make peace; Article 56, however, requires the consent of the National Assembly in these matters. Under Article 86 other important military matters, including the appointment and removal of service chiefs, are referred to the State Council but final decision rests only with the President. The Minister of National Defense represents the military establishment in the State Council. To assure civilian control of the military, Article 84 of the Constitution provides that state ministers may not be military men on active duty. This prohibition applies even to the Minister of Defense (though not to lesser positions within this Ministry). for example, General Park Chung-hee retired from the Army in August 1963, before running for the presidency (see ch. 13, The Governmental System; ch. 14, Political Dynamics).

The President is assisted and advised on security matters by the National Security Council which includes the President (as chairman), the Prime Minister, the Minister of Economic Planning, the Minister of Foreign Affairs, the Minister of Home Affairs, the Minister of Finance, the Minister of National Defense, one of the two ministers without portfolio (appointed by the President), and the Director of the Central Intelligence Agency. The Chairman of the Joint Chiefs of Staff although not a statutory member, is authorized to participate in the meetings.

The Joint Chiefs of Staff, composed of the chiefs of staff of the three services and an appointment chairman, formulates policies affecting the three services and thus exercises general control over the combined armed forces. The Commandant of the Marine Corps may act as a regular member when Marine Corps matters are discussed. The Chairman is directly responsible to the President on these matters, but the group is administratively subordinate to the Minister of National Defense. Each Chief of Staff is directly subordinate to the Minister of National Defense for the administration, organization, and training of his respective service.

Operational control of the Republic of Korea military field units is exercised by the Commander in Chief of the United Nations Command headquartered in Seoul. The United Nations Command was established on July 7, 1950, by a resolution of the United Nations Security Council in response to the unprovoked attack from the north by Communist troops across the 38th parallel. The Commander in Chief of the 16-nation United Nations forces concurrently holds the post of Commander of the United States Force in Korea and Commander of the United States 8th Army.

THE MILITARY ESTABLISHMENT AND THE NATIONAL ECONOMY

A significant percentage of the government's revenue is devoted to support the armed forces. Budget expenditures for fiscal year 1967 were 48 billion wŏn (272 wŏn equaled U. S. $1 as of May 1967), up 18.4 percent from 1966. Fiscal year 1968 budget estimates are expected to exceed 61 billion wŏn, or about 30 percent of the government's total budget.

The national economy has been growing steadily. The gross national product averaged an 8.5 percent annual increase in real terms over the five-year period from 1961 to 1966, with an extraordinary 13.4 percent in 1966. The 1967 rate was held to 8.5 percent only by a drought-damaged rice crop. Nevertheless, a large Korean military force, beyond Korea's capacity to finance, remains needed not only in Vietnam but also at home, especially with the increase in threats from the north to both internal and external security.

Consequently, the armed forces are dependent on aid from foreign sources—principally from the United States. The share of the military budget assumed by the Republic of Korea government has steadily risen from 27 percent in 1962 to 64 percent in 1968. Had it not been for the renewed threats from the north, reliable estimates indicate that the Republic would be able to assume all of its military costs, other than imported military goods, by 1971, the end of its Second Five-Year plan.

The necessity for a large military defense establishment has had a positive influence on the national economy. The introduction of aid funds for any purpose bolsters the economy since these funds represent revenues that the government would not be receiving from other sources. The funds which are allocated to the military budget provide a sizable sector of the economy with abnormal cash assets that eventually filter down to local economies. Another boost to the economy comes from the increased United States military purchasing for Vietnam and from remittances by soldiers and civilian technicians working in Vietnam.

The armed forces operate numerous technical schools and also send men to foreign technical training programs, particularly to the United States. Most of these servicemen are taught modern technologies which can be carried with them into civilian life upon discharge from the military. Such specialties as jet aircraft mechanics, electronics, communications, and heavy vehicle maintenance, as well as the more mundane clerical skills, are all important contributions to a rapidly expanding economy. Civilian business enterprises are often invited to attend courses in management techniques taught by the Army. The total impact of military education and training is significant and vital to the overtaxed civilian educational institutions.

The Republic of Korea armed forces frequently participated in construction and aid projects. The Army, for example, has completed or repaired hundreds of miles of roads, transported thousands of refugees, given medical aid to a like number, built nearly 200 new classrooms for primary schools, and contributed much equipment for civilian projects. Men frequently volunteer or are assigned to assist in transplanting rice seedlings, delivering grain, or implementing insect extermination programs. Senior officers are very much aware of the necessity for a healthy military-civilian relationship and, more importantly, the vital role it plays in the national economy.

The general policy of using the armed forces and their facilities to render emergency aid in disaster-stricken areas and to assist in public projects, such as flood control and road construction, has raised the prestige of the servicemen in the minds of many civilians. Although not completely accepted, the soldier is no longer as low on the social scale as he was in traditional Korean society. The new statute, derived from the importance and increased general understanding of the basic mission of the armed forces and their democratic composition, is emphasized in the government's public information program.

MISSION AND ORGANIZATION OF THE ARMED FORCES

The Army

The Chief of Staff of the Army commands all ground force units, but operational control of the field army, corps, divisions, and the antiaircraft artillery brigade is exercised by the Commanding General, United States 8th Army, who is subordinate to the Commander in Chief, United Nations Command. The major commands of the Republic of Korea Army consist of the First Army, the Second Army, the Logistic Base Command, and a newly established Military Combat Development Command.

The First Army is continually in a high state of combat readiness. Its troops are deployed along the 150-mile truce line between south and north Korea. The Second Army is made up of four military district commands and is responsible for the administration and training of the reserve divisions in the rear areas. It also manages and operates the Recruit Training Center and the Combat Arms Center. The Logistical Base Command has seven technical base depots that receive, store, and distribute supplies for the entire Army. The Combat Development Command was established to develop new tactics, strategies, and organizational innovations for future threat possibilities. In February 1968, the Army manpower ceiling was raised from 550,000 to 600,000, primarily in response to the increased infiltration from north Korea.

Military equipment has also been upgraded. Most of the World War II equipment has been replaced with up-to-date hardware such as M-48 tanks, M-79 grenade launchers, and integrated military communication networks. In addition, a Hawk missile unit and a Nike-Hercules missile battalion has been activated and placed under First Army jurisdiction. Meanwhile, in Vietnam, Republic of Korea combat troops have been supplied with the high-powered, rapid firing M-16 rifles as well as with other currently inventoried military equipment.

The Navy

The Chief of Naval Operations commands all naval units and installations but operational control of the fleet is exercised by the Commander, United States Naval Forces, Korea, who is subordinate to the Commander in Chief, United Nations Command. The small size of the Navy limits its capabilities mainly to coastal patrolling, minesweeping, and small-scale amphibious operations. Its headquarters are at Seoul and its principal base is at Chinhae, the site of its supply, storage, maintenance, and training facilities.

The Korean Navy has the fleet command, two combat groups, two independent squadrons, and a training group. It has recently upgraded its maintenance and operational equipment in order to increase its combat effectiveness. The current Korean five-year plan calls for augmenting the naval forces with new naval vessels having improved mission capability.

The Marine Corps

The Marine Corps, subordinate to the Navy, functions in a manner similar to that of a United States Marine Corps division. With its personnel strength as of mid-1968 exceeding that of the Navy, the Marine Corps consists of one division with three brigades, the 1st, 2nd, and 5th. The "Blue Dragon" 2nd Marine Brigade has been in South Vietnam since October 1965 and has compiled an enviable combat record. The 5th Marine Brigade was activated in November 1966 and is rapidly achieving combat readiness. The 1st Marine Brigade (Provisional) and the Marine Inland Security Unit form the major portion of the Security Forces which perform security missions among the home islands along the west coast. The Marine Corps headquarters are located at Seoul, the main Marine Corps base at Chinhae, and auxiliary bases at P'ohang and Kimp'o. The Marine Corps division is charged with the responsibility of the defense of Seoul, the capital. Its equipment is continually being modernized and its training is at a high level of proficiency.

The Air Force

The Air Force is commanded by the Chief of Staff of the Air Force, and, as in the other two services, operational control is exercised by the Commander in Chief, United Nations Command, through the Commander, United States Air Forces, Korea. Its principal components include the Combat Air Command, consisting of three fighter wings; two all-weather fighter interceptor squadrons; a tactical reconnaissance squadron; an air service wing; an air-sea squadron; and an aircraft control and warning group. The flying training wing and the technical training wing are also within the Combat Air Commands. In November 1966, the Air Logistic Command was established to manage and operate the Air Material depot at Taegu, with its extensive maintenance and supply facilities, the Aeromedical Center, near Yŏngdŏngp'o, and other support missions. The Air Force is steadily being re-equipped with modern aircraft such as the F–5 Freedom Fighter and the F–4 Phantom supersonic jets.

MANPOWER

The 1966 population census reflects a figure of 29,207,856 (preliminary), of which approximately 5,500,000 are men of military age. The current average of men reaching the military age of 18 is about 300,000 annually. By 1970 this number should increase by 10 percent for each succeeding year. Of the total 18 year olds, about 70 percent are considered physically fit (see ch. 4, Population and Labor Force).

Under the Military Service Law of 1949, as modified by the National Assembly or government decree, all physically fit male citizens of the country can be conscripted after reaching age 18. In early 1966, the Minister of National Defense announced that the military service term for enlisted men would be shortened from 2 years 10 months to 2 years 6 months and 15 days. The same decree also lowered the maximum draft age from 40 to 31 years.

Deferments are granted to qualified students attending universities and advanced schools, bona fide hardship cases, and to certain persons in occupations or positions regarded as essential to national security. Outright exemptions are given only for health reasons or for serious physical disabilities.

The quality of the manpower is attested to by the combat record of the armed forces during the Korean conflict and the conflict in Vietnam. They have demonstrated that, on the whole, Koreans make tough fighters when properly trained and led. The Korean is inured to hardship and is capable of sustained effort over long periods of time on a meager ration that would be considered barely a subsistence diet by the average Western soldier. Although he is small, averaging only about 5 feet 4 inches, he is wiry and sturdy and has a good physique.

Trained from childhood to fit himself into a hierarchical society, the Korean adjusts readily to military discipline. He may attempt to evade military service, but once inducted he accepts the authority of his officers and learns the fundamentals quickly.

Procurement and Training of Officers

The Army, Navy, and Air Force depend mainly on their academies (Military, Naval, and Air Force Academies, respectively) for their new officers. Cadets completing the four-year course of instruction are commissioned and in many cases are given some advanced or specialized training before assignment to units. The three services, however, conduct officer candidate schools and special branch schools to provide a supplemental source of officer strength derived from qualified enlisted men, college students, or civilian specialists.

Schools offering advanced and refresher courses for career officers are conducted mainly by the Army, but a limited number of officers from the other services frequently attend each course. The Command and General Staff College prepares selected field grade officers for command and staff duties at division, corps, and army levels. The National Defense College patterned after the United States National War College, trains a limited number of selected senior officers of the three services and some civilian government officials for the highest command and staff positions.

The Armed Forces Staff College was activated in May 1964 for senior officers from the Army, Navy, Air Force, and Marine Corps. Situated in the same compound with the National Defense College, the Staff College conducts courses in joint and combined organizations, plans, and related aspects of military operations, while the National Defense College concentrates on national safety and security problems.

The Navy conducts its own Naval War College for outstanding senior officers. Most of the Air Force officers selected for advanced military career training are sent to the Air Force College at Seoul. A few are sent to the National Defense College or to the Armed Forces Staff College.

The Reserve Officers Training Corps for college students was established in 1961 on a voluntary basis at 16 institutions and has since been extended to 36 colleges and universities. The program is designed to provide junior officers for the armed forces. Until 1968, this was wholly an Army program. In 1968, the Air Force and the Marines began to conduct programs for their branches of the service at selected institutions. The programs are taught by military personnel assigned to the schools. During the summer vacations, cadets are given five weeks of field training at Army, Air Force, or Marine installations. Upon completion of the two-year program, they are commissioned second lieutenants in their respective armed services and assigned to active duty units. At this time the newly commissioned officer must complete a company grade school in the particular branch of his services. After completion of the required active duty obligation the officer is assigned to a reserve unit nearest his residence and continues his military training on a part-time basis.

Procurement and Training of Enlisted Personnel

The 1949 Military Service Law provides most of the soldiers for the Army through its conscription mechanism; the Marines receive about a third. The men drafted for the Army and Marines serve a two-year, six-month period, while Air Force and Navy personnel who are all volunteers, serve for three years. The conscription system, supplemented by voluntary recruitment, is satisfactorily meeting the replacement needs of the armed forces.

The Second Republic of Korea Army, with headquarters at Taegu, is the training arm of the Korean Army. Here, the three Ready Reserve infantry divisions, seven Rear Area Security divisions, and a score of service schools are located. Unlike the recruits of the Korean conflict who received only 10 days of training, individuals now receive at least six weeks of intensive realistic training in squad to company tactics and operation of small arms and light crew-served weapons. Following this the army soldier may attend one of the branch schools or join his unit for on-the-job training. Volunteers may also go to airborne school and attend Ranger training courses.

Another means of providing well-trained specialists and skilled technicians is the Korean Augmentation to the United States Army, many of whom are now on full-time duty with United States Army combat and support units. Completely integrated into United States units, they live in the same barracks, eat the same food, perform the duties, and train with their United States counterparts.

The in-country training establishment and United States programs are supplemented by training of selected noncommissioned officers through the Military Assistance Training Program in almost every Army training school in the United States. For example, Korean soldiers operating the Hercules and Hawk missile battalions received their training at the United States Army Missile and Munitions Center, Redstone Arsenal, Alabama, and United States Army Air Defense Center, Fort Bliss, Texas. Their competence is evidenced by their fine academic records and outstanding missile firing performance at McGregor Range, New Mexico. The Korean Women's Army Corps has its school near Seoul and trains its students to serve as clerk typists, telephone and teletype operators, and radio broadcasters in psychological warfare operations.

The Naval Training Center at Chinhae conducts a school in which all enlisted men receive three months of recruit training. Further training is given in schools offering courses in radio, quartermaster, and engineering subjects. Additional schools provide training in cargo handling, firefighting, and damage control on ships of the fleet. The Marine Corps base at Chinhae has its recruit training center and conducts several schools offering instruction in the special features peculiar to Marine Corps operations.

Air Force training is conducted mainly by the Technical Training Wing at Taejon, and all airmen are attached to the Wing for training before being assigned to units. The Wing has three schools: Basic Military Training, Air Technical Training, and Communications and Electronics. Instruction includes a variety of courses, such as air operations, basic flying instructions, aircraft maintenance, weapons operation and maintenance, air traffic control, photographic interpretation, communications equipment operation and maintenance, and supply administration. This instruction, including pilot instruction, is continued by on-the-job training in the units to which the students are subsequently assigned.

Homeland Reserve Force

On April 1, 1968, the 2,270,000 reservists and veterans were organized into regional units down to the village level. The objective was to arm the heretofore unarmed reservists for the purpose of defending the cities, villages, and countryside from Communist infiltrators and guerrillas from the north. A government decree legalized the arming of the reservists and it is planned that 1 million reservists will be armed with M–1 and carbine rifles by the end of the first year. Formal training will consist of no more than seven days per year, supplemented by local drill and target practice. The law creating the regional reserve forces stipulates that the members of the reserve force should not participate in political activities as a group. The establishment of a "home guard" appears to be popular among the people, as shown through successful fund drives to purchase rifles and the volunteering of some 3,000 women for the reserve force. Political opposition, however, brings out the fear of rifles in relatively untrained hands, lack of arms control, and possible increase in crime, along with charges of "war hysteria."

CONDITIONS OF SERVICE

Life for the servicemen, particularly the enlisted man, has improved significantly since the 1950's. The major turning point is generally recognized to be the successful military coup in 1961. The resulting purges both inside and outside the Army were instrumental in altering the old military pattern of factionalism and favoritism. The Korean military service, although still hardly of an ideal standard, is receiving a more equitable distribution of funds allocated for pay, subsistence, and recreation.

Food

Food provided for the armed forces is not lavish but is in keeping with the simple dietary demands of the Koreans. From time to time the quantity and quality of the rations are subject to criticism but while some of this criticism seems to stem from the soldier's propensity to gripe, an effort is being made to ensure that rations are adequate. Rice remains the main staple food, usually

447

accompanied by fish and vegetables such as potatoes, cabbage, and bean sprouts. Meat or meat substitutes are becoming more available but still represent a small percentage of the Korean soldiers diet. Frequently available, especially during field condition, are "K" rations which are considered a balanced diet by Western standards and are much favored by Korean soldiers. Some United States items are issued as supplements to the rice and fish diet in Korean units; these include, at times, canned meats, vegetables, fruits, sweets, including sugar, and condiments. The Korean national dish "kimchi" in canned form is now being issued to Republic of Korea troops in Vietnam.

Off-Duty Activities

There is no restriction on religious services and practices; service personnel attend services conducted by chaplains (Christian and Buddhist) in their units or attend religious services in the civilian community. Members of the armed forces are, however, prohibited by law from joining any political party or engaging in any political activity. Recreational facilities are provided for baseball, football, basketball, and swimming to varying degrees, depending on the particular installation. The popular Armed Forces baseball league has seen spirited competition between the services. Other inter-service athletic competition is well supported and encouraged. Postal service is adequate and there is generally no censorship of troop mail. Leave policies are good and special efforts are made to assure short leaves for troops occupying truce line positions. Servicemen are eligible for reduced rates on railroads, motion pictures, and certain special events.

Military Justice

Discipline to a Korean means strict obedience to constituted authority. From birth he has been subject to rigid disciplines starting in his home, where the father exercised a sometimes arbitrary authority, and continuing with the rigid customs and prohibitions of the community and the outside controls of the police. All of these restraints have at times borne heavily upon him, and punishments have been frequent and, in many cases, harsh. But the pattern of his life has been to respect and accept authority. When the Korean enters military service he does not have to learn to adjust himself to its discipline (see ch. 12, Social Values).

Discipline is normally not a serious problem for unit commanders. Willful disobedience of orders and insubordination reportedly are rare offenses. Unauthorized absences and petty violations seem to be within reasonable limits. Serious crimes are rare.

Violators, depending upon the nature and seriousness of their offenses, may be tried by one of the three types of court-martial

—summary, special, or general. Under Constitution Article 106, military tribunals may be established as special courts to exercise appellate jurisdiction over military trials, and the Supreme Court has final appellate jurisdiction over the military courts. During periods of martial law, military tribunals may try civilians involved in espionage and in crimes, as defined by law, pertaining to offenses against sentinels, sentry posts, and prisoners of war and to the provision of harmful food.

Responsibility for the administration of justice rests with the judge advocate general of each of the services. Death sentences require approval of the President of the Republic before execution.

Medical Care

The Korean soldier is in a much better medical environment than is his civilian counterpart. The armed forces have an effective immunization program and modern medical facilities, as well as instruction in personal hygiene. The normal Korean military structure provides medical coverage similar to that in the United States forces, but to a lesser degree. For example, in 1964 the South Korean Air Force opened the Aeromedical Center, near Seoul, which has a 110-bed hospital, physiological training facilities, and altitude chambers and which is considered one of the best of its kind in the Far East. Normal sanitation requirements imposed by the military on the Korean soldier have effectively upgraded his general health. The Korean Army mobile surgical hospital, one of the first increments of the Dove unit to be sent to South Vietnam, had received the respect of not only its American counterpart but also of the Vietnamese people it has consistently aided.

Veterans Benefits

The Office of Veterans Administration was established in July 1961 to cope with the increasing number of veterans being released from the armed forces each year. The main task is to provide assistance and pensions to veterans disabled during their service, bereaved families of the war dead, and other persons who have been disabled in the service of their country.

The Veterans Administration furnishes 5,000 wŏn monthly for crippled veterans unable to work, 8,000 wŏn for totally disabled veterans requiring attendants, and varying sums for other categories of veterans. In addition, it administers the law requiring all government and private businesses with more than 16 employees to hire 3 to 8 percent of their work force from among wounded veterans, relatives of the war dead, and other recipients of pensions. The Veterans Administration also operates a veterans' hospital to accommodate ex-servicemen.

Children of deceased servicemen and policemen are assured of secondary education by law and the government plans to extend the benefits to the college level in the near future. In addition to exemption from school fees, education subsidies are provided.

According to the Military Personnel Insurance Law, all servicemen over the rank of Staff Sergeant must be covered by a military personnel insurance policy. The insured pays 200 wŏn on a monthly premium of 300 wŏn and the remainer is paid by the government. When the insured leaves the armed forces, he receives a premium refund.

Veterans retired from service after more than 10 years of active duty are eligible for a loan of up to 500,000 wŏn from the Veterans Administration for housing and farming purposes. Families of the war dead are eligible for loans up to ten times the amount of the war pensions they are entitled to.

RANK, PAY, AND INSIGNIA

The rank and grade structure of the armed forces corresponds closely to that of the United States. Similarly, the organizational responsibilities of the various ranks are generally the same as in the United States military (see table 26).

The pay scales have been a source of dissatisfaction for the serviceman despite efforts by the government to keep pace with rising cost of living. In 1966, for example, a 100 percent increase was given to conscripted soldiers and a 60 percent to the career soldier (whose pay scale is normally higher); in 1967, a 30 percent increase was granted to both groups, and another 30 percent had been promised for fiscal year 1968. It is evident that the pay problem is recognized as an important factor affecting morale and adjustments are being made as the pressures and budgets are increased.

Uniforms and Decorations

The uniforms of the country's military services are similar in color and style to those of the United States forces, particularly officers' uniforms. The Army and Air Force noncommissioned officers' uniforms are buttoned to the top of the tunic; the Navy noncommissioned officers wear the United States-type seaman's blouse.

There are numerous Korean decorations that are awarded to Korean or allied military personnel, most of them comprising several classes or grades denoting levels of achievement and degree of recognition or distinction conferred. They are highly regarded and coveted by Korean officers and men, as well as by the United Nations personnel serving in the Republic of Korea. Korean authorities have exercised considerable discretion and judgment in conferring distinctions, with the result that the various decorations

Table 26. Insignia and Pay Scale of the Armed Forces, Republic of Korea, 1967

Army, Air Force, and Marine Corps	Navy	Insignia	Monthly pay rate (in wŏn[1])
General of the Army	Fleet Admiral	Five silver stars	n.a.
General	Admiral	Four silver stars	64,000
Lieutenant General	Vice Admiral	Three silver stars	54,140
Major General	Rear Admiral	Two silver stars	41,610
Brigadier General	Commodore	One silver star	37,050
Colonel	Captain	Three silver hibiscus [2]	31,160
Lieutenant Colonel	Commander	Two silver hibiscus [2]	24,700
Major	Lieutenant Commander	One silver hibiscus [2]	19,190
Captain	Lieutenant	Three silver diamonds	13,010
First Lieutenant	Lieutenant Junior Grade	Two silver diamonds	10,210
Second Lieutenant	Ensign	One silver diamond	10,170
Warrant Officer	Warrant Officer	One golden diamond	10,350
Master Sergeant	Chief Petty Officer	One arc above three chevrons	
Sergeant First Class	Petty Officer 1st Class	Three chevrons	8,860
			8,490
Staff Sergeant	Petty Officer 2d Class	Two chevrons	2,940–1,520
Sergeant	Petty Officer 3d Class	One chevron	460
Corporal	1st Seaman	Three rockers	410
Private First Class	2d Seaman	Two rockers	340
Private	Seaman	One rocker	300

n.a.—Not available.

[1] 272 wŏn equaled U.S. $1 as of May 1967.

[2] The hibiscus is the national flower of the Republic of Korea.

—although awarded with reasonable liberality—have preserved their significance.

The first four awards are conferred for combat duty or duty in immediate support of combat operations against the enemy and denote outstanding service beyond the call of duty or meritorious service of national importance. These four awards have three classes, each denoted by the addition of a star affixed to the ribbon: a gold star for first class; silver star for second class; and without star for the third class. The level of responsibility of the individual and the achievement determine the class of the decoration.

Korean service personnel of all grades highly prize combat awards and decorations; they not only raise the individual's morale, but they gain for him much prestige among his comrades. As a rule the soldier is decorated before his company or other unit with much formal ceremony, no matter how small the award. The decoration is worn in the same way as in the United States services. Combat ribbons are displayed on the uniform even on occasions after separation from the service. Many former servicemen wear their military decorations while serving on the National Police Force.

Bibliographies

Section I. Social

RECOMMENDED FURTHER READING

Among the sources consulted in the preparation of this section, the following are recommended as additional reading on the basis of quality and general availability.

Chung, Hae-jong. "Encounter of Traditional and Foreign Thoughts." *Korea Journal*, VIII, No. 2, February 1968, 7–12, 53–62.

Crane, Paul S. *Korean Patterns*. Seoul: Hollym Press, 1967.

Hapdong News Agency. *Korea Annual, 1967*. Seoul: 1967.

———. *Korea Annual, 1968*. Seoul: 1968.

Henderson, Gregory. *Korea, The Politics of the Vortex*. Cambridge: Harvard University Press, 1968.

Kim,T'ae-gil. "The Changing morals of Korean students." *Korea Journal*, VI, No. 3, March 1966, 11–15.

Lee Sang-yun. "Confucian Thought from the Viewpoint of Humanist Contemporary Thought and the View of Human Nature Expressed in the Conception of *Jen*." *Koreana Quarterly*, IV, No. 2, Winter 1962, 122–133.

McCune, Evelyn. *The Arts of Korea, An Illustrated History*. Rutland, Vermont: Charles E. Tuttle Company, 1962.

McCune, George. *Korea Today*. Cambridge: Harvard University Press, 1950.

McCune, Shannon. *Korea: Land of Broken Calm*. Princeton: D. Van Nostrand Company, Inc., 1966.

———. *Korea's Heritage: A Regional and Social Geography*. Rutland, Vermont: Charles E. Tuttle Company, 1956.

Osgood, Cornelius. *The Koreans and Their Culture*. New York: The Ronald Press, 1951.

Republic of Korea. Bank of Korea. *Economic Statistics Yearbook, 1968*. Seoul: 1968.

Yim, Syŏng-hi. "Changing Patterns in Korean Family Structure." *Korea Journal*, VI, No. 8, August 1966, 4–7.

OTHER SOURCES USED

Byŏng, Doo Young. "International Higher Education in the Far East During the Period: 57 B.C.—668 A.D." *Koreana Quarterly*, VI, No. 2, Summer 1964, 8–112.

Canada Department of Mines and Technical Surveys. Geographical Branch. *Korea, A Geographical Appreciation*. Foreign Geography. Information Series No. 4. Ottawa: 1951 (pamphlet).

Centre for East Asian Cultural Studies. *A Short History of Korea*. Honolulu: Eest West Center Press, 1963 (pamphlet).

Choe, Chae-sŏk. "The Characteristics of Korean Society with Emphasis on its Family System." *Asiatic Research Bulletin*, VII, No. 6, September 1964, 1–4.

————. "Process of Change in Korean Family." *Korea Journal*, III, No. 1, October 1963, 10–15.

Chŏng, Tae-yum. "Korea Has 411 Different Family Names." *Korean Report*, VIII, No. 1, January-March 1968.

Chung, Chŏng-yang. "Women's Organizations and Their Activities." *Korea Journal*, IV, No. 2, February 1964, 14.

Chung, Tae-shi. "*Yesterday of Korean Education.*" *Korea Journal*, III No. 4, April 1963, 16–19, 38.

Clark, Allen D. "Protestant Work in Korea." *Korea Journal*, II, No. 6 June 1962, 9.

Clark, Charles A. *Religions of Old Korea*. New York: Fleming A. Revell Co., 1932.

"Development of Christianity." *Korea Journal*, II, No. 6, June 1962, 5 (editorial).

Hall, Ardelia Ripley. *Korean Monuments of Architecture and Sculpture*. Seoul: Republic of Korea and the Korea Society, n.d.

Heyman, Alan C. *Dances of the Three-Thousand-League Land*. Seoul: Dong-a Publishing Company, Ltd., 1966.

Hwang, Su-yong. "The Pagoda as an Art Form and Object of Faith in the Three Kingdoms Period." *Korea Journal*, VI, No. 4, April 1966, 16.

Hyŏng, Jin-yoo. "Private Educational Institutions in Korea—A Study on the Sowon System." *Koreana Quarterly*, III, No. 3, Summer 1961, 126–159.

Kang, Yoon-hi. "Basic Structure of Han'gul." *Korea Journal*, III, No. 7 July 1963, 8–13.

Kim, Doo-bun. "Historical Review of Korean Family Life." *Korea Journal*, III, No. 10, October 1963, 8.

Kim, Jyŏng-kyu. "Chinese Character and Korean Language." *Korea Journal*, III, No. 7, July 1963.

Kim, Jung-hak. "Ethnological Origin of Korean Nation." *Korea Journal*, III, No. 6, June 1963, 5–8.

Kim, Min-su. "Problems of the Modernization of Korea." *Asiatic Research Bulletin*, VI, No. 1, April 1963, 1–4.

Lee, Hang-nyŏng. "Korean Thought and Its Natural Features." *Koreana Quarterly*, IV, No. 2, Winter 1962, 117–120.

Lee, Hyo-chai. "Sociological Review of Population Growth in Korea." *Koreana Quarterly*, V, No. 1, Spring 1963, 135–151.

Lee, Ki-yŏng. "Buddhism and Modern Man." *Korea Journal*, VII, No. 10, October 1967, 14.

Meade, E. Grant. *American Military Government in Korea*. New York: Columbia University Press, 1951.

Na, Je-sin. "Physical Characteristics of Korean Nation." *Korea Journal*, III, No. 6, June 1963, 9–12.

Nelson, Frederick M. *Korea and the Old Orders in Eastern Asia*. Baton Rouge: Louisiana State University Press, 1945.

Oh, Chae-kyŏng. *A Handbook of Korea*. New York: Pageant Press, 1957.

Oliver, Robert F. *Syngman Rhee: The Man Behind the Myth*. New York: Ronald Press, 1951.

"Overseas-Trained Students Play Vital Roles." *Korea Journal*, II, No. 1, January 1962, 21.

Paik, Hyŏn-ki. "Population Increase and Educational Problems." *Korea Journal*, IV, No. 8, August 1964, 14–17.

————. "The Social Structure of Korea and Its Implications for Korean Education." *The Korea Journal*, VIII, No. 3, March 1968, 11–15.

Park, Chŏng-hong. "Postwar Currents of Thought and New Ethics." *Korea Journal*, IV, No. 12, December 1964, 4–8.

Republic of Korea. Economic Planning Board. (Bureau of Research and Statistics.) *Preliminary Population Count of the Simplified Census*. Seoul: 1966.

————. ————. *Economic Survey, 1967*. Seoul: 1967.

————. ————. *Korea Statistical Yearbook, 1966*. Seoul: 1967.

————. ————. The Second Five-Year Economic Development *Plan, 1967–1971*. Seoul: July 1966.

————. Manpower Development Research Board. *Handbook of Manpower Statistics, 1968*. Seoul: 1968.

————. Ministry of Education. *Education in Korea, 1966*. Seoul: 1966.

————. ————. *Education in Korea, 1967*. Seoul: 1967.

Republic of Korea. Ministry of Education. *Statistical Yearbook of Education, 1967*. Seoul: 1967.

————. Ministry of Public Information. *Korea, 1967*. Seoul: 1967.

Rhee, Jŏng-mo. "A Study of Population Problems in Seoul." *Korean Affairs*, IV, No. 1, May 1965.

Sŏng, Kyŏng-rin. *Graceful Music of Korea.* Seoul: Republic of Korea, Office of Public Information, August 1959.

United States Department of Defense. *A Pocket Guide to Korea* (DOD Publication No. DOD PAM 2-8A). Washington D.C.: Government Printing Office, 1962.

Vinache, Harold M. *Far Eastern Politics in the Postwar World.* New York: Appleton-Century-Crofts, 1956.

Yi, Hŏng-jik. "The Characteristics of Korean Society—A Historical Study of Korean Society." *Asiatic Research Bulletin,* VII, No. 9, December 1964-January 1965, 1-5.

Yi, Mun-yong. "The Modernization of Korea and Public Administration." *Asiatic Research Bulletin,* VI, No. 3, May 1963, 1-8.

Yoo, Yong-yul. "Catholicism in Korea." *Koreana Quarterly,*VI, No. 4, Winter 1963, 83.

(Also used in the preparation of this section were various issues of the following periodicals: *Asiatic Research Bulletin,* June 1963; *Korea Journal* [Seoul], from 1962 through March 1965; and *Koreana Quarterly* [Seoul], from 1962 through Summer 1964.

Section II. Political

RECOMMENDED FURTHER READING

Among the sources consulted in the preparation of this section, the following are recommended as additional reading on the basis of quality and general availability.

Crane, Paul S. *Korean Patterns.* Seoul: Hollym Press, 1967.

Douglas, William A. "South Korea's Search for Leadership." *Pacific Affairs,* XXXVII, No. 1, Spring 1964.

Han, Ki-uk. "Influence of Traditional Factors on Effectiveness of Mass Communications in Korea." *Korea Journal,* VIII, No. 2, February 1968.

Hapdong News Agency. *Korea Annual, 1966.* Seoul: 1966.

———. *Korea Annual, 1967.* Seoul: 1967.

———. *Korea Annual, 1968.* Seoul: 1968.

Hapdong T'ongsin-sa (Hapdong Annual). Seoul: 1966, 161; 1967, 111.

———. Seoul: 1968.

Henderson, Gregory. *Korea: The Politics of the Vortex.* Cambridge: Harvard University Press, 1968.

Kim, C. I. Eugene (ed.) *A Pattern of Political Development: Korea.* Detroit: The Korean Research and Publication, Inc., 1964.

Lee, Hwa-soo. "An Analysis of the April Revolution in Korea." *Koreana Quarterly*, VIII, No. 2, Summer 1966, 96–110.

Mobius, J. Mark. "The Japan-Korea Normalization Process and Korean Anti-Americanism." *Asian Survey*, VI, No. 4, April 1966, 241–248.

Moon, Ch'ang-joo. *A Study of Korean Politics*. Seoul: Ilcho-gak, 1965.

Mun, Hong-joo. "The History of Korean Constitution." *Koreana Quarterly*, VII, No. 3, Autumn 1965.

Pak, Chi-yŏng. "The Third Republic Constitution of Korea: An Analysis." *Western Political Quarterly*, XXI, No. 1, March 1968.

Pak, Mun-ok. *A Study of Korean Government*. Seoul: Bakyong-sa, 1967.

Republic of Korea. Ministry of Public Information. *Facts About Korea, 1968.* Seoul: 1968.

U.S. Department of State. United States Embassy, Seoul. *The Labor Situation in Korea.* Seoul: 1968 (pamphlet).

OTHER SOURCES USED

Allen, Richard C. *Korea's Syngman Rhee*. Tokyo: Charles E. Tuttle, 1960.

Che, Yuk-dae, "An analysis of the 6th Presidential Election." *Sindong-a*, No. 34, June 1967.

Cho, Soon-song. "Japan's Two-Korea Policy and the Problems of Korean Unification." *Asian Survey*, VII, No. 10, October 1967, 708.

––––––. "Korea: Election Year." *Asian Survey*, VIII, No. 1, January 1968.

––––––. "The Politics of North Korea's Unification Policies." *World Politics*, XIX, No. 2, January 1967.

Choe, Chun. "Politics and the Press in Korea." *Korean Affairs*, III, No. 3, December 1964.

Choe, Sang-mi. "The Federation of Agricultural Cooperatives." *Sasanggye*, XIV, No. 4, April 1966.

Chung, Chong-sik. "Political Parties and Funds in Korea." *Korean Affairs*, III, No. 31, December 1964, 286–295.

Democratic Republican Party. *DRP Bulletin*, II, No. 7, July 1967; II, No. 1, January 1967; II, No. 3, March 1967; II, No. 9, September 1967; III, No. 3, March 1968; III, No. 4, April 1968.

"Election Strategies of the DRP and the NDP." *Sindong-a*, No. 37, September 1967, 215–217.

Far Eastern Economic Review Yearbook, 1966. Hong Kong: 1966, 297–306.

Hahm, Pyŏng-jun. "Korea's Mendicant Neutrality." *Foreign Affairs*, XLIII, No. 1, October 1964.

Hakwŏn-sa, Ltd. *Korea: Its Lands, People and Culture of All Ages.* Seoul: Hakwŏn-sa, 1960.

Hong, Sŏng-chick. "Political Diagnosis of Korean Society: A Survey of Military and Civilian Values." *Asian Survey,* III, No. 5, May 1967, 329–340.

――――. "Post-Independent Changes in the Values of South Koreans." *Ase-a Yon'gu,* X, No. 2, June 1967.

――――. "Thoughts and Attitudes of the South Korean Intellectuals." *Sindong-a,* No. 46, June 1968.

Kang, Pŏm-sŏk. "Chosŏn daehakkyo" (Chosŏn University). *Chungang,* June 1968, 160–167.

Kim, C. I. Eugene. "Korea in the Year of Ulsa." *Asian Survey,* VI, No. 1, January 1966, 36, 37.

――――. "Significance of the 1963 Korean Elections." *Asian Survey,* IV, No. 3, March 1964.

Kim, Chŏng-han. "Korea's Diplomacy Toward Africa." *Orbis,* XI, No. 3, Fall 1967, 885–887.

Kim, Chŏng-rim. "Political Behavior of Election Losers." *Sindong-a,* No. 37, September 1967.

Kim, Dae-soo. "The Zaibatsu and the Public Interest." *Sedae,* IV, No. 11, November 1966.

Kim, Hak-joon. "The Zaibatsu and Mass Media." *Sedae,* IV, No. 11, November 1966.

Kim, Ki-bum. "Operation of the Presidential System in Korea." *Ase-a Yon'gu,* X, No. 2, June 1967.

Kim, Ki-doo. "The Question of Independent Judiciary." *Sinsajo,* I, July 1962.

Kim, Sam-kyu. *Truths About Korea.* Tokyo: Chisei-to, 1960.

Kim, Sŏng-tae. "Politics and the Press." *Sindong-a,* No. 39, November 1967.

Kim, Sŏng-sik. "Youth-Student Movement in Korea." *Korea Journal,* IV, No. 4, April 1964, 24–27, 31.

Kim, T'ae-gil. "The Changing Morals of Korean Students." *Korea Journal,* VI, No. 3, March 1966.

Kim, Yong-sam. "Crisis of Parliamentary Politics." *Sindong-a,* II, No. 42, February 1968, 90–98.

Koh, Myŏng-sik. "Development of the Korean Press." *Korean Affairs,* III, No. 3, December 1964.

Kondo, Ryunosuke. "Korea Diary." *Sekai,* No. 262, September 1967.

Korea, Main Series N.S. No. 145. *The British Survey,* April 1961.

Lee, Chŏng-sik. "Korea: In Search of Stability." *Asian Survey,* IV, No. 1, January 1964.

――――. "Korea: Troubles in a Divided State." *Asian Survey,* V, No. 1, January 1965.

McCune, George M. *Korea Today*. Cambridge: Harvard University Press, 1950.

Mendel, Douglas H., Jr. "Japan Reviews Her American Alliance." *Public Opinion Quarterly*, Spring 1966, 4.

"Military Purification Movement Leads to 1961 May Revolution." *Korean Report*, II, No. 4, May 1962.

Morley, James W. *Japan and Korea: America's Allies in the Pacific*. New York: Walker and Company, 1965.

Oh, Byŏng-hon. "How to Rescue the National Assembly." *Sindong-a*, V, No. 21, April 1966.

"Organizational Structure of Our Party." *Educational Reader*, No. 2. Seoul: Minju K'ong wha-dang, 1966.

Paige, Glenn D. "1966: Korea Creates the Future." *Asian Survey*, VII, No. 1, January 1967, 26.

Pak, Kyŏng-sŏk. "President, Assemblymen, and Election Funds." *Sindong-a*, V, No. 33, April-May 1967, 202–214.

Pak, Kyŏng-sŏk and Nam, Shi-uk. "Factions in South Korean Parties." *Sindong-a*, No. 30, February 1967.

Park, Il-kyŏng. "Review of Fourteen-Year History of Korean Constitutional Government." *Koreana Quarterly*, IV, No. 4, Winter 1962.

Reeve, W. D. *The Republic of Korea*. London: Oxford University Press, 1963.

Republic of Korea. Haengjong baekso (Administrative White Paper). Seoul: 1968.

————. The Civil Code, Article I.

————. The Commercial Code, Article I.

————. Manpower Development Research Institute. *Handbook of Manpower Statistics, 1968*. Seoul: 1968.

————. Ministry of Foreign Affairs. *The Military Revolution in Korea*. Seoul: 1961.

————. ———— *The Unification of Korea*. Seoul: 1961, 37, 39.

————. Ministry of Home Affairs. *Local Government in Korea*. Seoul: Local Government Research Committee, 1966.

————. Ministry of Public Information. *Intensified Aggression in Korea*. Seoul: 1968, 29, 46.

————. ————. *Let Us Defend Our Land with Our Own Forces: Independent National Defense*. Seoul: 1968, 26–27.

Republic of Korea. Ministry of Public Information. *Republic of Korea Forces in Vietnam*. (Korean Information Series No. 10) Seoul: n.d.

————. ————. *Results of Nationwide Survey of Public Opinion on Anti-Communist Policies*. Seoul: 1968, 234, 295.

————. National Assembly. *Constitution of the Republic of Korea*, Article 7.

Republic of Korea. Ministry of Public Information. *Law Concerning Political Funds*, Articles 4–5.

_____. _____. *Political Party Act.*

_____. Supreme Council for National Reconstruction. Ministry of Public Information. Revolution's First Two Months' Achievements. Seoul: n.d.

_____. Supreme Court. *Korean Legal System*. Seoul: 1964.

Rhi, Sang-kyu. "The Structure of the Government." *Korean Affairs*, III, No. 1, April 1964.

Sasanggye. XVI, No. 6. Seoul: June 1968.

Shigeru, Oda. "The Normalization of Relations Between Japan and the Republic of Korea." *American Journal of International Law*, January 1967, 51.

Sin, Sang-cho, "Policies Aimed at One-Person Domination of Korean Politics." *Sasanggye*, XIII, No. 7, July 1965.

Song, Hyo-bin. "Central Headquarters of the New Democratic Party." *Sedae*, V, No. 4, April 1967.

U.S. Department of State. *A Historical Summary of United States-Korean Relations*. Washington, D.C.: Government Printing Office, 1962.

_____. *North Korea: A Case Study in the Techniques of Takeover*. Washington, D.C.: 1961, 12–13.

U.S. Department of State Bulletin. Washington, D.C.: July 3, 1950, 5.

Widaehan chonjin (Great Step Forward). Seoul: Koryŏ Publishing Company, 1967.

Yi, Mun-yong. "Presidency and the Destruction of Division of Administrative Functions." *Sasanggye*, XIV, No. 7, September 1966.

Yi, Sang-yu. "Powers of the Executive and the Legislature." *Sedae*, IV, No. 11, November 1966.

Yoon, Chŏn-joo. *An Introduction to the Korean Political System*. Seoul: Mun woon-dang, 1962.

(Various issues of the following periodicals were also used in the preparation of this section: *Chosŏn Ilbo* [Seoul], *Dong-a Ilbo* [Seoul], *Han'guk Ilbo* [Seoul], *Korean Report* [Seoul], and *New York Times*, from March 1963 through July 1968.)

Section III. Economic

RECOMMENDED FURTHER READING

Among the sources consulted in the preparation of this section, the following are recommended as additional reading on the basis of quality and general availability.

Chase-Manhattan Bank. Economic Research Division. *Korea: Determined Strides Forward.* New York: May 1967.

Crane, Paul S. *Korean Patterns.* Seoul: Hollym Press, 1967.

Embassy of Korea. Korean Information Office. *Korean Report,* Washington, D.C.: VI, No. 3, July-September 1966; VII, No. 3, July-September 1967; VII, No. 4, October-December 1967; VIII, No. 1, January-March 1968.

Hapdong News Agency. *Korea Annual, 1964.* Seoul: 1964

———. *Korea Annual 1965.* Seoul: 1965.

———. *Korea Annual, 1966.* Seoul: 1966.

———. *Korea Annual, 1967.* Seoul: 1967.

———. *Korea Annual, 1968:* Seoul: 1968.

Korean Reconstruction Bank. *Industry in Korea, 1967.* Seoul: 1967, 299.

McCune, Shannon. *Korea: Land of Broken Calm.* New York: Van Nostrand & Company, 1967.

Republic of Korea. Bank of Korea. *Economic Statistics Yearbook, 1968.* Seoul: May 1968.

———. ———. *Economic Progress in Korea.* Seoul: 1967.

Republic of Korea. Economic Planning Board. *Economic Survey, 1967.* Seoul: 1967, 105, 106.

———. ———. *Overall Resources Budget, 1968.* Seoul: August 1967.

———. ———. *A Summary of the Second Five-Year Economic Development Plan, 1967–1971,* Seoul: 1966 (pamphlet).

———. Ministry of Agriculture and Forestry. *Annual Report on Agriculture, 1965.* Seoul: September 1966.

U.S. Agency for International Development. South Korea: *Economic Background Highlights.* Washington, D.C.: 1968 (pamphlet), Revision No. 206.

U.S. Department of Commerce. "Basic Data on the Economy of the Republic of Korea." *Overseas Business Reports.* Washington, D.C.: Government Printing Office, June 1968.

University of Wisconsin. International Cooperative Training Center. *Study of Agricultural Cooperatives in Korea.* Seoul: March 1966.

OTHER SOURCES USED

Chao, Hak-chung. "The Interest Rate Structure in Korea." *Korean Affairs,* II, Nos. 3–4, 1963, 362–368.

Ch'oe, Ung-sang. "Korean Agriculture at the Crossroads." *Korea Journal,* VI, No. 9, September 1966, 4–14.

Chu, Suk-kyŏn. "Farm Modernization in Korea." *Koreana Quarterly,* VI, No. 3, 1964, 42–49.

Consulate General of the Republic of Korea. *Foreign Capital Inducement Law.* Los Angeles: May 1967 (pamphlet).

461

"Deep Sea Fishing." *Korea Journal,* May 1967.

Economic Annual, 1968. Seoul: Hapdong News Agency, 1968.

Federation of Korean Trade Unions. *Activities Report for 1966.* Seoul: n.d.

Fees, Mark C. "Korea Develops New Look." *International Commerce,* August 7, 1967, 104.

First National City Bank. Foreign Information Service. *Republic of Korea; Economic Gains Spur New Confidence.* September 1967 (pamphlet).

Foreign Exchange Bank of Korea. *Monthly Economic Review,* I. No. 3, October 1967, 2; I, No. 5, December 1967, 1–6.

International Bank for Reconstruction and Development. Asia Department. *Recent Statistical Information Obtained from the Government of Korea* (Table 1). Seoul: April 11, 1968 (pamphlet).

——————————. *World Bank Atlas,* September 1967, 1967 edition.

Korea Chamber of Commerce. *A Summary Status of Foreign Investments As of January 1, 1967.* Seoul 1967.

Korea Exchange Bank. *Annual Report, 1967.* Seoul: 1967, 4–7.

——————. "Customs Laws Amended." *Monthly Review,* I, No. 5, December 1967.

——————. "Foreign Direct Investment in Korea." *Monthly Review,* I, No. 2, September 1967.

——————. "Guidelines for Foreign Loans to Korea." *Monthly Review,* II, No. 1, January 1968.

——————. "The Import Finance System in Korea." *Monthly Review,* I, No. 4, November 1967.

——————. *Monthly Economic Review,* II, No. 4, April 1968, 27.

Korea Trade Promotion Corporation. *Korea Trade Guide.* Seoul: 1967.

——————————. "Korea's Export Trade in 1968." *Korea Trade,* XXV, No. 2, 1968, 8.

——————————. *Invitation to KOTRA.* Seoul: 1968.

Korean Reconstruction Bank. *The Korean Reconstruction Bank: Its Functions and Activities.* Seoul: 1967, 5–6.

——————————. *Report on Sample Survey for Mining and Manufacturing Establishments.* Seoul: 1967.

Korean Traders Association. *Korean Trade Directory.* Seoul: 1967 (1967 edition).

Lim, Jong-chul. "Economic Development in Korea and U.S. Economic Mission's Reports and Advice." *Koreana Quarterly,* IX, No. 4, Winter 1967, 49–50.

Ogle, George. *Development of the Korean Labor Movement.* University of Wisconsin, 1966 (master's thesis, n. pub.).

Oh, Chae-kyŏng. *A Handbook of Korea*. New York: Pageant Press, Inc., 1957.

Reeve, W. D. *The Republic of Korea*. London: Oxford University Press, 1963.

Republic of Korea. Bank of Korea. *Economic Statistics Yearbook, 1967.* Seoul: May 1967.

_____. _____. *Monthly Statistical Review*, XXI, No. 2, November 1967, 3, 7–20, 25–26, 30–33.

_____. Economic Planning Board. *Indicators on Korean Economy*. Seoul: 1967–1968 (pamphlet).

_____. _____. *Investment Guide to Korea*. Seoul: 1967, 24–27.

_____. _____. *Major Economic Indicators*. Seoul: 1967.

_____. Korean Legal Center. *Laws of the Republic of Korea*. Seoul: 1964.

_____. Ministry of Agriculture and Forestry. *Agriculture in Korea*. Seoul: 1965, 143–154.

Republic of Korea. Ministry of Transportation. *Statistic Yearbook of Transportation, 1967*, Seoul: 1967.

Rhi, Sang-kyu. "The Structure of the Government." *Korean Affairs*, III, No. 1, April 1964, 38.

"South Korea 'Takes Off' — An Asian Success Story." *U.S. News & World Report*. October 31, 1966.

U.S. Agency for International Development. *U.S. Economic Assistance Programs Administered by the Agency for International Development and Predecessor Agencies*. February 1968, 47.

_____. *U.S. Foreign Aid in East Asia*. Washington, D.C.: 1968 (pamphlet).

U.S. Department of Agriculture. *Agricultural Policies: The Far East and Oceania*. Washington, D.C.: November 1967 (pamphlet).

_____. *The Far East and Oceania Agriculture Situation; Review of 1967 and Outlook for 1968*. Washington, D.C.: April 1968 (pamphlet).

U.S. Department of Commerce. Bureau of International Commerce. "New Korean Law Offers Variety of Incentives to Investors." *International Commerce*, August 7, 1967.

U.S. Department of State. United States Embassy, Seoul. *The Labor Situation in Korea*. Seoul: 1968.

U.S. Information Service. *Korea Builds: United States Aid Program in Korea*. Seoul: November 1966 (pamphlet).

Section IV. National Security

RECOMMENDED FURTHER READING

Among the sources consulted in the preparation of this section, the following are recommended as additional reading on the basis of quality and general availability.

Hapdong News Agency. *Korea Annual, 1967.* Seoul: 1967.

_____. *Korea Annual 1968.* Seoul: 1968.

Henderson, G. *Korea, The Politics of the Vortex.* Cambridge: Harvard Press, 1968.

Pak, Pyŏng-hya. "The National Police of the Republic of Korea." *Korea Briefing Book.* Seoul: 1968.

Republic of Korea. *Korea Air Force Yearbook, 1963.* Seoul: 1963.

_____. *Korea Army Yearbook, 1967.* Seoul: 1967.

_____. *Korea Marine Corps Yearbook, 1967.* Seoul: 1967.

_____. *Korea Today.* Seoul: May 1967.

_____. Korean Legal Center. *Laws of the Republic of Korea.* Seoul: 1964.

U.S. Agency for International Development. "Public Safety Assistance to KNP." *Korea Briefs.* Washington, D.C.: Government Printing Office, 1968.

OTHER SOURCES USED

Allen, Richard C. *Korea's Syngman Rhee.* Tokyo: Charles E. Tuttle, 1960.

Democratic Republican Party. *DRP Bulletin,* III, No. 3, March 1, 1968; III, No. 4, April 2, 1968.

Embassy of Korea. Korean Information Office. *Korean Report,* VII, Washington, D.C.: July-September 1967.

Embassy of Korea. Korean Information Office. *Korean Report,* VIII, No. 1, Washington, D.C.: March 1968.

Metcalf, J. E. "Republic of Korea Economic Gains Spur New Confidence." *Foreign Information Services* (First National Bank). New York: September 1967.

Pak, Ch'an-kuk. (Commodore, Republic of Korea Naval Attache). Letter, Washington, D.C.: July 1968.

Republic of Korea. Bureau of Research and Statistics. *Preliminary Count of Population.* Seoul: October 1966.

_____. Economic Planning Board. *Korea Statistical Yearbook, 1966.* Seoul: August 1966.

U.S. Agency for International Development. *U.S. Foreign Aid in East Asia.* Washington, D.C.: U.S. Government Printing Office, February 1968.

U.S. Army Chief of Information Office. *Army Digest.* Washington, D.C.: U.S. Government Printing Office, May 1967.

U.S. Department of Defense. *Uniforms of Seven Allies.* Document GEN–30. Washington, D.C.: U.S. Government Printing Office, February 1968.

U.S. Naval Institute. "Lord of the Turtle Boats." *U.S. Naval Institute Proceedings,* XCIII, No. 12. Annapolis, Maryland: December 1967.

U.S. News & World Report, October 2, 1967.

GLOSSARY

Ch'angga Hakhoe—Value Creation Learning Society; a recently introduced form of Buddhism with professed political ambitions (Japanese: Soka Gakkai).

che'myŏn—Personal honor, "face," as perceived by the individual and recognized by others; preserved by observance of Confucian standards of conduct. Individual *che'myŏn* is bound to the family honor, or *kamyŏng*.

Ch'ŏndogyo—An indigenous monotheistic religion stressing the equality of man and the unity of man and universe. Formerly Tonghak, it was revived and renamed in 1906.

ch'ŏnmin—Traditionally, the "despised" or "lowborn" people, including many useful trades and professions. Distinctions are lessening, but members of this class still experience some discrimination.

Chosŏn—Ancient name for Korea, derived from that of a tribe living in the northwestern portion of the peninsula.

chungbo—Standard measure of land area; 1 chungbo equals 2.45 acres.

chungmae—Professional matchmakers. The custom of arranging marriages through a broker has persisted into the 20th century though it is now diminishing in urban areas.

Ch'usŏk—Harvest festival, celebrated in late September.

do—Province; used in combined form, as Kangwon-do, Kangwon Province. There are eight mainland provinces and one island province in the Republic.

Gukmu hoeui—The State Council of the Republic of Korea, comprising 10 to 20 members and presided over by the President.

han'gab—The 60th birthday, an important day in traditional Korean family life, marking the end of the first life cycle and release from many family obligations. Persons over 60 are accorded great reverence.

han'gul—A Korean phonetic vernacular writing system developed in the 15th century and still in use; Han'gul Day (Alphabet Day) is celebrated on October 9.

hanyak—The ancient Korean system of medicine which is based on Confucian concepts and entails acupuncture and the use of herbs. Practitioners are licensed by the government.

Hŏnpŏp—The first Constitution of the Republic of Korea, promulgated on July 17, 1948, a date celebrated each year as Constitution-Making Day.

hwajŏnmin—Literally, "fire-field people;" farmers who clear the land by burning, leaving the ashes for fertilizer. Erosion is thus accelerated, and the land is depleted and eventually abandoned. Over 120,000 acres are under fire-field cultivation.

hwarang—An elite group of noble youths, political and military leaders of the Korean kingdom of Silla (A.D. 676–935) devoted to the highest Confucian and Buddhist ideals. The spirit of *hwarang* was revived in 1950, and the name is given to one of the country's four distinguished service medals.

kabujang—The head of the extended patrilinear family, traditionally having complete authority over, as well as responsibility for, the clan members.

kamyŏng—Family honor, dependent upon recognition by the community that every member of the family is conforming to Confucian standards of right conduct.

kan—Standard unit of area measure, approximately 8 to 9 feet square (64–81 square feet).

kayakeum—Traditional Korean stringed instrument, in popular use today. Other traditional instruments include: drum (*chwage*), tartar pipe (*hyang p'iri*), harp (*komungo*), lute (*hyang pip'a*), and bamboo flute (*taegum*).

kimch'i—A highly spiced dish of vegetables, fruits, nuts, and fish, served at every meal.

kisaeng—Traditional female entertainers, comparable to Japanese geisha; the *kisaeng* lost their former status during the Japanese occupation, but since 1945 have become active in repertory companies.

kongmuwŏn—The Civil Service of the Republic of Korea; national and local government employees appointed by executive agencies of the government.

Koryŏ—An early dynasty (935–1392) whose name was later transformed into "Korea."

KOTRA—Korean Trade Promotion Corporation; a government agency for the promotion of export trade.

ku—A ward, or subdivision of a large urban area; divided into *tong* (blocks).

kun—A county, administrative subdivision of a province; divided into towns (*ŭp*) and townships (*myŏn*), but does not include cities, which are under direct administration of provinces.

li—A Chinese word (Korean *ye*) denoting the Confucian standard for ideal conduct; involves righteousness and benevolence in superiors, humility and loyalty in inferiors, and, particularly, loyalty to the family and to rulers.

mudang—Female practitioners of shamanism, believed to cure diseases caused by evil spirits. Though feared and despised ("lowborn"), they are still called upon in times of crisis; believed to be more powerful than male shamans or *paksu*.

myŏn—Rural townships; administrative subdivisions of counties.

No Ch'ong—Federation of Korean Trade Unions, the major labor Organization in the Republic, composed of 16 unions with a total membership of 375,000.

paksa—Doctor; an honorific used toward a man having scholarly attainment.

paksu—A male shaman, counterpart of the *mudang*.

Samil—Independence Day (March 1), commemorating massive peaceful demonstrations in 1919 against Japanese oppression.

sangin—Commoners; the largest segment of traditional Korean society, distinguished from *yangban* (nobles) and *ch'onmin* (lowborn).

sangyong—Rice tea, taken after all meals.

sarangbang—The main room of the Korean house, opening on a central courtyard.

shamanism—Spirit worship, an indigenous animistic religion; though not officially favored, it persists in many rural areas.

si—A city (population 50,000 or over) ; under direct administration of the province.

Sirhak—Literally, Practical Learning; an intellectual and social movement started in the 17th century by scholars discontented with government discrimination.

Sŏhak—Literally, Western Learning; the name given to Christianity (particularly Catholicism) and to Western scientific knowledge in general.

sŏnsaeng—Teacher, or senior; a form of respectful address.

sul—Rice wine.

Tan'gun—Legendary founder of Korea, according to ancient folklore; the offspring of the divine creator and a bear who was transformed into a maiden.

Tano—A festival marking the end of plowing; celebrated in mid-June.

tong—Urban neighborhood association (covering roughly one block), a subdivision of the *ku*; headed by influential community leaders.

Tonghak—Eastern Learning; an indigenous religious movement, largely anti-foreign, spearheading the popular rebellion of 1894. Later renamed Ch'ŏndogyo.

turumagi—A long, flowing white coat worn by men on ceremonial occasions.

ŭp—A town having a population of 20,000 to 50,000, subdivision of a *kun*.

wŏn—Monetary unit of the Republic of Korea; in 1967 the official exchange rate was 100 wŏn = U.S. $.367, or 272 wŏn = $1.00.

yangban—The traditional nobility or ruling class of Korea. Membership, though largely hereditary, depended upon land ownership.

ye—See *li*.

Yong-gam—Honorable Sir; an honorific used toward men of advanced age or elevated station, particularly in high levels of government.

INDEX

censorship: 278–281; of press, 221

Central Election Management Committee: 202–203, 219, 232–234, 237

Central Federation of Fisheries Cooperatives (see also cooperatives, fishery): 403, 407

Central Intelligence Agency: 190, 237, 240, 440; and foreign policy-making, 267

Central Region: See topographic regions

ceramics: 329; clay deposits, 322 (figure 8); industry, 326 (table 16)

ceremonies and celebrations: 93, 105, 156, 179; national holidays, 46, 292

Ch'ae Man-sik (author): 132

Chang Myŏn (President): 54, 210–211, 213–214; government of, 160, 213–215, 229, 250; unification policy, 259

Chang Sung-op (artist): 129

Ch'angga Hakhoe Buddhism: 160

Chase-Manhattan Bank: 408

Cheju (Jeju) island and province: 12, 18, 19 (figure 4); airport, 24, 364; area and population density, 20 (table 3); Communist rebellion, 47; dialect, 66; population, 56, 65

chemical industry (see also fertilizers, petrochemicals): 21, 299, 328–329; firms and employees engaged in, 326 (table 16); government development of industry, 403; growth of, 319

Chiang Kai-shek: 47

children (see also education, juvenile delinquency): day care of, 107; early marriage of, 86; percent of minors in total population, 56; traditional upbringing, 88–90

China (see also Communist China, Republic of China): Cairo Declaration, 48; current attitudes toward, 264; dynasties, 25, 26, 27–28, 33, 34, 35, 39; history and cultural influence, 2, 25–42, 74, 125, 126–141 passim, 163–174 passim; influence on government, 176; Korean independence of, 43; Korean Provisional Government in, 47; Manchu invasions and domination, 25, 35, 39; Mongol

invasions, 25, 31, 33–34, 436; proximity to, 8, 20; religious and philosophical influence, 149–153; repatriation from, 58; Sino-Japanese wars, 42, 47

China, Republic of (Nationalist China): 47; ASPAC, 254–255; attitude toward, 264–265; Bank of Taiwan, 411; relations with, 247, 248

Chinese: language and characters, 25; living in Korea, 65; in news media, 272, 273

Ch'ing dynasty (Manchu); 39; scholars, 40

Chinhae (city): 24

Cho Bong-am (political leader): 210–211

Cho Byŏng-ok (political leader): 210, 212

Ch'oe Che-u (scholar): 42, 155

Ch'oe Chin-wun (author): 132

Ch'oe Ch'ung-hŏn (general): 33

Ch'oe Tu-sŏn (premier): 220

Cho-hung Bank: 407

Chŏlla Province, North and South: 19 (figure 4); area and population density, 20 (table 3)

Ch'ŏndogyo religion (see also Tonghak): 2, 45, 149, 154–156

Chŏng Chung-bu (general): 33

Chong Hyok Lee (sculptor): 142

Chonju (city): 21

Chongju (city): 10, 21

Ch'ŏngp'yŏng (city): 334

Chŏng Yŏ-rip (political leader): 38

Chŏnnam National University: 101

Chōsen University (Japan): 254

Chosŏn (ancient Korea): 26, 34

Chosun Brewery: 359

Chosŏn University: 101

Christian Science Monitor: 270

Christianity (see also Catholicism, Protestant): 2, 26; impact on Confucian tradition, 93; missions and schools, 39, 41, 45, 75, 77, 109, 112–113, 153–154, 159–160; persecution of Christians, 41; 17th century missions in Korea, 39, 41; Sohak, 153

Chu Hsi (see also Confucianism): 140

Ch'unch'on (city): 21, 334

Chungang University: 100

Economic Cooperative Administration: 375 (table 23)
economic policy: aims, 297, 304, 321
economy: 1, 4–6; character and structure of, 297–304; effects of Korean conflict, 300; effect of partition on, 297, 300–301; government development of, 297, 304, 319–332; growth since 1963, 301, 301–303; under Japanese domination, 298–300; labor force by economic sector, 62 (table 8)
education (see also medical training, military training, vocational training): 4, 6, 72, 109–123; attitude toward, 121–123, 125, 145–147, 167; civil service, 203–205; classical Buddhism, 152; classical Confucianism, 5, 31, 74–76, 109, 110–112, 150; coeducation, 93–94, 114; colleges and universities, 115, 120–121; for foreign service, 267; hanyak medical school, 99; Japanese influence, 47, 67, 94, 109–110, 113–114; legal training, 425; literacy, 67–68; medical training, 100; military, 441, 444–447; mission schools, 77, 109, 112–113, 154; modern elementary, 116–118, 122; modern goals, 116, 121–123; modern private schools, 115–116; modern secondary, 118–120; modern technical and vocational training, 60, 63, 110, 119–120, 122, 123, 335, 339; and monthly earnings, 342 (table 19); 19th century reforms, 43, 45; opportunities in cities, 6, 59–60; private academies (Sowon), 38, (Sodang), 110–111; rural-urban differences, 94–95, 119; since 1945, 114–121; structure and finance of, 115–116, 117 (figure 5), 116; teachers' colleges, 118, 119, 120–121; voluntary contributions to, 397; and women, Confucian, 75
Education Law: 114, 116
elections: Central Election Management Committee, 202; election irregularities, 224, 240; of 1948, 50; of 1960, 1963, 1967, 54, 240, 242–243; since World War II, 3, 4
electoral system: 200–202
electric power (see also power, hy-droelectric and power, thermal): 6, 300, 302; development of, 303
electrical and electronics industry: 302, 323 (table 15), 330–331
emigration: 46, 57, 58, 94, 178, 290–291; and Korean Provisional Government at Shanghai, 47; of students, 121
employment (see also labor, labor force, unemployment): conditions of, 340–344; persons employed by occupation, 338 (table 18); in urban centers, 6
engineering works: irrigation projects, 22, 306, 353; Naktong basin development project, 377; rehabilitation of public utilities, 97; road and bridge construction, 364
England: See Great Britain
English: teaching of, 119, 120
entertainment: See cultural activities
Ethiopia: participation in Korean conflict, 52
ethnic groups: Korean, 2, 26, 65; other groups, 65
etiquette: Confucian, 75, 88, 89–90
Ewha Women's University: 100, 112
executive powers: 187–191
expenditures: government, 386–388; private, 104 (table 9)
exports (see also imports, foreign trade): 4, 5; agricultural commodities, 315; fishing industry, 316; government promotion of, 4, 304, 320, 351, 378–379, 380 (table 24); growth since 1963, 302, 304; manufactured goods, 302; quality control by government, 361

factionalism: 29, 35, 37–39, 48, 234–236
family (see also Confucianism, social structure): conflict with Western ideas, 164, 288; familism, 85–86; foreign influences on, 93; influence on political attitudes, 290; kinship system, 85; modern trends in, 95–96; patriarchal system, 87; relationships, 87; size of, 83, 95; structure and living patterns, 83–96; traditional Korean, 2, 84
farmers (see also agriculture, peasants): government aid to, 313–

316; percent of total working force, 338 (table 18); and political activity, 230; taxation of, 315–316

farming: *See* agriculture, rural areas

Federation of Agricultural Cooperatives (*see also* National Agricultural Cooperatives Federation): 238

Federation of Financial Associations: 313–314

Federation of Korean Industries: 239, 326

Federation of Korean Trade Unions: *See* No Ch'ong

feldspar: 321, 330

fertilizers (*see also* chemicals): 16, 328–329; chemical fertilizers, 16, 299; development of industry, 301, 303; fish products used as, 317; government ownership of industry, 325; growth of industry, 328 (table 17)

festivals: *See* ceremonies and celebrations

feudalism: 85

fiber products: 328, 332

films (*see also* motion picture industry): 277–278

financial cooperatives: 313–314, 402–403

financial institutions: *See* banks and banking

financing (*see also* banks and banking): methods of, 413–414

firefield cultivation (*see also* agriculture): 16, 40, 46, 308

First City Bank of Korea: 407

First National City Bank of New York: 408

First Republic: *See* Republic of Korea

fiscal policy: 4, 304, 401–414

fish and fishing: 4, 7, 16, 302–303; cooperatives, 191, 317, 403, 407; definition of territorial waters, 252, 253, 262, 317; development under Japanese, 299; in diet, 311; government development of, 317; industry, 316–317; recent growth, 302; schools specializing in marine activities and fisheries, 120

Five-Year Economic Plans (*see also*

industrialization; industry, government development of): 23, 24, 241, 242, 304, 362; and fiscal policy, 387, 391

flag: 293

floods and flood control (*see also* irrigation): 313

flourite: 321, 322 (figure 8); production, exports and reserves, 323 (table 15)

food: *See* diet

Food and Agriculture Organization: 259

food and beverage industry: 317, 326 (table 16), 327, 328 (table 17)

foreign aid (*see also* United Nations, United States): 303, 373, 375 (table 23); in industrialization, 303; in reconstruction, 301, 303; as supplier of government revenue, 396

Foreign Capital Inducement Law: 304, 379, 391

foreign exchange: 381

foreign investment: 297, 301, 304, 372–373, 379

foreign policy (*see also* anticommunism, foreign relations, unification): attitude toward, 259–263; Foreign Ministry Organization, 266 (figure 6); goals, 245–247; organization and operation, 265–266

foreign relations (*see also* foreign policy and specific nations and regions): 245–265

foreign service: training of, 267

foreign trade (*see also* exports, imports): 6, 46, 299, 369–380; government promotion of, 378–381; growth since 1963, 304; invisible transactions, 371–373; under Japanese domination, 46, 299; organization of, 377–378

foreigners: attitude toward, 263–265

forests (*see also* vegetation, timber): 7, 15–16, 313; depletion and reforestation, 302, 313; forestry, 303

France: attitude toward, 264–265; 1886 trade treaty, 42; Geneva conference, 257; influence on

Third Republic Constitution, 183; participation in Korean conflict, 52; relations with, 248
Frazar International: 359
Free World (periodical): 284
fuel: coal as source of, 362; expenditures for, 104 (table 9); petroleum products, 330; timber as source of, 15, 16; use of in dwellings, 103
funerals: 92–93

Gabon: relations with, 248, 256
Gangneung (city): climate, 14 (table 2), 14
gardening: art of, 130
General Agreement on Tariffs and Trade (GATT), 378
Geneva: conference on Korean question, 257–258; Korean mission to, 6, 248
geographical features (*see also* mountains, rivers, topography): 9
geological data: 9
geomancers: 141, 159
Germany (and Germany, Federal Republic of): aid, 376; attitude toward, 264; 1883 trade treaty, 42; missionaries from, 77; proposal to neutralize Korea, 42; relations with, 248; trade, 370
Ghana: relations with, 248, 256
ginseng: 146, 311; government monopoly, 352, 360–361, 396
glass products: 319, 329–330; size of industry, 326 (table 16), 328 (table 17)
glossary: 467–470
Goesan (city and power plants): 334
gold: 17, 321, 322 (figure 8), production, exports, and reserves, 323 (table 15)
goods and services: balance of payments, 374 (table 22)
government (*see also* civil service, Confucianism, constitution, Park administration): aid to private enterprise, 297; budget, 384–386; centralization of, 175; constitutional system, 181–185; contemporary attitudes toward, 245, 290–291, 293–296; expenditures, 386–388; goals, 207, 247; history prior to Third Republic, 176–178, 208–

220; and industry, 4, 319, 334–335; investment in industry, 297, 304, 353; local, 198–200; price controls, 351; structure and functions, 187–198; system of, 1, 3, 4, 175–205 *passim*; and trade, 365–366
government subsidies: 304, 308, 353
grain loans (*see also* government subsidies): 30
grains (*see also* barley, millet, rice, wheat): distribution of, 354–355; imported, 312; production of, 310 (table 13), 312 (figure 7), 311–312, 353
graphite: 17, 299, 321, 322 (figure 8); production, exports and reserves, 323 (table 15)
Great Britain: aid, 376; alliance with Japan, 44; attitude toward, 264–265; Cairo Declaration, 48; 1883 trade treaty, 42; Geneva conference, 257; participation in Korean conflict, 52; relations with, 247, 248; trade, 370
Greece: participation in Korean conflict, 52; relations with, 248
gross national product: 303; growth, 297, 304; percentage breakdown, 303 (table 12)
Gulf Oil Corporation: 330

Haein-sa (temple): 34
Han dynasty (Chinese): 26–27
Han Musuk (author): 133
Han River: 11 (figure 3), 10, 13 (table 1), 27, 28, 33
handicrafts: 55, 298, 332; percent of work force employed in, 338 (table 18)
han'gul alphabet (*see also* education, literacy): 36, 67–68, 75, 112, 132, 290; in news media, 270, 273
Hanil Bank: 407
hanyak practitioners: 99
harbors: *See* ports
Hawaii: emigration to, 46
health (*see also* disease, hospitals, physicians and surgeons): 97–101
herbalists: 100
Hermit Kingdom: *See* isolationism
highways: *See* roads and highways
history: 1–3, 25–54; armed forces, 436–438; current study of, 142; effect on character of society, 25–

reclamation): 16, 21–23, 306, 308, 353; cooperative associations, 313–314, 315; in rice bowl area, 315
islands: *See* cheju, fish and fisheries
isolationism: 39, 41, 129
Israel: aid, 376
Italy: trade treaty, 42
Ivory Coast: relations with, 248, 256

Japan: 1, 3, 25, 27; and agriculture, 45, 46, 78; aid from, 376; annexation by, 3, 25, 35; attitude toward, 246, 264–265; and civil service, 77; and cultural activities, 126, 127–130 *passim*, 133; domination 1910–1945, 45, 48, 288; and economy, 45, 57, 298–300; Federation of Labor (DOMEI), 347; guerrilla activities against, 437; influence on educational system, 113–114; influence on Korean banking system, 45, 401–403; impact on political attitudes, 291; intervention between Korea and China, 41; invasions by, 35, 39, 40, 436; Normalization Treaty, 220–222, 235, 252–254, 376; press censorship by, 45; proximity to, 8; Russo Japanese rivalry, 25, 44; Sino-Japanese Wars, 42, 47; trade with, 5, 23, 302, 367; Treaty of Commerce with, 41; and urbanism, 58, 78
Japan, Sea of: 1, 8 (figure 2), 9, 10, 44
Japanese: language taught in schools, 113, 114; living in Korea, 55, 65; repatriation of, 56, 66
Jeju (island province): *See* Cheju
Jesuit missions: *See* Catholicism
Jinju (city): 21
Joint Commission: *See* Moscow Agreement
Journalists' Association of Korea: 347
judicial system (*see also* legal system): 196–198; military, 448–449
juvenile delinquency: 420, 423, 433; reformatories, 431; rehabilitation, 107

Kamsung industrial combine: 325
Kanghwa (island): 33, 34

Kangwŏn Province: 19 (figure 4), 23; area and population density, 20 (table 3)
kaolin (*see also* ceramics, clay): 302, 321
Kija (ruler *c.* 1122 B.C.): 131
Kil Chae-ho (political leader): 234, 236
Kim, family of: 29
Kim, Chong-pil (political leader): 215, 218, 233, 234, 235, 236; charges of election fraud against, 224–225; defection from political party, 234; delegation to Japan, 220; director of Central Intelligence Agency, 217
Kim, Namjo (poet): 133
Kim, Pu-shik (scholar): 35
Kim, Richard (author): 132
Kim, Song-kon (political leader): 234, 236
Kim, Tong-ha (political leader): 217
Kim, Yong-tae (political leader): 235, 236
kimchi (national dish): 101–102, 311
Kimpo International Airport (Seoul): 24, 364
kindergartens: 116, 122
kinship: *See* family
kisaeng entertainers: 36, 71, 77; under Japanese occupation, 139; since 1945, 146
Koguryŏ (Korean kingdom): 27–28, 31
Korea Air Lines: 24, 191, 364
Korea Broadcasting System: 274–275, 275 (table 11)
Korea Cement Manufacturing Company: 359
Korea Coal Corporation: 191
Korea Electric Company: 191, 334
Korea Exchange Bank: 379, 381, 403, 404–414 *passim*
Korea Housing Bank: 407
Korea Housing Corporation: 191
Korea Motion Picture Producers Association: 145
Korea Newspaper Ethics Association: 279
Korea Painting Society: 142
Korea Shipbuilding Corporation: 191
Korea Shipping Corporation: 191

481

7, 15–16; reform, 79, 307–308; tax, 392; tenure, 84–85, 307–308; topography and climate, 9–15; use and development, 7, 305–306, 354

land reclamation (*see also* agriculture, irrigation): 7, 10, 21–23, 306, 353

languages: dialects, 66, 81; *han'gul* alphabet, 36; *idu* script, 31; Japanese suppression of Korean language, 47; Korean, 2, 66; other languages used, 66–67, 120; social connotations of, 68, 81

Latin American nations: relations with, 245, 247–248

law (*see also* legal system, penal system): attitude toward, 416–419, 423, 432–433; civil, 185–187; commercial, 185; Confucian attitude toward, 185, 287–288, 416–417; criminal, 185–186, 419–421; system of, 415, 419

lawyers: 425; Korean Bar Association, 196, 240; legal training, 425

lead: 17, 302, 321, 322 (figure 8)

Lee Ki-pung (political leader): 211, 212

Lee Tong-won (Foreign Minister): 221

legal system (*see also* judicial system): 185–187, 419–432 *passim*; attitude toward, 419, 432–433; Confucian, 185, 416–417; courts and legal personnel, 424–425; impact of West on traditional, 417, 419–420 *passim*; Japanese influence, 417–418; reform of 1894, 417

legislature: *See* National Assembly

leisure patterns (*see also* ceremonies and celebrations, cultural activities): 105–106

Leninism: 178

li: *See* Confucianism

Liberal Party: 54, 209–213 *passim*, 218, 232

life expectancy: 97

limestone: 302, 321, 330

Li-po (Chinese poet): 137

liquor industry: 394; growth of industry, 328 (table 17)

literacy (*see also* education): 67–68, 109

literature (*see also* poetry, publishing): 125, 130–135, 140–141, 142, 143–144; folk, 134–135

livestock: 311, 315

living conditions: 6, 54, 97–107, 351

Local Autonomy Law: 198, 211

local government (*see also* government, constitution): 198

Lolang culture: 27–28

lotteries: public, 396

loyalty: to family and rulers, 168, 170–171, 291

Lucky industrial combine: 325

lumber: *See* timber

Luxembourg: participation in Korean conflict, 52

machinery: imports from Japan, 299; manufacture of, 304, 330–331; production, 326 (table 16), 328 (table 17)

Madagascar: relations with, 248, 256

magazines (*see also* periodicals): 273

Mahayana (*see also* Buddhism): 28, 149, 152

Malawi: relations with, 248, 256

Malaysia: relations with, 248; ASPAC, 254–255

Manchu: Ch'ing dynasty, 39; invasion of Korea, 25, 35, 39

Manchuria: history, 2, 27, 28; Japanese industry in, 47; migration to, 58; as possible origin of Korean people, 26

manganese: 17, 321, 322 (figure 8)

manpower resources: civil servants, 205; labor, 61–63; military, 444

manufacturing (*see also* imports, exports): 324–331; growth, 328 (table 17); growth since 1963, 6, 301, 302, 304; industrial combines, 325–326; labor utilization, 324–325; marketing of products, 351, 353, 355–357; percentage of GNP, 303 (table 12); representative industries, 326 (table 16); structure of industry, 325–327

Mao Tse-tung: 47

maps: mineral locations, 322 (figure 8); physiographic regions, 11 (figure 3); political subdivisions, 19 (figure 4); Republic of Korea,

monsoons: 13, 15
Moscow Agreement: 49–50
motion picture industry: 144–145, 269, 277–278
mountains: 7, 9, 10
mudangs (sorceresses): 77, 99, 157, 158
music: 135–140 *passim*, 143, 145–146
mutual aid companies: *See* financial cooperatives
Myonch'ong (political leader): 38

Naktong River: 10, 11 (figure 3); Naktong River Basin, 12, 377
Nam Jun Paik (musician): 143
names: 68–69
National Academy of Arts: 115, 142
National Academy of Science and Letters: 115, 142
National Agricultural Cooperatives Federation (*see also* Federation of Agricultural Cooperatives): 191, 313–315, 359, 403, 404, 406
national anthem: 293
National Assembly: 4, 188–192 *passim*, 192–196; and foreign policy, 265–266
National Assembly Law: 195
National Civil Service Law: 204
National Council of Fishery Cooperatives (*see also* cooperatives, fishery): 191
National Defense College: 438, 445
National Defense Constabulary: 435, 438
National Examinations (*see also* civil service): 73
National Federation of Medium and Small Industry Cooperatives: 359
National Land Administration: 307
National Library: 115
National Medical Center: 100
National Museum: 115, 142
National Music Conservatory: 142
National Public Health Institute: 100
National Public Servant Law: 199
National Rehabilitation Center: 100
National Science Center: 115
National Security Act: 240
National Security Council: 190, 440; and foreign policymaking, 266
National Security Law: 186, 211–212

nationalism: 125, 219, 245, 246–247, 287–294 *passim*
Nationalist China: *See* China, Republic of
nationalization of industry: 191, 334, 352, 360–361; mines, 324; radio, 274; railways, 363
natural resources: 15–17
Naval Academy: 444–445
navigation: *See* shipping
Navy (*see also* military): 422, 435, 438, 442–443, 444–445
Netherlands: aid, 52
New Democratic Party: 4, 214, 236–237, 223–243 *passim*; attitude on foreign policy, 259–263; and national defense, 295; in 1967 election, 241–242
New Korea Party: 222, 236, 237
New Politics Party: 218
New York Times: 270
New Zealand: aid, 52; ASPAC, 254–255, relations with, 248
news agencies: 272–273
newspapers: 45, 211–212, 261, 269–272; national and local, 271 (table 10)
Newsweek (magazine): 274
nickel: 322 (figure 8)
Nigeria: relations with, 248, 256; trade, 370
nobility (*see also* yangban): 30
No Ch'ong: 337–350 *passim*; affiliated unions, 346 (table 20)
Normalization Treaty (*see also* Japan): 220–222, 252–254
nurses: 100

Office of National Tax Administration: 391
oil: *See* petroleum
Opium War: 41
organizations (*see also* political parties): business and trade, 326; international, 256–259; labor, 346 (table 20); professional, 116, 197, 239–240; welfare, 106–107; women's, 209, 239–240
Oriental Development Corporation: 402

Paekche (Korean Kingdom): 27–29
Paek, Nak-chon (political leader): 233

484

Paek, Nam-ok (political leader): 234

pagodas (see also temples): 128, 130

Pak, Chang No Kyo: 149

Pak, Sun-ch'on, Mme. (political leader): 210, 218, 221–222, 233, 237

Pak, T'ae Sŏn (religious leader): 160–161

Pakistan: relations with, 248, 256

paper industry: 326 (table 16), 328 (table 17), 331

parallel, 38th: See partition of Korean peninsula

Park administration (see also government): 1, 4, 54, 220–226; agriculture, 230, 241; anticommunist propaganda, 269, 283–284; attitudes toward, 164–165, 242, 291, 293–295; banking, 401; budget, 384–387; and class distinctions, 80; constitution, 182–185, 187–200; courts and legal system, 415; and cultural expression, 142–147, 294; and Democratic Republican Party, 207–208; democratization, 6, 288–289; and education, 4, 63, 110, 115–123 passim; and emigration, 291; export and foreign trade promotion, 4, 304; and fisheries, 316–317; foreign aid, 54–100, 101, 303–304; foreign investment, 301, 304; foreign policy, 5, 245–247; goals of, 4, 246–247, 304; and housing, 103; industry, development of, 4, 54, 301–303, 319–335, passim; industry, government ownership of, 334–335; and inflation control, 304, 315, 321, 383; and Japan, 220–221, 251–254; and labor, 337; and living conditions, 53–54; military coup d'etat, 54, 215–220; and ministries, 190; political stability of, 6, 53; and population growth, 56–57, 60, 61; and public health and welfare, 54, 97–98, 101, 107; and religious freedom, 159, 160–161; and smuggling, 222–223; and State Council, 188–190; and taxes, 390–391; unification policy, 4, 247, 259; and United States, 248–251; and Vietnam involvement, 222

Park Chung Hee, General: 1, 4; and Democratic Republican Party,

234, 236; election in 1963, 54, 219–220; in 1967, 224, 240–242; military coup d'etat, 215–220

parliamentary government: 179, 180, 181

Partition of Korean peninsula (see also Korean conflict): 1, 3, 18, 25, 48; effect on economy, 297, 300–301

peasants (see also agriculture, farmers): 30; firefield farming, 40; and political activity, 228, 230–231, 238, 241; revolts by, 33, 39

Peking: capital of Yüan Empire, 33–34; Radio Peking, 285

penal system: 420–421, 430–431; and U.S. Military Government, 430–431

People's Friends Party: 218–219

People's Party: 221, 236, 237

periodicals: 211–212, 223, 231, 269, 273–274

pest control: 97, 101, 309; pesticides, 328

petrochemicals: 319, 329

petroleum industry: 319; firms and employers engaged in, 326 (table 16); imports, 5, 321; refineries, 5, 325, 327, 330

pharmacists and pharmaceutical training: 100

Philippines: aid, 52, ASPAC, 254–255; relations with, 248

physical environment: 7–24; climate, 12–15; location, xvi (figure 1), 8–9; map of Far Eastern setting, 8 (figure 2); topographic regions, 7–12 passim

physicians and surgeons: 100; hanyak practitioners, 99

plastics industry: 327; growth, 328 (table 17)

plywood industry: See timber

poetry: 130–131, 133

police (see also Korean National Police): 415, 417–419; attitude toward, 415; control of by Rhee government, 419; training of, 415–416, 422

political activity (see also political parties, politics, students): 207–243 passim

political administrative divisions:

17–18, 19 (figure 4), 20 (table 3);
population in, 56 (table 4)
political leaders: 207–243 *passim*
political parties: 231–238; factionalism in, 234–236; requirements for formation of, 232–233; trend toward two-party system, 231
Political Party Act and Law: 217, 225, 232–233, 237
Political Purification Law: 217
politics (*see also* political leaders, political parties, students): businessmen and financiers in, 231, 239; Confucian attitude toward, 287; contemporary attitudes, 207, 226–227, 289–291; in First Republic, 208–213; during Japanese colonial period, 288; and labor, 238–239; and the military, 228; and peasants, 230–231, 238; and political stability, 6, 297; and the press, 229–230; rural-urban differences, 289; in Second Republic and interim governments, 213–220; sources and aggregations of power, 227–231; and students, 228–229; in Third Republic, 220–226
polygamy: 73, 77, 85, 86–87
population (*see also* urbanism: 2, 55–61; attitudes toward birth control, 60–61; density by province, 20 (table 3); emigration and repatriation, 56, 121; ethnic origin 2; growth, 56–57, 57 (table 5), 297; and incidence of crime, 431 (table 25); and labor force, 55, 61–63; in major cities, 59 (table 6); by major political divisions, 56 (table 4); mobility, 57; problems and attitudes, 60–61; settlement patterns, 7, 18; structure of, 55–56; total population, 2
Portsmouth (N.H.), Treaty of: 44
Potsdam Conference: 48
ports: 7, 18–21, 24, 365; small coastal or fishing, 10
postal service: 214, 259, 362
postwar occupation: 48–51
potatoes: 311, 312; production, 313 (table 14)
potterymaking: 332
power: attitude toward, 171–172
power generating facilities (*see also*

hydroelectric power, thermal power): 333–334
president: 187–189
press: 269–274; Japanese control of, 45, 47; self-regulation of, 270, 279–280
prestige: *See* status
price controls (*see also* inflation): 351, 354, 360–361
Prime Minister: in Second Republic, 180, 214
primogeniture: 84, 307
printing (*see also* publishing): early, 34, 290; industry, 326 (table 16)
prisons (*see also* reformatories): 417
private enterprise, 297, 334
private expenditures: 104 (table 9), 104–105
private investment: 304, 372; growth of, 303
private schools: 115–116
Progressive Party: 210–211
propaganda (*see also* anticommunism): 269, 283–284, 289
property: ownership as sign of status, 77; ownership or control by women, 76
Protestantism (*see also* Christianity): 45, 154, 159–160
provinces: *See* political administrative divisions
public debt: 398–399
public finance (*see also* banks and banking): 383–399
public health (*see also* health, welfare): 100–101
public information: 269–285; anticommunist propaganda, 283–284; attitudes and effectiveness, 281–283; censorship and controls of, 231, 278–281; channels of distribution, 270–278; Communist propaganda, 285; foreign materials, 284–285; government agencies and activities, 283–284; propaganda, 269, 283–284; rural-urban differences toward, 281–282
Public Law 480: *See* United States
public office: attitude toward, 203
public order and safety: 415–433; attitudes toward, 415, 432–433
public service (*see also* civil service): 203–205

public utilities (see also engineering works): 361–362; reconstruction of, 97
publishing (see also literature): 143–144, 273–274, 326 (table 16)
Pueblo, USS: 251
Pulguksa, Temple of: 128
punishment (see also penal system): 416–417; family responsibility for, 94
Pusan (city): 7; area and population density, 20 (table 3); autonomous status of, 18; in Korean conflict, 51, 52, 210; population, 18, 20, 59 (table 6); power plants in, 334; rail and harbor facilities, 20; transportation, 23–24
Pusan National University: 101
Puyo tribe: 27

radio: 231, 269, 274–277, 362; stations, 275 (table 11)
Radio Moscow: 285
Radio Peking: 285
railways (see also transportation): 23–24, 363–364; government subsidies, 353; government-owned, 363–364; rehabilitation and modernization, 301, 363–364; Seoul-Pusan line, 20
rainfall: See climate
Reader's Digest (magazine): 274
rebellions: peasants' revolts, 33, 39; students' revolution of 1960, 54, 212–213; Tonghak, 42
reconstruction (see also Korean conflict): 3, 53–54, 301, 319, 373; foreign aid in, 301, 303; Law Concerning Extraordinary Measures for, 180–181; of schools, 117–118
recreation: See cultural activities
Red Cross: Calcutta Agreement, 254
Reform of 1894: 42–43, 177
reformatories: 430–431
refugees: 49, 55, 56, 57, 59, 95, 301, 441
religion (see also Buddhism, Ch'angga Hakhoe, Ch'ondogyo, Christianity, Confucianism, Pak Chang No Kyo, spirit worship, Tonghak): 2, 28–29, 34, 35, 36–37, 41, 42, 44–45, 149–161; and artistic achievement, 126–127 passim; and

education, 109, 146; history, 28–45 passim; and medicine, 99; modernization of dogma, 146; and relief work, 106; religious freedom in Third Republic, 159
repatriation (see also refugees): 49, 55, 56, 58, 59, 254
Republic of Korea, formation of (see also Constitution): First, 175, 179, 208; Second, 180–181, 213; Third, 181–185, 220
Republic of Korea, maps of: xvi (figure 1), 8 (figure 2); mineral locations, 322 (figure 8); physiographic regions, 11 (figure 3); political subdivisions, 19 (figure 4)
reservoirs: See irrigation
retail trade (see also domestic trade, trade): 302, 303 (table 12), 358–359, 358–361 passim
Reuters (British news agency): 273
revenue, government: 384, 388–398
Rhee, Syngman: 3, 52–54, 207–214 passim, 232, 287–289; assumption of power, 208; attitude toward rural electorate, 230–231; control of communications, 278; elections, 50–51, 209–210, 210–211; emigration in 1960, 213; Japan policy, 263; and Korean Provisional Government, 47; and labor unions, 239; martial law under, 212–213; and National Assembly, 209; and religious sects, 160; "Rhee line," 252–253; unification policy, 247, 258–259
rice (see also agriculture): 4, 21–23, 309, 310, 312; in barter and commerce, 309; double cropping, 298, 306, 310; exports, 315; exports to Japan, 298; imports of, 315, predominance in agricultural economy, 298, 306, 353; production, 310 (table 13), 312 (figure 7)
rivers: 9, 12, 13 (figure 1)
roads and highways (see also transportation): 23–24, 353, 363–364
rubber manufacture: 326 (table 16), 328 (table 17), 331
rural areas (see also villages): 306, 308–309
rural population (see also agriculture, migration): 6; living condi-

wages and salaries: 6, 341–343; average earnings, 342 (table 19); military pay scale, 450, 451 (table 26); payment in kind, 341, 355
Wang Kon (general): 31
wangul: See fibre products
warehousing: See storage facilities
water (*see also* hydroelectric power, irrigation): coastal, 4, 7, 10, 16; transportation, 10, 23, 365
wealth: distribution of, 72, 81; and government service, 80; and social class, 71, 73, 75
Weekly Review (periodical): 284
Weimar Constitution: influence of, 179
welfare (*see also* public health): 99, 100, 106–107
West: 2, 3, 39–40, 41, 45, 71, 72, 127, 367; aid, 106–107; attitudes in 1960's, 113; conflict with classical education, 109, 110, 112–113; conflict with Confucian values, 164–165, 167, 173–174, 288; impact of East-West conflict, 263; influence on art, 129–130, 139, 141–146 *passim*; influence on constitutional government, 178, 179; and political values, 287, 288–289 *passim*, 291; and religion, 149, 153–155, 159–160; and social structure, 77–81, 174; and traditional family patterns, 93–95; Western Learning (Sohak), 40–41
Whashin industrial combine: 325
wheat: 101, 298, 310, 312; imported, 305, 312; production, 310 (table 13)
wholesale trade (*see also* trade): 302, 303 (table 12), 356, 361
Wiman (general): 26
women: attitudes toward, 45, 73, 75–77 *passim*, 85–92 *passim*; education of, 93–94, 95, 112–113, 114, 119; equality of in Buddhism, 152; in government, 63, 95; *kisaeng* girls, 77; in labor force, 61–63 *passim*, 342 (table 19); organizations, 209, 240; in police force, 422
working conditions: 343–344

World Health Organization: 98, 259
writing: *See* literacy
Wu Tao-tzu (artist): 128
Wu Ti (Chinese emperor): 26–27

Yalu River: 25, 27, 44, 52, 149–150
yangban (aristocracy): 32, 36, 38, 38, 71, 73–75, 79–80, 84; education of, 110–112
Yellow Sea: 1, 8 (figure 2), 9, 10, 13, 20
Yi dynasty: 18, 35–45
Yi Kwang-su (author): 132
Yi Kyu-po (poet): 131
Yi Pŏm-sŏk (premier): 209, 218, 223
Yi Pyŏng-chol (industrialist): 222, 223
Yi Shi-ae (political leader): 38
Yi Sŏng-gye (*see also* Yi dynasty): 34, 35
Yi Sun-sin (admiral): 39, 290, 293, 436–437; and ironclad ships, 436
Yi Tong-won (Foreign Minister): and Status of Forces Agreement, 421
Yi Wan-yong (Prime Minister): 44
Yi Yu-song (legend): 134
Yongwol (city and power plant): 334
Yonsei University: 80
Yosu (city): climate, 14 (table 2), 14–15, 51
Young Poong Trading Co., Ltd.: 360
Young Women's Christian Association: 106
youth organizations: 209; efforts to combat delinquency, 433
Yu Chi-jin (author): 144
Yu Chin-o (scholar and statesman): 179–180, 223, 237
Yüan Empire (Mongol): 33–34
Yun Po-son (political leader): 201, 213, 214; and Civil Rule Party, 220; and New Democratic Party, 237, 240, 242; and normalization treaty, 261; presidential candidacy, 218–220, 223–224

zinc: 17, 302, 321

PUBLISHED AREA HANDBOOKS

550–65 Afghanistan
550–44 Algeria
550–59 Angola
550–73 Argentina
550–20 Brazil

550–61 Burma
550–83 Burundi
550–50 Cambodia
550–26 Colombia
550–60 Communist China

550–91 Congo (Brazzaville)
550–56 Congo (Kinshasa)
550–90 Costa Rica
550–22 Cyprus
550–54 Dominican Republic

550–52 Ecuador
550–29 Germany
550–78 Guatemala
550–82 Guyana
550–21 India

550–39 Indonesia
550–68 Iran
550–31 Iraq
550–25 Israel
550–30 Japan

550–34 Jordan
550–56 Kenya
550–41 Republic of Korea
550–58 Laos
550–24 Lebanon

550–38 Liberia
550–85 Libya
550–45 Malaysia and Singapore
550–76 Mongolia
550–49 Morocco

550–64 Mozambique
550–88 Nicaragua
550–81 North Korea
550–57 North Vietnam
550–48 Pakistan

550–72 The Philippines
550–84 Rwanda
550–51 Saudi Arabia
550–68 Senegal
550–86 Somalia

550–55 South Vietnam
550–27 Sudan
550–47 Syria
550–62 Tanzania
550–53 Thailand

550–89 Tunisia
550–80 Turkey
550–74 Uganda
550–43 United Arab Republic
550–71 Venezuela

550–75 Zambia
550–   Peripheral States of the
        Arabian Peninsula

☆ U.S. GOVERNMENT PRINTING OFFICE:1970—O-436-793#1